On the Road around Normandy, Brittany and The Loire Valley

THOMAS COOK

On 5 July 1841 Thomas Cook, a 33-year-old printer from Market Harborough, in Leicestershire, England, led a party of 570 temperance enthusiasts on a railway outing from Leicester to Loughborough which he had arranged down to the last detail. This proved to be the birth of the modern tourist industry. In the course of expanding his business Thomas Cook and his son John invented many of the features of organised travel which we now take for granted. Over the next 150 years the name Thomas Cook became synonymous with world travel.

Today the Thomas Cook Group employs over 10,000 people worldwide, with more than 1600 locations in over 100 countries. Its activities include travel retailing, tour operating and financial services – Thomas Cook is a world leader in traveller's cheques and foreign money services.

Thomas Cook believed in the value of the printed word as an accompaniment to travel. His publication *The Excursionist* was the equivalent of both a holiday brochure and a travel magazine. Today Thomas Cook Publishing continues to issue one of the world's oldest travel books, the *Thomas Cook European Timetable,* which has been in existence since 1873. Updated every month, it remains the only definitive compendium of European railway schedules.

The *Thomas Cook Touring Handbook* series, to which this volume belongs, is a range of comprehensive guides for travellers touring regions of the world by train, car and ship. Other titles include:

Touring by train
On the Rails around France (1995)
On the Rails around Britain and Ireland (1995)
On the Rails around Europe (Second Edition Published 1995)
On the Rails around the Alps (1996)
On the Rails around Eastern Europe (1996)
Touring by car
On the Road around California (1994)
On the Road around Florida (1995)
On the Road around New England (1996)
Touring by ship
Greek Island Hopping (1996)

For more details of these and other Thomas Cook publications, write to Passport Books at the address on the back of the title page.

ON THE ROAD AROUND

Normandy,
Brittany and
The Loire Valley

A Comprehensive Guide
to Northern France
by Car

Edited by Roger Thomas

PASSPORT BOOKS
a division of NTC *Publishing Group*

Published by Passport Books,
a division of NTC Publishing Group
4255 West Touhy Avenue,
Lincolnwood (Chicago),
Illinois 60646-1975 USA.

Text:
© 1996 The Thomas Cook Group Ltd
Maps and diagrams:
© 1996 The Thomas Cook Group Ltd

ISBN 0-8442-9011-4
Library of Congress Catalog Card
  Number: 95-71675

Published by Passport Books in conjunction
with The Thomas Cook Group Ltd.

Managing Editor: Stephen York
Project Editor: Deborah Parker
Map Editor: Bernard Horton
Editorial Assistant: Kevin Flynn

Cover illustration by Michael Bennallack-
  Hart
Text design by Darwell Holland
Text typeset in Bembo and Gill Sans using
  QuarkXPress
Maps and diagrams created using Aldus
  Freehand and GST Designworks
Paris Metro map © RAPT
Printed in Great Britain by Albert Gait Ltd,
  Grimsby

Written and researched by
Lucy Koserski
John Lloyd
Elisabeth Morris
Matthew Hayes
Nia Williams

Book Editor: **Roger Thomas**

Series Editor: **Melissa Shales**

ABOUT THE AUTHORS

Roger Thomas has written and edited many books on travel, walking and historic sites, including *Thomas Cook Travellers Provence* and *On the Rails around France, Belgium, The Netherlands and Luxembourg*. He also writes for magazines and newspapers in the UK and USA. He enjoys driving classic cars, playing music and exploring his favourite countries – France, America, Ireland and Wales. He lives in the Brecon Beacons National Park in Wales with his wife and two sons.

Lucy Koserski, originally from Toronto, has lived in England since 1970. She began her career as a reporter on a daily newspaper in Hamilton, Ontario. In England she was deputy editor of *In Britain* magazine and became a freelance writer/editor in 1991, focusing on Britain and France. A member of the British Guild of Travel Writers, she contributes to guidebooks, magazines and newspapers. Her pastimes include exploring off-the-beaten-track, reading about historic links and visiting small museums.

John Lloyd is a freelance travel writer and photographer whose love-affair with France began some 25 years ago when he visited Brittany. Since then he has travelled extensively by car, bicycle and foot throughout the country in search of new experiences. His writings on Normandy have appeared in various travel guides as well as national and regional newspapers and magazine, both in Britain and the US. John is also editor of a monthly outdoor leisure magazine.

Elisabeth Morris was born in France and studied languages in London and at Lille University. She married an Englishman and settled in London, working as a freelance writer. Having been commissioned to write a series of books on the regions of France she turned to writing travel guides.

Since returning to France she has written a number of guidebooks, including *Thomas Cook Travellers Brittany*. She has travelled throughout Europe and North Africa, and her hobbies are classical music, history and discovering new horizons.

Matthew Hayes has lived in Paris for four years and works at the British Embassy. Having spent a year riding buses in India and scrubbing the decks of yachts in the South of France, he studied History and Art History at Nottingham University. A year out in Champagne then led him to Paris, where he now spends his time selling Champagne, tasting wine, and scouring the countryside for rare and tasty fungi. He is author of a guide to Liverpool.

Nia Williams has been a freelance writer and editor for the past 9 years. She has contributed to a number of travel books covering Britain and France.

ACKNOWLEDGEMENTS

5

The authors and publishers would like to thank the following people and organisations for their assistance during the preparation of this book:

André Bernicot, Association Pays des Abers-Côte des Légendes, Ploudalmézeau; Brittany Ferries; Victoria Coleman, Blue Badge Driver Guide; Comité Départmental de Tourisme for Calvados, Eure, Manche, Orne and Seine-Maritime; Sylvie Coguic, Office du Tourisme du Pays de Lorient, Lorient; Mlle Jacob, Office du Tourisme, Huelgoat; Sarah Jarvis; Mme Elodie Lampe; Monique Le Quéré, Office de Tourisme du Pays de Vannes, Vannes; Paul Ligtenberg, Comité Régional du Tourisme des Pays de la Loire; Stena Line; and the staff of all the Tourist Offices who so generously gave their time and expertise.

CONTENTS

ROUTES AND CITIES

In alphabetical order. For indexing purposes, routes are listed in both directions – the reverse direction to which it appears in the book is shown in italics.
See also the Route Map, p. 8, for a diagrammatic presentation of all the routes in the book.
To look up towns and other places not listed here, see the Index, p. 348.

7

REFERENCE SECTION

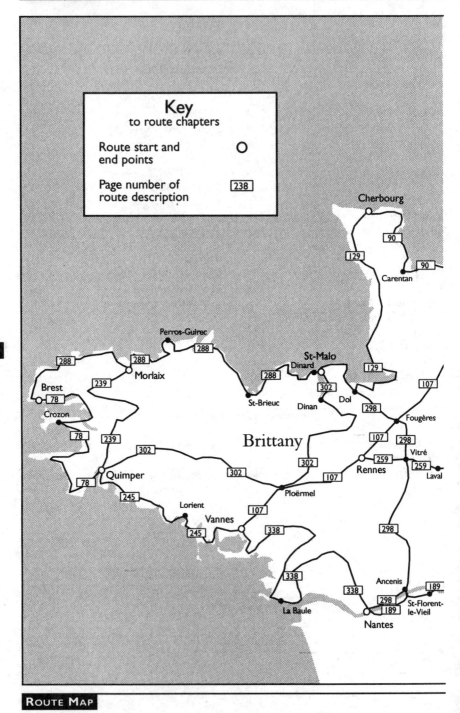

Key
to route chapters

Route start and
end points   O

Page number of   238
route description

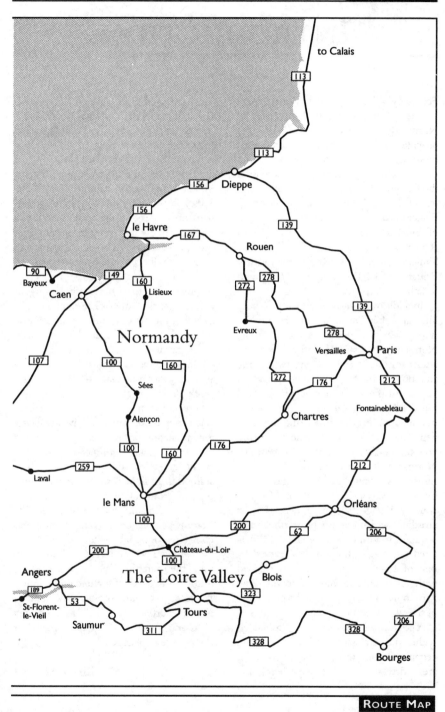

INTRODUCTION

For many visitors, this part of France represents a baptism of sorts. The roads of Normandy, Brittany and the Loire often provide the first experience of Continental motoring. It's easy to see why. A plethora of cross-Channel ferries (not to mention the Channel Tunnel) whisk you in a matter of hours from Britain to northern France. From London and the South-East of England, it's now quicker to get to Rouen or Paris than to much of Scotland. Similarly, direct crossings into the heart of Brittany make the journey as easy and straightforward as catching a bus.

In addition to those who are perhaps a little apprehensive about driving on the wrong side of the road for the first time, Normandy, Brittany and the Loire also attract seasoned travellers who return time and time again to this tempting part of France. At the outset, it should be pointed out that the area covered by this book is not an homogenous entity (the independent Bretons, for one, would not thank you for confusing them with Parisians). Normandy is an area of sweeping – and sometimes sophisticated – beaches backed by a flattish landscape of rich farming country. Rugged Brittany is defined by its coastline, which consists of breathtakingly beautiful headlands, savage cliffs and sheltered sands. The Loire Valley, carved by one of France's great rivers, is studded with châteaux and historic towns. And Paris, quite simply, is one of the great cities of the world.

Yet for all the diversity contained within the covers of this book, there are certain common threads. For much of this area, drivers will not experience the incessant grind of heavy traffic. France has about the same population as Britain but is four times larger. On cross-country routes, the traffic density is light. Along the coast – especially in the far-flung west – there are few bottlenecks, though popular spots can become busy in summer. The Loire Valley is a major communications artery, so main routes tend to be busy. But this book is not about getting from A to B in the quickest time (though we do try to give you a direct alternative to our meandering scenic routes). If you do have the flexibility, try to come in the spring or autumn, or the early or late summer (thus avoiding the brief but intense high season when every French family, lemming-like, is programmed to rush to the coast).

So motoring can still be a pleasure in France, as long as you do a little homework. You can also eat extremely well, wherever you travel. Though French cuisine is not as pre-eminent as it once was – a combination of Gallic complacency and increasing culinary competence in other countries – it's still pretty good. The seafood in Brittany is superb, and the butter and cream of Normandy underpin a rich and delicious regional cuisine. The Loire is famous for its wines, Paris for its choice of cosmopolitan cooking.

If you are driving in France for the first time, the routes in this book will ease you into the discovery of a wonderful country If you have been before but now want to venture further, you will find enough ideas and information on these pages for the next ten holidays.

Roger Thomas

HOW TO USE THIS BOOK

ROUTES AND CITIES

On the Road around Normandy, Brittany and The Loire Valley provides you with an expert selection of 30 recommended routes between key cities, towns and attractions of North-western France (plus the channel port of Calais and the capital, Paris), each in its own chapter. Smaller cities, towns, attractions and points of interest along each route are described in the order in which you will encounter them. Additional chapters are devoted to the major places of interest which begin and end these routes. These route and city chapters form the core of the book, from page 47 to page 342.

The routes have been chosen to take in as many places of interest as possible. Where applicable, an alternative route which is more direct is also provided at the beginning of each recommended route chapter. This will enable you to drive more quickly between the cities and towns at the beginning and end of the route, if you do not intend to stop at any of the intermediate places. To save space, each route is described in only one direction, but of course you can follow it in the reverse direction, too.

The arrangement of the text consists of a chapter describing a city or large town first, followed by chapters devoted to routes leading from that place to other major destinations; e.g. the port of St-Malo is described in one chapter (pp. 284–287), followed by routes from St-Malo to Brest (pp. 288–297), St-Malo to Nantes (pp. 298–301), and St-Malo to Quimper (pp. 302–306).

The key towns and city chapters are ordered alphabetically, followed by routes leading out from that starting point. Thus the first city is Angers (pp. 47–52) followed by the route from Angers to Saumur (pp. 53–56), followed Blois and a route from Blois, etc. To find the page number of any route or city chapter quickly, use either the alphabetical list on the **Contents** pages, pp. 6–7, or the master **Route Map** on pp. 8–9.

The routes are designed to be used as a kind of menu from which you can plan an itinerary, combining a number of routes which take you to the places you most want to visit.

WITHIN EACH ROUTE

Each route chapter begins with a short introduction to the route, followed by driving directions from the beginning of the route to the end, and a sketch map of the route and all the places along it which are described in the chapter. This map, not drawn to scale, intended to be used in conjunction with the driving directions, summarises the route and shows the main roads and road numbers; for a key to the symbols used, see p. 13.

DIRECT ROUTE

This will be the fastest, most direct, and sometimes, predictably, least interesting drive between the beginning and end of the route, usually along autoroutes and N roads.

SCENIC ROUTE

This is the itinerary which takes in the most places of interest, usually using secondary and minor roads. Road directions are specific; always be prepared for detours due to road construction, etc. The driving directions are followed by sub-sections describing the main attractions and places of interest along the way. You can stop at them all or miss out the ones which do not appeal to you.

Always ask at the local Tourist Office (Office du Tourisme) or tourist information centre (usually Syndicat d'Initiative) for more information on sights, guided tours, accommodation and places to eat at.

⇱ SIDE TRACK

This heading is occasionally used to indicate departures from the main route, or out-of-town trips from a city, which detour to worthwhile sights, described in full or highlighted in a paragraph or two.

CITY DESCRIPTIONS

Whether a place is given a half-page description within a route chapter or merits an entire chapter to itself, we have concentrated on practical details: local sources of tourist information; getting around in city and town centres (by car, by public transport or on foot as appropriate); accommodation and dining; communications; entertainment and shopping opportunities; and sightseeing, history and background interest. The largest cities have all this detail; in smaller places some categories of information are less relevant and have been omitted or summarised. Where there is a story to tell which would interrupt the flow of the main description, we have placed **feature boxes** on subjects as diverse as 'Megaliths', 'Parish closes' and 'Camembert'.

Although we mention good independently owned lodgings in many places, we always also list the hotel chains which have a property in the area, by means of code letters to save space. Many travellers prefer to stick to one or two chains with which they are familiar and which give a consistent standard of accommodation. The codes are explained on p. 344, and central booking numbers for the chains are also given there.

MAPS

In addition to the sketch map which accompanies each route, we provide maps of major city centres as well as smaller towns and ports. At the end of the book is a section of **colour road maps** covering the whole area described in this book, which is detailed enough to be used for trip planning. The **key to symbols** used on all the types of map in this book is shown on p. 13.

THE REST OF THE BOOK

At the front of the book, the **Contents** and **Route Map** pages have already been mentioned above. **Travel Essentials** is an alphabetically arranged chapter of general advice for the tourist new to France, covering a wide range of subjects from accommodation and currency to facilities for disabled travellers and telephones. **Driving in France** concentrates on advice for drivers on the law, rules of the road, and so on. **Background** gives a concise briefing on the history and geography of the three diverse regions covered in this book. **Touring Itineraries** provides ideas and suggestions for putting together an itinerary of your own using the selection of routes in this book. At the end of the book, **Driving Distances** is a tabulation of distances between main places, to help in trip planning. The

Hotel Codes and Central Booking Numbers page has already been described. To assist those with little knowledge of French, the **Language** section provides a number of useful phrases, together with phonetic spellings for ease of pronunciation. The **Conversion Tables** decode weights, measures and sizes for those outside continental Europe. Finally the **Index** is the quick way to look up any place or general subject. And please help us by completing and returning the **Reader Survey** at the very end of the text; we are grateful for both your views on the book and new information from your travels in Normandy, Brittany and the Loire Valley.

KEY TO MAP SYMBOLS

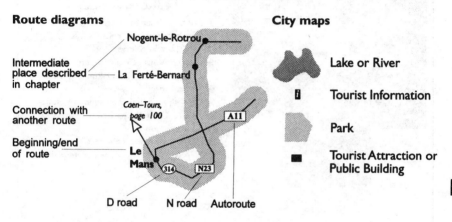

Route diagrams

Nogent-le-Rotrou

Intermediate place described in chapter — La Ferté-Bernard

Connection with another route — Caen–Tours, page 100

Beginning/end of route — Le Mans

A11

314   N23

D road   N road   Autoroute

City maps

Lake or River

🛈 Tourist Information

Park

■ Tourist Attraction or Public Building

13

KEY TO PRICE DESCRIPTIONS

It is impossible to keep up to date with specific tariffs for lodging and accommodation or restaurants, although we have given some general advice under 'Accommodation' in the Travel Essentials chapter on p. 15. Wherever possible, we have given the admission price to the sights mentioned under 'Sightseeing' in any city or place description, or the cost of any tours, boat-trips etc., but do remember that these are liable to change. The price quoted is usually the price per adult; if there is a price in brackets after the full price, then that is the cost per child.

ABBREVIATIONS USED IN THE BOOK
(For hotel chains, see p. 344)

av.	avenue		pl.	place
blvd	boulevard		r.	rue
Fr.	Franc		rte	route
hr(s)	hours		sq.	square
km	kilometres		tel:	telephone
m	metres		Jan, Feb are January, February, etc.	
min(s)	minute(s)		Sun, Mon are Sunday, Monday etc.	

T85

THOMAS COOK TRAVELLERS

This series of 192-page compact (192mm x 130mm) guides, each fully illustrated in colour and with completely new research and mapping, has been created for the holidaymaker of the 1990s by Thomas Cook Publishing and leading guidebook publishers AA Publishing.

Features include

★ Facts at your fingertips
★ Background information on history, politics and culture
★ Descriptions of major sights plus snippets about lesser known places
★ A 'get-away-from-it-all' section
★ A shopping and entertainment guide
★ An A-Z help list packed with practical information
★ Tips on 'finding your feet'
★ Up to 10 city walks or excursions with full-colour maps

Other titles in the series include:

☐ALGARVE ☐AMSTERDAM ☐BELGIUM ☐BERLIN ☐BOSTON & NEW ENGLAND ☐BUDAPEST ☐BRITTANY ☐CALIFORNIA ☐CANARY ISLANDS ☐CHINA ☐CRETE ☐CYPRUS ☐DELHI, AGRA AND RAJASTHAN ☐EASTERN CARIBBEAN ☐EGYPT ☐FLORENCE & TUSCANY ☐FLORIDA ☐GREECE (Mainland) ☐HAWAII ☐IRELAND ☐JAMAICA ☐JAVA & BALI ☐KENYA ☐LONDON ☐THE LOIRE VALLEY ☐MADEIRA ☐MALLORCA ☐MALTA ☐MEXICO ☐MIAMI & CARIBBEAN CRUISING ☐MOROCCO ☐MUNICH & BAVARIA ☐NEW YORK ☐NORMANDY ☐ORLANDO ☐PARIS ☐PRAGUE ☐PROVENCE ☐ROME ☐SINGAPORE & MALAYSIA ☐SOUTH AFRICA ☐SYDNEY & NEW SOUTH WALES ☐THAILAND ☐TUNISIA ☐TURKEY ☐VANCOUVER & BRITISH COLUMBIA ☐VENICE ☐VIENNA

Available in the UK from Thomas Cook shops, book shops, or by mail order from Thomas Cook Publishing, Dept (TPO/OWN), P.O. Box 227, PETERBOROUGH PE3 8BQ, UK. ☎ (01733) 505821/268943. These guides are published in the USA as Passport Illustrated Guides from Thomas Cook, and are available from bookstores.

TRAVEL ESSENTIALS

The following is an alphabetical listing of helpful tips for those planning a holiday to Normandy, Brittany and the Loire Valley.

ACCOMMODATION

This part of France offers all kinds of accommodation at all price ranges, from spartan youth hostels to unashamed five-star luxury. The Continental practice of paying by the room – as opposed to per person – can help budget travellers. Room rates can vary considerably. If you choose an upmarket Normandy resort or popular tourist spot along the Loire you can expect to pay more than for comparable accommodation in parts of inland Brittany or less fashionable stretches of the coast. Rural areas are good value for money, though competition in many resorts helps to keep prices down. In this book, we have identified *budget, moderate* and *expensive* accommodation. There are no hard-and-fast price bands. The descriptions relate to the area in which the accommodation happens to be located – for example, there might be little to choose, price-wise, between a 'moderate' Parisian hotel and an 'expensive' place elsewhere.

By law, the room rate must be displayed at the reception and in the rooms. A small supplement may be charged for three or four persons sharing a room. Breakfast (*petit déjeuner*) is generally extra. Hotels and restaurants may offer half board (*demi-pension*) and full board (*pension*). Local authorities classify hotels on a five-star grade scale. 'IC' (*Instance de Classement*) against a hotel in information leaflets means that the establishment is waiting for its grade to be awarded. Hotels that are unstarred (*sans étoile*) don't have the facilities required for one star, but might still represent good value for budget travellers: look at a room before taking it.

To give you some guidance in relation to prices, at time of going to press (spring 1996) an average price (based on the whole of France) for a comfortable two-star hotel would be around Fr.260–380 for a room for two. In Paris, the cost could be Fr.450–500 for equivalent accommodation.

If you are travelling out of season (along the coast in particular), it's wise to book ahead. Many resort hotels still abide by a strict season, closing for the winter as soon as the summer rush is over. The tourist offices mentioned in the text will usually help you find, and often reserve, hotel and other accommodation. This is almost always your best starting point if you haven't pre-booked. Don't be afraid to make clear to them your price horizons.

If you prefer to reserve some or all of your hotel rooms in advance, this can usually be arranged by Thomas Cook or another good travel agent (best done at the same time you buy your air ticket, if you are travelling from outside Europe). For those travellers who like to stay in hotels belonging to one of the branded international or national chains, we have indicated in the text which chains are represented in a town or city by means of initials in the 'Accommodation' section: e.g. *BW, Hd, Nv* means that the city has Best Western, Holiday Inn and Novotel properties (the initials used are explained on p 344). Further details can then be obtained from the chain's central reservation number in your own country (also on p. 344), or through your travel agent.

Camping

There are good campsites right across the area covered by this book (the French have a passion for camping, and even the smaller towns have good local sites). Facilities range from basic (clean toilets and showers) to luxury sites with dining rooms and swimming pools and even vast complexes of permanent tents aimed at package tourists with children. The various overseas French Government Tourist Offices (see Tourist Information) can provide listings. It's a good idea to book ahead or avoid popular areas in August, when the French flock to the coast. If you prefer to trust your luck, make sure that you always arrive in a new town with plenty of daylight to spare and ask at the local tourist office when you get there.

Don't camp uninvited or on private land; always check with the owner and obtain permission first, or you may be liable to prosecution for trespassing.

Gîtes, Cottages and Farmhouses

Gîtes are a very French form of accommodation, popular with those on a budget. They started up when the French government encouraged owners of redundant rural properties to convert them into holiday homes. Gîtes can be cottages, converted barns or farmhouses. Originally perceived as basic accommodation, many are now extremely comfortable. Details from **Gîtes de France**, *178 Piccadilly, London W1V 9DB; tel: (0171) 493 3480.*

The Thomas Cook France brochure offers farmhouse, cottage and campsite accommodation in the region

Chambres d'hotes are the French equivalent of the British bed and breakfast.

Hostelling International (HI)

The best bet, for those on a tight budget, is to join HI (Hostelling International), the new name for the IYHF (International Youth Hostel Federation). There is no age limit, membership of a national association will entitle you to use over 4,500 HI member association hostels in more than 60 different countries, and, next to camping, they are often the cheapest form of accommodation. Sleeping arrangements are usually in dormitory-style rooms, though some hostels also have smaller one- and two-bedded rooms. Many also have excellent-value dining, cooking and, in some cases, laundry facilities.

Membership for those over/under 18 is currently: A$44.50/$22.30 (Australia); C$25/$12 (Canada); NZ $30/$11 (New Zealand); £9.30/£3.20 (England and Wales); £6/2.50 (Scotland) $25/$10 (USA). A directory, *Hostelling International Europe* (£6.99), is available, listing addresses, contact numbers, locations and facilities of all HI member associations in Europe. Buy this upon joining, or from bookshops.

Hostels are graded according to their standard of comfort and facilities. Some, especially those in larger cities, are open 24 hours daily, while others have lock-out times. You are usually allowed to stay in a hostel for as long as you require but in peak periods, if you have not already booked to stay for more than three days, you may be asked to vacate your place to make way for newcomers.

Although it is not usually compulsory to reserve accommodation, hostels are often full in summer so you should book as far ahead as possible. In winter (except around Christmas) bookings can be slow, so it's worth asking if they have any special price deals. For information, to join, and to book accommodation in advance:

Australia *tel: (02) 565 1699*; Canada *tel: (613) 237 7884*; New Zealand tel: *(09) 379 4224*; UK *tel (0171) 836 1036*; USA *tel: (0202) 783 6161*.

Details of hostels are given in the accommodation section of individual town entries which appear either as major destinations at the start of routes or along the routes themselves. If no hostel is mentioned, it is still worth checking to see if this form of accommodation is available locally.

CHILDREN

Most popular tourist destinations are reasonably well adapted for children, with hygienic facilities, plenty of baby food and nappies. Baby-sitters are not that hard to find if you ask around – try the local tourist office or possibly the church. Many hotels will offer family rooms or provide a cot in a normal double. If you can't find suitable restaurants, you can always call at a coffee shop, snack bar or fast-food place which serves a children's menu or, at the very least, the sort of food they'll be inclined to try. Many sights, hotels and forms of transport will accept babies for free, and those under 12 for half-price.

CLIMATE

The climate in this part of France is not renowned for its excesses, especially along the coast. Summer in Brittany and along the shores of Normandy is usually pleasantly warm without being stifling, and winters are not unbearably cold. Inland, temperatures can vary more.

The Loire Valley, influenced by the climate of central France, can be hotter than the coast in summer.

The western seaboard comes under the influence of the Atlantic, so don't expect the guaranteed summer sun of the South of France.

CLOTHING

Most tourist spots in France are very informal these days and, unless you are planning to take society by storm, you'll rarely need evening clothes, or even a smart suit. You should make sure that you have some smart casual clothes (not jeans and trainers) for evening wear. People wearing shorts or sleeveless tops may be excluded from some churches, the most traditional of which still expect you to cover your head, so pack a long-sleeved shirt or blouse and a shawl or large scarf. You can encounter rain or cool weather no matter where you go, as at least one sweater or jacket and some sort of rainwear are essential.

CURRENCY

The currency of France is the French Franc (Fr.), which is divided into 100 centimes. There are 5, 10, 20 and 50 centime coins, and Fr. 1, 2, 5, 10 and 20 coins. Notes come in Fr. 20, 50, 100, 200 and 500 denominations (the old Fr.20 note is being replaced by the new Fr.20 coin).

European Union countries place no limit on the import/export of currency between member states (though you may be asked to declare large amounts – over Fr.50,000 for example – at French customs). That said, it is never advisable to carry more cash than necessary, and it is sensible to take most of money in the form of Eurocheques, travellers' cheques and credit cards. The latter are particularly convenient and widely accepted for most transactions, and often represent the best value in terms of commissions/charges.

Take travellers' cheques in Francs. You can cash travellers' cheques at most major banks and hotels (the bank Société Générale does not charge commission on Franc-denominated cheques). The Thomas Cook offices listed in this book will cash any type of Eurocheque/travellers' cheque and will replace Thomas Cook travellers' cheques if yours are lost or stolen. In case of loss or theft of Thomas Cook travellers' cheques *tel: 05 90 83 30* (toll-free 24-hr line).

CUSTOMS

As in most parts of the world, the importation of offensive weapons, pornography and narcotics is prohibited. If you are taking a prescribed drug on a regular basis, carry something (such as a doctor's letter) that will prove it is legitimate.

Duty-free allowances entering France and returning to EU countries

For those travelling between EU member countries, there are to all intents and purposes no restrictions in respect of goods bought in ordinary shops as long as they are intended for personal use. However, you may be questioned if you have excessive amounts. The indicative limits (which apply to anyone aged 17 or over) for tobacco and alcohol are:

800 cigarettes, 200 cigars, 400 cigarillos and 1 kg tobacco

+ 90 litres wine (max. 60 litres sparkling)

+ 10 litres alcohol over 22% volume (e.g. most spirits)

+ 20 litres alcohol under 22% volume (e.g. port and sherry)

+ 110 litres beer.

These allowances also apply when re-entering the UK or another EU country.

Duty-free allowances returning to non-EU countries

Allowances for those returning home to other parts of the world are as follows:

Australia: goods to the value of A$400 (half for those under 18) plus 250 cigarettes or 250 g tobacco and 1 litre alcohol.

Canada: goods to the value of C$300,

provided you have been away for over a week and have not already used up part of your allowance for that year. You are also allowed 50 cigars plus 200 cigarettes and 1 kg tobacco (if over 16) and 40 oz/1 litre alcohol.

New Zealand: goods to the value of NZ$700. Anyone over 17 may also take 200 cigarettes or 250 g tobacco or 50 cigars or a combination of tobacco products not exceeding 250 g in all, plus 4« litres of beer or wine and 1.125 litres spirits.

South Africa: 400 cigarettes, 250 g tobacco, 50 cigars; 1 litre spirits, 2 litres wine; 50 ml perfumeand 250 ml toilet water.

USA: goods to the value of US$400 as long as you have been out of the country for at least 48 hrs and only use your allowance once every 30 days. Anyone over 21 is allowed 1 litre alcohol plus 100 (non-Cuban) cigars and 100 cigarettes.

DISABLED TRAVELLERS

France, in theory, provides more facilities for the disabled traveller than most parts of the world. In practice, those facilities that do exist often fall short of real needs and expectations, and there is often a shortage of helpful bystanders to make up the difference. Travel is feasible, but it may be more expensive; for instance it is usually only the more upmarket hotels which have adequate access for guests in wheelchairs.

Holders of the Orange Badge in the UK will find that some concessions are made to cars displaying it; these vary from locality to locality. In Paris, for instance, disabled people are exempt from street parking charges and can claim a 75% discount on car park charges. Although there are no generally applicable parking concessions in France, police are expected to be sympathetic to the special parking needs of cars whose drivers or passengers have limited mobility – provided the parking is in a reasonable place.

More detailed advice can be obtained from:

UK: RADAR (Royal Society for Disability and Rehabilitation), Unit 12, City Forum, 250 City Road, London EC1V 8AF, tel: (0171) 250 3222 publishes a useful annual guide called *Holidays and Travel Abroad* (£5 inclusive of post and package). This gives details of facilities for the disabled in different countries.

For useful reading try: *The AA Guide for the Disabled Traveller* (AA Publishing, £3.95 – free to AA members); Alison Walsh, *Nothing Ventured: A Rough Guide Special* (Penguin, £7.99); Gordon Couch and Ben Roberts, *Access in Paris* (Quiller Press, £6.95).

USA: SATH (Society for the Advancement of Travel for the Handicapped), 347 5th Avenue, Suite 610, New York NY 10016; tel: (212) 447 7284.

Equivalent national organisations for disabled people in other countries will be able to offer advice and information to intending travellers with impaired mobility.

DISCOUNTS

Reductions are available on public transport and on entrance fees for senior citizens, students and the young. Some proof of your eligibility is usually required. Students should obtain an International Student Identity Card (ISIC) from their union, as this is recognised everywhere and offers a wider range of discounts than the national union card.

ELECTRICITY

The French system is 220V, using Continental two-pin round plugs. If you are taking any sort of electrical gadget, you will need a travel adaptor (these are inexpensive and widely available). It is unlikely that you will face power cuts, but a small torch (flashlight) is a useful back-up and essential if camping.

EATING AND DRINKING

Eating out is one of the great pleasures of France. Although in recent years a little complacency – and a touch of Euro-standardisation – has crept in, France can still offer superb eating experiences. If you are unlucky, you will wonder what all the fuss was about and come away with a jaded view of French cuisine. On the other hand, if you avoid the obvious tourist traps, you can eat extremely well for surprisingly few francs, especially if you choose the set-price menus, usually based on three courses. Overall, there is still a discriminating attitude to food in France and a love of good cooking which sets the country apart from other nations. When the food in France is good, it's very good. You will find that lunchtime set-price meals often offer better value than their evening equivalent. If you're on a budget, try to avoid the coffees, drinks and snacks eaten outside on the terrace. It may be enjoyable to sit back and watch the world go by, but it can be prohibitively expensive, especially if you are travelling as a family.

Breakfast, served in cafés and restaurants, is usually a light meal – a baguette or croissant with butter or jam, and coffee or hot chocolate. Lunch is served from midday until around 1400, and for dinner restaurants take orders from about 1700, with the rush coming between 2000 and 2100. Outside major tourist centres it's unusual for orders to be taken after 2100. Sunday lunch is a very busy time for most restaurants – book ahead if you can.

Brasseries tend to be more flexible than

restaurants, though they offer a more limited choice of food. Cafés usually charge less to eat or drink while standing at the counter (*comptoir*) than to sit at a table (*salle*) or outside (*terrasse*). Restaurants offer a range of set-price meals (*menu*) as well as the full menu choice (*à la carte*), which is usually more expensive. In some restaurants, especially in summer and in prime tourist locations, only the more expensive set-price menus are on offer if you sit outside.

Prices displayed outside restaurants should include all charges, including service (usually 15%). Customers can leave tips if they are especially pleased with the service.

Under recent legislation, smoking is restricted in cafés and restaurants, which are supposed to provide non-smoking areas – but don't count on it.

France has its own well-established fast-food tradition – baguette sandwiches at cafés, *crêpes* (pancakes) and *frites* (chips) at roadside stalls; the Quick chain is a French answer to McDonalds and Burger King, though these ubiquitous multinationals have a firm foothold in major cities.

HEALTH

There are no compulsory vaccination requirements for France. However, it is always advisable to keep your tetanus and polio protection up to date. You must be able to produce a certificate against yellow fever if you have been in a yellow fever endemic zone in the six days before entering Europe. It is a good idea to visit your dentist for a check-up before you leave home.

If you are a UK citizen, you can fill in Form E111 before you leave (available from your local health authority/doctor/post office). This form entitles you to treatment under the reciprocal arrangements that exist across most of Europe. However, the procedure is a bureaucratic one and you may have to pay up-front for treatment and reclaim the costs when you return home; additionally, you are only covered for medical care, not repatriation, so you are strongly advised to take out travel insurance (which will also cover you for holiday cancellation and other items – see 'Insurance').

If you happen to feel unwell while you re away, try visiting the pharmacy first before you make an appointment with the doctor, as French pharmacists tend to be well trained and may be able to advise you and prescribe treatment on the spot.

Dangers

Holiday romances are all very well, but don't get so carried away that you forget all about AIDS, which is as prevalent in France as anywhere else. Rabies exists across much of Continental Europe and, while the risk is very small, you should be wary of stray and wild animals. French tap water is safe to drink.

INSURANCE

You are strongly advised to take out travel insurance that covers your health as well as your belongings. It should also give cover in case of cancellation and include an emergency flight home if something goes really wrong. If you are likely to do something that might be classified as risky (e.g. drive a moped, dive), make sure that your insurance covers you for the activity concerned. The Thomas Cook Independent Traveller Insurance Package offers comprehensive medical insurance and is available from all Thomas Cook retail travel shops in the UK.

The Green Card which gives you comprehensive motoring cover is no longer required by law. But without it, you only have basic third-party cover, which is less in France than in Britain. You are therefore strongly advised to have Green Card cover – contact your insurance company for details.

LANGUAGE

Quite a few people can speak or understand a little English, particularly in Paris. But you should not rely on the efforts of others. Even if you only have the most rudimentary grasp of the language, your efforts to speak it will be appreciated, so don't be too self-conscious. A few of the most needed phrases can be found on pp. 345–346.

It's sensible to have a pen and paper handy at all times, so that you can ask people to write down figures such as times and prices.

OPENING HOURS

Banks open Monday to Friday or Tuesday to Saturday 0900–1200 and 1400–1600 or 1700. They usually close early on the day before a public holiday.

Museums are generally open 1900–1600 (extended evening hours may operate in the summer). Almost all national museums are closed on Tuesdays (except Versailles and Paris's Musée d'Orsay, which are closed on Mondays). Many municipal museums tend to close on Monday. On Sunday, entrance is often free or reduced in some museums. All museums tend to close on public holidays, Easter Sunday and Monday, and at Christmas.

Shops open Monday to Saturday 0900–1200 and 1430–1830; food shops tend to open earlier and on Sunday mornings. Large supermarkets and shopping complexes will stay open all day.

Please note that the times given are only intended as a rough guide. Don't, for instance, assume that every bank will be open during the banking hours listed – and you may find some that actually stay open longer. Although Sunday is the usual closing day for shops and businesses, many tourist attractions remain open – but will close on Monday or Tuesday. Timings are also subject to huge seasonal variations, with many places closing altogether in winter. Wherever possible we have detailed opening times of attractions in the text.

PASSPORTS AND VISAS

British and Irish visitors to France need a full valid passport. Non-European travellers may also need visas, especially if they are intending to stay for more than 90 days – check with your nearest French Consulate well before departure.

POST OFFICES

These open Monday to Friday 0800–1200 and 1430–1900, Saturday 0800–1200. Offices in town and city centres don't usually close for lunch. They are easily recognised by their yellow signs with *La Poste* in blue. Post boxes, small metal boxes fixed to the wall, are also in yellow.

There can be long queues at post office counters, but many now have self-service franking machines which weigh letters and packages and print franked stickers (there's usually an English-language instructions option). Stamps can also be bought from shops and cafés showing the red diamond-shaped Tabac sign. A postcard or letter (up to 20 g) from France costs Fr.2.80 to EU countries, Fr. 4.30 to overseas.

You can have post sent for collection c/o Poste Restante, Poste Centrale, in most towns you intend to visit (offices will hold the mail for up to a month). To collect you have to show proof of identity – usually a passport or driver's licence – and pay a small fee.

PUBLIC HOLIDAYS

France has 11 official public holidays, most of which mark religious occasions, though some celebrate historical events.

New Year 1 January; Easter Monday late March or early April; Labour Day 1 May; VE Day 8 May; Ascension Day five weeks after Easter Day; Whit Monday late May; Bastille Day 14 July; Assumption 15 August; All Saints 1 November; Armistice Day 11 November; and Christmas Day 25 December.

Holidays are sometimes extended by shops and cafés if they fall on Tuesday or Thursday to include the preceding Monday or following Friday.

SALES TAX

TVA, Value Added Tax (VAT in the UK) is automatically added to most goods in France. Non-residents can claim the tax back, though there is the deterrent of the usual impenetrable bureaucracy to contend with. Refunds can be reclaimed on major items of expenditure. If you spend more than Fr.2000 in one shop, ask for a TVA reclaim form which must be completed and stamped by the sales person (not all shops operate this service). When you leave France you will need to present the form(s) at Customs for verification before reclaiming any refund.

SECURITY

The best way to avoid becoming a victim of theft is to try and give the impression that you are not worth robbing (e.g. do not flash expensive jewellery or rolls of banknotes). Use a hidden money-belt for your valuables, travel documents and spare cash. Never carry a wallet in your back pocket or leave your handbag open, and use a bag with a shoulder strap slung hori-

zontally. In all public places – especially crowded markets – take precautions with anything that is obviously worth stealing. Never leave luggage unattended – even if it isn't stolen, France nowadays is very terrorist-conscious, and chances are that it will be reported as a possible bomb.

Mugging is a problem in some areas, but as a rule it is not rife in city centres, although pickpockets are a real risk there. If you are attacked, it is safer to let go of your bag or hand over the small amount of obvious money – you are more likely to be attacked physically if the thief meets with resistance. If you do run into trouble, you must report it to the local police, even if it is only to get a copy of their report for your insurance company.

Finally, take half a dozen passport photos (useful for all kinds of purposes) and photocopy the important pages and any visa stamps in your passport. Store these safely, together with a note of the numbers of your travellers' cheques, credit cards and insurance documents (keep them separate from the items themselves). If you are unfortunate enough to be robbed, you will at least have some identification, and replacing the documents will be much easier.

TELEPHONES

The French telephone system, run by the state-owned France Telecom, is considered one of the best in the world. Public phone boxes, which are widely available, are free-standing clear glass cabins with *Téléphone* signs or the France Telecom logo (a digital dialling pad enclosed in an oval) on the handle. In city centres and major tourist centres phones have instructions in English and French (including current tariff and international dialling codes). There are a few coin-operated phone boxes but most now take only

---

New phone numbers

From 18 October 1996 the following new telephone numbers will come into operation in France:

1. The existing eight-figure number will be replaced by a ten-figure number, consisting of two new figures added before the existing number – 01 Paris and outskirts, 02 North-West France, 03 North-East France, 04 South-East France, 05 South-West France.
2. To dial from Paris to the Provinces and vice versa, you will dial the new ten-figure number. Numbers 16 and 161 will no longer be used.
3. To dial abroad from France, 19 will be replaced by 00 followed by the country dialling code (e.g. 0044 for the UK).

---

phone cards (*télécartes*), sold at post offices and newsagents. A 50-unit card costs Fr.40, a 120-unit card Fr.96.

The following describes the current phone number system in France, and is valid until 18 October 1996. After that, see the box below.

There are two telephone regions within France: Paris and the Provinces. All numbers have eight digits. Paris numbers start with a 4, numbers in the Paris outskirts with a 3 or a 6. The prefix for calls from Paris to the Provinces is 16, and from the provinces to Paris 161. Domestic calls are cheaper on weekdays between 2230 and 0800, and at weekends after 1400 on Saturday. For the operator dial 13, for directory enquiries dial 12.

International calls can be made from phone boxes and some large post offices have a metered call service where you book a booth, make the call and then pay. To phone abroad dial 19 and wait for the dialling tone, then dial the country code

(44 for the UK, 353 for Ireland, 1 for USA or Canada, 61 for Australia, 64 for New Zealand, 27 for South Africa) and finally the area code (excluding any initial 0) and number. For the international operator, dial 00, wait for the dialling tone and then dial 33 12 and the country code. British Telecom produces a helpful free booklet, *A Guide to Calling the UK from Abroad*. There is also a France Telecom leaflet, *Call Home with a Télécarte*.

To phone France from abroad dial your own international code, e.g. 00 from the UK, then 33 (except for Paris, which is 331), then the eight-digit number.

Emergency calls are free. For the police dial 17; for the fire service (*Pompiers*) dial 18; and for ambulance and emergency medical care (*SAMU*) dial 15.

TIME

France is GMT (Greenwich Mean Time) + 1 hr in winter, GMT + 2 hrs in summer. Thus it is always 1 hour ahead of the UK (apart from a week in October when France is still on summer time and UK already on winter time).

TOILETS

Toilets are usually single-sex (Men *Messieurs*, Women, *Dames*), but automatic coin-operated unisex cabins are now a familiar feature in streets and parks. In public places such as stations there is often an attendant collecting money at the entrance; you may be expected to pay for toilet paper.

TOURIST INFORMATION

In France, a wide network of tourist offices provides information on local accommodation, where to eat, attractions, transport and entertainment. In most towns, they are known as *Syndicats d'Initiatives* or *Offices de Tourisme*; offices in

23

larger centres are called *Acceuil de France*. These offices are the best places to help you get your bearings in a new town, especially if you don't speak any French. English is often spoken, and services include free literature and hotel booking.

Useful Addresses in the UK

Consulate General, *21 Cromwell Road, London SW7 2EN; tel: (0171) 838 2000*. Maison de la France (Tourist Office), *178 Piccadilly, London W1V 0AL; tel: 0891 244 123* (calls charged at 39p per minute cheap rate and 49p per minute at all other times).

Useful Addreses in the Republic of Ireland

Embassy, *36 Ailesbury Road, Dublin 4; tel: (1) 694 777*. French Government Tourist Office, *35 Lower Abbey Street, Dublin 1; tel: (1) 77 18 71*.

Useful Addresses in the USA

Embassy, *4101 Reservoir Road NW, Washington DC 20007; tel: (202) 944 6000*. French Government Tourist Office, *610 Fifth Avenue, New York, NY 10020-25452; tel: (212) 757 1125*.

Useful Addresses in Canada

Embassy, *42 Promenade Sussex, Ottowa, Ontario K1M 2C9; tel: (613) 512 1715*. French Government Tourist Office, *1 Dundas Street West, Suite 24005, Box 8, Toronto, Ontario; tel (416) 593 4722*.

Useful Addresses in Australia

Consulate, *31 Market Street, Level 26, Sydney NSW 2000; tel: (2) 261 5779*. French Government Tourist Office, *BNP House, 12 Castlereagh Street, Sydney NSW 2000; tel: (2) 231 5244*. Thomas Cook Limited, *175 Pitt Street, GPO Box 3590, Sydney NSW 2000; tel: (2) 229 6611*.

Useful Addresses in South Africa

Consulate, *35th Floor, Carlton Centre, Commissioners Street, Johannesburg 2001; tel (11) 333 468*. French Government Tourist Office, *PO Box 41022, Craig Hall, Johannesburg 2024; tel (11) 880 8062*.

USEFUL READING

The *Thomas Cook Travellers* worldwide series, published in the USA and Canada as *Passport's Illustrated Travel Guides*, includes volumes on Normandy, Brittany, The Loire Valley and Paris. These colour-illustrated guides are available from any UK branch of Thomas Cook and most bookshops in the UK, USA, Canada, Australia, New Zealand and South Africa. UK standard price is £7.99, US $12.95. Most other established guidebook series also contain titles on the regions covered in this book. Travellers looking for very detailed coverage of cultural, historical and architectural sights will find either the Michelin Green Guides or the Blue Guides (A & C Black) worth seeking out.

WHAT TO TAKE

The dilemma for holidaymakers taking their own cars across the Channel from the UK and Ireland is that although they can pack nearly their entire household in the car (and many seem to do just that), this conflicts with the desire to leave as much free space as possible for the return trip to carry large-scale purchases of the low-price wine, beer and foodstuffs without which seemingly no trip to France is complete. If you are tempted to include everything you might conceivably need, bear in mind that much of it will have to be left in the car every day, with the attendant risks of theft, not to mention the inconvenience. Visitors from overseas who are planning to hire a car will encounter the baggage restrictions of the air trip.

DRIVING IN FRANCE

This chapter provides practical advice for those taking to the road in France. First-timers will find that any early apprehension soon disappears, as the roads are generally good and often surprisingly empty. Visitors from overseas will be used to driving on the right, although speeds on major roads may be higher than those they are accustomed to.

BASIC REQUIREMENTS

To drive in France you must carry a full and valid driver's licence and, if you take your own car, a vehicle registration document. If the car is not registered in your name you will need a letter of authorisation from the owner. You should also carry an insurance certificate and display a nationality plate.

If driving your own car, you should carry an International Insurance Certificate (green card), which can be obtained from your insurers; this provides immediate proof of insurance in case of an accident. Green cards are issued for periods of eight, 15 or 30 days.

It is advisable to carry a warning triangle (compulsory for cars towing a caravan or trailer). It is strongly advised that you carry a complete spare-bulb set, as it is illegal to drive with faulty lights. You must have headlamp converters to deflect the beams on left-hand drive cars. Yellow-tinted headlights are not compulsory for tourist vehicles.

DISTANCES AND SPEEDS

In France these are always in kilometres (km) and kilometres per hour (k.p.h.) and these units are used throughout this book. A kilometre is 0.6 of a mile; a mile is 1.6 km. For further conversions, see the table on p. 347.

ROADS

France has an excellent system of motorways and major roads, and even the minor roads in most areas are well maintained. They are classified by letter and number: A roads, *autoroutes*, are motorways (freeways); other main roads carry the prefix N, for *route nationale*; other roads are designated by D, for *départementale*, i.e. maintained by local government; hence the number may change as you cross into a new *département*.

In recent years there have been several changes to the numbering system, making N roads D roads (sometimes retaining the same number, sometimes gaining a new one) – but up-to-date maps and guides will give a clear idea of the current system. New roads are providing links between Paris and the Channel Tunnel (A16); between Calais and Rouen (A28) and between Calais, Rouen and Le Havre and eastern France (A29).

Main roads from Paris and other big cities are best avoided just before and just after public holidays and near Assumption Day (15 August); the outer and inner ring roads around Paris are always very busy. A leaflet is distributed at motorway offices listing the most congested days and routes. The government's *Bison Futé* scheme (see 'Information and Maps' below) is designed to divert tourist traffic from the roads most prone to congestion and on to speedier through-routes.

25

Autoroutes

Except for limited stretches of road approaching cities and large towns, most autoroutes are toll roads. Toll booths (*péages*) may be situated at motorway exits, or at the point where a free stretch of road begins, or where one network meets another. Some credit cards are accepted for sums over Fr.50. As you enter the toll road, collect a ticket (you may need to press a button first) from a machine on the right hand side; hand this in at the booth at the exit. The attendant will tell you the sum due, if you haven't worked it out from the ticket, and usually you can also read it on an electronic display. On some networks smaller sums are paid at automatic, change-giving machines or maybe thrown (exact money only) into large nets. Tolls vary according to the type of vehicle: motorcycles pay less and cars with caravans more than single cars. Near many toll stations there are picnic areas, and most have toilets and phones.

Every 10 km or so along the motorways are *aires*, or rest places, some of which have eating and play areas and even exercise circuits and sports facilities. Several have phones, operated with phonecards, and in some places there are nappy-changing and feeding caravans. Several *aires* have snack bars, open only during the peak summer months; other kiosks and restaurants are sited along motorway routes, providing service ranging from basic to semi-luxurious. All-year snack bars open at least 14 hours a day; some stay open all night and there is a chain of drive-in cafés. You'll find snack areas in a few petrol stations, a few of which offer cooked meals. Self-service restaurants (*cafétéria*) tend to open 16 to 17 hours a day; some are open 24 hours. Restaurants (*grill*) are rather more formal, with table service, set menus and *à la carte*,

and are more expensive than the self-service variety. They usually open for three to four hours in the middle of the day and for three hours in the evening, but some are restricted to lunchtimes outside the peak tourist season.

Autoroutes are generally considered to be safer than other roads, as well as faster, but naturally drivers wanting to linger and enjoy the scenery should opt for the *routes nationales* (N roads) and *routes départementales* (D roads).

ROAD SIGNS

Standard international European road signs are used throughout France, except for the odd corners of remote regions where older versions still display local place-names in wood or stone. International signs indicate their meaning by their shape: triangular for hazard warnings; circular for instructions and rectangular for general information.

To reach a town or city centre, follow the *Centre Ville* sign. Avoid roads marked with signs reading *seulement riverains* (residents only) or *sauf riverains* (except for residents): these indicate private roads and are mainly found in smaller towns and villages. Market towns also have signs to specify market days, and you should avoid driving into the square or parking there before stalls are set up.

RULES OF THE ROAD

The minimum age for driving in France is 18. Seatbelts must be worn by the driver and front- and back-seat passengers. Children under ten cannot travel in the front of a vehicle unless the child is in a specially approved fitted seat facing backwards.

Driving is on the **right**. Priority is usually given to traffic approaching from the right. In built-up areas drivers must give way to cars turning out of side roads on

Common Road Signs

absence de marquage no road markings	*ralentir/ralentissez* slow down
aire (de repos) rest area	*rappel* remember – a reminder of
cédez le passage give way (yield)	restrictions applying to your route, such
chantier/travaux road works	as speed limits
chausée déformée uneven surface	*renseignements* information
chausée glissante slippery road	*restez sur votre file* stay in your lane
dépassement interdit no overtaking	*route barrée* road closed
déviation diversion (detour)	*sens unique* one-way street
gravillons loose chippings	*sens interdit* no entry
péage toll	*servez la droite/gauche* keep to your right/left
périphérique ring road (around a city)	*stationnement interdit* no parking
priorité aux piétons pedestrians have right of	*toutes directions* through-traffic route
way	*voie de détresse* escape road
prochaine sortie next exit	*voie rétrécie* road narrows

the right. However, a yellow diamond and the words *passage protégé* (right of way) means that the main road has priority over secondary roads merging from the right; but if a black line runs through the diamond, the main road has no priority and traffic approaching from the right has precedence. At roundabouts (traffic circles/rotaries) where a sign shows a circle of arrows and the words *cédez le passage* (give way), priority is given to cars already on the roundabout (traffic circle or rotary), rather than those waiting to enter. If there are no such signs, assume that traffic entering has priority over traffic already on the roundabout.

If a driver flashes his headlights in France, he is usually indicating that he has priority and that you should give way (unlike in Britain, where it can mean the opposite).

Never overtake on the right. If you do overtake a car, return immediately to the right-hand lane. Overtaking where there is a solid single centre line is heavily penalised.

Speed limits

Unless otherwise stated and on dry roads:
130 k.p.h. on toll motorways (110 k.p.h. on wet roads). There is a minimum speed requirement of 80k.p.h in clear weather in the outside (left-hand) lanes of motorways. **110 k.p.h.** on non-toll motorways and dual carriageways (divided highways) – 100 k.p.h. on wet roads. **90 k.p.h.** on other roads (80 k.p.h. on wet roads). **50 k.p.h.** in towns (the town name starts the limit, a bar through the town name is the derestriction sign). There is a **50 k.p.h.** limit on motorways in foggy conditions when visibility is less than 50 m.

POLICE AND SECURITY

Heavy on-the-spot fines can be imposed by French police for driving violations. Those without the ready cash to pay can sometimes offer vouchers if they have insurance cover. Drivers who wish to argue their innocence can choose to pay a deposit – an *amende forfaitaire* – and take a

27

receipt in exchange. Anyone arrested by the police has the right to contact their consulate (for addresses and phone numbers, see p. 225).

Drink-driving laws are strictly enforced: the limit is 80mg per 100ml of blood and police operate random breath tests. Failure of the test can lead to a large fine or a ban from driving in France. Fines can also be handed out for speeding, not wearing a seat belt and failing to stop at a red light.

In towns and cities the police are eagle-eyed and thorough when it comes to illegal parking. Again they have the power to deliver on-the-spot fines, or to have the offending car towed away or clamped.

The biggest security problem for motorists is theft from cars; those carrying foreign number plates are particularly vulnerable. Never leave luggage or other valuables within sight in the car; if your tape deck or radio is detachable, always remember to lock it in the boot before leaving your vehicle. If anything is stolen from your car phone 17 for the police: you must report the theft in person and sign a written statement at the nearest *gendarmerie* (police station). Contact your insurance office at the first opportunity. Car theft is less prevalent, though it has been an increasing problem during recent years in the larger cities and especially in Paris.

(for addresses and phone numbers, see p. 225).

ACCIDENTS AND BREAKDOWNS

If you are unlucky enough to break down, move your car off the road and onto the roadside. All motorists should carry a red warning triangle; place this 30–50 m behind the car and flash your hazard warning lights. On major roads there should be no problem finding an emergency phone: orange *postes d'appel d'urgence* are placed every 4 km on main routes and every 2 km on the motorways. Some motorway phones are equipped with flashing lights to warn drivers of approaching hazards. To operate the phone, press the button and wait until you hear a reply before speaking. If your French is up to it, give exact details of your location, your car model and, if possible, of the cause or nature of the problem. Local garages are open for breakdown services every day of the week, including holidays, 24 hours a day. Their charges for towing and car repairs are set by the state and specified on the emergency phones. An extra 25 per cent is charged for night-time, weekend and holiday repairs.

In the event of a breakdown on a remote country road, open the bonnet of the car and tie something white to the door handle or the radio aerial.

If you are involved in an accident you have to inform the police: dial the emergency number, 17, to reach them and the ambulance service. You will need to provide a signed statement of events (a *constat á l'aimable* – you may need a translator for this), and to swap your insurance details with any other motorist involved. Make sure you keep copies of any documentation to present as evidence to your insurance company.

Thomas Cook (in the UK) and some motoring associations offer breakdown assistance abroad. Most schemes provide roadside help and alternative travel and accommodation arrangements, and some can meet the cost of transporting the car back home. The AA operates an English-speaking emergency centre at Lyon, which is open 24 hours a day, every day of the year.

CAR HIRE

Booking a car in advance can be cheaper than hiring on the spot, especially as part of a fly-drive or train-car package, best organised through travel agents in your home country. Most international car hire companies have offices in the major French cities and at airports, ferry ports and large railway terminals. It is also possible to hire from French national, regional and local companies – their details are usually available from French Government Tourist Offices. French car hire firms with several city branches include **Citer, Dergi Cie Location** and **Mattei**. On the whole, the smaller the company, the more restricted the service. For example, you may have to return the car to the same office; and during holidays and peak travel times there may be few or even no cars available.

To hire a vehicle in France you have to be over 21 (25 with some hire companies) and in possession of a valid driving licence with one or two years' driving experience. Credit cards are preferred for most bookings (otherwise the company will demand a substantial cash deposit. Some firms impose a maximum age ranging between 69 and 75.

Fee options vary and can include a per-day, per-kilometre charge (often with a free allowance of kilometres each day); or flat rates on a daily, weekly or monthly basis. Collision damage waiver also adds to the price, and it may be worth checking whether your own insurance covers this option (though many major hire companies include the waiver charge automatically). Personal accident insurance is only necessary for those not covered by a general policy.

Make sure your hired car is equipped with a spare tyre and jack, and preferably with a first aid kit, torch, warning triangle and petrol container.

INFORMATION AND MAPS

Members of motoring associations – the AA in the UK, AAA in the USA and their international equivalents – can obtain a fairly wide range of information and advice before starting out. They can draw up pre-planned travel itineraries designed to avoid the most congested and busy routes; they will also book accommodation and provide a route map, and members can ring an information line for recorded details of the traffic conditions abroad.

The routes in this book often use a maze of minor roads and although the driving instructions and route diagrams provide the basic information, and the colour maps at the end of the book give an overview of the road system, good road maps will be essential. Road maps are published by some motoring clubs and by Michelin, who produce national and regional maps as well as a series of sectional 'close-up' maps. Probably the best maps are those of the official IGN (Institut Géographique National) – for more details see the Thomas Cook offer on pp. 30–31.

Scales of 1:200,000 are the best options for route planning, but larger scales will be needed for detailed exploration.

Information points are stationed at the first and last toll booths of each motorway network. Most provide free motorway maps showing the *Bison Futé* fast routes, avoiding areas prone to traffic hold-ups, as well as information centres, restaurants, garages and hotels. Maps can also be obtained from garages showing the *Bison Futé* sign, from tourist offices and from **Autoroutes Information,** *3 rue Edmond Valentin, 75007 Paris (47 05 90 01).* Phone information about roadworks is available (in French), tel. *Paris 48 94 33 33.* Electronic displays placed a couple of kilometres before some motorway exits give the latest news about traffic conditions on the next route.

Discover Northern France with IGN mapping

Thomas Cook Publishing gives you easy access to the best maps of the region

The maps of the Institut Géographique National, France's official cartographers, are renowned for their clarity and detail, making them ideal companions for the touring motorist.

These full-colour relief maps carry a wealth of information, including minor roads, villages, sightseeing features and scenic viewpoints

Thomas Cook Publishing can supply both the Red series of regional touring maps and the Green series ('Série Verte') of larger-scale local maps for the places covered in this book.

Simply choose the maps you want, and order directly from Thomas Cook Publishing by phone, fax or post, quoting the reference numbers on the display opposite.

Send your order, stating delivery address, to:

IGN Map Offer
Thomas Cook Publishing
P O Box 227
Peterborough
PE3 8BQ   Phone: 01733 (International +44 1733) 505821
United Kingdom   Fax: 01733 (international +44 1733) 267052

Methods of payment:
- Sterling cheque drawn on a UK bank
- Eurocheque in £ sterling
- Credit Card: Mastercard · Visa · American Express
Please quote card number, expiry date, cardholder name and address.
Prices include postage and packing. Please allow 14 days for delivery.

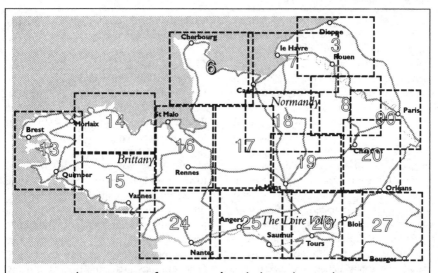

Please quote *reference numbers* below when ordering.

Red Series
Regional Touring Maps 1:250,000 (1 cm=2.5 km/1 in.= 10 miles)

Normandy *102* · Paris and Île-de-France *103* · Brittany *105*
Loire Valley *106*

Green Series
Local Excursion Maps 1:100,000 (1 cm=1 km/1 in.= 4 miles)

Abbéville to Rouen *3* · Cherbourg Peninsula *6* · Rouen to Caen *7*
Rouen to Paris *8* · Brest and Quimper *13* · Brittany North Coast *14*
Brittany South Coast *15* · St-Malo to Rennes *16* · Argentan to Laval *17*
Caen to Alençon *18* · Chartres to Le Mans *19* · Chartres to Orléans *20*
Châteaubriant to Nantes *24* · Angers to Chinon *25* · Orléans to Tours *26*
Orléans to Bourges *27* · Paris region *90*

Price per map (either series)
inclusive of postage and packing to

UK	Continental Europe	Outside Europe
2nd class post	Airmail	Airmail
£4.69	£5.39	£5.99

PARKING

Peak-season parking can be something of a nightmare in towns and cities. The easiest option is probably to head for an underground or covered car park, indicated with a blue 'P' sign. If you do park on the street, go for the more inexpensive short-stay parking in *stationnement payant* areas. Parking meters and ticket machines take coins, so equip yourself with plenty of small change. On-street parking may be restricted in some areas to one side of the road, every other day (odd or even dates). These zones are indicated with signs reading *côté du stationnement, jours pairs/impairs*.

Parking is forbidden on roads where the kerb is marked with yellow paint. Cars found in illegally parked are clamped or towed away to *fourrières* (pounds) and not released until the driver has paid a hefty fee, as well as the parking fine.

FUEL

Petrol (gas), or *essence*, is supplied in three basic grades: *gazole* (diesel), *essence super* (98 octane leaded petrol) and *super sans plomb* (98 octane unleaded petrol). Minimum filling is 5 litres. Large supermarkets generally sell petrol at lower prices than other stations. Costs may be lower in provincial towns and in the countryside. On the whole motorway stations are pricier than others. In rural areas stations are fewer and tend to shut on Sundays and public holidays; not all of them sell unleaded fuel. On the motorways petrol stations are usually open 24 hours a day, and may have many other facilities.

32

Driving vocabulary

Unleaded (lead-free)/Standard/Premium Sans plomb/normal/super *Sahng plong/normall/sewpehr*
Fill the tank please. Le plein s'il vous plaît. *Ler plahng seelvooplay.*
How do I reach the motorway/main road? Pour aller jusqu'à l'autoroute/la route principale? *Poor ahleh zhewskah lowtohroot/lah root prahngsipahl?*
I've had a breakdown at . . . Je suis tombé(e) en panne à . . . *Zher sewee tombay ahng pan ah . . .*
I am on the road from . . . to . . . Je suis sur la route de . . . à . . . *Zher sewee sewr lah root der . . . ah . . .*
I have a flat tyre. J'ai un pneu crevé. *Zhai ang punerr krervay.*
The windscreen (windshield) has smashed/cracked. Le pare-brise est cassé/fendu. *Ler pahrbreez ay kahseh/fahngdew.*

There is something wrong with the engine/brakes/lights/steering/gearbox/clutch/exhaust. Il y a un problème avec le moteur/les freins/les feux/la direction/la boîte à vitesses/l'embrayage /le pot d'échappement. *Eeleeyah ang problairm ahvek ler mowturr/leh frahng/leh fur/lah deerehk-seeawng/lah bwahtahveetess/lahngbrayyazh/ler poh dehshahpmahng.*
It won't start. La voiture ne démarre pas. *Lah vwahtewr ner dehmahr pah.*
Will it take long to fix? La réparation prendra longtemps? *Lah rehpahrasseeawng prahngdrah lohngtahng?*
Can you help me? There has been an accident. Vous pouvez m'aider? Il y a eu un accident. *Voo poovay mayday? Eelyaew ang akseedahng.*
Please call the police/an ambulance. Appelez la police/une ambulance s'il vous plaît. *Ahperlay lah poleess/ewn ahngbewlahngss seelvooplay.*

BACKGROUND

The three regions that occupy the north-western quarter of France take in a surprisingly wide variety of landscapes. Brittany and Normandy, strung along the Atlantic seaboard, are still popularly defined by their ancient duchy boundaries, despite being split into administrative *départements*. The Loire Valley, made up of the historic provinces of Orléanais, Touraine, Maine, Anjou, Poitou and Berry, straddle the country's longest river as it cuts across this swathe of France from north-west to south-east. Sharp contrasts of scenery characterise the Breton coast, known as *Armor* ('on the sea'), ranging from brooding, craggy cliffs and fierce seas in the north and western Finistère to the quiet, sandy bays of the south. Innumerable islands are scattered off its shoreline, some fertile and accessible – such as Belle-Île, the largest island, which lies off Quiberon – others remote and barren. Further inland, Brittany becomes the *Argoat* ('woodlands') – a land of forests and gorse, growing gentler towards the Loire in the south. Its air of legend and mystery, based on a strong Celtic heritage, is enhanced by the prehistoric megaliths that survive throughout the region (see p. 34).

The Normandy coast enjoys a rather more elegant reputation in resorts such as Fécamp and Deauville, and combines the bustle of working ports with cheerful tourism in towns such as Dieppe. The aftermath of the region's central role in the German occupation and D-Day battles of World War II can be seen at Le Havre, with its rebuilt post-war centre, and in the many cemeteries and war museums. The agricultural hinterland has fed and watered the residents of Paris for centuries, and its wealth of historic monuments, castles and religious buildings recall a vigorous past of empire-building and territorial tugs-of-war.

Parts of the Loire Valley are equally productive, servicing the cities from their vineyards, forests and cornfields. The valley embraces the so-called Granary of France, the rich Beauce, as well as the more infertile country of muddy and sandy flatlands nearer the river itself. Prone to heavy flooding, the Loire is protected by a raised bank – a *levée* – which runs from the old royal town of Blois east to Angers. The region is built on dark shale to the east, in 'Black Anjou', and on white tufa further to the west in Touraine – the striking rock used in the Loire Valley's ostentatious châteaux, which, with their proud towers and turrets, reflect the area's historic significance as a focus of French royal power.

Brittany, Normandy and the Loire Valley have been at the turbulent heart of French history. Politically and geographically attached to the French state, Brittany and Normandy are still conscious of their own distinct pasts and cultures, heavily influenced by their positions along the north-western coast. The provinces of the Loire Valley were an integral part of the web of possessions and rivalries spun out by medieval monarchy, and provided the power-base of the Plantagenet dynasty.

But resistance both to the crown and to the post-revolutionary secular state has

33

marked the history of all three regions. All have been the battlegrounds of warring kings and nobles; their territories have been subject to the kings of France and of England, to dukes and to counts, passed from hand to hand in treaties, dowries and invasion. Each region, in its heyday, has enjoyed a taste of power or independence; and each has been the scene of violent clashes when that power has been threatened or destroyed.

BRITTANY

Brittany's dramatic, often bleak landscapes provide an appropriate setting for some of the earliest **megalithic sites** in Europe. These vast slabs of stone, arranged in avenues or in circles, free-standing or as 'tables' of horizontal rocks laid across vertical columns, are evidence of a rich prehistoric civilization, though their original purpose remains a mystery. Theories have ranged from ancestor-worship to astronomy to an excuse for a community jamboree. As the earliest stones (at Carnac, about 5700 BC) and the latest are five millennia apart, it seems likely that their role may have varied considerably across the years. Theorists also come up against the inconvenient effects of time, elements and humanity on the stones, which have been moved, pilfered for new buildings or simply battered by the winds and rains of many centuries. The biggest single stone of all, near Locmariaquer, is one such victim, now lying prone and in pieces. Many are carved with Christian symbols, marking the absorption of pagan faith by a new religion. Whatever their true origins, these sites are of intense interest to archaeologists. Their Celtic names are applied to similar structures all over Europe: *menhir* ('long stone'), *dolmen* ('table stone') and *cromlech* ('rounded slab').

Present-day Brittany still bares strong traces, in its language and culture, of the **Celtic settlement** that took place between the 5th and 7th centuries, after the decline of Roman influence, as British tribes fled from waves of Pictish, Saxon and Angle invasion. The striking similarities between the Celtic languages of Breton, Cornish and Welsh are a legacy of the emigration that gave the region its name of 'Little Britain'. Among the emigrants were Christian missionaries, who laid the foundations of a devoutly religious society; British legends were another import, linking Brittany, Cornwall, Wales and Ireland in their associations with King Arthur, Merlin and other heroic figures of Celtic folklore.

Brittany was brought under the control of the Frankish monarchy in the 8th century and presented with a governor, Nominoë, who promptly declared independence and set himself up as the region's king. After fending off the incursions of its powerful Norman neighbours, the region became a feudal duchy, destined to be piggy-in-the-middle in the centuries of conflict that followed between the kings of France and of England. The **Middle Ages** were a time in all three regions of switching allegiances, betrayals and bargains in the power-struggle between royal and noble families, linked with each other by a bewildering network of marriage and succession. In 1341 Duke Jean III of Brittany died, leaving two rival heirs: his step-brother Jean de Montfort, and his niece, Jeanne de Penthièvre, to battle it out. In the thick of the **Hundred Years' War** between England and France, the two claimants became a focus for the emnity of the monarchs, Montfort being backed by Edward III of England and Penthièvre by her husband's uncle, Philippe VI of France. The ensuing **War of Succession** was long and brutal: 2000

34

inhabitants were massacred at Quimper and Nantes was besieged and pelted with the heads of its captured fugitives, before the duchy finally passed to the English candidate.

Brittany remained a threat and a goal for the French crown, and in 1488 Duke François II was defeated by King Louis XI's forces at St-Aubin-du-Cormier. The king's reward was to pick the husband of François' daughter, Anne, who was eventually married to the succeeding French monarch, Charles VIII. Although Anne insisted that the Bretons maintain their fiscal and judicial rights, the French monarchy had effectively won the power-game; and by 1532 the union between France and Brittany was complete.

The region retained its character and separateness. Rebellions such as the *nu-pied* peasant revolt of 1639, against salt tax, and the riots of 1675 against more war taxation, were a constant reminder of Breton grievances against the crown. Nevertheless, when the king was overthrown by the Estates in 1789, their revolutionary agenda was not well received by the Bretons. This was – and still is – a strongly Catholic community, famous for its *pardons* (solemn pilgrimages in honour of local saints) and its elaborate parish closes (decorated 16th- and 17th-century graveyard buildings). The Revolution's emphasis on the secular and its attacks on established religion were fiercely opposed and the royalists made Brittany their base for an attempted counter-insurgency. This failed when reinforcements from Britain were cornered and killed at Quiberon, and resistance was reduced to occasional guerilla-style attacks.

Brittany's recent history has again been one of protest and resentment against central government. Bretons complain that Paris has neglected the region, failing to help a struggling economy, based on fishing and agriculture, while people have flocked away from the countryside to the cities. The apparent indifference of the state to Breton identity was underlined when Nantes, the old capital, was sliced off by the borders of new administrative regions in the 1960s.

Separatism is still an issue of debate – not confined to the ranks of Breton terrorists whose sporadic bombing campaigns have made headlines since the 1930s. In 1973 Brittany regained a certain degree of autonomy in the government cautious moves towards decentralising power, but the region's sense of identity generally focuses on its ancient language, still spoken, especially in coastal Lower Brittany, and on periodic surges of interest in Breton folklore and culture.

NORMANDY

Normandy was always a land open to invasion and before the 9th century it was occupied successively by Romans, Franks, Celts and Saxons. But it was in 820 that its reputation as the home of warriors and conquerors really began, with the arrival of the **Viking Norsemen**, who established their own state there under the Christianised chief Rollo, who, in 911, was granted the title of Duke of Normandy by the French King, Charles the Simple. Rollo's descendants were fighters and explorers, who brought the Norman empire to its zenith in the 11th century, with territories settled in Sicily and the Near East and the crown of England snatched by the illegitimate Duke William in 1066. As the Normans extended their power, they left a network of sturdy castles to protect their gains, but this was also a period of religious and intellectual vigour, which left its own legacy in monasteries, cathedrals and churches such as Bayeux, Coutances and Mont-St-Michel.

The close ties built by William and his successors between England and Normandy were to lead to more than a century of war as the English kings asserted their claim to the French throne. The **Hundred Years' War** started in 1346 when Edward III, King of England, invaded Normandy, claiming succession through his mother, Isabella, daughter of Philippe IV of France. By this time Normandy's golden age had passed; in 1204 the duchy had been surrendered to King Philippe Auguste, and the title of Duke of Normandy was revived only in 1333, by Philippe IV for his son Jean de Valois. During the 14th and 15th centuries the province again became a setting for invasions and counter-invasions, its residents suffering from siege and pillage as soldiers roamed the country between set battles. When the French king, Jean II, was captured at the Battle of Poitiers, Edward III demanded Normandy in lieu of ransom only to renounce it under the **Treaty of Brétigny** in 1360.

In 1417 Henry V of England started a new and devastating campaign, winning back the Norman territories piece by piece and finally taking Rouen after a six-month siege. It was here in 1431 that **Jeanne d'Arc** (Joan of Arc) was tried and burned after reviving the French cause and seeing the hapless Dauphin crowned Charles VII. Twenty years later, the English had been driven out of Normandy altogether.

After the ravages of war, the province began to prosper, with the building of new ports such as Le Havre, and ships set out from Dieppe and Cherbourg to join the race for colonies in Canada, Florida and Brazil. But troubles returned to Normandy as France succumbed to the religious upheaval that was affecting every

major European state. In the 16th century, the influence of Martin Luther's Protestant movement had spread to France and into the ranks of the royal household, triggering a bitter period of in-fighting and persecution. Hostility towards the Protestants, known as Huguenots, was at its height in 1572, when thousands were killed or tortured in the **St Bartholomew's Day Massacre**. Although Henri IV's **Edict of Nantes**, issued in 1598, guaranteed freedom of worship to Protestants, sectarian violence continued to be part of daily life. In 1685 the country's longest-reigning monarch, Louis XIV, the Sun King, revoked the Edict of Nantes, sparking off a new wave of conflict within France and with its neighbouring powers. Normandy suffered badly during this period, having become a centre of Protestant life and employment. Louis XIV's policy caused an exodus of alarmed Normans, which in turn dealt the important Huguenot textile industry a heavy blow.

The **French Revolution** brought yet more fighting to the province, where early support for the Estates' cause was replaced with open hostility after the execution of Louis XVI. In 1793 a counter-revolutionary force was roundly defeated at Cotentin, putting an end to the royalists' rebellion.

Normandy entered the 19th century a prosperous and developing region, growing over a tenth of the whole country's agricultural produce, and with the building of the railways, later in the century, came the influx of tourists heading for new resorts on the coast.

The natural beauty of the province was celebrated by artists such as Claude Monet, who created his stunning gardens at Giverny, and Normandy enjoyed a period of relative calm and wealth which came to an abrupt end with the wars of the 20th century – most particularly **World War II**. On 6 June 1944 – **D Day** – British, American and Canadian forces landed on a string of Normandy beaches and began the advance against occupying German troops that eventually culminated in the liberation of Europe. The campaign known as the **Battle of Normandy** was completed on 19 Aug, when American and Canadian soldiers made contact at Chambois, having previously isolated the enemy on the northern Cotentin peninsula. Hundreds of thousands of lives were lost in the course of the campaign which marked as the beginning of the end of a terrible global war.

THE LOIRE VALLEY

The wide, shallow Loire river was, not surprisingly, an attractive area to early Gallic tribes, whose existence is recalled in the names of valley provinces such as Touraine (from the Turones) and Poitou (from the Pictones). It was in Poitou, the province south of the river now split into the *départements* of Vienne, La Vendée and Deux-Sèvres, that the Frankish king Clovis I defeated Alaric, the leader of the Visigoths, before converting to Christianity and setting up his court in Paris. Over 300 years later, in a kingdom weakened by the rivalry of the Frankish descendants, the invading Saracens had reached the provincial capital, Poitiers, when they were driven back by Charles Martel. Poitou was swallowed up by the Duke of Aquitaine and passed on to Henry II of England by his charismatic wife, Eleanor of Aquitaine.

The province then became a pawn in the long contest between French and English crowns, being regained by Philippe Auguste, then by the English after the Black Prince had overcome superior numbers and captured the French king at the 1356 **Battle of Poitiers**. After 13 years the city had fallen into the hands of the formidable Bertrand du Guesclin, the Breton captain who led French troops to several famous victories. The territory was eventually granted to the Dauphin who was crowned Charles VII in 1423.

To the north and north-west of Poitou, the provinces of Touraine and Anjou provided more pieces in the jigsaw of the developing French nation-state. For 200 years from the 9th century, Anjou (now Maine-et-Loire) was ruled by a dynasty of counts including Fulk the Red and Fulk the Black. In 1126 the marriage of Count Geoffrey Plantagenet to Queen Matilda of England ensured the inheritance of an amalgam of French territorial possessions by their son when he became Henry II of England. This Angevin king took the throne in 1154 with Normandy, Maine (between Touraine, Anjou, Brittany and Normandy) and Anjou tucked under his belt. Half a century later, King John of England had bungled his forays into France and forfeited the lands to Philippe Auguste. The Counts of Valois adopted the title of Duke of Anjou and Maine from the late 13th century, so that, when Philippe de Valois was crowned Philippe VI in 1328, soon to be challenged by Edward III of England, the two provinces were absorbed into the royal domain. The Valois kings had their palaces built in adjoining Touraine (Indre-et-Loire), at Chambord, Chenonceau, Amboise and Blois – though this province became crown territory only in the late 10th century.

The duchy of Orléans, north of the Loire, had a long history of close association with the French royal family. The Duke of Orléans was the son of Philippe I of Valois; he left no direct heir to the duchy. In the early 15th century Louis, the

37

ambitious younger brother of the Valois king Charles VI, added the duchy to his existing title of Duc de Touraine. Named regent when his brother succumbed to the hereditary Valois insanity, Louis was ambushed and killed by the followers of his arch-rival, the Duke of Burgundy. The emnity between the two factions reached its climax when the Burgundians, allied with the English, laid siege to Orléans, while the feeble 14-year-old Dauphin struggled to maintain his status. In 1429, Jeanne d'Arc, driven by the voice of God to be an inspiring leader of men, spurred the Dauphin's troops to raise the siege and saw him crowned Charles VII before her capture by the Burgundians. In 1498 the son of Charles of Orléans became Louis XII of France. He married the previous king's widow, Anne of Brittany, continuing the process of expansion and consolidation of territory that was transforming the French monarchy into a strong centralised force.

The 16th and 17th centuries brought more conflict and suffering to the Loire Valley, as the Protestant communities of Poitou and Maine were targeted in the **Wars of Religion**. In the revolutionary years of the late 18th century, these royal territories kept up their opposition to the new anti-monarchist state. Resistance was maintained by the rebel Chouans in Maine from 1793 to 1800, and in Poitou there were two further risings in support of the monarchy: during the '100 Days' of Napoleon's bid for absolute power in 1815, and in 1832, in support of the Duchesse de Berry, widow of the last duke of that province, who had been assassinated in Paris two years earlier.

The Loire Valley provinces were not entirely anti-revolutionary, however. Philippe of Orléans, known as Philippe Égalité, was a member of the National Convention who voted in favour of Louis XVI's execution, and who was guillotined himself a year later. His son, Louis-Philippe, was taken up as the leader of the **July Monarchy** in 1830, bringing the region once again into the forefront of royalist activity – only to be overthrown in the uprising of 1848, when a much larger electorate voted in the Second French Republic.

During the **Franco-Prussian war** of the late 19th century, an army from the Loire tried to head off the Prussian invaders at Le Mans and Tours, but were eventually forced to retreat. In early 1871 the Prussians captured Tours and an armistice was signed on 28 January.

Tours was to become a military and administrative headquarters during the 20th century's two world wars. The US army made its base there in 1917 and billeted its troops along the Loire; and in June 1940 the French government moved there before decamping to Bordeaux. That year saw the destruction of the Loire's bridges and towns by German bombs, and in October 1940 **Marshal Pétain** agreed to collaborate with Hitler when they met at Montoire. Until the end of the war in 1945 the Loire was an active centre of resistance to Nazi rule, and German movements along the valley were frequently sabotaged.

Since the war years the Loire has become a prosperous region, with a steadily developing industrial base. The first nuclear power station in France opened at Avoine-Chinon in 1963 and in 1974 the new A10 motorway provided a fast link between Paris and Tours. Cities such as Tours, Angers and Orléans, with their lively economic and business communities, and the appeal of the Loire's countryside and castles all help attract investment from the capital, and go to make this a forward-looking, self-confident region.

TOURING ITINERARIES

For those who like to follow specific themes – as part of their holiday, or for the entire trip – here we have listed six themed itineraries based on châteaux, inland highlights (eastern), inland highlights (western), coastal highlights, food and drink, and prehistoric sites. Using the routes and information in this book, you can adapt the themed idea to suit your own tastes.

The tours as presented last from three to twelve days, but please don't think that you have to follow them in their entirety from start to finish. They represent a distillation of notable sites featured in the book and can be tailored to suit your own inclinations and time available. You might, for example, want to follow only a short leg of the château or coastal tour.

Similarly, the contents of each daily leg are based on a full day's sightseeing (all major sites are listed in bold). On any given day, you might want to concentrate on just one site, skipping the next or leaving it for another time (this applies in particular to châteaux – please see the note at the beginning of the tour). The keynote here is on flexibility. These tours give you a framework with which to plan your own personal itinerary. You can follow them in their entirety, dip into them on a selective basis, or combine a few.

The term 'châteaux' includes ancient fortresses, adapted fortresses and the Renaissance-style, purpose-built 'pleasure palaces'. This tour is based on a varied cross-section of châteaux, and allows a maximum of two per day. This gives a total which perhaps only the most dedicated château-goer will achieve. Most visitors might prefer to travel at a less intensive pace and visit fewer sites.

Day 1: **St-Malo** (p. 284). The square medieval castle now houses the town hall and two museums – one in the formidable 15th-century keep, the other in a tower on the north-west wing built by Anne de Bretagne. **Combourg** (p. 304). Impressively preserved medieval fortress which belonged first to the Du Guesclin family and later, in the 18th century, to the Count of Chateaubriand, father of the romantic poet François René, who spent two solitary years of his childhood here. Visit his gloomy bedroom in the Tour du Chat (Cat Tower).

Day 2: (Please note that this day involves a detour from the main route of the tour, but it does take you to two outstanding châteaux. Alternatively, you might want to proceed directly to Day 3.) **Château de Caradeuc**, Bécherel (p. 305). This château, built in classical style and sometimes called the 'Breton Versailles', has a magnificent park with shaded landscape gardens, pools and statuary. **Château des Rohans**, Josselin (p. 305). A superb fortress castle in a picturesque setting on the banks of the River Oust. It has three great circular towers linked by curtain walls and topped with high, pointed roofs.

Day 3: **Fougères** (p. 110). Set high on a promontory dominating the high Nançon Valley, the medieval fortress commands the frontier between Brittany and Normandy. **Châteaugiron** (p. 298). An impressive fortified castle with moat, 13th-

39

century keep, 14th-century pepperpot roof and 15th-century clocktower.

Day 4: **Vitré** (p. 260). This triangular granite fortress dominates the beautifully preserved medieval town which is built high on a spur above the River Vilaine. **Château des Rochers-Sévigné** (p. 261). Built in the 15th century and remodelled in the 17th century, this was the home of the Marquise de Sévigné, whose letters have provided us with a vivid picture of 17th-century society. Madame de Sévigné's personal possessions are on view,

Day 5: **Châteaubriant** (p. 301). This fine castle, part medieval and part Renaissance, stands on the borders of Brittany and Anjou, with gardens stretching down to the Chère River. **Château de la Motte-Glain** (p. 301). In a lakeside setting, this château was originally built to defend the borders of Brittany. It was remodelled in 1496 in Renaissance style.

Day 6: **Château de Serrant, St-Georges-sur-Loire** (p. 192). Beautifully situated by a large lake, this often underestimated château was built between the 16th and 18th centuries and was designed by Délorme, the architect of the Tuileries (the famous gardens in Paris). **Angers** (p. 51). This fine feudal fortress dates from the early 13th century and dominates the city with its 17 red and white towers.

Day 7: **Château de Brissac, Brissac-Quincé** (p. 55). This vast seven-storey Renaissance building, flanked by two old fortress towers, has been lived in by the Brissac family for five centuries. It stands in a pretty park by the Aubance River. **Saumur** (p. 307). The castle, set on a steep hill looking down on the rivers Loire and Thouet, was begun in the 14th century, finished by Louis XII, and remodelled in the 15th century by René of Anjou.

Planning an Itinerary

Planning an itinerary can be a large part of the pleasure of your holiday, but remember a few golden rules:

1. Unless you have accommodation pre-booked, plan to arrive in your overnight stop in plenty of time to find your lodging. Make the tourist information office your first call.

2. Don't plan in too much detail. Detours are part of the enjoyment, and even if you stick to your planned route, you may find that one sight is much more interesting and time-consuming than you imagined, or that traffic makes the going slower than anticipated.

3. Allow extra time on the last two days to avoid a dash back to your ferry or airport.

Day 8: **Le Lude** (p. 204). A wonderful château, much remodelled over five centuries, yet its different façades blend harmoniously together. It has one of the best son et lumière shows in France. **Villandry** (p. 313). The main reason for a visit here is to wander in the unique and beautiful gardens, often called the finest in France. They are on three levels comprising water garden, ornamental garden and vegetable garden.

Day 9: **Blois** (p. 57). The city is built around the château, which has four wings dating from different eras. The courtyard staircase is a striking feature. **Chambord** (p. 63). Built by François I to impress his fellow monarchs. The château skyline is a profusion of towers, turrets and chimneys. The huge spiralling staircase around which the château is built is magnificent.

INLAND HIGHLIGHTS – EASTERN

Day 1: **Bayeux** (p. 91). Home of the famous Bayeux Tapestry and the Battle of Normandy Memorial Museum. **Liseux** (p. 161). Celebrated home and last resting place of Ste- Thérèse. Visit the magnificent Basilique Ste- Thérèse, consecrated in 1954, and other sites connected with her life and death.

Day 2: **Falaise** (p. 101). The Château Féodal, situated on a rocky spur, was in 1027 the birthplace of William the Conqueror. **Suisse Normande** (p. 102). Located west of Falaise, this is a beautiful area of wooded slopes, streams and rivers.

Day 3: **Haras du Pin, Le Pin** (p. 163). This is France's National Stud. Set in beautiful buildings and grounds, the Stud was established by the finance minister of Louis XIV to improve the stock of French horses. **Le Mans** (p. 170). Car lovers can enjoy driving along the N138, D140 and D139 which are in June part of the Le Mans 24-hour racetrack. Visit the Bugatti Circuit and excellent motor museum.

Day 4: **Le Lude** (p. 204). Magnificent château overlooking the River Loir with one of the most dramatic son et lumière presentations in France. The **Sologne** (p. 327). Bounded by Blois, Orléans, Gien and Vierzon, a vast area often called the 'Hunting Forest of France'. Consists of forest, heathland, lakes and streams.

Day 5: **Vendôme** (p. 201). Delightful town with colourful history dating back to pre-Roman times. Enjoy a walking tour of the town and of the Forêt de Vendôme. **Chartres** (p. 121). The twin towers of Chartres' Notre Dame Cathedral can be seen for miles across the plain of Beauce. Superb 12th- and 13th-century stained glass. Many other places to visit within the old town.

Day 6: **Giverny** (p. 281). Claud Monet's house and gardens are now a museum dedicated to his life and work. **Château Gaillard, Les Andelys** (p. 280). Evocative ruins of Richard the Lionheart's 12th-century château.

Day 7: **Rouen** (p. 264). The city has Normandy's largest concentration of medieval buildings. Visit the Notre Dame Cathedral and sights connected with Joan of Arc. **Jumièges** (p. 169). The abbey here is an atmospheric ruin saved for the nation in 1852.

INLAND HIGHLIGHTS – WESTERN

Day 1: **Roscoff** (p. 296). Interesting old granite town. **Lampaul Guimiliau, Guimiliau, St Thégonnec** (p. 243). Three villages with impressive parish closes. The close is a unique expression of Breton art and faith. **Huelgoat** (p. 241). Travel through the Monts D'Arrée (the highest mountain range in Brittany, rising to 490 m) to Huelgoat, sited between lake and woodland. Explore the forest paths past formations of granite boulders.

Day 2: **Lac de Guerlédan** (p. 306). A reservoir formed by the waters of the Blavet River, one of the finest sights of inland Brittany. **Josselin** (p. 305). Superb fortress castle of the Rohans, overlooking the River Oust.

Day 3: The **Forêt de Paimpont** (p. 305). This beautiful forest, the ancient Brocéliande, legendary home of Merlin and the fairy Viviane. It originally extended from Rennes to Carhaix. **Dinan** (p. 303). Historic town with ramparts and castle standing on a plateau overlooking the River Rance.

COASTAL HIGHLIGHTS

Day 1: **Dieppe** (p. 136). Lively port and seaside resort. **Fécamp** (p. 158). Situated between two chalk cliffs – hence the name

41

'Alabaster' for this stretch of coast – Fécamp is a fishing, freight and pleasure port. Visit the Palais Bénédictine to taste the famous liqueur, first distilled here by the monks of the Benedictine Order. Étretat (p. 157). Set at the foot of a wooded valley with steep weathered cliffs to the north and south, Étretat has the most beautiful location on the Alabaster Coast.

Day 2: Honfleur (p. 150). This picturesque port, with tall, slate-roofed houses overlooking the harbour, has provided inspiration for famous poets and painters. Deauville (p. 152). Most fashionable resort in northern France. Famous for horse racing, American film festival, and superb beach and boardwalk. Cabourg (p. 154). Elegant seaside resort with a wide symmetrical street pattern which escaped damage in World War II. The author Marcel Proust spent time writing here.

Day 3: Caen (p. 85). Successfully rebuilt after the devastation of 1944. Many old buildings have been preserved including the Abbaye aux Hommes (Men) and the Abbaye aux Dames (Women). From Caen, drive via Arromanches (p. 95) to Carentan (p. 97) along the coast where the D-Day Landings of 1994 took place.

Day 4: Le Mont-St-Michel (p. 135). This fortress town, perched on its pinnacle of granite, is an unforgettable sight. Visit the ramparts, monastery and 11th-century abbey. St-Malo (p. 284). Attractive resort on the rocky, picturesque Emerald Coast, surrounded by ramparts.

Day 5: St Cast-le-Guildo (p. 291). Superb views from the Pointe de St-Cast of the Emerald Coast and the Fort la Latte on its rocky promontory. Cap Fréhel (p. 289). Dramatic headland, home of gulls, fulmars, cormorants and guillemots.

Day 6: Cap Erquy (p. 291). Magnificent views over the bay of St Brieuc and the Ile de Bréhat. St-Quay-Portrieux (p. 292). Set on the Côte Goëlo. Pretty resort with excellent seafood restaurants. Boat trips to Ile de Bréhat.

Day 7: Tréguier (p. 293). The Cathedral of St Tugdual is one of the finest in Brittany. Perros Guirec to Trégastel (p. 294). The most beautiful stretch of the lovely Pink Granite Coast, with its jumble of strangely shaped pink rock formations. Pointe de Primel (p. 295). A peninsula 10 km due north of Morlaix (p. 243). Visit the Cairn de Barnenez, a huge tumulus covering 11 dolmens.

Day 8: Plouguerneau (p. 297). From this village discover the Côte des Abers – Aber Wrac'h, Aber Benoît, and Aber Ildut – a low rocky coast broken up by shallow estuaries famous for its seaweed. Brest (p. 73). This city is well situated for touring the wild peninsulas of Crozon and Cap Sizun. Visit Océanopolis, which re-creates the undersea world.

Day 9: Crozon Peninsula (p. 80). Part of the Parc Regional d'Amorique which opens out into the wild Atlantic. Menez Hom (p. 81). The 300-m summit gives superb views of Brest, Pointe de Penhir and Douarnenez Bay. Camaret (p. 80). Unpretentious seaside resort in wonderful setting.

Day 10: Cap Sizun (p. 83). A promontory which ends in Pointe du Raz overlooking jagged rocks and the savage tide race Raz du Sein. Also tour the other headlands with spectacular views and visit the Réserve du Cap Sizun (a bird sanctuary). Quimper (p. 235). The oldest Breton city full of historic buildings and traditional Breton atmosphere.

Day 11: Vannes (p. 334). A beautiful old city on the shores of the Golfe du Morbihan surrounded by inlets and creeks. Golfe du Morbihan (p. 340). An inland

42

sea studded with islands, best explored by boat. A haven for seabirds.

Day 12: **Guérande Peninsula** (p. 341). An area of contrasts – rocky shores, fishing villages and resorts like La Baule with its 7-km sweep of sand. Visit the unique marshes of La Grande Brière and the salt pans just north of La Baule. **La Baule** (p. 341). One of the most fashionable seaside resorts in Brittany.

FOOD AND DRINK

The seafood from the coastal areas of Brittany and Normandy is renowned. Try homarde (lobster), langouste (crayfish), and the less expensive but delicious langoustine (scampi) and tourteau (crab). A plate of moules (mussels) or huItres (oysters) is equally tasty, and a seafood platter fresh from the shell is a culinary must. The choice of 'wet' fish is also excellent – try cotriade, a succulent Breton fish stew, or a fresh sole from Dieppe in a creamy sauce. The hinterland of Brittany produces lamb raised on salt pasture, kig sal (a salty bacon), and superb artichokes and cauliflowers. Traditional Breton pancakes – crêpes and galettes – with sweet and savoury fillings, are served in the many crêperies throughout the region. Norman cooking is rich, making good use of the butter, cream and cheeses of the region such as Camembert and Pont l'Evéque. The Loire Valley, called the 'Garden of France', produces early vegetables and a profusion of fruits including apples, pears, strawberries and bitter cherries. Freshwater fish taken from the river like perch, pike and salmon appear on many menus and local game abounds. The fruit of Normandy is put to good use in the pâtisseries. The Loire region produces noted white wines – Muscadet, Sancerre, Anjou (also a famous rosé) and the sparking wines of Saumur and Vouvray. Touraine,

Bourgueil and Chinon produce distinctive red wines. Muscadet and Gros Plant are made in the Nantes area, while cider is drunk throughout both regions, as is the warming apple brandy, Calvados. Round off a meal with a final toast of Benedictine liqueur from Fécamp.

Day 1: **St-Malo** (p. 284). Seafood specialities in walled town. **Cancale** (p. 135). Famous for oyster production. Visit Musée de HuItres et du Coquillage (Oyster and Shellfish Museum). **Rennes** (p. 253). Huge choice of gastronomic restaurants. The Saturday market is called the finest in France.

Day 2: **Nantes** (p. 182). Good range of restaurants and food shops. Taste dishes àla Nantaise (white wine and butter sauce) and cakes like pain de Nantes and gateau Nantais.

Day 3: **Chalonnes-sur-Loire** (p. 191). Excellent wine-tasting centre. Train takes visitors on vineyard tour.

Day 4: **St-Barthélémy** (p. 54). Cross to the outskirts of Angers to visit the well-signposted Distellerie Cointreau. **Château de Brissac, Brissac-Quincé** (p. 54). Sample the château's own wine as part of the tour. **Saumur** (p. 307). Famous for its sparkling wine. Visit Maison du Vin for regional wines and information on vintages and local vineyards. Also call in at Distellerie Combier for fruit-based liqueurs.

Day 5: **St-Hilaire-St-Florent** (p. 55). In a suburb of Saumur, visit Musée Champignons (Mushroom Museum) for guided tour. **Tours** (p. 316). The Vieux Ville (Old Town) has an excellent variety of restaurants. Pork dishes are a local speciality. The town also has a wide choice of charcuteries, pâtisseries and cheese shops.

Day 6: **Thoré-la-Rochette** (p. 202). A train touristique makes a round trip to **Trôo**, ending in a wine-tasting at Thoré's

43

converted station, called Maison de Vin et de Produits des Terroirs Vendômois (Centre of Vendôme Food Products and Wine). Also visit Musée de la Vigne et du Vin (Wine and Vineyard Museum). **Chartres** (p. 121). Good for regional specialities – game and fish from the River Eure, partridge and duck paté. Eat at La Cave à Fromage cheese restaurant. Day 7: **Dreux** (p. 275). Musée du Vin Flora Gallica (Museum of Regional Wine Production). **Rouen** (p. 264). Good choice of restaurants, including Gill, one of the top restaurants in Normandy. Rouen's speciality is duck. Day 8: **Neufchatel-en-Bray** (p. 142). Neufchatel cheese farms dotted around the town. **Dieppe** (p. 136). Good choice of places to eat, including an expensive fish restaurant, La Marmite Dieppoise.

PREHISTORIC SITES

This area is a delight for those fascinated by megalithic sites. The most widely held theory concerning these sites is that they were the work of a seafaring race of late Neolithic times and the early Bronze Age. The reasons why they were constructed are still hotly debated. There are far too many prehistoric sites in this area to include them all – these are some of the best. Day 1: **Mont Dol** (p. 300). A 673-m-high mound of granite overlooking a great plain. The remains of prehistoric animals and numerous flint tools have been found on its slopes. **Dol-de-Bretagne** (p. 300). The 9.5 m Menhir de Champ Dolent has given rise to many local legends. One tells of the stone being hurled from heaven to separate two warring brothers and their armies, hence the name Champ Dolent (Field of Pain). **La Roche-aux-Fées** (Fairies' Rock) (p. 301). One of the finest megalithic monuments in Brittany, with a massive entrance from which a low-ceilinged corridor leads to a large high divided chamber. Day 2: **Rochefort-en-Terre** (p. 339). Sited east of this charming old town is the Parc de la Préhistoire which provides reconstructions of prehistoric scenes in a woodland setting. Gavrinis Tumulus (p. 340). Many islands in the Golfe du Morbihan have megalithic sites. Take a boat trip to Gavrinis Island to see the 6-m-high and 50-m-round stone tumulus which contains a covered passage leading to a burial chamber. The stones of the passage are covered with carvings. **Er Lannic** (p. 340). It is not possible to land on this tiny island, but the two adjoining circles of menhirs can be seen by boat. Day 3: **Carnac** (p. 251). A must for those interested in prehistory. The site has a host of megalithic monuments, including the Alignements du Menec (the Ménec Lines), 1,099 menhirs arranged in 11 lines and a semi-circle of 70 menhirs; the Alignements de Kerlescan, 540 menhirs in 13 lines and a semi-circle of 39 menhirs; the Alignements de Kermario, 982 menhirs in ten lines; and the St Michel Tumulus, a huge mound of earth and stones covering two burial chambers and 20 stone chests (the artefacts from this tumulus can be seen in the museums in Carnac and Vannes). In Carnac itself, visit the **Musée de la Préhistoire** (p. 251), which traces the evolution of civilisation in the Carnac area between 450,000BC to AD86, and contains jewellery, casts of carvings from the megalithic monuments, reconstructions of tombs, etc. Day 4: **Locmariaquer** (p. 252). See the Dolmen de Mané-Lud, Dolmen de Mané-Rethual, the Grand Menhir and the Table des Marchands (Merchants' Table) which consists of three flat stones and a large flat stone serving as a lid. Many of the stones are carved.

SEA CROSSINGS

This page lists the main ferrries operating between Britain/Ireland and France at the time of going to press. Frequencies and journey times from port to port are those of the summer season.

FROM...TO	SAILINGS	JOURNEY TIME	OPERATOR	TEL. FOR DETAILS
CORK to				
Le Havre	1 per week	21 hrs	Irish Ferries	*(01) 855 2222*
Roscoff	2 per week	14 hrs	Brittany Ferries	*(0990) 360360*
Roscoff	1 per week	17 hrs	Irish Ferries	*(01) 855 2222*
St-Malo	1 per week	18 hrs	Brittany Ferries	*(0990) 360360*
DOVER to				
Calais (catamaran)	14 per day	35 mins	Hoverspeed	*(01304) 240241*
Calais (catamaran)	7 per day	45 mins	Stena Line	*(0990) 707070*
Calais	25 per day	75 mins	P&O European Ferries	*(0990) 980980*
Calais	20 per day	1 hr 30 mins	Stena Line	*(0990) 707070*
Calais	14 per day	1 hr 30 mins	SeaFrance	*(01304) 204204*
FOLKESTONE to				
Boulogne	6 per day	55 mins	Hoverspeed	*(01304) 240241*
NEWHAVEN to				
Dieppe	2 per day	4 hrs	Stena Line	*(0990) 707070*
Dieppe (catamaran)	3 per day	2 hrs 15 mins	Stena Line	*(0990) 707070*
PLYMOUTH to				
Roscoff	1 per day	6 hrs	Brittany Ferries	*(0990) 360360*
POOLE to				
Cherbourg	2 per day	4 hrs 15 mins	Truckline	*(0990) 360360*
St-Malo	4 per week	8 hrs	Brittany Ferries	*(0990) 360360*
PORTSMOUTH to				
Cherbourg	3 per day	5 hrs	P&O European Ferries	*(0990) 980980*
Le Havre	3 per day	5 hrs 30 mins	P&O European Ferries	*(0990) 980980*
Ouistreham (Caen)	2 per day	6 hrs	Brittany Ferries	*(0990) 360360*
St-Malo	1 per day	9 hrs	Brittany Ferries	*(0990) 360360*
ROSSLARE to				
Cherbourg	2 per week	17 hrs	Irish Ferries	*(01) 855 2222*
Le Havre	3 per week	21 hrs	Irish Ferries	*(01) 855 2222*
Roscoff	2 per week	17 hrs	Irish Ferries	*(01) 855 2222*

45

The Channel Tunnel

The tunnel has been a long time coming. Napoleon approved plans for a tunnel in 1802, and the British began digging one in 1880 only to abandon work for fear of a military invasion. The idea was revived after World War II, but it was not until July 1987 that work began on Europe's most ambitious construction project of the century: a 50 km tunnel, one of the longest undersea tunnels in the world, between France and Britain. On 6 May 1994, the tunnel was officially opened, a ceremony that marked the linking of Britain to Continental Europe for the first time since the Ice Age.

The undersea link is not, in fact, one tunnel but three – two for rail tracks and one service tunnel for maintenance work – situated side by side 25 to 45 km below the sea bed.

Le Shuttle

The vehicle-carrying service known as Le Shuttle operates between the two terminals at Cheriton (near Folkestone) and Coquelles (near Calais), both situated on their respective countries' motorway networks. Using the world's largest passenger-carrying rail vehicles (each train can carry 180 cars in carriages 5.6 m high), Le Shuttle runs 24 hrs a day, 365 days a year, with up to four departures every hour taking 35 mins from platform to platform. Motorists simply drive onto the train at one terminal and off at the other, staying with their vehicles in the air-conditioned carriages throughout. The carriages have toilet facilites but no refreshments. With border formalities all completed at the boarding terminal, motorists can drive straight off the train and onto the motorway on completion of the crossing. The aim is to offer a service with a total journey time, inclusive of waiting, loading and unloading, of no more than one hour. Travellers can book in advance or simply 'turn up and go'.

Both terminals have restaurants and duty-free shops. A special package known as Le Swap, which includes return Le Shuttle tickets, allows motorists to hire a right-hand drive car from Hertz in the UK (or take their own), swap the car on arrival in Calais for a left-hand drive model without any further paperwork, and swap it back on the return journey.

For Le Shuttle details and reservations *tel: 0990 35 35 35*.

Eurostar

This is the brand name of the new generation of high-speed trains connecting London to Paris and Brussels via the Channel Tunnel. Operated by European Passenger Services (EPS), in collaboration with French and Belgian railways, Eurostar trains regularly run at speeds of up to 300 kph on the *ligne à grande vitesse* (high-speed line) between Calais, Lille and Paris, putting the French capital just 3 hours away from London. When the Belgian and British high-speed lines are completed around the turn of the century, journey times will be further reduced.

Two classes of accommodation are provided aboard the quarter-mile-long trains. First-class passengers are served a meal at their seats, while two buffet-bars and a mobile refreshment service are available to all passengers.

As the number of daily services increases, so too do the possibilities for using Eurostar as a part of longer itineraries. The Brussels trains serve Lille Europe station, from which French TGV trains run direct to Lyon and the Mediterranean, obviating the need to change stations in Paris. From summer 1996, there will also be direct TGV trains from Lille Europe to **Le Mans, Rennes**, and **Nantes**. For information *tel: 0990 186 186*; for bookings *tel: 0345 881 881*.

ANGERS

Charm is the overall impression achieved by Angers, despite its size (population of 146,000), and its forbidding château. A modern, prosperous city, it owes its congenial air to its vivacious centre and historic artistic mantle. There are visually arresting statues in its streets and parks and a legacy of tapestry making – a craft that continues in the city today – the showpiece attraction of which is a remarkable 13th-century tapestry of the Apocalypse. Once the capital of the Anjou region, Angers has a splendid position on the banks of the wide River Maine, a tributary of the Loire, which it joins some 8 km away.

TOURIST INFORMATION

Tourist Office: *pl. du Président Kennedy, 49000 Angers; tel: 41 23 51 11.* Open Mon–Sat 0900–1900, Sun and public holidays 1000–1300, 1400–1800. It has a good range of information in English and makes bookings for hotels and *chambres d'hôtes* for a fee (Fr.8 in Angers, Fr.15 in the region, Fr.25 rest of France). Its bureau de change is open daily during its office hours (June–Sept), Mon 1000–1830, Tues–Sat 0930–1830, Sun 1000–1300 (Oct–May).

ARRIVING AND DEPARTING

To approach Angers from the south-east (from Saumur) take D952 straight into the town on *r. Volney*, continuing on *r. Paul Bert* and *blvd du roi Renée* to the château, where there are parking spaces.

GETTING AROUND

There are six main car parks, including a spacious free one at *pl. la Rochefoucauld*, which is on the river bank on the north side of the River Maine, a district called *La Doutre*, pleasant to explore and with a modern tapestry museum. To get to the main city centre means a walk across one of two bridges – either **Pont de Verdun** or **Pont de la Haute Chaîne**. City centre attractions are easily reached on foot as they are mostly around the cathedral, the château and the commercial centre, *pl. du Raillement*.

Public transport

COTRA bus, *pl. Lorraine; tel: 41 33 64 64.* One ticket good for an hour is Fr.5.50; a booklet of five, Fr.27. Linking the *La Doutre* district and the main centre are bus nos 21, 22, 23 and 25 which go over *Pont de Verdun*; no. 24 goes over *Pont Haute de la Chaîne*.

STAYING IN ANGERS

Accommodation

There is a wide selection of two-star hotels, six three-star hotels plus numerous unclassified hotels. There is a good choice around the rail station and nearby streets, otherwise hotels are scattered throughout the centre and the outskirts. Chain hotels include *Ba, BW, Ca, Ct, F1, IH, Mc, RC.*

HI youth hostel is at *3 r. Darwin; tel: 41 72 00 20.* Campsite: **Camping du Lac de Maine**; *tel: 41 73 05 03.*

Eating and Drinking

Lively Angers, with a large university stu-

47

dent population, has a wide choice of places to eat, especially in the streets leading off *pl. du Ralliement* (including *r. St-Laud, r. Lenepveu, r. du Pilori*) and there are many *crêperies*, pizzerias, bar-brasseries, cafés and snack bars. Cuisines represented include American, Chinese, Thai, Vietnamese, Greek, Turkish, Indian, Mexican, Lebanese. Regional specialities are plentiful in most restaurants.

For cheeses, pâtés and snacks, a good place to browse is the covered **Les Halles** (central market), *pl. de la Republique.* Open Tues–Sat afternoon. There are good eating places around *Les Halles.* Benches for picnic snacks are at *Bout du Monde* terrace beside the château and the park at *allée du Haras,* which has a play area.

Communications
Main **post office** is at *1 r. F. Roosevelt.* Open Mon–Fri 0800–1900, Sat 0800–1200, it has bureau de change and poste restante.

Money
Many banks are open on the often difficult days, Mon and Sat. Branches of all the major banks are found in the shopping and restaurant districts.

A listings brochure, published every two months, is available free from the Tourist Office. *Angers Poche* is a monthly listing. The **Grand Théâtre**, *pl. du Ralliement; tel: 41 24 16 40,* is a splendid backdrop for a wide array of drama. **Les Mardis Music-aux** (musical Wed evenings, mid-month) include piano recitals, duos, quartets and ensembles. Tickets from the theatre or the CD/bookshop **fnac**, *r. Lenepveu; tel: 41 24 33 33*; open Mon–Sat 1000–1900. **Nouveau Théâtre d'Angers**, *12 pl. Imbach; tel: 41 87 80 80,* has a repertory

company creating productions which then go on tour. Musical, theatrical and dance events also take place with visiting companies and artists.

There are four cinemas but the *Version Originales* (marked *V.O.* to indicate original language films) are shown at **400 Coups**, *12 r. Claveau; tel: 36 68 00 72.*

Nightlife is lively at weekends and there are discotheques in the centre as well as one on a boat, **Topaze**, *quai des Carmes* (facing the château from the other side of the river); *tel: 41 88 30 01.* There are half a dozen piano bars and café-theatres.

Events
The **Festival d'Anjou**, each July, brings together theatre, music, poetry, comedy and dance. Information: *tel: 41 88 14 14.* Cinema inspires two festivals, European cinematography (end of Jan) and African cinema (April); there is a music and folkore festival (Sept).

The pedestrianised streets, like *r. Lenepveu,* have good quality fashion and interior decoration shops. Larger stores, including **Nouvelles Galeries**, are on *r. d'Alsace.* The *La Doutre* district has a small shopping area, best for food.

Markets take place daily except Mon in various locations, including bric-a-brac on Sat at *pl. Imbach.* This large market also has flowers, fruit, vegetables and clothing in the *blvd. de la Resistance,* sold to the beat of music played from CD stalls.

Angers is well served for sightseeing on foot, made interesting thanks to the many plaques, in French and English, outside important buildings. This can be supplemented by a free leaflet in English, *Art and History in One Town,* which outlines three

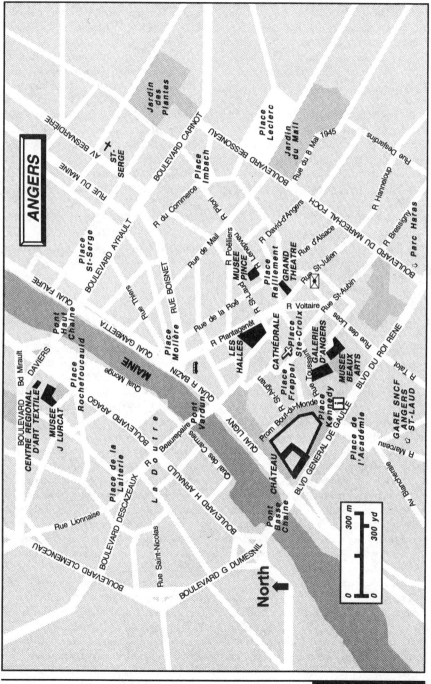

ANGERS

49

'strolls'. These take in the town centre, the gardens and architectural façades of town buildings and **La Doutre**. Guided tours, in French, Mon–Sat and one in English, Wed, 2100 (mid June–mid-Sept). Fr.25. Tickets from the Tourist Office, starting points vary.

Le Petit Train takes in the old centre and the *La Doutre* district which has the best views of the Angers skyline, particularly lovely when illuminated at nightfall. Commentary is in French. The train leaves from *pl. Kennedy*, opposite the château, Mon–Sat 1415, 1530, (end June–July, Sept); Mon–Sat 1100, 1400, 1515, 1630, 1745, Sun, public holidays 1400, 1515, 1630 (July–Aug). Fr.28. Evening rides take place Wed, Fri 2100 (July–Aug). Fr.35.

Batallerie Promenade (boat cruises), *cale de la Savatte; tel: 41 42 12 12,* run a 2-hr cruise on the river Maine, departing from *quai de la Savette,* Sat, Sun, 1630 (end June–mid-Sept). Also on Thurs, Fri (mid-July–first week of Sept). Fr.45. An all-day picnic cruise leaves Sun 0930 (returns 1615). Fr.76. A combination 'little train' ride and cruise, lasting 3½ hrs, leaves *pl. Kennedy* Thurs–Sat 1515. Fr.68. Other cruises are available including a dinner cruise Fri, 1930 (July–Aug). Fr.200.

Walking around Angers is a delight, thanks to sculptures in the streets and gardens. Look for *Fontaine du Dialogue* (two men in earnest conversation) at *pl. Louis de Romain;* a coy, scantily dressed prophetess, *Velleda,* in the sylvan setting of the garden of the **Jean Lurçat** museum; and the defiant *Nicholas de Beaurepaire,* the lieutenant colonel who died in 1792 during the Revolutionary war, at *pont de Verdun.*

The most important statue is *Le Roi René,* facing the château, a bronze made by the city's famous son, David d'Angers, in 1846, of a much-loved Duke of Anjou who inspired a rich cultural life in the 14th century. There is a statue of David himself, made in 1949, in *pl. Lorraine.* In the **Jardin des Plantes** are several striking examples. An illustrated, free brochure, *Les Statues dans La Ville* (town statues) pinpoints the finest examples. There are picturesque buildings such as the half-timbered **Maison d'Adam**, *r. Toussaint,* and the **Maison Bleue** (the blue house), *blvd Mar. Foch,* an art deco apartment building built 1927.

A steep flight of stairs from the river leads impressively to the entrance of **Cathédrale St-Maurice**, *4 r. St-Christophe; tel: 41 87 58 45.* This 12th–13th-century cathedral has stained glass from the 12th–16th centuries and a collection of hundreds of tapestries, a few of which hang along the sides of the nave.

Angers has a *billet jumelé* (combination ticket) which allows entry into its museums and the château, Fr.50. The ticket allows for three days' free parking.

The cathedral is a couple of streets away from the **Château d'Angers**, *promenade du Bout du Monde; tel: 41 87 43 47.* Open daily 0900–1900 (June–mid-Sept); daily 0900–1230, 1400–1830 (Palm Sunday–May); 0930–1230, 1400–1800 (mid-Sept–Palm Sunday) Fr.32 (child Fr.21). Cafeteria open Apr–Sept. A terrace at the end of the street by the drawbridge entrance offers a good view of the river.

An exterior of dark-grey slate banded by white limestone layers, 17 no-nonsense towers and walls, built 1230–38, and a narrow drawbridge entrance staunchly proclaim the château's fortress function. It was built during a war with the Duke of Brittany. Although now truncated, the walls were strengthened in the 15th century to resist English attack and the chapel in Flamboyant Gothic design was built in the courtyard, which is surprisingly pretty thanks to the medieval garden. Inside the

Logis Royal (royal apartments) are 15th-century *Milles-Fleurs* tapestries, decorated with many flowers. Guided visits given in English; self-guided tours in the tapestry gallery.

The **Apocalypse** tapestries, depicting scenes described in St John's revelations, are 100 m long and divided into 70 sections. They were made in the late 14th century for Louis I of Anjou and are in a specially-built gallery. Remarkably, they survived being thrown away during the Revolution.

Museums

The municipal museums of Angers, described in the following paragraphs, are open daily 0930–1230, 1400–1900 (mid-June–mid-Sept); Tues–Sun 1000–1200, 1400–1800 (mid-Sept–mid-June).

Musée des Beaux Arts, (Fine Arts Museum) *10 r. du Musée; tel: 41 88 64 65; Fr.10.* Housed in the **Logis Barrault**, the collection includes paintings and sculpture by Fragonard, Boucher, Delacroix and Raphael. Nearby is the **Galerie David d'Angers**, *33 bis r. Toussaint; tel: 41 87 21 03; Fr.10.* Many civic statues of local dignitaries and heroes were made by David, born and educated in Angers, 1788–1856. On display are his plaster models, 30 full-size figures, seen in the natural light which comes through the glassed-over ceiling of the **Toussaint Abbey** building. Most striking is the model of the Marquis de Bonchamps (see p. 191) who had saved the sculptor's father among other Revolutionary prisoners threatened with execution. There are also busts and medallions. Replicas of 100 medallions are on sale and there is a pretty garden in the cloisters.

A Renaissance building with a fine façade houses a collection of Etruscan and Greek vases as well as Japanese and Chinese ceramics, bronzes, lacquer ware,

tapestries and engravings, the collection of a 19th-century mayor Turpin de Crissé; **Musée Pincé**, *32 bis r. Lenepveu; tel: 41 88 94 27. Fr.10.* **Musée d'Histoire Naturelle**, *43 r. Jules Guitton; tel: 41 86 05 84*, is in a fine late 17th-century building.

To complement the city's tapestry theme, it is important (and pleasant) to cross the river to **Musée J. Lurçat et de la Tapisserie Contemporaine**; *4 blvd Arago; tel: 41 87 41 06. Fr.20.* It is right beside the free car park. The 12th-century building, once **l'Hôpital St-Jean** (St John's hospital), is in a charming garden and houses a modern series of stunning tapestry works in dramatic colours on black backgrounds – *Le Chant du Monde* (the song of the world). It is the work of Jean Lurçat, 1892-1966, who began the project in 1957 and helped revive the art of tapestry-making. Sometimes echoing the Apocalypse image of the historic tapestries in the château, Lurçat's striking images include *L'homme d'Hiroshima* (Hiroshima inhabitant) and the artist's own favourite *Le grand Charnier* (the Great Charnel House) depicting a post-bomb 'dance of death'. There are also joyous pieces and the crazily vivid *Conquête de l'Espace* (Conquest of Space). In a separate building at the back is the **Centre Regional d'Art Textile**, *3 blvd Daviers; tel: 41 87 10 88*, where temporary exhibitions are held and it is possible to see crafts people making tapestries (Mon, Tues, Thur, Fri 1000–1200, 1400-1700). **La Doutre** has some pleasant streets around *pl. de Laiterie* and the Holy Trinity church.

⚡ SIDE TRACKS FROM ANGERS

Les Sables d'Olonne is a delightful coastal town, with pastel-hued buildings and the air of a stylish resort from the fashionable era of the 1920s, despite

51

its modern facilities. Its long, curving beach of fine white sand is a great attraction for families. Because the N160 road leads directly to the resort from Angers, 163 km, a seaside break on the Atlantic coast is easily possible: a change of pace from the châteaux and forests of the Loire Valley. For an overnight stay, there is a very wide range of hotels and restaurants. Nightlife includes a couple of casinos as well as discos and and clubs. There is a marina, an old fishing quarter, an ancient fort and a museum about the Vendée region and its history. **Tourist Office**: *r. Mar. Leclerc; tel: 51 32 03 28.*

The whole coast has good sandy beaches. Excursions from Sables d'Olonne can include the **Île de Noirmoutier** (16 km on the D38) which is an island for part of the day. Cars cross the mud track at **le Gois** at low tide or go over the modern toll bridge at **Fromentine**. The quiet island has ten hamlets with red-roofed white houses, a fort, a fishing port, woodland and more than 30 km of beaches. It is fertile farmland and has oyster and mussel beds just off shore. There are a handful of hotels and restaurants. **Tourist Office**: *tel: 51 39 80 71.* ⓐ

Châteaux Gardens

There is an unexpected surprise for visitors who look over the stone wall into the dry moat of the Angers château, for tucked within the tight confines of one corner is a small classically laid out *parterre*, planted at the beginning of the 1990s. This is a token nod to the way many grand châteaux developed formal gardens as part of the Renaissance influence, planning them as part of the architectural concept. A *parterre* describes the garden as a whole, which would then be divided into squares planted in different geometric patterns, often squares, circles, diamonds, crosses as well as scrolls. Angers château also pays tribute to the natural park idea by keeping a herd of deer on the other side of the moat, below the entrance. Many chateaux would have wanted an area where hunting and horse-riding could take place. With these gardens in the moat, Angers is the only one of the seven main Loire Valley towns to recreate some of the heritage of grand garden planning which is so amazingly in evidence at Chenonceau, Chambord, Le Lude and Villandry, as well as Fontainebleau and Versailles, near Paris, where expanses of water are as important in the layout as the formal plantings.

Courtly life in the châteaux used for summer sojourns demanded a grand garden, not just as a pleasant background for daytime walks and romantic meetings, but for the evening entertainments when blazing torches illuminated the grounds and fireworks often turned the night into a spectacle. The lavishly costumed ladies and their equally resplendent admirers also sought out the cool, scented gardens as a break from the hectic pace of the ballroom and for further flirtations in shadowy corners.

Although the Renaissance brought formality to gardens, with an obsessive zeal for symmetery, proportions and exact measurements, the medieval age was more interested in aromatic and medicinal plants and herbs. To appreciate how the formal gardens looked when first laid out, a good place to visit is the **Château de Chamerolles** (see p. 213). The Villandry gardens were restored at the beginning of the century and include vegetable plots as part of the decorative scheme.

ANGERS–SAUMUR

There is a very pretty stretch of riverside from St-Mathurin to Saumur on this route which also goes inland to take in two well-furnished châteaux which have belonged to the same families for generations – one is privately owned, another belongs to a duke. Interesting museums en route cover such topics as slate-quarrying, modern-day communications and the history of masks, and there is the chance to visit the cave dwellings which are numerous in the region. The low-key towns of Gennes and Les Rosiers make pleasant stops.

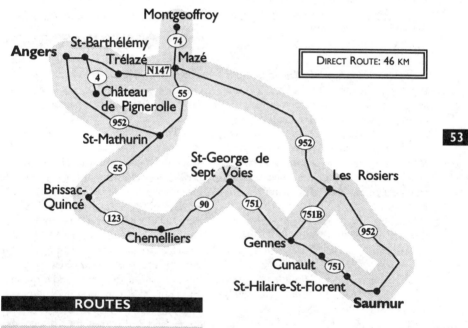

DIRECT ROUTE: 46 KM

53

ROUTES

DIRECT ROUTE

Take the D952 north of the Loire, 46 km.

SCENIC ROUTE

To start this 83.5 km route, take N147 turning right onto D117, then left to **Château de Pignerolle**. After, return to D117 for **St-Barthélémy** and signposts to the Cointreau distillery. Then continue on D117 to **Trélazé**. Turn left onto D4 to rejoin N147, turn right to **Mazé**, then turn left onto D74 to **Montgeoffroy**. Return to Mazé on the same road, then turn right onto D55 to **St-Mathurin-sur-Loire** to cross the river. Continue on D55 to **Brissac-Quincé**. Then take D123 to **Chemellier**, turn left onto D90 and then turn right to **St-Georges-des-7-Voies** and the D751 (about 1 km). Turn right onto D751 to **Gennes**. For a slight detour, cross the river on D751B to Les Rosiers. After, return to Gennes by the same road. Turn left onto D751 to **Cunault**. Continue on D751 to **St-Hilaire-St-Florent** and Saumur.

ST-BARTHÉLÉMY

Set in a pleasant park is the **Musée de la Communication**, *Château de Pignerolle, Parc de Pignerolle; tel: 41 93 38 38*. Open daily 1000-1230, 1430–1830 (July-Oct); Sun 1000-1230, 1430–1830 (Nov–Mar); Tues–Sun 1030–1230, 1430–1830 (Apr–June). Fr.50; (children Fr.40). English leaflet for self-guided visit. The museum is about the development of radio, television and satellite communications and also covers transport. It is expensive but the special effects include a recreated submarine, which portrays the adventures of Jules Verne. In the grounds there is a pretty tea room in a conservatory based around a steam engine as well as miniature steam train rides.

A short drive away and well-signposted is the famous **Distillerie Cointreau**, *Carrefour Molière, St-Barthélemy; tel: 41 43 25 21*, in an industrial zone. Tours are Mon–Fri 1000, 1100, 1400, 1500, 1600, 1700, Sat–Sun 1500, 1630 (mid-June–mid-Sept); Mon–Fri, 1000, 1100, 1400, 1500, 1600, 1700, Sun 1500, 1630 (mid-Sept–mid-June). Fr.20. Guided tours only (some English possible) last 1½ hrs. Founded in 1849, this aromatic, liqueur-making establishment has 19 giant copper stills. Tastings of Cointreau end the tour.

TRÉLAZÉ

Musée de l'Ardoise (slate museum), *32 ch. de la Maraîchère, 49800 Trélazé; tel: 41 69 04 71*. Open Tues–Fri 1000–1200, 1400–1800, Sun 1400-1800 (July–mid-Sept); Sun, public holidays 1400–1800 (mid-Feb–June, mid-Sept–Nov). Fr.28; (Fr.23). The Loire Valley châteaux are enhanced by roofs made of blue-grey slate which came from the region's quarries. Industrial heritage is poignantly shown off at these disused quarries. Features include a walk around the old workings, now full of water and overgrown with vegetation. Retired slate workers demonstrate their skills in a little theatre and there is a slate-clad museum with tools of the past.

MAZÉ

Tourist Office: *Mairie, Mazé, Montgeoffroy 49250; tel: 41 80 60 19*. Open Mon–Fri 0900–1200, 1400–1700, Sat 0900–1200 (all year). There are *chambres d'hôtes* and rural *gîtes* but no hotels. The Tourist Office does not make bookings.

Château de Montgeoffroy, *49250 Beaufort-en-Vallé, Mazé; tel: 41 80 60 02*. Open daily 0930–1200, 1430–1830 (Palm Sunday–mid-June, mid-Sept–Oct). Open daily 0930–1830 (mid-June–mid-Sept). Guided visits (English). Fr.40, (Fr.30). Little has changed at this charming château since the Maréchal de Contades rebuilt an existing château, decorating and furnishing it in Louis XVI style during 1772–76. It is a very liveable place, still enjoyed by his descendants and a treat for visitors who can appreciate original, unrestored furniture, tapestries and curtains.

BRISSAC-QUINCÉ

Tourist Office: *Brissac-Quincé 49320; tel: 41 91 21 50*. Open 1015–1230, 1430–1845 (May–Sept). There is information about accommodation but no bookings are made. Brissac has one hotel.

Château Brissac; *tel:41 91 22 21.*
Open daily 1000-1800 (July–mid-Sept);
Tues–Sun 1000–1200, 1415–1715 (Apr–
June, mid-Sept–Oct). Fr.40, (Fr.30).
Guided visits only (in French with English
leaflet).

In a romantic setting, the seven-storey
château, topped with jumble of narrow
chimneys, is the residence of the 13th
duke of Brissac, whose ancestor acquired
the building in 1502. Framing the ornate
façade of the mainly 17th-century building
are the two medieval towers from the
fortress originally on the site. The grand
staircase tower adds to the busy look of the
façade with its display, floor by floor, of
the five orders of classic architecture showing, from the bottom, Tuscan, Doric,
Ionic, Corinthian and Composite pillars.
Samplings of the château's own wines are
part of the visit.

The grand **Salle des Gardes** (guardroom) has huge walls with fine tapestries
and an ornate open-beamed ceiling which
is gilded, carved and painted. The château
is handsomely furnished and has its own
18th-century *belle époque* theatre.

ST-GEORGES-DES-SEPT-VOIES

L'Orbière, *49 St-Georges-des-Sept-Voies;
tel: 41 57 95 92.* Open daily 1100–2000,
(May–Sept). Open daily 1400–1900
(Oct–Apr). Fr.20 (Fr.15). This is the most
unusual of the cave dwelling attractions of
the area because it is a giant work in
progress by the artist Jacques Warminski,
who has carved out tunnels, staircases and
striking outlooks – even an amphitheatre.
The first sight of the complex, thanks to a
bevy of clucking hens near the entrance,
does not give a hint of this modern artistic
achievement with a science fiction feel to
it. A wall of press cuttings attests to the
artist's achievement.

GENNES

Tourist Office: *sq. de l'Europe 49350; tel:
41 51 84 14.* Open 1000–1300, 1500–
1900 (Apr–Sept). It has regional leaflets
and makes hotel bookings. There are a
handful of pleasant hotels and restaurants.
Open 0930–1230, 1500–1800 (May–
Sept). Beside the bridge on the river front
is **Camping Municipal**, *tel: 41 38 04 67.*

This quiet town was a Roman settlement. Excavations in 1985-93 revealed an
oval-shaped amphitheatre which could
seat 5000. About half of this **Amphi-
théatre Gallo-Romain** is on view in a
wooded setting, with an exhibition about
it at the nearby **Musée Archéologique** in
*Château de la Roche, rte de Louerre; tel: 41 51
83 33.* Both are open Sunday 1500–1800
(Apr–June, Sept); daily 1000–1200, 1430–
1830 (July–Aug). Fr.16 (Fr.10).

The ruined 12th-century **Église St-
Eusèbe** has wonderful views of the Loire
where occasional fishermen stand serenely
on its banks. Open Sun, public holidays
1500–1830 (Easter–June, Sept); daily
1500–1830 (July–Aug). Guided visits only
(English possible). It has painting exhibitions (free). Entry to the bell tower, Fr.6.

A prehistoric relic is the neolithic stone
dwelling, the **Dolmen de la Madeleine**,
in the outskirts of the town.

LES ROSIERS-SUR-LOIRE

Tourist Office: *pl. du Mail 49350; tel: 41
51 90 22.* Open Mon–Sun 0930–1230,
1500–1900 (June–Sept), it makes bookings. In the flat countryside settting by the
Loire, this village is a pleasant detour across
the river for an undemanding stroll. It has
seven restaurants and hotels, including one
rated highly by foodies, **Jeanne de Laval**,
rte Nationale; tel: 41 51 80 30.

ST-HILAIRE-ST-FLORENT

On the road to this Saumur suburb is the

55

Église Prieurale (priory church), *tel: 41 67 92 44*, at Cunault which is considered to be a masterpiece of Romanesque art, with more than 200 carved capitals and murals.

Caves line the long street which forms the town of St-Hilaire St-Florent. Notable among them is the **Musée Champignon** (mushroom museum), *tel: 41 50 61 94*. Open daily 1000-1900 (mid-Feb-mid-Nov). Fr.32; Fr.28. Guided tours only (in English). Watching mushrooms grow sounds an odd way to spend a sightseeing hour or so but this well-presented view of the industry is fascinating, explaining the region's geology and how the quarry business created a maze of caverns with cool, constant temperatures. There is a recreated laboratory which prepares mushroom spores for cultivation and more than 220 different varieties of mushrooms are grown, some in specially prepared compost beds, others in bags and boxes. The weirdly-shaped *pleurotus* variety comes in pretty colours while the Japanese *shiitake* mushrooms are grown in tree trunks. A café with an outdoor terrace overlooking the Loire serves grilled and stuffed mushrooms with a variety of sauces as well as Saumur blanc des blancs wine.

St-Hilaire-St-Florent has a variety of attractions. Among the wine caves, there is the **Musée-galerie Bouvet Ladubay**, *r. Ackerman; tel: 41 50 11 12*. Open daily 1000–1200, 1400-1800 (mid-June-mid-Sept); Mon-Fri 1400-1800, Sat-Sun 1000-1200–1400-1800 (mid-Sept-mid-June). Fr.10.

Musée du Masque (mask museum), *r. de l'Abbaye; tel: 41 50 75 26*. Open daily 1000-1230, 1430–1830 (Easter–mid-Oct); Sat-Sun 1000–1230, 1430–1830 (week before Easter, mid-Oct-mid-Dec). Fr. 25 (Fr.20). A collection of masks from 1870 is displayed, some on costumed figures to show off their decorative, theatrical and fashionable uses. Most importantly above the town is **L'École Nationale d'Équitation et le Cadre Noir** (national academy of riding), *Saumur Terrefort; tel: 41 53 50 60*. Here the black-uniformed riders display their prowess at regular performances, with commentary (English). See also Saumur, pp. 307–310. Open Mon afternoon–Sat morning 0930–1100, 1430–1600 (Apr–May, Sept); Mon–Sat 1430–1600 (June–Aug). Fr.30 (mornings); Fr.20 (afternoons).

Cave Dwellings

In curious contrast to the high concentration of fanciful châteaux in the Loire Valley are the carved out caves of the cliffsides. These **troglodytiques** are homes, wine cellars, businesses, restaurants, mushroom farms or tourist attractions in a 1000 km stretch. The highest concentration of such dwellings in France is in the Anjou region, many of them cheerfully lining the banks of the Loire.

Since the 12th century people have been living in these mellow excavations, left behind by the quarrying of stone to build châteaux, churches and cathedrals. These underground dwellings included some baronial halls, workshops and chapels. The **tufa** (limestone) is so pliable that even furnishings, such as beds, tables and seats, could be carved. The dwellings were safe, insulated, economical to maintain, easily expanded and versatile.

It is possible to find accommodation in a troglodyte cave dwelling. **The Central Booking Agency for Gîtes in Maine-et-Loire**, *BP 2147, 49021 Angers; tel: 41 23 51 23*. **Les Perrières Reception Centre**, *545 r. des Perrières 49700 Doué-La-Fontaine; tel: 41 59 71 29*.

BLOIS

A handsome town where the cliff-top château and cathedral are reflected romantically in the wide River Loire, Blois (population 60,000) is interesting for the royal intrigues when it was an important court, for its secret huddle of ancient streets and for its animated enclaves of restaurants and shops. It is excellently placed for visiting the very grand châteaux nearby.

TOURIST INFORMATION

Tourist Office: *Pavillion Anne de Bretagne, 2 av. Jean Laigret, 41000 Blois; tel: 54 74 06 49.* Open Mon–Sat 0900–1230, 1400–1900, Sun and public holidays 1030–1230, 1630–1900 (Apr–Sept); Mon–Sat 0915–1200, 1400–1800 (Oct–Mar). It makes hotel bookings for a fee (within Blois Fr.5; outside Blois Fr.10) and has a bureau de change. There are tourist information desks at the château and in the pedestrianised area, daily 1000–1900 (July–Aug).

Le Comité Départemental du Tourisme, *5 r. de la Voûte du Château; tel: 54 78 55 50,* open Mon–Fri 0900–1200, 1400–1800, has information about the region.

ARRIVING AND DEPARTING

The part of the N152 that links Orléans and Tours runs through Blois. To approach the city from the south-west, follow N152 along the Loire until *quai Abbe Gregoire,* which leads to *quai de la Saussaye,* with parking on the left side.

GETTING AROUND

Parts of the town, such as the little streets behind the cathedral, are impossible for cars and are best appreciated on foot. But sightseeing should be paced as the cobbled streets can be tiring, especially as there are more hillside streets around the château. There is a car park underneath the château and parking beside the river banks.

TUB bus, *2 av. Victor Hugo; tel: 54 78 15 66.* Open Mon 1330–1730, Tues–Fri 0830–1200, 1330–1730, Sat 0900–1200. Single ticket is Fr.5.70; a booklet Fr.38.

STAYING IN BLOIS

Accommodation

There is a reasonable selection of hotels in the three- and two-star range, some around the rail station, some along the river banks on both sides of the Loire. Chain hotels include: *Ba, Ca, Co, F1, Ib, Mc, Nv, RC.*

HI: youth hostel is in *Les Grouëts* (4 km away) on the Tours road; *tel: 54 78 27 21.*

Camping Municipal de La Loire, *rive gauche D 951; tel: 54 74 22 78.* Sharing the same site is **Camping-Caravaning du Lac de Loire**; *tel: 54 78 82 05.*

Eating and drinking

Restaurants, brasseries, pizzerias, *crêperies* and snack bars are plentiful. A lively corner of reasonably priced eating brasseries with partial views of the Loire is at *pl. de la Résistance.* The ambiance is more charming at the bottom of the web of steep streets next to the cathedral, especially *r. de la Foulerie.* There is a pleasantly isolated but prettily located brasserie next to the cathedral at *pl. St-Louis.* Besides regional specialities, cuisines represented in Blois include American, Chinese, Vietnamese, Moroccan and Thai.

A well-shaded garden with a fountain and park benches for picnics is at *pl. Victor Hugo*, even though it is at the hub of traffic-filled streets including *av. Jean Laigret*. A steep street up to the looming château is on one side of the garden and **St-Vincent's** church is on the other. There are also benches in the terraced gardens of the former bishop's palace beside the **cathedral**.

Communications
The **main post office** is at *122 r. Michel Bégon*. Open 0800–1900, Sat 0800–1200, with bureau de change and poste restante.

Money
Banks are closed on Sat afternoon and Mon; use the Tourist Office or post office.

ENTERTAINMENT
Concerts and theatre events are staged at the modern **la Halle aux Grains**, *pl. de la République*; *tel: 54 56 19 79*. There are three cinemas, showing films mostly in French. Nightlife is not extensive, but there is a discotheque or two and late-night bars in the restaurant areas.

Events
A multi-cultural festival is held mid-June; a cinema festival based on films from Quebec takes place at the beginning of Oct; a comic book festival is also held in Oct. A street festival, July–Aug, stages many free musical events throughout the town. One of the joys of Blois in the summer is coming across a quartet playing perhaps in the Ste-Anne pavilion within the château, or in the cloisters of St-Saturnin, when the locals might also set up a home-made food and wine buffet table for the evening.

SHOPPING
The pedestrianised streets, laid out in flat tiles of pastel pink and blue, are pleasant for shopping as they are gently sloping rather than steeply cobbled, especially *r. Porte-Chartraine* and *r. du Commerce*. There are many fashion and home decor shops. The department store **Le Printemps** is on *r. D. Papin*.

A special market of local produce (*foie gras*, honey, jams, cheese, chocolates, cakes and also pottery) is held in the *pl. du Château*, Thur 1500–2100, (Aug–mid-Sept). Markets are held on Tues, Thur, Sat mornings at *pl. Louis XII*.

SIGHTSEEING
Guided walking tours leave the château Thur 1430 (July, Aug). Also themed walks (topics vary) Mon–Wed, Fri–Sun at 1000. Tickets on sale at the château; *tel: 54 78 06 62* or *54 74 16 06*, price Fr.42 (children Fr.26)

The free walking-tour leaflet in English, *Blois – Town Visiting Circuits*, divides the town into three areas which is the sensible way to tackle the hilltop town. The **château district** straddles the hillside and there are some pedestrianised streets. The **cathedral quarter** is beside a higgledy-piggledy patch of very steep, narrow streets, mostly residential, which are linked by passages of steps. Across the river over the Pont Gabriel is **Blois Vienne**, which is flat and less picturesque but excellent for views looking back on the main town.

The Château district
Overlooking the town in splendid style is the **Château de Blois et Musée des Beaux-Arts**; *tel: 54 78 06 62*. Open daily 0900–1830 (mid-March–mid-June, Sept–mid-Oct); daily 0900–2000 (mid-June–Aug); daily 0900–1230, 1400–1730. Fr.32 (Fr.22). Self-guided tours and guided visits

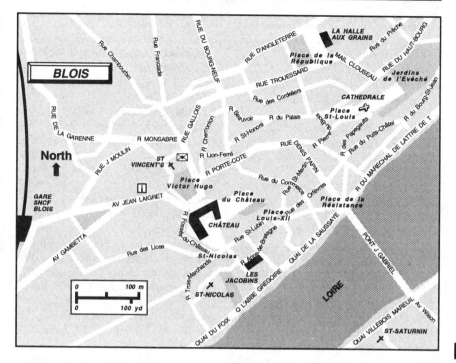

in English. In-depth, 60 min, guided tours 'from cellar to attic' take place daily 1030, 1500, 1730 (mid-June–Aug); Sat, Sun 1500 (mid Mar–mid-June, Sept–mid-Oct). Fr.42 (Fr.26).

The **Musée Lapidaire** (Museum of Stonework) displays some of the château's original statues as renovation in the last century removed them from the façade to replace them with copies.

A *son et lumière* display takes place at the end of May–mid Sept; times vary depnding on nightfall. *Tel: 54 78 72 76.* Fr.60. Ticket holders can visit the château between 1800–2000, then leave for dinner in town and return for the show at nightfall. Note that there is no seating at the display, so pace sightseeing in the steep, cobbled streets to allow for tired feet.

The **château** was an important royal residence up to 1598, when the court moved to Paris, so it has witnessed many royal events including a strategic murder. The staircase alone is a delightful sight in the cosy courtyard, always bustling with visitors, reminiscent of its heyday as a thriving court. It was built between 1515 and 1524. Restoration work, which started in 1900, has brought out the luminous glow of the limestone façade. The château interior is richly decorated with carvings, painted wooden beams and wallpapers in deep colours, all based on Renaissance designs as researched by a 19th-century restorer, Félix Duban. There is little furniture as the court would have travelled extensively, taking the necessary furnishings each time to set up residence anew. However, there are tapestries and many paintings depicting scenes which took place within the rooms of the château.

There are four wings from different eras – the medieval is centred in the **Salles des États Généraux,** (the meeting hall of the States General, which met here in 1756 and 1588); the Louis XII wing combines a Gothic style of architecture with Renaissance inspiration; the François I wing is a full-blown Renaissance masterpiece; and the Gaston d'Orléans wing was built by the exiled brother of Louis XIII in the classical style.

Most interesting are the royal chambers used by Catherine de Medici, including a study with 237 carved panels, some of which hide once-secret cupboards. The novelist Alexandre Dumas imagined them to hide poisons but Honoré de Balzac described them as holding state secrets necessary for Catherine's strong command of affairs during the Wars of Religion. In the king's bedroom the assassination of the Duke of Guise took place as commanded by Henri III in 1588. The duke had been planning a *coup d'état,* and the assassination became the subject of many paintings.

Musée d'Histoire Naturelle, (Museum of Natural History). *Les Jacobins, r. Anne de Bretagne; tel: 54 74 13 89.* Open Tues–Sun 1400–1800 (Jan–May, Sept–Dec); Tues–Sun 1000–1200, 1400–1800 (June–Aug). Free. Also housed in the former convent at Les Jacobins is the **Musée des Arts Religieux;** (Museum of Religious Art); *tel: 54 78 17 14.* Open Tues–Sat 1400–1800. Free.

To the south of the château, a small staircase, **Les Petits Degrés du Château,** leads to Quartier St-Nicolas, an area extensively damaged in World War II, although the centrepiece, the medieval church of St-Nicholas, was mostly unscathed. Confusingly, it is sometimes referred to by its original name of St-Laumer, when it was a Benedictine abbey church.

Recently opened nearby and run by enthusiastic volunteers is the **Musée Résistance, Déportation, Libération du Loir et Cher,** *1 pl. de la Greve; tel: 54 56 07 02.* Free.

Cathedral district

Cathédrale St-Louis was built in the 16th century, then rebuilt in Gothic style after a hurricane destroyed most of it in 1678. The cathedral stands detached from the town centre but the area around it is a must for visitors who appreciate a fine garden with splendid views and who enjoy sauntering down quiet old streets with crumbling façades. The viewpoint at **Jardins de L'Eveche** is from a landscaped terrace, once part of the bishop's palace (now the town hall) beside the cathedral. Beside an equestrian statue of **Joan of Arc,** it overlooks a terrace of roses, the grandly flowing river, and red-roofed houses. The steep old streets start immediately next to the cathedral at the well-preserved, handsome, half-timbered house called **Maison des Acrobates,** whose woodwork includes figures of acrobats and jugglers. The steps beside it lead to r. *Pierre de Blois,* r. *du Papegaults* and r. *du Puits-Châtel.* There are intriguing glimpses into the courtyards of grand townhouses such as the **Hôtels de Saumery, Belot** or **Sardini.**

Although there are several little staircase-style streets, the wide, 19th-century **Escaliers Denis Papin** is splendid, overlooking the city and leading down directly to *pl. de la Résistance* and the river.

Blois Vienne

Blois Vienne retains vestiges of its time as a busy port although it is now a rather dilapidated residential area. Before the 18th century, it boasted the main road from the east as there were none from

Forests

It might come as a surprise to many visitors to the Loire Valley but their holiday albums may well end up displaying as many photos of forests as of river scenes. Some sightseeing routes are completely monopolised by woodland rather than the River Loire or its tributaries. The region's legacy as a retreat for the royal court, which enjoyed hunting as a pastime, ensured that the forest landscape survived. Around Blois and Orléans, or Amboise and Montrichard, Loches and Chinon, the maps show green forest areas and even close to Paris, the château at **Fontainebleau** is visible only after a 6 km drive through a regimented forest of oaks, pines and beeches. Some of the most charming places to visit are within the forest boundaries, such as the artists' village of *Barbizon* or the tiny hamlet of *Milly-la-Forêt*.

Some of the best walking routes are through forests and the most scenic drives include roads from which forest views are seldom absent, such as the road from Chinon to Azay-le-Rideau. Because the forests are cultivated and well tended, the roads are straight and well defined, suiting cyclists especially. Some forests have hides from which to see animals such as deer and wild boar. Generally, Tourist Offices will have leaflets outlining good walks in the forests, which tend to be well marked. Maps with circular routes are the most useful enabling a return to the car. Enquire at Tourist Offices about cycle hire to really enjoy the quiet, sylvan landscape. There are usually some picnic tables but the wide verges are ideal for picnics.

Between Blois and Gien lies the **Sologne** (see page 327), often described as the royal hunting forest of France. Some 40 per cent is woodland with much of the rest being heathland. It is rich hunting territory, a fact brought home especially in autumn when wild boar, roebuck, or partridge are suspended in butchers' shops. Much of the wildlife, including beavers, otters or salamanders, relies on a watery environment .

61

Orléans on the other side of the river
There are some half-timbered houses in *r. de la Chaîne* and the one at the corner of *Gaston d'Orléans* and *r. 1er Septembre* was once an inn.

The main sights include **Église St-Saturnin**, dating to the 15th–16th centuries. Opposite it is a charming little cloister with its passages covered by a timber, barrel-shaped ceiling. Stone columns are topped with carvings of bizarre figures, including skeletons. It has become the home of statuary fragments from 13th–18th century monuments which were destroyed in World War II. **Au Cloître St-Saturnin**, *r. Munier; tel: 54 74 16 06.* Open daily 1000–1230, 1400–1830 (June–Sept); Sat, Sun, public holidays (mid-May–June, Oct–Nov). Château

ticket includes entry to the cloisters. The main reason for strolling on this side of the river is for the wonderful view of Blois itself from the embankment which has some bars and restaurants. There are park benches by the willow trees on the bank at **Port de la Creusille,** one of the old berths once used by sailing boats.

Blois is well connected by road to **Chartres** (see p. 121) and its attractions which include the **Nôtre-Dame** cathedral. Take D924 to Châteaudun, then follow N10 to Chartres, a journey of 101 km. Chartres is conveniently placed to extend a visit to Paris (see **Le Mans–Paris**, pp. 176–181) or as the starting point for a journey between Chartres and Rouen (see **Rouen to Chartres**, p. 272).

BLOIS–ORLÉANS

Mostly on back roads away from the Loire, this route goes through much flat countryside, not dramatically beautiful but mysteriously isolated, a part of the Sologne (see p. 327) which includes stretches of treeless and dreamily featureless landscape. The only real town, Beaugency, where the Loire is splen-didly expansive, is a lovely and lively contrast. Surprisingly, the route includes the Loire Valley's largest château, Chambord, as well as quiet roads in its large forest. Smaller châteaux, such as Talcy and Meung, have literary connections.

62

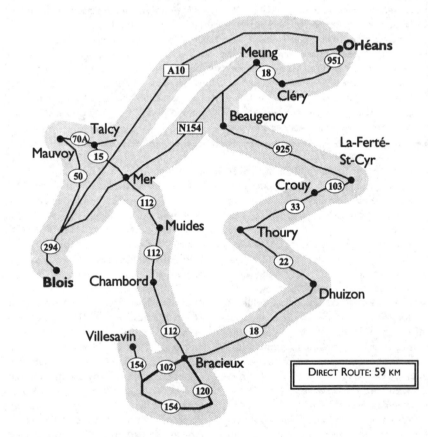

DIRECT ROUTE: 59 KM

ROUTES

DIRECT ROUTE

➡️ Take D924 north out of Blois, turning right on to N252 to join the motorway A10, north of the river, to rejoin N152 at Orléans for the city centre, 59 km.

SCENIC ROUTE

➡️ Take the ring road to N152, to join D50, which goes direct, albeit not straight, to **Mauvoy**. Turn right onto D70A to **Talcy**. From here, take D15 to Mer to join D112 to cross the river heading for Muides-sur-Loire, continuing south on D112, which veers right to enter the Parc de **Chambord**, part of the forest of Boulogne. D112 heads for the château de Chambord. After visiting the château, continue on D112 through the forest to **Bracieux**, turn right onto D102, then right again onto D154 to cross the river Beuvron for the **Château de Villesavin**. Afterwards, return to D154, continuing on it until it joins the D102; turn left back towards Bracieux, take D923 to **Neuvy**, then turn left onto D18. Turn eft at **Dhuizon** onto D22 towards Thoury, turn right onto D33 to **Crouy-sur-Cosson**, continuing on D103 to **La-Ferté-St-Cyr**. Turn left onto D925 to cross the river into **Beaugency**. After Beaugency, take N152 to **Meung-sur-Loire**. From here, take D18 to recross the river to **Cléry St André**. Then take D951 to **Orléans** centre.

TALCY

Château de Talcy; *tel: 54 81 03 01.* Open-0930–1200, 1400–1800 (Apr–Sept); daily 1000–1200, 1400–1630 (Oct–Mar). Fr.21 (Fr.14 child). English leaflet. Guided visits only with English text. Aficionados of small châteaux will enjoy 16th-century Talcy, austere outside, intimate indoors, and set in an isolated hamlet in the flat, open farmland of the Beauce plain. Florentine banker Bernardo Salviati, a cousin of Catherine de Medici, added crenellation to this fortress in 1520 but despite his Italian origins did not indulge in many Renaissance details. The courtyards are charming, the first with a fine well covered by a cupola, the second boasting a finely preserved dovecote. In the barn is a 400-year-old wine press.

It has romantic literary connections. The poet, Pierre de Ronsard, fell in love with Salviati's 16-year-old daughter, courting her in the rose garden. Although she rejected him then, and again 20 years later when she was a widow, he dedicated 183 sonnets to her, called *Les Amours de Cassandre*. Her niece, Diana, later inspired another poet, Agrippa d'Aubigné, who was also a satirist of early 17th-century court life.

63

CHAMBORD

Tourist Office: next to the château; *tel: 54 20 34 86.* Open 1000–1900 (Apr–Sept). It books accommodation and has leaflets on the area. There is a snack bar and cafeteria and even a hotel, **Du Grand St-Michel**; *tel: 54 20 31 31.*

SIGHTSEEING

Domaine National de Chambord (the estate of Chambord), *41250 Chambord; tel: 54 50 40 00.* The château is open daily 0930–1815 (Apr–June); daily 0930–1915 (July–Aug). daily 0930–1215, 1400–1715 (Oct–Mar) Closed 1 Jan. 1 May, 1 and 11 Nov 25 Dec. Fr.35; Fr.22.

Deep in the conifer forest of Boulogne, the tiny village of Chambord, like the château (which is the largest in the Loire Valley), is preserved by the state. Drive carefully on the straight roads, which are intersected by ramps. Regular one-hour guided tours of the château (in English), daily, free, except July and Aug. No booking is required; the times are posted at the entrance. Special 1½-hr guided tours (English) take in rooms usually closed to the public, daily, July–Aug, Fr.20 (plus the entrance ticket); book a place at the entrance. There is a good English leaflet, Fr.3, with a map of the park, which is 35 km in circumference. Parking Fr.5.

François I set out to build a sumptuous hunting pavilion combining the features of a fortress with the silhouette of a romantic palace. It makes a dramatic impact after the seven-mile forest drive. His emblem, the crown hovering over a salamander, appears 700 times throughout the building.

Work started in 1519 and, surprisingly for such an extravagant building with 440 rooms, the architect is unknown, although Leonardo da Vinci may have been involved, as there is an ingenious double staircase which allows a person to climb to the top without meeting anyone descending the steps.

The walk along the roof terraces, with the crazy multitude of turrets, lantern towers, spires, cupolas and chimneys, is an exhilarating architectural treat with sweeping views of the River Cosson, a tributary of the Loire. Apparently, François had considered diverting the Loire to flow past his showpiece home.

A *son et lumière* show is staged evenings Fri, Sat, public holidays (mid-Apr–mid-June, second week Sept–mid-Oct); daily (mid-June–first week Sept); *tel: 54 20 34 86*. Starting times vary, from 1915–2230, during the season as nightfall changes. Fr.55; (Fr.45). A horse show with traditionally dressed riders is held at the Maréchal de Saxe stables, daily (May–Sept); *tel: 54 20 31 01*.

The château is set in a national hunting park, composed of mostly oak and pine trees but also with elm, chestnut, birch, alder and willow trees. There are four observatories from which to watch wildlife which includes deer, boar, foxes and many birds such as ducks, herons, buzzards, woodcocks and pheasants.

The park has three signed footpaths and one *grande randonée* (long-distance) footpath. Horses can be hired at the stables; *tel: 54 20 31 01*. Fr.45. There are seven parking and picnic areas and the public must stay within authorised areas. Bicycles can be hired from Fr.25 for one hour to Fr.80 for four hours.

BRACIEUX

The craftsmen who built Chambord created this compact village which has a fine wooden market hall with an exterior staircase up to its granary, a 12th–13th century church and two rivers, the Beuvron and Bonneure.

Nearby is the **Château de Villesavin**, *Tour-en-Sologne, 41250 Bracieux; tel: 54 46 42 88*. Open daily 1000–1200, 1400–1900 (Mar–Apr); daily 1000–1900 (May–Sept); daily 1400–1700 (Oct–third week Dec). Fr.25 (Fr.20). Guided tours only (in French with English text).

This privately owned château was built by Jean le Breton, finance secretary to François I. Since le Breton was in charge of the building of Chambord, he used the top craftsmen on his own home built in Italian Renaissance style, perhaps overgrandly as the rooftops overwhelm the ground floor which is arranged around a *cour d'honneur*, a courtyard with a fountain, sculpted in Carerra marble. One theory suggests it was intended for Chambord and diverted here, another that the sculptors he gave so much work to presented it to le Breton. There are also vintage cars, a chapel and a dovecote for 3000 birds.

BEAUGENCY

Tourist Office: *pl. du Dr Hyvernaud 45190 Beaugency; tel: 38 44 54 42.* Open Mon–Sat 0930–1200, 1430–1800 (Oct–May; also Sun 1000–1200 May); Mon–Sat 0930–1230, 1430–1830, Sun, public holidays 1000-1200 (June-Sept). It books accommodation. Information leaflets include a good walking route in English.

ACCOMMODATION

There is a reasonable selection of hotels, including a former abbey on the river front. **Camping Municipal du Val de Flux**; *tel: 38 44 50 39.*

SIGHTSEEING

There is parking by the river bank near the bridge. The narrow streets mean that this pretty medieval town, crowded in summer, is best explored on foot. Interesting buildings include the **Hôtel-de-Ville** (town hall), a 16th-century building with an intricate façade. The **Tour de l'Horloge** (clock tower) is part of the city walls. *R. de l'Évêché* evokes the Middle Ages and the *r. du Rû* is a flower-bedecked, stone-cobbled path by a stream. This was a fortress town and its 14th-century stone bridge was the only crossing between Blois and Orléans until modern times. It was captured four times during the Hundred Years' War with the English.

The residents take part with gusto in two spectacles in one evening, which take place the last two weekends of June (sometimes overlapping into July); Fr.20. The first, at 2100 in the historic centre, is akin to street theatre. The later *Soirée Spectacle* takes place at 2230 in the square, flanked by the château and abbey church. Fr.60. Tickets from the Tourist Office.

In the **Église Abbatiale Notre-Dame** (abbey church of Our Lady), a 17th-century building, an event took place which affected English and French history. Here, in 1152, the wedding of Eleanor of Aquitaine and François VII was annulled, thus leaving her free to marry Henry Plantagenet, later Henry II of England, whose kingdom stretched from the Scottish border to the Pyrenees. Their belligerent sons included Richard the Lionheart and King John.

At the atmospheric *pl. St-Firmin* is the 15th-century **Château de Dunois**, now housing the **Musée Dunois**; *tel: 38 44 55 23.* Open Wed-Mon 1000–1200, 1400–1830 (Apr–Sept); 1000–1200, 1400–1700 (Oct–Mar). Fr.20 (Fr.15). This museum highlights the arts and traditions of the Orléans region and its people, with themed galleries covering such subjects as traditional costume, children's toys, archaeology and furniture. The one-time owner of the château, the Count of Dunois, was a comrade in arms of Joan of Arc and led many battles to drive the English out of France.

MEUNG-SUR-LOIRE

Tourist Office: *42 r. Jean de Meung, 45130 Meung-sur-Loire; tel: 38 44 32 28.* Open Mon, 1000–1200, 1400–1730, Tues–Sat 0900–1200, 1400–1830, Sun 1000–1200 (Apr–Sept); Mon, 1000–1200, 1400–1730, Tues–Sat (0900–1200, 1400–1830 (Nov–Mar). It has information in English and makes hotel bookings.

A Loire tributary, the little Mauve, runs in rivulets between the old streets of this well-preserved, medieval town, known for its literary associations. The long *Roman de la Rose*, mostly by the 13th-century poet, Jean de Meung, influenced Chaucer and eventually became one of the first books to be printed. The poet François Villon was imprisoned for burglary in the château, which is right in the centre of the town next to the church. He

65

was fortunate in being pardoned by the king. A famous line from one of his ballads is often quoted. 'But where are the snows of yesteryear?'

The rather grim-looking château was used by the bishops of Orléans from 1200 to 1789. **Château de Meung-sur-Loire**, *tel: 38 44 36 47*, was used as headquarters by the English army during the latter part of the Hundred Years' War. Open daily 1000–1200, 1400–1730 (Easter–June); daily 0900–1230, 1300–1830 (July–Aug); 1000–1200, 1400–1700 (Sept–Oct); Sat, Sun, public holidays 1000–1200, 1400–1700 (Nov–Mar.). Guided tours only (English). Fr.30 (Fr.10). It has a complex of dungeons and *oubliettes*, cone-shaped holes where prisoners were lowered half-way down and left with little food so that they starved to death without the involving the bishops in passing an official death sentence.

CLÉRY-ST-ANDRÉ

This village was once an important stop in the pilgrimage route to Santiago de Compostela in north-western Spain. It has a church of cathedral proportions, the **Basilique de Notre-Dame**; *tel: 38 45 70 05*. Open 0900–1200, 1400–1900 (Apr–Oct); 0900–1200, 1400–nightfall (Nov–Mar). No charge but donation welcome. This 15th-century Flamboyant Gothic church has some curious features, including the Chapelle St-Jacques with a spiral staircase and small window which allowed the king to worship without being seen. The opening to Louis XI's burial vault is left open to show the macabre sight of the dissected skulls of the king and his wife.

Châteaux

Renaissance is the buzz word which dominates château-sightseeing. The word describes a European movement, from about the 14th century to the mid 17th century, which inspired great changes in the arts, sciences and architecture. It started in Italy, where building went back to the basic principles of proportion used in Roman times and spread to other countries, notably France, where input from local craftsmen developed the ideas.

Royalty, aristocrats and the wealthy showed off their wealth and status by building their 'pleasure palaces' in the fashionable Renaissance style. Here they pursued such courtly interests as hunting, falconry, banqueting, fêtes champêtres (country festivals), musical evenings, masked balls, poetry readings and romantic encounters, events which are today remembered by the *son et lumière* productions popular at some top châteaux.

Some owners simply adapted the fortresses which were on their properties already. These were solid buildings with defensive features such as look-out towers, moats and drawbridges but usually blessed with dramatic views thanks to their commanding position of strategic points on the Loire or a tributary. Many were built during the Hundred Years' War, 1337-1453.

Today's sightseeing thus includes ancient fortresses, the combination fortress-and-pleasure palace, and the purpose-built, show-off château in full-blown Renaissance style. It is the large number of these grand buildings which make the Loire Valley unique although the pleasant landscape, the vineyards and the majestic river would always make the region, between Nantes and Orléans, a popular place for modern-day tourists. Seeing inside every château on any route is impossible: choose ones which appeal because of their history, artistic and architecural merits or because of their gardens or museums, alternating the large and small. Admire the others from outside as man-made wonders in harmony with nature's backdrop.

BOURGES

Its very pretty streets with old houses give the historic centre of the town (population 76,000) a cosy air, despite the traffic whizzing around its circuit of busy streets. It has a magnificent cathedral. Its other showpiece is not a château, but a grand 15th-century mansion built for the famous charismatic, town merchant and royal diplomat, Jacques Coeur (see p. 211). The rivers Yèvre and Auron flow by but do not make their presence felt in the centre. The Yèvre runs through an intriguing flat marshland which makes a peaceful and definitely off-the-beaten-track walk even though it is right beside the lively town.

TOURIST INFORMATION

Tourist Office: *21 r. Victor Hugo. BP 145, 18003 Bourges; tel: 48 24 75 33.* Open Mon–Sat 0900–1900, Sun, public holidays 1000–1830 (July–Sept); Mon–Sat 0900–1230, 1330–1800, Sun 1000–1230 (Oct–June). In July–Aug, there are tourist information kiosks at the motorway (A71) junctions into the town. It has good leaflets in English and organises guided walks, and will book accommodation in the town and immediate area. There is an in-depth exhibition about the region.

ARRIVING AND DEPARTING

The A71 motorway bypasses Bourges just to the west of the town. To approach Bourges from the north (from Paris via Gien), take the D940 from Gien until it becomes *av. de Gén. de Gaulle* on the outskirts of town, and continue straight onto *av. Marx Dormoy* and across a little bridge onto *r. E. Vaillant.* At *pl. St-Bonnet*, at the edge of the old town, there is parking.

GETTING AROUND

There are many car parks in Bourges and the tourist office has a good map clearly showing which ones are free (14 out of 24) including the ones on the ring road around the centre (*cours Anatole France, pl. St-Bonnet, blvd de la République*). It is just a few minutes' walk to the town centre attractions. Car parks right in the centre are not free. The centre is very pleasant to explore on foot, thanks to the many pedestrianised streets.

CTB has many bus routes. Information from **Boutic-Bus**, *cours Avaricum; tel: 48 50 82 83.* Open Tues–Sat 0900–1230, 1400–1800. One journey ticket is Fr.6.20, booklets of ten, Fr.47. The centre is so compact that it is not necessary to take a bus.

STAYING IN BOURGES

Accommodation

Hotels are not plentiful in Bourges and it can be difficult to stay in the centre during festivals and special events. Booking ahead is a good idea. It has a couple of three-star hotels and a sprinkling of two-star hotels, some near the rail station but the others are dotted sporadically, some in streets leading away from the town (*r. E. Vaillant*). Hotel chains include: *Ct, Ib, Cn, IH*

HI youth hostel: *r. Henri Sellier* (on the banks of the Aurun); *tel: 48 24 58 09;* **Le**

67

Foyer de Jeunes, *La Charmille, 17 r. Félix Chédin* (near the rail station); *tel: 48 70. 63 90*. **Camping Municipal**, *blvd de l'Industrie* (beside the River Auron); *tel: 48 20 16 85*.

Eating and Drinking

Restaurants are plentiful, especially lining the pedestrian streets such as *r. Bourbonnoux*, but also in squares like the shaded *r. Maurice de Bourges* and the *pl. Cujas*. There are reasonably priced pizzerias, *crêperies* and brasseries. A good local dish is *galettes de pomme de terre* (potato pancakes).

Other food specialities include *forestines* (soft-centred sweets inside a hard sugar coating), *bûchettes du Berry* (chocolate sticks), *sablés* (shortbread), *croquets* (crisp almond biscuits), terrines, goat's cheese, especially the *crottin de Chavignol*, wine and liqueurs. A good place to find them is at **Maison des Forestines**, *3 pl. Cujas, 1 r. Moyenne; tel: 48 24 00 24*. Local wines include those made in Sancerre and its near neighbour Menetou-Salon, which is said to have been owned by the local historic character, Jacques Coeur.

The central covered market **Les Halles**, *pl. St-Bonnet*, is open Tues–Sat 0730–1300, 1500–1930; Sun 0800–1300. There are markets Wed morning at *r. G. Eiffel*, Thurs morning at *pl des Maronniers* and at *St-Germain du Puy*.

Many shops are closed Mon, but the STOC supermarket within the department store **Aux Nouvelles Galeries**, *r. Moyenne*, is open Mon–Sat 0900–1900.

A good picnic place is beside the River Yèvre, off *blvd de la République*, on a shaded walk lined with plane trees, although the park benches actually face away from the river. They face instead a large, exuberantly laid-out garden, the **Jardin des Prés-Fichaux**, with pools, *parterres* and an open-air theatre. Open daily 0800; closing times vary but as late as 2200 in June–July.

Communications

Main **post office**, *r. Moyenne*. Open Mon–Fri 0800–1900, Sat 0800–1200; it has bureau de change and poste restante.

Money

Banks are closed on Mon, except **Crédit Agricole**, *69 r. d'Auron*, open Mon–Fri 0830–1200, 1345–1730; closed Sat. There are no bureaux de change open Sun.

ENTERTAINMENT

A free listings leaflet *Culture Bourges* (published every two months) details main events in a town which has a lot going on. There are concerts and theatrical events at **La Maison de la Culture**, *pl. André Malraux; tel: 48 67 06 07*. Other events take place at the **Palais des Congrès**, *blvd Lamarck; tel: 48 70 11 22*, or **Théâtre Jacques-Coeur**, *r. Jacques-Coeur; tel: 48 70 59 36*. There are two cinema complexes (*r. Pelvoysin, r. Littré*) showing French films only.

Nightlife revolves around eating out, 'pub' style drinking places, a couple of discotheques and a café-theatre (*pl. Gordaine*).

Events

Music festivals include **Le Printemps de Bourges**, at the end of Apr, and **Ballades de Bourges**, mid-July–mid-Aug. It has many individual events all summer, sometimes in the museums or the cathedrals; the Tourist Office makes bookings.

SHOPPING

The main shopping streets are *r. Moyenne*, which has a couple of department stores, *r. Coursalon*, and just a little off the main centre, the semi-pedestrianised *r. Auron* which leads to the River Auron. This road is

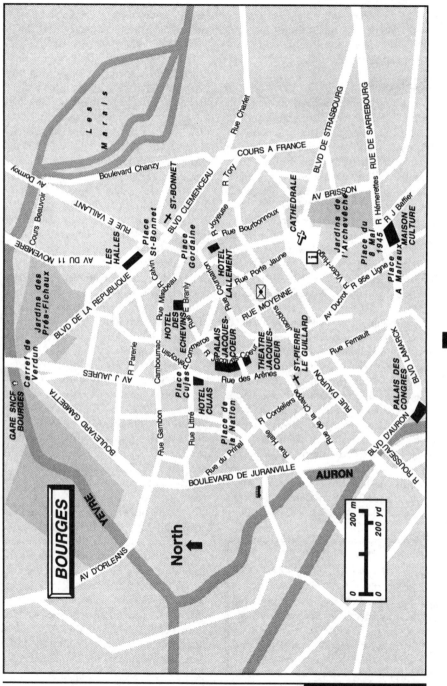

BOURGES

Les Marais

Boulevard Chanzy

Av Dormoy

Cours Beauvoir

RUE E VAILLANT

AV DU 11 NOVEMBRE

Jardins des
Prés-Fichaux

BLVD DE LA REPUBLIQUE

LES
HALLES

ST-BONNET

BLVD CLEMENCEAU

Place
St-Bonnet

Place
Gordaine

Rue Mirebeau

Rue Calvin

Rue Branly

HOTEL
DES
ECHEVINS

Rue Commerce

Cambournac

R Moyson

AV J JAURES

R Parerie

BOULEVARD GAMBETTA

GARE SNCF
BOURGES

Carrel de
Verdun

Rue Gambon

Rue Littré

HOTEL
CUJAS

Place
Cujas

Place de
la Nation

Rue du Prinal

Rue Charlet

Rue Tory

COURS A FRANCE

R Joyeuse

Rue Bourbonnoux

Coursarlon

HOTEL
LALLEMENT

RUE MOYENNE

Rue Porte Jaune

PALAIS
JACQUES-
COEUR

Place
Jacques Coeur

THEATRE
JACQUES-
COEUR

Rue des Arènes

Rue de la Chappe

R Cordeliers

Rue Halle

CATHEDRALE

BLVD DE STRASBOURG

AV BRISSON

Jardins de
l'Archevêché

R Victor-Hugo

Place du
8 Mai
1945

Av Ducrot

R 95e Ligne

RUE DE SARREBOURG

R Hémerettes

R J Baffier

Place
A Malraux

ST-PIERRE
LE GUILLARD

RUE D'AURON

Rue Ferrault

MAISON
CULTURE

PALAIS DES
CONGRES

BLVD LAMARCK

BLVD D'AURON

R ROUSSEAU

BOULEVARD DE JURANVILLE

AURON

YEVRE

BOURGES

North

AV D'ORLEANS

200 m
200 yd
0
0

pleasantly decked out with flower tubs and with interesting small shops (pottery, antiques, clothes) as well as *pâtisseries, chocolatiers* and *charcuteries*.

SIGHTSEEING

Guided tours in French, 90 min, around the old quarter take place each Sat 1500; daily (mid-Apr–mid-May). There are themed walks on subjects such as the cathedral's stained glass, half-timbered houses and in the footsteps of Jacques Coeur; days vary (Apr–Nov). The walks leave from the Tourist Office. They usually cost Fr.35; (concessions Fr.20).

During the Hundred Years' War when English raiders posed a constant threat, Bourges became the capital of the duchy ruled by Jean de France, son of King Jean le Bon. Until the duke's death in 1416, the Berry region prospered as described in the famous illuminated manuscript called *Les Très Riches Heures du Duc de Berry*.

The delightful town centre has picturesque streets lined with 15th–16th century houses, in particular *r. Bourbonnoux* (look for the **House of the Three Flutes** at the corner of *r. Joyeuse*), *r. Mirabeau* and *pl. Gordaine*. There are many narrow, quiet passages linking the old streets. Look also for the old **tithe barn** at *r. Molière* and *r. des Trois-Maillets* (an entry point for the remains of the Gallo-Roman ramparts).

Cathédrale St-Étienne is open 0800–1830 (Apr–Nov); 0800–1800 (Dec–

Mar). Guided tours in French and English of the crypt Mon–Sat 0900–1130, 1400–1830, Sun 1400–1800 (Apr–Nov); 0900–1130, 1400–1630 (Dec–Mar). Fr.27 (which includes entry to one of the towers). Started in 1192 by Henri de Sully, it is one of France's great Gothic cathedrals. In 1992, the cathedral was placed on Unesco's list of World Heritage Monuments. The west façade has a remarkable doorway with 13th-century stone carvings of the Last Judgement. There are five naves of descending heights and stained-glass windows from the 13th century to the Renaissance. An extravaganza of flying buttresses, this fabulous building, although huge, can come as a surprise, as it seems to appear suddenly when approached from one of the narrow streets such as *r. Molière*. It looks splendid seen from the other side thanks to the landscaped garden **Jardin de l'Archevêché** (Garden of the Archbishops). Its main entrance faces a more spacious square leading to *blvd de Strasbourg*. In the crypt is the funeral monument of Jean, Duke of Berry.

Palais Jacques Coeur, *r. Jacques Coeur; tel: 48 24 06 87.* Open 0900–1110, 1400–1719 (Easter–Oct); 0900–1110, 1400–1610 (Nov–Easter). Admission Fr.27 (Fr.18). Guided tours only, in French with English leaflet. A merchant banker and renowned businessman of his time, Jacques Coeur (see p. 211) became famous for his wheeling and dealing from Northern Europe to the Mediterranean, trading and selling silks, spices, carpets and furs. His sense of humour is shown on the façade of the great mansion he built for himself in Bourges. There are stone figures carved in relaxed poses looking out of fake windows. The house has fine wooden vault ceilings; the one in the chapel is lavishly painted. Although unfurnished, the stone and wood is richly carved including

> *Stop press – admission free!*
>
> Shortly before publication, it was announced that admission to **all museums** in Bourges (with the exception of the Palais Jacques Coeur and the Musée d'Histore Naturelle) will now be free of charge.

many vignettes of daily life, such as three ladies preparing their fashionable outfits to attend Mass. Everywhere are the family emblems – a scallop and a heart – and his punning motto, *A vaillant coeur rien impossible* (nothing is impossible for a valiant heart). He fell from power after losing royal favour and died in exile in 1456.

Museums

Musée Estève, *L'Hôtel des Échevins, 13 r. Edouard-Branly; tel: 48 24 75 38.* Open Wed–Sat 1000–1200, 1400–1800; Sun 1400–1800. Fr.18 (Fr.9);.free Wed. Built in 1489 as a meeting place for mayor and aldermen (the *échevins*), this handsome building has modern paintings by Maurice Estève, donated by him to Bourges. Guided visits in French and English.

Musée du Berry, *Hotel Cujas, 4. des Arènes; tel: 48 70 41 92.* Open Wed–Sat 1000–1200, 1400–1800, Sun 1400–1800; Admission Fr.18 (Fr.9), free Wed. Built in 1585, the building houses Gallo-Roman and ancient Greek and Egyptian collections, plus a permanent collection about Berry traditions. Most notable are the Gothic statues of prophets as mourners from the Duke of Berry's tomb.

Musée d'Histoire Naturelle (Museum of Natural History), *r. René-Ménard; tel: 48 57 82 44.* Open daily 1400–1800; Fr.18 (Fr.9). **Musée des Arts Décoratifs** (Museum of Decorative Arts), *Hôtel Lallemant, 6 r. Bourbonnoux; tel: 48 57 81 17:* Open Tues–Sat 1000–1200, 1400–1800, Sun 1400–1800; Fr.18 (Fr.9), free Wed. The recently opened, **Musée des Meilleurs Ouvriers de France**, *Ancien Archevêché, pl. Étienne Dolet; tel: 48 57 81 15,* features contemporary objects such as award-winning furniture. Open daily 1400–1800; Fr.18 (Fr.9), free Sun afternoon. **Musée de l'École** (Schoolroom Museum), *2. r. de la Thaumassière; tel: 48*

24 31 03. Open Wed 1400–1700; admission free. Built in 1887, this schoolroom has blackboards, wooden tables and benches, an abacus, purple ink in the inkwells and other schoolday relics.

Les Marais

The flat marshland and water meadows with allotment gardens, right beside the town, make an unusual rural stroll in a secret landscape. The Tourist Office will certainly tell visitors about the *marais* but there are no maps or special walks leaflets. However, make sure to ask for the city map which includes the pedestrianised *blvd du Gén. Chanzy* (off *blvd G. Clémenceau*) as this does not appear on the map in the English colour brochure *Bourges – the City of Hearts*. This quiet backwater street edges the *marais* and houses soon have water-edged frontages. Within 20 mins, the walker will be in the middle of the *marais*. The street leads to the bridge crossing the River Yèvre. Cross the bridge to the cluster of shops and bars on the busy *av. Marx Dormoy* and take the fourth turning on the right down the intriguingly named, pedestrian-only passage *r. de Babylone* which goes straight into the middle of the *marais*, past fertile allotments of flowers and vegetables with ramshackle garden sheds and the occasional gardener tending his patch. Water channels often divide the gardens. Surprisingly there is a little restaurant **La Courcillière**, *r. de Babylone; tel: 48 24 41 91.* Closed Tues afternoon, Wed.

From this flat area, the cathedral looms large on the horizon to the right. On the left is another large building in the distance, the **convent** of the *Soeurs de Charité* (sisters of charity). Where the *r. de Babylone* ends at the River Voiselle, turn right onto the riverside path which leads to a little wooden bridge. After crossing that, the path meanders back to the top end of the *blvd de Gén. Chanzy.* The garden plots have fences or *privé* (private) signs down their paths so it is not easy to stray into really private property.

If doing the walk in reverse, the entrance into the *marais* on *blvd Chanzy* (opposite *r. des Bouchers*) really does look as if it leads only to private homes but there is a big map just outside the entrance beside a phone booth. Note that the *r. Babylone* does not have a street sign where it meets the river but it is the first straight, wide passage leading left (and the convent will be looming on the right).

⬏ SIDE TRACK
FROM BOURGES

Because Bourges is so far south in the Loire Valley region, it is possible to reach wonderful volcanic mountain scenery by taking the good motorway link, A71, to Clermont-Ferrand, 188 km away.

CLERMONT-FERRAND

Tourist Office: *69 blvd Georgovia, 63000 Clermont-Ferrand; tel: 73 93 30 20.* Open Mon–Sat 0830–1900, Sun 0900–1200, 1400–1800 (June–Sept); Mon–Fri 0845–1830, Sat 0900–1200, 1400–1800 (Oct–May). Good English information available. Industrial Clermont has an extensive, charming old town and a wide choice of moderately priced hotels plus many good places to eat in all price brackets. It looks towards **Le Puy de Dôme**, 1465 m, the highest of the surrounding mountain peaks, which is a pleasant drive away and has panoramic views, Roman ruins and an information centre with an exhibition. *Tel: 73 62 21 46.* Open daily 0900–1900 (June–Sept); 0830–2000 (July–Aug).

A short drive away are two lively mountain towns, **La Bourboule** and **Le Mont Dore.** ⬛

Activities for children

Swimming, pedaloes, canoeing, windsurfing and other watersports are found in the Loire Valley but often around man-made or natural lakes rather than the river and its tributaries. Most main towns have a nearby *parc de loisirs* (leisure park), often with a swimming pool as well as other sporting facilities. There is usually equipment for hire and a café/bar, restaurant and picnic area. Tourist Offices will have details.

Hiring bicycles to enjoy the air is easily managed in the Loire Valley, which is well-suited for cycling excursions as so many of the main châteaux and their associated attractions lie close together. There are many quiet roads in well-tended forests.

Some châteaux have more child appeal than others. At St-Brisson, there are demonstrations of the real-sized battering-rams, catapults and medieval weapons which children will have seen in Robin Hood movies. At Ussé, the tableaux focus on the *Sleeping Beauty* theme. At Montrichard, a ruined keep is used for flying demonstrations of birds of prey. At Amboise, computer buffs can visit Leonardo da Vinci's home to see computer-designed realisations of his inventions worked out from his original drawings.

Some historical attractions are curiosities such as the many cave dwellings, some of which (besides the ubiquitous wine caves) are open to the public. In St-Hilaire-St-Florent, the caves include a mushroom cultivation museum with weird-looking mushrooms growing in oddly-shaped containers. A bit of forward planning means sightseeing need not be all art and history.

BREST

Brest occupies a prime position inside one of the most impressive natural harbours in the world. During World War II, the town paid dearly for the privilege of being France's most prestigious naval port and, since then, its maritime image has drastically changed. In spite of being hurriedly rebuilt after the war, the heart of the city was well planned with vast open spaces, wide avenues, an imposing university complex and cultural centre. No longer relying exclusively on its maritime activities to provide economic growth, Brest has become a leader in the field of advanced technology and oceanographic research. However, traditions die hard and, for the first time in July 1992, Brest welcomed an armada of ships from all over Europe to an extraordinary festival of colour, music and rejoicing. This popular meeting is expected to bring the town's maritime past to life every four years, during a week of continuous festivities.

TOURIST INFORMATION

Tourist Office: *8 av. G. Clémenceau, 29200 Brest* (opposite town hall); *tel: 98 44 24 96, fax: 98 44 53 73.* Open Mon–Sat 1000–1230 and 1400–1800, Sun 1000–1200 and 1400–1600 July–Sept; otherwise closed Sun morning.

Reservation service for a selection of hotels, restaurants and furnished accommodation; booking service for boat trips, guided tours, Océanopolis and various shows.

Bureau d'Information de la Jeunesse (Young People's Information Office), *1 r. d'Harteloire, 29200 Brest; tel: 98 43 01 08.* Contact them direct or inquire at the Tourist Office where the latest information is available.

ARRIVING AND DEPARTING

Airport

Located 10 km north-east of the city centre, along the N12 dual carriageway, the **Aéroport International de Brest-Guipavas**, *tel: 98 32 01 00,* is the main regional airport with direct daily flights to and from London and connecting flights via Paris to and from European destinations, New York and Miami.

By Car

The N12 linking Rennes and Brest by the northern route and the N165 linking Nantes and Brest along the south coast, lead straight to the centre of town; follow the signs for *Centre ville.* The centre of activity is the *pl. de la Liberté* and the adjacent wide avenues, *av. G. Clémenceau* and *r. de Siam.* There is free parking available in some side streets, but along main arteries parking spaces are marked *payant* and there are ticket dispensers nearby. The maximum time available is two hours so you may prefer to leave your car in the car park situated in the *pl. de la Liberté*, which never closes.

GETTING AROUND

The main sights are all within walking

73

distance of the *pl. de la Liberté*, except **Océanopolis** and the **Botanical Gardens**. Walking from the centre down to the château is quite pleasant as there are splendid views of the harbour along the way. As an alternative, there is an efficient bus service called **Bibus**, information *pl. de la Liberté; tel: 98 80 30 30*. A day card, allowing unlimited travel on the whole network, is available from bus drivers for Fr.18. Bus nos 2, 3, 7, 8, 11 and 12 connect all the main sights. Océanopolis and the Botanical Gardens are on the way out of town towards Quimper and can easily be reached by car; both have large car parks.

To call a **taxi**, call either *tel: 98 80 43 43* or *98 42 11 11*.

Accommodation

There is a good selection of reasonably priced two- and three-star hotels in the vicinity of the *pl. de la Liberté*, as well as a few good value one-star hotels such as **Hôtel Pasteur**, *29 r. Louis Pasteur; tel: 98 46 08 73*. There are cheaper hotels outside the town centre, especially on the way to the airport. Very good value for money, if you are just passing through, are the low-priced *BB, F1* and *NH* chain hotels.

Hotel chains in and around Brest offer a wide price range and include *BB, Ca, Ct, F1, Hd, Ib, Mc, Nv*.

For a memorable stay, try the three-star **Belvédère Hôtel**, *Ste-Anne du Portzic, 29200; tel: 98 31 86 00*, offering panoramic views of Brest roadstead and the Crozon Peninsula across the narrow entrance to the roadstead.

The **Youth Hostel** is near Océanopolis, *r. de Kerbriant, Port de Plaisance du Moulin Blanc* (bus no.7); *tel: 98 41 90 41*.

There are two **campsites** a short distance from the town centre: **Camping du Goulet**, *Ste-Anne du Portzic*, (bus nos 7, 11, 12 and 26 to *Rte du Conquet* stop); *tel: 98 45 86 84*, where there are rooms and mobile homes to let, and **Camping Municipal de St-Marc**, *45 r. de Kérampéré*, (near the Port de Plaisance du Moulin Blanc); *tel: 98 02 30 64*.

For information about graded holiday homes in the Brest region, *tel: 98 44 50 18* or *fax: 98 44 53 73*.

Eating and Drinking

There is a wide choice of restaurants serving traditional French cuisine and quite a few specialising in fresh fish and seafood. The higher price bracket includes two gastronomic establishments, **Le Nouveau Rossini**, *22 r. Commandant Drogou; tel: 98 47 90 00*, and **Le Vatel**, *23 r. Fautras; tel: 98 44 51 02*, as well as **L'Océania**, *82 r. de Siam; tel: 98 80 66 66*, and **Le Poulbot** (at the Belvédère Hôtel). More reasonably priced, but still very refined, are **Le Ruffé**, *1 r. Y. Collet; tel: 98 46 07 70*, famous for its fresh seafood, and **L'Osso Buco**, *3 pl. J. Gouez; tel: 98 45 97 87*. Cheaper and very good value for money restaurants are also easy to find: two of them, specialising in seafood, **L'Abri des Flots** and the **Maison de l'Océan**, are situated along the *quai de la Douane*, very fashionable with the locals; a third, specialising in grilled meat, is significantly called **La Boucherie** (the Butcher's), *164 r. J. Jaurès; tel: 98 43 64 68*.

Crêperies – a flourishing Breton tradition – offer a wide choice of fillings, savoury and sweet; a couple of *crêpes* and a bottle of cider make up a reasonably priced meal, but be prepared for a fairly long wait if the place is crowded. Try **Aux Crêpes du Roi Gradlon**, *19 r. Fautras; tel: 98 80 17 28*, **Crêperie de Cornouaille**, *9 r. St-*

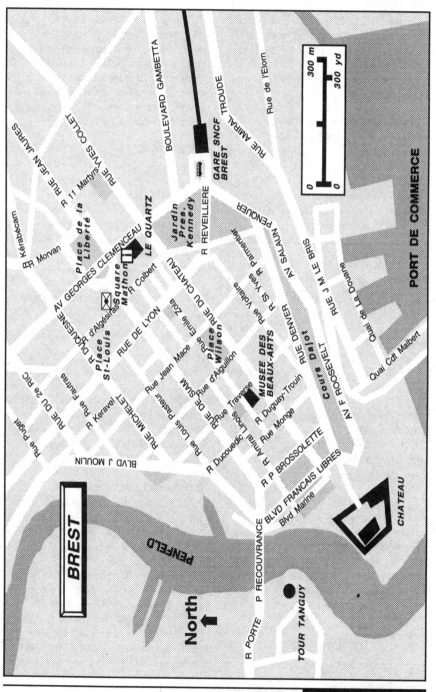

Marc; tel: 98 80 01 91, and **Crêperie Moderne,** *3 r. Algésiras; tel: 98 44 44 36.*

There are two excellent covered markets in the town centre (*pl. St-Martin* and *pl. St-Louis*) where you can buy fresh food for picnics.

Communications and Money

Situated at the junction of *r. de Siam* and *sq. Mathon*, the main **post office** is open Mon–Fri 0900–1900, Sat 0900–1200, closed Sun.

The **Banque de France** is open Mon–Fri, while **Crédit Agricole** is closed Mon and open Sat morning. There are a number of cash dispensers in the town centre.

ENTERTAINMENT

Cultural events normally take place in the Cultural Centre known as **Le Quartz,** *2-4 av. Clémenceau; tel: 98 44 33 77.* There are also concerts in the auditorium of the music conservatory, *16 r. du Château; tel: 98 44 45 74,* but during July and Aug, the focus is on the Jeudis du Port (see under 'Events').

Besides the usual discotheques, such as **La Chamade,** *2 r. Kérivin; tel: 98 80 18 71,* Brest offers a good choice of cabarets with live music and singing; two of them have become the favourite haunts of young people: the **Arizona Café,** *228 r. J. Jaurès; tel: 98 46 52 67* and **Le Club 26,** *26 r. Magenta; tel: 98 46 38 20.*

The popularity of Irish pubs underlines the strength of the Celtic connection in this most Breton part of Brittany: **The Dubliners,** *28 r. M. Donnart; tel: 98 80 20 99,* and **Tara Inn,** *1 r. Blaveau; tel: 98 80 36 07,* are among the liveliest.

Events

Every Thur during July and Aug, the harbour echoes the sounds of music and rejoicing: **Les Jeudis du Port** stage open-air performances of jazz, folk and pop music, plays and a variety of street entertainment graciously offered by the town.

Every four years in July, Brest is the meeting place of boats from all over Europe during a week of continuous festivities. Enquire at the Tourist Office.

SHOPPING

R. de Siam, r. J. Jaurès and *av. G. Clémenceau* are the main shopping streets. There is a useful shopping centre at *91 r. J. Jaurès; tel: 98 44 28 20,* with 120 boutiques and snack bars. Specialist shops include **La Boutique du Port,** *34 quai Cdt Malbert; tel: 98 43 46 13,* which sells gifts all connected with the sea, and **Les Lutins,** *5 r. de Siam; tel: 98 44 34 01,* with a wide choice of souvenirs, sailing clothes and Quimper pottery (see Quimper p. 235).

SIGHTSEEING

Although the town itself is no great tourist attraction, it is situated at the heart of the most rugged coastal area of western Brittany, within easy reach of the Côte des Abers (see St-Malo–Brest p. 288), Crozon Peninsula and Cap Sizun (see Brest–Quimper p. 78). It is also close to the fascinating Ouessant Island.

Roadstead and Islands

A walk along the **cours Dajot,** a short distance from the *pl. de la Liberté,* is a good introduction to the splendid panoramas Brest **roadstead** has to offer. The roadstead is the vast, sheltered expanse of water that surrounds Brest harbour. The 600-m-long seafront promenade overlooks the harbour and the docks with the vast expanse of the roadstead in the distance. A pink granite tower commemorates the American landings in 1917; destroyed by bombing in 1941, it was rebuilt in 1958.

Boat trips round the naval harbour, regular crossings to the Crozon Peninsula and trips up the Aulne and Elorn rivers, are organised by **Société Maritime Azénor**, *Port de Plaisance du Moulin-Blanc BP 40, 29281 Brest Saint-Marc; tel: 98 41 46 23* and **Vedettes Armoricaines**, *1er Eperon Port de Commerce BP 88, 29268 Brest Cedex; tel: 98 44 44 04*. It is also possible to discover the wild seascapes of **Ouessant Island**, 20 km offshore, and the sandy beaches of **Molène Island**; apply to **Compagnie Maritime Penn Ar Bed**, *1er Eperon Port de Commerce, 29607 Brest Cedex; tel: 98 80 24 68*, who run regular crossings all year round.

If you enjoy going back in time, then sailing round the roadstead in an authentic cargo ship formerly used to carry wine is definitely for you. Enquire at the Tourist Office for details.

Recouvrance District

Situated on the west bank of the Penfeld River, **Recouvrance** is all that is left of pre-war Brest. Guided tours start from the Tour Tanguy (see below); information from the Tourist Office.

Facing the château across the Penfeld river, the **Tour Tanguy**, *tel: 98 00 88 60*, houses a museum devoted to Brest's history; open daily 1000–1200 and 1400–1900 (June–Sept), otherwise Wed, Thur, weekends and afternoons only; free.

Museums

The **Musée des Beaux-Arts** (Fine Arts Museum), *22 r. Traverse; tel: 98 44 66 27*, is mostly famous for its collection of Breton painting from the 19th and 20th centuries, including the Pont-Aven School (see Quimper–Vannes p. 245); open daily except Tues 1000–1145 and 1400–1800, Sun 1400–1845; admission free.

Housed in the **château** extended by Vauban (Louis XIV's military architect), is one of the few buildings left standing at the end of World War II. The **Musée de la Marine** (Naval Museum), *tel: 98 22 12 39*, contains a fine collection of model ships, paintings and instruments. Open daily except Tues 0915–1200 and 1400–1800; Fr.27 (Fr.15 child).

Océanopolis

Shaped like a giant crab, **Océanopolis** *Port de Plaisance du Moulin Blanc; tel: 98 34 40 40*; is a centre of oceanographic research aimed at helping visitors to learn all about the sea in an environment which recreates the undersea world. Discover the secrets of tides and currents, the beautiful marine flora and fauna off the coast of Brittany, fish-farming, etc. Open daily 0930–1800 (May–Sept), 0930–1700, closed Mon morning (Oct–Apr); Fr.50, (Fr.30).

Parks and Walks

There are two beautiful parks on the outskirts of Brest. The **Bois de Kéroual** (north-west on the road to Guilers) is the favourite Sunday haunt of the locals, with 50 hectares of woodland with marked paths, lakes, a castle, games and picnic areas and the inevitable *crêperie*. The **Vallon du Stang-Alar** (south-east on the way to Quimper) is even more attractive because this privileged environment houses the **Conservatoire Botanique National de Brest** (Brest's Botanical Gardens), dedicated to the protection of endangered species from all over the world; open daily 1400–1700, free.

The west bank of the **Penfeld River** offers pleasant walks in the footsteps of Châteaubriand, the Romantic poet who spent some time in Brest at the impressionable age of 14.

BREST–QUIMPER

Western Finistère has the most deeply indented coastline in Brittany and two magnificently rugged peninsulas, Crozon and Cap Sizun, which offer wild seascapes and crumbling cliffs, sheltered creeks and vast open bays, granite villages and colourful fishing ports. The long coastal route reveals many facets of Breton life from the peaceful villages of Locronan or Le Faou to the bustling fishing ports of Douarnenez or Le Guilvinec. Allow three days at least, more if you take a boat trip to Sein Island.

DIRECT ROUTE: 66 KM

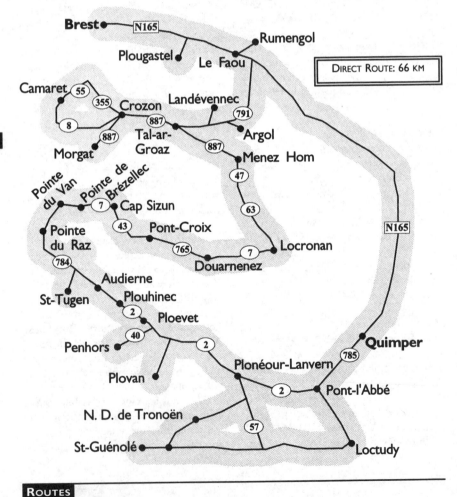

ROUTES

DIRECT ROUTE

➡ There are only 66 km between Brest and Quimper, less than an hour's drive, via the fast N165 dual carriageway. Take the ramp down to the harbour and follow the *r. J.M. Le Bris* and the *Rte du Vieux St-Marc* eastwards; alternatively follow the *r. J. Jaurès* from the *pl. de la Liberté* and turn right at the *pl. de Strasbourg* along the route de Quimper. Leave at the exit signposted *Quimper Centre*.

SCENIC ROUTE

➡ The 377-km coastal route including side-tracks explores the **Crozon Peninsula** and follows the coast of Cornouaille, one of the last bastions of Breton traditions, from Douarnenez right round to Pont-L'Abbé. Leave Brest as indicated above along the N165 to **Plougastel-Daoulas** and **Le Faou**. Turn right and drive along the D791 and D887 to Crozon, then bear right onto the D355 and follow the coast to **Camaret**. From there drive back across the Crozon Peninsula along the D8 and D887 to **Ménez-Hom** and turn south on the D47 towards **Locronan**. Continue to Douarnenez along the D7, the follow the D765, D43, D7 and D784 right round **Cap Sizun** via Pont-Croix, Pointe du Raz, **Audierne** and Plouhinec. Turn right onto the coast road to Penhors, drive south to Plonéour-Lanvern, N.D. de Tronoën and St-Guénolé, then follow the coast round to **Pont-l'Abbé** via Le Guilvinec, Lesconil and Loctudy. From Pont-l'Abbé, drive north on D785 the 35 km to Quimper.

PLOUGASTEL-DAOULAS

Tourist Office: *4 bis pl. du Calvaire, 29470 Plougastel-Daoulas; tel: 98 40 68 85;* open weekdays and Sun morning (summer), closed Sun, Mon and Thurs afternoon (winter).

ACCOMMODATION AND FOOD

There are only two very cheap hotels in the village but *Ba, Ib* and *IH* have establishments just outside. There are several restaurants and a *crêperie* within a few mins' walk of the centre; gourmets will want to try the **Chevalier de l'Auberlach**, *5 r. M. Thomas; tel: 98 40 54 56.*

SIGHTSEEING

The traditional **Fête des Fraises** (Strawberry Festival), which takes place on the second Sun in June, is famous throughout Brittany.

Being so close to Brest and only a few hundred metres from the fast flowing N165, this peaceful village comes as a surprise; in fact, the Plougastel Peninsula remained isolated from the mainland until the 1930s when the **Albert Louppe Bridge** linked it to Brest. Hedges, narrow winding roads and tiny chapels are characteristic of the countryside around Plougastel-Daoulas. In the centre of the village stands a monumental **calvary**, one of the most beautiful in Brittany (see Quimper–Morlaix p. xxx); damaged by allied bombing during World War II, it was restored with the generous help of an American officer.

Nearby, the excellent **Musée du Patrimoine de Plougastel**, *tel: 98 40 21 18*, is devoted to local history and culture.

From the extremity of the peninsula (8.5 km from Plougastel), known as the **Pointe de Kerdéniel**, there is a panoramic view of the Brest roadstead.

LE FAOU

Tourist Office: *10 r. du Gén. de Gaulle, 29580 Le Faou; tel: 98 81 06 85* (open all year).

The town's two hotels, **La Vieille Renommée**, *tel: 98 81 90 31*, and **Le Relais de la Place**, *tel: 98 81 91 19*, both have restaurants and are quite reasonably priced. There is a *crêperie* next door and another one in the high street.

Nestling deep inside the Brest roadstead, the town has retained some beautiful samples of 16th- and 17th-century architecture. In those days Le Faou (pronounced 'Fou') was a prosperous port shipping timber from the nearby Cranou forest to Brest for the famous shipyards of *La Royale* (the French Navy). The **corbelled houses** along the main street are faced with slates and have pointed gables. The beautiful **Église St-Sauveur** (St Saviour's church) has an elegant Renaissance steeple.

Two important *pardons* (religious celebrations, see Quimper–Vannes p. 245) take place in the picturesque village of **Rumengol** situated 3 km east of Le Faou (and now officially joined to it) on the Sun after Whitsun and on 15 Aug.

CROZON PENINSULA

Tourist Information: Maison du Tourisme, *BP 45, 29160 Crozon; tel: 98 26 17 18, fax: 98 26 21 63*; information service about classified holiday homes in the whole area. **Tourist Offices** open all year: **Camaret-sur-Mer**, *tel: 98 27 93 60*; **Crozon-Morgat**, *tel: 98 27 07 92*. **Tourist Offices** open in summer only: **Argol**, *tel: 98 27 75 30*; **Landévennec**, *tel: 98 27 72 65*; **Telgruc-sur-Mer**, *tel: 98 27 78 06*. Some beaches on the peninsula are dangerous; if in doubt inquire at any Tourist Office. The Crozon Peninsula forms part of the **Parc Naturel Régional d'Armorique**; for information *tel: 98 21 90 69*.

The Tourist Office also provide information on walking tours, guided nature walks, boat trips, outdoor activities, market days and events.

ACCOMMODATION

There is a good selection of one- and two-star hotels in Camaret-sur-Mer and Crozon-Morgat, with restaurants and the possibility of opting for half or full board. The higher price range is limited to the **Thalassa** in Camaret, *tel: 98 27 86 44* and the **Grand Hôtel de la Mer** in Crozon, *tel: 98 27 02 09*. There are several very well appointed campsites, again in and around Camaret and Crozon-Morgat, but also south at Telgruc-sur-Mer.

EATING AND DRINKING

Restaurants offer the usual choice of traditional French cuisine, delicious seafood, crêpes and other Breton specialities, such as fish soup and *homard à l'armoricaine*, lobster served with a tasty sauce made from tomatoes, garlic and cognac. For a gastronomic treat, try the restaurant of the **Hôtel Julia** in *Morgat, tel: 98 27 05 89* , the **Hostellerie de la Mer** in *Le Fret, tel: 98 27 61 90*, or **La Voilerie** in *Camaret-sur-Mer, tel: 98 27 99 55*.

ENTERTAINMENT

Breton festivities called **Fest Noz**, accompanied by traditional music and folk dancing, take place during the summer. There are also various sea festivals and the **Jeux Nautiques Interceltiques**, a sporting and cultural event open to seven Celtic countries (for information, *tel: 98 52 04 80*). The main musical event of the area is **Les Lundis Musicaux** (Musical Mondays) in Camaret-sur-Mer, July and most of Aug.

SIGHTSEEING

There is no coastal road as such, but a series of minor roads radiating from the main D791 and D887 which meet at the narrowest point of the peninsula. Leave Le Faou on the D791, which offers lovely views of the Aulne estuary. Five km after the picturesque **Pont de Térénez** (Térénez Bridge), look out for a left turn to the **Musée du Cidre,** (Cider Museum) *tel: 98 27 35 85,* and the village of **Argol** with an interesting 16th-century church, monumental arch and the **Musée des Vieux Métiers** (Museum of Ancient Crafts), *tel: 98 27 07 92.* Return to the main road, turn left then right 500 m further on to **Landévennec** and the site of the ruined abbey, founded in the 5th century by the Welsh monk St-Gwennolé and rebuilt several times before being finally abandoned at the end of the 18th century. Its interesting museum relates the life and cultural contribution of the monks during the Middle Ages (*tel: 98 27 35 90).*

Crozon is a lively resort with hotels and holiday homes. Before going on to Camaret-sur-Mer, make a detour on the D887 to **Morgat,** a fashionable seaside resort, to visit the **Grottes Marines,** a group of caves accessible by boat only; visits depend on tidal conditions (*tel: 98 27 10 71).* The D355 goes north from Crozon towards the **Pointe des Espagnols,** which offers panoramic views of the entrance to the Brest roadstead, right round to Camaret.

Sheltered inside a small semi-circular bay, **Camaret** is the liveliest and most attractive resort of the Crozon Peninsula as well as a busy fishing port famous for its lobsters and a pleasant port of call for yachts and cabin cruisers. On a narrow sandbank jutting out into the bay stand the 16th-century **Chapelle Notre-Dame de Rocamadour** and the **Tour Vauban,** built in the 17th century to protect the port from English and Dutch attacks. Cliffs, spectacular reefs and sheltered sandy creeks alternate along the picturesque coast

around Camaret. It is possible to take a boat trip round the **Pointe du Toulinguet** to the rugged **Pointe de Penhir** and the famous **Tas de Pois,** an alignment of pointed reefs emerging from the sea like giant stepping stones. Alternatively, these can be reached by road from Camaret; notice on the roadside between Toulinguet and Penhir, several rows of megaliths known as the **Alignements de Lagatjar,** dating from 2500 BC (see Quimper–Vannes p. 245). The **Musée Mémorial de la Bataille de l'Atlantique,** *tel: 98 27 92 58,* is housed in a bunker, on top of the windswept cliffs of the Pointe de Penhir; it traces the history of the Allied and German merchant navies during World War II.

Go back to Crozon and follow the D887 all the way to the foot of **Ménez Hom** (330 m). A 2-km long narrow road leads to this isolated peak guarding the entrance to the Crozon Peninsula. The view from the top takes in the whole of Crozon and extends across the Baie de Douarnenez to the northern coast of Cap Sizun and inland to the Monts d'Arrée.

Tourist Information: Syndicat d'Initiative, *pl. de l'Église, 29550* **Plomodiern***; tel: 98 81 27 37.* **Tourist Offices: Ploëven,** *tel: 98 81 51 84;* **Plonevez–Porzay,** *tel: 98 92 53 57.*

There is a splendid but expensive hotel on the beach at Ste-Anne-la-Palud, where one of the most picturesque *pardons* (religious festivals) takes place at the end of Aug: **Hôtel de la Plage,** *tel: 98 92 50 12.* More reasonably priced and still very attractive is the 17th-century **Manoir de Moëllien,** just south of *Plonévez-Porzay,* *tel: 98 92 50 40.* On the other hand, the **Relais de Tréfeuntec,** *tel: 98 92 50 03,*

81

and the **Hôtel du Prieuré** in *Locronan, tel: 98 91 70 89*, are quite good value for money in the middle price range.

The best **campsite** is in **Kervel**, *tel: 98 92 51 54*, on the coast between Ste-Anne-la-Palud and Douarnenez.

At **Ste-Marie-du-Ménez-Hom**, have a look at the Renaissance chapel before driving on to Plomodiern and Ploëven and turning right towards **Ste-Anne-la-Palud**. Lost among the sand dunes, the 19th-century chapel contains a granite statue of St Anne dating from 1548. During the *Grand Pardon*, which lasts for three days and attracts thousands of people, services are held in the open just outside the chapel.

LOCRONAN

Tourist Office: *pl. de la Mairie, 29180; tel: 98 91 70 14.*

Situated 8 km to the south-east, **Locronan** is an architectural gem. Substantial 16th–18th-century granite houses surround the *Grande Place* and line the paved streets radiating from it. They once belonged to rich cloth merchants who made the town prosperous. The interesting **Musée Municipal** is devoted to the history of the town and its ancient crafts. It also contains a collection of paintings on Breton themes. Many craftsmen have settled in Locronan and offer a choice of Breton specialities. The imposing 15th-century **church** dominates the square; the adjoining **Chapelle du Pénity** contains the grave of St Ronan, the Irish monk who lived as a hermit in the nearby forest of Nevet. A colourful *pardon*, known as **La Grande Troménie**, takes place every six years in July; the procession follows an ancient Druidic route and ends on top of Locronan 'mountain' crowned by **Chapelle St-Ronan**. The last of these *pardons* this century took place in 1995. A

Fishing

It is still true to say that the majority of Bretons are either fishermen or farmers, often both. This is not surprising, considering that Brittany has some 3000 km of coastline, deeply indented and offering ideal shelter to a great number of fishing ports of all sizes which harbour 2650 boats representing half the fishing fleet of France!

But fishing practices have changed considerably and the Terre-Neuvas who left St-Malo to fish for cod along the shores of Newfoundland now belong to Breton legends. Today, Lorient (first fishing port in Brittany), Concarneau and Douarnenez practise 'industrial' fishing: Large trawlers leave port bound for the coast of central Africa, returning with thousands of tonnes of tuna, frozen on board and later processed in canneries all over Brittany. However, local fishing for a variety of fresh fish as well as lobster is on the increase. The foremost French port for this kind of traditional fishing is Le Guilvinec in Bigouden country in south Finistère, which has the highest concentration of fishing ports along the whole coast of Brittany.

shorter version, called **La Petite Troménie**, takes place every year in July.

DOUARNENEZ

Tourist Office: *BP 216, 29172 Douarnenez Cedex; tel: 98 92 13 35, fax: 98 74 46 09.* Open daily except Sun.

ACCOMMODATION

Linked to the hydrotherapy centre, the **Thalasstonic**, *tel: 98 74 45 45*, is a fairly expensive hotel, situated near the Sables Blancs beach. A more reasonable and certainly charming alternative is the **Ty Mad**, *tel: 98 74 00 53*, overlooking the St-Jean beach. The recently renovated **Hôtel de France**, *4 r. J. Jaurès, tel: 98 92 00 02*, situated in the old part of town, is ideal as a stopover. All three hotels have fine restaurants and there are many more to choose from in the town and near the harbour.

SIGHTSEEING

Guided tours of the fishing harbour, of canneries and of the town are organised by the Tourist Office during July and Aug. For boat trips round the bay, apply to **Vedettes Rosmeur**, *tel: 98 92 83 83*. Regattas take place regularly and there are all day events at the open air Port-Musée. The international film festival is now well established and appreciated.

Douarnenez has three harbours: the fishing harbour, an impressive sight early in the morning when the auction sale begins; the elegant and well appointed marina; and the **Port-Musée**, *tel: 98 92 65 20*, a vast museum housing a rich collection of boats, about 200 on land and 50 afloat, among them a Thames river barge. However, the museum is under threat of closure due to financial problems. Open daily 1000–1900; Fr.50, (Fr.25 children).

CAP SIZUN

Tourist Office: *pl. de la Liberté, 29770 Audierne; tel: 98 70 12 20, fax: 98 75 01 11* (open all year, reservation service, booking service for excursions and boat trips). **Tourist Office**, Pont-Croix; *tel: 98 70 40 38* (open July and Aug)

ACCOMMODATION

There are plenty of reasonably priced hotels, but those close to the sea have the edge over the others: **Le Goyen**, *Audierne, tel: 98 70 08 88*; **Au Roi Gradlon**, *Audierne, tel: 98 70 04 51*; **L'Horizon**, *Audierne, tel: 98 70 09 91*; **Breiz Armor**,

Penhors-Plage, tel: 98 51 52 53; **La Baie des Trépassés**, *Plogoff, tel: 98 70 61 34*; **Hôtel de l'Iroise**, *Pointe du Raz, tel: 98 70 64 65*.

Campsites are mainly situated inland except the **Camping de Kersiny**, in *Plouhinec, tel: 98 70 82 44*, which is one of the better appointed ones.

SIGHTSEEING

Cap Sizun offers the ideal environment for outdoor activities both inland and on the water, but its architectural heritage is by no means negligible and a good way to discover its fine churches and chapels is to attend the **Festival du Cap Sizun** (traditional music, Breton tales and legends, in July and Aug). It is possible to hire boats from the **Club Nautique**, *tel: 98 70 21 69*.

Leave Douarnenez on the D765 towards Audierne. The charming village of **Pont-Croix** has one of the most beautiful medieval churches in Finistère, **Notre-Dame-de-Roscudon** (guided tours daily except Sun in July and Aug), with a finely carved porch and a spire which served as a model for those of **Quimper Cathedral**.

Soon after leaving Pont-Croix turn right towards the north coast of Cap Sizun. The greater part of the **Réserve Naturelle du Cap Sizun** (bird sanctuary) is freely accessible, the rest is open from mid-Mar–Aug. Cormorants, seagulls, petrels, fulmars and guillemots cohabit on the rocky cliffs and islands. The **Pointe de Brézellec** and **Pointe du Van** with its tiny **Chapelle St-They** offer magnificent views of the Crozon Peninsula across the Baie de Douarnenez. The sombre rock omnipresent at the extremity of Cap Sizun conveys an impression of wild austerity; one million visitors a year have severely damaged the unique environment of the

83

Breton costumes

There is no single 'Breton national costume' but a considerable number of regional costumes with strong characteristics and subtle variations from one area to another, a source of great pride at a time when parishes found the need to assert their individuality. Costumes gradually became more ornate and were soon considered as an essential element of traditional events such as *pardons* and *fest-noz* (folk festivals). Women add a splash of colour to processions and gatherings with their richly embroidered dresses and aprons and men look handsome with their large-brimmed felt hats and bright-buttoned jackets. But *coiffes* (headdresses) are undoubtedly the most original element of Breton costumes. They are made of fine lace starched into unusual shapes: with graceful wings in Pleyben and Pont-Aven or cylindrical and rising high above the head as in Bigouden Country.

Pointe du Raz, which is being carefully restored.

Just before reaching Audierne, turn right towards **St-Tugen** to admire the Flamboyant Gothic chapel. In **Audierne** go straight to the harbour which specialises in lobster fishing. Boat trips to **Sein Island** take 1 hr 10 mins.

Continue on the D784 and turn right in Plouhinec.

BIGOUDEN COUNTRY

Tourist Office: *29120 Pont-l'Abbé; tel: 98 82 37 99* (open daily 0900–1215 and 1500–1900, Sun 1000–1230). There are smaller offices in Le Guilvinec, Loctudy and Plonéour-Lanvern. Pont-l'Abbé is the main town in this area south of Audierne and Quimper in south-west Finistère.

ACCOMMODATION

There are two expensive *châteaux-hôtels* in the area, **Manoir de Kerhuel**, Plonéour-Lanvern, *tel: 98 82 60 57* and **Château de Kernuz**, just south of Pont-l'Abbé, *tel: 98 87 01 59*. A more conventional and cheaper choice would be **Hôtel de la Mer**, St-Guénolé, *tel: 98 58 62 22* or **Hôtel du Port**, Le Guilvinec, *tel: 98 58 10 10*. There are plenty of other comfortable hotels and well appointed **campsites** all along the coast.

SIGHTSEEING

Many traditional events, often connected with the sea, take place in the area; among the liveliest and most colourful is the **Fête des Brodeuses** (Festival of Embroidery, Pont-l'Abbé, second Sun in July).

Leave Penhors towards Plonéour-Lanvern; just after Plovan, don't miss the lovely ruins of the **Chapelle de Languidou** on the left. In Plonéour, turn right towards **N.D. de Tronoën**, the oldest calvary in Brittany and one of the finest then **St-Guénolé** and its picturesque pink rocks. Just before reaching St-Guénolé, stop at the **Musée de Préhistoire Finistérienne** (Museum of Prehistory in Finistère, open June–Sept). The ports situated along the south coast are all picturesque and colourful resorts as well as lively fishing ports.

At Loctudy, drive north towards Pont-l'Abbé. Two km before reaching the town, visit the **Maison du Pays Bigouden,** an open-air museum housed in an old farm (open June–Sept daily except sun). The **Musée Bigouden** in Pont-l'Abbé occupies part of the medieval castle and contains a remarkable collection of furniture and costumes (open Easter–Sept daily except Sun). Ask the Tourist Office for mapped itineraries of excursions in and around Pont-L'Abbé.

CAEN

The capital of Basse-Normandie (Lower Normandy), Caen has grown rapidly since World War ll, and is now one of the most lively modern commercial centres in Normandy. It occupies a position at the centre of the Caen Plain, from which Caen stone, a particularly attractive type of sandstone, has been quarried for many centuries. The stone was used in the building of both Westminster Abbey and Canterbury Cathedral, but these days it is used only for special projects such as Caen's Mémorial Museum and the restoration of medieval buildings originally constructed from the material.

TOURIST INFORMATION

Tourist Office: *pl. St-Pierre, 14000 Caen; tel: 31 27 14 14.* Open Mon–Sat 0900–1900, Sun and public holidays 1000–1230 and 1500–1800 (May–Sept); Mon 1000–1230 and 1400–1830, Tues–Sat 0900–1230 and 1400–1830, Sun and public holidays 1000–1230 (Oct–Apr).

ARRIVING AND DEPARTING

By Car

A dual carriageway links Caen with its ferry port at Ouistreham (14km to the north-east) and this leads directly to the town centre.

The *Boulevard Périphérique* links the A13 from Paris and Rouen to the N13 Caen to Cherbourg road, skirting the town to the north. Driving from Paris, the best exit is

at the end of the autoroute at Mondeville or at St-Jean immediately before the Viaduc de Calix. From the west, take the second exit after the Mémorial Museum, a distinctive landmark to the left.

By Ferry

Brittany Ferries operate a car ferry service from Portsmouth to Caen, docking at Ouistreham. **Bus Verts**, *tel: 31 44 77 44,* operate an express bus service between Ouistreham and Caen, which links with ferry departures and arrivals.

GETTING AROUND

All the town's main sights are located close to the centre, apart from the Mémorial Museum which is beside the *Boulevard Périphérique* to the north. The Tourist Office has a good street map of the centre showing the main sights, which is free. For a broader view showing the Mémorial in relation to the centre, ask the tourist office for their hotel and restaurant guide (also free). Bus Verts operate an extensive network of bus routes throughout the town and its suburbs, with route nos 12 (Mon–Fri) and 14 (Sat–Sun) going to the Mémorial from *pl. Courtonne.*

STAYING IN CAEN

Accommodation

Caen has a large proportion of two-star hotels, but also a choice of one- and three-star and unclassified or *économique* hotels, as well as one four-star. Most are located near the centre, a few of them near the station, while a number of modern business hotels have sprung up alongside the *Boulevard*

Périphérique, especially around the southeast approaches, and to the north near the Mémorial Museum.

Hotel chains include *Ca, Fr, Ib, Me, Nv*. The most expensive place to stay is the modern and elegant **Relais des Gourmets**, *15 r. de Geôle; tel: 31 86 06 01*, facing the château. Just as classy and also located in the centre, though a little cheaper, is the **Hotel Moderne**, *116 blvd Mar. Leclerc; tel 31 86 04 23*. Rooms are soundproofed against traffic noise, while a sauna offers additional relaxation. Far more reasonable is the **Ibis Centre Paul Doumer**, *33 r. de Bras; tel: 31 50 00 00*, which, though a typically characterless modern hotel, is ideally positioned in the centre of town. The **Hotel Friendly**, *2 pl. de Boston, Hérouville-St-Clair; tel: 31 44 05 05*, rated three-star, is the best of the hotels in the outskirts, though rooms are expensive. There is also a good quality restaurant.

HI: the **Auberge de Jeunesse de Caen – Residence Robert Rème**, *68 r. Eustache-Restout; tel: 31 52 19 96*, is in the south of the town, not far from the station, but is only open June–Sept.

Campsite: the **Camping Municipal**, *Rte de Louvigny; tel: 31 73 60 92*, has 130 pitches and is open late Apr–early Oct.

Eating and Drinking

Caen has an excellent choice of restaurants, offering mainly traditional French cuisine, though there is a fair selection of a more exotic nature – Italian, Mexican and Far Eastern. Most restaurants are in the centre of town, with particular concentrations around *pl. Courtonne* and *quai Vendeuvre* near the marina, and the delightful *r. du Vaugueux*, a street of ancient gabled buildings located just beneath the castle. The town's speciality is *tripes à la mode de Caen* – tripe cooked in

the Caen fashion, which is stewed for hours – but it is not to everyone's taste. It can be found at its best at **La Bourride**, *15–17 r. du Vaugueux; tel: 31 93 50 76*, the top restaurant in town, if not in Normandy. Very expensive.

L'Étoile, *90 blvd Mar. Leclerc; tel: 31 86 07 00*, is one of a handful of brasseries in Caen. Snacks are available in the downstairs bar, while more substantial meals are served in the first floor dining room which can be quite busy at lunch-time. Good value.

Communications

Main **post office** at *pl. Gambetta*, is open Mon–Fri 0800–1900, Sat 0800–1200.

Money

The Tourist Office has change facilities, open Mon–Sat 1000–1215 and 1300–1800, Sun 1030–1230 and 1500–1700. In addition **Crédit Agricole** has a kiosk next to their branch in *blvd Mar. Leclerc*, open daily 0900–1300 and 1400–1845.

ENTERTAINMENT

There are a couple of listings publications: the monthly *Le Mois à Caen* has cultural information, and *Caen Loisirs*, which comes out fortnightly and has a broader range of information. Both are available free from hotels and the Tourist Office, which also produces its own monthly listings leaflet.

The **Théâtre de Caen**, *135 blvd Mar. Leclerc; tel: 31 30 76 20*, offers the most extensive programme of entertainment, with plays, opera and classical concerts. Other venues offering a mixture of theatre and music include the **Comédie de Caen**, *32 r. des Cordes; tel: 31 46 27 29* and **Espace Puzzle**, *28 r. de Bretagne; tel: 31 50 04 52*.

As well as the Théâtre de Caen, the

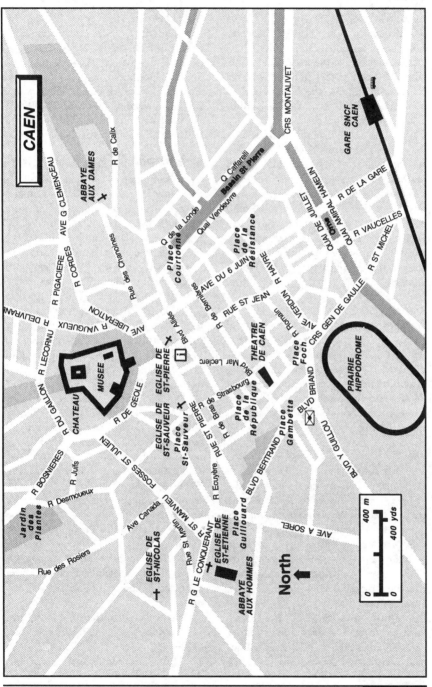

87

Conservatoire, *1 r. du Carel; tel: 31 50 05 64*, frequently hosts classical concerts, either in the Grand Auditorium for which there is a charge, or the Petit Auditorium, which are free. For rock and jazz, with big names from the UK and USA as well as home grown bands, head for the **Zénith**, *r. Joseph Philippon; tel: 36 68 68 37*.

Caen has two mainstream **cinemas**, the **Pathé Lumière**, *15 blvd Mar. Leclerc; tel: 36 68 20 22*, and the **Pathé Malherbe**, *55 r. des Jacobins; tel: 36 68 20 22*. Each has seven screens and shows a mixture of French, American and British films. All foreign films are dubbed into French. The **Lux**, *av. Ste-Thérèse; tel: 31 82 29 87*, shows various foreign language films in their original form, with French subtitles.

Sport

Spectator sports on the whole consist of soccer and horse-racing. Caen's football team plays at the **Michel d'Ornano stadium**, *tel: 31 29 16 00*, while the **Prairie Hippodrome**, *blvd Aristide Briand; tel: 31 85 42 61*, on a vast open tract of land on the southern edge of town, hosts trotting and flat racing.

SHOPPING

The main shopping area, one of the best in Normandy, comprises the pedestrianised *r. St-Pierre*, which among other shops has a good selection of *chocolatiers* (chocolate shops) and *pâtisseries* (cake shops), as well as *r. St-Jean* and the *blvd Mar. Leclerc* along with the various interlinking streets. Most of the big national stores are represented, with the **Nouvelles Galleries** in *blvd Mar. Leclerc*, **Monoprix** at *r. de Bernières* and **Printemps** in *r. St-Jean*. The **Centre Paul Doumer**, *r. de Bras*, houses a number of fashion stores as well as **fnac**, a leading bookstore and music centre.

Markets are held every Fri and Sun morning. The largest is Friday's traditional market, which centres on *Fossés St-Julien* and spreads along *r. Pémagnie* to *pl. St-Sauveur*. This one is best for enjoying the ambience of French market life as well as for the purchase of farm produce, whereas the Sunday market, in *pl. Courtonne*, is better for clothing and bric-à-brac.

SIGHTSEEING

Capital of Basse-Normandie and of the *département* of Calvados, Caen is a modern town, a large part of it having been destroyed in Allied bombardments following the D-Day landings of 1944. However, the main historical landmarks have survived and there are a few small reminders of medieval Caen to be seen. It was William the Conqueror's favourite town and the curtain walls of his **castle** (grounds open daily 0600–2130 summer, 0600–1930 winter; admission free) still stand in the centre, enclosing two museums. Housed in the former Governor's lodgings, the **Musée de Normandie**, *tel: 31 86 06 24*, (open Wed–Fri 1000–1230 and 1330–1800, Sat–Mon 0930–1230 and 1400–1800, closed Tues; admission Fr.10) recalls the region's history, crafts and costume, and the **Musée des Beaux-Arts**, *tel: 31 85 28 63*, (open daily except Tues 1000–1800, admission Fr.20) has a wide representation of Flemish, Italian and French art.

The **Musée de la Poste**, *52–54 r. St-Pierre; tel: 31 50 12 20*, (open Tues–Sat 1330–1730, admission Fr.10) is housed in a 16th-century half-timbered building and illustrates the history of post and telecommunications.

The **Musée d'Initiation à la Nature**, *Hôtel de Ville, tel: 31 30 43 27*, open Wed 1400–1730 (Oct–Mar); Mon–Fri 1400–1730 (Apr–Sept) admission free, provides a first step towards discovering Normandy's fauna and flora.

Fast becoming Caen's most famous attraction, the **Mémorial**, *Esplanade Eisenhower; tel: 31 06 06 44* (open daily 0900–1900, admission Fr.61, Fr.51 for over 60s and students, free to World War II veterans and under 10s), is described as a museum for peace. The simple, windowless building, on the windy plain north of town, is a high-tech museum which charts world history from 1918 to the present day. It has an excellent specialist bookshop and a restaurant.

There are several churches of interest in Caen, most notably the two abbeys (one either side of town), built by William the Conqueror and his wife Mathilda as an act of penitence for their marriage, which the Pope had objected to as the couple were cousins. What is left of William (said to be only a thighbone after the grave was desecrated during the Revolution and his remains thrown in the river) is buried in the beautiful **Église de St-Étienne** (St Stephen's Church), *r. G. le Conquérant*, (open daily 0815–1200, 1400–1930) at the vast **Abbaye aux Hommes** (Men's Abbey), while Mathilda is buried at the **Abbaye aux Dames** (Ladies' Abbey), *r. des Chanoines; tel: 31 06 98 98*, (open daily 1430–1600), in the chancel of the Romanesque-style **Église de la Trinité** (Holy Trinity Church). The 18th-century monastery buildings attached to the Abbaye aux Hommes now house the Town Hall. Other churches include the 14th-century **Église St-Pierre**, *pl. St-Pierre*, richly decorated and beautifully restored after the wartime bombardments, the Gothic **Église St-Sauveur**, *r. St-Pierre*, which has two naves, side by side, and the Romanesque **St-Nicolas**, *r. St-Nicolas*, which has remained unaltered since completion in the late 11th century.

Several Renaissance merchants' houses can still be seen in Caen, and the best of them, the **Hôtel d'Escoville**, which is entered via a magnificent courtyard, lies behind the Office de Tourisme.

Canal Cruises

L'Hastings carries up to 80 people on mini cruises between Caen and Ouistreham. Boarding point is at the *quai Vendeuvre* in the **Port de Plaisance** (Pleasure Harbour), *bookings tel: 31 96 00 55*, right in the centre of town, and a round-trip to Ouistreham and back, passing through the port of Caen, past Bénouville Château and the famous Pegasus Bridge, takes 2 hrs 15 mins, fare Fr.68, Fr.120 for a couple, Fr.25 for a child.

OUT OF TOWN

A drive north past the castle via the D7 towards Langrune-sur-Mer leads to **Douvres-La-Délivrande** within about 13 km, a village famous for its **basilica**. The tall twin spires of this 19th-century neo-Gothic building can be seen for miles around, but it is for the highly-venerated 16th-century statue of the **Vierge Noire** (Black Virgin) that people visit. A grand pilgrimage takes place every year on the first Thur after Aug 15. Just across the square from the basilica at *78 r. Gén. de Gaulle*, there is an interesting pharmacy built in the art nouveau style.

From the *pl. de la Basilique*, take the road sign posted Luc-sur-Mer and Ouistreham, but then follow the signs along the D7, right onto D404 and first right onto D83 for the **Musée Radar de Douvres**; *tel: 31 37 74 43*, open daily 1000–1900 (Easter–Oct), admission Fr.30 adults, Fr.15 children. The first museum dedicated to the history of radar, it is housed in the concrete bunkers of a former German radar station.

89

CAEN–CHERBOURG

The direct route between Caen and Cherbourg, N13, is dual carriageway virtually all the way now and you have to leave the road to visit any towns of interest. The scenic route meanders along the coast made famous by the D-Day landings of 1944, with, here and there, a diversion to take in other points of interest.

DIRECT ROUTE: 115 KM

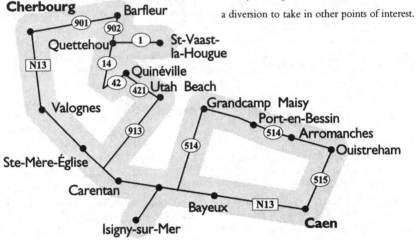

ROUTES

DIRECT ROUTE

➡ Roads out of Caen are well-signposted to Cherbourg via the *Boulevard Péripherique*, but try to avoid the busy periods 0730–0930, 1200–1400 and 1630–1830. The total journey is 115 km and takes around 1 hr 30 mins. Take the N13 westwards across the Caen Plain and then follow the ring road round **Bayeux**. Around **Carentan**, which is now bypassed, the N13 passes through the marshlands of the **Parc Régional des Marais du Cotentin** to Ste-Mère-

Église, before reaching the higher, more undulating *bocage* (hedged fields) en route for **Valognes**, also bypassed, beyond which the road descends into Cherbourg.

COASTAL ROUTE

➡ Leave Caen via the *av. de la Libération*, following the signs for **Ouistreham** and **Le Car-Ferry**. Initially the road is designated D515, but shortly becomes D514 and remains so through the ribbon of coastal resorts until beyond **Grandcamp-Maisy**, when it joins the N13. Stay on this for about 10 km and beyond Carentan take the D913 to **Utah**

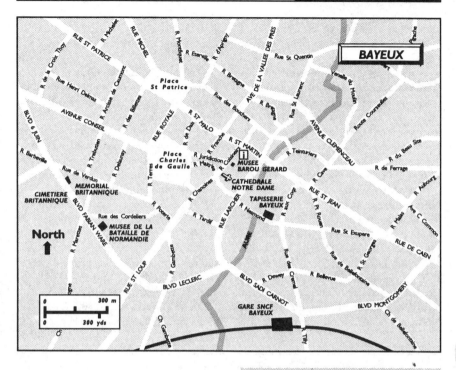

Beach. At the coast take the D421 northwards, turning left at **Quinéville** onto D42 and then take D14 to **Quettehou**, from which a short diversion along D1 leads to **St-Vaast-la-Hougue**. Returning to Quettehou, the route goes via D902 to **Barfleur** and then 901 to Cherbourg.

The road is slow at the best of times, but is especially so in high season between Ouistreham and **Arromanches**. Total distance is 185 km and will take a minimum of 3 hrs 30 mins to drive, though if you want to take in all the D-Day sights and the diversions that this route offers, allow at least two days.

BAYEUX

Tourist Office: *Pont St-Jean, 14403 Bayeux; tel: 31 92 16 26*, has information on accommodation and sightseeing in the area.

ACCOMMODATION

Bayeux has a good choice of hotels, mainly two-star, though there are several three-star too. In the town centre, the **Hôtel Churchill**, *14–16 r. St-Jean; tel: 31 21 31 80*, is a comfortable three-star hotel with an excellent restaurant, though is somewhat on the expensive side. Far more moderate is the **Hôtel Notre-Dame**, *44 r. des Cuisiniers; tel: 31 92 87 24*, also in the town centre, which has a good restaurant specialising in regional cuisine. Campers and caravanners will find flat, leafy pitches at **Camping Municipal**, *blvd Eindhoven; tel 31 92 08 43*, just off the ring road.

SIGHTSEEING

The capture of Bayeux by the British the day after D-Day meant that the town was one of the few Norman towns to survive World War II intact, and as a result its streets still have a very strong medieval feel. A much earlier invasion, that of England by the Normans in 1066, is commemorated by the **Tapisserie de la Reine Mathilde** (Bayeux Tapestry, see box below), *Centre Guillaume le Conquérant, r. de Nesmond; tel: 31 92 05 48,* open daily 0900–1230 and 1400–1830 (Sept–Oct, Mar–Apr); 0900–1900 (May–Sept); 0930–1230, 1400–1800 (Oct–Mar), admission Fr.33 (Fr.14 children, students).

The **Musée de la Bataille de Normandie** (Battle of Normandy Memorial Museum), *blvd Fabian Ware; tel: 31 92 93 41,* open daily 0930–1230 and 1400–1830 (Mar–May, Sept–Oct); 1000–1230 and 1400–1800 (Oct–Mar); 0900–1900 (June–Aug), admission Fr.28 adults, (Fr.12 children and students), has documents and weapons from the Battle of Normandy, which took place between 6 June and 22 Aug 1944, and stands opposite the largest **British War Cemetery** in Normandy.

The **Musée Baron Gérard**, *pl. de la Liberté; tel: 31 92 14 21,* open daily 0900–1900 (June–Sept), 1000–1230 and 1400–1800 (Sept–May), admission Fr.19 (Fr.10), housed in the former Episcopal palace of Bayeux, has an important collection of lace and porcelain, as well as paintings, prints and furniture. The **Mémorial Géneral de Gaulle**, *10 r. Bourbesneur; tel: 31 92 45 55,* open daily 0930–1230 and 1400–1800 (Mar–Nov), admission Fr.15 (Fr.10), has memorabilia of France's wartime leader in the form of photographs, documents and personal effects. The **Cathédrale Notre-Dame**, *r. Lambert-Leforestier,* open 0900–1215 and 1430–1900 (Sept–June), 0800–1900 (July–Aug), is a mixture of Romanesque and

Bayeux Tapestry

Commissioned by Odo, Bishop of Bayeux, the Bayeux Tapestry is believed to have been made in England sometime between the Battle of Hastings in 1066 and the consecration of Bayeux Cathedral in 1077, where it was first displayed. In actual fact an embroidery and not a tapestry, the work, made up of coloured wool on a narrow strip of linen 70 m long, tells the story leading up to the Battle of Hastings and of the battle itself. There are 58 panels in all, and the story begins with Harold being sent by the King of England, Edward the Confessor, to inform William that he will succeed to the English throne.

On landing in Normandy, Harold is taken prisoner by Guy de Ponthieu, but William pays a ransom for his release. Harold then joins William in battle with Conan, Duke of Brittany, whom they defeat, and Harold is knighted by William. At Bayeux, Harold swears allegiance to William and returns to England.

Shortly afterwards, Edward dies and Harold is crowned king. When William hears how he has been deceived, he orders a fleet of longships to be built and an army to be prepared. The ships are loaded with supplies and then set sail, landing at Pevensey. Eventually the two armies meet and though, at one point, the invaders are almost routed when they believe William has been killed, he lifts his helmet to rally his men and they go on to cut the English army to pieces, Harold dying from an arrow in the eye.

The tapestry is a fascinating work of art with the main story told in vivid detail, while above and below are numerous picture comments, some humorous, some tragic, on various aspects of medieval life and the battle.

Gothic architecture, but of the original church completed for Bishop Odo in 1077, only the crypt and parts of the west towers survive. Various additions were made in the 13th, 15th and 19th centuries, one of which was a small hermit's house on the roof.

STE-MÈRE-ÉGLISE

Tourist Information: Syndicat d'Initiative, *1 pl. Gén. de Gaulle, 50480 Ste-Mère-Église; tel: 33 21 00 33,* has information about local attractions.

ACCOMMODATION

The hotel choice is not extensive: the modern **Hôtel Le Sainte-Mère,** *RN13; tel: 33 21 00 30,* is the best bet and moderately priced. A few less attractive hotels are located in the town centre.

SIGHTSEEING

This small town, captured by American paratroopers in the early hours of 6 June 1944, was the first French town to be liberated in World War II. An effigy of one of the paratroopers hanging by his parachute from the church tower, graphically recalls the scene depicted in the film *The Longest Day.* **Kilometre 0,** the first symbolic kilometre-stone on the Liberty Way taken by American forces on their way to Metz and Bastogne, is outside the town hall. The **Musée des Troupes Aéroportées** (Airborne Museum), *pl. du 6 Juin; tel: 33 41 41 35,* open daily 1000–1200 and 1400–1800 (Feb–Mar and Oct–Nov); 0900–1200 and 1400–1845 (Apr–May, Sept); 0900–1845 (June–Sept); Sat–Sun 1000–1200 and 1400–1800 (Nov–Dec); closed Dec–Jan, admission Fr.18 (Fr.7), houses beneath its parachute-shaped roof an American glider and Douglas tow-plane as well as weapons, uniforms and documents of the period.

VALOGNES

Tourist Office: *pl. du Château, 50700 Valognes; tel: 33 40 11 55.*

ACCOMMODATION

Most attractive of the town's hotels are the ivy-covered **Hôtel de l'Agriculture,** *16 r. Léopold-Delisle; tel: 33 95 02 02,* and the **Grand Hôtel du Louvre,** *28 r. des Religieuses; tel: 33 40 00 07,* with similarly priced rooms and excellent restaurants.

SIGHTSEEING

Struggling now to maintain its image as the 'little Versailles of Normandy', Valognes still has one of two 18th-century corners remaining as a reminder of its past glories. Principally, however, it serves as a good overnight halt with three or four inexpensive hotels from which to choose. There is a good market on Fri in the *pl. du Château.*

The **Hôtel de Beaumont,** *tel: 33 40 12 30,* open daily 1430–1830 (July–Sept) is the most prestigious of the town's 18th-century *hôtels particuliers* (mansion houses) and contains a monumental staircase, ceremonial rooms and private chambers, all richly furnished and decorated, and French-style gardens. More sober in style, the **Hôtel de Granval-Caligny,** *32 r. des Religieuses; tel: 33 40 01 75,* open Wed–Sat 1100 and 1430–1800 (June–Sept), was once the home of the writer Jules Barbey-d'Aurevilly. The **Musée Régional du Cidre** (Cider Museum), *r. de Petit-Versailles; tel: 33 40 22 73,* located in the 15th-century **Logis du Grand Quartier,** includes apple presses from the 16th–20th centuries, and displays of local pottery, costume and furniture.

OUISTREHAM-RIVA-BELLA

Tourist Office: *Jardin du Casino, 14150 Ouistreham; tel: 31 97 18 63,* though small,

D-DAY BEACHES

To see the quiet holiday resorts and beautiful beaches that stretch for some 80 km between the eastern Cotentin and the Caen Canal it is difficult to appreciate the mayhem that befell them a little more than 50 years ago. Just after midnight in the early hours of June 6, 1944, British and American paratroopers made there silent way to earth to secure the eastern and western flanks of what were to become known as the D-Day beaches.

The Germans were expecting an invasion but were convinced it would come in the Pas de Calais and so Normandy was defended by second-rate army units. Even when the defenders became engaged with the paratroopers they thought it was nothing more than a diversionary raid.

The main landings commenced at dawn at Utah Beach and progressed eastwards with the rising tide along the four other code-named beaches, Omaha, Gold, Juno and Sword. The invasion fleet consisted of 7000 vessels, which landed 200,000 men – Americans on Utah and Omaha, British on Gold and Sword and Canadians on Juno. Although the Germans put up stiff opposition, the troops landing on Utah, Gold, Juno and Sword managed to secure the beaches fairly quickly and with far fewer casualties than were envisaged. The problem came on Omaha, where less than a third of the men survived the landing and it was evening before the last of the beaches was secured.

The battle for Normandy, however, was to last another 11 weeks. Two 'Mulberry' harbours were assembled, one at Arromanches and the other on Omaha, and though the latter was destroyed in a storm shortly afterwards, they helped to land more than two million men. Gradually the Germans were forced to retreat and finally on August 22, at the Battle of the Falaise Pocket, the last of the German army in Normandy was annihilated by a combined force of British, American, Canadian, Polish and French armoured divisions.

has plenty of information and will book rooms.

ACCOMMODATION

There are two clusters of hotels, those in Ouistreham in or near *av. M. Cabieu*, those of Riva Bella leading up from the seafront near the Casino to *av. Gén. Leclerc*. The resort's top hotel is the modern three-star **Hôtel Les Thermes**, *av. du Commandant Kieffer; tel: 31 96 40 40*, which has *thalassothérapie* (sea-water therapy) available; expensive. Closest to the ferry port is the more moderate **Hôtel Delta**, *37 r. des Dunes; tel: 31 96 20 20*, which is modern and characterless but is comfortable and has a good restaurant. Among budget-priced hotels are the

Hôtel du Commerce, *19 Grande-Rue; tel: 31 97 14 31*, and **Hôtel Roulis**, *104 av. M. Cabieu; tel: 31 97 17 95*.

SIGHTSEEING

Though often known simply as Ouistreham, this ferry port and holiday resort's full name reveals that it is two places in one: old Ouistreham slightly inland, modern Riva-Bella beside the sea and at the eastern extremity of the D-Day beaches.

Ouistreham's 12th-century **St-Samson church**, *pl. A. Lemargnier*, has a stained-glass window commemorating the landing of British and French commandos in 1944. A more comprehensive reminder of the event is on display at the **Musée du**

Débarquement No 4 Commando (No. 4 Commando Landing Beaches Museum), *pl. Alfred Thomas; tel: 31 96 63 10*, open daily 0900–1800 (June–Sept); Sat, Sun 0930–1800 (Mar–May), admission Fr.20 adults, Fr.10 children. Not far away the **Musée du Mur de l'Atlantique** (Atlantic Wall Museum), *av. du 6 Juin; tel: 31 97 28 69*, open daily 1000–1200 and 1400–1800 (Feb–May and Oct–Nov), 0900–1900 (June–Sept), admission Fr.25 (Fr.15), occupies a former Nazi bunker commanding gun batteries overlooking the Orne Estuary.

SWORD, JUNO AND GOLD BEACHES

Tourist Offices: Lion-sur-Mer, *6 blvd du Calvados; tel: 31 96 87 95*, **Luc-sur-Mer**, *r. du Docteur Charcot; tel: 31 97 33 25*, **Langrune-sur-Mer**, *pl. du 6 Juin; tel: 31 97 32 77*, **St-Aubin-sur-Mer**, *Digue Favereau; tel: 31 97 30 41*, **Bernières-sur-Mer**, *159 r. Victor Tesnière; tel: 31 96 44 02*, **Courseulles-sur-Mer**, *r. de la Mer; tel: 31 37 46 80*, collectively have extensive information about the area and places to stay.

ACCOMMODATION

An extensive choice of hotels along the coast means there should be little difficulty finding a room for the night. Worth considering are the **Hôtel de la Plage**, *2 blvd du Calvados, Lion-sur-Mer; tel: 31 97 21 66*, the **Hôtel Beau Rivage**, *1 r. du Docteur Charcot, Luc-sur-Mer; tel: 31 96 49 51*, both of which are moderately priced and right by the sea. A little more expensive, the **Hôtel des Thermes et du Casino**, *3 r. Guynemer, Luc-sur-Mer; tel: 31 97 32 37*, is a modern hotel of 48 rooms with a first-class restaurant serving seafood specialities. Courseulles has no less than four *LF*, any of which will provide a good night's sleep

and an excellent evening meal to boot. They are the **Hôtel la Belle Aurore**, *Bassin de Plaisance; tel: 31 37 46 23*, **Hôtel la Crémaillère**, *blvd de la Plage; tel: 31 37 46 73*, **Hôtel Le Gytan**, *blvd de la Plage; tel: 31 37 95 96*, and **Hôtel de Paris**, *pl. du 6 Juin; tel: 31 37 45 07*.

SIGHTSEEING

These are the British and Canadian sectors of the D-Day beaches and comprise a ribbon of resorts between the rivers Orne and Seulles. Although considerably damaged during the landings, they have been restored and some of the resorts have expanded with modern holiday apartments. There are no museums relating to the landings, but there are numerous memorials, many erected for the 50th anniversary commemorations in 1994.

Other than enjoying the resort atmosphere within an historical context, there is little to divert your attention. At Luc-sur-Mer, the **Maison de la Baleine** (House of the Whale), *Jardin Public de la Mairie; tel: 31 97 55 93*, open daily 1000–1200 and 1400–1900 (June–Sept); 1400–1800 (Sept) Sat–Sun 1430–1800 (Oct–May), admission Fr.15 (Fr.9), is a museum about the life and protection of the whale. Aspects of the sea continue at the **Musée Aquarium**, *pl. du 6 Juin, Courseulles-sur-Mer; tel: 31 37 92 58*, open Tues–Sun 1000–1200 and 1400–1800 (Oct–Apr); daily 0900–1300 and 1400–1900 (May–June, Sept); daily 0900–1900 (July–Aug), admission Fr.34 (Fr.24), where there are displays on the life of shellfish and oysters as well as the opportunity to walk through a perspex tunnel under the sea.

ARROMANCHES

Tourist Offices: *4 r. du Mar. Joffre, 14117 Arromanches; tel: 31 21 47 56*, and *pl. du Groupe Lorraine; tel: 31 22 36 45*.

ACCOMMODATION

Arromanches has five hotels. All have moderately priced rooms, though two of them, the friendly **Hôtel Mulberry**, *r. M. Lithare; tel: 31 22 36 05*, and the **Hôtel Normandie**, *pl. du 6 Juin; tel: 31 22 34 32*, have rooms at the economy level. The best positioned is the **Hôtel Marine**, *quai du Canada; tel: 31 22 34 19*, which looks directly out onto the sea.

SIGHTSEEING

Arromanches proved to be the key to the success of the D-Day landings when the famous prefabricated **Mulberry Harbour** was towed across the English Channel and assembled within days of the invasion, allowing troops and equipment to disembark until a proper harbour – Cherbourg – was captured from the Germans. The remains of the concrete breakwater can still be seen offshore and the view from the calvary overlooking the town gives an excellent idea of the enormity of the undertaking.

Until 1994, the 50th anniversary of the D-Day landings, the town's sole attraction was the **Musée du Débarquement** (Landings Museum), *pl. du 6 Juin; tel: 31 22 34 31*, open daily 0900–1200, 1400–1800 (Sept–Apr); 0900–1900 (May–Aug), admission Fr.30 (Fr.15), which explains how the harbour was secretly built in England, towed across the Channel and assembled. Models and film show what it was like during its brief existence, when it was the largest port in the world.

Since the anniversary there has been a new attraction in a dome near the *table d'orientation* (viewpoint indicator) on the cliffs, beside the D514 entering the town from the east. **Arromanches 360**, *chemin du Calvaire; tel: 31 22 30 30*, open daily 0910–1840 (Easter–Sept), 1010–1640 (Oct–Easter), admission Fr.20 (Fr.17), is a

cinema with 360-degree projection, enabling you to feel as though you are in the middle of the Normandy landings. Archive footage is mixed with present day images and each showing runs for 18 mins.

PORT-EN-BESSIN

Tourist Office: *r. du Croiseur-Montcalm 14520 Port-en-Bessin; tel: 31 21 92 33*.

An attractive and lively fishing port, this is a useful point for an overnight halt. The **Hôtel de la Marine**, *quai Letourneur; tel: 31 21 70 08*, has been entirely renovated and has 16 modernised rooms and a superb, largely seafood restaurant overlooking the sea. Moderate. A little outside the town, the **Mercure Omaha Beach**, *tel: 31 22 44 44*, is located beside a 27-hole golf course and has a swimming pool, billiards room and tennis court. Expensive.

A little outside Port-en-Bessin is the **Musée des Épaves Sous-Marines** (Museum of Under-Sea Wrecks), *rte de Bayeux; tel: 31 21 17 06*, open daily 1000–1300 and 1400–1900 (June and Sept); 1000–1900 (July–Aug), admission Fr.30 (Fr.10), which has displays of tanks, aircraft parts, ships' equipment and personal documents salvaged from the sea in the years following the D-Day landings.

OMAHA BEACH

Tourist Information: Syndicat d'Initiative, *Vierville-sur-Mer; tel: 31 22 43 08*.

ACCOMMODATION

The **Hôtel du Casino**, *Vierville-sur-Mer; tel: 31 22 41 02*, is a moderately priced chalet-style *LF* which looks out over the length of Omaha Beach. Simple rooms, quiet, and a good restaurant.

SIGHTSEEING

The wartime code name for the section of coast between **Port-en-Bessin** and the

Pointe du Hoc, Omaha Beach looks peaceful enough now, but in the hours following the D-Day landings it suffered the greatest number of casualties.

The **American Military Cemetery**, just off the D514 at Colleville-St-Laurent, stands on top of the cliffs overlooking Omaha Beach and contains the graves of more than 9000 men, their gleaming white marble crosses laid out in endless rows. The peacefulness of the place is in stark contrast to the horrors that took place on the beach. On the D517 at St-Laurent-sur-Mer, the **Musée Omaha Beach 6 Juin 1944**, *tel: 31 21 97 44*, open daily 0930–1230 and 1430–1830 (Mar–June, Sept–Oct); 0930–1900 (July–Aug), admission Fr.20 (Fr.10), has displays of uniforms, weapons and military vehicles as seen in action on this sector of the landing beaches. Some 10 km further west, a turning off the the D514 to the right leads to the **Pointe du Hoc**, a heavily fortified German gun emplacement which was captured by US Rangers under the command of Colonel Rudder, who scaled the cliffs in the early hours of 6 June, 1944. The site, heavily pockmarked by shell craters, is still surrounded by rolls of barbed wire. Several of the bunkers are open to visitors.

GRANDCAMP-MAISY

Tourist Office: *quai Crampon, 14450 Grandcamp-Maisy; tel: 31 22 62 44.*

ACCOMMODATION

Though a fairly unattractive fishing port, Grandcamp-Maisy has a couple of moderately priced hotels.

The **Hôtel Duguesclin**, *4 quai Crampon; tel: 31 22 64 22*, is a comfortable two-star *LF* on the seafront close to the harbour. Its restaurant offers regional cooking with special emphasis on seafood.

SIGHTSEEING

The **Musée des Rangers**, *quai Crampon; tel: 31 92 33 51*, open Tues–Sun 1000–1300 and 1500–1800 (Apr–May and Sept–Oct); daily (except Mon morning) 1000–1900 (June–Aug), admission Fr.15 (Fr.7), tells the story of the assault on the Pointe du Hoc.

A 65-seat covered boat, the **Colonel Rudder**, bookings: *11 r. A. Briand; tel: 31 21 42 93*, carries out cruises of 1–6 hours from the harbour to view Pointe du Hoc, Omaha Beach, Utah Beach, Port-en-Bessin, the gun batteries at Longues-sur-Mer and Arromanches, from the sea. Other excursions take in the Îles St-Marcouf, Carentan and Isigny-sur-Mer.

Opposite the harbour, a short excursion along the D113 leads to La Cambe, once on the N13, but now bypassed. At the old N13 turn left into the village and then turn right, again on the D113, following the signs for the **Cimetière Militaire Allemand** (German Military Cemetery). The largest of the World War ll cemeteries in Normandy, it contains more than 21,000 graves, each group of tablets in the lawn marked by five dark granite crosses. A much larger cross stands on a mound overlooking it all.

ISIGNY-SUR-MER

Tourist Office: *1 r. Victor Hugo, 14230 Isigny-sur-Mer; tel: 31 21 46 00*, has details of local points of interest and accommodation.

Although the town itself has little of interest, it does have a good two-star *LF*, the **Hôtel de France**, *r. E. Demagny; tel: 31 22 00 33*, if you are in need of somewhere inexpensive to stay.

CARENTAN

Tourist Office: *blvd de Verdun, 50500 Carentan; tel: 33 42 33 54*, has a broad range of material covering many towns in the *départements* of Manche and Calvados.

ACCOMMODATION

There are a couple of hotels worth considering in the town. The two-star **Hôtel le Vauban**, *pl. Vauban; tel: 33 71 00 20*, lacks a restaurant, but is comfortable and moderately priced. A little cheaper, the **Hôtel du Commerce et de la Gare**, *34 r. de la Gare; tel: 33 42 02 00*, is an attractive ivy-clad building with fairly basic rooms and a restaurant offering simple, reasonably priced menus. Beside the ring road and opposite the station, it is subject to a certain amount of noise. To the north of the town, close to the canal leading to the sea, the three-star **Camping Le Haut Dick**, *chemin du Grand Bas Pays; tel: 33 42 16 89*, has flat and shaded pitches for tents and caravans.

SIGHTSEEING

A busy market town, Carentan has some late 14th-century arcades of a former covered market, while the spire of the 12th-century **Église Notre-Dame** (Church of Our Lady) is a dominant landmark over the surrounding area. The **Port de Plaisance** (Pleasure Harbour), *quai de Caligny*, is a popular halt for sailing boats. Standing in the heart of the **Parc Naturel des Marais du Cotentin** (Nature Park of the Cotentin Marsh), Carentan also has boat excursions along the marshland waterways, a particular attraction for birdwatchers. Embarkation points are at St Hilaire-Petitville on the River Taute, just east of Carentan, *tel: 33 55 18 07*, departures daily 0930 and 1430 (May–Sept); and at Port-Jourdan on the River Douve, north-west of the town, *tel: 33 71 55 81*, departures Sun 1500 (May–June and Sept); Sun–Fri 1500 (July–Aug); Sat 0930 (May–Sept).

UTAH BEACH

Tourist Information: **Syndicat d'Initiative**, *Mairie, Ste-Marie-du-Mont; tel: 33 42 04 03.*

ACCOMMODATION

There is little accommodation along Utah Beach, though there are two hotels at opposite ends of the price scale worth investigating. The **Hôtel l'Estaminet**, *Ste-Marie-du-Mont; tel: 33 71 57 01*, is a charming stone-built hotel with floral balconies overlooking the village square. It also has its own restaurant. Economically priced. At the northern end of Utah Beach is the 18th-century **Hôtel Château de Quinéville**, *Quinéville; tel: 33 21 42 67*, which offers 24 rooms and an elegant restaurant with seating for 80. Pricey. There are also a couple of campsites at Ste-Marie-du-Mont, a couple more at Ravenoville and a fifth at Quinéville. The best of them is the three-star **Camping Le Cormoran**, *Ravenoville; tel: 33 41 33 94*, which has 230 pitches and excellent facilities, including a swimming pool, restaurant and shop.

SIGHTSEEING

There are several D-Day monuments along this stretch of coast, notably one on the road from Ste-Marie-du-Mont to the sea dedicated to the 800 Danish seamen who took part in the landings, several American ones at **la Madeleine**, and one farther north in memory of Gén. Leclerc. Also at la Madeleine is another landmark kilometre post on the Liberty Way, **Kilometre 00**, and the **Musée d'Utah Beach**, *Utah Beach; tel: 33 71 53 35*, open daily 1000–1200 and 1400–1800 (Mar–June, Oct–Nov); 0930–1830 (July–Sept); 1000–1200 and 1400–1700 (Nov–Mar); admission Fr.25 (Fr.10), which occupies a former German bunker and includes models, archive film and other material describing the American landings here. Most of the museums along the D-Day beaches document the landings themselves, but one museum that looks at the period from a different standpoint is the **Musée de la Liberté** (Liberty Museum), *av. de la Plage, Quinéville; tel: 33 21 40 44*, open daily 1000–1200 and 1400–800 (Apr–May, Oct); 0930–1830 (June–Sept), admission Fr.30 (Fr.20). Here, with the aid of life-size street reconstructions, posters and photographs, the focus is on civilian life under German occupation.

ST-VAAST-LA-HOUGUE

Tourist Office: *quai Vauban, 50550 St-Vaast; tel: 33 54 41 37.*

ACCOMMODATION

Of the St-Vaast hotels, the most popular among British visitors is the **Hôtel de France et des Fuchsias**, *18 r. Mar. Foch; tel: 33 54 42 26*, a two-star moderately priced *LF*, with comfortable rooms, a delightful frontage and an excellent restaurant. Nearby, the more expensive three-star **Hôtel la Granitière**, *74 r. Mar. Foch; tel: 33 54 58 99*, has luxuriously furnished rooms, though restaurant prices tend to be more on a par with its neighbour. For something at the economy level try the **Hôtel Vauban**, *tel: 33 54 42 46*, just up from the harbour.

SIGHTSEEING

A picturesque fishing port and yachting harbour, St-Vaast is also famous for its oyster farms. The great military architect Vauban built fortifications to protect the harbour. **Fort de la Hougue** is occupied by the army, but on the nearby island of **Tatihou** the fortifications can be visited, as can the **Musée Maritime,** which tells the story of the Battle of La Hougue in

1692, when a French fleet of 44 vessels, assembled to invade England and return James II to the throne, was attacked by a superior Anglo-Dutch fleet. As the French fleet tried to break away, they were caught in the fierce current and ran onto the rocks off Tatihou, suffering huge losses. Tickets for the return boat journey to the island are available from **Accueil Tatihou**, *quai Vauban; tel: 33 23 19 92*, daily departures every half-hour at high tide and every hour at low tide 1000–1230 and 1400–1700 (May–Sept); Sat, Sun 1000–1230, 1400–1700 (Oct–Apr), admission and fare inclusive Fr.50; children under 10 free.

BARFLEUR

Tourist Office: *2 Rd Point le Conquérant, 50760 Barfleur; tel: 33 54 02 48.*

ACCOMMODATION

Barfleur has a couple of moderately priced hotels, the **Hôtel Le Conquérant**, *18 r. St-Thomas; tel: 33 54 00 82*, with its pretty courtyard garden at the rear, and the now renovated **Hôtel du Phare**; *42 r. St-Thomas; tel: 33 54 10 33*, which is marginally cheaper than Le Conquérant but, unlike its neighbour, has a restaurant.

SIGHTSEEING

The picturesque harbour is surrounded by granite houses and overlooked by a small 17th-century **church** with a stubby tower. William the Conqueror sailed from here on his way to invade England, an event commemorated by a plaque at the harbour entrance. A short distance away, at the Pointe de Barfleur, is the **Phare de Gatteville** (Gatteville Lighthouse), open daily 0900–1200 and 1400–1830, admission free (key from house at right), which, at 71 m, is one of the tallest lighthouses in France. From the top, views extend the length of the Cotentin Peninsula.

99

CAEN–TOURS

The road from Caen to Tours is a major north–south route linking a number of significant and historical towns. Some have connections with William the Conqueror, others were important milestones in the latter days of the Battle of Normandy in World War II.

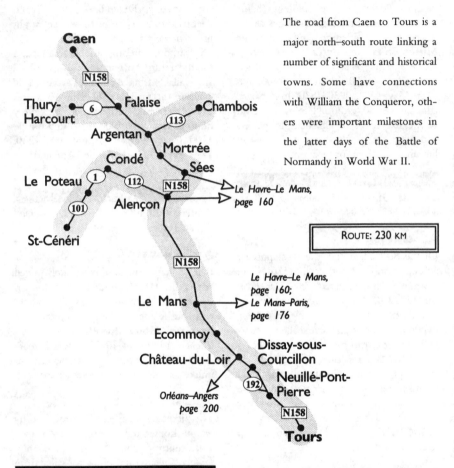

ROUTE: 230 KM

ROUTE

Follow N158 dual carriageway south from Caen towards **Falaise**, crossing the Caen Plain en route. Falaise can be bypassed if you wish, but it is well worth a stop. From there N158 continues through more undulating countryside to **Argentan** and then **Sées**. From Sées, join the partially dualled N138 to **Alençon**. Continuing south, N138 follows a largely straight,

though undulating, course to **Le Mans** (described on p.170). Stay on N138, driving along the **Mulsanne Straight**, part of the motor circuit. The road passes through **Ecommoy, Château-du-Loir** and **Dissay-sous-Courcillon**, where for a change of scenery you could turn right onto D192, later becoming D6 and D28 and following the **Escotais Valley** through **St-Christophe-sur-le-Nais** and **St-Paterne-Racan** to **Neuille-Pont-Pierre**. Just south of St-Paterne-Racan is the 17th-century **La Roche-Racan Château**, perched on a rock. At Neuille-Pont-Pierre, rejoin N138 for the final 20 km to Tours. Total route distance is 230 km.

FALAISE

Tourist Office: *blvd de la Libération, 14700 Falaise; tel: 31 90 17 26*, open daily 0930–1800 (Apr–Sept); Mon–Sat 0930–1230 and 1330–1800, Sun 1100–1230 and 1330–1600 (Oct–Mar), has information about the town and surrounding area.

ACCOMMODATION

Falaise has a handful of hotels, nearly all of them moderately priced and graded two-star. **Hôtel de la Poste**, *38 r. Georges Clémenceau; tel: 31 90 13 14*, is a post-war *logis* on the N158 and so subject to traffic noise, but it is convenient and comfortable. It also has a very good restaurant. The **Hôtel de Normandie**, *5 r. Amiral Courbet; tel: 31 90 18 26*, is marginally cheaper and being off the main road is quieter too. The restaurant is recommended. Another hotel just off the main road and close to the centre is the **Hôtel de la Place**, *1 pl. St-Gervais; tel: 31 40 19 00*.

Falaise has an excellent **campsite** beneath the walls of the castle, the three-star **Camping Municipal du Château**; *tel: 31 90 16 55*.

SIGHTSEEING

Falaise was badly damaged during the latter stages of the Battle of Normandy in 1944 as the Allied armies closed in on the retreating German army, and so much of what can be seen today is modern. However, parts of the old town have survived, most notably its **Château Féodal**

(feudal castle), *tel: 31 90 17 26*, open daily 1000–1800, admission Fr.12 adults (Fr.8 children), where William the Conqueror was born in 1027. (There is a magnificent statue of William on horseback in the *pl. Guillaume-le-Conquérant*). Its imposing keep stands on a rocky spur on the edge of the town, while next to it is the 13th-century **Talbot Tower**. Beneath the keep, in the valley of the Ante, is a small spring, the **Fontaine d'Arlette** (Arlette's fountain), where Robert, the younger son of Richard II, Duke of Normandy, met and fell in love with Arlette, a young woman washing clothes in the spring. Their son, William, was known first as the Bastard, and later the Conqueror.

A lesser known château in Falaise is the 18th-century **Château de la Fresnaye**, which lies next to the main road through the town. Napoleon is said to have stayed there a night. The grounds are open all year round, but the interior can only be visited during the exhibitions held in the summer.

Opened in 1994, **Automates Avenue**, *blvd de la Libération; tel: 31 90 02 43*, open daily 1000–1800 (Apr–Sept); Sat–Sun and bank holidays 1000–1800 (Oct–Mar), admission Fr.29 (Fr.16), is one of the most charming museums in Normandy. Visitors walk the streets of Paris in the first half of the century, past delightful automated window displays which are not only fascinating for children, but contain much humour for adults too.

Not far from the château, the **Musée Août 1944** (Museum of August 1944), *chemin des Roches; tel: 31 90 37 19*, open daily 1000–1200 and 1400–1800 (June–Aug); Wed-Sun 1000–1200 and 1400–1800 (Apr–May and Sept–Oct), admission Fr.30 (Fr.10), tells the story of the Battle of the Falaise Pocket in the final stages of the

101

Battle of Normandy. Churches in Falaise include **Église de la Trinité** (Trinity Church), *pl. Guillaume-le-Conquérant*, **Église St-Gervais**, *r. Georges Clémenceau*, a mixture of Romanesque and Gothic styles, and **Église Notre-Dame de Guibray**, *r. Notre-Dame*, which is built in the Romanesque style.

SIDE TRACK FROM FALAISE

SUISSE NORMANDE

To the west of Falaise, the Suisse Normande is an area of hills and gorges bordering the River Orne. Just north of Falaise, the D6 leads to **Thury-Harcourt**, a pleasant tourist centre on the northern edge of the region. Its main attraction is the **Parc et Jardins du Château d'Harcourt**, *pl. du 13 Août 1944; tel: 31 79 65 41*, open daily 1430–1830 (May–Sept); Sun and public holidays 1430–1830 (Apr and Oct), admission Fr.23 (Fr.7). The gardens are beautiful at any time of year, while at their heart stand the eerie ruins of the early 17th-century château, destroyed in 1944 by the retreating German army.

To the south, **Clécy** is regarded as the capital of the Suisse Normande and is a superb centre for hiking, climbing, cycling, canoeing, fishing and hang-gliding. The banks of the Orne here are lined with cafés and restaurants. There are two museums, the **Musée du Chemin de Fer Miniature** (Model Railway Museum); *tel: 31 69 07 13*, open daily 1000–1200 and 1415–1800 (Apr–Sept); Sun 1400–1700 (Mar and Oct–Dec), admission Fr.18 (Fr.15), which claims to be the most extensive miniature railway in Europe, and the **Musée Hardy**, *pl. de la Mairie; tel: 31 69 79 95*, open daily 1000–1200 and 1400–1800 (Apr–Sept), admission Fr.12 (Fr.6), which has more than 100 works of local scenes by the Impressionist painter **André Hardy**.

There is a good choice of hotels in both Thury-Harcourt and Clécy, with further options at Pont-d'Ouilly and Putanges continuing south along the Orne Valley.

ARGENTAN

Tourist Office: *pl. du Marché, 61200 Argentan; tel: 33 67 12 48*, has information about where to stay in and around the town.

ACCOMMODATION

Although Argentan has nothing startling in terms of hotels, there are two or three worth mentioning for their restaurants. The modern **Hôtel La Renaissance**, *20 av. de la 2e-Division-Blindée; tel: 33 36 14 20*, gets no less than four stars for its restaurant, though, surprisingly, menus are modestly priced. Two others are part of the *LF* group, the **Hôtel de France**, *8 blvd Carnot; tel: 33 67 03 65*, and its neighbour **Hôtel des Voyageurs**, *6 blvd Carnot; tel: 33 36 15 60*. Both *logis* have restaurants and all three have moderately priced rooms.

There is a two-star municipal **campsite**, **Camping du Parc de la Noë**; *tel: 33 36 05 69*, which is south of the town centre and close to a lake and the River Orne.

SIGHTSEEING

Argentan was another Norman town to be badly hit in the closing stages of the Battle of Normandy in 1944 and there isn't a great deal to be visited, though the town centre is pleasant enough. The **Église St-Germain** (St Germanus Church), dominates the town centre, but is still undergoing restoration from war damage.

Across the *pl. du Marché*, where the market is held every Tues, the imposing 14th century castle now serves as the law courts. Argentan was once a renowned lace making centre, and although the art has declined it is still made by the nuns at the **Abbaye des Bénédictines**, *2 r. de l'Abbaye; tel: 33 67 12 01*. There is a permanent exhibition of Argentan lace at the abbey, open Mon–Sat 1030–1200 and 1430–1630 (all year), admission Fr.10.

SIDE TRACK FROM ARGENTAN

MONT-ORMEL

Thirteen km north-east of Argentan along the D113, the little village of **Chambois** played an important part in the final stages of the Battle of Normandy, when Polish, Canadian and American forces met on Aug 19 1944 cutting off the escape of the German 7th Army in the Falaise Pocket. A memorial next to the angular **donjon** (keep) in the middle of the village commemorates the event. With French and British troops completing the pincer movement, the German armour was destroyed in two days of fierce fighting at the foot of **Mont-Ormel**, a hill a further 5 km along D113.

At the summit, overlooking the battlefield, stands a monument to all the Allied armoured divisions involved in the fighting, and, opened in 1994, the **Mémorial de Mont-Ormel**; *tel: 33 pn67 38 61*, open daily 0900–1800 (May–Sept); Wed, Sat and Sun 1000–1700 (Oct–Apr), admission Fr.20 adults (Fr.5), a museum with archive film and sound vividly describing the events. Commentary is available in any of five languages, including English.

MORTRÉE

No more than a straggling village on N158 between Argentan and Sées with neither a tourist office or accommodation, it could be very easy to miss its great attraction, one of the most beautiful châteaux in Normandy, the simply named **Château d'O**, *route d'Almenêches; tel: 33 35 34 69*, open Wed-Mon 1430–1800 (Apr–Oct); 1430–1700 (Nov–Mar), admission Fr.25 (Fr.15). Reached by turning left in Mortrée onto D26 to Médavy, the château, which is inhabited, is built in Renaissance style, its earliest part dating from the 15th century. In its grounds is a dovecote and an excellent though rather pricey restaurant, the **Restaurant de la Ferme d'O**; *tel: 33 35 35 27*.

SÉES

Tourist Office: *pl. Gén. de Gaulle, 61500 Sées; tel: 33 28 74 79*, open Mon 1000–1200, 1400–1800, Tues–Fri 0900–1230, 1400–1830, Sat 1000–1200, 1400–1700.

ACCOMMODATION

Though small, Sées has quite an attractive selection of hotels, including several rated two stars and moderately priced. One of the best known is the **Hôtel du Cheval Blanc**, *1 pl. St-Pierre; tel: 33 27 80 48*, a *LF* overlooking a leafy square just off the road to Alençon. Another *logis*, the **Hôtel du Dauphin**, *31 pl. des Halles; tel: 33 27 80 07*, stands opposite the old covered market and is rather pricier, both for rooms and in the restaurant. A good alternative with more rooms is the **Garden Hotel**, *12 bis r. des Ardrillers; tel: 33 27 98 27*. More economic options are the **Hôtel Le St-Louis**, *9 r. Billy; tel: 33 27 89 43*, which has its own restaurant, and the **Hôtel Normandy**, *20 pl. Gén de Gaulle; 33 27 80 67*, which has a *crêperie* attached.

There is a two-star **campsite**,

Camping Essi le Clos Normand, *rte d'Alençon; tel: 33 28 74 79*, open May–Sept.

Apart from its magnificent **cathedral** which stands as a landmark for miles around, there is little to keep the visitor in Sées for long. The cathedral, the fifth to be built in the town, was built in the 13th and 14th centuries in Norman Gothic style. During the summer it is beautifully lit at night and during July and Aug presents music and light spectaculars on Fri and Sat evenings. Bookings can be made through the tourist office. The **Anciennes Halles** (old covered market), *pl. des Halles,* is an unusual building dating from the 19th century and although part is used as a library, it is possible to see the old timber-work roof supported by stone columns facing the Hotel du Dauphin. The only museum is the **Musée Départemental d'Art Religieux** (Religious Art), *pl. Gén de Gaulle; tel: 33 81 60 00*, open Wed–Mon 0930–173 (June–Sept), admission Fr.10 adults, Fr.7 children.

ALENÇON

Tourist Office: *Maison d'Ozé, pl. Lamagdelaine, 61003 Alençon; tel: 33 26 11 36*, housed in a 15th century mansion behind the church, has extensive information on Alençon and the Orne *département*, and can make hotel bookings for visitors. Daily guided tours are organised in July and Aug at 1430 and 1630, plus 2030 on Fri, price Fr.25 adults, children free. Information from Musée des Beaux-Arts et de la Dentelle; *tel: 33 32 40 07*.

ACCOMMODATION

Being the capital of the Orne départe-ment, Alençon has a wide choice of hotels, a large proportion of them rated two stars,

all of which are moderately priced. Several are located close to the centre. One of the best of these is the **Hôtel du Grand-Cerf**, *21 r. St-Blaise; tel: 33 26 00 51*, which has a good restaurant and happens to be easy to find too. Rather more diffi-cult to find because of Alençon's compli-cated one-way streets, but worth it if you make it, is **Hôtel le Grand St-Michel**, *7 r. du Temple; tel: 33 26 04 77*. Located in a quiet side-street, this *LF* has comfortable rooms and one of the best restaurants in town. The most modern of the town cen-tre hotels is the **Hôtel Ibis**, *13 pl. Poulet-Malassis; tel: 33 26 55 55*, which is typical of its type but has no restaurant. The **Brasserie des Ducs** next door; *tel: 33 26 37 49*, however, has a good choice of main courses. Another *logis* with a good restaurant is the unromantically named **Hôtel de l'Industrie**, *20 pl. Gén de Gaulle; tel: 33 27 19 30*. Its drawback is that it stands beside a busy roundabout on the town's inner ring-road and so is rather noisy.

Alençon has two **campsites**, one north and one south of the centre. The northern one, the two-star **Camp Municipal du Stade**, *av. de Quakenbrück; tel: 33 29 23 29*, open all year, is close to the N12, but the other one, the three-star **Camping de Guéramé**, *r. de Guéramé; tel: 33 26 34 95*, open May–Sept, is agreeably located beside the River Sarthe.

SIGHTSEEING

Alençon lies just on the Normandy side of the boundary with the Western Loire region, and despite the attentions of World War II there is still plenty of the old town to see. All the main sights are close to the centre and within easy walking dis-tance of each other. The town is princi-pally famous for two things – **lace** and **Ste-Thérèse of Lisieux** who was born there in 1873. Alençon was already well-known for lace-making in the mid 1600s, when Venetian lace became fashionable in the French court. It was thought that France could profit more from its skills and further investment was bestowed on Alençon's lace-makers. Today, the town still has a lace-making school and there are two museums with excellent collections.

The first of these is the **Musée des Beaux-Arts et de la Dentelle** (Museum of Fine Arts and Lace), *r. Charles Aveline; tel: 33 32 40 07,* open Tues–Sun 1000–1200, 1400–1800 (all year), admission Fr.18 (Fr.15), which has an excellent display of lace from the major lace-making centres of Italy, Belgium, England and France. In addition there are collections of mainly French paintings and drawings as well as Cambodian works of art. The other lace museum is the **Musée de la Dentelle au Point d'Alençon**, *31 r. du Pont-Neuf; tel: 33 26 27 26,* open Mon–Sat 1000–1130 and 1400–1730 (all year), admission Fr.18 (Fr.10), where a film is shown depicting the history of lace and the technique involved in producing Alençon needlepoint. It is possible to buy items of lace at this museum. The building in which the museum is housed was used by the French Gen. Leclerc as his headquarters when he liberated the town in Aug 1944 and to commemorate the 50th anniversary of the event part of the building was opened as the **Musée Leclerc**, *31 r. du Pont-Neuf; tel: 33 26 27 26,* open Mon–Sat 1000–1130 and 1400–1730 (all year), admission Fr.12 (Fr.6). (Admission to both museums can be combined at Fr.23 adults, Fr.13 children). The displays consist mainly of documents and photographs from the period.

The **Église Notre-Dame**, *pl. Lamagdelaine,* open 0900–1200 and 1400–1730, was built in the 14th and 15th centuries in Flamboyant style. It has an elegant porch and a side chapel in which Ste Thérèse was baptised. Above the font is the embroidered robe in which she was christened. The **Maison Natale de Ste-Thérèse** (Birthplace of St Teresa), *50 r. St-Blaise; tel: 33 26 09 87,* open Wed–Mon 0900–1200, 1400–1800 (June–Sept); 0930–1200, 1430–1700 (Oct–Dec and Feb–May), admission free, where **Thérèse Martin** was born of a lacemaker and a watchmaker, is a short walk away. Adjoining the house is a small chapel dedicated to the saint. To the west of the town centre is the former **château**, *pl. Foch,* built in the 14th and 15th centuries by the first Duke of Alençon, which now serves as a prison.

⏩ **SIDE TRACK FROM ALENÇON**

THE ALPES MANCELLES

Leave Alençon on the D112 towards Mayenne and within 4 km turn left at Condé onto the D1. Within another 3 km bear left again, at Le Poteau onto the D101, which leads to **St-Cénéri-le-Gérei**, a delightful little village tucked into a fold of the Alpes Mancelles, an exaggerated name for a nevertheless attractive range of hills. Looking down on a deep valley carved by the River Sarthe, St-Cénéri has inspired many artists and poets, among them Corot, Courbet, Oudinet and Baudelaire.

In the 11th-century Romanesque church at the top of the village there are some faded frescoes, while a footpath leads past the church to the 15th-century **Chapel of St-Cénéri**, which stands picturesquely in a meadow beside the Sarthe. Another 5 km south of St-Cénéri, **St-Leonard-de-Bois**

105

occupies another attractive spot beneath steep, leafy hills beside the Sarthe. It is a popular base for hiking and cycling and has several hotels, the three-star **Touring-Hotel**; *tel: 43 97 28 03*, in a pretty location beside the Sarthe, the one-star **Hôtel de France**; *tel: 43 97 92 29*, and the unclassified **Hôtel Bon Laboureur**; *tel: 43 97 28 02* and **Hôtel Grand Cerf**; *tel: 43 97 28 04*, plus a **campsite**, the two-star **Camping des Alpes Mancelles**; *tel: 43 33 81 79*.

Mountain bikes can be hired from the Bar des Alpes Mancelles, opposite the church; *tel: 43 97 28 11*. ▣

CHÂTEAU-DU-LOIR

Tourist Information: Maison du Tourisme, *2 av. J. Jaurès, Parc Henri Goude, 72500 Château-du-Loir; tel: 43 44 56 68.*

ACCOMMODATION

The best hotels are the two-star **Grand Hôtel**, *pl. de l'Hôtel de Ville; tel: 43 44 00 17*, and the one-star **Hôtel de la Gare**; *tel: 43 44 00 14*; both *LF*. Moderately priced, both have restaurants, the latter offering cheaper set menus. There is one **campsite**, **Camp Municipal de Coëmont**, *av. des Déportés; tel 43 79 44 63*, a two-star site on the banks of the River Loir.

SIGHTSEEING

This pleasant old town is gathered round the church of **St-Guingalois**, which, as well as a 17th-century terracotta pietà, has a wooden figure of the Scouring of Christ. All that remains of the château that gave the town its name is the **donjon** (keep), which stands in public gardens. From the top there are fine views of the surrounding landscape.

The Normans

Normandy gets its name from the Northmen, the Vikings, who began raiding the French coast at the beginning of the 9th century. Within a few years they had settled along the banks of the River Seine, although the marauding didn't stop immediately, with Paris and later Evreux coming under siege in the latter years of the century.

The leader of the Vikings at this point was Rollo, and he was proving such a thorn in the side of the French king, Charles the Simple, that in 911 Charles drew up the Treaty of St-Clair-sur-Epte, giving Rollo the land around Rouen and Evreux. This allowed Charles to enjoy the rest of his kingdom in peace, while Rollo became the first Duke of Normandy.

In subsequent years, the duchy expanded its borders, taking over the Cotentin, the Channel Islands and fixing the frontier with Brittany along the Couesnon River, where it still stands. Under William, the bastard son of Robert the Devil, the expansion continued, the province of Maine being annexed in 1062. Then in 1066, believing he was rightful heir to the English throne, William cast his sights across the Channel. Assembling an army of 7000 men and more than 600 longships, he sailed across the English Channel, landed at Pevensey Bay and defeated Harold at the Battle of Hastings. The Conqueror was crowned King of England on Christmas Day 1066.

For another 138 years, England and Normandy were inextricably linked until 1204 when King John's indifference towards Normandy allowed Phillippe-Auguste to seize the duchy for France. However, the Channel Islands remained with England and to this day the English monarch retains the title of Duke of Normandy.

CAEN–VANNES

This is a mixture of main routes and quieter more meandering roads. Once beyond the Caen plain the route passes through some really lovely countryside, much of it the typical *bocage* of Normandy - small fields enclosed by hedges and trees. There are several points along the route where a short diversion will show off the landscape at its best.

ROUTE: 280 KM

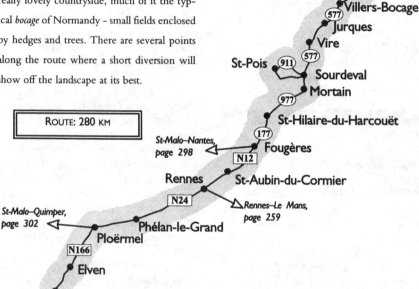

ROUTE

From the *Boulevard Périphérique* take N175 towards Avranches. This is dual carriageway until 5 km after **Villers-Bocage** the route bears left onto the D577 to **Vire**. D577 continues beyond Vire and at **Sourdeval** becomes D977. A delightful excursion from Sourdeval would be to take D911 along the **Vallée de la Sée** to **St-Pois**, returning via **St-Michel-de-Montjoie**, from where, on a clear day, the views extend to **Le Mont-St-Michel**.

Back at Sourdeval, follow D977 south through **Mortain**, immediately after which it turns right to **St-Hilaire-du-Harcouët**. Within another 7 km, as the road crosses from Normandy into Brittany, it becomes D177 en route to **Fougères**. At this ancient town, take N12 via **St-Aubin-du-Cormier** to **Rennes** and then N24 towards Lorient, but at **Plélan-le-Grand**, take the old N24 just south of the **Forêt de Paimpont** to **Ploërmel**. From there, the dualled N166 passes **Elven** and the imposing ruins of the feudal fortress of **Largoët** en route to **Vannes**.

107

Much of the route is fast and though the total distance is around 280 km, it could driven, if wished, in 3–4 hrs.

JURQUES

Just after this village, about 12 km beyond Villers-Bocage, the D165A, a right turn off the D577, leads to the **Zoo de Jurques** (or **Parc Zoologique de la Cabosse**); *tel: 31 77 80 58,* open daily 1000-1900 (May–Aug); 1000–1800 (Mar–Apr and Sept–Oct); 1330–1730 (Jan–Feb and Nov). Located in a 15-hectare wooded park, it contains more than 500 wild animals from around the world.

VIRE

Tourist Office: *sq. de la Résistance, 14500 Vire; tel: 31 68 00 05,* open Mon–Sat 1000–1200 and 1400–1800.

ACCOMMODATION

Vire has three good two-star hotels located in the centre and one or two more on the outskirts. All are moderately priced, though two are at the more expensive end of the scale – the **Hôtel de France**, *4 r. d'Aignaux; tel: 31 68 00 35,* and the **Hôtel St-Pierre**, *20 r. du Gén Leclerc; tel: 31 68 05 82,* which both offer comfortable en suite rooms and restaurants. Also centrally located is the **Europ'Hotel**, *2 pl. de 6 Juin 44; tel: 31 67 19 82,* while a good alternative on the way to the railway station is the **Hôtel des Voyageurs**, *47 av. de la Gare; tel: 31 68 01 16,* which has excellent, moderately priced menus in its restaurant.

There is a small riverside **campsite**, **Camping La Piscine**; *tel: 31 67 20 34,* by the D175 south of the town.

SIGHTSEEING

On a hilltop overlooking the Norman *bocage,* Vire is a very old town famous for its culinary contribution to Norman din-

ner tables, *andouilles* (chitterlings). Though much of the town has been rebuilt following wartime devastation, it still has a number of ancient landmarks, among which is the **Porte Horloge**, *pl. du 6 juin 44; tel: 31 68 00 05,* open Mon–Sat 1430–1830 (all year), admission Fr.10 adults, (Fr.5 children). A 15th-century **clock tower** standing atop a 13th-century gateway, it is the former main entrance to the walled town. This, and two towers nearby, the **Tour St-Sauveur** and **Tour aux Raines**, are all that remain of the town walls.

Behind the clock tower is the 13th-century **Église Notre-Dame** (Church of Our Lady), while beyond that, standing amid gardens on a rocky promontory is all that remains of the 12th-century feudal château, the **donjon** (keep). The steep valley beneath the keep, the **Vau de Vire**, was busy with clothmakers in the 14th and 15th centuries, and one of the workers, **Olivier Basselin**, wrote many songs, which later led to the coining of the word *vaudeville.*

Beside the River Vire just south of the centre, the **Musée Municipal**, *2 pl. Ste-Anne; tel: 31 68 10 49 or 31 68 06 94,* open Wed–Mon 1000–1200 and 1400–1800 (May–Sept); Wed–Mon 1400–1700 (Oct–Apr) admission Fr.20 (Fr.12), is devoted to local life and contains a number of craftsmen's workshops, furniture, Norman headdresses, and paintings and sculptures by local artists.

MORTAIN

Tourist Office: *Grande-Rue, 50140 Mortain; tel: 33 59 19 74.*

ACCOMMODATION

This small town has a couple of hotels to choose from, the two-star **Hôtel de la Poste**, *1 pl. des Arcades; tel: 33 59 00 05,* a well-appointed *LF* with an excellent restaurant, and the one-star **Hôtel du Cheval Blanc**, *14 av. de l'Abbaye-Blanche; tel: 33 59 00 60*. Both are moderately priced but the latter is slightly cheaper, both for rooms and its restaurant.

Mortain has a small **campsite** by the River Cance, **Camping Les Cascades**, *pl. du Chateau; tel: 33 59 00 51*, open Apr–Oct.

SIGHTSEEING

Another Norman town to suffer devastation in 1944, Mortain has been rebuilt on its ruins. Some parts, however, survived, most notably the **Église St-Évroult**, *Grande-Rue*, a 12th-century church with a fine Romanesque door and a 7th-century Anglo-Irish beechwood and copper casket in its treasury. From the church, a road winds uphill to the **Chapelle St-Michel** or **Petite Chapelle** (St Michael's or Little Chapel), which was built in 1852 and contains a 16th-century polychrome of the Last Supper. Nearby is a small monument to the American soldiers who died liberating Mortain. From the chapel there are also superb views over the surrounding countryside, which on a clear day extend as far as Mont St-Michel.

Just north of Mortain is the **Abbaye Blanche** (White Abbey), *av. de l'Abbaye Blanche; tel: 33 59 00 21*, open Mon–Sat 0930–1130 and 1430–1700, Sun 1500–1730 (all year), admission free, a 12th-century Cistercian abbey with a chapter house, cloister, abbey church and store rooms, all open to the public. From June–Sept there are guided tours which include a video presentation and an exhibition of religious art.

On the other side of the road from the abbey, the River Cance descends through a leafy setting and a path leads to the **Grande Cascade** (Great Waterfall),

which crashes through rocks for 82ft (25m). The path continues downstream to the **Petite Cascade** (Small Waterfall).

ST-HILAIRE-DU-HARCOUËT

Tourist Office: *pl. de l'Église, 50600 St-Hilaire-du-Harcouët; tel: 33 49 10 06*.

ACCOMMODATION

Although there is nothing of interest to see in this busy market town (market day Wed), its position at a crossroads makes it a useful place to stay and it has a choice of three two-star hotels. The best of them is the **Hôtel Le Cygne**, *67 r. Waldeck-Rousseau; tel: 33 49 11 84*, a moderately-priced *LF* with a good but rather pricey restaurant. Cheaper rooms are available at the **Hôtel Le Relais de la Poste**, *11-13 r. de Mortain; tel: 33 49 10 31*, and you get good value for money in the restaurant too. With similarly priced rooms, the **Hôtel de l'Agriculture**, *79-81 r. Waldeck-Rousseau; tel: 33 49 10 60*, offers the cheapest choice of menus.

A three-star **campsite**, **Camping La Sélune**, is located by the River Sélune just west of the town, off the N176. Its season runs from Apr–Sept.

> ↰ **SIDE TRACK FROM ST-HILAIRE-DU-HARCOUËT**
>
> Take N176 out of St-Hilaire-du-Harcouët towards Avranches and Le Mont-St-Michel and after about 7 km, turn left at Les Biards, following signs for La Mazure. The road descends into the leafy valley of the River Sélune which, to the west, has been dammed to form the **Lac de Vezins**, a serpentine lake some 11 miles (18 km) long. **La Mazure** is a leisure centre; *tel: 33 89 19 50*, where a wide range of outdoor activities is available, including walking, canoeing, mountain biking,

109

sailing, horse-riding, windsurfing, fishing and climbing. The centre has gîte-style accommodation as well as camping and there is also a good restaurant, **Le Pic Epeiche**; *tel: 33 48 02 45*. It is also possible to join cruises along the lake aboard the *Sélune*; *tel: 33 50 16 36*, daily at 1500 and 1700 (July–Aug); Sun and public holidays 1500 and 1700 (Apr–June and Sept), price Fr.50 adults, Fr.30 children for a one-hour cruise. Other options include two-hour lunch and dinner cruises departing Sun and bank holidays 1200 (May–Sept) and Sat 1930 July–Aug respectively.

Continue on down the Sélune Valley and you come to **Ducey**, where there are a couple of good hotels, a two-star *LF*, the moderately priced **Auberge de la Sélune**, *2 r. St-Germain*; *tel: 33 48 53 62*, which stands by the river and has an excellent restaurant, and the three-star **Hôtel Moulin de Ducey**, *1 Grande-Rue*; *tel: 33 60 25 25*, a modernised former mill without restaurant. Moderate to expensive.

FOUGÈRES

Tourist Office: *1 pl. Aristide-Briand, 35500 Fougères*; *tel: 99 94 12 20*, has a wide selection of information on the town and the département of Ille-et-Vilaine. Open 0900–1900 in summer.

ACCOMMODATION AND FOOD

Fougères is a large town at a major cross-roads, with roads converging from Caen, Alençon, Tours, Rennes and St-Malo, and as a result has a fair number of hotels, some in the town itself, others on the main roads out of or circling the town. None has more than two-stars and one of the nicest in town is the **Hôtel Les Voyageurs**, *10 pl. Gambetta*; *tel: 99 99 18 21*. It has a three-star restaurant, comfortable rooms

and off-road parking, useful since the road outside is very busy. For that reason it is worth requesting a room at the back of the hotel. Not far away, the **Hôtel Balzac**, *15 r. Nationale*; *tel: 99 99 42 46*, is in a much quieter setting, though the rooms are not so cheerful. Cheaper town centre options include the one-star **Hôtel Commerce**, *3 pl. de l'Europe*; *tel: 99 94 40 40*, and the **Hôtel Bretagne**, *7 pl. de la République*; *tel: 99 99 31 68*, both of which are near where the railway station used to be.

Fougères' **campsite**, the three-star **Camping Municipal de Paron**; *tel: 99 99 40 81*, open Mar–Nov, lies about 1.5 km east of the town on the D17 towards La Chapelle-Janson.

There is a good choice of restaurants in Fougères, moderately priced, serving a range of gourmet cuisine, traditional dishes and snacks.

SIGHTSEEING

Fougères has played many roles in its long history – defender of the duchy of Brittany from the rest of France; stronghold of the Chouans' rebellion which attempted to restore the monarchy following the 1789 Revolution; and since the early 19th century, an industrial base specialising in the manufacture of shoes. Today, however, it isn't the industry that the visitor notices, but the massive 12th-century **château**, *pl. P. Symon*; *tel: 99 99 79 59*, open daily 0900–1900 (June–Sept); 1000–1200 and 1400–1730 (Sept–June), admission Fr.20, which dominates the town, albeit from its position tucked into the valley of the River Nançon, a loop of which almost surrounds it. One of the largest and most impressive feudal fortresses in Europe, it is in a remarkable state of repair despite regular sieges and capture. A walk around the ramparts gives good views of the château and the town and there are several towers topped with slate 'witches' hats' which can be visited, including one, the Raoul Tower, which contains a small museum on the town's shoe-making history.

The town's only other museum, the **Musée Emmanuel de la Villéon**, *r. Nationale; tel: 99 94 88 60*, open daily 1030–1230 and 1430–1830 (June–Sept); Wed–Sun 1400–1700 (Sept–May), admission free, housed in a 16th-century half-timbered building supported by pillars, is dedicated to the work of Emmanuel de la Villéon. One of the last great Impressionist artists, he was greatly inspired by Brittany's landscape and people.

Just along the *r. Nationale* is one of the town's churches, the **Église St-Léonard**, which dates largely from the 15th and 16th centuries, with next to it, the 16th-century **Hôtel de Ville** (town hall). From the church's belfry there are exceptional panoramas over the town. Behind the church, the **Jardin Public** (Public Garden) provides a splendid view over the lower town and château. The *r. des Vallées*, which skirts the gardens, leads by way of the Duchess Anne's stairway and a bridge over the River Nançon to the medieval quarter around the *pl. du Marchix*. With several attractive groupings of half-timbered buildings, it is popular with photographers and artists. Off the *r. Le-Bouteiller* stands the **Église St-Sulpice**, which has some imposing altar pieces.

ST-AUBIN-DU-CORMIER

Midway between Fougères and Rennes, this small town makes a quiet place to stop for those wishing to avoid the bustle of its larger neighbours, though there isn't much choice. Cheap and fairly basic is the best way to describe the **Hôtel du Bretagne**, *68 r. de l'Ecu; tel: 99 39 10 22*, but it does have a restaurant.

Campers and caravanners can pitch at the two-star **Camping Municipal**, *r. du Four Banal; tel: 99 39 10 42* or *99 39 18 22*, open Apr–Oct, just below the castle ruins.

St-Aubin-du-Cormier was the site of a major battle in 1488 when the Breton army was defeated by the French, following which Brittany renounced its independence and became part of France. What remains of the town's once great **château**, demolished after the battle, stands between a small lake and a ravine on the edge of the town.

RENNES

For details, see p. 253.

FORÊT DE PAIMPONT

Lying immediately north of the N24 west of Rennes, the 70 sq km Forêt de Paimpont once extended 136 km to the west. It was also said to be **Brocéliande**, the magical forest of Arthurian legend where the sorcerer **Merlin** lived. For further details, see the St-Malo–Quimper chapter, p. 302.

PAIMPONT

Tourist Information: *tel: 99 07 84 23.*

ACCOMMODATION AND FOOD

In the heart of the forest is the lakeside village of **Paimpont**. A delightful place to stay in the village centre is the two-star **Hôtel Relais de Brocéliande**; *tel: 99 07 81 07*, which has a super restaurant and a beer-drinking parrot to entertain customers in the bar. Room and menu prices are moderate. If you want to go a little up-market, the three-star **Hôtel le Manoir du Tertre**; *tel: 99 07 81 02*, occupies an old manor-house signed off D71, 4 km north of the village. Rather pricier, it is a hotel of character and, again, has a very good restaurant.

SIGHTSEEING

North of Paimpont is the **Château de Comper**; *tel: 97 22 61 12*, where **Viviane** is supposed to have been born. Its park is open Wed, Thur, Sat–Mon 1000–1900 (Apr–Sept), while the château is home to the **Centre Arthurien**, which organises events and exhibitions on the Arthurian theme. Also worth a visit, if only to view from the outside, is the **Château de Trécesson**, a real medieval-looking moated castle south-west of Paimpont.

At nearby **Tréhorenteuc**, the **church**; *tel: 97 93 05 12*, open daily 1100–1900 (Apr–Oct); Sat–Thur 1400–1800 (Mar–Apr and Nov), admission Fr.5, has several mosaics and paintings depicting the Knights of the Round Table and the legends of the Valley of No Return and the Barenton Fountain, plus a stained glass window of the Holy Grail.

PLOËRMEL

Tourist Office: *5 r. du Val, 56800 Ploërmel; tel: 97 74 02 70.*

ACCOMMODATION

There are a couple of *Logis de France* in the town, both of them close to the centre. The three-star **Hôtel Le Cobh**, *10 r. des Forges; tel: 97 74 00 49*, has moderately priced rooms as well as some on the more expensive side, plus a good restaurant with a full range of menus from the very reasonable to the expensive. The two-star **Hôtel du Commerce**, *70 r. de la Gare; tel: 97 74 05 32*, is moderately priced too, both in its rooms and its restaurants, but doesn't rise to the expense of the other.

There is a good two-star **campsite**, **Camping Le Lac**; tel: 97 74 01 22, beside the Lac au Duc, just north of Ploërmel. Reached via the D8 towards Taupont, it is open Apr–Sept.

SIGHTSEEING

Ploërmel was once the seat of the Dukes of Normandy, but time hasn't been so kind to it as it has to nearby Josselin (see St-Malo to Quimper route, p. 302). There were frequent battles between the two in the Middle Ages. In the early years of the Hundred Years War, when Ploërmel was garrisoned by a mainly English force, the two towns arranged a battle, known as the Battle of the Thirty, with 30 knights apiece. Ploërmel lost, with nine of its men killed and the rest captured. Today, the battle site, beside the N24, is marked by a stone column. The town still has some medieval houses near the church, particularly in *r. des Francs-Bourgeois* and *r. Beaumanoir*, in one of which James II is said to have sheltered for a while during his exile.

The 16th-century **Église St-Armel**, at the end of *r. des Francs-Bourgeois*, is worth a visit for its 16th- and 17th-century stained glass windows and carved doors. Statues of two of the Dukes of Brittany can be seen in one of the chapels. The church is dedicated to St Armel, the Irish missionary who founded the town in the 6th century.

Opposite the church stands the **Maison-Mère des Frères de Ploërmel** (Mother-house of the Brothers of Ploërmel), the abbey for a religious order founded in 1819. It houses a museum, the **Musée La Mennais**; *tel: 97 74 06 67*, open daily 0930–1200 and 1400–1730 (Apr–Sept), which has displays about the order and its founder, Jean-Marie de la Mennais, and an **astronomical clock**.

Out of town, the **Lac au Duc**, 2.5 km north, has a beach and water sports centre. The largest natural lake in Brittany, it is a popular place for relaxation. A mapped walk around the lake is available from the Tourist Office.

CALAIS–DIEPPE

Most people arriving in Calais from England immediately join the A16 autoroute south, but this route along the coast passes through some of the delightful villages and countryside so often overlooked by British visitors.

Not surprisingly on the nearest French coast to England, nearly every town of any size has historical connections, peaceful and otherwise, with the British, from William of Normandy's departure for Hastings to today's day-tripping invasions in the opposite direction.

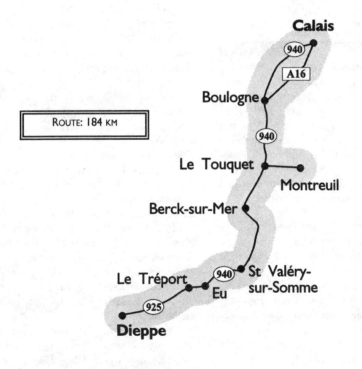

ROUTE: 184 KM

113

ROUTE

From Calais' *pl. d'Armes* take *r. de la Mer* towards the beach and turn left onto *av. du Gén. de Gaulle*, which becomes the D940 coast road. This passes both **Cap Blanc-Nez** and **Cap Gris-Nez** and through attractive coastal villages such as **Wissant**, **Audresselles** and **Wimereux** before reaching **Boulogne-sur-Mer**.

From there D940 heads inland for a while until reaching **Étaples**, at the mouth of the River Canche, and its more upmarket neighbour, **Le Touquet-Paris-Plage**. From here, there is a good diversion inland to **Montreuil**. Otherwise stay on D940, heading south past seaside resorts at **Stella-Plage** and **Merlimont-Plage** to **Berck-sur-Mer**. Again, D940 heads inland, skirting **Rue** to **Le Crotoy** and then looping round the **Somme Bay** to **St-Valéry-sur-Somme**, from where it continues to **Eu**. D940 then heads along the north side of the River Bresle to **Mers-les-Bains** and **Le Tréport**, south of which it joins D925 to **Dieppe**. Total distance is 184 km.

CALAIS

Tourist Office: *12 blvd Clémenceau, 62100 Calais; tel: 21 96 62 40,* open Mon–Sat 0900–1930, Sun and bank holidays 1000–1300 and 1630–1930 (July–Aug); Mon–Sat 0900–1230 and 1430–1830 (Sept–June), has extensive information on Calais and the Pas-de-Calais, as well as a hotel booking service and a bureau de change. An excellent indexed street map is available free.

ARRIVING AND DEPARTING

Calais has more ferry movements per day than any other French Channel port. In addition the Channel Tunnel (*Tunnel sous la Manche;* see p. 46) emerges beside the A16 motorway south-west of Calais.

Stena Line: from Dover, frequent services all year round, with a 45-min high-speed catamaran service starting early 1996; *tel: 21 46 80 22.*

P & O European Ferries: provice the fastest of the conventional ferry crossings from Dover; *tel:21 46 04 40.*

Hoverspeed: 35-min crossing by hovercraft from Dover; *tel: 21 46 14 14.*

Le Shuttle: the Channel Tunnel rail crossing from Folkestone takes an hour

from motorway to autoroute; *tel: 0990 35 35 35.*

ACCOMMODATION

There is no shortage of one- to three-star hotels in Calais. One of France's earliest luxury hotels, in business since 1771, the **Meurice**, *5 r. Edmond Roche; tel: 21 34 57 03,* was rebuilt after the war but still offers a high degree of sophistication. Room prices range from moderate to expensive. Its restaurant, **La Diligence**; *tel: 21 96 92 89,* mirrors room prices in its menus. Another top-notch hotel, with slightly less expensive rooms, is the **George V**, *36 r. Royale; tel: 21 97 68 00,* a comfortable, modernised *logis*. It has two restaurants, a gastronomic three-star option and a more economic one.

Two-star hotels worth investigating include the **Victoria**, *8 r. du Commandant Bonningue; tel: 21 34 38 32,* and its near-neighbour, the **Windsor**, *2 r. du Commandant Bonningue; tel: 21 34 59 40,* which are both close to the ferry port. While neither has its own restaurant, they are within a short walk of the restaurants of the *pl. d'Armes* and the *r. Royale*.

Most of Calais' hotels are hidden from the sea, but two that face the beach are the **Hôtel du Golf**, *digue Gaston Berthe; tel: 21 96 88 99,* and the **Climat de France**, *digue Gaston Berthe; tel: 21 34 64 64,* which are similarly priced modern two-star hotels.

The Golf has no restaurant, but there are a couple of good if pricey ones on the seafront, the **Aquar'Aile**, *255 r. Jean Moulin; tel: 21 34 00 00,* which has wonderful panoramic views of the beach, and the **Côte d'Argent**, *digue Gaston Berthe; tel: 21 34 68 07.* Both specialise in seafood but have other dishes, too.

Calais has two **campsites**, neither particularly inviting. Biggest by far is the

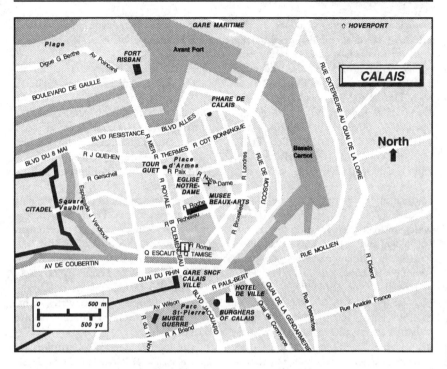

Camping Municipal, *av. Raymond Poincaré; tel: 21 97 89 79*, which is close to the beach beside the 16th-century **Fort Risban** overlooking the harbour entrance, but tends to get crowded. The other, **Camping Les Peuplier**s, *394 r. du Beau-Marais; tel: 21 34 03 56*, is near industrial areas off the N1 heading towards Dunkirk. Both remain open all year.

SIGHTSEEING

Calais is known as 'the most English town in France', which isn't surprising since it was in English hands for more than 200 years from 1347, following an eight-month siege, until the French retook it in 1558. Then in the early 19th century, Nottingham lacemakers arrived to create a lace industry, which thrives today. And, of course, every ferry arrival brings another influx of day-trippers from England. Most come to buy cheap wine and beer and to enjoy a meal at the town's many restaurants. The town, drab and modern, has few places of interest, but it does have a vast beach of fine, golden sand.

Calais's most famous landmark is the **Hôtel de Ville** (Town Hall), *pl. du Soldat-Inconnu*, built in the 1920s in 15th-century Flemish style, complete with a 75m belfry. Before it, amid colourful flower beds, stands Auguste Rodin's famous bronze statue, **the Burghers of Calais**, which honours six citizens who surrendered themselves to the English in 1347 to prevent a massacre.

Over the road, in the **Parc St-Pierre**, stands one of the town's two museums, the **Musée de la Guerre** (War Museum); *tel: 21 34 21 57*, open daily 1000–1700 (Mar–Dec), admission Fr.15 adults (Fr.10 children). Housed in a well-camouflaged

German naval command bunker which the RAF failed to hit despite flattening much of the town, it contains local memorabilia from World War II. The other museum, the **Musée des Beaux-Arts et de la Dentelle** (Museum of Fine Arts and Lace), *25 r. Richelieu; tel: 21 46 62 00,* open Wed–Mon 1000–1200 and 1400–1730 (all year), admission Fr.10, (Fr.5), free Wed, has large displays of lace, 15th- to 20th-century art and local history.

The few remnants of pre 20th-century Calais include the **Église Notre-Dame** (Church of Our Lady), *r. Notre-Dame;* which was completed during the English occupation and displays English influence. Charles de Gaulle married a local girl, Yvonne Vendroux, here in 1921.

Elsewhere, the **Citadelle**, *sq. Vauban,* built on the ruins of a medieval castle in the 16th century and improved by Vauban a century later, is now used as a sports stadium, while the **Tour de Guet** (Guet Tower), *pl d'Armes*, was built as a watchtower in 1229 and became a lighthouse in the early 19th century.

A proper lighthouse, the **Phare de Calais**, *pl. Charles Bourgeois; tel: 21 34 33 34,* open Mon–Fri 1000–1200 and 1400–1830, Sat–Sun 1400–1830 (June–Sept); Mon–Fri 1000–1200 and 1400–1700 (Oct–May), admission Fr.10 (Fr.5), opened in 1848 to take over from the watchtower. It stands 53 m high and provides good views over the town and harbour.

BOULOGNE-SUR-MER

Tourist Office: *quai de la Poste, 62200 Boulogne; tel: 21 31 68 38.*

ARRIVING AND DEPARTING

At one time several ferry companies sailed into Boulogne, but now that all efforts are being directed towards Calais, only the **SeaCat** high speed catamaran travels there from Folkestone; *tel: 21 30 27 26.*

ACCOMMODATION

Boulogne is not quite so well off for hotels as Calais, but there is a good choice of two-star options. The only three-star is the **Metropole**, *51 r. Adolphe Thiers; tel: 21 31 54 30,* located in the centre, though fairly quiet and with off-road parking. Expensive. The **Faidherbe**, *12 r. Faidherbe; tel: 21 31 60 93,* is a comfortable modern two-star on a busy street leading up from the quayside. Prices are moderate.

Few of Boulogne's hotels have restaurants, but two that do are the **Ibis**, *blvd Diderot; tel: 21 30 12 40,* and the **Ibis Plage**, *170 blvd Ste-Beuve; tel: 21 32 15 15.* **The Ibis Plage**, opposite Nausicaa, is the smaller of the two, but nevertheless has 42 rooms, and is a little more expensive than the Ibis.

The massive three-star **Camping du Phare**, *quai de la Violette; tel: 21 31 69 20,* is on the south-western edge of town at Le Portel. Open Apr–Sept.

SIGHTSEEING

Boulogne is effectively in two parts, the lower town, the modern shopping centre near the port (said to be the largest fishing base in Europe), and the upper town (La Ville-Haute), which is enclosed by ramparts and is by far the most interesting part. That's if you exclude **Nausicaa** (the Centre National de la Mer or National Sea Centre), *blvd Ste-Beuve; tel: 21 30 98 98,* open daily 1000–2000 (June–Sept); Mon–Fri 1000–1800, Sat–Sun 1000–1900 (Sept–May), admission Fr.50 (Fr.35), Boulogne's most popular attraction and the largest sea experience museum in Europe. The aquarium contains an amazing array of fish, 6000 or so representing more than 300 species ranging from

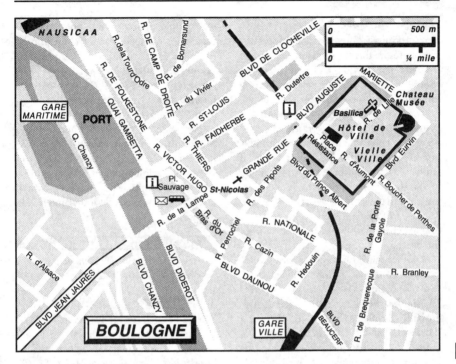

simple plankton to fearsome-looking sharks. The centre is strongly educational and tackles environmental issues too.

The smell of fish is very strong by the harbour and the only real escape is to head for the **Ville-Haute**, the walls of which were built in the 13th century on the site of a Roman fortified town. There are good views of the town from the ramparts. Many visitors wander up for the excellent choice of restaurants, but there are several places to visit too. The **Basilique Notre-Dame**, *r. de Lille*, was built in the mid 1800s over the crypt of a Romanesque church that stood on the site. The crypt itself, open Tues–Sun 1400–1700 (all year), admission Fr.10, contains some interesting statues and relics and painted pillars.

A short walk away is the **Château-Musée** (Castle Museum), *r. de Bernet; tel:* *21 80 00 80,* open Mon–Sat 0930–1230 and 1330–1815, Sun 0930–1230 and 1430–1815 (May–Sept); Mon–Sat 1030–1230 and 1400–1700, Sun 1030–1230 and 1430–1730 (Sept–May), admission Fr.25, which includes among its displays items from Egypt, ancient Greece and the Gallo-Roman era, medieval and Renaissance sculptures, and an unusual collection of Eskimo masks. Also within the walls is a 13th-century **beffroi** (belfry), *pl. Godefroy de Bouillon,* open daily 0800–1230 and 1400–1700, admission free.

LE TOUQUET-PARIS-PLAGE

Tourist Office: *Palais de l'Europe, pl. de l'Hermitage, 62520 Le Touquet-Paris-Plage; tel: 21 05 21 65,* open Mon–Sat 0900–1230 and 1400–1830, Sun 1000–1200, has plenty of local information and will also make hotel bookings.

ACCOMMODATION

Not surprisingly, for what is the most fashionable resort this far north in France, Le Touquet has a wide range of hotels to choose from, including several bearing four stars. The top hotels go back to the Edwardian heyday, among them the **Westminster**, *av. du Verger; tel: 21 05 48 48*, where you can indulge yourself in luxury in exchange for a large number of francs. A little cheaper, but still coming within the expensive price band and bearing just three stars is the **Bristol**, *17 r. Jean Monnet; tel: 21 05 49 95*, restored to its original charm and just a short walk from the beach.

Another star down, with a corresponding drop in price to a more moderate level is the **Red Fox**, *r. de Metz; tel: 21 05 27 58*, another hotel which has been modernised. Similarly priced is the **Ibis Thalassa**, *Front de Mer; tel: 21 09 87 00*, which has exceptional views along the beach. Even more moderate are **Robert's Hotel**, *66 r. de Londres; tel: 21 05 52 88*, and the **Victoria**, *11 r. de Paris; tel: 21 05 02 11*.

Three-star **camping** is available at **Camping Stoneham**, *av. Godin; tel: 21 05 16 55*, open Feb–Nov.

SIGHTSEEING

It is for the extensive sandy beach and the shops - mainly along *r. St-Jean* - that most people visit Le Touquet. At low tide it is a long hike to the sea, but then the land-yachts take to the sands.

The main seafront attraction is the **Aqualud**, *Front de Mer; tel: 21 05 63 59*, open daily 1000–1900 (July–Aug); 1000–1800 (Sept–June), admission Fr.70, an aquatic leisure complex with a wave pool, giant waterslides, outdoor pools and a sauna. Other activities available at Le Touquet include golf, horse-riding and windsurfing. For evening entertainment there are a number of night-clubs (mostly along *r. St-Jean*) and two casinos, the **Casino du Palais**, *Palais de l'Europe, pl. de l'Hermitage; tel: 21 05 01 05*, and the **Casino des Quatre Saisons**, *26 r. St-Jean; tel 21 05 16 99*.

For quieter moments there is the **Musée du Touquet**, *av. du Golf; tel: 21 05 62 62*, open Wed–Sun 1000–1200 and 1400–1800 (closed June and Sept), admission Fr.10 adults, Fr.5 children, which contains the works of local painters and sculptors.

MONTREUIL

Tourist Office: *pl. Dametal, 62170 Montreuil; tel: 21 06 04 27.*

ACCOMMODATION

The place to head for luxury rooms and dining is the château-hotel near the citadel, the **Château de Montreuil**, *4 chaussée des Capucins; tel: 21 81 53 04*. Very popular with the British, despite expensive rooms and menus.

In the centre of town, the **les Hauts de Montreuil**, *21-23 r. Ledent; tel: 21 81 95 92*, is in a building dating back to 1537, though the inside has been renovated to provide the comforts of its two-star classification. Again, expensive, but at a more affordable level than the château-hotel. More moderate is the **Bellevue**, *6 av. du 11 Novembre; tel: 21 06 04 19*, a 12-room *Logis de France*.

Camping Municipal la Fontaine des Clercs; *tel: 21 06 07 28*, open all year, provides three-star **camping** on the banks of the River Canche.

SIGHTSEEING

This delightful and peaceful town was once the port of French kings. Now it is stranded some 16 km inland and is well worth the diversion to see it. Standing on a hill overlooking the Canche Valley, it is enclosed within medieval walls from which there are fine views over the surrounding countryside. Standing guard is the 16th-century **citadel**, which replaced an earlier castle and was improved by Vauban. Around the **Église St-Saulvé**, *pl. Gambetta*, there are several cobbled lanes where craftsmen work in half-timbered houses.

BERCK-SUR-MER

Tourist Office: *5 av. F. Tattegrain, 62600 Berck-sur-Mer; tel: 21 09 50 00.*

ACCOMMODATION

Berck is a down-market version of Le Touquet and this is reflected in its hotels, most of which are two- or one-star. There are three moderately priced *logis* worth investigating, the **Flots Bleus**, *17 r. du Calvaire; tel: 21 09 03 42*, the **Littoral**, *36 pl. de l'Entonnoir; tel: 21 09 07 76*, and the **Hôtel de l'Entonnoir**, *av. Francis Tattegrain; tel: 21 09 12 13*. All have restaurants, again moderately priced. For a hotel offering more economically priced rooms try the **Concorde**, *39 r. Gabriel Péri; tel 21 09 01 76*. There is a wide choice of **campsites** here. Two close to the beach include **Camping de la Manche**; *tel: 21 09 36 29*, and the much bigger **Campilu**; *tel: 21 09 65 00*.

SIGHTSEEING

As well as the usual beach activities, Berck has an indoor activity centre, **Agora**, *Esplanade Parmentier; tel: 21 09 01 81*, open daily 1000–2000 (July–Aug); Fri– Sun and Tues–Wed 1000–2000 (Sept– June), complete with swimming pool, slides, sauna and gym. There is also a museum, the **Musée Municipal**, *60 r. de l'Impératrice; tel: 21 84 07 80*, open Wed–Mon

1500–1800 admission free, which contains a collection of art and items illustrating Berck's seafaring traditions.

ST-VALÉRY-SUR-SOMME

Tourist Office: *23 r. de la Ferté, ; tel: 22 60 93 50.*

ACCOMMODATION

Moderately-priced hotels are the order of the day in St-Valéry, one of the best being a two-star *LF*, the **Relais Guillaume de Normandy**, *40 quai de Romerel; tel: 22 60 82 36*, which has a château-like appearance and a superb restaurant serving such specialities as seafood and lamb from the Somme salt-marshes. A slightly cheaper neighbour is the **Colonne de Bronze**, *43 quai de Romerel; tel: 22 60 80 07*, while offering more economically priced rooms is the **les Pilotes**, *62 r. de la Ferté; tel: 22 60 80 39*.

SIGHTSEEING

Pretty St Valéry was William the Conqueror's last port of call before he sailed across the Channel to invade England, and since then it has been occupied by the English on at least two occasions, most recently during World War I.

Effectively, it is two towns – the busy lower town (**basse-ville**) and port, and the medieval upper town (**haute-ville**), which still has fortifications, including the **Porte de Nevers** (Nevers Gate) and the **Porte Guillaume** (William's Gate).

The upper town is overlooked by the Gothic **Église St-Martin**, while from the *pl. de l'Ermitage* a path leads to the unusual **Chapelle des Marins** (Sailors' Chapel), with its sandstone and flint chequerboard walls. There are good views from here overlooking the Somme Bay.

Worth a visit in the lower town is the **Musée Picarvie**; *tel: 22 26 94 90*, open

119

daily 1400–1900 (May–Aug); Wed–Mon 1400–1900 (Feb–Apr and Sept–Dec), which reconstructs life as it was in the area before the advent of the industrial age.

EU

Tourist Office: *41 r. Paul Bignon, 76260 Eu; tel: 35 86 04 68.*

ACCOMMODATION

If you want to live in style make for the three-star **Château-Hôtel du Pavillon de Joinville**, *rte du Tréport; tel: 35 86 24 03*, which was once part of **King Louis-Philippe's** estate. There is a helicopter pad for those who also wish to arrive in style. Rooms are expensive, as is the restaurant.More moderately priced are the **Hôtel de la Cour Carrée**, *rte de Dieppe; tel: 35 50 60 60*, and the **Hôtel de la Gare**, *20 pl. de la Gare; tel: 35 86 16 64*, a *logis* with a good restaurant. The most economically priced rooms are at **L'Étoile**, *37 blvd Thiers; tel 35 86 14 89*.

SIGHTSEEING

William the Conqueror married Mathilda of Flanders at Eu in 1050, though nothing remains of the castle where the ceremony took place. The present **château** was built in the 16th century and became the favourite residence of Louis-Philippe, who was visited there twice by Queen Victoria. Her first visit was the first time an English monarch had set foot on French soil since Henry VIII's meeting with François I at the Field of the Cloth of Gold in 1520.

The château now serves as the Town Hall and also houses the **Musée Louis-Philippe**; *tel: 35 86 44 00*, open Wed–Mon 1000–1200 and 1400–1800 (Apr–Oct), which has a section on the glass-making industry based in Eu and the Bresle Valley. Facing the château is the Gothic **Église Notre-Dame et St-Laurent**, dedicated to St Lawrence O'Toole, an Archbishop of Dublin, who died in Eu in the 12th century. The crypt beneath the church contains an effigy of the saint.

LE TRÉPORT

Tourist Office: *Esplanade de la Plage, 76470 Le Tréport; tel: 35 86 05 69.*

ACCOMMODATION

Le Tréport has a reasonable range of economically and moderately priced hôtels. The **Le Riche Lieu**, *50 quai François 1er; tel: 35 86 26 55*, is one of the best located, its modernised rooms facing the harbour. Its restaurant is also worth trying, though it has to compete with the seafood restaurants on the quay. A good alternative is the **Hôtel du Casino et de la Plage**, *15 Espl. de la Plage; tel: 35 86 06 70*, close to the beach and harbour entrance.

Le Tréport has two four-star **campsites, Camping Municipal les Boucaniers**, *av. des Canadiens; tel: 35 86 35 47*, and the **Parc International du Golf**, *route de Dieppe; tel: 35 86 33 80*. Both are open Apr–Sept.

SIGHTSEEING

In an attractive setting beneath high cliffs, Le Tréport is a busy fishing port as well as a lively holiday resort. Its church, the **Église St-Jacques**, *pl. de l'Église*, built in the 16th century and extensively restored in the 19th, looks out over the harbour. The one museum is the **Musée des Enfants du Vieux Tréport**; *tel: 35 86 13 36*, open Sat–Sun, bank holidays 1000–1200 and 1430–1800 (Apr–Sept), admission free, which recalls the earlier seafaring days of the port. From the clifftop **Calvaire des Terrasses** (Terrace Calvary) views extend inland along the Bresle Valley and north to the Somme.

CHARTRES

Chartres lies on the Beauce Plain about 89 km south-west of Paris. Today's visitors have just the same view on their approach as that of pilgrims over the centuries – the twin spires of the Notre-Dame Cathedral, one of the finest in Europe, towering over endless fields of wheat.

TOURIST INFORMATION

Tourist Office: *pl. de la Cathédrale, BP 289, 28005 Chartres; tel: 37 21 50 00,* open Mon–Fri 0930–1845, Sat 0930–1800, Sun 1030–1230 and 1430–1730 (June–Sept); Mon–Fri 0930–1830, Sat 0930–1800, Sun 1030–1230 and 1430–1730 (Mar–May and Oct); Mon–Fri 0930–1800, Sat 1000–1700, Sun 1030–1230 and 1430–1730 (Nov–Feb).

ARRIVING AND DEPARTING

Chartres lies just off the A11 *autoroute* from Paris to Nantes, with exits linking with the N10 east and south of the city. It is a major road junction, with the N10 Paris to Bordeaux road, the N154 from Rouen to Orléans and the N23 from Nantes all meeting at Chartres, along with a number of *départmental* roads

GETTING AROUND

Most of sightseeing Chartres is within the inner péripherique and so the main attractions are all within reasonable walking distance of one another.

The Tourist Office has a useful town centre plan (free) that will help you locate most of the sights.

Buses

STAC operates the nine-route **Filibus** service from the centre of Chartres to all the outlying suburbs. Their head office is at *57 r. de la Beauce, Lucé; tel: 37 35 68 02,* but they also have a kiosk in the *pl. des Épars; tel: 37 36 26 98,* where you can buy tickets. Tickets can also be purchased at most *tabacs* (tobacconists) in the city. All the services pass through the *pl. des Épars* and the *pl. de la Gare.* An excellent map showing the routes and a street-indexed plan of central Chartres is available free from the STAC kiosk or from the Tourist Office.

Taxis

Two taxi services operate in Chartres, **Taxi 2000,** *pl. Pierre Sémard; tel: 37 36 00 00,* and **Chartres Radio-Taxi,** *17 r. Charles Brune; tel: 37 21 91 62.*

STAYING IN CHARTRES

Accommodation

There is a good selection of one-, two- and three-star hotels close to the city centre or around the periphery. Chartres is a popular centre, however, and it is advisable to book in advance, especially in the high season. If you experience difficulty, the Tourist Office will assist in finding accommodation.

Hotel chains in Chartres include *Ba, BW, Co, Ct, F1, Ib, Mc, Mp, Nv.*

Top hotels in town are the three-star **Le Grand Monarque,** *22 pl. des Épars; tel: 37 21 00 72,* which has 54 rooms, a restaurant and private car-parking facilities, and is on the inner ring road (expensive), and the **Mercure-Châtelet**, *6-8 av. Jehan de Beauce; tel: 37 21 78 00*, which is near the railway and bus stations and has 48 rooms and no restaurant (moderate-expensive). Another three-star-hotel, the **Novotel**; *av. Marcel Proust; tel: 37 34 80 30*, is located on the eastern edge of Chartres on the road to Paris, and is complete with restaurant and swimming pool. Moderate-expensive.

Nearest to the **cathédrale** is the two-star **Le Boeuf Couronné**, *15 pl Châtelet; tel: 37 18 06 06*. This has 27 rooms and a restaurant. Moderate. Lying north of the *cathédrale*, the two-star **Ibis-Centre**, *14 pl. Drouaise; tel: 37 36 06 36*, has the largest number of rooms in town and is reasonably moderate. Also close to the railway station, the **Jehan de Beauce**, *19 av. Jehan de Beauce; tel: 37 21 01 41*, has 46 rooms ranging from economy to moderate. One of the cheapest options is the one-star **St-Jean**, *6 r. du Faubourg St-Jean; tel: 37 21 35 69* which has 16 rooms.

The only **campsite** is the three-star **Camping des Bords de l'Eure**, *r. de Launay; tel: 37 28 79 43*, which is signed from the N154 on the south-eastern outskirts and lies on the banks of the River Eure. Open Apr–Sept.

Auberge de Jeunesse (youth hostel): *23 av. Neigre; tel: 37 34 27 64.*

Eating and Drinking

The choice of restaurants here is excellent, mainly French traditional, but there are several Italian and Asian restaurants and even one specialising in cheese and another in vegetarian meals, still relatively rare in France. Specialities from the region include game such as partridge, pheasant, hare, venison and wild boar, while the River Eure is an excellent source of fish, especially trout. Partridge and duck paté are also specialities of the area.

One of the more expensive places in town is **La Truie qui File**, *12 r. de la Poissonnerie; tel: 37 21 53 90*, housed in a beautiful half-timbered building dating from around 1500. Creativity and imagination are the hallmarks of the menu. Closed Sun evening and Mon. A near neighbour, **L'Estaminet**, *4 r. de la Poissonnerie; tel: 37 21 11 48*, offers simple cuisine with little originality but in a relaxed atmosphere and at far more affordable prices. Closed Mon. In a charming setting beside the River Eure, the **Moulin de Ponceau**, *21 r. de la Tannerie; tel: 37 35 87 87*, has terrace seating.

Just below the cathedral, **Le Pichet**, *19 r. du Cheval Blanc; tel 37 21 08 35*, has a moderately priced menu and a warm welcome. Specialities include boiled chicken. Nearby, **Le Méditerranéen**, *6 r. du Cheval Blanc; tel: 37 36 28 00*, serves couscous specialities, along with Algerian and Moroccan wines.

The cheese restaurant is **La Cave à Fromages**, *24 r. de la Porte Morard; tel: 37 30 18 64*, which includes among its specialities *Fondue Normande*, made from camembert and cider, and *Fondue Royale*, which uses champagne. Closed all day Mon and Tues lunchtime. **Le Verger**, *12 r. de la Clouterie; tel 37 36 78 31*, is the vegetarian restaurant and is economically priced. Open only for lunch Mon–Fri.

Communications

The main **post office** is located at *1–3 blvd. Maurice Violette; tel: 37 27 40 70*, open Mon–Fri 0830–1900 and Sat 0830–1200.

Money

Several of the usual banks are located around the shopping area leading from the *pl. des Épars* and most have automatic cash dispensers. **Crédit Agricole**, *pl. des Halles*,

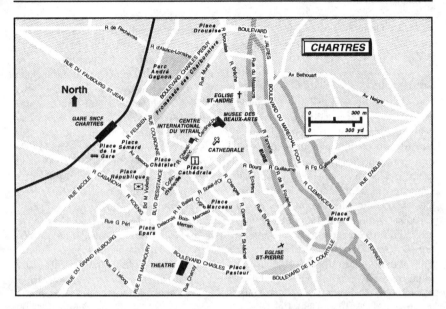

has a 24-hr cash dispensing facility. A change office is also located at *pl. de la Cathédrale*, open daily 1000–1800 (Mar-Oct).

ENTERTAINMENT

Although much of the entertainment in Chartres leans towards the cultural, there are also several night-clubs and meeting places. The Tourist Office publishes details of the major events, which include annual musical festivals, taking place mainly between June–Sept at various venues around the city. One of the most popular is the **Festival d'Orgue** (Organ Festival) in which international organists perform at the cathedral on Sunday afternoons throughout the summer. Admission is free.

The **Théâtre**, *blvd Chasles; tel: 37 21 57 29*, has a varied programme of concerts, dance and plays. There are two cinemas, **Les Enfants du Paradis**, *11 pl. Pasteur; tel: 37 35 99 28*, and the **ABC**, *10 av. Jehan de Beauce; tel; 37 36 14 67*.

Foreign language films are dubbed in French.

For night owls there are several late bars and night-clubs. **L'Académie de la Bière**, *8 r. du Cheval-Blanc; tel 37 36 90 07*, has more than 120 different beers to choose from. **Le Saxophone**, *20 pl. des Halles; tel 37 36 05 05*, and **Le Duke**, *32 r. des Comtesses; tel: 37 35 68 82*, both have live music from time to time. Among night-clubs are **Les Caves du Saxo**, *20 pl. des Halles; tel: 37 36 05 05* and **Le Lido Club**, *15 av. Marcel Proust; tel: 37 34 41 41*.

The **Hippodrome de Chartres** (Chartres Racecourse), *r. Jean Mermoz; tel: 37 34 93 73* features steeplechase and trotting races, mainly on Sun during the season.

SHOPPING

The principal shopping area, which is largely pedestrianised, spreads from *pl. des Épars* along *r. du Bois Merrain* and *r. Noel Ballay* to *pl. du Cygne*, *pl. Marceau* and *pl.*

des Halles. Street markets take place on Sat mornings in the *r. des Changes* and *pl. Billard.*

SIGHTSEEING

Personal cassettes in English can be hired from the office for a one-hour self-guided walk through old Chartres, price Fr.35 for one or two people, plus deposit. Other organised sightseeing possibilities include a tourist train with commentary, which will take you on a 35-min trip around old Chartres, departing from *pl. de la Cathédrale,* daily 1000–1900 (Apr–Nov), price Fr.30 adults (Fr.15 children), or horse-drawn carriages which also depart from in front of the cathedral, offering two tours, one of 40 min, the other of 70 min, around old Chartres. There are regular departures daily 1030–1830 (July–Sept), price Fr.30 adults (Fr.18), with commentaries in English.

If you wish to wander the **old town**, you should head roughly east and northeast of the cathedral down to the River Eure, where old humpback bridges add an attractive element to the scene. It is from the river that some of the best views of the cathedral can be had, while the *r. des Écuyers* features some particularly attractive restored houses.

The town's greatest attraction is the **Cathédrale de Notre-Dame**, open daily 0730–1900 (Oct–Mar), 0730–1930 (Apr–Sept). One of the finest cathedrals in Europe, it was built in the Gothic style between 1194 and 1225 after its Romanesque predecessor had been burned down in a disastrous fire that also destroyed much of the town. Especially worth seeing are the **Portail Royal** (Royal Doorway) at the front of the cathedral, and the magnificent **stained glass windows**, more than 160 of them, most dating from the 12th and 13th centuries.

These are currently in the process of being cleaned and restored, with dazzling results. The north and south doorways are also impressive, while other attractions include the **trésor** (treasury), open Tues–Sat 1000–1200 and 1400–1800, Sun 1400–1800 (all year), admission free, a visit to the **New Bell Tower**, open Mon–Sat 0930–1130 and 1400–1730, Sun 1400-1730 (Apr–Sept); Mon-Sat 1000–1130 and 1400-1600, Sun 1400-1600 (Oct–Mar), admission Fr.14 (Fr.7), and the **crypte** (crypt), the longest in France, entered via the **Maison de la Crypte**, *18 cloître Notre-Dame; tel: 37 21 56 33,* 30-min guided tours only (in French but with a written English translation) daily 1100–1615 (all year), admission Fr.11 adults, Fr.8 children. Guided tours of the cathedral in English, conducted by Malcolm Miller, an English expert on Chartres, are available at 1200 and 1445 (Mar–Nov), price Fr.30 adults, Fr.20 children.

Other churches worth a visit include **Église St-André** (St Andrew's Church), *r. St-André,* a Romanesque collegiate church, which has been badly damaged over the years and is now used for art exhibitions and concerts, **Église St-Pierre** (St Peter's Church), *pl. St-Pierre,* formerly part of a Benedictine monastery, and **Église St-Aignan**, *pl. St-Aignan,* which has a wooden barrel-vault roof and a lavishly decorated interior. The latter two also have stained-glass windows dating from the 14th and 16th centuries.

Next to the cathedral, the **Musée des Beaux-Arts** (Fine Arts Museum), *29 cloître Notre-Dame, tel: 37 36 41 39,* open Mon, Wed–Sat 1000–1200 and 1400–1700, Sun 1400–1700 (Nov–Mar); Wed–Mon 1000–1800 (Apr–Oct), admission Fr.10 adults (or Fr.20 if a major temporary exhibition is being held), Fr.5

children, is housed in the former **Palais Épiscopal** (Bishop's Palace), a largely 17th- and 18th-century edifice. The museum has an important collection of paintings covering the 16th to 19th centuries, with works by Boucher, Chardin, Holbein, Teniers and Vlaminck among others, as well as sculptures, earthenware and pewterware, harpsichords, tapestries, and 12 enamels of the Apostles, made in the 16th century for François I by Léonard Limosin. Every May, a harpsichord festival is held at the museum.

Just a short walk from both the cathedral and fine arts museum, the **Centre International du Vitrail** (International Stained Glass Centre), *5 r. du Cardinal Pie; tel: 37 21 65 72*, open Mon–Fri 0930–1230 and 1330-1800, Sat–Sun 1000–1230 and 1430–1800 (Oct–Mar); daily 0930–1800 (Apr–Oct), admission Fr.15 adults, Fr.10 children, is housed in the renovated 12th-century **Grenier de Loëns** (Loëns granary). In the courtyard of the old chapter house, it was once used to store grain and wine, but is now home to displays of medieval, Renaissance and modern stained glass, not only from France, but from around the world. There are also exhibits showing stained glass history, production and restoration.

Not to be confused with the nearby **Galerie du Vitrail** (Stained Glass Gallery), *17 cloître Notre-Dame; tel: 37 36 10 03*, where there are exhibitions of contemporary stained glass which can be purchased.

The **Musée des Sciences Naturelles et de Préhistoire** (Natural Science and Prehistory Museum), *blvd de la Courtille, sq. Noël Ballay; tel: 37 28 36 09*, open Wed and Sun 1400–1700 (Sept–June); Sun–Fri 1400–1800 (June–Sept), admission free, is just off the ring road near the theatre and has collections of fossils, insects from around the world and stuffed French fauna.

The **Maison de l'Archéologie** (Archaeology Museum), *16 r. St–Pierre; tel: 37 30 99 38*, open Wed and Sun 1400–1800 (Oct–May); Wed–Mon 1400–1800 (July–Sept), admission Fr.5, contains remains discovered during archaeological excavations in the city.

Near the railway station and housed in a former steam engine shed, the **Conservatoire de l'Agriculture** or **COMPA** (Agricultural Museum), *1 r. de la République; tel: 37 36 11 30*, open Tues–Fri 0900–1230 and 1330–1800, Sat–Sun 1000–1230 and 1330–1900 (all year), admission Fr.25 adults, Fr.10 children, is the first museum of its kind in France and brings together a splendid collection of agricultural machines and tools, some of them unique. There is an audiovisual display (in French) explaining history of agriculture, plus a gallery introducing major characters who were instrumental in bringing new ideas to agriculture over the centuries.

The **Musée de l'École** (School Museum), *1 r. du 14 Juillet; tel: 37 34 46 97*, open Mon–Fri 1000–1200 and 1400–1800 (Sept–June), admission Fr.15 adults Fr.10 children, has displays of educational material and classroom furniture from times gone by.

Undoubtedly one of Chartres' most unusual sights, the **Maison Picassiette** (Picassiette House), *22 r. du Repos; tel: 37 34 10 78 and 37 36 41 39*, open Wed–Mon 1000–1200 and 1400–1800 (Apr–Oct), admission Fr.10 adults, Fr.5 children, was home to Raymond Isidore who built it over a period of around 30 years earlier this century. An amazing example of *Art Naïf* (Naive Art), the house, inside and out, including its furniture, plus the gardens and various monuments, are decorated with mosaics made from broken crockery and pieces of coloured glass. Monuments include a chapel, a tomb crowned with a representation of Chartres Cathedral, and the Wall of Jerusalem.

On the northern outskirts of Chartres, the **Grenier de l'Histoire** (History Loft), *1 bis r. des Grands Prés, Lèves; tel: 37 21 77 77*, open Wed–Sun 1430–1800 (Apr–Sept), admission Fr.20 (Fr.10), creates scenes at various times through history using wax figures.

⟁ SIDE-TRACK FROM CHARTRES

The drive south of Chartres on the N10 takes you across the **Beauce Plain**, an area renowned for it windmills. In the mid 1800s there were more than 800 punctuating the landscape, but within 50 years this number had fallen to no more than 100, and little by little the numbers have been further depleted. A notable one beside the N10 is **Le Moulin Pelard**, *Le Bois de Feugères; tel 37 96 31 08*, open Sat–Sun 1400–1830, admission Fr.10 (Fr.5 children), which dates from 1796 and following restoration is in full working order.

Some five miles farther to the south is **Bonneval**, a small town which still retains some of its medieval town walls and towers. It also has some attractive abbey buildings dating from the 13th and 15th centuries which now serve as a hospital.

Another nine miles to the south is **Châteaudun**, (tourist information; **Office de Tourisme**, *1 r. de Luynes; tel: 37 45 22 46*). Built on a rocky spur overlooking the Loir Valley, the town has a **château**, *tel: 37 45 22 70*, open daily 1000–1145 and 1400–1600

(Oct–Apr); 0930–1145 and 1400–1800 (Apr–June and Sept); 0900–1845 (July–Aug), admission Fr.27, built in Gothic and Renaissance styles, with one of the best preserved 12th century keeps in Europe. Jehan de Dunois, a companion in arms to Joan of Arc, lived there for while. Below the château are several medieval streets that escaped the fire which destroyed most of the town in 1723. One of them, *r. St-Lubin*, lined with half-timbered houses, still has its central water channel.

Of the handful of churches, the most interesting is the **Église de la Madeleine** (Church of St Mary Magdalene), *pl. Cap de la Madeleine*, which was built into the ramparts in the 12th century but never completed.

Worth a visit is the **Musée des Beaux-Arts et d'Histoire Naturelle** (Fine Arts and Natural History Museum), *3 r. Toufaire; tel: 37 45 55 36*, open daily 1000–1230 and 1330–1830 (July–Aug); Wed–Mon 1000–1230 and 1330–1830 (Apr–June and Sept); Wed–Mon 1000–1200 and 1400–1700 (Oct–Mar), admission Fr.16 (Fr.10), which has important collections on Egyptology, Far Eastern art and weapons and local archaeology as well as a remarkable ornithological display containing around 3000 bird specimens. Below the *Promenade du Mail*, from where there are fine views, are the **Grottes du Foulon** (Foulon Caves), *r. des Fouleries; tel: 37 45 19 60*, open daily 1000–1200 and 1400–1900 (May–Sept); Tues–Sun 1400–1800 (Oct–Apr), admission Fr.25 (Fr.15), a series of limestone caves formed by the waters of the River Loir. A visit ends with a *son et lumière* display of the 18th-century town fire ⬛.

CHERBOURG

At the tip of the Cotentin Peninsula, the commercial port of Cherbourg was developed as a naval base, first by the military architect Vauban in the 17th century and then by Napoleon.

TOURIST INFORMATION

Maison de Tourisme, *2 quai Alexandre III, 50100 Cherbourg; tel: 33 93 52 02.* Open daily 0900–1200, 1400–1800 (June–Aug); Mon 1400–1800, Tues–Fri 0900–1200, 1400–1800, Sat 0900–1200 (Sept–May).

ARRIVING AND DEPARTING

Most traffic enters Cherbourg from the south, via N13 from Caen and Paris. A link road now takes ferry traffic east of the town, avoiding city-centre congestion.

Cherbourg has a greater choice of UK and Ireland **ferry** connections than any other French port. **Stena Line** from Southampton (May–Dec only, limited service outside summer months); *tel: 33 20 43 38.* **P&O European Ferries**: from Portsmouth (year-round, but limited Jan–Mar); *tel: 33 88 65 70.* **Truckline** (Brittany Ferries): from Poole (year-round, limited Jan); *tel: 33 22 38 98.* **Irish Ferries**: from Cork (June–Aug) and Rosslare; *tel: 33 44 28 96.*

GETTING AROUND

Most sights are close to the centre, where car parking is difficult.

Local **bus services** are operated by **Zéphir Bus**; *tel: 33 22 40 58*, while services elsewhere in the Manche *département* are operated by **STN**; *tel: 33 44 32 22.* The **Gare Routière** (bus station) is oppo-

site the **Gare SNCF** (rail station) on *av. J.-F. Millet.* There are two **taxi** ranks, one at the end of the *quai de Caligny*, the other in front of the rail station; *tel: 33 53 36 38.*

STAYING IN CHERBOURG

Accommodation

There are several hotels, mainly around the centre. Nearly all are two-star and moderate. Hotel chains include Ca, IH. The best hotel is the modern three-star **Mercure**, *Gare Maritime; tel: 33 44 01 11.* Expensive, it has a restaurant.

Hotels with more character are found along the *quai de Caligny*, among them the moderately priced **Ambassadeur**, *at no. 22; tel: 33 43 10 00*, (no restaurant) and the **La Régence**, at *no. 42; tel: 33 43 05 16*, a two-star *LF* with most rooms overlooking the fishing harbour (moderate to expensive). It has an excellent restaurant.

Youth hostel: *av. Louis-Lumière; tel: 33 44 26 31*, open Apr–Oct.

Eating and Drinking

Most restaurants serve seafood and traditional Norman cuisine. *Quai de Caligny* has several to choose from: the **Café de Paris**, at *no. 40; tel: 33 43 12 36*, and the slightly more expensive **Le Cotentin**, at *no. 30; tel: 33 43 51 80.* More economic is **La Pizza Café Caligny**, at *no. 48; tel: 33 43 15 17.* Elsewhere, another favourite is **Le Grandgousier**, *21 r. de l'Abbaye; tel: 33 53 19 43*, famed for its ambiance.

Communications

The main **post office** is at *r. de l'Ancien Quai; tel: 33 08 87 01.*

127

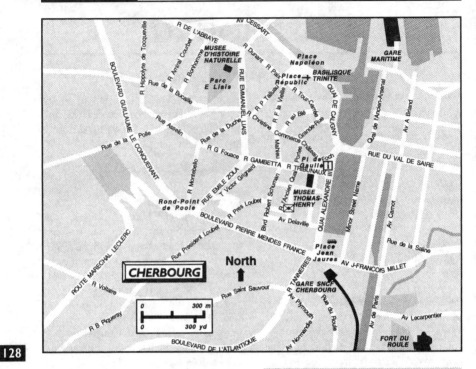

Consulates

Republic of Ireland: *Gare Maritime; tel: 33 44 11 11*. **UK**: *Gare Maritime; tel: 33 88 65 60*.

ENTERTAINMENT

Apart from clubs and bars, often frequented by sailors from the naval base, places of entertainment are fairly thin on the ground. **Théâtre de Cherbourg**, *pl. Gén. de Gaulle; tel: 33 88 55 55*, has drama and operatic productions and concerts.

SHOPPING

Most shops are located on the pedestrian streets adjacent to the *pl. Gén. de Gaulle*; **Printemps** is the main department store. There are markets in the square every Tues and Thur. For hypermarkets, the **Continent** is off the *av. J-F Millet* and the **Auchun** on N13 at La Glacerie.

SIGHTSEEING

Musée Thomas-Henry, *Centre Culturel, r. Vastel; tel: 33 23 02 23*, open Tues–Sat 0900–1200, 1400–1800, Sun 1000–1200, 1400–1800, contains fine paintings, including works by Millet, and sculptures. The **Musée d'Histoire Naturelle et d'Ethnographie** (Ethnography and Natural History Museum), *r. Emmanuel-Liais, tel: 33 53 51 61*, open Tues–Sat 1000–1145, 1400–1645, Sun 1400–1645, has scientific collections, while the park in which it stands has plants and trees from around the world. The **Basilique de la Trinité**, *r. de l'Église*, open daily 0800–1900, dates from the 14th century. **Musée de la Libération**, *Fort du Roule; tel: 33 20 14 12*, opens daily 1000–1800 (Apr–Sept), Tues–Sun 0930–1200 and 1400–1730 (Oct–Mar) has displays on the D-Day landings and the liberation of Cherbourg.

CHERBOURG–ST MALO

This is a delightful part of rural Normandy, where the traveller sees some of the best scenery typical of these parts – small enclosed fields – as well as attractive coastline. The scenic route along the coast takes in some of Normandy's finest beaches.

DIRECT ROUTE: 202 KM

129

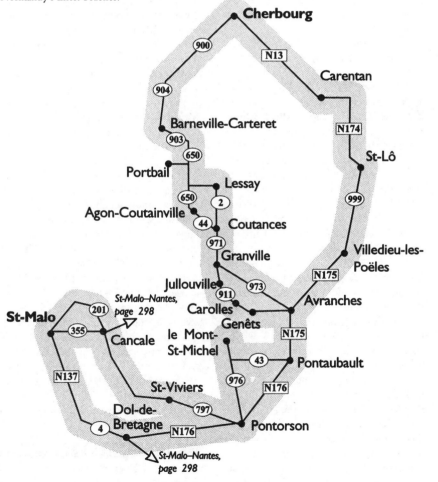

ROUTES

DIRECT ROUTE

➡ The quick way to St-Malo is via the N13 from Cherbourg to **Carentan**, before bearing right onto the N174 to **St-Lô**. From there the D999 goes to **Villedieu-les-Poêles**, where it joins the N175 to **Avranches** and **Pontorson**. The N176 continues to **Dol-de-Bretagne**, where the D4 branches off, joining the N137 just south of **St-Servan-sur-Mer** for the final leg into St-Malo.

Total distance is 202 km and the driving time 2hrs 30 mins.

SCENIC ROUTE

➡ From Cherbourg take the D900 and then D904 to **Barneville-Carteret**. From there, continue on the D903 for 7 km, then about 2 km after bearing right on the D650, turn right to **Portbail**. The D650 continues south and just after the **Ay estuary**, a short diversion left on the D652 leads to **Lessay**. Here, a choice of routes, directly on the D2 or via **Agon-Coutainville** on the D650 and then D44, leads to **Coutances**.

The D971 then leads to **Granville** and from there the dead straight D973 goes to **Avranches**. A more picturesque alternative is the D911 along the coast via the small resorts of **Jullouville**, **Carolles** and **Genêts**, from where guided walks are possible across the sandbanks to **Le Mont-St-Michel**.

At **Avranches**, take the N175 for 8 km to **Pontaubault**, then branch off on the D43 to **Le Mont-St-Michel**. From there, the D976 heads inland to **Pontorson**, then the D797 returns to the coast at **Le Vivier-sur-Mer** and continues to **Cancale**. The D355 goes direct to **St-Malo**, the much prettier D201 winds

along the coast. Total distance around 154 246 km; driving time 4-5 hrs.

ST-LÔ

Tourist Office: *2 r. Havin, 50000 St-Lô; tel: 33 05 02 09.*

ACCOMMODATION

Most hotels are modern, but in the suburb of Agneaux is a 13th-century château-hotel, **Hôtel du Château d'Agneaux**, *av. Ste-Marie; tel: 33 57 65 88*. Expensive. Two central hotels are the moderately priced **Hôtel Les Voyageurs**, *5-7 av. Briovère; tel: 33 05 08 63*, and **Hôtel Ibis**, *1 av. Briovère; tel: 33 05 10 84*. Les Voyageurs has a restaurant, the Ibis a sauna/solarium.

A small **campsite**, **Camping Municipal de Ste-Croix**, *av. de Paris; tel: 33 55 16 14*, open Apr–Oct, lies to the east, close to the D972.

SIGHTSEEING

The administrative centre of Manche, St-Lô was almost totally destroyed in 1944. The oldest quarter, the Enclos, is in the upper town and comprises administrative buildings and the bomb-damaged **Église Notre-Dame**. The **Musée des Beaux-Arts** (Museum of Fine Arts), *pl. du Champ de Mars; tel: 33 57 43 80*, open Wed–Mon 1000–1200 and 1400–1800 (Apr–Oct), admission Fr.10 adults (Fr.5 children), contains tapestries of Gombault and Macée, and paintings by Boudin, Millet and Corot. The **Haras National** (National Stud), *r. Mar. Juin; tel: 33 57 14 13*, open daily 1000–1200 and 1400–1700 (July–Feb), houses 120 stallions and a museum of horse breeding.

VILLEDIEU-LES-POÊLES

Tourist Office: *pl. des Costils, 50800 Villedieu-les-Poêles; tel: 33 61 05 69.*

ACCOMMODATION

Villedieu has three moderately priced two-star hotels, all with their own restaurant, the **Hôtel St-Pierre et St-Michel**, *12 pl. de la République; tel: 33 61 00 11*, the **Hôtel Le Fruitier**, *pl. des Costils; tel: 33 90 51 00*, and the **Hôtel des Visiteurs**, *57 r. du Gén. Huard; tel: 33 61 01 13*.

Camping Municipal le Pré de la Rose; *tel: 33 61 02 44*, open Apr–Sept, is close to the centre.

SIGHTSEEING

Villedieu, a craft centre since the middle ages, has several places where you can see skills performed. These include the **Fonderie de Cloches** (Bell Foundry), *10 r. du Pont-Chignon; tel: 33 61 00 56*, open daily 1000–1200, 1400–1800 (June–Sept); Tues–Sat 1000–1200, 1400–1700 (Oct–May), admission Fr.15; the **Atelier du Cuivre** (Copper Workshop), *54 r. du Gén. Huard; tel: 33 51 31 85*, open Mon–Sat 0900–1200, 1400–1830, Sun 1000–1200, 1430–1830 (July–Aug); Mon–Sat 0900–1200, 1400–1800 (Sept–June), admission Fr.15; and the **Maison de l'Étain** (House of Pewter), *15 r. du Gén. Huard; tel: 33 51 31 85*, open Mon–Sat 0900–1200, 1400–1830, Sun 1000–1200, 1430–1830 (July–Aug); Mon–Sat 0900–1200, 1400–1800 (Sept–June), admission Fr.15.

Museums include the **Musée du Cuivre et Maison de la Dentellière** (Museum of Copperware and Lacemaker's House), *Cour de Foyer, 25 r. du Gén. Huard; tel: 33 90 20 92*, open Wed–Mon 1000–1200 and 1400–1830, Tues 1400–1830, admission Fr.15 (Fr.5), where visitors can see lace made; the **Musée du Meuble Normand**, *9 r. du Reculé; tel: 33 61 11 78*, which contains antique Norman furniture; and the **Royaume de l'Horloge** (Kingdom of the Clock), *50 r.*

Carnot; tel: 33 90 95 38, open Mon–Sat 0900–1230, 1400–1830, admission Fr.18 (Fr.10), which has clocks and watches going back four centuries.

AVRANCHES

Tourist Office: *2 r. Gén. de Gaulle, 50300 Avranches; tel: 33 58 00 22.*

ACCOMMODATION

One of the best located hotels is the **Hôtel du Jardin des Plantes**, *10 pl. Carnot; tel: 33 58 03 68*, a simple, moderately priced *logis* with an inexpensive restaurant. Others include the 17th-century **Hôtel de la Croix d'Or**, *83 r. de la Constitution; tel: 33 58 04 88*, and the modern **Hôtel Les Abrincates**, *37 blvd du Luxembourg; tel: 33 58 66 64*. More economical is the **Hôtel Renaissance**, *r. des Fossés; tel: 33 58 03 71*.

SIGHTSEEING

General Patton started his break-through against the German Army from Avranches in July 1944, and the square named after him is now American territory.

The **Musée Municipal**, *pl. Jean de St-Avit; tel: 33 58 25 15*, open Wed–Mon 0930–1200 and 1400–1800 (Apr–Oct), is housed in a 15th-century mansion and contains medieval sculptures and goldsmith work. The real treasure is the **Mont-St-Michel manuscripts**, magnificent works of art from the 8th–15th centuries, kept in the old library at the **Mairie** (town hall), *pl. Littré; tel: 33 68 33 18*, open daily 1000–1200, 1400–1800 (July–Aug); Wed–Mon 1000–1200, 1400–1800 (June).

The **Église St-Gervais**, *pl. St Gervais*, open Wed–Mon 1000-1200 and 1400–1800 (June–Aug), an imposing 19th-century church, contains the skull of St Aubert, founder of Le Mont-St-Michel,

131

complete with a hole in the crown said to have been made by St Michael. Admission to all three sights is Fr.20 (Fr.10).

In the old town is a 10th-century **castle keep**, while at the end of the r. *Office*, in a small garden on the site of the former cathedral, where Henry II made public penance in 1172 for the murder of Thomas à Becket. There are good views here but even better ones from the **Jardin des Plantes** (Botanical Gardens), *pl. Camot*.

Just outside Avranches at Le Val St-Père, the **Musée de la Seconde Guerre Mondiale** (Museum of World War II); *tel: 33 68 35 83*, open daily 0930–1900 (Apr–Oct); Sat–Sun 1000–1200 and 1400–1900 (Nov–Mar), admission Fr.35 (Fr.10), is dedicated to Patton's breakthrough.

PONTORSON

Tourist Office: *pl. de l'Église, 50170 Pontorson; tel: 33 60 00 18.*

If you don't want to stay too close to Le Mont-St-Michel, Pontorson has no fewer than six *LF*. Two favourites are the **Hôtel Montgomery**, *13 r. Couesnon; tel: 33 60 00 09*, (moderate to expensive), and the **Hôtel Le Bretagne**, *59 r. Couesnon; tel: 33 60 10 55*, (moderate).

A good place to stay, but with nothing to see other than the **Église Notre-Dame**, a church founded by William the Conqueror as thanksgiving for his army's rescue from local quicksands.

DOL-DE-BRETAGNE

Tourist Office: *Grande-Rue des Stuarts; tel: 98 48 15 37.*

For further details of this town, an important religious centre in the Middle Ages, with its 13th-century cathedral, see St-Malo to Nantes route p. 298.

BARNEVILLE-CARTERET

Tourist Office: *10 r. des Écoles, 50270 Barneville; tel: 33 04 90 58*, and *pl. Flandre Dunkerque, 50270 Carteret; tel: 33 04 94 54.*

ACCOMMODATION

The best hotel is the three-star **Hôtel de la Marine**, *11 r. de Paris; tel: 33 53 83 31*, looking out on the Gerfleur estuary. Rooms and restaurant expensive. More moderate is the **Hôtel L'Hermitage**, *4 promenade Abbé Lebouteiller; tel: 33 04 96 29*. An option at Barneville-Plage is the **Hôtel Les Isles**, *9 blvd Maritime; tel: 33 04 90 76*, a two-star *LF* facing the beach. Barneville has the more economic **Hôtel de Paris**, *pl. de l'Église; tel: 33 04 90 02.*

Among several three-star **campsites** are **Camping de la Gerfleur**; *tel: 33 04 38 41*, and **Camping Les Vikings**; *tel: 33 53 84 13.*

SIGHTSEEING

Carteret, the prettiest part of this three-in-one resort, has some of the best sandy beaches in Normandy, but beware of strong currents. Excursions include fast catamaran services to the Channel Islands with **Émeraude Lines**, *Gare Maritime; tel: 33 52 61 39*, and a scenic rail journey to Portbail with the **Train Touristique du Cotentin**, *Clos St Jean, St-Jean-de-la-Rivière; tel: 33 04 70 08.*

The old market town of Barneville, slightly inland, has the 11th-century **Église St-Germain**, *pl. de l'Église*, with its 15th-century fortified tower, while Barneville-Plage has an extensive beach backed by villas.

PORTBAIL

Tourist Office: *26 r. Philippe Lebel ; tel: 33 04 03 07.*

ACCOMMODATION

Portbail has one hotel, the one-star **Hôtel La Galiche**, *pl. Edmond Laquaine; tel: 33 04 84 18*, recommended only for its economic prices.

Campers and caravanners have two three-star **campsites, International Camping le Vieux Fort**, open Apr–Oct, and **International Camping le Vieux Puits**, open July–Aug; *tel: 33 04 81 99*.

SIGHTSEEING

Portbail, straddling a broad inlet via a 13-arched bridge, has a long history, and excavations behind the town hall have revealed a Gallo-Roman **baptistry**. Guided tours of that and the 11th-century **Église Notre-Dame** are possible Mon–Sat 1000–1130 and 1600–1830, Fr.10; *tel: 33 04 03 07*.

Émeraude Lines; *tel: 33 04 86 71*, operate ferries to Jersey from the harbour (May–Aug).

LESSAY

Tourist Office: *Mairie; tel: 33 46 46 18*.

Lessay has a small riverside **campsite, Camping Municipal du Val d'Ay**; *tel: 33 46 46 18*.

The 11th-century Romanesque **abbatiale** (abbey church), open daily 0800–1900 (guided tours July–Aug), destroyed in 1944 but rebuilt from the rubble, holds concerts during spring and summer (details from the tourist office). Lessay's major event is the thousand-year-old **Ste-Croix Fair** (2nd weekend in Sept), a picturesque mixture of animal market and fairground.

AGON-COUTAINVILLE

Tourist Office: *pl. du 28 Juillet, 50230 Agon-Coutainville; tel: 33 47 01 46*.

ACCOMMODATION

The best hotels are the three-star **Hôtel Neptune**, *Promenoir de Jersey; tel: 33 47 07 66*, with excellent sea views, and the **Hôtel Hardy**, *23 pl. du 28 Juillet; tel: 33 47 04 11*, a smart two-star *LF*. Rooms are similarly priced (moderate) but the Hardy has a restaurant. More economical is the **Hôtel les Minquiers**, *5 r. du Dr. Viaud; tel: 33 47 05 33*.

Best of several **campsites** is **Camping Le Marais**, *blvd Louis Lebel-Jehenne; tel: 33 47 25 72*, open June–Sept. Nearest to the beach is the two-star **Camping Les Mouettes**, *r. du Dr. Viaud; tel: 33 45 38 63*, open Apr–Sept.

SIGHTSEEING

With a sandy beach stretching 8 km, Agon-Coutainville is also famous for oyster farming. At the end of the beach is the **Pointe d'Agon** nature reserve. The resort has a **casino**, *av. Franklin D. Roosevelt; tel: 33 47 06 88*, open daily 1100–0300.

COUTANCES

Tourist Office: *pl. Georges Leclerc, 50200 Coutances; tel: 33 45 17 79*.

ACCOMMODATION

The two-star **Hôtel Cositel**, *Route d'Agon-Coutainville; tel: 33 07 51 64*, is a modern *logis* with a superb view of the town. Moderate. More central are the **Hôtel Le Parvis**, *pl. du Parvis; tel: 33 45 13 55*, (moderate), and the **Hôtel de Normandie**, *2 pl. Gén. de Gaulle; tel: 33 45 01 40*, which has rooms starting at more economic prices. All three have restaurants.

The two-star **Camping Les Vignettes**; *tel: 33 45 43 13*, open all year, lies next to the Hotel Cositel.

133

SIGHTSEEING

The overall view of Coutances on a hill crowned by the spires of its cathedral and churches is best seen from the Agon-Coutainville road. The Norman Gothic **Cathédrale de Notre-Dame**, *pl. du Parvis*, built on the remains of its Romanesque predecessor, is one of the most beautiful in France. Vauban, the 17th-century military architect, described its lantern tower as 'the work of a sublime madman'. The cathedral is flanked by two 15th- and 16th-century churches, the **Église St-Pierre**, *r. Geoffroy de Montbray*, and the **Église St-Nicolas**, *r. St-Nicolas*.

The **Musée Quesnel-Morinière**, *2 r. Quesnel-Morinière; tel: 33 45 11 92*, open Mon–Sat 1000–1200 and 1400–1700, Sun 1400–1700, admission Fr.10, contains paintings by Rubens and Le Sueur, and a collection of Norman ceramics. Behind the museum, the **Jardin des Plantes**, *r. Quesnel-Canveaux*, open daily 0900–2330 (July–August); 0900–2000 (Apr–June and Sept–Oct); 0900–1700 (Oct–Mar), has 47,000 plants and rare trees.

In May, the town hosts the week-long international **Jazz sous les Pommiers** (Jazz under the Apple-trees).

GRANVILLE

Tourist Office: *4 Cours Jonville, 50400 Granville; tel: 33 91 30 03.*

ACCOMMODATION

Granville has plenty of hotels, though none in the old town. Top choice is the three-star **Hôtel des Bains**, *19 r. Georges Clémenceau; tel: 33 50 17 31*, which has a restaurant. Prices range from moderate to expensive.

Others include the **Hôtel Normandy-Chaumière**, *20 r. Paul-Poirier; tel: 33 50 01 71*, a *logis* with a particularly delightful restaurant (prices

moderate), the charming **Hôtel Michelet**, *5 bis r. Jules Michelet; tel: 33 50 06 55*, (economical to moderate), tucked away above the town but without a restaurant (not a problem with the town's wide choice), and the **Hôtel de la Mer**, *74 r. du Port; tel: 33 50 01 86*, opposite the port. Prices moderate, both for rooms and restaurant.

SIGHTSEEING

Granville comprises the fortified upper town built by the English in the early 15th century as a base to attack Le Mont-St-Michel, and the more modern and lively commercial town below. Amid the upper town's granite houses are two museums, the small **Musée du Vieux Granville** (Museum of Old Granville), *2 r. Lecarpentier; tel: 33 50 44 10*, open Wed–Sun 1000–1200 and 1400–1800, admission Fr.10 (Fr.6), in the fortified gatehouse, which retells the town's seafaring days, and the **Musée Richard Anacréon**, *pl. de l'Isthme; tel: 33 51 02 94*, open Wed–Mon 1000–1200 and 1400–1800 (July–Sept); Wed–Mon 1400–1800 (Oct–June), admission Fr.10 (Fr.6), containing original editions of famous 20th-century writers and paintings illustrating modern French art.

The austere **Église Notre-Dame** dates from the 15th century, while nearby, the **Pointe du Roc** has an aquarium and museum complex. **L'Aquarium du Roc** contains fish from around the world; **La Féérie des Coquillages** (Shell Fairyland) has fabulous scenes created from shells; **Le Palais Minéral** (Museum of Rocks and Minerals) displays works of art made from precious stones; and the **Jardin des Papillons** (Butterfly Garden) has spider and beetle species as well as colourful butterflies. The complex; *tel: 33 50 03 13*, is open daily 0900–1200 and 1400–1900

(Apr–Oct); Sun 1400–1900 (Nov–Mar), admission Fr.50 adults, Fr.30 children.

In the lower town, the **Historial Granvillais**, *79 r. Couraye; tel: 33 50 03 74*, open Mon–Sat 0900–1200 and 1400–1800 (June–Sept), admission Fr.30 (Fr.22), has tableaux depicting Granville's historical events. Also in the lower town is the **casino**, *pl. Mar. Foch; tel: 33 50 00 79*, open daily 1100–0400.

Overlooking the beach, the **Jardin Christian Dior** (Christian Dior Gardens), *r. d'Estouteville*, belonged to the family of the fashion designer, who was born in the town. His former home is now the **Musée Christian Dior**, *Villa les Rhumbs; tel: 33 61 48 21*, open Tues–Sun 1000-1200 and 1430–1830 (June–Sept), admission Fr.20 (Fr.15).

From the harbour (Gare Maritime), **Émeraude Lines**; *tel: 33 50 16 36*, **Channiland**; *tel: 33 51 77 45*, and **Jolie France**; *tel: 33 50 31 81,* sail to the Channel Islands and/or Îles Chausey.

LE MONT-ST-MICHEL

Tourist Office: *Corps de Garde des Bourgeois, 50116 Le Mont-St-Michel; tel: 33 60 14 30.*

ACCOMMODATION

Le Mont-St-Michel has several hotels, almost all expensive, though most have one or two more moderately priced rooms. Best known is the **Hôtel de la Mere Poulard**, *Grande Rue; tel: 33 60 14 01*, famous for the omelettes served in its restaurant. On the ramparts is the **Hôtel la Croix Blanche**, *Intra Muros; tel: 33 60 14 04*, while more moderately priced is the **Hôtel de Guesclin**, *Intra Muros; tel: 33 60 14 10*, a two-star *LF*. Several modern hotels are located at the end of the island's causeway.

SIGHTSEEING

Le Mont-St-Michel, the most popular tourist sight outside Paris, is crammed with visitors in summer. Most climb its steep medieval streets and stairways to the **Benedictine Abbey**; *tel: 33 60 14 14*, open daily 0900–1800 (May–Sept); 0930–1145 and 1345–1700 (Feb–May and Sept–Nov); 0930–1145 and 1345–1615 (Nov–Feb), admission Fr.36 (Fr.10), at the summit. For a highly atmospheric visit with fewer visitors, the abbey re-opens Mon–Sat 2200–2400 (June–Sept), admission Fr.60 adults, Fr.35 youths, free for children, when, with appropriate music, chapels, crypts, cloisters, gardens etc., are specially lit.

There are several museums; the **Musée Grevin** tells the history of Le Mont-St-Michel with wax figures; **Archéoscope** has multi-media presentations to trace the island's history and legends; the **Musée Maritime** explains the dangers and difficulties of the surrounding bay. All three museums; *tel: 33 60 14 09*, are open daily 0900–1800 (Feb–Nov), admission for each is Fr.45 adults, Fr.30 children, or a combination ticket is available, Fr.75 (Fr.45).

Another museum, the **Logis Tiphaine**; *tel: 33 60 23 34*, open daily (Feb–Nov), admission Fr.20, the 14th-century home of Bertrand du Guesclin and his wife Tiphaine de Ragunel, contains period furniture and tapestries.

CANCALE

Tourist Office: *44 r. du Port, tel: 99 89 63 72.*

Cancale is a picturesque town renowned for its oyster production, with a number of harbourside hotels. For fuller details of accommodation and sightseeing in the town, see St-Malo to Nantes route, p. 298.

135

DIEPPE

France's oldest seaside resort, Dieppe attracts many weekend visitors from Paris and from across the English Channel. It was the scene of a disastrous raid by Canadian Commandos in 1942, but the lessons learned led to the success of the D-Day landings two years later.

TOURIST INFORMATION

Tourist Office: *Pont Jehan-Ango, quai de Carénage, 76204 Dieppe; tel: 35 84 11 77.*

ARRIVING AND DEPARTING

By Ferry

Until 1994, ferries from England moored next to the *Grande-Rue*. Now, a new ferry terminal has been built at the entrance to the harbour, which, though a little farther east of the centre, is better sited for motorists who want to avoid the town centre.

Stena Line: sails from Newhaven (year-round); *tel: 35 06 39 00.*

GETTING AROUND

All of Dieppe's attractions are within easy walking distance of the centre. The Tourist Office has some excellent free maps to help you find your way around.

Buses

Local bus services are operated by **Stradibus**, *1 pl. Ventabren; tel: 35 84 49 49*, with a flat fare of Fr.6.

Taxis

Radio Taxis Dieppois, *Pont Jehan Ango;* *tel: 35 84 20 05*, operate a 24-hr service (sample fare from the ferry terminal to town centre is Fr.30).

STAYING IN DIEPPE

Accommodation

Dieppe has a reasonable choice of hotels, half of them with restaurants. Most fall within the moderate price range, but there are one or two expensive ones and several in the economy range.

Hotel chains in the town include *Ca* and *Ib*.

Most of the best hotels are on the *blvd de Verdun* facing the sea and include the three-star **Hôtel La Présidence**; *tel: 35 84 31 31* (expensive), **Le Grand Hôtel**, *3 blvd de Verdun; tel: 35 82 33 60* (expensive), and **Hôtel Aguado**, *30 blvd de Verdun; tel: 35 84 27 00* (moderate), as well as the two-star **Hôtel Windsor**, *18 blvd de Verdun; tel: 35 84 15 23* (moderate), **Hôtel Epsom**, *11 blvd de Verdun; tel: 35 84 10 18* (moderate) and the new **Hôtel de l'Europe**, *63 blvd de Verdun; tel: 32 90 19 19* (moderate).

At the economy end of the scale try **Hôtel la Pêcherie**, *3 r. du Mortier d'Or; tel 35 82 04 62*, in the back streets near the fishing harbour.

The **HI** youth hostel is **Auberge de Jeunesse**, *48 r. Louis Fromager, Quartier Janval; tel: 35 84 85 73.*

Dieppe has two **campsites**; the three-star **Camping Vitamin**, *Les Vertus; tel: 35 82 11 11*, just off the N27, 3 km south of the town, and the two-star **Camping du Pré St-Nicolas**, *Rte de Pourville; tel: 35 84 11 39.* Both are open all year.

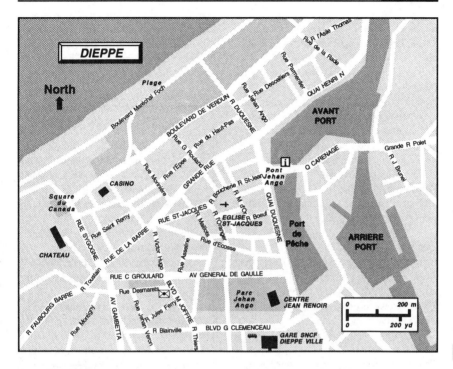

Eating and Drinking

Dieppe may be small but it has no shortage of restaurants – around 100 at the last count. Seafood features strongly and there are one or two specialist restaurants. **L'Ankara**, *18 r. de la Rade; tel: 35 84 58 33*, for instance, serves Turkish food and also has a vegetarian menu at quite moderate prices.

An excellent, though pricey, fish restaurant is **La Marmite Dieppoise**, *8 r. St-Jean; tel: 35 84 24 26*, named after a town speciality, a kind of fish stew. For cheap eats, there are a number of possibilities along the *quai Henry IV*, but if it is value for money you seek and you're not in a hurry, try **Les Tourelles**, *43 r. de Cdt Fayolle; tel: 35 84 15 88*.

Communications

The main **post office** is at *2 blvd Mar.*

Joffre; tel: 35 04 70 14, open Mon–Fri 0800–1800, Sat 0800–1200.

Money

Most of the major banks are in or close to *Grande-Rue*. Generally they open Tues–Sat 0900–1200 and 1400–1730.

ENTERTAINMENT

Two publications free from the Office de Tourisme, *A Taste of Dieppe* and *The Dieppe Shopper*, both list places worthy of a late-night visit. Still a popular meeting place, the 17th-century **Café des Tribunaux**, *pl. de 9 Puits-Salé*, has scarcely changed since its Belle Époque heyday. Among those to have passed through its portals are Oscar Wilde, Monet, Renoir and Pissarro. Elsewhere, the **Casino**, *blvd de Verdun; tel 35 82 33 60,* has gaming and a nightly discotheque, while the British-run **Select Hotel**, *1 r. Toustain; tel: 35 84 14 66*, has a late-night bar with live music on Fri.

The **Centre Jean Renoir**, *1 quai Bérigny; tel: 35 82 04 43*, at Dieppe's cultural heart, has a theatre renowned for innovative productions, and a cinema which often shows undubbed English language films. The four-screen **Rex**; *tel: 35 84 22 74*, is a more mainstream cinema.

The **Hippodrome** (Racecourse) *Rouxmesnil-Bouteilles; tel: 35 84 12 02*, has a programme of flat, jump and trotting races during July and Aug.

Events

Attracting entrants from all over the world, a colourful international kite festival is held on the lawns beside the *blvd de Verdun* every other (even) year for two weeks in mid-Sept.

SHOPPING

The main shopping area comprises the pedestrianised **Grande-Rue**, where the Saturday market takes place, and the *r. St-Jacques*.

SIGHTSEEING

The **Château-Musée** (Castle Museum); *tel: 35 84 19 76*, is open daily 1000–1200 and 1400–1800 (June–Sept), Wed–Mon 1000–1200 and 1400–1700 (Oct–May); admission Fr.13 adults (Fr.7.50 children). The 15th-century castle, overlooking the seafront, contains exceptional collections of carved ivory and the works of several artists, among them Sickert, Renoir, Boudin, Pissarro and Braque.

Église St-Jacques (St James' Church), *pl. Nationale*, dates from the 14th century.

The **Cité de la Mer** (City of the Sea), *37 r. de l'Asile Thomas; tel: 35 06 93 20*, open daily 1000–1230, 1400–1900 (Apr–Sept); 1000–1200, 1400–1800 (Oct–Mar),

admission Fr.25 adults (Fr.15 children), explains the workings of ships and the sea. English Channel sea-life is displayed in large aquariums.

Drink

Unusually for a French region, Normandy has no vineyards and so it does not produce its own wine. What it does grow in huge quantities, however, are apples, and from these come cider and calvados.

Norman cider is generally light and refreshing and many locals consider it an excellent accompaniment to their meals. In *crêperies* it is usually offered as a matter of course.

Calvados is apple brandy, often served as a digestif at the end of a meal. Its traditional role, however, is as the *trou Normand*. Norman meals often extend to five or six courses, but the digestive powers of calvados is such that a shot taken half way through a meal is said to clear the way for the next dish. More often these days it is poured over a baked apple or apple-flavoured sorbet.

A cross between cider and calvados is *pommeau*, which is deliciously refreshing when chilled. It is normally served as an apéritif.

Another digestif from Normandy is *Bénédictine*, a liqueur made at Fécamp, which lies 75 km west of Dieppe. Twenty-seven aromatic plants and spices go into its making, though the exact formula is a closely guarded secret. Originally produced by monks at Fécamp's monastery in the 16th century, the recipe was lost at the time of the French Revolution but rediscovered in 1863 by Alexandre Le Grand, who perfected the drink as it is known today.

DIEPPE–PARIS

These two routes run more or less parallel to each other, the quieter, more northerly route following attractive river valleys, the other carrying heavier traffic. There are numerous opportunities to switch from one route to the other along the way.

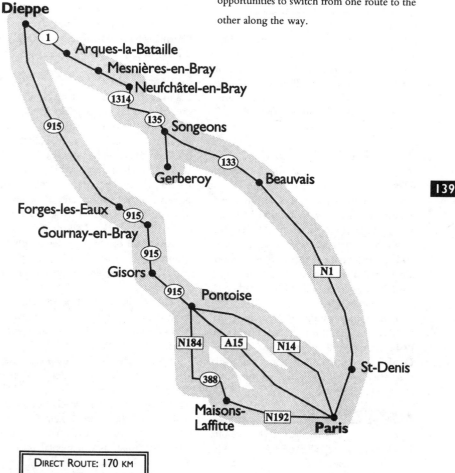

139

DIRECT ROUTE: 170 KM

ROUTES

DIRECT ROUTE

Take the N27 road out of Dieppe towards Rouen and just outside Dieppe bear left at a roundabout onto the D915, which passes through only the occasional village before reaching **Forges-les-Eaux**. From there continue on the D915 via **Gournay-en-Bray** to **Gisors** and then south-east to **Pontoise**.

The quick route into Paris is along the A15 motorway or N14 dual carriageway, though the alternative N184 into the **Forêt de St-Germain** leads via the D308 to **Maisons-Laffitte**. From there, the D308 links with the N192 into Paris. Distance is 170 km, driving time about 2 hrs.

SCENIC ROUTE

Leave Dieppe via the *r. Bonne-Nouvelle*, which becomes the D1 to **Arques-la-Bataille** and continues via **Mesnières-en-Bray** to **Neufchâtel-en-Bray**, From there, take the D1314 but within 5 km bear left on the D135 which leads to **Songeons** – from where a short diversion leads to the fortified village of **Gerberoy** – then on to the cathedral town of **Beauvais**.

The journey south of Beauvais is via the N1, cutting through the **Forêt de l'Isle-Adam** and passing through **St-Denis** before reaching the Paris ring road. Distance covered is 177 km, journey time about 2 hrs 30 mins.

FORGES-LES-EAUX

Tourist Office: *r du Mar. Leclerc, 76440 Forges-les-Eaux; tel: 35 90 52 10.*

ACCOMMODATION

A modest selection of hotels includes a two-star *LF*, the **Hôtel La Paix**, *15 r. de* *Neufchâtel; tel: 35 90 51 22*, and the three-star **Relais du Bois des Fontaines**, *route de Dieppe; tel: 35 09 85 09*, both of which have rooms at moderate prices.

Offering rooms at moderate to expensive prices is the **Hôtel Continental**, *av. des Sources; tel: 35 09 80 12*. For rooms in the economic price range try the **Sofhotel**, *57 r. du Mar. Leclerc; tel: 35 90 44 51*, or the **Hôtel St-Denis**, *1 r. de la Libération; tel: 35 90 50 70*.

There is a municipal campsite, **Camping La Minière**, *3 blvd Nicolas Thiesse; tel: 35 90 53 91*, open Apr–Sept.

SIGHTSEEING

If a town can be encapsulated in its name, then that town is Forges-les-Eaux. Until the 15th century it was famous for metal foundries, but since the mid 1600s its fame has been based on being a spa resort. The waters, which are only used for drinking, have a high iron content. The **spa park** is perfect for relaxation and contains the grotto where Louis XIII and Anne of Austria used to take the waters. It also has a **casino**, one of very few inland casinos in France, which has the usual gaming rooms, dancing, jazz, a piano bar and restaurants.

The town has three museums, all located in the grounds of the **Hôtel de Ville** (town hall), *r. du Mar. Leclerc; tel: 35 90 52 10*.

The **Musée de la Faïence** (Museum of Ceramics), is open Mon–Sat 1000–1200 and 1400–1800, Sun 1100–1230 (July–Aug); Mon–Sat 1000–1200 and 1400–1700 (Sept–June). It contains 18th- and 19th-century ceramics made in the town, such as ornamental plates and barbers' dishes.

The **Musée des Maquettes** (Model Museum), open Tues–Sat 1400–1700, Sun 1430–1800 (Apr–Oct), has 80 models of agricultural machinery and horse-drawn carriages depicting rural life at the turn of the century.

The **Musée de la Résistance** (Museum of the Resistance), open daily 1400–1800 (Mar–Oct), admission Fr.10, has more than 1000 items of World War II memorabilia along with several newsreels of the time.

GOURNAY-EN-BRAY

Tourist Office: *Pavillon de la Porte de Paris, 76220 Gournay-en-Bray; tel: 35 90 28 34.*

ACCOMMODATION

Gournay has three hotels close to the centre. The **Hôtel Le Cygne**, *20 r. Notre-Dame; tel: 35 90 27 80*, and the **Hôtel de Normandie**, *pl. Nationale; tel: 35 90 01 08*, are both moderately priced two-star establishments. The **Hôtel des Touristes**, *10 r. Docteur Duchesne; tel: 35 90 03 33*, is unclassified but has economically priced rooms.

SIGHTSEEING

This busy town on the River Epte is known for producing one of Normandy's lesser known cheeses, Petit Suisse. Worth a visit is the **Église St-Hildevert**, a largely 12th-century church, which contains polychromed wooden statues of St-Hildevert and the Virgin.

GISORS

Tourist Office: *3 r. Balechoux, 27140 Gisors; tel: 32 55 13 09.*

ACCOMMODATION

Visitors with economy in mind will be happy with the choice of hotels in Gisors. A moderately priced *logis*, the **Hôtel Moderne**, *pl. de la Gare; tel: 32 55 23 51*, is the most expensive, but other hotels in the town have rooms at economy prices. Choose from the **Hôtel de Dieppe**, *1 av. de la Gare; tel: 32 55 25 54*, the **Hôtel La Houblonnière**, *15 r. de Dieppe; tel: 32 55 11 17*, the **Hôtel de Paris**, *52 r. de la Libération; tel: 32 55 22 63*, and the **Hostellerie des Trois Poissons**, *13 r. Cappeville; tel: 32 55 01 09*.

Lakeside camping and caravanning is available at **Camping La Ferme de Vaux**; tel: 32 55 12 42r, about 1 km from the town on the D181.

SIGHTSEEING

On the banks of the River Epte, Gisors is the capital of the **Normandie Vexin**, a rich agricultural plateau lying between the Seine, Andelle and Epte rivers. Its strategic location was noted early on by the dukes of Normandy, and a **château fort**; *tel: 32 27 30 14*, open Wed–Mon 1000–1200 and 1400–1800 (Apr–Sept); Sat–Sun 1000–1200 and 1400–1700 (Feb–Mar and Oct–Nov), admission Fr.25 adults, (Fr.15 children) for guided tours. It was built in the late 11th and 12th centuries as a defence against the French, started in 1097 by King Willliam Rufus. There are commanding views over the town from the keep, which now stands at the centre of a public garden within the former curtain wall.

141

In the town itself, the **Église St-Gervais et St-Protais** originally dates from the 13th century, though the decorated nave is a 16th-century restoration. The building has superb Renaissance decoration around the main door, while inside there is a quaint spiral staircase and magnificent stained-glass windows. Several old houses can be seen in the *r. de Vienne*, which leads to the *Fossé aux Tanneurs*, a flower-lined quayside alongside the canal, where tanners used to soak animal skins.

MAISONS-LAFFITTE

Tourist Office: *41 av. de Longueil; tel: 39 62 63 64.*

ACCOMMODATION

Surprisingly, given its close proximity to Paris, Maisons-Laffitte is not over-endowed with hotels, but there are two good moderately priced hotels. By far the largest is the **Hôtel Climat de France**, *2 r. de Paris; tel: (1) 39 12 20 20*, while the other is the strangely named **Hôtel Le Pur Sang** (Hotel of the Thoroughbred), *2 av. de la Pelouse; tel: (1) 39 62 03 21*. Both have restaurants, the latter offering better value meals.

There is also a very large campsite, one of the better ones within reasonable distance of the Paris centre, the leafy four-star **Camping Caravaning International de Maisons-Laffitte**, *r. Johnson; tel: (1) 39 12 21 91*, which lies on an island in the Seine. Open all year.

SIGHTSEEING

The town is built around the **Château de Maisons**, *2 av. Carnot; tel: (1) 39 62 01 49*, open Mon–Sat 1000–1800, Sun 1000–1900 (Apr–Oct); Mon–Sat 1000–1700, Sun 1000–1800 (Oct–Mar), admission Fr.26, constructed in the mid 1600s for René de Longueil, Governor of the royal chateaux at Versailles and St-Germain-en-Laye. It is considered one of the finest examples of French classical architecture. Louis XlV, the Sun King, attended the chateau's inauguration when only 13 and was a frequent visitor. The richly decorated interior is unfortunately devoid of furniture.

The town is also famous for its **hippodrome** (race-course), one of the most important in France. Laid out just before the Revolution under the orders of Louis XVl's brother, the Comte d'Artois, who

later became Charles X, it has one of the longest straights in Europe.

ARQUES-LA-BATAILLE

The **Manoir d'Archelles**; *tel: 35 85 50 16*, is a small modernised manor-house off the D1 just south of Arques, and though fairly basic, it does have moderate prices, both for rooms and in the restaurant.

SIGHTSEEING

Arques-la-Bataille is noted for its **château**, admission free, which is regarded as one of the most important feudal ruins in Normandy. Built on a chalk promontory, the castle, dating from the 12th century, was the scene of a famous battle in 1589 between Henri lV and the vastly superior forces of the Duke of Mayenne during the Religious Wars. The Protestant forces under Henri overcame those of the Duke and the Catholic League, and it was this battle that gave the town its suffix of 'la Bataille'.

MESNIÈRES-EN-BRAY

Mesnières, too, has its **château**; *tel: 35 93 10 04*, open daily 1400–1830 (mid-July–Aug); Sat–Sun 1400–1830 (Apr–mid-July and Sept–Oct), admission Fr.15, a 15th-century edifice built in Renaissance style and flanked by impressive towers not unlike some in the Loire Valley. Guided tours take in several rooms and galleries, the main chapel and the main courtyard.

NEUFCHÂTEL-EN-BRAY

Tourist Office: *6 pl. Notre-Dame, 76270 Neufchâtel-en-Bray; tel: 35 93 22 96.*

ACCOMMODATION

Though quite small Neufchâtel has a fair number of hotels from which to choose, all with restaurants. They include two two-star *LF*, the **Hôtel Les Airelles**, *2* *passage Michu; tel: 35 93 14 60,* and the **Hôtel du Grand Cerf**, *9 Grande Rue Fosse Porte; tel: 35 93 00 02,* which are the most expensive hotels in town though prices still fall within the moderate category.

Also good value is the **Hôtel du Lion d'Or**, *17–19 pl. Notre-Dame; tel: 35 94 77 94,* while those in search of economy should try **Chez Jean-Pierre**, *8 Grande Rue St-Jacques; tel: 35 93 02 91.*

There is a three-star campsite beside the River Béthune, **Camping de Ste-Claire**; *tel: 35 93 03 93,* open Apr–Oct.

A largely modern town following its virtual destruction in 1940, Neufchâtel is renowned for its cheese, the oldest in Normandy, which has been produced in the area since around 1035. It comes in a variety of shapes, most usually heart-shaped, and is produced in farms within 30 km of the town.

One of the older remaining buildings in the town, a 16th-century manor house, is home to the **Musée Mathon-Durand**, *Grande Rue St-Pierre; tel: 35 93 06 55,* open Tues–Sun 1500–1800 (July–Aug); Sat–Sun 1500–1800 (Sept–June), admission Fr.10. Five rooms are devoted to popular traditions and arts of the Bray region, including glassware, furniture, pottery and cheese-making. The **Église Notre-Dame**, *pl. Notre-Dame,* built in 1130, has been completely restored since suffering serious bomb damage in 1940.

BEAUVAIS

Tourist Office: *1 r. Beauregard, 60000 Beauvais; tel: 44 45 08 18.*

There is no shortage of hotels in Beauvais and several more on the main approach roads. In town, the one-star **Hôtel de la Poste**, *19–21 r. Gambetta; tel: 44 45 14 97,* is a comfortable logis with economical to moderate prices, while a near neighbour, the **Rustic Hotel**, *68 r. Gambetta; tel: 44 45 10 43,* has marginally cheaper rooms. Both have good restaurants. Economy prices are possible at the one-star **Hôtel Le Brazza**, *22 r. de la Madeleine; tel: 44 45 03 86,* but there is no restaurant.

If you prefer a place with somewhere to eat, try the **Hôtel Bristol**, *58-60 r. de la Madeleine; tel: 44 45 01 31,* where room prices range from economy to moderate.

The two-star **Camping Municipal**, *r. Binet; tel: 44 02 00 22,* open June–Aug, is located to the south of the town centre.

The **Cathédrale St-Pierre**, *r. St-Pierre; tel: 44 48 11 60,* reached its huge proportions as a result of cathedral builders' efforts to outdo each other, and despite collapsing on two occasions, its choir today has the highest Gothic vault in existence. In 1569 its spire was completed, giving the building a height of 502ft, but this, too, collapsed four years later and now the cathedral has neither spire nor towers. Inside the cathedral is a huge **astronomical clock**, constructed in the 1860s with 90,000 parts.

Next to the cathedral, the **Musée Départemental de l'Oise** (Oise Department Museum), *r. du Musée; tel: 44 48 48 88,* open Weds–Mon 1000–1200 and 1400–1800, admission Fr.20 (Weds free), has collections of religious sculptures, local ceramics and 16th-, 17th-, 18th- and 19th-century paintings of the French and Italian schools as well as reconstructions of a potter's studio and art nouveau dining rooms. Also nearby is the **Galerie Nationale de Tapisserie**

143

(National Tapestry Gallery); *tel: 44 05 14 28*, open Tues–Sun 0930–1200 and 1400–1830 (Apr–Sept); Tues–Sun 1000–1200 and 1400–1700, admission Fr.20, which follows the history of tapestries since the 15th-century. Remains of the town's Roman walls are incorporated within the modern building.

ST-DENIS

Tourist Office: *1 r. de la République; tel: 42 43 33 55.*

ACCOMMODATION

St-Denis has several two-star hotels to choose from including two **Hôtel Campaniles**, one at *2 quai de St-Ouen; tel: 48 20 29 88*, the other at *14 r. Jean Jaurès; tel: 48 20 74 31*. Both are moderately priced. Other options are the **Sovereign Hotel**, *54 quai de Seine; tel: 40 12 91 29*, which has similarly priced rooms, and the **Hôtel Moderne**, *4 bis r. Gabriel Péri; tel: 48 20 17 15*, which has the cheapest rooms on offer.

SIGHTSEEING

The main attraction is the **Basilique St-Denis** (St Denis Basilica), open daily 1000–1900 (Apr–Sept); 1000–1700 (Oct–Mar), which was built in the 12th century in Gothic style and restored in the 19th century by the ecclesiastical architect Viollet-le-Duc. The cathedral is especially noted as the mausoleum of the Kings of France and though attempts were made to destroy the tombs during the Revolution, the most important ones survived. A span of 1200 years is represented by the tombs and effigies, from Dagobert I to Louis XVIII. Among other tombs in the cathedral is that of Bertrand du Guesclin who, born in Brittany, was a formidable opponent of the English during the Hundred Years' War, and became Constable of

France. A chapel in the crypt contains the remains of Louis XVI and Marie-Antoinette. A short distance from the basilica, the **Musée d'Art et d'Histoire** (Art and History Museum), *22 bis r. Gabriel Péri; tel: 42 43 05 10*, open Mon, Wed–Sat 1000–1730, Sun 1400–1830 (all year), admission Fr.20, is housed in a 16th-century former Carmelite convent. Among its exhibits are documents and audio-visual displays relating to the Paris Commune of 1871.

Another museum worth visiting is the **Musée Christofle**, *112 r. Ambroise-Croizat; tel: 49 22 40 00*, open Mon–Fri 0900–1700 (all year), which displays the work of a local gold and silverware manufacturer as well as rarities spanning a period from Gallo-Roman times to the 1960s.

Flamboyant Gothic

Throughout Normandy, Brittany and the Loire Valley, many churches and cathedrals have been built in the Gothic or Flamboyant Gothic styles.

The Gothic style was the predominant type of architecture in Europe from the 12th to the 16th centuries, and the cathedral at Chartres (see p. 124) is regarded as perhaps the finest example. The style is characterised by the ribbed vault, the pointed arch and the flying buttress, as well as the use of stained-glass windows and wood and stone carving

Flamboyant Gothic is the style, characteristic of 14th- and 15th-century French architecture, that developed after the end of the Hundred Years' War, a further development of the Gothic style. The adjective flamboyant refers to the wavy, flame-like lines of window tracery and the elaborate carving that is typical of the period.

LE HAVRE

Le Havre was the most bombed French port in World War II, and its rapid rebuilding in the 1950s left it looking rather soulless. However, maturity seems to be having a positive effect, especially around the centre, though it will never be able to compensate for the huge petro-chemical installations lining the River Seine.

TOURIST INFORMATION

Tourist Office, *Forum de l'Hôtel de Ville; tel: 35 21 22 88.* Open Mon–Sat 0845–1215 and 1330–1900 (Apr–Sept); Mon–Sat 0845–1215 and 1330–1830 (Oct–Mar).

Other offices are located at the P&O European Ferries terminal, *quai de Bostrom*, the Irish Ferries terminal, *blvd J.F. Kennedy*, and at the railway station, *cours de la République*. Opening times at the terminals coincide with arrivals and departures (June–Sept).

ARRIVING AND DEPARTING

Airport

The **Aéroport du Havre-Octeville**; *tel: 35 46 09 81*, located 5 km north of the town centre on the D940 to Étretat has flights to London Gatwick. **Auto-Cars Gris**; *tel: 35 28 16 04*, run an irregular bus service between the airport and the **Gare Routière** (bus station), *blvd de Strasbourg; tel: 35 26 67 23*. Journey time is 15 mins.

By Car

Most traffic enters and leaves Le Havre by the A131 and N15. Signposting in both directions is good.

By Ferry

Le Havre has ferry connections, operating from separate terminals, with both the UK and Ireland. A shuttle bus operates between the harbour and the station.

P&O European Ferries: from Portsmouth (year-round); *tel: 35 19 78 50*.

Irish Ferries: from Cork (May-Sept only) and Rosslare (year-round); *tel: 35 22 50 28*.

GETTING AROUND

Le Havre is not renowned for its sights, but what few there are are somewhat scattered and some would certainly require transport to get to them. In any case, apart from one or two small pockets in the centre, the town is hardly the most attractive to walk through. If you need maps, the Tourist Office is a good source of free ones, their *Plan Guide* indicating the main attractions.

Buses

The local bus service is operated by **Bus Océane**, *115 r. Jules Lecesne; tel: 35 19 75 75*, its network of 12 routes linking the centre with the suburbs. Tickets, based on zones, can be bought when boarding the bus, or *carnets* of 10 tickets can be purchased from the address above or the **Bus Océane** kiosk at the **Hôtel de Ville** (town hall). A validated ticket provides an hour's unrestricted travel within each zone. A free map showing the routes is available from the same sources as the tickets.

Bus services beyond the suburbs are operated from the Gare Routière by **Bus Verts du Calvados**; *tel 31 44 77 44*, to Caen, and by **CNA**; *tel: 35 71 23 29*, to Rouen.

Taxis

Taxis are operated by **SCHLT**, *65 r. François Mazeline; tel: 35 25 12 33*, and, from the railway station, **Radio-Taxis**; *tel: 35 25 81 81*. The latter also offer tours, using English-speaking drivers, through Le Havre and the surrounding area, a 2-hr tour of the town for up to four passengers costing Fr.250, excluding admission to attractions. This service can also be booked through the Tourist Office.

STAYING IN LE HAVRE

Accommodation

For a town not very high on the list of Normandy tourist attractions, Le Havre has a surprising number of hotels to choose from – more than 40 of them. Three are rated three-star, the rest are fairly evenly divided between two- and one-star and unclassified hotels. There should be little difficulty finding a room at any time of the year, but the Tourist Office will help if necessary.

Hotel chains in Le Havre include *BW, Ca, Ct, F1, Ib, Mc*.

The **Hôtel Mercure**, *chaussée d'Angoulême; tel: 35 19 50 50*, is a typical three-star example of the chain with comfortable rooms, garage parking and a good restaurant. Not far from the ferry terminals, it is the most expensive hotel in town. More moderately priced, the other three-star hotels are the **Hôtel Bordeaux**, *147 r. Louis Brindeau; tel: 35 22 69 44*, right in the town centre, and the **Hôtel Marly**, *121 r. de Paris; tel: 35 41 72 48*, between the centre and ferry terminals.

Neither has garage parking or a restaurant.

There are several two-star hotels near the railway station, including the moderately priced **Hôtel Green**, *209 blvd de Strasbourg; tel 35 22 63 10*, which has double glazing and easy parking, and its near neighbour, the **Grand Hôtel Parisien**, *1 cours de la République; tel: 35 25 23 83*. Though neither has a restaurant, there are several close by. More economic neighbours are the one-star **Hôtel Britania**, *5 cours de la République; tel: 35 25 42 51*, which has its own brasserie, and the hospitable **Hôtel Yport**, *27 cours de la République; tel: 35 25 21 08*. Cheaper still, but quite basic and a little farther from the station is the unclassified **Hôtel Le Relax**, *97 cours de la République; tel: 35 26 53 07*.

Good economy/moderate alternatives nearer the centre are the one-star **Hôtel Séjour-Fleuri**, *71 r. Emile-Zola; tel: 35 41 33 81*, and the two-star **Hôtel Richelieu**, *132 r. de Paris; tel: 35 42 38 71*.

There is no **youth hostel** as such, but hostellers can usually find lodging at **Union Chrétienne des Jeunes Gens**, *153 blvd de Strasbourg; tel: 35 42 47 86*.

Camping is available at a four-star municipal site, **Camping de Montgeon**; *tel: 35 46 52 39*, on a hill in the **Forêt de Montgeon**, 3 km north-east of the town centre. Open Apr–Sept.

Eating and Drinking

Le Havre is as well served with restaurants as it is with hotels, many of them brasseries offering traditional and regional food. There are only one or two more exotic restaurants serving Far East or Lebanese dishes, and just a handful of fast food and pizza restaurants. Recommendations include the moderate to expensive **La Petite Auberge**, *32 r. de Ste-Adresse; tel: 35 46 27 32*, which offers good down-to-earth French food (booking advised),

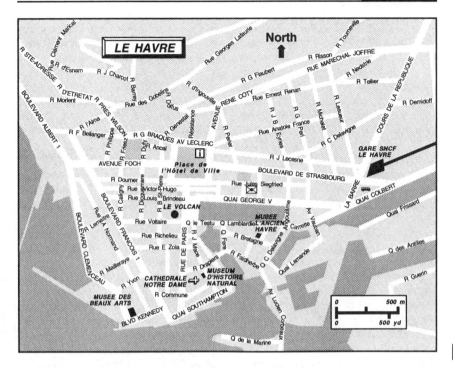

Lescalle, *39 pl. de l'Hôtel de Ville; tel: 35 43 07 93*, with its opulent decor and Sat evening dancing (moderate), and the Grignot, *53 r. Racine; tel: 35 43 62 07*, a brasserie with outdoor tables and a moderately priced menu. For a light lunch, try Le Lafayette, *6 av. René Coty; tel: 35 43 32 16*, which has a good choice of salads.

Communications

The main post office is at *62 r. Jules Siegfried; tel: 35 92 59 10*, open Mon–Fri 0800–1900, Sat 0800–1200.

Money

The main banks are found around the shopping area, but outside banking hours there is a bureau de change near the ferry terminals at *41 blvd J. F. Kennedy; tel: 35 21 53 98*, open Mon–Sat 0700–2000, Sun 0900–1200 and 1400–1800 (July–Aug); Mon–Sat 0700–1230 and 1330–2000, Sun 1000–1200 and 1400–1800 (June, Sept); Mon–Sat 0700–1230 and 1330–1900, Sun 1000–1200 and 1400–1700 (Oct–May).

Consulates

Belgium: *6 r. Dupleix; tel: 35 21 09 90*.
Germany: *7 r. Pierre Brossolette; tel: 35 21 11 22*.
Republic of Ireland: *Gare Maritime, quai de Southampton; tel: 35 22 50 24*.
Netherlands: *71 r. Jules Siegfried; tel: 35 21 50 70*.
South Africa: *109 blvd de Strasbourg; tel: 35 21 75 75*.
UK: *124 blvd de Strasbourg; tel: 35 42 27 47*.

ENTERTAINMENT

Useful sources of information about what is going on in town are the Tourist Office and a record shop called L'Audito, *104 r.*

Victor Hugo; tel: 35 42 13 38. The cultural centre is **Le Volcan,** *espace Oscar Niemeyer; tel: 35 19 10 10,* a strange building rather like a concrete cooling tower, which hosts plays, dance and music concerts, mainly classical but sometimes featuring jazz. Other theatres are the **Théâtre des Bains Douches,** *22 r. Louis Lo Basso; tel: 35 47 63 09,* and **Théâtre de l'Hôtel de Ville,** *pl. de l'Hôtel de Ville; tel: 35 19 45 74.*

There are several cinemas, among them the eight-screen **Colisée,** *123 blvd de Strasbourg; tel: 35 43 45 44,* the **Sirius,** *5 r. Duguesclin; tel: 35 26 52 15,* and the **Eden,** *espace Oscar Niemeyer; tel: 35 19 10 10,* which shows some films in their original language. Other entertainment options include **bowling** at *47 r. François Mazeline; tel: 35 24 32 52,* and several **discotheques,** one of them, **Le Cap,** *quai George V; tel: 35 42 71 94,* on board a boat in the Bassin du Commerce.

Le Havre football club enjoys first division status in the French League and plays at **Stade Jules-Deschaseaux,** *r. du Commandant-Abadie; tel: 35 47 12 44.*

SHOPPING

The main shopping area centres on the *pl. de l'Hôtel de Ville,* taking in *av. René Coty, r. de Paris* and *pl. des Halles,* where there is a covered market. Major stores include **Le Printemps** and **Monoprix,** both in *av. René Coty,* and **Les Nouvelles Galeries,** in *r. de Paris.* *Av. René Coty* is also the scene of a market on Mon and Wed mornings and all day Fri, while another market is held at *cours de la République* on Tues, Thur and Sat.

SIGHTSEEING

The **Salamandre** sails from the *quai de la Marine; tel 35 42 01 31* daily at 1500 (July–Aug), Fr.64 (Fr.50 children), on a sightseeing trip of 1 hr 15 min around the port.

One of the oldest remaining buildings is the **Cathédrale Notre-Dame** (Cathedral of our Lady) , *r. de Paris,* which was built between 1575 and 1630 in a mixture of Gothic and Renaissance styles.

Le Havre's most important attraction is the **Musée des Beaux Arts André Malraux** (André Malraux Fine Arts Museum), *blvd J. F. Kennedy; tel: 35 42 33 97,* open Wed–Mon 1000–1200 and 1400–1800 (all year), admission Fr.10 adults and children over 12. Paintings are largely from the Dutch, Flemish and French schools between the 17th and 20th centuries, with a particularly fine collection of Impressionist works; Boudin, Renoir, Pissarro, Sisley and Monet all being represented. Raoul Dufy, born in the town, has 70 works at the museum.

If you would like to see what Le Havre was like before the war, head for the **Musée de l'Ancien Havre** (Museum of Old Le Havre), *1 r. Jérôme Bellarmato; tel: 35 42 27 90,* open Wed–Sun 1000–1200 and 1400–1800 (all year), admission Fr.10 adults and children over 12. Housed in a restored 18th-century building, it tells the history of the town from its founding in 1517 to the present day.

Shipping played a major part in Le Havre's history and the **Musée Maritime et Portuaire** (Maritime and Harbour Museum), *Dock Vauban, quai Frissard; tel: 35 25 37 39,* open Wed–Mon 1000-1200 and 1400–1800 (all year), admission Fr.20 (Fr.10), has an interesting collection of merchant navy and port artefacts.

The **Muséum d'Histoire Naturelle** (Natural History Museum), *pl. du Vieux Marché; tel: 35 41 37 28,* open Mon, Thur, Fri 1430–1730, Wed, Sat and Sun 1000–1130 and 1430–1730 (all year), has rooms on prehistory, mineralogy, ornithology and zoology, plus paintings by the 19th-century naturalist Alexandre Lesueur.

LE HAVRE–CAEN

Once clear of Le Havre's industrial skyline and across the Seine Estuary, this route stays close to the Côte de Grâce and Côte Fleurie (Floral Coast), where magnificent coastal scenery combines with picturesque greenery. The lively and fashionable resorts en route are very popular and can be somewhat crowded in summer

DIRECT ROUTE: 83 KM

149

ROUTES

DIRECT ROUTE

The most direct route is to take the A131 motorway out of Le Havre and then cross the Seine via the new **Pont de Normandie** (Normandy Bridge – toll). This links with the D579 to **Pont-l'Évêque**, where you can join the A13 straight to Caen. Distance is 83 km, driving time about an hour.

SCENIC ROUTE

Take the same route out of Le Havre and cross the **Pont de Normandie**, but at the far side take the D513 to **Honfleur**. From there, continue on the D513 via **Villerville** to **Trouville**. Cross the River Touques and, still on the D513 pass through **Deauville**, **Blonville-sur-Mer**, **Villers-sur-Mer**, **Houlgate**, **Dives-sur-Mer** to **Cabourg**. There, the D513 heads inland to Caen, but the D514 keeps closer to the coast for a while to **Merville-Franceville Plage** before heading up the Orne Valley to **Ranville** and crossing the **Pegasus Bridge** to **Bénouville**. From there, join the D515 dual carriageway into the centre of Caen. Time taken for the 80 km is around 2 hrs.

PONT-L'ÉVÊQUE

Tourist Office: *r. St-Michel, 14130 Pont-L'Évêque; tel: 31 64 12 77.*

ACCOMMODATION

The **Hôtel Le Lion d'Or**, *8 pl. du Calvaire; tel: 31 65 01 55*, has reasonable rooms at a moderate price and an excellent restaurant. Just out of town at the lakeside leisure centre on the D48, the two-star **Hôtel Climat de France**; *tel: 31 64 64 00*, has moderately priced rooms. Also beside the lake is the large four-star **Camping La Cour de France**; *tel: 31 64 17 38*, which is open Mar–Oct. A second campsite, the two-star **Camping du Stade**, *rte de Beaumont; tel: 31 64 15 03*, has fewer pitches and is open, Apr–Oct.

SIGHTSEEING

Pont-l'Évêque, famous for the cheese of the same name since the 13th century, looks rather sad these days under the grime of traffic from the N175, which passes through the town. The best of what little remains of the the old town can be seen in *r. St-Michel* and *r. de Vaucelles*. The most interesting sights are outside the town and include the **Château de Betteville**, which was built in the mid-1800s in the Renaissance style. It houses the **Musée Automobile La Belle Époque** (Vintage Motor Museum); *tel: 31 65 05 02*, open daily 1000–1900 (July–Aug); 1000–1230, 1330–1900 (Apr–June, Sept); 1400–1800 (Oct–Nov), admission Fr.35 (Fr.18 children), which displays more than 100 luxury cars dating from 1898–1950. Opposite the château, a 59-hectare lake is the venue for a **Centre de Loisirs** (Leisure Centre); *tel: 31 64 00 02*, where various water activities are available.

On the other side of the town, the **Musée du Calvados et des Metiers Anciens** (Museum of Calvados and Ancient Crafts), *rte de Trouville; tel: 31 64 30 31*, open 1000–1230 and 1430–1830 (Mar–Oct), admission Fr.15 adults, free to children, housed in the Père Magloire calvados distillery, highlights the legacy of local crafts and traditions.

HONFLEUR

Tourist Office: *pl. Arthur-Boudin, 14600 Honfleur; tel: 31 89 23 30.*

ACCOMMODATION

Such is the popularity of Honfleur that hotels tend to be more expensive than elsewhere. There are two four-star and eight three-star hotels, and though most two-star hotels have moderately priced rooms, some rise to expensive levels. Very, very expensive is the four-star **Hôtel La Ferme-St-Simeon**, *rte A- Marais; tel: 31 89 23 61*, which, when it was a farm, was the meeting place of Impressionist artists. Now largely frequented by American tourists, it is worth a visit for its past associations. Most moderately priced of the three-star options close to the harbour are the **Hôtel du Cheval Blanc**, *2 quai des Passagers; tel: 31 81 65 00*, the **Tilbury Hôtel**, *30 pl. Hamelin; tel: 31 98 83 33*, and the **Hôtel La Diligence**, *53 r. de la République; tel: 31 98 81 80*. One of the best value hotels is the unclassified **Hôtel des Cascades**, *17 pl. Thiers; tel: 31 89 05 83*. The two-star campsite, **Camping du Phare**, *blvd Charles V; tel: 31 89 10 26*, opens Apr–Sept.

SIGHTSEEING

Despite not having a beach, Honfleur is popular with tourists, who are largely drawn to the **Vieux Bassin** (old harbour) area, surrounded by 18th-century, slate-fronted high-rise houses. At one end of the harbour, the **Lieutenance** combines what remains of the 16th-century Governor's House and the Caen Gate, one of the old gates to the town. On the east side of the harbour, the former Église St-Étienne is now the **Musée de la Marine**, *quai St-Étienne; tel: 31 89 14 12*, with displays of local sailing craft and information on the port's history. Nearby, the **Musée d'Art Populaire** (Folk Art Museum), *r. de la Prison; tel: 31 89 14 12*, housed in the old prison, has a reconstruction of a Norman house interior along with a large number of objects once part of local everyday life. Both museums are open daily 1000–1230, 1400–1830 (July–Sept); daily 1030–1230, 1430–1830 (Apr–June); Mon–Fri 1430–1800, Sat–Sun 1030–1230, 1430–1800 (Feb–Mar, Oct–Dec), admission Fr.25 (Fr.15). On the other side of the harbour is the unusual **Église Ste-Catherine**, *pl. Ste-Catherine*, built at the end of the Hundred Years' War entirely of wood. The belfry stands apart from the church and contains fine displays of religious art. The square itself is the venue for a colourful market on Sat mornings. Round the corner, the **Musée Eugène Boudin**, *pl. Erik Satie; tel: 31 89 54 00*, open Wed–Mon 1000–1200, 1400–1800 (Mar–Sept); Wed–Fri, Mon 1430–1700, Sat–Sun 1000–1200, 1430–1700 (Oct–Mar), admission Fr.18 (Fr.15), contains works by famous 19th- and 20th-century painters, including Boudin, who was born in the town, Monet and Dufy.

TROUVILLE

Tourist Office: *32 quai F. Moureaux, 14360 Trouville; tel: 31 88 36 19.*

ACCOMMODATION

Although only the River Touques separates Trouville from Deauville, there is a gulf between hotel prices and Trouville has a greater choice of hotels at the lower end of the moderate price scale. Two three-star hotels near the casino are the **Beach Hôtel**, *quai Albert ler; tel: 31 98 12 00*, and the **Hôtel Mercure Trouville**, *pl. Foch; tel: 31 87 38 38*. Both are expensive and both have restaurants. Much better value are the moderate **Hôtel Les Sablettes**, *r. P.-Besson; tel: 31 88 10 66*, the **Hôtel Les Charmettes**, *22 r. de la Chapelle; tel: 31 88 11 67*, and the **Hôtel Le Trouville**, *1 r. Thiers; tel: 31 98 45 48*.

There are two campsites, both fairly large, the two-star **Camping Hamel**, *55 r. des Soeurs de l'Hôpital; tel: 31 88 15 56*, and the one-star **Camping Chant des Oiseaux**, *11 rte de Honfleur; tel: 31 88 06 42*. Both open Apr–Sept.

SIGHTSEEING

Originally a fishing port at the mouth of the River Touques, Trouville became a holiday resort around 150 years ago. Fishing boats moor at the quay alongside the *blvd F. Moureaux*. There is also a huge sandy beach backed by the **Promenade des Planches** (boardwalk). Not far from the northern end of the beach, the **Musée de Trouville**, *64 r. Gén. Leclerc; tel: 31 88 16 26*, open Wed–Mon 1415–1815, at the 19th-century **Montebello Villa**, has works by artists such as Boudin, Dufy and Truffaut. One room is devoted to the history of sea bathing. An annex at the Tourist Office holds temporary exhibitions. Also close to the beach is the **Aquarium Écologique**, *17 r. de Paris* (entrance from beach); *tel: 31 88 46 04*, open daily 1000–1930 (July–Aug); 1000–1200, 1400–1900 (Apr–June, Sept–Oct); 1400–1830 (Nov–Mar), admission Fr.30 (Fr.20), displays fish from around the world in as natural a habitat as possible. At the end of the beach and overlooking the harbour is the **casino**, *quai Albert 1er; tel: 31 87 75 00.*

DEAUVILLE

Tourist Office: *pl. de la Mairie, 14800 Deauville; tel: 31 88 21 43.*

ACCOMMODATION

The two top hotels near the beach are the **Normandy Hôtel**, *38 r. Jean Mermoz; tel: 31 98 66 22*, and the **Hôtel Royal**, *blvd Cornuché; tel: 31 98 66 33*, both massive affairs with 300 rooms apiece and high prices that more than match their four stars. Of the three-star hotels, the one with the most moderate starting price, though opening only May–Sept, is the **Park Hôtel**, *81 av. de la République; tel: 31 88 09 71*, but this is on the busy through-road from Trouville, where there are also several more moderately priced two-star hotels. Among them are the **Hôtel Le Chantilly**, *120 av. de la République; tel: 31 88 79 75*, and the **Hôtel Le Patio**, *180 av. de la République; tel: 31 88 25 07*.

SIGHTSEEING

It was horse-racing that put Deauville on the map, when, in 1825, the Duke of Morny saw the possibility of creating a racecourse on the vast plain of sand just across the river from Trouville. Thereafter, it mushroomed as a holiday resort and became the most fashionable holiday resort in northern France, a title it can still claim. The season is short, basically July–early Sept, when the town fills with the jet set in town for the horse-racing, world-championship polo and the **American Film Festival**. There are two race-courses, **Clairefontaine**, which has regular racing July and Aug, and **La Touques**, where there is a full month of racing in Aug, and a couple of meetings in Oct.

Deauville's beach is superb, its sands decorated with multi-coloured parasols and backed by the famous *planches*, the wooden promenade where visitors like to stroll. The beach huts here are decorated with the names of many of the stars who have attended the film festival. Behind the beach, the **casino**, *blvd Cornuché; tel: 31 98 66 66*, is the main source of entertainment for the rest of the year with stage shows and dancing as well as gaming tables and fruit machines.

VILLERS-SUR-MER

Tourist Office: *pl. Jean Mermoz, 14640 Villiers-sur-Mer; tel: 31 87 01 18.*

ACCOMMODATION

Villers has a handful of hotels, the best of which is the three-star **Hôtel La Bonne Auberge**, *1 r. Mal. Leclerc; tel: 31 87 04 64*, where prices are on the high side of moderate. Open Mar–Sept and weekends. The two-star **Auberge des Frais Ombrages**, *38 av. de la Brigade-Piron; tel: 31 87 40 38*, opens from Apr– mid-Nov, the unclassified **Hôtel Le Celtic**, *r. Mal. Leclerc; tel: 31 87 41 46*, from Mar–Nov. The only hotel open all year is the one-star **Chez Guy**, *15 r. du Mar. Foch; tel: 31 87 46 55*. All are moderately priced.

There are three campsites nearby, the best of which is the four-star **Camping Les Ammonites**, *rte de la Corniche; tel: 31 87 06 06*, on the clifftops (open Apr–Oct). Others are the three-star **Camping Bellevue**, *rte de Dives; tel: 31 87 05 21*, (open Apr–Oct) and the massive two-star **Camping Le Drakkar**, *av. de la République; tel: 31 87 52 41*, (open Apr–Sept).

SIGHTSEEING

Straddling the Greenwich meridian, Villers is an elegant resort with a large number of turn-of-the-century villas. Its beach extends for 5 km, ending at the **Falaise Vaches Noires**, where large numbers of fossils have been found. Many of these, along with stuffed birds and seashells, are exhibited in the **Musée de Paléontologie**, at the Tourist Office, *pl. Jean Mermoz; tel: 31 87 01 18*, open daily 0900–1900 (July–Aug); daily 0930–1230, 1400–1800 (Mar–June, Sept); Mon–Sat 0930–1230, 1400–1700 (Oct), admission free. The **casino**, *pl. Fanneau; tel: 31 87 01 07;* has gaming tables and night club.

HOULGATE

Tourist Office: *blvd des Belges, 14510 Houlgate; tel: 31 24 34 79* open all year, and *r. Henri Dobert; tel: 31 24 62 31*, next to the casino, open daily July–Aug.

ACCOMMODATION

Houlgate has eight or so hotels, all of them moderately priced, some with rooms at economical prices. Those nearest the sea are the **Hôtel La Plage**, *99 r. des Bains; tel: 31 28 70 60*, the **Hôtel du Centre**, *31 r. des Bains; tel: 31 24 80 40*, and the **Hôtel 1900**, *17 r. des Bains; tel: 31 28 77 77*, which has turn-of-the-century decor. The **Hôtel Mon Castel**, *1 blvd des Belges; tel: 31 24 83 47*, just up from the beach, is very welcoming and has a popular restaurant, as does the **Hôtel Le Normand**, *40 r. du Gén. Leclerc; tel: 31 24 81 81*.

There are three campsites, the best of which is the four-star **Camping de la Vallée**, *88 r. de la Vallée; tel: 31 24 40 69*. The others, rated two stars, are **Camping Municipal**, *chemin des Chevaliers; tel: 31 24 37 93*, and **Camping Plage**, *r. Henri Dobert; tel: 31 28 73 07*, near the casino. All are open Apr–Sept.

SIGHTSEEING

Houlgate, lying in the Drochon Valley, is a typical resort of the **Côte Fleurie**, ini-

tially making its mark in the late 19th century. It has a fine sandy beach and parasols similar to Deauville's, but is more noted for family holidays than its more fashionable neighbour. There are plenty of sporting activities available, while **Port Guillaume**, a huge marina being developed with Dives-sur-Mer and Cabourg, has moorings for 600 boats. The **casino**, *r. Henri Dobert; tel: 31 28 75 75*, open daily 1030–0300, fronts onto the beach and has a discotheque and cinema as well as gaming tables.

DIVES-SUR-MER

Tourist Information: **Syndicat d'Initiative**, *7 r. du Gén. de Gaulle; tel: 31 91 24 66*, or *Mairie; tel: 31 91 04 28*.

ACCOMMODATION

Three hotels worth investigating are the one-star **Hôtel de la Gare**, *pl. M. Tréfouel; tel: 31 91 24 52*, which has 16 rooms, ranging in price from economy to moderate, the two-star **Hôtel d'Hastings**, *6 r. d'Hastings; tel: 31 28 02 00*, (moderate), and the **Hôtel Le Bon Gite**, *71 r. du Gén. de Gaulle; tel: 31 91 24 39* (economic). Campers and caravanners have two two-star **campsites** to choose from, **Camping Municipal Les Tilleuls**, *rte de Lisieux; tel: 31 91 25 21*, open Apr–Sept, and **Camping de la Ferme du Golf**, *rte de Lisieux; tel 31 24 73 09*, open May–Sept.

SIGHTSEEING

Dives, wedged between Houlgate and Cabourg in the Dives Estuary, was a major port in the Middle Ages, and it was here that William the Conqueror gathered his fleet before sailing for England in 1066. Inside the massive **Église Notre-Dame**, a carved list names the barons who joined William for the invasion. Other medieval

153

buildings still surviving include the 14th- and 15th-century **halles** (covered market), *pl. de la République*, which has an immense roof of tiles supported by a magnificent oak frame (market Sat mornings), and the nearby **Manoir du Bois-Hibout**, built in the 16th and 17th centuries and all that remains of the Ste-Marie du Hibout Abbey. Also close at hand, the **Village Guillaume le Conquérant** (William the Conqueror Village) is a picturesque group of craft and antique shops built around the courtyard of a 16th-century inn.

CABOURG

Tourist Office: *Jardins du Casino, 14390 Cabourg; tel: 31 91 01 09.*

ACCOMMODATION

The **Grand Hôtel**, *promenade Marcel Proust; tel: 31 91 01 79*, facing the sea, is the most distinctive building in Cabourg and where the writer **Marcel Proust** frequently stayed between 1881 and 1914. There is an excellent restaurant, **Le Balbec** (the name given to Cabourg in one of Proust's novels), but, like the palatial rooms, it is expensive. The three-star **Hôtel Le Cabourg**, *5 av. de la République; tel: 31 24 42 55*, offers good value with moderately priced rooms but is further from the sea. Among two- and one-star hotels, worth considering are **Hôtel de Paris**, *39 av. de la Mer; tel: 31 91 31 34*, and **Auberge du Parc**, *31 av. du Gén. Leclerc; tel: 31 91 00 82*, a *LF* some way back from the sea. Both moderate.

Campsites include **Camping Plage**, *av. du Gén. de Gaulle; tel: 31 91 05 75*, a four-star site open Apr–Oct, the three-star **Camping Joli**, *5 chemin Cailloué; tel: 31 91 68 43*, open Apr–Sept, and two two-star sites, **Oasis Camping**, *av. du Gén. de Gaulle; tel: 31 91 10 62*, open May–Aug, and **Camping de la Pommeraie**, *av.*

Guillaume le Conquérant; tel: 31 91 54 58, open Apr–Sept.

SIGHTSEEING

Another of the Côte Fleurie's elegant resorts, Cabourg is at its best in July and August. Outside this period it reverts to being a ghost town. Developed in the mid-1800s, it was created with a geometrical symmetry, with streets radiating from the **Grand Hôtel** linked by crescent shaped avenues. The seafront has a 3 km promenade and there are various leisure activities on hand. These include the recently refurbished **casino**, *promenade Marcel Proust; tel: 31 91 30 30*, open daily 1100–0400, which has gaming tables, cinemas, discotheque, piano bar and a theatre of the Belle Époque, and the **hippodrome** (racecourse), which has a programme of evening horse-racing July–Aug, during a season that lasts from Apr–Oct.

MERVILLE-FRANCEVILLE PLAGE

Tourist Office: *pl. de la Plage, 14810 Merville-Franceville; tel: 31 24 23 57.*

ACCOMMODATION

The **Hôtel Chez Marion**, *10 pl. de la Plage; tel: 31 24 23 39*, is the best of this resort's few hotels, though prices may seem rather steep, especially in the restaurant. The food, however, is excellent, as might be expected of a three-star *LF*. Another *logis*, the half-timbered and two-star **Hôtel de la Gare**, *rte de Cabourg; tel: 31 24 23 37*, is more acceptable pricewise, but is not so well located, being beside a busy road. On the same road, the **Hôtel La Mer**, *71 rte de Cabourg; tel: 31 24 10 40*, has similarly moderately priced rooms, though some are marginally cheaper.

The resort has no fewer than eight

campsites to choose from. The top-rated is the three-star **Camping Le Point du Jour**, *rte de Cabourg; tel: 31 24 23 34*, open Feb–Dec, which has access to the beach. Another site with direct beach access is the two-star **Oasis Camping**; *tel: 31 24 22 12*, open Apr–Sept. **Camping du Relais**, *57 rte de Cabourg; tel: 31 24 22 82*, has two stars and is open Apr–Sept.

SIGHTSEEING

This quiet resort is famous for the German gun battery built here as part of the Atlantic Wall defences in World War II. The guns, with a range of 20 km, were considered a serious threat to allied forces landing on the beaches on D-Day, and on the night of June 5–6, 1944, were captured by British paratroopers. The **Musée de la Batterie**; *tel: 31 24 21 83*, open daily 0900–1900 (Apr–Sept), admission Fr.15 (Fr.8), installed in one of the four blockhouses, shows through various displays how the assault was carried out. Another defensive position, the **Redoute de Merville**, undergoing restoration, was built in 1779, to plans by Vauban, to protect the Orne Estuary.

Not far from the resort, **Sallenelles** is an important nature reserve designated a European site of special interest. The **Maison de la Nature et de l'Estuaire**; *tel: 31 78 71 06*, open daily 1400–1800 (June–Sept); Sun 1400–1800 (Apr–May and Oct), admission free, has an exhibition on the flora and fauna of the marshlands.

RANVILLE

Ranville has no hotels but there is a **campsite**, the two-star **Camping des Capucines**, *4 r. du Calvaire; tel: 31 78 69 82*, open all year.

Ranville is famed as the first village in France to be liberated, after paratroopers landed in the early hours of June 6, 1944

to capture the Merville gun battery. The village has one of the largest British **cemeteries**, holds the graves of 2151 soldiers.

BÉNOUVILLE

Tourist Office: *Mairie, 1 av. du 5 Juin 1944, 14000 Bénouville; tel: 31 44 62 01.*

ACCOMMODATION

The four-star **Manoir d'Hastings**, *18 av. de la Côte de Nacre; tel: 31 44 62 43*, is renowned for its restaurant, but it is expensive, as are the rooms. Much better value is the nearby **Hôtel La Glycine**, *11 pl. du Commando; tel: 31 44 61 94*, where two stars mean more moderate prices.

Also rating four stars is the one **campsite**, **Camping Les Hautes Coutures**, *rte de Ouistreham; tel: 31 44 73 08*, open Apr–Sept, which has a swimming pool.

SIGHTSEEING

Just outside the village is the **Pegasus Bridge**, a bridge across the Orne Canal linking Ranville with Bénouville, which was strategic to the success of the D-Day landings. On the night of June 5-6, 1944, paratroopers and glider-borne soldiers captured the bridge, and their emblem, Pegasus, was used to name the bridge. The original was removed in 1994 to make way for a similar but wider bridge to handle increased traffic. The café next to the bridge claims to be the first house liberated in France and inside there are many reminders of the time. More details about the landing and capture of the bridge are on display at the neighbouring **Musée des Troupes Aéroportées** (Museum of Airborne Troops), *10 av. du Commandant Kieffer; tel: 31 44 62 54*, open daily 0900–1900 (July–Aug); 0930–1230, 1400–1900 (June); 0930–1230, 1400–1800 (Apr–May, Sept–Oct), admission Fr.17 (Fr.12).

LE HAVRE–DIEPPE

This route passes along the northern edge of the Caux region, a rich and fertile plateau punctuated by tiny rivers and dry valleys where small resorts lie hidden. The coastline, made up of chalk cliffs, is known as the Côte d'Albâtre or Alabaster Coast.

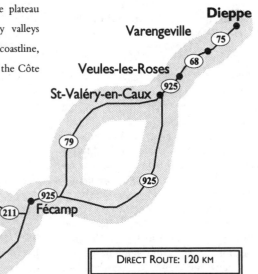

156

DIRECT ROUTE: 120 KM

ROUTE

Leave Le Havre on the D940, diverting briefly via **Ste-Adresse** and rejoining the D940, passing Le Havre-Octeville airport en route for **Étretat**. From this attractive resort, take the narrow and winding D11 (later D211) via **Bénouville**, **Vattetot** and **Vaucottes** to the little resort of **Yport**, which has some small hotels. Stay on the D211 and rejoin the D940 to

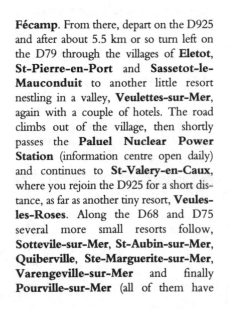

Fécamp. From there, depart on the D925 and after about 5.5 km or so turn left on the D79 through the villages of **Eletot**, **St-Pierre-en-Port** and **Sassetot-le-Mauconduit** to another little resort nestling in a valley, **Veulettes-sur-Mer**, again with a couple of hotels. The road climbs out of the village, then shortly passes the **Paluel Nuclear Power Station** (information centre open daily) and continues to **St-Valery-en-Caux**, where you rejoin the D925 for a short distance, as far as another tiny resort, **Veules-les-Roses**. Along the D68 and D75 several more small resorts follow, **Sottevile-sur-Mer**, **St-Aubin-sur-Mer**, **Quiberville**, **Ste-Marguerite-sur-Mer**, **Varengeville-sur-Mer** and finally **Pourville-sur-Mer** (all of them have hotels) before the road descends into Dieppe. The distance from Le Havre to Dieppe is approximately 120 km. Journey time is about 2 hrs 30 mins.

STE-ADRESSE

Tourist Office: *Forum de l'Hôtel de Ville, Le Havre; tel: 35 21 22 88*, has information on the resort. The one hotel in this resort, the **Hôtel des Phares**, *29 r. Gén. de Gaulle; tel: 35 46 31 86*, provides an inviting and quiet option to staying down the road in Le Havre. Rooms are economic to moderate and there is now a restaurant.

Ste-Adresse is just to the north of Le Havre and is really the resort suburb for the port. There is a beach backed by changing huts, while the town itself lies in terraces on the hillside behind. Overlooking all is **Ste-Adresse Fort**, from which there are panoramic views across the Seine Estuary and along the coast.

ÉTRETAT

Tourist Office: *pl. Maurice Guillard, 76790 Étretat; tel: 35 27 05 21.*

ACCOMMODATION

There is no shortage of hotels in Étretat, not surprisingly perhaps for a resort that was the St-Tropez of its day. The grandest hotel in the village itself is the **Hôtel de la Résidence**, *blvd de Président Coty; tel: 35 27 02 87*, a half-timbered mansion with rooms ranging in price from economic to expensive. Opposite, the **Hôtel les Falaises**, *blvd de Président Coty; tel: 35 27 02 77*, has a more moderate price range. Two near-neighbours, also with moderately priced rooms are the **Hôtel de Normandie**, *pl. Foch; tel: 35 27 06 99*, and the **Hôtel l'Escale**, *pl. Foch; tel: 35 27 03 69*, both of which have restaurants. For something a little special, try the **Hôtel le Donjon**, *chemin de St-Clair; tel: 35 27 08*

23, a chateau-hotel with just eight rooms, all of them expensive.

There is a three-star **municipal campsite**, *r. Guy de Maupassant; tel: 35 27 07 67*, open Apr–Sept.

SIGHTSEEING

At the turn of the century the pretty fishing village of Étretat was a magnet for writers and artists, and even today artists are often seen on the seafront capturing on canvas the strange cliff scenery of arches and pinnacles. Monet, Boudin, Matisse, Maupassant and the composer Offenbach all have associations with the resort. Fishermen still launch their boats from the beach and some of the traditional thatched fishermen's huts have been restored. The village itself contains some elegant half-timbered buildings and includes wooden **halles** (covered market), *pl. du Mar. Foch*, which now houses a number of souvenir shops. There is a small **casino** on the seafront, while tucked into the cliffs at Les Roches, the **Aquarium Marin**; *tel: 35 27 01 23*, open daily 1000–1900 (July–Aug); 1000–1200, 1400–1900 (Apr–June and Sept), admission Fr.12.50 adults (Fr.5 children), has more than 100 species of sealife from local, Mediterranean and tropical waters. Two distinctive features of the Falaise d'Amont (upstream cliff) seen from the promenade are the **Nungesser and Coli Memorial** and the **Notre-Dame de la Garde**, a seaman's chapel. The former marks the point where, in 1927, two French aviators crossed the coast en route from Paris in an attempt to be the first to fly the Atlantic. They were never seen again. Just across the road, the **Musée Nungesser et Coli**; *tel: 35 27 07 47*, open daily (June–Sept), Sat–Sun (Apr–May) 1000–1200 and 1400–1900, admission Fr.5.60 (Fr.3.80), contains personal mementoes of the two aviators. The

157

Château des Aygues, *r. Offenbach; tel: 35 28 92 77*, open daily 1400–1800 (July–Aug); Wed–Mon 1400–1800 (Apr–June and Sept–Oct), admission Fr.25, built in 1866, was the former summer residence of the Queens of Spain, and contains period furniture and Chinese objets d'art.

FÉCAMP

Tourist Office: *113 r. Alexandre le Grand, 76400 Fécamp, tel: 35 28 51 01.*

ACCOMMODATION

Most of Fécamp's hotels are moderately priced, though there are one or two with more economical rooms. The **Hôtel de la Mer**, *89 blvd Albert 1er; tel: 35 28 24 64*, faces the sea but has no restaurant. The nearby **Hôtel Les Embruns**, *73 blvd Albert 1er; tel: 35 28 31 31*, is slightly cheaper but does have a restaurant. Most economical is the **Hôtel Martin**, *18 pl. St-Etienne; tel: 35 28 23 82*. The large but excellent two-star **Camping Municipal de Reneville**; *tel: 35 28 20 97*, is on the clifftops just west of the town.

SIGHTSEEING

Fécamp has a long sea-going past and at one time was also one of the most important monastic centres in Normandy. Until 1204, it was the residence of the Dukes of Normandy and it was Richard I, the English King, who founded the **Église de la Trinité**, *r. des Forts*. Rebuilt several times since, it has the proportions of a cathedral and contains many treasures. Opposite are the remains of the medieval ducal palace.

The town's grandest building is the **Palais Bénédictine** (Benedictine Palace), *110 r. Alexandre le Grand; tel: 35 28 00 06*, open daily 0930–1800 (June–Aug); 1000–1200, 1400–1730 (Mar–May and Sept–Oct); guided visits only at 1030 and 1530 (Jan–Mar and Nov–Dec), admission Fr.25 (Fr.12.50). It was built in Gothic and Renaissance style in the late 19th century, not only as a distillery of the famous drink discovered by a monk from Fécamp Abbey in 1510, but to house the abbey's treasures which were dispersed after the Revolution. There are three parts to the palace: the **museum** containing religious art, ivory and alabaster carvings, and enamels: the **art gallery**, which houses temporary exhibitions; and the **distillery**, where visitors can see the manufacturing process for benedictine. At the end of the visit there is an opportunity to taste.

Two other museums in the town are the **Musée Centre des Arts** (Arts Centre Museum), *21 r. Alexandre Legros; tel: 35 28 31 99*, open Wed–Mon 1000–1200 and 1400–1730 (all year), admission Fr.20, housed in a former private mansion, with collections of Rouen earthenware, ivory carvings and 18th- and 19th-century works by French artists, and the **Musée des Terre-Neuvas et de la Pêche** (Nova Scotia and Fishing Museum), *27 blvd Albert ler; tel: 35 28 31 99*, open daily 1000–1200, 1400–1750 (July–Aug); Wed–Mon 1000–1200, 1400–1730 (Sept–June), admission Fr.20, recounts Fécamp's history in fishing the Nova Scotian cod banks. The admission ticket can be used for entry to both museums.

ST-VALERY-EN-CAUX

Tourist Office: *Maison Henri IV, quai d'Aval, tel: 35 97 00 63.*

ACCOMMODATION

St-Valery has a couple of LF, the two-star **Hôtel les Terrasses**, *22 Le Perrey; tel: 35 97 11 22*, which faces the sea and has rooms on the high side of moderately priced, and the **Hôtel de la Marine**, *r. St-Léger; tel: 35 97 05 09*, which has rooms at a more economic level. Others to choose from include the **Hôtel des Bains**, *15 pl. du Marché; tel: 35 97 04 32*, and the **Hôtel des Remparts**, *4 r. des Bains; tel: 35 97 16 13*, (both moderate), and the **Hôtel l'Escale**, *r. des Pénitents; tel: 35 97 04 98*, and the **Hôtel de la Poste**, *10 pl. du Marché; tel: 35 97 10 44*, which both have rooms at economic prices.

The nearest campsite is the two-star **Camping Falaise d'Amont**; *tel: 35 97 05 07*, but a better one is the four-star **Camping d'Etennemare**; *tel: 35 97 15 79*, just south west of the town, near the hamlet of Etennemare.

SIGHTSEEING

St-Valery competed with Fécamp as a port, but when it became clear its neighbour was winning the battle, St-Valery turned its attention to seaside holidays. Today, it is one of the liveliest resorts on the Alabaster Coast. The **Maison Henri IV**, *quai d'Aval; tel: 35 57 14 13*, which houses the Tourist Office, is a marvellous half-timbered house built in Renaissance style, with beautifully carved beams. It is also home to a small **local history museum**, open daily 1100–1300, 1500–1900 (July–Aug); Wed–Sun 1100–1300, 1500–1900 (June, Sept); Sat–Sun 1100–1300, 1500–1900 (Oct–May), admission Fr.10. On the cliffs are monuments to the 51st Highland Division and the French 2nd Cavalry Division who attempted to prevent German tanks over-running the town in June 1940. The French troops were on horseback. Another monument commemorates two aviators, Costes and Bellonte, who, in 1930, were the the first to fly from Paris to New York.

VEULES-LES-ROSES

Tourist Office: *11 r. du Dr. Girard, 76980 Veules-les-Roses; tel: 35 97 64 11.*

The **Hôtel Café Suisse**, *r. Victor-Hugo; tel: 35 97 63 44*, is a small ungraded hotel, moderately priced, with a restaurant.

Another haunt of writers and artists, aptly-named Veules-les-Roses has old-world charm with flower-covered thatched cottages, watermills, and a lovely walk beside the **Veules River**. The river rises in watercress pools in the village and is said to be France's smallest.

VARENGEVILLE-SUR-MER

Tourist Office: *Mairie, 76119 Varengeville-sur-Mer; tel: 35 85 12 46.*

ACCOMMODATION

The only hotel, the **Hôtel de la Terrasse**, *Vasterival; tel: 35 85 12 54*, a large two-star *LF* on the cliffs, is moderately priced, but visitors are obliged to take evening meals there.

SIGHTSEEING

A longtime favourite of artists, Varengeville is tucked away in leafy countryside only 8 km from Dieppe. Overlooking the sea is the 11th-century **church** and its small cemetery, where the artist Georges Braque is buried. The church has a Tree of Jesse stained glass window by Braque. Nearby, the **Bois des Moutiers**; *tel: 35 85 10 02*, open daily 1000–1200, 1400–1800 (Mar–Nov), admission Fr.25, is an English-style ornamental and botanical garden with a house at the centre designed by the English architect, Edwin Lutyens. Exhibits in the house include a tapestry by Burne-Jones. Just south of the village is the **Manoir d'Ango**; *tel: 35 85 12 08*, open daily 1000–1200, 1400–1800 (Apr–Oct), admission Fr.25, a Renaissance manor-house built around 1530 by Jéhan d'Ango, a shipowner who developed the ports of Le Havre, Rouen and Honfleur.

LE HAVRE–LE MANS

As well as taking in a number of interesting and attractive medieval towns, this route passes through some fascinating countryside, most notably the Marais Vernier (Vernier Marsh) just south of the Seine, and the undulating Perche region.

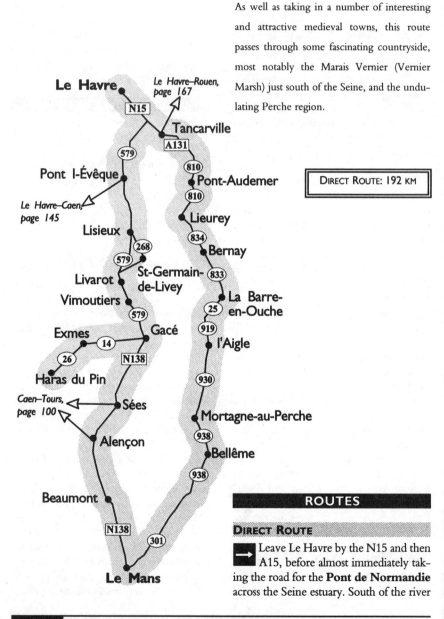

Le Havre

Le Havre–Rouen, page 167

N15

Tancarville

A131

Pont l-Évêque

579

810

Pont-Audemer

810

Le Havre–Caen, page 145

Lieurey

Lisieux

268

834

Bernay

579

St-Germain-de-Livey

833

Livarot

Vimoutiers

La Barre-en-Ouche

25

579

919

Exmes

Gacé

l'Aigle

14

26

N138

930

Haras du Pin

Caen–Tours, page 100

Sées

Mortagne-au-Perche

938

Alençon

Bellême

938

Beaumont

N138

301

Le Mans

DIRECT ROUTE: 192 KM

160

ROUTES

DIRECT ROUTE

Leave Le Havre by the N15 and then A15, before almost immediately taking the road for the **Pont de Normandie** across the Seine estuary. South of the river follow the D144 and then D579 via **Pont l'Evêque** to the pilgrimage town of **Lisieux**. Continue south on the D579 (a short diversion just south of **St-Martin-de-la-Lieue** via the D268 takes you past the pretty château of **St-Germain-de-Livet**, the D268A returning you to the D579) through first **Livarot** and then **Vimoutiers** before reaching **Gacé**. There, turn right onto the N138, which goes via **Sées**, **Alençon** and **Beaumont-sur-Sarthe** to Le Mans. Total distance is 192 km, driving time about 2 hrs 30 mins.

SCENIC ROUTE

Take the N15 out of Le Havre initially, then follow the autoroute signs for the A15, crossing the Seine at the **Pont de Tancarville**. South of the river, bear left on the A131, skirting the **Marais Vernier**, and then at the next exit take the D810 to **Pont-Audemer**. From there continue on the D810 to **Lieurey** and then join the D834 to **Bernay**. Leave Bernay on the D140 and within a short distance bear right on the D833 to **La Barre-en-Ouche** and from there take the D25 to **Chambord**, then the D114 to **Glos-la-Ferrière** and the D919 to **L'Aigle**. Then take the D918 south and within about 2 km or so bear right on the D930 which passes the edge of the **Forêt de la Trappe** close to the **Abbaye de la Trappe** where the Trappist order was founded in the 17th century. Continue on the D930 to **Mortagne-au-Perche**, from there taking the D938 to **Bellême** and then **Igé**. The road then continues as the D301, passing through **St-Cosme-en-Vairais** and bypassing **Bonnetable** before reaching Le Mans. Driving time for the 222-km journey is about 3 hrs 30 mins.

PONT-L'ÉVÊQUE

For details, see p. 150.

LISIEUX

Tourist Office: *r. d'Alençon, 14100 Liseux; tel: 31 62 08 41.*

ACCOMMODATION

A town of pilgrimage, Lisieux has plenty of hotels, most of them two-star, though there are some one- and three-star options. Two central three-star hotels are the **Azur Hôtel**, *15 r. au Char; tel: 31 62 09 14*, moderate to expensive, and the **Hôtel de la Place**, *67 r. Henry Chéron; tel: 31 31 17 44*, moderate. Neither has a restaurant, but there is also a handful of LF, all with reasonable restaurants. Worth considering are the **Hôtel de la Coupe d'Or**, *49 r. Pont Mortain; tel: 31 31 16 84*, and the **Hôtel La Bretagne**, *30 pl. de la République; tel: 31 62 09 19*, which are both in the centre, and the **Terrasse Hôtel**, *25 av. Ste-Thérèse; tel: 31 62 17 65*, on the road leading to the basilica. All are moderately priced. Also moderate are the **Hôtel de l'Europe**, *34-38 r. de la Gare; tel: 31 31 01 43* and the **Hôtel Regina**, *14 r. de la Gare; tel: 31 31 15 43*, both of which are a little distant from the centre but close to the station. Both have restaurants. Nearby, the **Hôtel de la Gare**, *8 pl. de la Gare; tel: 31 62 07 42*, offers a more economical option.

    Camping de la Vallée, *9 r. de la Vallée; tel: 31 62 00 40*, is a municipal campsite with 100 pitches. Open Apr–Sept.

SIGHTSEEING

The most important town in the Auge region, Lisieux relies mainly on the story of Ste-Thérèse for its tourist (often pilgrim) interest, as the many tacky souvenir shops on the *av. Ste-Thérèse* testify. Born in Alençon, Thérèse Martin moved to Lisieux after the death of her mother and entered a convent when only 15. She died

161

in 1897 at the age of 24 and was canonised in 1925. The house where she lived as a child, **Maison des Boissonnets**, *blvd Herbet-Fournet*, open daily 0900–1200 and 1400–1800 (July–Sept); 1000–1200 and 1400–1700 (Oct); 1000–1200 and 1400–1600 (Nov–Apr); 0900–1200 and 1400–1730 (Apr–June), admission free, contains mementoes of her childhood. The saint is enshrined at the **Chapelle du Carmel**, *r. Carmel*, open daily 0715–1900 (Apr–Oct); 0715–1800 (Nov–Mar), admission free, but her greatest memorial is the **Basilique Ste-Thérèse**, *av. Ste-Thérèse*, consecrated in 1954. Modelled on the Sacré-Coeur in Paris, it is one of the largest churches built this century. The crypt contains mosaics depicting the saint's life.

Also worth a visit is the **Cathédrale St-Pierre**, *r. Henry-Chéron*, a magnificent Gothic construction built between the 12th and 14th centuries. *Son et Lumière* displays are held between June and Sept. Tickets can be bought through the Tourist Office.

The **Musée du Vieux Lisieux** (Museum of Old Lisieux), *blvd Louis Pasteur; tel: 31 62 07 70*, open Wed–Mon 1400–1800, admission Fr.15 adults, housed in a beautiful half-timbered house, is devoted to local folk traditions and arts.

VIMOUTIERS

Tourist Office: *10 av. du Gén. de Gaulle, 61120 Vimoutiers; tel: 33 39 30 29.*

ACCOMMODATION

A small market town, Vimoutiers has only a few hotels, two of them *LF*. The best is the two-star **Hôtel L'Escale du Vitou**, *rte d'Argentan; tel: 33 39 12 37*, which has moderately priced rooms and a good restaurant. A little cheaper is the one-star **Hôtel Le Soleil d'Or**, *16 pl. de Mackau; tel: 33 39 07 15*, but cheaper still is the

CAMEMBERT

Camembert, the *pièce de résistance* of the French dinner table, is admired by cheese-lovers around the world. Watch how the experts study the cheese when it is presented at the table, carefully checking its consistency, its pungency. Watch them, too, in the supermarkets, lifting the lid of the famous circular wooden boxes, and prodding the contents carefully in the centre to see if they are ripe enough. However, if things had gone wrong 200 years ago during the French revolution, Camembert might never have been discovered.

The name existed then, but in the form of a tiny, hidden village. Even today, the village is well off the beaten track and has hardly altered, consisting of a church, a handful of half-timbered houses, a large town hall out of all proportion to the size of the place and, dominating all, Beaumoncel Farm. It was while milking cows at Beaumoncel that a young farmer's wife, Marie Harel, was approached by a desperate priest on the run from the revolutionaries. If he was caught, he pleaded, he would go the way of the aristocrats – to the guillotine. Risking the same fate, Marie hid the priest at Beaumoncel until, eventually, it was safe for him to leave.

To show his gratitude he gave her the recipe to a cheese that the priests made at the priory. The following year Marie Harel started producing Camembert in small quantities, little realising just how successful the new product would be.

Hôtel de la Couronne, *9 r. du 8 Mai; tel: 33 39 03 04*. Campers and caravanners should head for the two-star **Camping La Campière**, *blvd du Dr Dentu; tel: 33 39 18 86*, a riverside site open all year.

SIGHTSEEING

Largely rebuilt after the war, Vimoutiers is the main centre in Normandy for Camembert cheese production. The person credited with its invention was Marie Harel, a farmer's wife from the nearby hamlet of Camembert. During the Revolution she sheltered a priest and by way of thanks he gave her the recipe for the cheese (see box, left). There are two statues of Marie Harel in Vimoutiers. One, opposite the Église Notre-Dame, is headless, the head having been blown off during an American bombing raid in 1944 (appropriate reward, some locals thought, for someone who had helped a member of the establishment amid social turmoil), while the other, a replacement donated by a cheesemaker from Ohio, USA, stands opposite the town hall.

Not surprisingly, there is a museum, the **Musée du Camembert**, *10 av. du Gén. de Gaulle; tel: 33 39 30 29*, open Tues–Sun 0900–1200 and 1400–1800, Mon 1400–1800 (May–Oct); Mon 1400–1800, Tues–Fri 0900–1200 and 1400–1800, Sat 0900–1200 (Nov–Apr), admission Fr.15 adults (Fr.10 children), which includes a mock-up of a cheese farm, information on the history of Camembert and a collection of 1500 Camembert box labels from around the world.

GACÉ

Tourist Office: *Mairie, 61230 Gacé; tel: 33 35 50 24.*

ACCOMMODATION

The **Hôtel Le Morphée**, *r. Lisieux; tel: 33 35 51 01*, is a 19th-century mansion in its own grounds, with comfortable, moderately priced rooms. Another manor house of a similar period is the **Hôtel Hostellerie les Champs**, *rte d'Alençon-Rouen; tel: 33 39 09 05*, again moderately priced, though more expensive suites are available. Likewise, menus range from moderate to expensive. In the town itself, the **Hôtel L'Etoile d'Or**, *60 Grande Rue; tel: 33 35 50 03*, is more down-to-earth with economic to moderate prices.

A small two-star campsite, **Camping Le Pressoir**, *impasse Tahiti; tel: 33 39 96 01*, is open June–Aug.

SIGHTSEEING

Although a useful place to stay, Gacé is not a tremendously exciting town. It does, however, have a **château** which dates from the 12th and 15th centuries and houses the town hall as well as the **Musée de la Dame aux Camélias** (Museum of the Lady with Camelias); *tel: 33 35 50 24*, open Tues–Sun 1400–1745 (July–Aug), or by arrangement, admission Fr.15 adults, Fr.8 children. This museum celebrates the life of Alphonsine Plessis, a well-known 19th-century courtesan who was born at nearby Nonant-le-Pin and went on to the high life of Paris. She was the subject of Alexandre Dumas' *La Dame aux Camélias* and Verdi's opera *La Traviata* as well as numerous films, plays and ballets.

SIDE TRACK FROM GACÉ

HARAS DU PIN

Leave Gacé in a southerly direction on the N138 towards Sées and after about 1 km bear right on the D14. After about 10 km turn left at Exmes onto the D26, then at the junction with the N26 turn right. Shortly after, on the left of a bend, is the **Haras National du Pin** (National Stud); *tel: 33 36 68 68*, open daily 0930–1800 (Apr–Sept); 1000–1200 and 1400–1700 (Oct–Mar), admission Fr.25 (Fr.15). Known as the 'Versailles of the Horse World', it was

163

founded in 1715 on the instigation of Jean Baptiste Colbert and is the most famous stud farm in France. Around 80 thoroughbreds are stabled there and a tour takes visitors through the stables and past displays of carriages and harnesses. Horse racing takes place in Sept and Oct. ▣

SÉES

For details see Caen–Tours route, p. 100.

ALENÇON

See p. 104.

TANCARVILLE

For details, see p. 168.

PONT-AUDEMER

Tourist Office: *pl. Maubert, 27500 Pont-Audemer; tel: 32 41 08 21.*

ACCOMMODATION

If money is no object, the place to stay is the **Hôtel Belle-Isle-sur-Risle**, *122 rte de Rouen; tel: 32 56 96 22*, which offers four-star comfort and a gourmet restaurant on an island in the River Risle. Among its luxuries are a heated swimming pool, a sauna and solarium, tennis courts and a gym. Very expensive.

Popular with the British is the two-star **Auberge du Vieux Puits**, *6 r. Notre-Dame du Pré; tel: 32 41 01 48*, a picturesque 17th-century inn with 12 moderately priced rooms and an intimate dining room, but also some noise from the ring road. A one-star *LF*, the **Hôtel du Pilori**, *38 pl. Victor Hugo; tel: 32 41 01 80*, is surprisingly economical, as is its restaurant, but even more so is the riverside **Hôtel de l'Agriculture**, *84 av. de la République; tel: 32 41 01 23.*

There is a small lakeside campsite north of the town, the one-star **Camping des**

Carmes, *21 rte de Quillebeuf; tel: 32 41 17 36.*

SIGHTSEEING

Rather industrial on its outskirts, Pont-Audemer's centre still has many remnants of its past. Formerly a tanners' town, it lies largely between the River Risle and Lower Risle which are connected by small canals, giving it the nickname of 'Normandy's Little Venice'. Overhanging these waterways, which are interlinked by delightful narrow lanes, alleyways and tiny bridges, are tall timber-framed houses where the tanners used to live and work. Standing at the centre is the **Église St-Ouen**, *r. de la République*, which has parts dating from the 11th–16th centuries. It includes some magnificent Renaissance stained glass windows. The street outside is the venue for two colourful weekly markets, a general one (Mon) and a garden produce market (Fri).

A short walk from the church, the **Musée Canel**, *r. de la République; tel: 32 41 08 15* , has varied displays, but most notable are a collection of 10,000 beetles, and paintings of the late 19th and early 20th centuries.

BERNAY

Tourist Office: *29 r. Thiers, 27300 Bernay; tel: 32 43 32 08.*

ACCOMMODATION

There are a couple of reasonable hotels in the centre, the **Hôtel Lion d'Or**, *48 r. du Gén. de Gaulle; tel: 32 43 12 06*, a two-star logis with moderately priced rooms and menus, and the one-star **Hôtel Angleterre et du Cheval Blanc**, *10 r. du Gén. de Gaulle; tel: 32 43 12 59*. Again, prices are moderate.

The three-star **Camping Municipal**, *r. des Canadiens; tel: 32 43 30 47*, is located off the N138 2 km south-west of the town. Open May–Sept.

Bernay is an ancient town which grew up around its abbey in the 11th century. Some of its streets are lined with half-timbered houses, most notably along *r. Gaston Folloppe* (famous for its antique shops), *r. de Geôle* and *r. Auguste Leprevost*. Its most notable sight is the former **Église Abbatiale** (Abbey Church), *pl. Héon*, open Mon, Wed–Sat 1000–1200 and 1400–1900, Sun 1500–1730 (July–Aug); Mon, Wed–Sat 1000–1200 and 1400–1730, Sun 1500–1730 (Sept–June), which has splendid façades and arcades.

Next to it, the **Hôtel de Ville** (Town Hall) is housed in the 17th-century buildings of the former abbey. Also here is the **Musée Municipal**, *pl. de la République; tel: 32 46 63 23*, open Mon, Wed–Sat 1000–1200 and 1400–1900, Sun 1500–1730 (July–Aug); Mon, Wed–Sat 1000–1200 and 1400–1730, Sun 1500–1730 (Sept–June), formerly the abbot's residence, which has an extensive ceramics collection, 17th and 18th-century furniture and paintings of the French, Italian, Dutch and Flemish schools.

A smaller museum, the **Musée Charette**, *15 r. Gaston Folloppe; tel: 32 43 05 47*, open Mon–Sat 1000–1200 and 1400–1900 (all year), has items and documents relevant to 19th-century Normandy life.

Also worth visiting is the 14th-century **Église Ste-Croix**, *r. Thiers*, which contains works of art from the abbey at Bec-Hellouin. Opposite, there is an attractive **covered market**.

L'AIGLE

Tourist Office: *pl. Fulbert de Beina, 61300 L'Aigle; tel: 33 24 12 40.*

The hotel to stay at in L'Aigle is the three-star **Hôtel du Dauphin**, *4-6 pl. de la Halle; tel: 33 84 18 00*, where the rooms are expensive and so too are the meals, though the latter are well worth it. A more moderate alternative is the **Hôtel Artus**, *7 r. Louis Pasteur; tel: 33 24 52 01.*

The **Camping Municipal**, *r. Louis-Pasteur; tel: 33 24 32 79*, offers two-star camping and caravanning from May–Sept.

Although badly bombed in 1944, L'Aigle has a number of sights to attract visitors, not least of which is the market held every Tues morning. The largest in Normandy (and the third largest in France), it spreads through the streets linking the huge *pl. Boislandry*, the *pl. St-Martin* and the *pl. de la Halle*. Overlooking part of the market, the **Hôtel de Ville** (Town Hall), *pl. Fulbert de Beina*, was originally a château when built in 1690. Now, it and its outbuildings house several museums. The **Musée Juin 44** (June 1944 Museum); *tel: 33 24 19 44*, open daily 0900–1200 and 1400–1800 (Apr–Oct); 1000–1200 and 1400–1800 (Nov–Mar), admission Fr.20 (Fr.15) has a dozen scenes illustrating events during the Battle of Normandy with wax figures and authentic recorded voices of some of the main allied leaders. The **Musée des Instruments de Musique** (Museum of Musical Instruments); *tel: 33 24 44 99*, open Mon–Fri 0900–1130 and 1430–1700 (all year), admission free, has an interesting display of musical instruments from around the world, from the 16th century to the present day. The **Musée d'Archéologie** (Museum of Archeology); *tel: 33 24 12 40*, open Tues–Sat 1000–1130 and 1400–1730 (Mar–Oct), admission free, has prehistoric curiosities from the region.

The **Musée Les Bois Sculptés de Louis Verrières** (Louis Verrières Museum of Wooden Sculptures); *tel: 33 24 12 40*, which has a collection of miniature wooden models of religious monuments, is temporarily closed and due to re-open in 1996.

MORTAGNE-AU-PERCHE

Tourist Office: *pl. Gén. de Gaulle, 61400 Mortange-au-Perche; tel: 33 85 11 18.*

ACCOMMODATION

Considering it is the largest town in Normandy's Perche region, Mortagne has few hotels. The best of them, the **Hôtel du Tribunal**, *4 pl. du Palais; tel: 33 25 04 77*, a *LF* in a quiet part of town, has rooms at moderate prices. Rather cheaper is the **Hôtel du Grand Cerf**, *29 r. Ste-Croix; tel: 33 25 04 88*, while also worth investigating is the **Hostellerie Genty Home**, *4 r. Notre-Dame; tel: 33 25 11 53*, a restaurant offering four plush, moderately priced rooms. The **Camping Municipal**, *23 r. Ferdinand-de-Boyères; tel: 33 25 04 35*, has just 30 pitches and is open Apr–Aug.

SIGHTSEEING

A medieval hilltop town, now with little evidence of its ramparts, Mortagne is known for Percherons, the massive horses originally bred to carry knights in armour. More prosaically it is also famous of is *boudin noir* black pudding. A statue of a Percheron stands in the **Jardin Public** (public gardens), *r. Montacune*, carrying Cupid on its back who in turn carries Neptune's trident and the goddess Ceres. Black pudding fanciers head for the town in March when its international festival enables black pudding producers from around Europe to demonstrate their skills. The only sizable part of the town defences remaining is the **Porte St-Denis** (St

Denis Gate), while the nearby **Maison des Comtes du Perche**, *8 r. du Portail St-Denis; tel: 33 25 25 87*, a 17th-century mansion, houses two museums, the **Musée Percheron**, open Tues–Sun 1500–1800 (July–Aug), admission free, good for local history, and the **Musée Alain**, open Tues–Sat 1500–1800 (all year), admission free, named after the philosopher born in the town and containing a display of his belongings. The **Église Notre-Dame**, *r. Notre-Dame*, built in the early 16th century, has an interesting stained-glass window in one of the side chapels recalling the many citizens from Mortagne and the Perche region who emigrated to Canada in the 17th century.

BELLÊME

Tourist Office: *blvd Bansard-des-Bois, 61130, Bellême; tel: 33 73 09 69.*

ACCOMMODATION

Best choice in the town itself is the **Hôtel Le Relais St-Louis**, *1 blvd Bansard-des-Bois; tel: 33 73 12 21*, a moderately-priced one-star *LF* with an attractive restaurant. Below the town and adjoining its golf course, the also moderately-priced **Hôtel Domaine du Golfe**; *tel: 33 73 00 07*, bears three stars and has a large and excellent restaurant.

Bellême has one campsite, the two-star **Camping Municipal**, *rte de Mamers; tel: 33 73 02 21*, which is open Apr–Oct.

SIGHTSEEING

Though Mortagne is larger, it is Bellême that is considered the main town of Normandy's Perche region. It, too, stands atop a hill, overlooking the Bellême Forest, and like its neighbour has little left of its medieval walls. There is a gateway, however, comprising two rebuilt towers complete with portcullis grooves.

LE HAVRE–ROUEN

The route south of the Seine is the quick way to Rouen, the route north is the more leisurely one. It takes in a number of historic abbeys, the most famous of which is the ruined Jumièges.

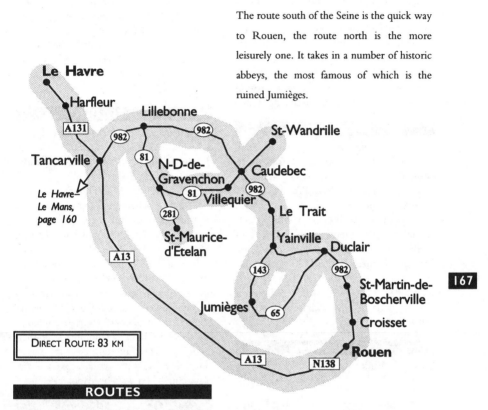

Le Havre
Harfleur
Lillebonne
St-Wandrille
A131
982
982
Tancarville
982
81
N-D-de-Gravenchon
Caudebec
Le Havre–Le Mans, page 160
81
281
Villequier
982
Le Trait
St-Maurice-d'Etelan
Yainville
Duclair
A13
143
982
St-Martin-de-Boscherville
Jumièges
65
Croisset
DIRECT ROUTE: 83 KM
Rouen
A13
N138

167

ROUTES

DIRECT ROUTE

→ The road out of Le Havre is well-signed via the *blvd de Léningrad* and beyond **Harfleur** leads to the A131 autoroute and the **Pont de Tancarville**, continuing south of the Seine to join the A13 autoroute near **Bourneville**. The route runs south of the **Forêt de Brotonne** and just beyond the ruined **Château de Robert-le-Diable** (Robert the Devil's Castle) exit 23 links with the N138 into Rouen. Distance is 83 km, journey time about an hour.

SCENIC ROUTE

⋯▶ The route north of the Seine follows the start of the direct route, but just before the **Pont de Tancarville** bear right onto the D982, passing under the bridge en route for **Lillebonne**. Just before **Lillebonne** you can bear left on the D982 into the town and continue to **Caudebec-en-Caux**, or bear right on the D81 to **Notre-Dame-de-Gravenchon** to join D281 to **St-Maurice-d'Etelan**. Beyond the village is the 15th-century

Château d'Etelan, which dominates the valley. At **Norville**, the route rejoins the D81 to Caudebec from where D982 goes through **Le Trait** to **Yainville** where you turn right onto D143 to **Jumièges**. Beyond the village, the D65 follows a loop of the Seine and rejoins D982 at **Duclair**. Stay on this road, passing through **St-Martin-de-Boscherville**, **Canteleu** and **Croisset** to Rouen. The route is around 104 km, drive time around 2hrs 30 mins.

TANCARVILLE

There is just one hotel at Tancarville, a *LF* at the foot of the bridge, the **Hôtel de la Marine**; *tel: 35 39 77 15*, which has comfortable rooms (moderate to expensive) looking out on the Seine.

Until the **Pont de Tancarville**, which dominates views hereabouts, was built in 1959, there was no bridge across the Seine between Rouen and Le Havre. Nearby are the ruins of the **château féodal** (feudal castle); *tel: 35 96 00 21*, admission FFr.10, parts of which date back to the 10th century.

LILLEBONNE

Tourist Office: *4 r. Pasteur; tel: 35 38 08 45.*

ACCOMMODATION

Lillebonne has a couple of hotels, the **Hôtel de France**, *1 bis r. République; tel: 35 38 04 88*, moderately priced, and the smaller **La P'tite Auberge**, *r. du Havre; tel: 35 38 00 59*. Both have restaurants.

SIGHTSEEING

Although Lillebonne is largely industrial, its history goes back to Roman times and from the *pl. de l'Hôtel-de-Ville* can be seen the layout of the 2nd- and 3rd-century, 10,000-seat **Amphithéâtre**; *tel: 35 71 78 78*, the largest Roman monument of its type north of the Loire. **Musée Jean-Rostand**, *Jardin Jean Rostand; tel: 35 38 53 73*, open Wed–Mon 1000–1200, 1430–1830 (May–Oct); Wed–Mon 1430–1830 (Nov–Apr), has exhibits relating to its Roman past and the more recent textile industry. The nearby ruined **château**, *r. Césarine*, is where William the Conqueror gathered his barons before setting out to invade England.

VILLEQUIER

The charming **Hôtel du Grand Sapin**, *12 r. Louis le Gaffric; tel: 35 56 78 73*, (moderate) has a terrace and balconies overlooking the Seine. .

Villequier is the first of the riverside villages to be reached on the north bank and occupies a beautiful setting beneath a wooded hill. The **Musée Victor Hugo**; *tel: 35 56 91 86*, open Wed–Mon 1000–1230, 1400–1830 (Apr–Oct); Wed–Mon 1000-1230, 1400–1800 (Nov–Mar), is in a house once owned by the Vacquerie family, whose son married Hugo's daughter Léopoldine. The couple were drowned in the Seine in 1843, six months after their wedding. The museum contains letters and drawings by the writer as well as displays connected with his daughter's life.

CAUDEBEC-EN-CAUX

Tourist Office: *pl. du Gén. de Gaulle, 76490 Caudebec-en-Caux; tel: 35 96 20 65.*

ACCOMMODATION

There are three *LF* in Caudebec, two overlooking the Seine. The **Hôtel Normotel-Marine**, *18 quai Guilbaud; tel: 35 96 20 11*, and the **Hôtel de Normandie**, *19 quai Guilbaud; tel: 35 96 25 11*, both two-star, look alike though the former has more expensive rooms. Restaurant and room prices are moderate. The one-star **Hôtel Cheval Blanc**, *4 pl.*

René Coty; tel: 35 96 21 66, lies back from the river and has cheaper rooms.

SIGHTSEEING

Because of a fire that swept through the town in 1940, Caudebec is mainly modern, only a handful of medieval houses and the **Église Notre-Dame**, *pl. du Marché*, once described as 'the most beautiful chapel in the kingdom', surviving. One of the old houses, the 13th-century **Maison des Templiers**, *r. Basin; tel: 35 96 00 21*, houses a local history museum, open daily 1000–1200, 1500–1800 (July–Aug); daily 1500–1800 (June and Sept), admission Fr.10. More interesting is the **Musée de la Marine de Seine** (Seine Maritime Museum), *av. Winston Churchill; tel: 35 96 27 30*, open daily 1400–1830 (July–Aug); Wed–Mon 1400–1830 (Sept–June), admission Fr.20, which has displays about life on the Seine.

ST-WANDRILLE

A turning to the left off the D982 just beyond the Pont de Brotonne leads to the village of St-Wandrille and its **abbaye** (abbey); *tel: 35 96 23 11*. Founded in 649, the original abbey was destroyed by Vikings, but was later rebuilt by Benedictine monks. The monks have come and gone over the years and most recently returned in 1931. Guided visits, Mon–Sat 1500 and 1600, Sun 1130, 1500 and 1600 (all year), admission Fr.15, are possible to parts of the partially ruined abbey, including the cloisters and the church. Gregorian chants can be heard, Sun 1000 and 1700, Mon–Sat 0925 and 1730 (Thur 1845).

JUMIÈGES

The **Auberge des Ruines**, *1 pl. de la Mairie; tel: 35 37 24 05*, has four economically priced rooms available for restaurant clients. There is a well-equipped three-star

campsite at the **Base de Plein Air et de Loisirs du Parc Regional de Brotonne**, on the D65 south of the village.

Considered the most evocative ruin in Normandy, the **Abbaye de Jumièges**; *tel: 35 37 24 02*, open Mon–Fri 1000–1200, 1400–1600, Sat–Sun 1000–1200, 1400–1700 (Nov–Mar); Mon–Fri 0900–1200, 1400–1700, Sat–Sun 0900–1830 (Apr–June, Sept–Oct); Mon–Fri 0900–1700, Sat–Sun 0900–1830 (June–Sept), admission Fr.26 adults (Fr.17 children), was built on the foundations of an earlier abbey destroyed by the Vikings. It was consecrated in 1067 at a ceremony attended by William the Conqueror and following the Revolution, was used as a quarry until saved for the nation.

ST-MARTIN-DE-BOSCHERVILLE

The Benedictine **abbey** at St-Martin-de-Boscherville was founded in 1144, but when the monks were driven out in the Revolution, its **Abbatiale Saint-Georges**; *tel: 35 32 10 82*, open Wed–Mon 0900–1900 (June–Sept); 0900–1200, 1400–1900 (Apr–June); 0900–1200, 1400–1700 (Oct–Mar), admission Fr.25 (Fr.20), became the parish church, thus saving it from the same fate as Jumièges. One of the finest churches in the Seine Valley, it stands in gardens currently undergoing restoration.

169

CROISSET

It was in Croisset that Gustave Flaubert wrote *Madame Bovary* and though his house no longer exists, the riverside pavilion in which he worked is now a small museum. The **Pavillon Flaubert**; *tel: 35 36 43 91*, open Thur–Mon 1000–1200, 1400–1800, Wed 1400–1800 (all year), admission Fr.5 (children free), contains furniture, personal curios and manuscripts.

LE MANS

Originally founded as Vindunum on the banks of the River Sarthe by the Romans in the 4th century, Le Mans still has one of the best surviving town walls from this period in western France. Yet, aside from its old quarter, it is an exciting and vibrant modern city, linked with the motor car since its invention more than a century ago, and host to one of the most famous motor races in the world, the Le Mans 24 Hours. Le Mans is the capital of the Sarthe *département*.

TOURIST INFORMATION

Tourist Office, *Hôtel des Ursulines, r. de l'Étoile, 72000 Le Mans; tel: 43 28 17 22*, open Mon–Fri 0900–1800, Sat 0900–1200 and 1400–1800, Sun 1000–1200, it has an extensive range of information covering Le Mans and the *département* of Sarthe. Hotel bookings can also be made.

ARRIVING AND DEPARTING

Le Mans lies immediately south-east of the junction between the A11 and A81 autoroutes linking Paris with Nantes and Rennes. Best exits for the centre are junctions 7 and 8 of the A11. Otherwise, Le Mans is at the crossroads of national routes, the N138 from Rouen to Tours, the N157 from Rennes to Orléans, and the N23 from Nantes to Chartres, as well as several departmental roads.

GETTING AROUND

Almost all of the city's sights are within walking distance of the tourist office, which has a number of excellent free maps to help you find your way around. The best of these is the *Plan Touristique*, which shows clearly on one side greater Le Mans and its main roads, and on the other side more detailed maps of the centre and **Le Vieux Mans** (old Le Mans). The map also shows the main sights, and indicates all car parks, stating whether they are free or if there is a charge. Basically, the closer the car parks are to the centre, the more expensive they are (around Fr.6 per hour). Another useful map comes with the Tourist Office's hotel and restaurant guide.

Buses

The city's bus service is operated by **Setram**, *av. de Gaulle; tel: 43 24 36 36*, while the bus terminal is located in the **Centre Commercial République** underground shopping centre beneath *pl. de la République*. Tickets can be purchased on board buses, at the Setram agency at the bus terminal, open Mon–Fri 0700–1900, Sat 0830–1830, or at one of 80 shops in the city designated **Pointbus** centres.

Taxis

Taxis are operated by **Le Mans Radio Taxi**, *2 av. du Gén. Leclerc; tel: 43 24 92 92*.

STAYING IN LE MANS

Accommodation

The choice of hotels in and around Le Mans is excellent. They are mainly two-star, but there is a handful of three-star hotels and several that bear one star or are

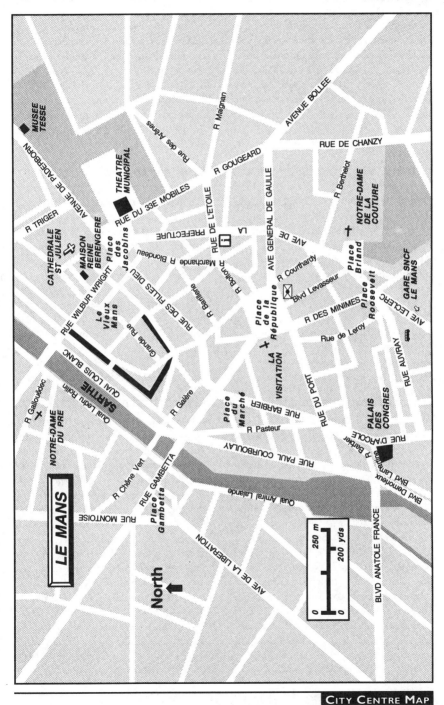

LE MANS

North

MUSEE TESSE

AVENUE DE PADERBORN

THEATRE MUNICIPAL

Rue des Arènes

R Maignan

AVENUE BOLLEE

RUE DE CHANZY

R GOUGEARD

R TRIGER

RUE DU 33E MOBILES

RUE DE L'ETOILE

R Berthelot

NOTRE-DAME DE LA COUTURE

CATHEDRALE ST JULIEN

MAISON REINE BERENGERE

Place des Jacobins

PREFECTURE

RUE DE

AVE GENERAL DE GAULLE

AVE DE

R Courthardy

Place Briand

GARE SNCF LE MANS

RUE WILBUR WRIGHT

Le Vieux Mans

Grande Rue

R Bollon

R Marchande R Blondeau

R Bellière

RUE DES FILLES DIEU

Blvd Levasseur

R DES MINIMES

Place Roosevelt

AVE LECLERC

RUE AUVRAY

Place de la République

Rue de Leroy

R Galère

LA VISITATION

Place du Marché

R Pasteur

RUE BARBIER

RUE DU PORT

PALAIS DES CONGRES

RUE D'AROULE

R Galouédec

QUAI LOUIS BLANC

Quai Lédru Rollin

NOTRE-DAME DU PRE

SARTHE

R Chêne Vert

RUE MONTOISE

Place Gambetta

RUE GAMBETTA

R Barbier

Blvd Lamartine

Blvd Demoreaux

RUE PAUL COURBOULAY

Quai Amiral Lalande

AVE DE LA LIBERATION

BLVD ANATOLE FRANCE

250 m

200 yds

0

0

171

unclassified. Rooms are difficult to find when major motor sporting events take place in April, Sept and especially mid-June during the **24 Heures du Mans** (Le Mans 24-hour sports car race). If you intend going to any of these races, you should book your accommodation well in advance.

Hotel chains in Le Mans include *Ca, Cn, Ct, F1, Ib, Nv.*

Two of the three-star hotels are close to the railway station. The 59-room **Hôtel Concorde**, *16 av. de Gén. Leclerc; tel: 43 24 12 30*, has its own parking, but is expensive, while the smaller (35 rooms) **Hôtel Chantecler**, *50 r. de la Pelouse; tel: 43 24 58 53*, also with its own parking, falls into the moderate to expensive category. Another three-star hotel, a modern one out of town, is the **Hôtel Closerie**, *Route de Laval; tel: 43 28 69 92*, which again is moderate to expensive, but has a swimming pool. All three have their own restaurants. A good two-star hotel is the **Hôtel Ibis Centre**, *quai Ledru-Rollin; tel: 43 23 18 23*, which is on the south bank of the river Sarthe, opposite the old town. Another, the **Central Hôtel**, *5–7 blvd René Levasseur; tel: 43 24 08 93*, is in the city centre, just off the *pl. de la République*. Both are moderately priced. Several cheaper hotels are located opposite the station, among them the **Hôtel d'Anjou**, *27 blvd de la Gare; tel: 43 24 90 45*, the **Hôtel Galaxie**, *39 blvd de la Gare; tel: 43 24 99 50*, the **Hôtel Commerce**, *41 blvd de la Gare; tel: 43 24 85 40*, and the **Hôtel Rennes**, *43 blvd de la Gare; tel: 43 24 86 40*. These are all a little distant from the centre and the old town (bus nos 3, 5 and 16 run from the station to *pl. de la République*) and a better placed economically priced hotel is the **Hôtel Select**, *13 r. du Père-Mersenne; tel: 43 24 17 74*.

HI: *23 r. Maupertuis; tel: 43 81 27 55.*

There are **no campsites** in Le Mans itself but two within a reasonable distance are **Camping Le Vieux Moulin**, *Neuville-sur-Sarthe; tel: 43 25 31 82*, a three-star riverside site a short distance from N138 9 km north of the city, and **Camping La Chataigneraie**, *Yvre l'Eveque; tel: 43 89 60 68*, a one-star site near the N23, 7 km east.

Eating and Drinking

Le Mans has a wide choice of restaurants, with mainly French-style traditional cooking available. Foreign speciality cooking is quite rare and even pizzerias few and far between. *Rillettes*, potted minced pork, is produced throughout France, but Le Mans has made it a speciality by adding goose and sometimes rabbit. Like tripe, it is an acquired taste but the best is bought from charcuteries that make their own. The wines of the region are Jasnières, reputed to be one of the best dry white wines in France, and Coteaux du Loir, which is produced in red, white and rosé varieties.

If you are seeking relatively cheap meals, the *pl. de la République* is the place to head. There are several brasseries to choose from as well as **McDonald's** and **Quick** burger bars. One of the more expensive restaurants is the nearby **Le Grenier à Sel**, *26 pl. de l'Eperon; tel: 43 23 26 30*, where menus start at Fr.120, while one of the cheapest is **La Brise**, *10 pl. de l'Eperon; tel: 43 28 20 52*. The best selection of restaurants, however, is in the old town, where quite literally, you are spoilt for choice. Most restaurants here start at moderate prices. Among those to choose from are **La Vie en Rose**, *55 Grande-Rue; tel: 43 23 27 37*, **La Tarantelle**, *Grande-Rue; tel: 43 87 06 27*, a pizzeria, **Le Belliny**, *Grande-Rue; tel: 43 24 65 60*, which has duck as a speciality, **Au P'ti Montmartre**, *9 r. des Trois*

Sonnettes; tel: 43 87 03 63, a popular spot, and a number of restaurants in *pl. St-Pierre*, all with outside terraces.

Communications

The **main post office** is located on the *pl. de la République*, open Mon–Fri 0800–1900, Sat 0800–1200. Another is in the *blvd de la Gare* next to the railway station (same opening hours).

Money

Major banks, including **Crédit Agricole**, **BNP** and **Crédit Lyonnais** have branches on the *pl. de la République* and most have cash dispensing facilities outside normal opening hours. Crédit Agricole also have cash dispensers in *r. Marchande*, just around the corner from the Tourist Office, and at the railway station.

ENTERTAINMENT

A useful little booklet available free from the Tourist Office is the French language *Le Mans Actualités* which lists three months' events at a time.

The most important sporting event of the year is the **24 Heures du Mans** (see p. 263), the world famous sports car race which was inaugurated in 1923. It takes place over a weekend in mid-June using a 13.6 km circuit located 5 km to the south of the city, part purpose-built but mostly using public roads, with speeds of over 300 kph being attained. Tickets for the general enclosures are not cheap, currently Fr.310; stands are extra, ranging from Fr.170 to Fr.470. Unreserved parking is Fr.90, while camping is possible for Fr.300 per pitch. All tickets are available from **Circuit des 24 Heures**, *Les Raineries, 72100 Le Mans; tel: 43 40 24 24*, or from the Tourist Office. Other motor sporting events are held on the shorter **Circuit Bugatti**, which is part of the main circuit, and

include a 24-hour motorcycle race in mid-April, the French motorcycle Grand Prix in mid-July, a 24-hr karting race in early Sept and a 24-hr truck race in early Oct.

Horse-racing takes place at **Les Hunaudières Racecourse** next to the motor racing circuit. Soccer fans are entertained by second division French league matches taking place at the **Stade Léon-Bollée**, *r. Claircigny; tel: 43 24 52 62*.

The main theatres are the **Palais de Congrès et de la Culture**, *r. d'Arcole; tel: 43 24 22 44*, and the **Théâtre Municipal**, *pl. des Jacobins; tel: 43 81 45 00*, which both have extensive programmes of music, dance, opera and plays.

There are four cinemas, all centrally positioned: **Les Ambassades**, *pl. des Comtes-du-Maine; tel: 43 24 83 46*, which has four screens; **Le Ciné-Poche**, *Centre Jacques-Prévert, 97 Grande-Rue; tel: 43 24 73 85*, one screen; **Le Français**, *26 r. Gambetta; tel: 43 28 29 87*, five screens; and **Le Colisée**, *r. du Port; tel: 43 28 90 90*, seven screens.

Several bars offer musical entertainment, among them **Le Stan**, *2 pl. de l'Eperon; tel: 43 28 31 34*, **Le Stendhal**, *46 r. des Ponts Neufs; tel: 43 24 89 56*, and its neighbour **Sunset-Boulevard**, *44 r. des Ponts Neufs; tel: 43 24 23 66*, all of which have jazz, and **Le Bacula**, *33 r. Jankowsky; tel 43 24 98 26*, **Le Caveau**, *32 r. du Dr Leroy; tel: 43 28 80 50*, and **Le Kentucky**, *7 pl. de l'Eperon; tel 43 77 17 93*, where rock dominates. For discotheques try **Ampelopsis**, *35 r. d'Orléans; tel: 43 24 21 45*, **La Limite**, *7 pl. St-Honoré; tel: 43 24 85 54*, and **Le Remyxon**, *26 r. du Port; tel: 43 23 20 02*.

Events

One of the most colourful festivals each year is **Les Cénomanies**, a 17th-century street spectacular of dance, music and

173

theatre taking place over the first weekend in July in *Le Vieux-Mans*. Tickets for the event available from the Tourist Office.

Very popular is the **Europa Jazz Festival**, held every year in the last two weeks of April, with participating bands from across Europe. The venues are the Palais de Congrès et de la Culture (for details see p. 173) and the 13th-century **Abbaye de l'Epau**, four km east of Le Mans.

SHOPPING

The main shopping area is centred on the *pl. de la République*, with some shops beneath the square in the **Centre Commercial République**. Several of the surrounding streets are pedestrianised. The **Centre Jacobins**, opposite the Tourist Office, contains large stores like **C&A** and **fnac**, while **Galeries Lafayette** is located at *r. des Minimes*.

A daily market is held at the covered halls of the *pl. du Marché*, and an open market is held Wed, Fri and Sun mornings at the foot of the cathedral in *pl. du Jet d'Eau*. There are also several hypermarkets, including **Carrefour**, *av. Georges Durand*, on the N138 road south to Tours.

SIGHTSEEING

Cruises on the River Sarthe are possible on the *Le Mans* excursion boat which moors at the port; *tel: 43 23 83 84*. Options range from a tourist trip of 1hr 30 min to all-day cruises and candle-lit dinner cruises in the evening.

Le Vieux Mans (Old Le Mans), overlooking the River Sarthe, is one of the most delightful old quarters of any city in France. Its narrow streets, lined with medieval carved and decorated timber-framed houses and Renaissance mansions, are enclosed within 3rd-century Gallo-Roman **walls**, 1300 m long, reputed to be

the best-preserved anywhere in Europe. The best way to soak in the atmosphere of the place is to use a map and wander the warren of streets off **Grande-Rue**. At several points, such as the staircase from *r. de Vaux* down to the River Sarthe, you can climb down through the walls to get a better view of them from the other side.

Look out for the **Maison du Pilier Rouge** (Red Pillar House), *r. Maison du Pilier Rouge*, a timber-framed house, used as an occasional exhibition centre, whose once brightly painted pillar has now rather faded, the **Maison d'Adam et Eve** (Adam and Eve's House), *Grande-Rue*, a superb Renaissance house and, from the same period the **Hôtel de Vaux**, *r. de Vaux*, a building set around a courtyard. The 15th-century **Maison de la Reine Bérengère** (Queen Berengaria's House), *13 r. de la Reine Bérengère*, open daily 0900–1200 and 1400–1800, admission Fr.14 (Fr.7 children), is named after Richard the Lionheart's wife – though it was actually built 200 years after her lifetime – and is now a regional history and art museum with displays of Le Mans folklore and ceramics.

Several attractive buildings grouped around *pl. St-Michel* include the much-photographed **Maison de la Tourelle**, with its Renaissance turret. Next to this is the **Grabatoire**, a rather sober example of Renaissance architecture now serving as the bishop's palace, while beyond that is the **Maison de Pèlerin** (Pilgrim's House), which is decorated with shells, the symbol of pilgrims on their way to the shrine of St Jacques at Santiago de Compostela in north-west Spain.

Occupying the north-east corner of the old town, and overlooking *pl. de Jet d'Eau* and *pl. des Jacobins,* is the **Cathédrale St-Julien**, open daily 0800–1200 and 1400–1900, which features a lofty Gothic chancel – almost as high as the Notre-Dame's in Paris – with some superb 13th-century stained glass windows, and a Romanesque nave. A *menhir* (standing stone) stands at one corner of the cathedral. A guided tour of the old town and cathedral starts at the Tourist Office, daily 1500 (July–Aug).

Other churches in Le Mans include **Notre-Dame de la Couture** (Our Lady of Culture), *pl. Aristide Briand*, which has a 13th-century façade and Plantagenet vaulting; the **Chapelle de la Visitation** (Church of the Visitation), *pl. de la République*, built in the baroque style; **Église Ste-Jeanne d'Arc** (Church of St Joan of Arc), *pl. Washington*, originally the Maison-Dieu de Coëffort, a hospital founded in the late 12th century by Henry II of England in penance for the murder of Thomas à Becket at Canterbury, which has elegant vaulting supported by thin columns; and the **Notre-Dame du Pré** (Our Lady of the Fields), *pl. du Pré*, which was part of a Benedictine convent.

Standing in a corner of *pl. des Jacobins* at the entrance to *r. Wilbur Wright*, the tunnel that passes under the old town, is a statue to Wilbur Wright, the American aviator who made one of his first flights in an aeroplane from the racecourse at Les Hunaudières in 1908. He was in the air for more than 1 hr 30 mins.

Not far from the cathedral, through a park off *pl. des Jacobins,* is the **Musée de Tessé**, *2 av. de Paderborn,* open daily 0900-1200 and 1400–1800, admission Fr.14, in the 19th-century former bishop's palace. The museum contains paintings from the 15th to 19th centuries, sculptures, furniture and an archaeological collection, including Egyptian artefacts as well as a piece of 12th-century enamel representing Geoffroi Plantagenet, father of Henry II, who was originally buried in the cathedral.

Beyond the museum's gardens is the **Jardin d'Horticulture**, said to be one of the best garden parks in France. Designed in 1851, it features a lake and cascading streams, a magnificent rose garden and a rockery.

The **Collégiale St-Pierre-la-Cour** (Collegiate Church of St Peter), *r. des Fossés St-Pierre; tel: 43 47 36 18,* a former 14th-century church, is now a venue for temporary exhibitions, open during exhibitions 0900–1200 and 1400–1800, admission free.

The **Musée Vert** (Green Museum), *235 av. Jean Jaurès,* open Mon–Fri 0900–1200, 1400–1800, Sat–Sun 1400–1800, is a museum of natural history housed in a 19th-century school and contains a collection of more than 160,000 geological, zoological and botanical specimens. It is planned to create an arboretum in the courtyard behind the museum.

While wandering around the pedestrianised shopping area around *pl. St-Nicolas,* watch out for a series of bronze plaques laid into the paving depicting hand and foot imprints of famous drivers who have won the 24-hr motor race, among them Derek Bell, Jacky Ickx, Henri Pescarolo and Jean-Pierre Jaussaud.

Not surprisingly for a city where car manufacturing began in 1873 and whose modern appeal is based on motor sport, Le Mans has a motor museum, the **Musée Automobile de la Sarthe** (Sarthe Motor Museum), *Circuit des 24 Heures du Mans; tel: 43 72 72 24,* open daily 1000–1900 (June–Sept); Wed–Mon 1000–1800 (Oct–Dec and Feb–May); Sat–Sun 1000–1800 (Jan–Feb), admission Fr.35 (Fr.26). The museum includes a large collection of road cars and famous sports cars that have raced on the neighbouring circuit, as well as hands-on displays describing motoring technology.

175

LE MANS–PARIS

This is a route crammed with culture, starting with the magnificent cathedrals of Le Mans and Chartres and taking in a series of grand châteaux, including Maintenon, Rambouillet, Dampierre and Versailles. The countryside varies from the undulating hills of the Perche around Nogent-le-Rotrou to the wheat plains around Chartres.

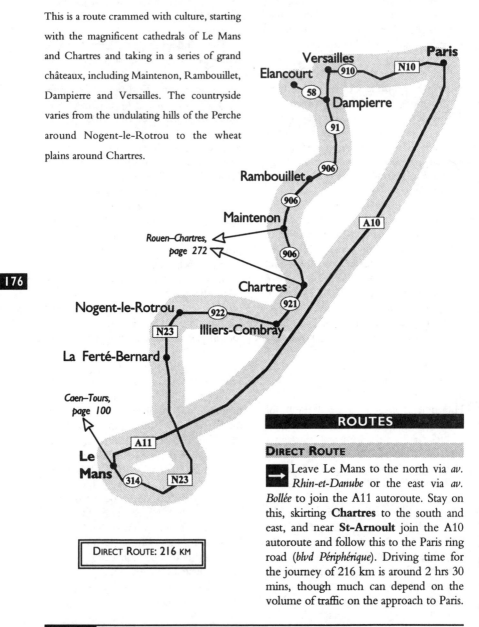

Rouen–Chartres, page 272

Caen–Tours, page 100

176

DIRECT ROUTE: 216 KM

ROUTES

DIRECT ROUTE

Leave Le Mans to the north via *av. Rhin-et-Danube* or the east via *av. Bollée* to join the A11 autoroute. Stay on this, skirting **Chartres** to the south and east, and near **St-Arnoult** join the A10 autoroute and follow this to the Paris ring road (*blvd Périphérique*). Driving time for the journey of 216 km is around 2 hrs 30 mins, though much can depend on the volume of traffic on the approach to Paris.

SCENIC ROUTE

▸ Take the *av. Bollée* out of Le Mans, joining first the D314 and then the N23 to **Connerré**, **La Ferté-Bernard** and **Nogent-le-Rotrou**. From there, take the D922 via **Thiron-Gardais** (where there is a large abbey-church) to **Illiers-Combray** and then join the D921 to **Chartres**. Leave the cathedral town by the *r. St-Maurice*, turning right onto the D906 to **Maintenon** and **Rambouillet** and continuing almost to **Cernay-la-Ville** before turning left on the D91 to **Dampierre** and **Versailles**. Depart Versailles by the *av. de Paris* (D10) to join the D910, then N10 to the *blvd Périphérique*. Distance is around 216 km, journey time about 3 hrs 30 mins.

LA FERTÉ-BERNARD

Tourist Office: *15 pl. de la Lice, 72400 La Ferté-Bernard; tel: 43 71 21 21.*

ACCOMMODATION

There are two large hotels at La Ferté-Bernard, both of them moderately priced, the **Hôtel Climat**, *43 av. du Gén. de Gaulle; tel: 43 93 84 70*, and the **Hôtel Gril Campanile**, *espace du Lac; tel: 43 71 15 05*, which is located at a leisure activity lake south of the town. Both have restaurants, as do the two *LF* in the town, the **Hôtel de la Perdrix**, *2 r. de Paris; tel: 43 93 00 44*, and the **Hôtel du Stade**, *21-23 r. Virette; tel: 43 93 01 67*. Again, both are moderately priced, though the Perdrix is the more expensive of the two. Its restaurant is particularly good.

    Camping Le Valmer, *espace du Lac; tel: 43 71 70 03*, is a three-star municipal campsite by the lake. Open Apr–Sept.

SIGHTSEEING

This medieval town was built on stilts in the middle of a marsh and with numerous canals and rivers passing through it has become known as 'the Venice of the west'. Guided tours through the town's 15th- and 16th-century streets are available (enquiries to the Tourist Office) and these take in the magnificent 15th- and 16th-century **Église Notre-Dame-des-Marais** (Church of our Lady of the Marshes), *pl. de la République*, and its treasury, the 15th-century **Porte St-Julien** (St Julian's Gate) at the entrance to *r. d'Huisne;* the **Halles** (covered market); *pl. de la Lice*, with its particularly impressive framework supporting the tiled dormer roof; a 15th–16th-century granite fountain between the market and the church; and the 14th-century **Chapelle St-Lyphard**. Motor boat trips are also available on the town's canals between May and Sept. Again, enquiries to the Tourist Office.

    Just south of the town is the lakeside **Municipal Leisure Activity Centre**; *tel: 43 71 04 41*, where there is a beach (supervised bathing July–Aug). Sailboards, catamarans, canoes and kayaks can be hired, mountain bike rental is also available and there are family picnic areas with barbecues.

177

NOGENT-LE-ROTROU

Tourist Office: *44 r. Villette-Gaté, 28400 Nogent-le-Rotrou; tel: 37 52 22 16.*

ACCOMMODATION

There is a good *LF* in Nogent, the two-star **Hôtel du Lion d'Or**, *28 pl. St-Pol; tel: 37 52 01 60*, which has moderately priced rooms and an excellent restaurant. A much larger alternative is the three-star **Hôtel Le Relais de Sully**, *12 r. des Niennes; tel: 37 52 85 00* (expensive), but more moderate is the **Hôtel L'Eldorado**, *2 pl. du 11 Août; tel: 37 52 01 78*. For economy rooms try the one-star **Hôtel La Gare**, *6 pl. de la Gare; tel: 37 52 39 96*.

Camping des Viennes, *r. des Viennes; tel: 37 52 80 51*, is a small two-star municipal campsite beside the river just north of the town. Open May–Sept.

SIGHTSEEING

A quite large town, Nogent lies on the River Huisne and is capital of the Perche region. Originally a Gallo-Roman town, it was rebuilt after the Hundred Years' War and parts of the old town, particularly the *r. Bourg-le-Comte* and the *r. St-Laurent*, display some Renaissance influence. Dominating the town is the **Château St-Jean**, *r. du Château St-Jean; tel: 37 52 18 02*, open Wed–Mon 1000–1200, 1400–1800 (May–Oct); 1000–1200, 1400–1700 (Nov–Apr), admission Fr.13 adults (Fr.7.50 children), the construction of which began in the 11th century. The circular enclosure and the seven defensive towers were built at the beginning of the 13th century. From 1624 until the Revolution it was owned by the Sully family, who built the attractive Louis Xlll pavilion. The château has been completely renovated over the last 30 years and now houses the **Musée Municipal** (Municipal Museum), which contains exhibits about country life in the Perche region as well as the history of the town. It also holds occasional temporary exhibitions. Sully, who was the Minister of France under Henri IV, is buried in a small mausoleum at the **Hôtel-Dieu**, *3 r. Gouverneur*. There are three churches worth visiting, the much restored 14th-century **Église Notre-Dame**, *r. Gouverneur*, the 15th-century **Église St-Laurent**, *pl. St-Laurent*, and the **Église St-Hilaire**, a 13th–16th-century church on the banks of the Huisne.

ILLIERS-COMBRAY

Tourist Information: Syndicat d'Initiative, *5 r. H. Germond; tel: 37 24 21 79*.

ACCOMMODATION

A three-star campsite, **Camping de Montjouvin**, *rte de Brou; tel: 37 24 03 04*, is located beside the River Thironne on the D921 south-west of the town.

SIGHTSEEING

This small market town is best known for its associations with the writer Marcel Proust, who, between the ages of six and nine, stayed with his aunt during school holidays. The **Maison de Tante Léonie** (Aunt Léonie's House) now houses the **Musée Marcel Proust**, *4 r. du Docteur Proust; tel: 37 24 30 97*, open for guided visits Tues–Sun at 1130 (in English), 1430, 1530, 1630 (July–Aug); 1430 and 1600 (Sept–June), admission Fr.25 adults, free children, which, as well as rooms with their original furnishings, contains portraits, documents and family mementoes. The house was immortalised, along with the town (which he called Combray), in his novel *A la Recherche du Temps Perdu*. Just south of the town on the D149, a landscaped garden, the **Pré Catelan**, also appears in the book as *Parc de Tansonville*.

CHARTRES

See the Chartres chapter, pp. 121–126.

MAINTENON

Tourist Information: Syndicat d'Initiative, *pl. Aristide Briand, ; tel: 37 23 05 04*.

ACCOMMODATION

Maintenon has a one-star *LF*, the **Hôtel St-Denis**, *5 pl. Aristide Briand; tel: 37 23 00 76*, which has moderate to expensive rooms and a rather pricey restaurant.

There are a couple of campsites to choose from, **Camping Municipal**, *rte de Bouglainval; tel: 37 23 09 11*, which is open all year, and **Camping Les Ilots de**

St-Val, *rte de Néron; tel: 37 82 71 30*, a quite large site 4.5 km north-west of the town. Open Feb–Nov.

SIGHTSEEING

A delightful town straddling the River Eure, Maintenon is best known for its **château**; *tel: 37 23 00 09*, open Mon, Wed–Fri 1400–1800, Sat–Sun 1000–1200 and 1400–1800 (Apr–Oct); Sat–Sun 1400–1700 (Nov, Feb–Mar), admission Fr.30 (Fr.17). Originally dating from the 11th century, the château was enlarged in Renaissance style in the early 16th century and then in the latter part of the 17th century it was purchased by the widowed Françoise Scarron. She farther enlarged and embellished the château and its park before secretly marrying Louis XIV in 1684. An aqueduct built in the grounds by Vauban was designed to carry water from the Eure to feed the fountains of Versailles but was never completed.

RAMBOUILLET

Tourist Office: *Hôtel de Ville, pl. de la Libération, 78120 Rambouillet; tel: 34 83 21 21.*

ACCOMMODATION

Rambouillet has several modern hotels located on or close to the N10, including the **Hôtel Climat de France**, *La Louvière; tel: 34 85 62 62*, the **Hôtel Ibis**; *tel: 30 41 78 50*, the **Resthotel Primevere**, *r. Jacquard; tel: 34 85 51 02*. All are rated two-star, have moderately priced rooms and restaurants. Also moderately priced but nearer the château is the **Hôtel de la Gare**, *17 r. Sadi Carnot; tel: 34 83 03 04*, a one-star *logis* with a restaurant offering attractively priced menus.

Camping L'Etang d'Or; *tel: 30 41 07 34*, is an attractive two-star municipal campsite, just off the N10 3 km south of the town and located near a lake in the **Forêt de Rambouillet**. Open all year.

SIGHTSEEING

Rambouillet's **château**, *pl. de la Libération; tel: 34 83 00 25*, open (unless the President of France is in residence) Wed–Mon 1000–1130 and 1400–1730 (Apr–Sept); Wed–Mon 1000–1130 and 1400–1630 (Oct–Mar), admission Fr.26 (Fr.13), may not be the most attractive of those around Paris, but some significant events in French history have taken place here, including the death of François I in 1547, the abdication of Charles X in 1830, and while staying there in Aug 1944 Gen. de Gaulle ordered the Leclerc Division to liberate Paris. For the last 100 years it has been used as the summer residence of the President. Only part of the château can be visited but includes reception rooms commissioned by the Comte de Toulouse and the Renaissance style Marble Hall.

The **gardens** are stunning and include formal gardens and water gardens in front of the château. Beyond that is the landscape garden which contains the **Pavillon des Coquillages** (Seashell Cottage) in which the walls are decorated with shells, marble and mother-of-pearl. Elsewhere in the park surrounding the château is the **Bergerie Nationale** (National Sheep Farm); *tel: 34 83 83 09*, open Sat–Sun and bank holidays 1400–1700 (July–Sept); Sun and bank holidays 1400–1700 (Oct–June), admission Fr.20 adults, free children, which was created by Louis XVI in 1786 when he had a flock of nearly 400 merino sheep driven across the Pyrenees from Spain to improve the quality of French cloth. There are now around 800 sheep at the farm. Nearby is the **Laiterie de la Reine** (Queen's Dairy); *tel: 34 83 02 49*, open Wed–Sat and alternate Sun–Mon 1000–1130, 1400–1730 (Apr–Sept);

179

1000–1130, 1400–1530 (Oct–Mar), admission Fr.13 adults, Fr.7 children, which Louis XVl had built for Marie-Antoinette to prevent her becoming bored during visits to Rambouillet.

In the town itself, the **Musée Rambolitrain**, *1 pl. Jeanne d'Arc; tel: 34 83 15 93*, open Wed–Sun 1000–1200 and 1400–1730 (all year), admission Fr.20, has a superb display of toy trains including a circuit that covers the second floor.

DAMPIERRE

Tourist Office: *Hôtel de Ville; tel: 30 52 53 70.*

The two-star **Auberge du Château**, *1 Grande Rue; tel: 30 52 52 89*, moderate to expensive, has a large restaurant.

Constructed of brick in the late 17th century, Dampierre's moated **château**; *tel: 30 52 53 24*, open Mon–Sat 1400–1800, Sun 1100–1200, 1400–1800 (Apr–Sept), admission Fr.45, is one of the smaller châteaux in the Paris outskirts but still has an elegant beauty. Still occupied by the Luynes family, only one of its two wings is open to the public, but it gives a useful insight into how the aristocracy lived. There are some impressive 17th and 18th-century furnishings. The estate includes a deer park and splendid floral gardens.

SIDE TRACK FROM DAMPIERRE

ELANCOURT

Leave Dampierre on the D58, crossing the N10 to Elancourt and **France Miniature**, *25 rte de Mesnil; tel: 30 51 51 51*, open daily 1000–1900 (Apr–May, Sept–Oct); Sun–Fri 1000–1900, Sat 1000-2300 (June); Sun–Fri 1000-2000, Sat 1000-2300 (July–Aug), admission Fr.68 (Fr.48), which on a 12-acre site shows the whole of France in relief along with nearly 2000 models of the country's major sights, including the Eiffel Tower, Le Mont St Michel and Futuroscope. Footpaths connect all the sights, while from the top of the Alps, which stand 9 m high, there is a good view over the whole country. ⬛

VERSAILLES

Tourist Office: *Hôtel de Madame de Pompadour, 7 r. des Reservoirs; tel: 39 50 36 22.*

ACCOMMODATION

There is no shortage of hotels in Versailles, but neither is there a shortage of visitors and you would be well advised to book in advance, particularly during July and Aug. Top hotel is the four-star **Hôtel Trianon Palace**, *1 blvd de la Reine; tel: 30 84 38 00*, which is renowned for its elegant turn-of-the-century decor. It has some 90 rooms, all of them very expensive, two restaurants and a tearoom. Even larger is the four-star **Hôtel Sofitel Château de Versailles**, *2 av. de Paris; tel: 39 53 30 31*. Prices are not quite so high, but it is still expensive. Menus in its restaurant are moderate to expensive. More moderately priced are the two-star **Hôtel Printania**, *19 r. Philippe de Dangeau; tel: 39 50 44 10*, and the **Paris Hôtel**, *14 av. de Paris; tel: 39 50 56 00*, but neither has a restaurant. Most economical of all is the **Hôtel Ménard**, *8 r. Ménard; tel: 39 50 47 99*, though it closes annually in July. Again there is no restaurant.

Just north of the château, in the suburb of Le Chesnay, there are several large modern hotels, among them the three-star **Novotel**, *4 blvd St-Antoine; tel 39 54 96 96* (expensive), the three-star **Hôtel Mercure**, *r. de Marly-le-Roi; tel: 39 55 11 41* (expensive) and the two-star **Hôtel Ibis**, *44 av. Dutartre; tel 39 63 37 93* (moderate). Only the *Nv* has a restaurant.

Campers and caravanners can stay at the two-star **Camping Municipal**, *r. Berthelot; tel: 39 51 23 61*. Open Apr–Oct, it is often crowded.

Visitors flock in their millions each year to Versailles to see its **château**, *pl. d'Armes; tel: 30 84 74 00*, open Tues–Sun 0900–1830 (May–Sept); 0900–1730 (Oct–Apr), admission Fr.40 adults, free children. Guided tours are an additional Fr.23. One of the largest and grandest châteaux in France, it is worth allowing at least one full day to give it justice. The château, along with its extensive grounds and trianons, was created in the reign of Louis XIV (the Sun King) in a huge undertaking that lasted from 1664 until 1710, and it remained the centre of government until the Revolution in 1789. The town itself was basically an annexe to house the many people who served at court. Because of the size of the estate a **petit train** (small motorised train) runs between the various sights from the terrace, daily (Mar–Nov), Sat–Sun (Dec–Feb), fare Fr.29. Alternatively bikes can be hired at park entrances (Mar–Nov), price Fr.29 per hour.

The château is entered via the vast cobbled courtyard at the front, in the middle of which is a fine equestrian statue of Louis XIV. Inside, the main areas of interest include the state apartments (among which are the Hercules Salon and the Hall of Mirrors), the King's Suite, the Royal Opera, the chapel and **Museum of French History**, which displays thousands of 16th–19th-century paintings and sculptures. The 250-acre **gardens** are laid out in formal French style with terraces, flowerbeds, footpaths, ponds and fountains all carefully aligned. At one side is the orangery, which contains orange trees and palms and is reached by two grand staircases. Beyond the gardens is the vast **park**, open dawn–dusk, admission free except Sun during May–Sept when fountain shows are held. Admission then is Fr.20. In a corner of the park, the **Chèvreloup National Arboretum**; *tel: 39 55 53 80*, open Sat–Mon 1000–1700 (Apr–Oct), admission Fr.12, has many unusual trees.

At the park's centre the 1.6 km **Grand Canal** and 1 km **Petit Canal** form a cross-shaped expanse of water where boats can be hired (Mar–Sept). Close to the northern end of the Petit Canal is the **Grand Trianon**, open Tues–Sun 1000–1830 (May–Sept); Tues–Fri 1000–1230 and 1400–1730, Sat–Sun 1000–1730 (Oct–Apr), admission Fr.21 adults, a more manageable palace built in 1687 to enable Louis XIV and his family escape the pressures of court life. Nearby, the **Petit Trianon**, open Tues–Sun 1000–1830 (May–Sept); Tues–Fri 1000–1230 and 1400–1730, Sat–Sun 1000–1730 (Oct–Apr), admission Fr.12 adults, was more an elegant townhouse built by Louis XV, though it was Louis XVI's wife Marie-Antoinette who used it most. Another of Marie-Antoinette's amusements was the **Hameau de la Reine** (Queen's Hamlet), a mock village of pretty thatched and slate-roofed cottages which lies a little farther north.

Other attractions around the town include the 17th-century **Jeu de Paume** (Royal Tennis Courts), *r. du Jeu de Paume; tel: 39 50 36 22*, open Sat pm or Sun am (July–Aug), the **Musée Lambinet**, *54 blvd de la Reine; tel: 39 50 30 32*, open Tues–Sun 1400–1800 (all year), admission Fr.19, which is housed in an 18th-century mansion and contains period furniture, ceramics, medieval religious art, paintings and sculptures. There are also displays concerning the Revolution.

NANTES

A big city, with 500,000 inhabitants, Nantes retains some of the atmosphere of its heyday as a great port when it had a ship-building industry as well as sea-going vessels off-loading goods from around the world. It is 50 km from the Atlantic. After the quaint charm of the Loire Valley villages, the city takes a bit of getting used to with its bustling, noisy streets and constant traffic. It has some down-at-heel quarters, a thriving shopping and restaurant scene, a busy nightlife and an impressive château and cathedral. The Loire flows expansively here, retaining an industrial air thanks to warehouses and mechanical cranes. But it is the cheerful tributary, the River Erdre, which provides excursions and watersports for the Nantais. The city was once the capital of Brittany but now is the chief town of a region called Loire-Atlantique.

TOURIST INFORMATION

Tourist Office Nantes-Atlantique: *pl. du Commerce, 44000 Nantes; tel: 40 20 60 00*. Open Mon–Fri 0900–1900, Sat 0900–1800 (June–Sept); Mon–Sat 0900–1800 (Oct–May).

An annexe is beside the château in *r. du Château*. Open daily 1000–1900 (July–Aug); Sat, Sun, public holidays 1000–1900 (Sept–June). The offices book accommodation, have bureaux de change, organise guided tours and sell tickets to many events (*tel: 40 47 61 77*).

ARRIVING AND DEPARTING

The A11 *autoroute* links Paris and Nantes. To approach Nantes from Angers and the east, follow N23 straight through to *rte de Paris*, then take *blvd Jules Verne, r. Gén. Buat,* and *r. du Mar. Joffre*, reaching the roundabout at *pl. Mar. Foch*. Go straight on to *r. de Verdun* which leads to *pl. St-Pierre* and the cathedral.

GETTING AROUND

Its size means that using the **SEMITAN** tram lines (backed with a bus system) is a good idea. The trams are modern, with ramps emerging automatically at carriage doors at each stop, making it easy for prams, strollers and cycles to board. Although traffic is busy in the centre, bicycle paths have been created, especially along the River Erdre, to reach scenic spots. There are two tram lines (*Ligne 1, Ligne 2*) which dissect the city into four.

TAN kiosk, *allée Brancas, cours Fr. Roosevelt; tel: 40 29 39 39*. Open Mon–Sat 0715–1900. For both bus and tram a single ticket is Fr.7; a book of 5 is Fr.30; a book of 10 is Fr.53. Each ticket is valid for 1 hr. A day ticket is Fr.19. Tram tickets must be purchased at machines before boarding. Main tram stations on the city centre edges have car parks. Most Nantes attractions are clustered in distinct areas and can be visited on foot.

STAYING IN NANTES

Accommodation

There is a wide range of hotels in all price ranges (but not four-star), with a good choice in the lower price brackets. There

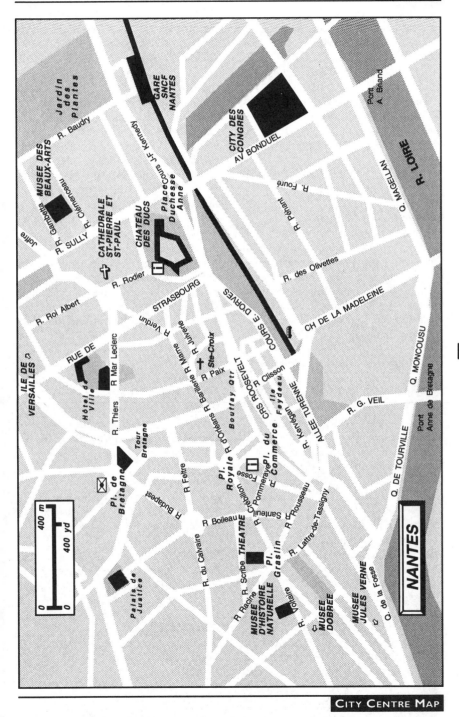

are some hotels in the streets near the rail station (the Accès Nord side) and some near the château (*pl. de la Duchesse Anne*). Chain hotels in Nantes include: *Ba, Ca, F1, Mc. Nv, Pr.*

There are two **HI: Foyers des Jeunes Travailleurs; Résidence Porte Neuve**, *1 pl. Ste-Elisabeth; tel: 40 20 00 80*, and **Port Beaulieu**, *9 blvd Vincent Gache; tel: 40 12 24 00.*

Camping; Val du Cens, *2 blvd du Petit Port; tel: 40 74 47 94.*

Eating and Drinking

The city centre is well endowed with places to eat in all price categories in almost every street. Cuisines represented include African, American, Belgian, Chinese, Greek, Indian, Italian, Spanish, Japanese, Turkish. The busiest areas are off *pl. du Commerce* and *pl. Royale* (especially the pedestrianised streets such as *r. Scribe, r. Ste-Croix, r. des Petites Écuries*.

La Cigalle, *4 pl. Graslin; tel: 40 69 79 41*, is an art nouveau extravaganza with beautiful floral tiling from floor to ceiling inside. It has an oyster and seafood stall outside, complete with oyster-opener in colourful apron.

A quiet corner with a pretty view is beside the château, along the cobbled *r. Prémion* and *r. des États*, where there are a couple of fashionable bars and restaurants and a second-hand bookshop (with some paperback thrillers in English). The outdoor seating facing the poplar-lined château moat and drawbridge makes dining pleasant at **Le Pont-Levis**, *17 r. des États; tel: 40 35 10 20*. Open daily.

Regional dishes are often served with a sauce *à la Nantaise* (white wine sauce enriched with butter). Muscadets are the local wines. Busy city workers often eat lunch on the run, a baguette in hand. A good choice of sandwiches, pizzas and cakes is found at **Chez Marie**, *23 r. de la Fosse; tel: 40 20 14 69.* Bread is baked in wood-fired ovens behind the counter. A speciality is *Le Tourton*, bread which can be sweet or savoury. *Pain de Nantes* is a small round cake flavoured with lemon or orange and filled with shredded almonds. *Gâteau Nantais* is a shortbread cake mixed with ground almonds or crystallised fruits and flavoured with kirsch or rum.

Places with benches for picnics include the tree-lined *r. Armand-Brossard* (which also has cafés and bars) and the **park** on *Île de Versailles* on the River Erdre. Opposite the *pl. du Commerce* and numerous busy streets is a small fountain square *pl. Juillet XIV* (beside the *Île de Feydeau* quarter).

Food markets take place Tues–Sun from 0500 in three covered halls *at r. Talensac*. Sandwiches, salads, biscuits and drinks are for sale at **Marks and Spencer**, *1 r. de Budapest; tel: 40 47 61 61.* Open Mon–Sat 0930–1900. There is a supermarket within the department store **Monoprix**, *2 r. du Calvaire; tel: 40 48 20 20.* Open Mon–Sat 0900–2100. Interesting cheeses are sold at a shop which includes a restaurant featuring cheese dishes: **Fromagerie du Val de Loire**, *51 r. Mar. Joffre; tel: 40 74 43 54.*

Communications

Main **post office** is at *pl. Bretagne.* Open Mon–Sat 0800–1900; Sat. 0800–1200. It has a bureau de change and poste restante.

Money

Banks are open on Mon–Sat morning. On Sun, the Tourist Office on *r. du Château* runs a bureau de change.

Consulates

UK:*5 r. des Cadeniers; tel: 40 63 16 02.* **Netherlands**: *7 blvd de Chantenay; tel: 40 58 56 57.*

ENTERTAINMENT

Opera and musicals are performed at the grand **Théâtre Graslin**, *pl. Graslin*; *tel: 40 69 77 18*. Its ostentatious façade with composite columns and statues of the muses dates to 1788. Classical concerts and ballets are held at the modern **Cité des Congrès**, *1 à 5 r. de Valmy*; *tel: 40 51 88 20*. Plays are staged at the **Maison de la Culture, Éspace 44**, *84 r. du Gén. Buat*; *tel: 51 88 25 25*.

Cabaret bars, karaoke and music pubs, dancing and strip bars and plenty of discothèques are part of the varied, lively nightlife. *Nantes des jours et des nuits* (Nantes by day and by night) is a free booklet which lists monthly events. Tobacconists sell the booklet *Nantes La Nuit* (Nantes by night). Fr.18.

Cinema includes the **Gaumont**, *12 pl. du Commerce*, with some films shown in the *Version Originale* (V.O.).

Events

Annual events include a carnival in Apr, **Les Allumées** in Oct and the Spring Arts Festival in May. At the **Fêtes de l'Été** in July many open-air events are held on stages specially set up in the château moat.

SHOPPING

The main shopping area is west of *pl. Royale* including department stores on *r. du Calvaire* and *r. de la Marne*. An attraction in its own right is the three-storey, 19th-century **Passage Pommeraye** (Pommeraye Gallery) with an ornate central staircase flanked by lamp-topped statues. It has antique print and bric-à-brac shops. Open 0800–2000.

SIGHTSEEING

There is a leaflet *A City to Discover*, published every two months, which lists in English the main museums and tourist activities. Guided walking tours are available in French/German daily 1500 (July–Aug); English-only tours Tues 1500, Sun 1500 (July–Aug). Fr.35 (Fr.25 children). Departure point is usually the Tourist Office, which also arranges guided tours in the vicinity by coach, boat or tram, lasting from 4 hrs to all day. A typical theme for a tram tour is the 3-hr *From the Gallo-Romans to le Corbusier*. Fr.65 (Fr.50) (tram tickets not included).

Horse and carriage tours leave from the château daily every hour 1000–2000 (Apr–Sept); **L'Omnibus de la Dame Blanche**; *tel: 40 38 34 16*. A **little train** tour leaves from the cathedral square daily 1000–1700 (July–Aug); 1400–1700 (Easter–June, Sept). *Tel: 40 60 78 88*; Fr.35. There are organised tours by bicycle and a **cycle hire** office at the *pl. du Commerce* 0900–1900 (July–Aug). Cost of tour Fr.25 plus cost of the cycle. Cycle hire charges start at Fr.20 for two hrs, up to Fr.40 for 5 hrs. A day's hire is Fr.50; two days is Fr.90; *tel: 40 12 02 07*.

A **Vélo+Tram** promotion allows cycles to be taken aboard trams free, Sat, Sun, public holidays (June–Sept). For information *tel: 40 29 39 39* or **Association Place au Vélo**; *tel: 40 48 15 87*.

Interesting gardens in Nantes include **Le Jardin des Cinq Sens** (Garden of the Five Senses), *r. Gaetan Rondeau* in the *Île Beaulieu* district, south of the Loire. Opposite the rail station is the **Jardin des Plantes** *blvd Stalingrad*, with 15 acres of spectacular landscaping including rare plants, medicinal herbs, camellia beds and a cactus greenhouse.

Château and Cathedral District

The *r. de M. Rodier* connects the cathedral and the château. **Cathédrale St-Pierre et St-Paul**; *tel: 51 88 95 47*. Open 0830 until nightfall (or 1900). The crypts are open Mon, Wed–Sat 1000–1230, 1400–1700, Sun 1400–1800. The gaunt cathedral, started in 1434 and completed in 1893, is Gothic with modern, patterned windows. The most impressive effigies are on the Renaissance tomb of François II and his wife, Marguerite de Foix.

Le château des Ducs de Bretagne, *1 pl. Marc Elder; tel: 40 41 56 56*, is open Wed–Mon 1000–1200, 1400–1800 (Sept–June); daily 1000–1200, 1400–1800 (July–Aug); admission Fr.10 (Fr.5), free Sun. Self-guided, 25-min tours with an audio-cassette commentary in English are Fr.20. Guided tours in French take place regularly; Fr.20. The courtyard and ramparts are open daily 1000–1900 (July–Aug). Historical events which took place here include the signing of the Edict of Nantes by Henri IV in 1598 granting Protestants religious freedom. Entry is by a pedestrian bridge over the moat. Major restoration work is nearing completion, creating a new gallery covering the archaeological and architectural history of the building and allowing access to the ramparts walkway.

Within the building are two museums. **Musée de l' Art Populaire Breton** (Breton folk art museum) which has costumes and artefacts of the region. The **Musée des Salorges** (marine museum) currently undergoing refurbishment, has displays about the city's navigational history, its colonial links and slave-trading past in the 18th–19th centuries. Nantes was the Loire Valley's gateway for overseas trade. Boats still bring cargoes of wood, iron, coal and grain but the main port for the Loire is now St-Nazaire.

Île Feydeau

No longer an island, this compact district opposite the *pl. du Commerce* has streets of 18th century buildings with crumbling façades and wrought iron balconies. Cafés and restaurants are on the cobbled *r. Kervégan*; a plaque marking the birthplace of Jules Verne, 1828–1905, is at *4 cours Oliver de Clisson*. (In the main town centre there are plaques on his former homes at nearby *2 cours des 50 Otages* and at *16 r. J. J. Rousseau*.)

Museums

Just off *pl. Graslin* are several top museums. **Musée Dobrée**, *pl. Jean V; tel: 40 71 03 50*. Open Tues–Sun 1000–1200, 1330–1730. This one site with a pretty garden includes three attractions: the 15th-century **Manoir de la Touche** with a display about the Vendée wars; **Palais Dobrée,** based on one collector's art treasures; and the **Musée Archéologique.** Open Mon, Wed–Sun 1000–1200, 1330–1730. Fr.20 (Fr.10). Free on Sun. Nearby is the **Musée d'Histoire Naturelle**, *12 r. Voltaire; tel: 40 41 67 67*. Open Tues–Sat 1000–1200, 1400–1800, Sun 1400–1800. Fr.30 (Fr.15).

Heading west out of the city there are a couple of interesting museums by the quayside. One is a ship, the **Musée Naval Maillé Brézé**, *quai de la Fosse; tel: 40 69 56 82*. Open daily 1400–1700. Fr.30; Fr.15 (with tour in French) or Fr.45; F25 (tour also includes the engine room). On a cliff-side edge overlooking the *quai d'Aiguillon* is a late 19th-century, three-storey house which is the **Musée Jules Verne**, *3 r. de l'Hermitage; tel: 40 69 72 52*. Open Mon, Wed–Sat 1000–1230, 1400–1700, Sun 1400–1700. Fr.19. Self-guided, with an English leaflet.

Verne himself did not live here, although his grandparents had a similar house in the area. Letters, first editions, cinema posters, theatrical flyers and board games of his books including the world-famous *Twenty Thousand Leagues Under*

The Sea, Journey to the Centre of the Earth and *Around the World in 80 Days* are among the displays. The parlour of his house in Amiens, with his own furniture, is recreated, as is his bedroom as a child. The window views over the Loire from this giddy height are stunning.

Close by is the **Planétarium**, *8 r. des Arcadiens; tel: 40 73 99 23*. Shows take place Tues–Sat 1030, 1415, 1545; Sun 1415, 1545. Fr.24 (Fr.12). The road leading up to the Verne museum has a terrace (a photo stop for coaches, although there is no parking area) at *pl. des Garennes* overlooking the Loire, its industrial quaysides and high-rise buildings. Occasionally adding a romantic sight is the three-masted tall ship *Bellem*, used as a training vessel for young people in ports around France. It returns regularly to Nantes where it was built in 1896.

Dotted around various locations are the fine arts museum and three special interest museums. **Musée des Beaux Arts** (Museum of Fine Arts), *10 r. G. Clemenceau; tel: 40 41 65 65*. Open Mon–Wed, Sat 1000–1800, Fri 1000–2100, Sun 1100–1800. Fr.20 (Fr.10). Free Sun. **Musée de la Poste** (postal museum), *10 blvd A. Pageot; tel: 40 29 93 08*, is open Mon–Fri 0900–1130, 1330–1600; admission Fr.10. **Musée de la Poupée et des Jouets Anciens** (doll and toy museum), *39 blvd St-Aignan; tel: 40 69 14 41*. Open Wed–Sun 1430–1730. Fr.20 (Fr.8). **Musée de l'Imprimerie** (museum of printing), *24 quai de la Fosse; tel: 40 73 26 55*. Open Tues, Thur, Fri 1400–1800, Wed, Sat 1000–1200, 1400–1800 (Sat until 1700); Fr.20 (Fr.10).

River Erdre

Île de Versailles is a man-made island (for pedestrians) on the River Erdre which has been turned into a park with a Japanese influence, including wooded and landscaped areas and a children's playground. It is a 15-min walk from the centre. Tram stop: *Minihel*. Open Mon–Sat 0800–0100, Sun, public holidays 0800–2000. On the river's edge is a Japanese restaurant **Le Torigaï**; *tel: 40 37 06 37*. Closed Sun.

Originally a marsh, the island was created with earth from the excavation of the Nantes–Brest canal in the early 19th century. It was a working-class site with ironworks, tanneries, joiners' shops and ship-building but from 1950 the site was abandoned until the city acquired the plots of land. Built in Japanese tea-house style, one building houses aquariums with local fish and an exhibition about the river as a natural habitat. The **Maison de l'Erdre**; *tel: 40 29 41 11*. Open Tues–Thur 1400–1800, Sat, Sun 1400–1900. Free. English leaflet.

Hire of electric, pedalo-shaped boats is available next to the cable footbridge; **Ruban bleu**; *tel: 51 81 04 24*. Hire for 30 min is Fr.70; 1 hr, Fr.120; 4 hrs, Fr.350. It is pleasant to reach the island by the little bridge off the *quai de Versailles* and leave it at the other end, via a cable bridge back to *quai de Versaille*, and then walk a little further to the **Pont de la Motte-Rouge** to cross the river to the boat terminus. From here, a 2-hr cruise aboard a smart, two-storey boat is run by **Bateaux Nantais**, *gare fluviale, quai de la Motte-Rouge (pl. Waldeck-Rousseau; tel: 40 14 51 14)*. Sun, public holiday 1500 (Apr, Sept), Sun public holidays 1700 (May); Wed, Sat, 1500, Sun 1500, 1700 (June); Mon–Sat 1500, Sun 1500, 1700 (mid-July–Aug). Fr.50. There are lunch and dinner cruises, with commentary (in English by request). Within the modern terminus building are an information desk, souvenir shop and a brasserie. Open Mon–Sat 0900–1900, Sun 1000–1300, 1400–1700. Free car park.

The boat sails past small châteaux and pretty scenery along the valley of Erdre.

To explore the **Erdre Valley**, a pack of leaflets *Errances – Circuits Découverte du Pays Nantais* (circular discovery routes in the Nantes countryside) includes routes for cars, cyclists and walkers. The descriptions are in French but include maps. Bases include such charming towns as **Sucé-sur-Erdre, Carquefou, Chapelle-sur-Erde** and **Ste-Luce-sur-Loire**.

The River Erdre is well endowed with facilities for canoeing, kayaking, dinghy sailing, windsurfing, rowing, water-skiing and fishing.

SIDE TRACK FROM NANTES

The N137 goes almost direct (144 km) to handsome, jaunty **La Rochelle**, an old harbour and seaside resort with a cathedral and strong links with North America. The **New World Museum** has displays about immigration and trade such as fur from 17th-century Canada. There are boat excursions to the islands of Ré, Aix and Oléron. The town has a good choice of accommodation especially in the two-star hotel category. **Tourist Office**: *Le Gabut, 17025 La Rochelle; tel: 46 41 14 68.*

Slightly closer to Nantes are the seaside resorts of **Les Sables d'Olonne** (reached via D178 and D978) or, at the mouth of the Loire, **St-Brévin-les-Pins** (take D723 and D77) and **La Baule** (via N165 and N171), **Pornic** (take D751), all with sandy beaches.

Cuisine of the Loire Valley

The Loire Valley, often called the 'garden of France', is famous for its asparagus, endive, miniature tomatoes, innumerable herbs, peas, beans, lettuce (often served with walnut oil) and a diversity of mushrooms such as the grey *pleurotes* and the button mushrooms grown in the natural vaults around Saumur; plus strawberries, plums, prunes, melons, apricots, pears and apples.

Charcuterie is popular, including *rillons* (pork breast, stewed, and then served cold), *rillettes* (a type of pâté made from minced pork), *andouillettes* (tripe sausages), crumbed pig's trotters, chicken liver terrine and a variety of sausages. Since this is hunting country, red and roe deer, partridge and pheasant appear on the menu, from *pâtés* to casseroles. Fish dishes include salmon, carp, shad, bream and eels simmered in wine. A sauce which often accompanies fish is *beurre blanc*, made with butter, vinegar and shallots.

Goat cheeses are a speciality, in particular the *crottin of Chavignol*, the cylinder-shaped Ste-Maure and the pyramid-shaped, charcoal-sprinkled *Valençay*. A popular salad features warm goat's cheese on toast served with *petits lardons* (small pieces of fried pork). Orchards mean apple and quince dishes such as the *cotignac*.

Desserts often use fruit-flavoured liqueurs, such as pancakes flavoured with the famous orange-scented Cointreau (see p. 54). The caramelised upside-down apple cake, *Tarte Tatin*, was invented in the Loire Valley. Some main dishes rely on sweet flavours, such as guinea fowl, rabbit, or a hen chicken called *géline*, prepared with heather honey or fresh fruits, lightly fried or roasted like vegetables. A popular dish is pork with prunes. Wine is another important ingredient in recipes such as veal in a white wine sauce or casseroled chicken in a red wine sauce.

NANTES–ANGERS

This undemanding drive through vineyard-lined countryside along the south bank of the river Loire makes a refreshing change from the grand châteaux-lined routes further up the river. The Loire looks at its best in the many grand vistas from pretty hill-top villages and it a good idea to stop to stroll through some of these rather than just drive through. There are no major towns. Highlights are the great Château Serrant designed with Versailles and Fontainebleau as its inspirations and the tiny Loire island of Béhuard, population 100.

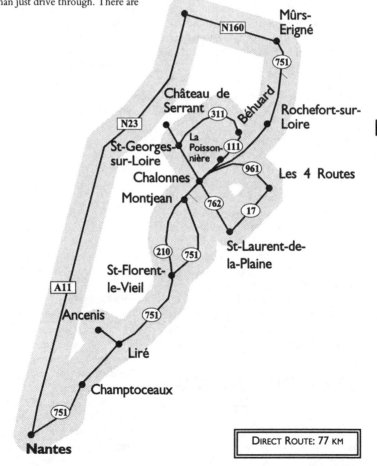

Angers

Mûrs-Erigné

N160

751

Château de Serrant

311

Béhuard

Rochefort-sur-Loire

N23

La Poisson-nière

111

St-Georges-sur-Loire

Chalonnes

961

Les 4 Routes

Montjean

762

17

210

751

St-Laurent-de-la-Plaine

St-Florent-le-Vieil

A11

Ancenis

751

Liré

Champtoceaux

751

Nantes

DIRECT ROUTE: 77 KM

ROUTES

DIRECT ROUTE

→ Take the motorway A11 to Beaucouzé, then N23 to Angers centre, 77 km.

SCENIC ROUTE

⇢ To start this 135.5 km route, take the D751 on the south side of Nantes to **Champtoceaux**, then continue on D751 to Liré, turn left onto D763 to cross the suspension bridge into **Ancenis** (see p. 301) then return over the same bridge to rejoin the D751 at Liré, turning left for **St-Florent-le-Vieil**. On leaving there, turn left onto D210 to **Montjean-sur-Loire**, and from there rejoin the D751 to **Chalonnes**.

There, turn right onto D762 to **St-Laurent-de-la-Plaine**. There, turn left onto D17 to **Les 4 Routes** to turn left onto D961 to Chalonnes, and cross the river to **St-Georges-sur-Loire**. Turn right there onto N23 for **Château de Serrant**.

Return to St-Georges-sur-Loire by the same route but at St-Georges-sur-Loire turn left onto D311 to **Savennières**.

Leave there by D106, then across the bridge to the island of **Béhuard**. Return to Savennières by the same route, turning left onto D111, passing **La Poissonnière** to rejoin the D961, then turn left to recross the bridge to Chalonnes. Turn left onto D751 (the 'Corniche Angevine') and continue on D751 via Rochefort-sur-Loire to **Mûrs-Erigné** to join the N160 into Angers centre.

CHAMPTOCEAUX

Tourist Office: *Le Champalud, 49270 Champtoceaux; tel: 40 82 57 49.* Open Tues–Sun 1000–1200, 1400–1800 (June–mid-Sept). **Mairie** (Town Hall): *tel: 40 83 52 31.* Open variable hours (mid-Sept–May).

Built on a truly impressive ridge overlooking the Loire, which divides into several channels around the islands, Champtoceaux possesses a ruined fortress and a scenic walk, **Promenade du Campalud**. Near the bridge is a ruined 13th-century ferry toll house, which used to take in fees from passing boat traffic when the Loire was a busy commercial waterway.

ST-FLORENT-LE-VIEIL

Tourist Office: *pl. de la Mairie 49410 St-Florent-Le-Vieil; tel: 41 72 62 32.* Open daily 1000–1200, 1500–1800 (mid-Apr–June); daily 1000–1300, 1400–1900 (July–mid-Sept); Mon 0800–1200, 1400–1800, Wed 0800–1200, Fri 1400–1800 (mid-Sept–mid-Apr). It gives information only and does not make hotel bookings. A good leaflet, with some English text, Fr.5, outlines a 20-30 min walking route along the village's leafy narrow cobbled streets. There is a music and dance festival during the first three weeks of July.

ACCOMMODATION

There is a hotel, a *chambre d'hôte* and a *gîte d'étape* in this village. Right on the bank of a peninsula on the river is **Camping L'Île Batailleuse**, *tel: 40 83 45 01.*

SIGHTSEEING

This pleasant hill-top village, with a market square, an impressive church and spectacular views of the wide Loire, is a must-stop for a taste of French history far removed from the aristocratic anecdotes of the Loire châteaux.

Despite its peaceful air, the village played a crucial role in the Vendéen uprising, 1793–1795, in which local peasants were whipped up into an army by the nobility to defy the Revolutionary forces of Paris and to restore the monarchy. It was also at this village, after their defeat at Cholet, that the Vendéens congregated in order to cross the river in their thousands on 18 October 1795. In revenge for the brutal behaviour of the Revolutionaries, they planned to kill some 4000 prisoners who were held in the immense church, but spared them at the request of their own mortally wounded leader, the Marquis de Bonchamps.

Although 80, 000 Vendéens crossed the river on a makeshift bridge of wood in just two days, 2000 were shot dead. Finally, one of the treaties to end the rebellion was signed at the village.

The events are explained in the **Musée d'Histoire Locale des Guerres de Vendée** (museum of local history and the Vendéen wars). Open Sat, Sun 1430-1830 (Easter-June); daily 1430-1830 (July-mid-Sept). Fr.15. It is housed within the 17th-century **Chapelle du Sacré-Coeur** (Chapel of the Sacred Heart), where five display areas show the uniforms of the combatants as well as local folk costumes and information about wildlife. In the enormous austere church, known as the **Abbaye**, is the white marble tomb of Bonchamps and a moving heroic statue of him carved in 1825 by the sculptor David d'Angers, whose father had been one of the reprieved prisoners in the church.

The village's royalist sympathies are also evident at the end of the tree-lined esplanade, where there is a grand column in honour of the visit of the Duchess of Angoulême, daughter of Louis XVI. From this terrace there are extensive views. It is possible to survey the Loire Valley some 15 km into Brittany.

The village name honours a 4th-century hermit, originally a Roman soldier, who inspired an abbey to be built here until the Norse invaders forced the monks to leave to found a new abbey at St-Hilaire-St-Florent further down the Loire, thus making this 'le vieil' (the old) St-Florent.

MONTJEAN-SUR-LOIRE

Tourist Office: *Quai des Mariniers 49570 Montjean-sur-Loire; tel: 41 39 07 10.* Open Wed–Mon 1000–11200, 1430–1800 (June–Sept). Mairie; *tel: 41 39 80 46.* Open Mon–Fri 0900–1200, 1300–1700 (Sept–May). It gives information but does not make hotel bookings.

There are about a dozen small hotels in the town.

This little town has a fine view acoss the river to **Camptocé**, where the castle, now in ruins, inspired the author Charles Perrault to write his story about Bluebeard in 1697. The castle's owner Gilles de Rais, 1404-1440, was a sinister personality who had been a marshal of France and a comrade of Joan of Arc but turned out to be a criminal who confessed to hundreds of murders and was hanged.

Montjean's riverbanks are quiet now but its boat-building and busy navigational era are the theme of the exhibits at an old forge by the riverside, the **Ecomusée de Montjean**. (open Tues-Sun 1500–1900, Apr–Oct, Fr.60/Fr.47). The visit includes an hour's trip in a small boat as well as admission to the museum, which shows off many old regional industries including hemp growing and sail making.

CHALONNES-SUR-LOIRE

Tourist Office: *pl de Layon; tel: 41 78 26 21.* Open Mon–Sat 1000–1230, 1430–1745, Sun 1430–1745 (mid-June–mid-Sept). Mairie; *tel: 41 78 13 22* Open Mon–Fri 0900–1230, 1330–1730, Sat 0900–1200 (mid-Sept–mid-June).

Extremely pretty river views along the

191

road lead to this lovely town, where there is parking next to the **Église St-Maurille**, the church right on the riverside and a little quay with pleasure and fishing boats. This is a nice place for a picnic.

Chalonnes is an important wine centre and its main attraction is tastings of the many local wines at the wine merchants. There is a **little train** which takes visitors along through some of the vineyards; *tel: 41 78 14 90*. Fr.34 (Fr.23 child).

Between Chalonnes-sur-Loire and Rochefort-sur Loire is the twisting road known as the *Corniche Angevine,* which gives lovely views of the Loire, including vineyards and marshy islands

ST-LAURENT-DE-LA-PLAINE

Tourist Office: *7 pl. Abbé Joseph Moreau; tel: 41 78 24 08.* Open daily 1000–1800 (Jan–Sept); Mon–Fri 1000–1800 (Oct–Dec). It gives information but does not make hotel bookings. There are no hotels in the town itself.

SIGHTSEEING

The town's main attraction is the Musée des Vieux Métiers (the museum of old trades). Open same hours as the tourist office. Fr.27 (Fr.22). Of all local crafts museums, this is the one to see. Some of the little buildings have been made by a local carpenter using traditional methods.

It is this carpenter who helped bring the museum about when he saw the local blacksmith about to throw some old tools away in 1968 and suggested instead that they be kept and put on exhibition to show how people worked in the past. The result was that the tools of many more crafts were donated and now the museum has volunteers scouring all of France for more and more everyday machines and tools, from weaving looms to forges, lace-making bobbins to printing presses. The

local theatre is often used to display overflow exhibits.

ST-GEORGES-SUR-LOIRE

The town's interest lies in the nearby **Château de Serrant**, *49170 St-Georges-sur-Loire; tel 41 39 13 01.* Open Wed–Mon 0900–1200, 1400–1730 (Apr–June, Sept–Oct); daily 0900–1200, 1400–1730 (July–Aug). Fr.40. Guided only, with English leaflet.

A connection with the Stuarts of Scotland is found here as it is in other corners of the Loire Valley. The château, built over the 16th–18th centuries, has a symmetrical façade and looks splendid reflected in its large lake. It has two solid domed towers, a fine moat and a large dovecote overlooking a rectangular pool. The courtyard is used for theatrical productions, including Shakespeare in French, during the **Festival of Anjou** – usually the first three weeks of July.

Inside there is a beautiful stone staircase with a finely decorated, barrel-vaulted ceiling. In the library, which has 10,000 books, is a painting of Bonnie Prince Charlie in conversation with Francis Walsh, the Irishman who was made Count of Serrant by Louis XV as a reward for his support of the Stuart cause in 1745. The château is still owned and lived in by his direct descendant, Prince Jean-Charles de Ligne.

There is a bedroom furnished for Napoleon's brief visit in 1808 with elaborate wall borders and Empire furniture although he didn't stay long enough to sleep here.

It is interesting to pick out the more modern conveniences throughout the château, such as the brass grilles of an underfloor heating system introduced around 1850 in the Grand Salon and a hand-operated lift of 1900.

BÉHUARD

Tourist Office: *Mairie; tel: 41 72 84 11.* Open Tues 1030–1900, Sat 0830–1200 (Jul–mid-Sept).

This lovely narrow island in the middle of the river has picture-postcard, 15th–16th-century houses.

Built high on a rock is the **Église de Notre Dame** (Church of Our Lady); *tel: 41 72 21 15.* Open daily 0900–1200, 1400–1900. In the chaplain's house is an exhibition of photographs, vintage and modern, of the village including shots of floods which occur regularly. A slate marker on the church indicates the high water mark of each flood. There had been an old shrine on the site for prayers for sailors in peril on the Loire. Louis XI built the present church when he was saved from a nearby shipwreck. He is depicted in the stained glass window. This is a lovely place to stop for a picnic or a restaurant lunch and a pleasant walk to the wide sandy beach.

ROCHEFORT-SUR-LOIRE

Tourist Office: *Grand Cour; tel: 41 78 81 70.* Open Mon–Sat 1000–1230, 1500–1800 (Jul–Aug). Mairie; *tel 41 78 70 24.* Open Mon–Fri 0900–1230, 1400–1700 (Sept–June).

There is a hotel and the tourist office gives information on local accommodation but does not make hotel bookings.

This nice little town has some castle ruins and old houses with turret silhouettes. Its quiet air is far removed from its brief time as a pirate hang-out in the late 16th century. It is famous for its sweet wines, Quarts de Chaume. Despite its name, the town is on the little tributary, the River Louet.

The Loire

Majestic, the adjective most often used about the River Loire, is apt both because of its grand, impassive pace and its royal connections. As France's longest river, it is the country's most important and historic waterway. It begins deep in the interior, in the volcanic hills of the Massif Central at Mont Gerbier de Jonc, and meanders for some 1000 km westwards to the Atlantic coast.

It was connected to the Seine by the canal at Briare from 1642 and was a working river, used as a highway, bustling with boats carrying passengers and cargoes such as coal until the rise of the railways. Local museums are full of displays about its heyday and the many navigational industries it supported. It has never been an easy river to navigate, owing to its unpredictable currents and many shallow sandy banks. However, its proximity to Paris made it popular with the royal family and their courtiers who built grand châteaux for their pleasurable pursuits. Then came wealthy merchants and the bourgeoisie, and now weekenders from Paris and holidaymakers from all over the world.

It can be a frustrating river, as likely to disappoint as it is to delight. In the height of summer it can dry up, so that the romantic waterside vistas portrayed in coffee table books become expanses of sand. Even in full flow, there is little navigation so the landscape can look empty and melancholy. However, the morning mists, the sunsets, an unexpected viewpoint transform it and one of the great pleasures is to sit on its banks in tranquil communion with Nature.

The Loire basin also contains a great network of river. Many are worth touring in their own right, especially the Indre, Vienne, Sarthe, Cher and the confusingly named Loir.

ORLÉANS

A sprawling city, Orléans, with a population of 105,000, has a stylish, easily manageable centre to explore, with an array of undramatic but pleasant attractions to visit. The city also has an emotional historical link with the great French heroine, Joan of Arc, who became known as the Maid of Orléans after saving the city from the English army during the Hundred Years' War. Its importance in royal times meant that the title Duke of Orléans was always bestowed on the second son of the monarch. The Loire sweeps grandly past but the hub of city life is away from its tree-lined banks.

TOURIST INFORMATION

Tourist Office: *pl. Albert 1er, 45000 Orléans; tel: 38 53 05 95*. Opens Mon–Sat 0900–1900, Sun 1000–1200 (Apr–June, Sept); Mon–Sat 0900–1900, Sun, public holidays 0930–1230, 1500–1830 (July–Aug); Mon–Sat 0900–1830, Sun 1000–1200 (Nov–Mar). It operates a bureau de change during limited hours (see under 'Money' p. 196) and makes hotel bookings in Orléans and the vicinity. English leaflets available include a walking route of the city.

ARRIVING AND DEPARTING

To approach Orléans from Paris and the north, follow N20 until it becomes the *av. de Paris*, going just past the rail station to *pl. d'Arc* adjoining *pl. Albert 1*, for parking and the Tourist Office.

GETTING AROUND

Traffic bypasses the city centre on wide streets (*blvds Alexandre Martin, Rocheplatte, J. Jaurès*) which were once the city walls. The main attractions are easily reached on foot from the central square *pl. du Martroi* or the cathedral. There are good car parks; those by the river banks are free.

SEMTAO is the bus service. Information from **Centre Bus** *pl. Albert 1er* (beside the rail station); *tel: 38 71 93 38*. Open Mon–Sat 0615–1915.

STAYING IN ORLÉANS

Accommodation

There are seven three-star hotels and a large number of two- or one-star hotels, distributed throughout the city and around the rail station.

Hotel chains in Orléans include *Ba, BW, Ca, Ct, F1, Ib, Mc, Nv, Pr, RS*.

There is a **youth hostel** at *14 Faubourg Madeleine; tel: 38 62 45 75*. **Camping r. de la Roche** is 3 km away at *St-Jean-de-Ruelle; tel: 38 88 39 39*.

Eating and Drinking

There are plenty of eating places in all price ranges. Cuisines represented include African, American, Australian, Chinese, Greek, Indian, Lebanese, Spanish, Tex-Mex and Turkish.

Gourmets will associate Orléans with its fine vinegars. Regional specialities include *andouillette de Jargeau* (pork sausages), venison and game from the Sologne, fruit liqueurs, Loire river salmon and *sandre* (a type of pike), asparagus, mushroom varieties such as *cèpes* and

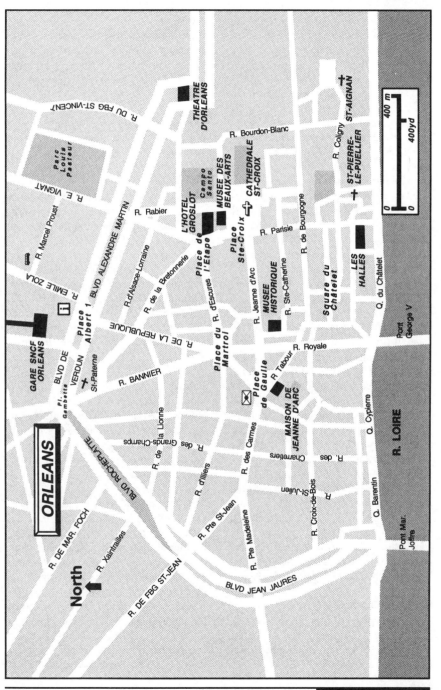

ORLEANS

North

CITY CENTRE MAP

girolles and cheeses such as the wood-ash coated *cendré d'Olivet* or the soft *frinault*.

The best choice of restaurants is along the pedestrianised *r. de Bourgogne*, jauntily decked out in bunting, and the nearby *r. Ste-Catherine* or *sq. du Châtelet*. This is the old quarter of the city. There is a lively cluster of open-air pizzerias and brasseries in the station area (*blvd Alexandre Martin*).

The *pl. du Matroi* has brasseries with umbrella-topped tables spread out along one side but the wide open square dominated by banks is a little soulless for people-watching, although there are usually tourists taking photos in front of the statue of **Joan of Arc** and locals waiting for buses. With its oyster and seafood bar, **La Chancellerie** is in a delightful Paris-style brasserie, *27 pl. du Martroi; tel: 38 53 57 54*. Open Mon–Sat 0700–0100.

Dotted throughout the centre are *pâtisseries, chocolatiers, charcuteries, boulangeries* (*r. Bannier*). A large roundel-shaped sweet made with quince paste, the pink *cotignac* is stamped with an image of Joan of Arc and comes in round wooden boxes. A good cheese and wine shop is **Philippe Olivier**, *228 r. de Bourgogne; tel: 38 68 07 88*. The covered central market, **Les Halles** is open Tues–Fri 0700–1900, Sat 0600–1900, Sun 0700–1200.

For picnics, there are park benches along the river bank but although the views are good the traffic makes it noisy; there are peaceful leafy corners found when following the walking route map, such as Jardin Jacques Boucher, cloître St-Aignan and Collégiale St-Pierre-le-Peullier (see Sightseeing, pp. 197–199).

Communications

The main **post office**, *pl. du Gén. de Gaulle*, opens Mon–Fri 0800–1900, Sat 0800–1200. It has bureau de change and poste restante.

Money

Banks are closed Mon but there is a bureau de change) at *pl. du Matroi* and at the post office. The Tourist Office will change travellers' cheques on Sat afternoon and Sun.

Consulates

Belgium, *29 4. Ch. Sanglier; tel: 38 53 91 50*.

ENTERTAINMENT

There is a lively choice of jazz clubs, rock music venues, discotheques and nightclubs, usually found around the restaurant streets.

Refurbished to create four venues for drama, dance, music and a wide range of cultural events is the **Théâtre d'Orléans**, *blvd Aristide-Briand; tel: 38 62 75 30*.

There are four cinemas but *version originale* (original language) films are shown at **Select Studios**, *45 r. Jeanne-d'Arc; tel: 36 68 69 25*.

Events

Joan of Arc inspires the annual **Fête de Jeanne d'Arc**. On 29 Apr, 7 and 8 May, her liberation of Orléans is re-enacted in remarkable detail, including the entry into the city, riding a white horse and accompanied by soldiers, of a girl dressed in armour and carrying a standard. On 7 May, this standard is presented to the people of Orléans by being handed to the bishop during a *son et lumière* show outside the illuminated cathedral. It all ends with a procession across the *pont George V* to the *quai du Fort des Tourelles*, site of the last of the English-held fortresses to be captured.

There is an annual jazz festival, early July, and a series of musical weekends during the year. Tickets for many events can be purchased at the record/bookshop **fnac**, *16 r. de la République; tel: 38 53 10*

196

10. Open Mon–Sat 1000–1900. Among many floral events, there is a rose festival at the beginning of Sept.

SHOPPING

A large shopping mall, the **Commercial Place d'Arc,** enlivens the rail station area of the city at *pl. Albert 1er,* The trains are tucked away at basement level. Inside are fashion, gift and speciality shops, restaurants, a cinema and a hypermarket, **Carrefour,** open Mon–Sat 0830–2100. The shopping mall faces the bus station, the Tourist Office, a restaurant area and the top end of the semi-pedestrianised *r. de la République,* which has a good range of fashion shops. It leads to *pl. du Matroi* where other shopping streets radiate, including *r. Royale* and *r. Adolphe-Thiers,* where the department store, **Les Galeries Lafayette** is located.

SIGHTSEEING

Guided walking tours are available (mid-Mar–Oct). Times and days vary. Themes include Roman and Gothic art; the Renaissance of Orléans, Joan of Arc. Fr.35 (Fr.17 child). Virtually the whole town centre, more than 3000 buildings, was destroyed in World War II so its elegantly rebuilt streets and historic houses are all the more remarkable.

Le petit train (little train) leaves *pl. Ste-Croix* daily 1430, 1545, 1645 June–Sept; also at 1800 July–Aug. Fr.25. There is a combination ticket for the train and entry to the towers of the cathedral valid Mon–Thurs (July–Aug) Fr.35.

Another combination ticket allows entry to four museums (fine arts, history, the Charles Péguy centre and Joan of Arc's house). Fr.40 (Fr.20).

Museums
The heart of Orléans is the spacious *pl. du*

Martroi with its dramatic bronze statue of the armoured **Joan of Arc** on horseback, sword lifted, and with flags flying on the four poles set around her – so inspirational a pose that it is easy to imagine an army gathering behind her. In high relief and fine detail, engravings around the plinth show the key moments in her life and her place in history. The bronze was made in 1855 by Denis Foyatier.

Nearby is the **Maison de Jeanne d'Arc** (Joan of Arc's house), *3 pl. de Gaulle; tel: 38 52 99 89.* Open Tues–Sun 1000–1200, 1400–1800 (May–Oct); Tues–Sun 1400–1800 (Nov–Apr); admission Fr.12 (Fr.6). Self-guided tour with English notices. Rebuilt in 1965, this timber-framed house is a faithful reproduction of the house where the girl-soldier stayed in 1429 as a guest of its owner, Jacques Boucher, who was treasurer to the Duke of Orléans. It has models to illustrate major events of the **Hundred Years' War.** Note the arcades of the handsomely decorated 16th-century house next door, the **Maison de la Porte-Renard,** named after a town gate which was destroyed in 1516. Beside it is the entrance to the small, shady **Jardin Jacques Boucher** (Jacques Boucher's garden) with its picturesque 16th-century ruin the **Pavillion Colas des Francs** (counting house).

Also just off *pl. du Martroi* is the **Musée Archéologique et Historique** (archaeology and history museum), housed in **Hôtel Cabu,** *pl. Abbé-Desnoyers; tel: 38 53 39 22.* Open Wed–Mon 1000–1200, 1400–1800; Fr.12 (Fr.6). It was beautifully restored after World War II to show off the ornate carved façade of the 16th-century house built for an Orléans lawyer, Philippe Cabu, whose coat of arms is on the building.

Nearby is another beautiful rebuilt 16th-century town mansion, built for

Euverte Hatte, a local merchant, now the **Centre Charles-Péguy, Hôtel Euverte Hatte**, *11 r. du Tabour; tel: 38 53 20 23.* Open Tues–Sun 1400–1800. Free. This has exhibits about the writer, Charles Péguy, 1873–1914, who was born in Orléans and wrote passionately on political and social issues. Look inside the courtyard to see a fine two-storey arcade.

Cathedral District

The showpiece of the old quarter is the **Cathédrale Sainte-Croix**, *pl. Ste-Croix; tel: 38 53 47 23.* Open 0900–1200, 1400–1800. A hotch-potch of architectural styles, the two 'wedding cake' towers date from 1829 but the main building dates from the 1600s. There were earlier cathedrals on the site, with the first one built in the 4th century. There are wide views of the city and the Loire from the top of the towers, Fr.25. The crypt and its treasure display is open daily 1500–1830. Fr.10. Beside the cathedral are the landscaped former archbishop's gardens.

Next to the cathedral is the **Musée des Beaux Arts** (Museum of Fine Arts), *pl. Ste-Croix; tel: 38 53 39 22.* Open Wed–Sun 1000–1200, 1400–1800. It has a rich collection of French paintings particularly from the 17th–20th centuries plus works by Rubens, Tintoretto, Corregio. Nearby is **L'Hôtel Groslot** (Groslot Mansion), *pl. de l'Étape; tel: 38 79 22 30.* Open Mon–Fri, Sun 1000–1200, 1400–1700. Free. Used previously as a royal residence, and then as town hall from 1790 to 1982, the heavily decorated and furnished rooms are open to the public. It was built in the 1500s for Jacques Groslot, bailiff. The first husband of Mary, Queen of Scots, the 16-year-old François II, died here in 1560.

The long and picturesque *r. Bourgogne* is the backbone of the old quarter but there are quiet streets close by to explore, with helpful small plaques as a guide. **Collégiale St-Pierre-le-Puellier**, *off r. de l'Université,* is open Tues–Fri 1000–1230, 1330–1800, Sat 1000–1200, 1400–1800, Sun 1400–1900; admission free. This pretty little redundant church, built between the 12th and 16th centuries, was used as a salt warehouse for a time but now makes a stunning backdrop for changing modern art exhibitions, particularly sculptures.

Off the same little square is **Musée de la Loire et du Bateau**, *2 cloître St-Pierre-le-Puellier; tel: 38 42 06 55.* Open (for guided tours only, in French) Wed, Sat 1415, 1515, 1615. Fr.10. It is difficult to find this little exhibition (on the left of the college) which displays models of boats used on the Loire for four centuries.

Somewhat disconcertingly, the quiet backwater streets in this area are a riot of graffiti. They lead to **Crypte St-Aignan** (St Aignan's crypt), *r. Neuve St-Aignan* (separate entrance from the main church at the back). Open daily 1030–1800 (June–Sept); free. Self-guided tour with English leaflet. Guided tour in French. With the rounded 10th–11th-century arches and tunnels glowing under gentle illumination, it is like a visit to a well laid out archaeological site and very evocative of the Romanesque era. It is in a quiet residential area beside a large tree-lined square.

Away from the centre are a couple of special interest museums. Near the rail station is the **Musée du Para**, *27 r. de la Bienvenue; tel: 38 88 12 14.* Open daily 1400–1800; admission Fr.30 (Fr.15). It has displays covering 55 years of military parachuting.

In a suburb 3 km away is **Musée Campanaire Bollée** (bell-making museum), *156 Faubourg Bourgogne, 45800, St-Jean-de-Braye; tel: 38 86 29 47.* Open Wed–Mon

1400–1730 (Oct–Mar); Wed–Mon 1000–1200, 1400–1900 (Apr–Sept); Fr.18.

South of the river is the **Jardin des Plantes et sa roseraie** (botanical and rose gardens), *av. de St-Mesmin*. Open daily 0730–1830 (Mar, Apr, Oct); daily 0730–2000 (May–Sept); 0800–1730 (Nov–Feb); free. Althought its origin is as a 17th-century apothecaries' garden, its layout dates to 1834 and there are more than 560 varieties of roses, earning Orléans the tribute 'city of roses'.

Further south, after a 15-min drive on the D14, is **Parc Floral de la Source**; *tel: 38 63 33 17.* Open daily 0900–1800 (Apr–mid-Nov); daily 1400–1700 (mid-Nov–Mar); entrance Fr.20 Laid out in the 1960s, the landscaped flower beds make a lovely setting for a family visit. Dahlias, chysanthemums, irises and especially roses are the best displays within the park which is laid out around the lake formed by the source of the River Loiret. A little train runs around the 35-hectare site, Mon–Thur, Sat, Sun afternoons (June–Sept); Fr.7. Bicycle-style vehicles for four are another way to get around; Fr.30. There is a small zoo, deers in the woods, a butterfly pavilion, flamingoes in the lake plus a snack bar, play area and picnic spots. The park is beside the university and its modern complex of buildings.

Legends of the Loire

The Loire Valley resounds with stories of the shepherdess, **Joan of Arc** and her inspired military campaign which led ultimately to the end of English rule in France but also to her own martyrdom at the age of 19 in May 1431 when she was burned at the stake in Rouen. Her image appears in stained glass and paintings and has inspired poets, playwrights and film directors. Her story is based on fact – with numerous plaques at Beaugency, Blois, Chinon, Gien and Tours marking her progress through the Loire Valley – but has transcended into mythology, thanks to the heavenly voices she heard, the knight in shining armour she became and her elevation to the sainthood in 1920.

Royal historical anecdotes also abound in the Loire Valley due to its popularity as a playground with the court. Its excesses are now the folklore of the châteaux, such as Chenonceau, where Catherine de Medici was notorious for her bevy of naked nymphs and satyrs emerging from the garden thickets as part of the entertainment. Young women adorned as mermaids in the moat welcomed merrymakers.

Literature has inspired many Loire stories as several famous writers were born or educated in the region, including Rabelais, Ronsard and Balzac. At Chinon, Rabelais turned a squabble about fishing rights on the Loire into a fantasy war in his novel *Gargantua*. At Talcy, Ronsard was smitten by the 15-year-old Cassandra and wrote flowery poems about his unrequited love. Children's literature has done rather well out of the Loire, too, with Charles Perrault's fairy tales about the Sleeping Beauty, Little Red Riding Hood and Bluebeard.

In the local museums of little villages, the River Loire is likely to be the subject of folklore especially about dangerous events such as the shipwrecks or floods. Local saints add colour, as in the story that when St Martin's relics were being transported from Auxerre to Tours the procession left cured invalids in its wake, even two who didn't want to lose their livelihood of begging. The Vendée wars in support of the monarchy inspired heroic deeds, whose histories are recorded in such places as St-Florent-le-Vieil.

ORLÉANS–ANGERS

The Loir flows at a placid pace for 300 km from south of Chartres to its confluence with the Loire tributary, the Sarthe, just outside Angers. Unlike its grand sister river, there is an intimate air to the Loir as it loops its way through handsome, quiet towns and villages with pretty bridges, past châteaux ruins, into small forests and along pastoral countryside.

This countryside lends itself well to horse-riding, cycling, walking, fishing and water sports. En route there are churches with medieval wall paintings, cave dwellings, many craft shops, a wonderful château at Le Lude and the charming birthplace home of the poet Pierre de Ronsard at La Possonnière

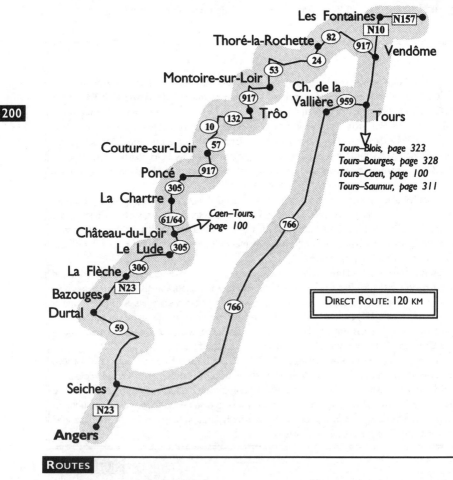

Orléans

Les Fontaines — N157

N10

Thoré-la-Rochette — 82   917   Vendôme

24

53

Montoire-sur-Loir   Ch. de la
Vallière   959

917   Trôo   Tours

132

10

Couture-sur-Loir   57   Tours–Blois, page 323
Tours–Bourges, page 328
Tours–Caen, page 100
Tours–Saumur, page 311

Poncé   917

305

La Chartre

61/64   Caen–Tours,
page 100

Château-du-Loir

Le Lude   305   766

La Flèche   306

Bazouges   N23

Durtal

59   766

DIRECT ROUTE: 120 KM

Seiches

N23

Angers

ROUTES

DIRECT ROUTE

There is no straightforward fast road from Orléans to Angers. This 120 km route is one of the most efficient. From Orléans, take N157 past Morée to N10, turn left and take N10 to Tours. Turn right to join D959 to Château-la-Vallière, then turn left on D766 to Seiches, then turn left on N23 to Angers.

SCENIC ROUTE

For this 202 km route, follow the N157 from Orléans to **Les Fontaines**, turn left on N10 to **Vendôme**, then turn right on D917 to D82, turn right to Thoré-la-Rochette. Continue on D82 to D24, then turn left to follow D53 to Les Roches-l'Evêque. Continue on D53 to **Montoire-sur-le-Loir**, turn right on D917 to **Trôo**, then continue on D917 to turn left at Sougé onto the road to Artins. Turn right on D10 to D57 to turn left for La Possonnière.

Return to D57, continuing to the river through **Couture-sur-Loir**. After crossing the river, turn left on D917 to **Poncé-sur-le-Loir**.

Follow D305 to cross the river into **La-Chartre-sur-le-Loir**. Continue on D305 through Marçon, turn right on D61 to Ste-Cécile, turn left on D64 to **Château-du-Loir**.

Then continue on D305 to cross river into **Le Lude**, then take D306 to **La Flèche**. After, take N23 to **Bazouges-sur-le-Loir**, then stay on N23 to cross river at **Durtal**.

Turn left onto D59 through the forest of Chambiers to Beauvau. Turn right on D109 to **Seiches-sur-le-Loir**. There, turn left onto N23, continuing on to Angers.

VENDÔME

Tourist Office: *Hôtel du Bellay-Le Saillant, Parc Ronsard, 41100 Vendôme; tel 54 77 05 07.* Open Mon–Sat 0900–1230, 1415–1830, Sun, public holidays 1000–1300 (May–Sept); Mon–Fri 0900–1230, 1415–1830, Sat 0900–1230, 1415–1800 (Nov–Mar). Also at **Abbaye de Trinité** (Trinity Abbey), daily 0900–1900 (June–Sept). The main Tourist Office gives out information, including *What's On In the Loir Valley*, an in-depth brochure in English. It will book hotels.

ACCOMMODATION

There is a good selection of small and medium-sized hotels in the town and plenty of *chambres d'hôtes*. **Camping des Grands Pres**, *r. Geoffroy Martel; tel: 54 77 00 27.*

SIGHTSEEING

Guided walking tours in French are held throughout the summer, Apr–Oct. Themes and days vary but subjects can include *Vendôme Through The Ages*, Fr.20; *Vendôme and its City Walls*, Fr.25; *The Abbey in the Days of the Monks*, Fr.25; and *The Art of Church Building in the Middle Ages*, Fr.25.

Vendôme's half-timbered houses with brick in-filling make a pretty background to the brightly coloured awnings of the many outdoor cafés and moderately-priced restaurants, especially in the *pl. St-Martin*, one of the town's market squares. This one is presided over by the statue of the town's famous son, the Marquis de Rochambeau, romantic hero of the American revolution who fought at Yorktown and who was born here in 1725. Next to it is the **Abbaye de la Trinité** with its remarkable façade of flame-shaped stone carvings. A 12th-century bell tower from an earlier church stands separately next to it. In the cloisters is **Musée de Vendôme**, *tel: 54 77 26 13.* Open Mon, Wed–Sat 1000–1200, 1400–1800. Fr.14, free on Wed. It has fine ceramics, archaeological finds and tableaux of local life of the past.

High above the town on a rocky outcrop are the ruins of the **château**; there is a shaded car park next to it on the *r. du Château* The building was pulled down in 1793 and its grounds are now laid out in landscaped walks and gardens. These are open daily 0900–2000 (Sept–May), 0900–2100 (June–Aug). *tel: 54 77 01 33.* The best surviving tower is the **Tour de Poitiers**.

Down in the town, the winding River Loir breaks up into various streams. A riverside walk goes past the **Lavoir des Cordeliers**, a half-timbered two-storey wash house with a drying room jutting out over the river, and continues past willow trees, weirs and mills. There are rowing boat trips, with a commentary in French. **Le Vieux Moulin** (the old mill); *tel: 54 72 29 10,* is open daily 1400–1900 (July–Aug); Sat, Sun, public holidays 1400–1900 (May, June, Sept). Fr.20. Outside the town, the **Forêt de Vendôme** has many sign-posted walks including some which pass bird-watching hides. There is a picnic area and children's playground. The Tourist Office sells guidebooks about the forest.

THORÉ-LA-ROCHETTE

Tourist Office: *Mairie; tel: 54 72 80 82.* Open Mon–Wed 0830–1200; Thurs–Fri 1500–1800. There is one hotel and the Tourist Office has information about *chambres d'hôtes,* but does not make bookings.

SIGHTSEEING

The town's main attraction is the **Train Touristique** (tourist train); trips take

place Sat, Sun, public holidays 1415 (June–Aug); additional trip Sun 0900 (mid-July–mid-Aug). Book at the Tourist Office. Fr.65 (Fr.50 children). This jaunty 1950s train chugs along a little track for a 36 km round trip to Trôo. The price includes entrance to the exhibition at Trôo and the wine museum at **Thoré**. The trip ends with wine tasting at the old rail station at Thoré which is converted into a **Maison de Vin et des Produits des Terroirs Vendômois**, a centre of Vendôme food products and wines. The centre is open daily 1500–1900 (June–Aug). Free entry. There is also a **Musée de la Vigne et du Vin** (wine and vineyard museum); *tel: 54 77 05 07.* Open Sat–Sun 1400–1900 (July–Sept). Free.

MONTOIRE-SUR-LE-LOIR

Tourist Office: *18 pl Clemenceau, 41800 Montoire; tel: 54 85 00 29.* Open Mon 1430–1730, Tues–Sat 1000–1200, 1430–1730 (May–Sept). Hours may be extended as the Tourist Office has only recently opened. There are five hotels and many *chambres d'hôtes.*

SIGHTSEEING

This is a rather plain town but with a pretty bandstand in its main square, *pl. St-Quentin*, and riverside walks along the left bank where there are some 16th–18th-century houses. Markets take place Wed afternoon and Sat morning. The **Chapelle St-Gilles** (priory chapel of St Gilles) has Romanesque paintings decorating the apse. Fr.10. Obtain the key from a nearby shop, *33A r. St-Oustrille*. Montoire stages an annual festival of folk music around 15 Aug and plans to open a **Musée-Spectacle Musiques Traditionelles** (museum of traditional folkloric music).

About 3 km outside the town is the **Parc Botanique de la Fosse**, *Fontaine-*

les-Coteaux 41800 Montoire; tel: 54 85 38 63. Tours only, in French, daily at 1430, 1630 (Easter-Sept); extra tour Wed-Fri at 1500 (Jul–Aug); daily 1500 (Oct-Easter). Fr.50. Since 1751, several generations of one family have planted thousands of trees and shrubs from all over the world.

TRÔO

Tourist Office: *tel: 54 72 51 27.* Opening times vary as the information is dispensed from a private home in this village, which has a do-it-yourself approach to tourism, with some residents opening their cave homes to the public, usually free, relying on the sale of postcards and guidebooks.

Riddled with troglodyte caves in its cliffsides, the village is unusual and includes the ruins of the **Maladerie Ste-Catherine**, an old leper house, opposite the town hall. To reach the caves, there is a steep walk up from the car park. On the other side of the river (reached by a bridge down the road) is the rather grand **Église St Jacques-des-Gerets** which has ancient wall paintings. Inside one of the caves is an exhibition about the village history. Open Mon–Fri 1400–1800, Sat–Sun 0900–1200, 1400–1900 (mid-May–mid-Sept). Free.

COUTURE-SUR-LE LOIR

Just outside this hamlet the romantic poet, Pierre de Ronsard, was born in 1524 at the **Manoir de la Possonière**; *tel: 54 72 40 05.* Open Sat, Sun, public holiday 1530, 1630 (Apr–Oct). In addition, Wed–Fri 1530 (mid June–Aug). Guided visits only, in French with English leaflet. Fr.30. The poet lived in this handsome manor house, with its mullioned windows and fine garden, until he was 12. He wished to be buried on the nearby willow-fringed **l'Île Verte** (the green island) where the River

Braye flows picturesquely into Le Loir. His parents are buried in the local church, with their effigies showing the elaborate costumes of the era. Ronsard eventually died at the priory at St-Cosmé, near Tours, but he often wrote about the beauty of this rural place.

PONCÉ-SUR-LE-LOIR

Tourist Office: *pl. de la Fontaine St-Julien; tel: 43 79 02 98.*

SIGHTSEEING

The town has an artistic reputation thanks to fashionable little crafts shops in the town, including one devoted to painted furniture. In a fine converted, 18th-century water mill is the **Centre d'Art et d'Artisanat, Tourisme, Pédagogie et Culture** (arts and crafts centre). **Moulins de Paillard** (Paillard Mill); *tel: 43 44 45 31.* Open Tues–Sat 0900–1200, 1400–1830; Sun, public holidays 1430–1830. Fr.24 (weekdays); Fr.18. (Sun, public holidays). Explanatory notices in English. Beside the river bank there is a picnic area with children's play area and cafeteria. The exhibition area includes expert craftsmen at work. Displays include furniture-making, leatherwork, glass blowing, ceramics, enamelling, hat and clothes designing, candle-making, pottery. There is an audio-visual room showing films on various crafts.

The town's 16th-century **château** is open Mon–Sat 1000–1200, 1400–1800, Sun 1400–1800 (Apr–Sept). Fr.24. The entry includes a museum within the château which has displays about traditonal art and folklore. There is a pretty walk to the old dovecote and a fine **church**, St Julien's, with 12th-century wall paintings. The craft workshops hold open days (July–Aug) and there is a festival of music at the end of June.

203

LA CHARTRE-SUR-LE-LOIR

Tourist Office: *Parking Central; tel: 43 44 40 04*. Open Mon–Sat 1000–1230, 1530–1800, Sun 1000–1230, (mid-June–Aug); Tues, Fri 1500–1700, Thur, Sat 1000–1230 (Sept–mid-June).

There are several hotels and numerous cafés and restaurants in this small town, especially along the handsome square, *pl. de la Republique.*

CHÂTEAU-DU-LOIR

Tourist Office: *2 av. Jean Jaurès, parc Henri-Goude 72500 Château-du-Loir; tel: 43 44 56 68*. Open Mon–Sat 1000–1200, 1400–1800, Sun 1000–1200 (June–mid-Sept); *Mairie, tel: 43 44 00 38* Open Mon–Fri 0800–1200, 1330–1730, Sat 0800–1200 (mid-Sept–May). There are four hotels, a campsite and several *chambres d'hôtes*. The Tourist Office will make bookings and there is a detailed English/French brochure about the town and its region.

For further details of the town, see Caen–Tours, p. 106.

LE LUDE

Tourist Office: *pl. François de Nicolay, 72800 Le Lude; tel: 43 94 62 20*. Open Mon 1400–1800, Tues–Sat 0900–1200, 1400–1800 (Easter–Sept). There are two hotels; the Tourist Office makes bookings.

SIGHTSEEING

The charming town has narrow streets, even more picturesque on Thur market days. It is justly known for its very fine château, with its fine collection of furniture, tapestries and paintings. **Château Le Lude;** *tel: 43 94 60 09,* open daily 1430–1800 (Apr–Sept); gardens open 1000–1200, 1400–1800; Fr.30. Guided tours only (including English). The entrance is in a sleepy back street of the town. Inside are two massive cylindrical towers of medieval proportions but with Renaissance decorative details. Le Lude's architecture spans several centuries and is richly furnished. The first one was built in the 10th century by the dukes of Anjou. In 1457 the Daillon family took over the property and built the present château. It is constructed on a square plan, rising from a wide dry moat. During the 19th century major renovations took place by the Talhouët-Roy family whose initials are found on the chimneys. Inside look for the wall paintings in the south-east tower. The Grand Salon is painted in pearl grey, a popular colour in the late 18th-century.

There is a cast of 350 costumed characters in its *son et lumière* show at 2230, days vary (end of June, July–Aug). Fr.85, probably the most splendid of all such shows. It has won awards including the French tourism 'Oscar' and other accolades. The performances take place on a grass-covered stage beside the water with many flood-lit fountains and the château in the background.

Costumed characters also enliven a visit to the château as they inhabit such rooms as the reception hall, drawing room, kitchens and stables. They are also present at afternoon tea accompanied by music. Fr.45. Information *tel: 43 94 67 27*. There are regular gardening weekends with demonstrations and talks (in French) at the beginning of June.

LA FLÈCHE

Tourist Office: *Hall Coppélia, 72200 La Flèche; tel: 43 94 02 53*. Open Mon–Sat 0930–1230, 1400–1845 (mid-June–mid-Sept).

ACCOMMODATION AND FOOD

The town has 20 small and medium-sized hotels and hotel restaurants and many *chambres d'hôtes.* The Tourist Office will make bookings.

SIGHTSEEING

The main attraction is the **Prytanée Militaire National** (national military academy), *tel: 43 94 03 96, extension 704.* Open second and third weeks 1400–1800 (Apr); daily 1030–1200, 1400–1830. Fr. 20 (during school holidays) Fr.15 (term time). Descartes was a pupil at this prestigious school, one of the most famous Jesuit colleges of the 17th century. Now a state school, it has a grand gateway into a fine courtyard. A visit includes the library, decorated with frescos, the great halls and the St-Louis chapel which has an urn containing the ashes of the hearts of Henri IV and Marie de Medici. The visits are sometimes guided by the pupils themselves (in French and English). Henry IV founded the school in 1603 to teach young people 'honour and virtue in order to serve the community'.

The school was revamped by Louis XV and then Napoléon.There is also the **Musée de la Providence**, *32 r de la Beufferie;* open Wed–Mon 1430–1800, 1700–1830; also first and third Sun of each month, 1500–1700. Free. It looks at the local history and the work of the religious communities.

BAZOUGES-SUR-LE-LOIR

Tourist Office: *Mairie; tel: 43 45 33 94.* Open Mon 1500–1800, Tues–Sun 1030–1230, 1500–1830 (mid-June–mid-Sept). It does not make hotel bookings.

The little town has two châteaux. One is the privately owned **Château de la Barbée**; *tel: 43 45 34 68.* Open daily 1500–1830 (July–Aug). Fr. 25. Guided visits in French only. The **Château de Bazouges**; *tel: 43 45 32 62.* Open Tues 1000–1200; Thurs, Sat, Sun 1500–1800

(mid-June–mid-Sept). château and gardens Fr.18; garden only Fr.5.

DURTAL

Tourist Office: *Mairie: tel: 41 76 30 24.* Open Mon 1500–1800, Tues-Sat 1000–1230, 1500–1800, Sun 1000–1230 (mid-June–mid Sept). There is one hotel and *chambres d'hôtes.* The Tourist Office does not make bookings.

SIGHTSEEING

There are a few antique shops in the little town, which stages a huge antique fair on the last Sun of Sept. Spanning the 11th–16th centuries the imposing **Château de Durtal**, perched on top of a rocky outcrop, is not furnished. Open Wed–Mon 1000–1200, 1500–1800, Sun 1500–1800. Guided tours in French only. Fr.10. The keys for the **Église de Nôtre Dame** are at *9 pl. des Terrasses.*

About 2 km outside the town is the conservation village and open-air museum of **Les Rairies**, famous for its terracotta clay works. To see the potters and kilns in action, visit **Maison de la Terre Cuite**, *rte de Fougeré; tel: 41 76 33 12.* Open Sun 1500–1900 (Easter-Oct); in addition Tues–Sun (June–Aug). Fr.10.

SEICHES-SUR-LE-LOIR

Tourist Office: *Mairie: tel: 41 76 20 37.* Open Mon–Fri 0830–1200, 1330–1800 (May-Sept). There is one hotel. The Tourist Office does not make bookings.

There are fabulous views over the Loir Valley. One of the churches, **La Chapelle de Nôtre Dame de la Garde** was a stopping point on the great pilgrimages to Santiago de Compostela in Spain and has a splendid 18th-century altar. There is a giant antiques centre, **Le Grenier Seichois**, *72 r. Nationale; tel: 41 76 60 42.* Open daily 0900–1830.

205

ORLÉANS–BOURGES

A variety of museums bring a change of pace to this route although there are still interesting châteaux, including the one at Sully which is partly a work site showing off its renovations, another which demonstrates medieval war machines and one with Scottish lineage. There is a pretty Victorian canal forming a ribbon of water over the Loire. The River Sauldre brings its charms to the river views which include the vineyard country of Sancerre.

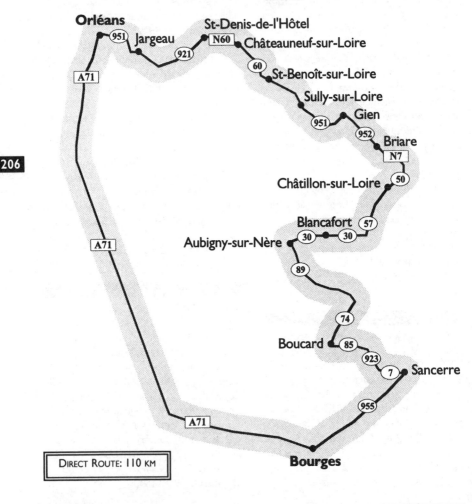

DIRECT ROUTE: 110 KM

ROUTES

DIRECT ROUTE

From Orléans take autoroute A71 the 110 km, to Bourges.

SCENIC ROUTE

From Orléans take the pretty D951 through Sandillon to **Jargeau**. Turn left to cross the Loire on the D921 to **St-Denis-de-l'Hôtel**. Turn right on N60 to **Châteauneuf-sur-Loire**. Take D60 to Germigny-Des-Près, then follow D60 through flat, tree-fringed countryside, to **St Benoît-sur-Loire** and then to **Sully-sur-Loire**, sometimes along the river. Take D951 towards **Gien**, turning left to cross the river into Gien. After Gien, follow D952 to **Briare**. From Briare, take N7 for 4.5 km to turn right onto D50 to cross the Loire in **Chatillon-sur-Loire**. Continuing on D50, turn right at la Fousserotte on to D57, then left on to D30 to **Blancafort**. Then take D30 to **St Aubigny-sur-Nère**. From the town, take D89 to the **Château de la Verrarie**, turning right at Le Noyer on to D74 to **Boucard**. Then take D85 to Menetou-Râtel to join D923, then D7 to **Sancerre**. From here. take D955 to Bourges, joining D7 at St Germain du Puy for the Bourges town centre.

JARGEAU

Tourist Office: *La Chanterie, blvd Carnot 45150 Jargeau; tel: 38 59 83 42.* Open Mon–Sat 0900–1200. 1400–1800, Sun, public holidays 1000–1200 (June–Aug); Mon–Sat 0900–1200, 1400–1800 (Sept–May). You will find a hotel, *a gîte d'étape, chambres d'hôtes* and a campsite on the river bank; *tel: 38 59 70 04*. The banner-waving statue of Joan of Arc in the *pl. du Matriot* honours her bloody victory over the English at Jargeau on 12 June

1429. The twisting main street (*r. Porte-Berry*) of this pleasant, flat town is not suitable for cars. A walk takes visitors past old houses, some leaning with age, or along the river with its wide views. Next to the Tourist Office is the **Musée Oscar Roty**; *tel: 38 59 80 13.* Fr.10. Open Sat 1430–1830, Sun 1000–1200, 1430–1830. Oscar Roty's work as an engraver appears on French francs with the graceful image of a female sower. There is also an exhibition dedicated to the Loire, the 'royal river'. Open daily 0900–1200, 1400–1800. Fr.5.

ST-DENIS-DE-L'HÔTEL

La Maison Maurice Genevoix *45550 St-Denis-de-l'Hôtel; tel: 38 59 02 24.* Open Sat, Sun 1000–1200, 1400–1800. Free. Next to the church in this neat hamlet is a small exhibition, which is as much devoted to the wildlife as it is to the novelist Maurice Genevoix, 1890–1980. He wrote movingly about nature and the wild animals and birds of the region in such books as *Rémi des Rauches* about a fisherman on the Loire and *Rabiolot* about a poacher in the Sologne countryside.

CHÂTEAUNEUF-SUR-LOIRE

Tourist Office: *pl. Aristide Briand 45110 Châteauneuf-sur-Loire; tel: 38 58 44 79.* Open Mon–Sat 0930–1230, 1400–1900; Sun 0930–1230 (May–Sept); Mon–Sat 1000–1230, 1500–1900 (Oct–Apr). Besides booking hotels, the office has a bureau de change Sat–Mon (May–Sept). There are campsites in and near the town. Although bombarded in World War II, the town with some cobbled streets leading to the château, has recovered well.

Château de Châteauneuf-sur-Loire *45110 Châteauneuf; tel 38 58 41 18.* Only the park and the **Musée de la Marine de Loire** (museum of navigation) inside the

207

château, owned by the town, are open. Sun 1400–1800 (Jan–Mar); daily 1400–1800 (June); Mon, Wed–Fri 1400–1800; Sat–Sun 1000–1200, 1400–1800 (July–Aug); daily (closed Tues) 1400–1800 (Sept); Sat, Sun 1400–1800 (Oct); Sun, public holidays 1400–1800 (Nov–Dec). Last admissions are at 1730. Fr.13.50; (Fr.7 children). Some 5000 items, including models, sculptures, paintings, engravings and fishing tackle, illustrate the work, pleasures and dangers that people living along the Loire have undertaken, enjoyed and endured. The pleasant park has a 900m rhododendron walkway (in bloom May, June) and an arboretum of rare trees. The latter was laid out by the botanist Huilard d'Hérou, influenced by English gardens. Inside the town's much restored, 15th-century **Église St-Martial**, note the flamboyant tomb of one of Louis XIV's ministers, Louis Phélypeaux de la Vrillière (1598–1681) with its grisly skeletons.

Just 4 km away is **Germigny-des-Près known for its Oratory**; *tel: 38 58 27 97*. Open daily 0800–2000 (Apr–Oct); daily 0930–1900 (Nov–Mar). Free. English leaflet. This simple church set amid cypress trees was built in 803 and is one of France's oldest churches. Inside there are intricate arches, alabaster-filled windows and a 9th-century mosaic from the emperor's palace at Ravenna. The adjoining shop sells English information (a leaflet, Fr.2; book, Fr.30).

ST-BENOÎT-SUR-LOIRE

Tourist Office: *44 r. Orléanaise 45730 St-Benoît-sur-Loire; tel: 38 35 79 00*. Open Mon 1430, 1830, Tues–Sat 0930–1200, 1430–1830 (March–Oct); Sat 0930–1200 (Jan–Feb). In the tourist office is a permanent exhibition about a local poet Max Gercob and the French Resistance as well as changing exhibitions about the Loire.

There are a couple of hotels and the **Camping Municipal 'Le Port'**; *tel 38 35 79 00*.

SIGHTSEEING

The **Basilique de Saint-Benoît** dominates the village. Open daily 0700–2200. Free (donation). From May–Sept, there are guided tours in French for visitors in groups of 10; the gathering point is outside the church, Mon–Fri 1100, 1500. Fr.15. English information available in the adjoining bookshop which sells handicrafts made by the monks. Originally there was an important abbey here and the present church was built between 1067 and 1150. The monks here were custodians of the relics of St Benedict which attracted many pilgrims, including Joan of Arc and Charles VII in June 1429. They were mainly driven out during the revolution but returned in 1944. It is moving to hear their Gregorian chants at various daily services, but always Mon–Fri at noon, Sun at 1100. Although gauntly simple, the church boasts clever, sometimes humorous, carvings of biblical scenes on the stone capitals in the vaulted porch. Their theme is paradise receiving souls.

SULLY-SUR-LOIRE

Tourist Office: *pl. Gen. de Gaulle 45600 Sully-sur-Loire; tel: 38 36 23 70*. Open Mon–Sat 0900–1900, Sun 1000–1200 (Apr–Oct); Mon–Sat 0900–1200, 1430–1830; Sun 1000–1200. (Oct–Mar). For a small town, it is well-served with hotels and other acommodation. **Château de Sully**, *45600 Sully-sur-Loire; tel: 38 36 36 86* is open daily 1000–1200, 1400–1700 (Mar–Apr, Nov); daily 1000–1200, 1400–1800 (May–mid June) Fr.15; (Fr.10). Self-guided tour with English leaflet. Guided visits in English available mid-May–Aug. 'Men at work' should be

208

one of the signs promoting the attractions of this huge château undergoing massive restoration since 1992. Visitors see the work in progress, with bits and pieces of decorated stone lying about as each room is taken apart. There is an exhibition about medieval building. An excellent 21-page English booklet guides visitors through each room, explaining its purpose and any historical events. The upper great hall has a remarkable timber-framed roof of chestnut The 14th-century château was transformed by Maximilien de Béthune, chief minister to Henri IV and better known by the title of Duc de Sully, which the king gave him in 1606. Voltaire was exiled here in 1716 for writing a satire about the regent Phillipe of Orléans and Joan of Arc was also imprisoned here for a time.

GIEN

Tourist Office: *pl. Jean Jaurès 45501 Gien; tel; 38 67 25 28.* Open Mon–Sat 1000–1900, Sun 1000–1300 (June–Sept); Mon–Sat 0900–1200, 1400–1800 (Oct–May). The riverside road is lined with cafés and restaurants.

The town was extensively restored in the regional style after the war. There are markets on Wed and Sat 0800–1300. **Musée International de La Chasse** (international museum of hunting) *45501 Gien; tel: 38 67 69 69* is open Tues–Sun 1000–1200, 1400–1700 (Oct–Dec, mid-Feb–Apr); Mon–Sun 0930–1830 (May–Oct). Fr.25. To join a guided tour in French, Fr.5. A thorough English leaflet is available. The marvellous brick-walled and timber-roofed great upper hall shows works by François Desportes. who painted hunt scenes for Louis XIV. There are galleries about falconry, hunting costumes and trophies from around the world. **Château de St Brisson**, *45500 Gien; tel: 38 36 71 29* is open Thur–Tues

1000–1200, 1400–1800 (Easter–mid-Nov). Fr.20. In the town centre, the stone château with brick patterned walls was commissioned by Anne of Beaujeu, eldest daughter of Louis XI, who was regent for her brother Charles VIII. In the dry moat are full-size replicas of medieval war machines including a battering ram and catapult. There are summer demonstrations of these weapons on Sun 1530 and 1630.

Since 1821, the town has been known for its manufacture of **faïence** pottery – note the street signs made by the pottery factory and the plaques of the stations of the cross as well as the scenes from the life of Joan of Arc in the modern church named after her, next to the château. The warrior saint rode through the town in 1429. The factory's invention is the *bleu de Gien*, a deep blue highlighted with yellow. Visit the **Musée de la Faïencerie** (ceramics museum), *78 pl. de la Victoire; tel 38 67 00 05.* Open daily Mon–Sat 0900–1200, 1345–1815, Sun, public holidays 1000–1145, 1400–1745. Fr.16; (Fr.13). It is housed in the paste storage cellar of the old factory, with hundreds of examples and a 10-min video (in English) about production techniques. There is a factory shop of seconds and end-of-line pieces. Open Mon–Sat 0900–1200, 1400–1800.

BRIARE

Tourist Office: *1 pl. Charles de Gaulle 45250 Briare; tel: 38 31 24 51.* Open Mon–Sun 1000–1230, 1500–1900 (Mar–Dec); Mon–Sat 1000–1200, 1500–1800 (Jan–Feb). It is a busy town known for its aqueduct. There are small hotels and *gîtes* as well as restaurants and on the riverside **Camping Le Martinet,** *45250 Briare; tel: 38 31 24 50* (turn right at the bottom of *r. des Grandes*).

The town's main sight is **Le Pont**

Canal (canal bridge), described as a ribbon of water. It carries the **Canal Latéral** across the Loire to connect with the 17th-century Briare canal. The navigation companies using the river Loire from the 14th and 19th centuries encountered unpredictable currents and very shallow waters so Henri IV's brilliant minister, the Duke of Sully, ordered the building of the Briare Canal in 1604. The 664-m iron aqueduct bridge, the longest in the world, was built in 1890–94 with the collaboration of the engineer, Gustave Eiffel, whose name is immortalised with his famous tower in Paris. In Briare, boats gliding over the Loire on this mid-air construction, lined with art nouveau lamps and with the forest-fringed banks in the background, are a photographer's delight. It is possible to stroll along the aqueduct path. It is better to park beside the aqueduct than in the busy town. There are a variety of boat trips, some with lunch or dinner, leaving the **Port de Plaisance**; *tel: 38 37 12 75*. The **Bâteau Yoline** is also a houseboat available for weekend (Fr.1300–Fr.1600) or five-day (Fr.2250–Fr.2600) trips; *tel: 85 74 74 85*. There is also a little **tourist train** leaving the Port de Plaisance at 1500, 1600, 1700. Sun (Apr–first week in July; daily (second week in July–Aug); Sun (Sept). Fr.25.

BLANCAFORT

Château de Blancafort, *18410; tel 48 58 60 56*. Open daily 1000–1200, 1400–1830 (last two weeks in May; Oct). daily 1000–1900 (June–Sept). (Mar–Nov); Sat, Sun 1000–1200, 1200–1600 (Nov–mid-Mar). Guided tours only (in French, with English leaflet). Fr.30. This is a neat town built around the church and a solid-looking, 15th-century château set beside a forest on the River Sauldre. It has a low-key history, finely-furnished rooms and a

charming garden, set out formally with the lawn cut into a scroll pattern.

AUBIGNY-SUR-NÈRE

Tourist Office: *r. de l'Église 18700; tel: 48 58 40 20*. Open Mon–Sun 1000–1200, 1430–1930 (May–Oct). Tourist information in winter is at the *Hôtel de Ville; tel: 48 81 50 00*. Open Mon–Fri 0800–1200, 1400–1800. Neither office makes hotel bookings but leaflets about the local hotels and several campsites.

SIGHTSEEING

Proud of its Scottish connections, it calls itself **La Cité des Stuarts**, even boasting a coat of arms – three gold buckles on a purple backdrop – borrowed from John Stuart of Darnley, Constable of the Scottish Army, who helped fight the English during the Hundred Years' War. He was awarded the town and land by Charles VII in 1423. The pretty town has half-timbered brick houses along *r. de Bourg-Coutant, r. des Foulons,* and *r. Camboumac,* so different from the limestone houses along much of the Loire to the west. The Nère flows through the town to join the Sauldre. Inside the town hall is **Musée de la Vieille Alliance** (Auld Alliance) between France and Scotland; *tel: 48 81 50 00*. Open daily 1000–1200, 1500–1900 (July–Sept). Fr.15. There are English leaflets and a 10-min video in English. There are also free exhibitions on the Resistance.

About 11 km away is **Château de la La Verrerie**, *18700 Aubigny sur Nère; tel: 48 58 06 91*. It has 12 *chambres d'hôtes*. Open daily 1000–1200, 1400–1900 (Easter–mid-Nov); last admission 1830 (May–Sept); 1530 (Mar, Apr, Oct, first two weeks in Nov). Fr.30 (Fr.20). The visit is partly guided with a 20-min commentary, including music in the chapel.

English leaflet. In the park is an *auberge* open for meals Apr–Oct (closed Tues, Wed morning); *tel: 48 58 24 27*. Reflected romantically in a placid lake and tucked into the verdant forest of Ivoy, this compact, well-furnished château was built at the end of the 15th century by Béraud Stuart, grandson of John Stuart who had been awarded the land. Scenes of family events are painted in frescos in the chapel. Later there was an English resident, the Duchess of Portsmouth, one of the mistresses of Charles II, the most flamboyant of the Stuart monarchs. Her descendants sold the castle to the Marquis of Vogüé, an ancestor of the present owner.

BOUCARD

Château de Boucard, *Le Noyer 18260; tel: 48 58 72 81.* Open Wed–Sun 1000–1145, 1400–1645 (Feb); Thur–Tues 1000–1145, 1400–1645 (Mar–May); daily 1000–1145,1400–1845 (June–mid-Aug); Thur–Tues 1000–1145, 1400–1730 (mid-Sept). Fr.30. First built in 1350, this small, many-turretted fortress on the River Sauldre has a formidable appearance. Crossing over the little stone bridge, visitors enter a fine Renaissance hall and the rooms once occupied by the Maréchal Duc de Navailles who was exiled here by Louis X1V. English leaflet.

SANCERRE

Tourist Office: *de Nouvelle Place 80300 Sancerre; tel: 48 54 08 21.* Open Mon–Fri 1000–1200, 1430–1830; Sat, Sun public holidays 1000–1200, 1500–1800 (June–Sept) Tourist information in winter from the *Hôtel de Ville* (Town Hall); *tel: 48 54 0026.* Open Mon–Fri 0900–1200, 1400–1900, Sat 0900–1200 (Oct–May). Neither office makes bookings for hotels but has leaflets. The delightful town has a good selection of small hotels and restaurants.

La route Jacques Coeur

Many a finance minister built a château but Jacques Coeur is the only one to have a tourist trail named after him. Son of a Bourges furrier, he was a financial wizard who built up a trading empire, became treasurer of Bourges in 1427 and eventually master of the mint to Charles VII. His place in French history includes mustering up the money to pay Joan of Arc's troops. He was a victim of plots against him and in 1451 he was exiled, dying five years later on a Greek island. Most Tourist Offices will have a leaflet outlining this route, which includes 18 scenic places associated with him. The leaflet is available in English, if not at every tourist office, certainly at the Bourges office. The scenic route outlined in this chapter includes some Jacques Coeur sites including Gien, Aubigny-sur-Nère, La Verrerie, Blancafort and Boucard.

On its hilltop surrounded by endless vineyards, Sancerre overlooks red-roofed houses and rolling countryside which, viewed from miles away, resemble a Tuscan landscape. Narrow steep streets have picturesque houses and shops where craftsmen make pottery and vintners display *Dégustation Gratuite* (free tasting) signs to sell the famous Sancerre wines. For views over the vineyards, park at the **Esplanade de la Porte César.** The region has been making fine wines since the 11th century, almost 80 per cent white from Sauvignon grapes and fruity red from Pinot grapes. It is a good base for visitors to explore wine villages such as Pouilly-sur-Loire, St-Thibault-sur-Loire, St- Satur and Chavignol (famous for its Côte de Mont Dâmné wines and Crottin de Chavignol goat's cheese).

ORLÉANS–PARIS

Although this route goes from built-up Orléans to the Paris conurbation, it offers some rural treats, including the sleepy but surprising forest village of Milly-la-Forêt, the picturesque artists' colony at Barbizon and the grand forest town, Fontainebleau, boasting one of the most important châteaux in France. The route includes the spanking new renovation of the Château de Chamerolles, with a perfume museum, and the largely, unchanged 350-year-old Château Vaux-le-Vicomte, which proved to be an ostentatious folly

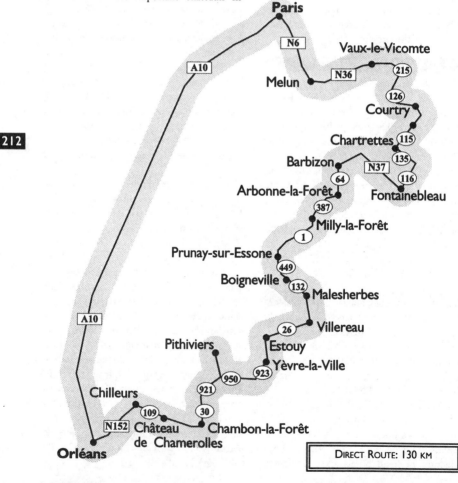

DIRECT ROUTE: 130 KM

ROUTES

DIRECT ROUTE

The direct road from Orléans to Paris is the A10, 130 km, just over 1½ hrs away.

SCENIC ROUTE

This scenic route is 178 km. Since Fontainebleau is easily a day out in its own right, this route can be spread out with an overnight stay so as to enjoy the slower pace of the smaller rural attractions.

At Orléans, leave on the N152 through the east side suburb of Saint-Jean de Braye. Keep on the N152 through the flat, forest countryside (with picnic tables), past **Loury**, to the cross-road village of **Chilleurs-aux-Bois**. Turn right on D109 and the château is almost immediately visible.

Continue on D109 until **Chambon-la-Forêt**, turn left onto D30, following it through the forest leading to D921 to **Pithiviers**.

After Pithiviers, take the little roads to **Malesherbes** – D950 to the first right turning, D923 past **Yèvre-la-Ville** and the ruins of Yèvre-le-Châtel to Estouy, then right on D26 to Villereau, then left on D25 to Malesherbes.

Then take the country roads to **Milly-la-Forêt**. First D132 to Boigneville, then straight onto D449. Just past Prunay-sur-Essone, cross the River Essone through the hamlet of **Buno-Bonnevaux**. The road leads to D1 to Milly-la-Forêt. After the village, follow D837 to Arbonne-la-Forêt, turn left on D64 to **Barbizon**. Then take the forest road past the Gorges d'Apremont which joins the N37 and the roundabout where the roads lead to **Fontainebleau**.

After Fontainebleau, take D116 towards Châtelet-en-Brie but turn left immediately after crossing the Seine at Massoury, onto D135 towards Melun. Turn right at **Chartrettes** onto D115, go past Sivry, then next left onto D126 to **Courtry**. Continue until it joins D215, turn left for the **Château de Vaux-Le-Vicomte**.

After visiting the château, take D215 to the N36 to the **Melun** ring road, then the N6 for the last 46 km to the centre of Paris.

CHILLEURS-AUX-BOIS

This is a crossroad village, whose main attraction is the château, a self-contained complex about 400m to the right. The château has an information desk (including details of other local attractions), a drinks machine, picnic area, toilets and telephone and an excellent gift shop.

Chamerolles Château de Promenades des Parfums *45170 Chilleurs-aux-Bois; tel: 38 39 84 66*. Open Sat–Thur 1000–1700 (Feb–Mar); 1000–1800 (Apr–Sept); 1000–1700 (Oct–Dec). Closed Jan. Fr.25 (Fr.15 children). At first glance, this rather stark château looks over-restored but it rewards a visit as it shows off rooms in deeply-coloured fabrics and furnishings, as rich and fresh as when the original rooms were first decorated in Renaissance grandeur.

It is also a museum of perfumes: there are buttons to press for a whiff of lavender as well as explanatory boards (in French) about bathing habits – in the 17th century water was considered so dangerous to health that personal hygiene required rubbing oneself with linen soaked in perfumes. There is a re-creation of a 19th-century perfume shop and a gallery devoted to today's perfumes in their designer bottles. The still-immature gardens have a perfumed walk and a picnic area. The château layout has remained the

213

same since rebuilding in 1500–30 but the building was a ruin until restored in the early 1990s by the local council. There is a good English leaflet.

PITHIVIERS

Tourist Information: *Mail-Ouest Gare Routière, Pithiviers 45300; tel: 38 30 50 02,* offers many leaflets in French including a walking route, and arranges accommodation. Open Mon 1400–1800; Tues 1000–1200, 1400–1830; Wed–Sat 9000–1200, 1400–1830.

ACCOMMODATION AND FOOD

A pleasant town, Pithiviers has tree-lined avenues (also used for car-parking) called *mails*, surrounding its centre. Hotel accommodation is in small family-run establishments. Restaurants include brasseries and pizzerias in the town centre which is based around the Gothic **Église Saint-Salomon Saint-Gregoire**. In the patisseries and cafés, look out for almond-based sweet specialities such as white-glacé fondants and pastry-topped pies (*feuilletées*). There is a seven-day supermarket in the centre – **Supermarché Champion**, *6 r. de Senives; tel: 38 30 03 59.*

SIGHTSEEIN

Archaeological specimens, local and from as far afield as Australia, are the showpieces of the **Musée Municipal** (town musuem), *17 r. de La Couronne; tel: 38 30 10 72.* Open Wed–Mon 1000–1200, 1400–1800 (1700 on Sat). Closed public holidays. Fr.10. It displays local ancient crafts including saffron cultivation and pottery. plus religious paintings. There is also the **Site Gallo-Romain** (an archaeological site and museum), 3 km away off D9237 in **Pithiviers-le-Vieil**; *tel; 38 30 25 12* Layouts show the temples and baths; the museum has pottery, coins and burial

artefacts. Open Sat, Sun, public holidays 1400–1800 (May–Sept).Fr.5.

Next to the town's rail station are twin attractions: the **Musée des Transports** (Train Museum), *r. Carnot; tel: 38 30 50 02.* Open Sun, public holidays 1400–1800 (May–3rd week Sept); daily 1400–1800 (July–Aug); and the **Chemin de Fer Touristique de Pithiviers** (Pithiviers Steam Railway). Open 1400–1800 Sun, public holidays (May–3rd week in Sept); also Sat 1500 and 1600 (July–Aug). Train and museum Fr.30 (children Fr.22); museum only Fr.15. A group of steam enthusiasts beat the scrap merchants to save this 4 km section of what was once the busy line between Pithiviers and Toury, on which steam trains transported both sugar-beet and passengers. The 600 mm gauge line, dating to 1892, takes on a jolly air for round-trip excursions from Pithiviers to the edge of the small Bellébat wood. In the sheds are 11 steam locomotives, dating from 1870 to 1945.

MALESHERBES

Tourist Office: *2 r.de la Pilonne 45330 Malesherbes; tel: 38 34 81 94.* Open Tues, Thur 1500–1800; Wed 0900–1200; Fri, Sat 1000–1200, 1500–1800; also on Sun 1000–1200 (May–Sept). There are a couple of small hotels in the town. and a fine town **château**; *tel: 38 34 80 18.* Open Wed–Sun 1400–1700 (Nov–third week in Mar); Wed–Sun 1430–1815 (end Mar–Oct). Fr.30 (Fr.15). The château park is open daily 0900–1900; free. In the furnished 15th-century building is a chapel where the owner's statue turns its back on that of his unfaithful wife; there is an imposing dovecote.

MILLY-LA-FORÈT

Tourist Office: *60 r. Jean Cocteau 91490 Milly-la-Forêt; tel: (1) 64 98 83 17.* Open

Mon, Wed, Sun 1000–1200, Thur–Sat 1000–1200, 1430–1730. It books accommodation, mostly in *chambres d'hôtes*; there is no hotel.

A walk around the small village is rewarding as it has a pretty river overlooked by a private château, the 15th-century **Église de Notre-Dame** (church of Our Lady) and a timbered, covered market place dating to 1479, where antique fairs are held every second Sun, 0700–1900 (Apr–Oct). There are sleepy streets with picturesque houses – a plaque marks the the one owned by writer, poet and artist Jean Cocteau.

Tucked into a forest path but near the village centre is **Le Cyclop**, a sculpture made in 1969 by Jean Tinguely. It is possible to climb inside the giant statue (only with a guide, but possibly with some English commentary): phone the Tourist Office. Visits are booked Fri–Sun 1100–1700 (mid-May–Oct). Fr.30. Another artistic sight is the **Chapelle de St-Blaise-des Simples** (St Blaise's chapel); *tel: (1) 64 98 84 94.* Open Wed–Mon 1000–1200, 1430–1800 (Easter–mid-Nov); Sat, Sun, public holidays 1000–1200, 1430–1700 (mid-Nov–Easter). Closed three weeks from mid-Jan. Fr.10. In the chapel is the tomb of Jean Cocteau, who lived in the village from 1946 until his death in 1963. He decorated the chapel's interior with paintings of the medicinal plants which have been cultivated for centuries locally. The plants themselves can be seen 1 km away at the **Conservatoire National des Plantes Medicinales et Aromatiques** (The National Conservatory of Medicinal and Aromatic Plants), *rte de Nemours 91490 Milly-la-Forêt; tel: (1) 64 98 83 77.* Open Mon–Fri 0900–1700 (Apr–Oct); Sat, Sun, public holidays 1400–1800 (May–mid-Sept). Fr.15. The gardens are laid out with herbs and plants once used for dyeing (woad, madder and broom) or for medicinal purposes (camomile, wormwood, belladonna) plus some aquatic varieties. A wooden 19th-century drying shed shows off old agricultural tools and demonstrates how plants were dried on hessian mats.

BARBIZON

Tourist Office: *55 Grande-rue, 77630 Barbizon; tel: (1) 60 66 41 87.* Open Wed–Mon 1000–1230, 1400–1700 (Oct–Mar); Wed–Mon 1000–1230; 1400–1800 (Apr–Sept). It provides leaflets (including an illustrated village map), accommodation and bureau de change. There are working artists' studios, antique shops and 18 hotels and restaurants, some quite smart, along what is basically one main street – **Grande-rue**. The Tourist Office is inside the **Maison de Rousseau**, once home of the artist Théodore Rousseau and now displaying changing exhibitions. Dubbed **Le Village des Peintres** (Village of Painters), this pretty, bustling place has been an attraction since it became an artist's colony in the 19th century, when the Ganne family welcomed artists to its inn, including Diaz, Daubigny, Jacque, Ziem, Barye and Corot, considered to be precursors of the Impressionists. The old inn is now the **Musée Ganne**, *88 Grande Rue; tel: (1) 60 66 22 27,* devoted to the landscapes of the *École de Barbizon* and is also the municipal museum. Open Wed–Mon 0900–1230, 1400–1800 (Apr–Sept); closes at 1700 (Oct–Mar). Fr.25. The **Maison de J. F. Millet**, *29 Grande Rue; tel: (1) 60 66 21 55,* once home of Jean-François Millet, famous for his peasants-in-the-fields paintings, is also a museum.

FONTAINEBLEAU

Tourist Office: *31 pl. Napoléon Bonaparte, 77300 Fontainebleau; tel: 64 22*

215

25 68. Open Mon–Sat 0930–1830, Sun 1000–1230 (July–Aug); Mon–Sat 0930–1230, 1345–1800 Sun Closed (Sept–June).

ACCOMMODATION AND FOOD

Usually visited on a day-trippers' itinerary from Paris, the town nevertheless has several hotels, ranging from two- to four-star. Chains include *Ib*. There are plenty of affordable restaurants and shops.

SIGHTSEEING

Musée National du Château Fontainebleau, *77300 Fontainebleau; tel: 60 71 50 70.* Open Wed–Mon 0930–1230, 1400–1700 (Oct–May) Wed–Mon 0930–1700 (June–Oct); until 1800 (July–Aug). Fr.31 (Fr.20 on Sun); Fr.20 children. The gardens are open daily from 0800 to dusk (free).

This sprawling château conveys a village-like air in summer, what with the snack-bars, ice-cream stands and souvenir shops, all of which comes as a jaunty surprise set in a busy town, especially after the quiet roads of the surrounding forest, which covers 20,000 hectares and has numerous footpaths.

Within the château, mostly commissioned by Francois I in the 16th century, are various sections, parts of which may be closed, especially the **Petits Appartements**, which were the private rooms. These rooms are only for guided tours (in French) on certain days (enquire at the information desk on arrival). The main sections include the **Musée Chinoise** (Chinese Museum) built and decorated for the Empress Eugénie and Napoléon III (allow 30 mins for a visit) and the **Grands Appartements**, which show off the lifestyles of French sovereigns and their courts from François I to Napoléon III (allow about an hour on a self-guided tour). The **François I Gallery** fulfils the king's grand vision of himself which he indulged fully by bringing in Florentine artists to create the allegorical frescoes.

Other outstanding rooms are the **Ballroom of Henri II**, the **Throne Room** and the **Chapelle de la Trinité** (chapel of the Trinity). The **Musée Napoléon I** has 15 rooms displaying paintings, furnishing and artefacts (allow about 45 mins) including Napoleon's abdication chamber and a tent-style recreation of his campaign quarters. Allow time to wander in the large gardens enhanced by lakes and fountains.

VAUX-LE-VICOMTE

About 8 km outside the village of **Maincy**, down a peaceful country road, rises the grandiose silhouette of the **Château de Vaux-Le-Vicomte**, *Maincy; tel: (1) 64 14 41 90.* Open daily 1000–1800 (Apr–Oct); also 1100–1500 (first two weeks in Nov). Fr.56.

Built in 1657–61 by the architect Le Vau for Louis XIV's finance minister, Nicholas Fouquet, it was decorated in sumptuous style by Le Brun and is the most important architectural work of the 17th century before Versailles, which was started in 1668.

The gardens, by Le Nôtre, show off formal terraces, lakes and fountains, with avenues punctuated by statues and embellished with crisply-cut box hedges.

Fouquet's château infuriated the young Louis XIV because its luxury surpassed the royal palaces. and his motto – *Quo non ascendam?* (What heights will I not reach?) – didn't help. His estates were confiscated and he died in gaol. Fouquet's château retains an intimate scale and is largely unchanged from when it was built. The tour is self-guided, with French information boards; the English guidebook is Fr.25.

PARIS

To the rest of the world Paris is the capital of France, but to the French it is the capital of world civilisation. Paris is a dynamic and vibrant city combining a glorious past with an unashamed love for the present. It is a city of imperial grandeur and bohemian chic, a result of 19th-century planning on a grand scale when Napoleon III's henchman Baron Haussmann razed medieval Paris to create a city of elegant boulevards and open vistas. Paris proudly retains this grandeur today, and its tree-lined avenues and endless squares provide the perfect contrast to today's quirky, and often controversial, monuments which put the city's elegantly shod feet firmly in the 21st century. Paris is a city with the proud and powerful force which seduces the heart of even the most cynical tourist.

TOURIST INFORMATION

Paris Convention and Visitors Bureau, 127 av. des Champs Élysées, 75008 Paris (near the Arc de Triomphe; metro: Charles de Gaulle/Étoile, George V); tel: (1) 49 52 53 54. Open daily all year (except 25 Dec, 1 Jan and 1 May), 0900–2000. Guides, catalogues and phonecards are on sale here, as well as tickets for leisure parks, trips, cabarets and museum passes. Leaflets on Paris and the rest of France are available on serve-yourself shelves. A bureau de change is open in the office Mon–Sat, 0900–1930, and there are SNCF (rail) and Disneyland Paris booking services. The office can also arrange hotel accommodation in the Paris region.

Another office at the **Eiffel Tower** (Tour Eiffel) opens in high season, also selling excursion tickets and phonecards (RER rail line C to Champs de Mars Tour Eiffel, metro: Bir Hakeim); tel: (1) 45 51 22 15. Open daily 1100–1800 (May–Sept).

ARRIVING AND DEPARTING

Airports

Roissy-Charles de Gaulle airport is a quick 26 km north-east of the city; it has a 24-hr answering service giving flight information, tel: (1) 48 62 22 80, a bureau de change and several cash dispensers (distributeurs automatiques). There is also a hotel reservation desk, tel: (1) 48 62 27 29, open daily 0700–1900

The **Roissy Rail** service runs to the Gare du Nord and Châtelet metro station every 15 mins; the station is reached by a shuttle (navette) outside the arrivals hall. Trains run 0530–2330, on RER line B3 and the journey takes 35 mins. **Roissy Bus**, tel: (1) 48 04 18 24, runs buses to the Opéra Garnier 0545–2300 taking between 40 mins and an hour, **Air France** coaches run every 12 mins to pl. Charles de Gaulle Étoile and porte Maillot. They run between 0540 and 2300 and take 1 hr. Regular buses are slower but cost less – no. 350 runs to the Gare du Nord and the Gare de l'Est, and no. 351 to pl. de la Nation.

A taxi should cost around Fr.200 to the centre of Paris. Major car-hire firms operating at Paris's airports include: **Avis**, tel:

217

(1) 46 10 60 60; **Europcar**, *tel: (1) 30 43 82 82;* **Eurorent**, *tel: (1) 44 38 55 55 and* **Hertz**, *tel: (1) 47 88 51 51*. All companies take international reservations. A look in *Pages Jaunes* (Yellow Pages) will offer better deals in Paris itself. By car follow signs to the A1 and Paris, not Lille, as you leave the airport. Journey time is 20–40 mins.

Orly Airport is 20 km to the south and also has a 24-hr answering service: *tel: (1) 49 75 15 15*. There is a *bureau de change* at Orly Sud, *tel: (1) 49 75 79 41* and a cash dispenser on the first level. **OrlyVal** connects the airport to the RER rail system at the *Gare Anthony* (RER line B), 0550–2350. The journey to central Paris takes 20 mins. **Orly Bus** departs to *Denfert-Rochereau* metro station every 15 mins 0630–2230, taking 30 mins (from Paris to Orly, 0600–2300). **Air France** coaches to the *Gare Montparnasse* and the *Gare des Invalides* leave every 12 mins, *tel: (1) 43 24 97 10*, 0550–2300. The **RATP** (Paris Urban Transport) has an information line, *tel: (1) 43 46 14 14;* see also 'Getting Around' p. 219 for more details

By Rail

Paris has six main line stations, all of which are connected to the metro system. Each has a tourist information office, *bureaux de change*, left luggage departments and cafés. General information about train times and tickets is available *tel: (1) 30 64 50 50;* for reservations, *tel: (1) 45 65 60 00*.

Paris Nord, *r. de Dunkerque; tel: (1) 49 95 10 00*, serves the UK, Belgium and Scandinavia; trains from Boulogne and Calais also arrive here. **Paris Est**, *pl. du 11 Novembre 1918; tel: (1) 40 18 20 00*, connects with north-east France, Germany, Switzerland, Austria and Luxembourg. **Paris St-Lazare**, *r. d'Amsterdam; tel: (1) 42 85 88 00* serves Normandy and Dieppe. **Paris Austerlitz**, *7 blvd Hôpital;*

tel: (1) 45 84 14 18, links with the Loire, the South West, Spain and Portugal. **Paris Lyon**, *pl. Louis Armand; tel: (1) 40 19 60 00* serves the Auvergne, Provence, southeastern and eastern France, the Alps, Italy and Greece. **Paris Montparnasse**, *17 blvd de Vaugirard; tel: (1) 40 48 10 00* connects with Brittany and the south-west coast.

By Car

The quickest way to Paris by car is inevitably by motorway. All the major *autoroutes* lead right up to the city's umbilical cord, **la périphérique**. They are fast and comparatively clear outside rush hour and Fri and Sun evenings.

Those arriving from the **Channel Ports** and the **north** will arrive on the A1, entering Paris by *Porte de la Chapelle* or *Porte de Clignancourt*. (Follow signs for *périph. est/ouest*).

Travellers from **Le Havre** and **Normandy** enter on the A13. To join the *périphérique* follow the signs *périph. nord/sud*, depending on your heading; for central Paris follow the signs to *Paris centre*, entering Paris along the right bank of the Seine.

Cars coming from **Brittany** (A11) join up with those coming from the **Loire** and **Bordeaux** on the A10 as it approaches Paris; the A10 in turn joins the A6 and enters Paris at either *Porte d'Orléans* (west Paris) or *Porte d'Italie* (east Paris). For central Paris follow signs to *Paris centre*, which will bring you to the left bank and the *Île de la Cité*.

Those driving to Paris from **central France**, **Burgundy**, **Lyon**, **Provence** and the **Côte d'Azur** will also arrive on the A6.

Visitors from **Eastern France** and **Germany** arrive in Paris on the A4 at *Porte de Bercy*. If you are heading to the north of Paris, or to the north of France follow the signs to *périph. nord*; for the southern half of Paris follow *périph. sud*; for central Paris continue straight on and you will arrive on the banks of the Seine just below Bastille, from where the road follows the river up to Châtelet and the Hôtel de Ville (town hall).

When arriving in the city it is generally easiest to use the exits on the *périphérique* and the wide roads on the banks of the Seine as reference points before submerging yourself into the often labyrinthine streets of Paris proper. Pin-point the place you want to reach by reference to the nearest metro station and work towards this.

GETTING AROUND

As in any major city a car is more of a luxury than a necessity and Paris has an extremely effective public transport system. It may be best to park your car and continue on foot, by metro or bus (see p. 222 for information on parking). Having said that, a car is extremely useful at night when the streets are emptier, parking easier and certain metro lines and stations potentially less safe.

The **RATP** runs the metro (underground/subway), buses and the RER suburban rail link – see the map facing inside back cover. Metro stations can often provide free street maps. The RATP has a general information line: *tel: (1) 43 46 14 14*, open 0600–2100.

Tickets

Within the city centre, the same tickets can be used on buses, metro and RER. Greater Paris is divided up into several zones, and crossing zones requires more than one ticket; bus routes are divided into more zones than the metro and RER and thus use more tickets. A single ticket costs

Fr.7.50, but better value is a ten-ticket **carnet** (booklet) at Fr.41.

For several journeys in the same day buy a **Formule 1** card from the central Tourist Office or any metro station. This offers unlimited travel for one day and can cover anything from the city centre to five zones including the airports (Fr.28–Fr.95). It is valid on buses, metros and the RER.

Paris Visite is an all-encompassing tourist ticket covering three or five consecutive days and is available at metro stations, airports, railway stations and the central Tourist Office. However, bear in mind that if you have a car its extended coverage may well be wasted. The card does have the advantage of discounts to some tourist attractions and allows you to bypass queues, but at a cost of between Fr.95–285, a weekly (Mon–Sun) **Carte Orange hebdomadaire** may be a wiser choice (Fr.63, zones 1–2; Fr.139, 5 zones). A Carte Orange for a month (*coupon mensuel*) costs Fr.230 for the two central zones, and both need passport photos. They are available at all metro stations.

Metro

The impressive and extensive metro system runs every few minutes between 0530 and 0030 (last departure). Lines are known by their final destination and number; they are colour coded on the metro maps. Orange signs on platforms indicate connecting lines (*correspondances*). Slot your ticket into the automatic barrier, retrieve it and and follow the signs to your platform. The names of all stops are shown on blue panels by the platform.

Buses

Buses make less sense to the car driver, but are a pleasant enough way to cover small sections of Paris. Buses generally run 0630–2030. There are also hourly night

219

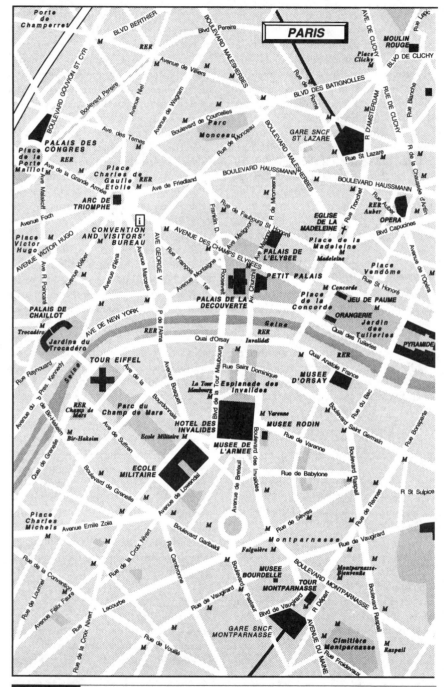

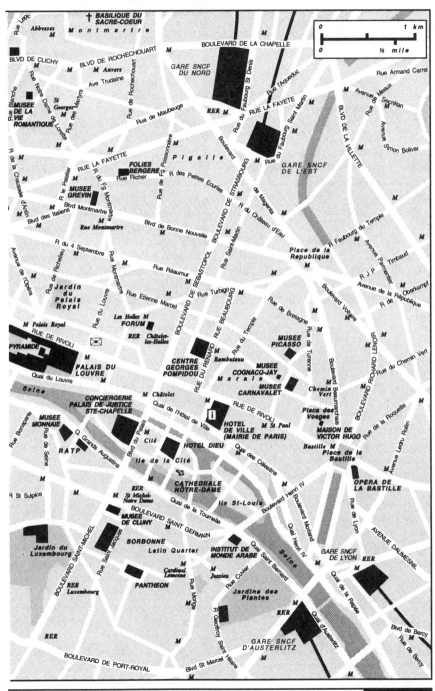

buses following ten routes from *pl. du Châtelet*, near the Hôtel de Ville. They run 0100–0500.

Driving in Paris

For getting around, the best and clearest means of information is a pocket *Plan de Paris*, dividing Paris up into its sixteen *arrondissements*. The best is produced by Éditions Leconte, and costs around Fr.35 from newspaper kiosks and bookshops; it includes an extensive list of useful addresses and has a map of the *Île de France* (greater Paris region) which is essential for trips out of town.

Traffic in Paris moves at a startling pace, but the quality of driving is generally good although motorists used to a less frenetic pace might find the experience intimidating. Careful non-French drivers may find Parisian habits *au volant* (at the wheel) worrying to say the least; the *périph.* seems to be used as a private race track (speed limits entirely ignored) and car horns used to intimidate at every opportunity. However, horns are an essential part of the Parisian automobile experience, and if you are honked hold your ground – you may be growled at, but you will be avoided – it it just bolshy Parisian bravado. Above all, remember that traffic from the right almost always has priority, so if in doubt, give way.

Parking will be the biggest problem for the car driver in Paris. Free parking is almost non-existent; most streets have pay-and-display meters and the word **payant** is marked out on the tarmac. These meters charge Fr.5–10 per hour for a maximum of 2 hours. Between 1900 and 0900 daily, at weekends and during August in *most* areas, parking is free (it will state on the meter if not). Do not park in bus lanes, yellow marked areas or where you see a sign marked *stationnement gênant*.

Amnesty

One of the most impressive things in France is the apparent power of the citizen. Nowhere is this better illustrated than in the French driver's attitude to parking tickets. In general, and especially in Paris, these are left unpaid, gathering dust in the glove compartment. The reason for this is largely historical: until very recently the French President annulled all speeding and parking tickets every 14th July, which effectively meant that no one ever bothered paying any. The rules have changed and now the amnesty only comes once every seven years. An amnesty would also have been good news for the tourist, but don't hold your breath: the good Monsieur Chirac has just annulled everything and his amnesty may have been the last.

In general, if no one else is parked there don't risk it.

There are plenty of of underground car-parks throughout Paris, and these offer a certain security, especially to foreign cars. They are marked by the international white-on-blue 'P' sign and are not too exorbitant. Average prices start at Fr.13 for one hour, Fr.45 for 4 hrs to Fr.90 for 24 hrs.

Parking tickets are as much an accessory to Parisian cars as the obligatory dent (see box above). The fines are graded according to the infringement, starting at Fr.75 and rising to Fr.900. Tickets are payable by *timbre fiscal* bought at a *tabac* (tobacconist's). A fine for parking in a *payant* zone is cheaper than a day's parking, but you risk being towed away. If you are towed, you will pay your ticket *and* the cost of towing, around Fr.500. Cars are impounded at *fourrières*.

STAYING IN PARIS

Accommodation

Finding accommodation in Paris is only a problem in the busiest season (usually May, June, Sept and Oct); there are plenty of options in all price ranges.

Hotel chains in Paris include *BW, Ca, Cn, Co, Dm, DV, Ex, GT, Hd, Hn, Hy, Ib, IH, Mc, Md, Mp, Nv, Pu, QI, RC, Rm, RS, Sf* and *TH*. A car allows swift access into central Paris and your only real problem will be deciding where to stay.

If money is no object you could treat yourself to a night at the **Hôtel de Crillon**, literally an 18th-century palace, *10 pl. de la Concorde, 75008; tel: (1) 44 71 15 00*, or the **Ritz**, *pl. Vendôme, 75001; tel: (1)42 60 38 30*, where nerves can be calmed with a Fr.1000 cognac.

Cheap accommodation can be found around the student area of *St-Michel* on the left bank and the *r. Faubourg Montmartre* on the right. Areas around the Gare du Nord and St-Lazare also have cheaper hotels although they tend towards the seedy at night.

St-Germain on the left bank and the beautifully bourgeois *Île St-Louis* have many hotels in the medium bracket. Three good bets are the **Hôtel Lutèce**, *65 r. St-Louis en l'Île, 75004* (metro: *Pont Marie*) *tel: (1) 43 26 23 52*; **Hôtel Marronniers**, *21 r. Jacob 75006* (metro: *St-Germain des Prés*); *tel: (1) 43 25 30 60*; **Hôtel d'Angleterre**, a one-time British embassy, *44 r. Jacob, 75006; tel: (1) 42 60 34 72* (metro: *St-Germain des Prés*)

Moving across the river, the *1st* and *2nd arrondissements* are well located but dull in the evenings. Down river, the ancient and preserved *Marais* district is close to Pompidou, Bastille and shopping at Les Halles. All price ranges are catered to, and the area is one of Paris's hippest.

Montmartre to the north has plentiful accommodation and a village atmosphere. Good bets are the **Timhôtel Montmartre**, *11 r. Ravignan, 75018* (metro: *Abbesses*); *tel: (1) 42 55 74 79* and the **Ermitage**, *24 r. Lamarck, 75018* (metro: *Lamarck-Caulaincourt*); *tel: 42 64 79 22*.

The so-called *Beaux Quartiers* of the 16th and 17th *arrondissements* are residential in the extreme but surprisingly disquieting at night; despite their chic residents, these areas have a high incidence of agression.

If you are planning a longer stay, self-catering apartments can be found through **Paris Séjour Réservation**, *90 av. des Champs Élysées, 75008; tel: (1) 42 56 30 00*; or **Bed and Breakfast 1**, *7 r. Campagne Première, 75014; tel: (1) 43 35 11 26* (self-catering and bed and breakfast).

The **Fédération Unie des Auberges de Jeunesse**, *27 r. Pajol, 75018; tel: (1) 46 47 00 01*, has a list of its youth hostels in Paris and the rest of France. International Accommodation Centres offer sightseeing trips and cheap beds; a free list is available from **UCRIF (Union des Centres de Rencontres Internationales de France)**, *72 r. Rambuteau, 75001* (metro *Les Halles*); *tel: (1) 40 26 57 64*. The **AJF (Acceuil des Jeunes de France)** also caters for the youth hostelling crowd. They will sell you the card which entitles you to make use of their services. Their central office is at Beaubourg, *119 r. St-Martin, 75004* (metro: *Châtelet, Hôtel de Ville*); *tel: (1) 42 77 87 80*. They provide university beds during the summer and you may even find yourself in an *hôtel particulier* in the Marais. They also have offices at *139 blvd St-Michel, 75006* (metro: *Port Royal*); *tel: (1) 43 54 95 86* and the Gare du Nord; *tel: (1) 42 85 86 19*.

Information on camping around Paris and the Île de France can be found at the **Féderation Française de Camping-**

223

Caravaning, *78 r de Rivoli, 75004;* (metro: *Hôtel de Ville*); *tel: (1) 42 72 84 08;* open Mon–Fri 0900–1230 and 1330–1730.

There is a campsite within Paris itself in the Bois du Boulogne on *allée du Bord de l'Eau, 75016,* (metro: *Porte de Maillot*) but it is heavily booked up in summer. There are also three campsites just to the east of the city: **Camping du Tremblay**, *quai de Polangis, Champigny sur Marne, 94500; tel: (1) 42 83 38 24;* **Campings Île de France**, *blvd Alliés, Champigny sur Marne, 94500; tel: (1) 43 97 43 97;* and **Camping du Camp des Cicognes**, *bord de Marne, Créteil, 94000; tel: (1) 42 07 06 75.* Further out of the city, **Disneyland Paris** offers **Camp Davy Crockett**, which has wild-west style cabins to rent from Fr.369 per night for six people. *Disneyland Paris, Marne la Vallée (autoroute A4; périph. Porte de Bercy).*

Eating and Drinking

Paris flaunts its reputation as the world capital of gastronomy and there is certainly much to praise. There is also much to criticise as burger and pizza empires increase their stakes in the city. Price is not always a guarantee of quality and you can eat well for relatively little. Food available ranges from a quick *crêpe* on a street corner right up to a three-star binge at **La Tour d'Argent**, *15–17 quai de la Tournelle, 75005; tel: (1) 43 54 23 31* (metro: *Maubert-Mutualité*). Menus are displayed on the outside of restaurants and often have a variety of fixed *formules* at different prices.

There is a strict hierarchy for bars. A simple café is lower than a bar, which is lower than a salon de thé, which is lower than a brasserie, and prices follow accordingly. Brasseries such as **La Coupole** in Montparnasse and **Brasserie Lipp** on the *blvd St-Germain* are veritable institutions. If you are watching your wallet it pays to stand at the bar, for the closer to the street you get the more you will pay.

For night life and people-watching the bars of the Marais and Bastille are excellent, especially the *r. de Lappe* and *r. Vieille du Temple*. St-Germain des Prés and Montmartre have a quainter atmosphere which touches on the Paris of the past.

The side streets of the Marais, Montmartre and Montparnasse have a host of cosmopolitan restaurants at reasonable prices, and the area around the *r. des Rosiers* is exceptionally good for Jewish and North African food, whilst *Belleville* is good for Chinese and Vietnamese specialities.

Away from these areas you can eat just about anything you want simply by strolling through the busiest districts. Beware of major tourist areas such as the *Champs Élysées* where price will almost certainly outclass the quality. The listings magazines *Pariscope* and *Figaroscope* (each Wed) have extensive restaurant guides listed by nationality and speciality.

Communications

The main **post office** (*La Poste*) is at *52 r. du Louvre, 75001* (metro: *Louvre, Rivoli*); *tel: (1) 40 28 20 00.* It is open 24 hrs, but after 1900 only for telephone, emergency cash withdrawal and poste restante services. Stamps can also be bought at tobacconist's shops (*tabacs*). Post boxes are yellow and fixed to the wall.

Phonecards can be bought at post offices, tourist offices, most metro and RER stations, France Télécom offices and tabacs.

To phone abroad from Paris dial *19* and the country code, followed by the number. To call elsewhere in France dial *16* plus the eight-figure number. To phone

Paris from the provinces dial *16* plus *1*, then the eight-figure number.

Money

Money can be exchanged at most banks or at *bureaux de change* throughout the city. **Thomas Cook bureaux de change** can be found all over the centre of Paris, including most main rail stations (see box, right). They offer money-changing facilities plus a range of other services, such as information and phonecards.

Consulates

Australia: *4 r. Jean Rey, 75015; tel: (1) 40 59 33 00* (metro: *Bel Hakeim*).
Canada: *35 av. Montaigne, 75008; tel: (1) 47 23 01 01* (metro: *Franklin D Roosevelt*).
Republic of Ireland: *4 r. Rude, 75016; tel: (1) 45 00 20 87* (metro: *Étoile*).
New Zealand: *7ter r. L. da Vinci, 75016; tel: (1) 45 00 24 11* (metro: *Victor Hugo*).
UK: *16 r. d'Anjou, 75008; tel: (1) 42 66 91 42* (metro: *Madelaine*).
USA: *2 r. St-Florentin, 75001; tel: (1) 42 96 14 88* (metro: *Concorde*).

ENTERTAINMENT

Organised entertainment usually comes at a cost. Some of the cheapest high quality events are in the field of classical music, but it is also worth looking out for student and fringe entertainment. You can get a copy of the monthly *Paris Sélection* and the annual *Saisons de Paris* from the Tourist Office, which also has a 24-hr information line: *tel: (1) 49 52 53 56*. Two inexpensive listings magazines are *l'Officiel des Spectacles* and *Pariscope* (with an English language *Time Out* section). *Boum!Boum!* is a freebie available at most *boulangeries,* which offers ticket reductions to many shows and events.

Theatre tickets can be bought half price for same-day performances from the

Thomas Cook

Thomas Cook bureaux de change in Paris are open seven day a week and have extended opening hours. As well as encashing Thomas Cook Travellers' Cheques free of commission charges, and providing emergency assistance in the case of lost or stolen Thomas Cook Travellers' Cheques and to holders of MasterCard, they offer foreign exchange facilities. In addition most sell maps and Thomas Cook publications.

Thomas Cook bureaux can be found at the following locations in Paris:

Champs Élysées:
> 52 av. des Champs Élysées
> 73 av. des Champs Élysées
> 125 av. des Champs Élysées

Montmartre:
> 84 blvd de Clichy
> 2 r. Lepic
> 14 r. Norvins
> 8–10 r. Steinkerque

Rail stations:
> Gare St-Lazare
> Gare du Nord
> Gare de l'Est
> Gare Montparnasse
> Porte Maillot

Halles-Rivoli:
> 194 r. de Rivoli
> 36–42 r. Rambuteau

St-Michel:
> 4 blvd St-Michel

Opéra:
> 25 blvd des Capucines
> 8 pl. de l'Opéra

Tour Eiffel:
> Bateaux Parisiens
> Tour Eiffel

225

kiosks at *15 pl. de la Madeleine, 75008* (metro: *Madeleine*), open Tues–Sat 1230–2000, Sun 1230–1600; and at RER *Châtelet-Les Halles* station, *75001*, open 1230–1930, closed Sun, Mon and public holidays.

Clubs and Discos

The club scene is lively and varied; just about all tastes from techno to rumba are catered for, although at some clubs you may be affronted by a haughty door policy. Most get going towards midnight and entrance often includes a first drink – just as well as bar prices tend towards the extortionate.

In mainstream disco-land the large **Loco,** *90 blvd de Clichy, 75018* (metro: *Blanche*), *tel: (1) 42 57 37 37*, has music for all tastes. For the hip and beautiful, **Les Bains-Douches,** an ancient Turkish bath house, is the place to be seen. *7 r. Bourg-l'Abbé, 75003*, (metro: *Étienne Marcel*) *tel: (1) 48 87 01 80*. For something outrageous try **Queen,** *102, av. des Champs-Élysées, 75008* (metro: *George V*); *tel: (1) 42 89 31 22*. The name rather gives the game away, but this Paris success story throws the most outrageous 'parties' in the city, and the cast is there to be seen.

For ballroom dancing and Latin hip swinging try **La Java,** *105 r. du Faubourg du Temple, 75010* (metro: *Belleville*); *tel: (1) 42 02 20 52*, or **Le Slow Club,** *130 r. du Rivoli, 75001* (metro: *Châtelet-Les Halles*); *tel: (1) 42 33 84 30*.

Paris is the European capital of jazz with plenty of visits from big-name performers. There are concerts each night of the week; check the listings magazines for details of venues and performers.

Cabarets and Floor Shows

The flesh-and-feather shows passed off as essential Parisian culture are geared to tourists and businessmen. Tickets are expensive and may include food and a token half-bottle of tepid champagne, or, just the show. The best known are: **Le Moulin Rouge,** *83 blvd de Clichy, 75018* (metro: *Blanche*); *tel: (1) 46 06 00 19*; **Crazy Horse Saloon,** *12 av. George V, 75008* (metro: *George V*); *tel: (1) 47 23 32 32*; **Le Lido de Paris,** *116 bis av. des Champs-Élysées, 75008* (metro: *George V*); *tel: (1) 40 76 56 10*; **Folies-Bergères,** *32bis r. Richer, 75009* (metro: *Cadet, r. Montmartre*); *tel: (1) 44 79 98 98*. **Chez Michou,** *80 r. des Martyrs, 75018* (metro: *Abbesses, Pigalle*); *tel: (1) 46 06 16 04*, is a popular drag show venue and has a constant sprinkling of stars in the audience. Most shows, dinner included will cost between Fr.400 and Fr.700.

Classical Music

Free concerts are regular features in churches and museums and there is also a free recital each Sun evening at 1745 at the cathedral of **Notre-Dame**; see listing magazines for details. Otherwise there is a surprisingly spartan programme for a major capital city. Concert halls include **Théâtre Musical de Paris Châtelet,** *2 r. Edouard Colonne, 75001* (metro: *Châtelet*); *tel: (1) 42 33 00 00*; the all-new **Cité de la Musique,** *223 av. Jean Jaurès, 75019* (metro: *Pantin*); *tel: (1) 44 84 45 00*. and **La Maison de Radio France** (Salle Olivier Messiaen), *116 av. du Président Kennedy, 75016*; (RER: *Maison de la Radio*; metro: *Passy*); *tel: (1) 42 30 22 22*.

Opera is well catered for and not as expensive as in the UK. The controversial **Opéra de Paris-Bastille,** *120 r. de Lyon, 75012* (metro: *Bastille*); *tel: (1) 44 73 13 00*, has seats from Fr.60–370 and the histrionics continue offstage with plenty of political intrigue and melodrama. The **Opéra-Comique** plays at the *Salle*

Favard, 5 r. Favard, 75002 (metro: *Richelieu-Drouot*); *tel: (1) 42 96 12 20.* See listings magazines for other occasional performances.

Classical ballet is performed by the *Ballet de l'Opéra de Paris* at the wonderful neo-Baroque **Opéra Garnier**, *8 r. Scribe, 75009* (metro: *Opéra*). At the time of writing the opera house was being restored and performances have been transferred to the Opéra Bastille. Modern dance performances are listed in the weekly listing magazines.

Theatre

Classical French drama by Molière, Racine etc., is the main repertoire at the stiffly classical **Comédie Française**, *Salle Richelieu, 2 r. de Richelieu, 75001* (metro: *Palais Royal*); *tel: (1) 40 15 00 15.* Remainder tickets can be bought for same day performances. **The British Council**, *11-13 r. de Constantine, 75007*, gives details of English language performances in and around Paris (metro: *Invalides*); *tel: (1) 49 55 73 00.* The new **American Center**, *51 r. de Bercy, 75012*, hosts visiting art exhibitions, dance and theatre in an exciting new building (metro: *Bercy*); *tel: (1) 44 73 77 77.*

Cinema

Finding a good film in Paris is no problem, even if you speak little or no French. The *Champs Élysées* and *blvd des Italiens* are lined with cinemas showing the latest French and foreign releases. Look out for the letters VO (*Version Originale*) or *Sous-titres Français*; these mean the films are in their original language. Seats are cheaper on Mon and there are reductions for children, students and senior citizens.

A glance in the listing magazines will lead you to more off-beat venues where, no doubt, that film you always wanted to see is showing. Old movies are shown at the **Cinémathèque Française**, *Palais de Chaillot, pl. de Trocadéro, 75016* (metro: *Trocadéro*); *tel: (1) 45 53 21 86* and videos covering almost everything imaginable can be viewed Tues–Sun, 1230–2300, Sat 1000–2300 at the **Videothèque de Paris**, *Forum des Halles, Porte St-Eustache, 2, Grande Galerie, 75001* (metro: *Les Halles*); *tel: (1) 40 26 34 30.*

Spectator Sports

Details of clubs and sporting events are listed in the *Sports-Loisir* section of *Pariscope*, and on the **Allô-Sport** information line, *tel: (1) 42 76 54 54.*

Soccer and international rugby matches are held at the **Parc des Princes**, *24 r. du Cmt Guillbaud, 75016* (metro: *Porte de St-Cloud*); *tel: (1) 42 88 02 76*; horse races at the *hippodromes* of **Longchamp** and **Auteuil**, and anything from ice skating to stock-car racing at the **Palais Omnisports Paris Bercy**, *8 blvd de Bercy, 75012* (metro: *Bercy*); *tel: (1) 44 68 44 68.*

The French Open tennis championships are held at Roland Garros stadium towards the end of May each year. **Stade Roland Garros**, *2 av. Gordon Bennett, 75016* (metro: *Porte d'Auteuil*); *tel: (1) 47 43 48 00.*

Events

The most famous event in the French calendar is **Bastille Day**, each 14 July, which commemorates the storming of the Bastille prison and the start of the French Revolution. There are big parades culminating in a firework display on the **Champs de Mars** near the Eiffel Tower (also at Château de Chantilly, see p. 233). The last or penultimate Wed in June sees the increasingly popular **Fête de la Musique** with musicians giving free concerts, where they like, and as loud as they like, well into the early hours. The finale of the **Tour de France** takes place on the *av. des Champs Élysées* towards the end of July and there is a **Festival de Jazz** at the end of Oct. *Paris Saisons*, available from the Tourist Office, details other events and festivals.

SHOPPING

Paris is a high temple of fashion and shopping, and the two combine to produce a heady cocktail of dazzling window displays and astronomical price tags. To wonder at graceful *haute couture* head for the *av. Montaigne* and the *r. du Faubourg St-Honoré*. To actually buy some clothes head to *St-Germain* and the *r. de Rennes* or the *r. de Commerce*, or search the rag-trade district around **Sentier** (metro: *Sentier*). The most famous department stores are **Galeries Lafayette**, *40 blvd Haussmann, 75009* (metro: *Chaussée d'Antin*); tel: (1) 42 82 34 56; **Printemps**, *64 blvd Haussmann, 75009* (metro: *Havre Caumartin*); tel: (1) 42 82 50 00, and on the left bank, **Au Bon Marché**, *38 r. de Sèvres 75007* (metro: *Sèvres Babylone*); tel: (1) 42 60 33 45.

Markets are big business in Paris and the Tourist Office provides a free list. The best known flea-market (*marché aux puces*) is at the **Porte de Clignancourt** (périph. exit and metro: *St-Ouen, Porte de Clignancourt*); Sat–Mon 0730–1900. Bargains in this huge warren of junk, clothes and antiques are scarce but it is worth a visit. Better is the chaotic **Puces de Montreuil** just off the *périphérique* to the east (*périph.* exit and metro: *Porte de Montreuil*); Sun–Mon, 0730–1900. For food, visit the daily markets in **r. Mouffetard** (metro: *Censier Daubenton*), **r. de Buci/r. de Seine** (closed Mon; metro: *Mabillon*) and on Sat, the exotic international market at **La Chapelle** (metro: *La Chapelle*). A visit to the

bouquinistes (booksellers) on the left bank of the Seine near the **Pont Neuf** combines an interesting walk with stimulating reading. They sell anything from Tintin to ancient volumes of Proust.

SIGHTSEEING

As most museums and monuments in Paris charge hefty entrance fees it is worth considering a **Carte Inter-Musée**, or museum pass, sold at the Tourist Office and major metro and RER stations. This gives access to most of the popular museums for one, three or five days, costing Fr.70, Fr.140 and Fr.200 respectively. Student cards give reductions in some places. Children and senior citizens benefit from reduced rates but may need some proof of age.

Museums run by the city tend to close on Mon and give free entry to permanent collections on Sun. National museums usually close on Tues, except the Musée Rodin and Musée d'Orsay (Mon).

Daily walking tours of the city's monuments, on various themes, are run by the **Caisse Nationale des Monuments Historiques et des Sites**, *Hôtel de Sully, 62 r. St Antoine, 75004* (metro: *St-Paul*); tel: (1) 44 61 21 50. See also the section *Monuments et Visites* in the listings magazines.

If you leave the car, cycling tours (only for the fearless) are organised by **Paris by Cycle**, *2 r. de la Jonquière, 75017* (metro: *Porte de Clichy*); tel: (1) 42 63 36 63; and by **Mountain Bike Trip**, *6 pl. Étienne Pernet, 75015* (metro: *Félix Faure*); tel: (1) 48 42 57 87. Numerous companies run bus tours of Paris including **Cityrama**, *4 pl. des Pyramides, 75001* (metro: *Palais Royal*); tel: (1) 42 60 30 14; and **France Tourisme/Paris Vision**, *214 r. de Rivoli, 75001* (metro: *Tuileries*); tel: (1) 42 60 31 25. Both run hourly services. The big red

Paribus, leaving from *pl. du Trocadéro* and the Eiffel Tower, allows you to get on and off as you like during two days. Tickets cost Fr.120 for adults, Fr.60 for children, with commentaries in English and French. The RATP's **Balabus** takes a meandering route past the major sights between La Défense and the Gare de Lyon each Sun (1230–2000, 19 Apr–27 Sept). The journey takes 50 mins; join at any stop marked *Balabus Bb*.

Paris is a compact city and most popular sights are within walking distance of each other. Most of the stately monuments are on the **Rive Droite** (Right Bank), whereas the **Rive Gauche** (Left Bank) has a more casual, intimate character. The middle of the Seine, with its two islands, **Île de la Cité** and **Île St Louis**, is the oldest part of Paris and the centre of ancient Lutetia.

The Right Bank *(La Rive Droite)*

Parking is easier on the right bank, with several large car parks and space between the bottom of the Champs Élysées and the river. Try the car parks at *pl. de la Madelaine* and *Louvre/r. de Rivoli*.

The **Arc de Triomphe**, *pl. Charles de Gaulle/Étoile* (metro: *Charles de Gaulle-Étoile*) crowns the Champs Élysées and has excellent views from the top. Built by Chalgrin to celebrate Napoleon's victories, it now forms the half-way point of **la Voie Triomphale** (Triumphal Way, see p. 233) which runs between the Louvre and Mitterrand's **Grande Arche de la Défense**. A ride to the roof of the Arc de Triomphe costs Fr.31; open daily 0930–1830, Fri until 2200 (summer); 1000–1700 (winter).

At the bottom of the Champs Élysées is the vast **pl. de la Concorde** where many a noble head was chopped off by the Jacobins in 1789. The 3000-year-old pink **obelisk** was a gift to King Louis-Philippe from the Viceroy of Egypt in 1831. It weighs 230 tonnes and on AIDS day in 1994 was covered by a 23 m condom.

Directly across the square is the 16th-century **Jardin des Tuileries**, re-landscaped by Le Nôtre in the 17th-century in the heavily formal French style. It is a pleasant park to wander around, with sculpture and cafés dotted amongst the trees. The gardens are the settings for two art galleries: the **Jeu de Paume**, with a changing programme of modern art; *20 r. Royale, 75008* (metro: *Concorde*); open Tues 1200–2130, Wed–Fri 1200–1900, Sat–Sun 1000–1900, Fr.35; and the **Orangerie**, *pl. de la Concorde, 75008* (metro: *Concorde*), open 0945–1715, closed Tues; Fr.27, which houses the Walter and Paul Guillaume collection, including works by Renoir, Matisse, Derain, Picasso and, downstairs, Monet's entrancing panoramic waterlilies.

As you continue through the Tuileries towards the Louvre, be sure to see the splendid **pl. Vendôme** on the left. The column at its centre was cast from the bronze of captured Turkish cannon and Napoleon casts a discerning eye on Paris's smartest jewellers.

The vast **Musée du Louvre**, *cour Napoléon or Pavillon de Flore, r. de Rivoli, 75008* (metro: *Louvre*), has been revamped in recent years with I.M. Pei's controversial glass pyramid as its best known addition. One of the world's oldest art galleries, the Louvre's 30,000 works cover everything from ancient Egypt, Rome and Greece, to the Renaissance and 19th-century European paintings. Amongst its best known works are the *Mona Lisa* and Géricault's *Raft of the Medusa*. Don't expect to do it in one go and beware, the crowds are as tiring as the legwork. Enter through Pei's pyramid; open Wed–Mon

229

0900–1800, until 2145 Mon and Wed (Fr.40 till 1500; Fr.20 after 1500 and all Sun).

Further down river is the **Marais**, one of Paris's oldest and best preserved quarters. Wander the streets and peer into courtyards to see the 17th-century *hôtels particuliers* (mansions) before arriving at the oldest square in Paris, the **pl. des Vosges**, with its elegant colonnades and central garden. The **Maison de Victor Hugo**, *Hôtel de Rohan Guéméné, 6 pl. des Vosges, 75004* (metro: *St Paul, Chemin Vert*); open Tues–Sun 1000–1745, Fr.17, records the writer's life through drawings and other memorabilia. Also in the Marais is the **Musée Picasso**, *Hôtel de Juigué-Salé, 5 r. de Thorigny, 75003* (metro: *St Paul, Chemin Vert*), open Wed–Mon 0930–1800 (summer), 0930–1730 (winter), Fr.27, Fr.18 on Sun. The collection, a gift to the state in lieu of death duties, covers Picasso's whole life and career and includes many famous works. Another 17th-century *hôtel particulier* (mansion) houses the **Musée Carnavalet**, *23 r. de Sévigné, 75003* (metro *St Paul, Chemin Vert*). The museum traces the history of Paris from its earliest days to the 20th century, and has some beautifully reconstucted interiors next door in the Hôtel le Peletier. The Tourist Office has details of the principal mansions in the Marais, and walks are advertised in the listing magazines. Try *r. des Francs Bourgeois* for good shopping and the *r. des Rosiers* for Jewish deli-style food.

Between the Marais and the Louvre is the **Centre National d'Art et de Culture Georges Pompidou**, *r. Rambuteau / r. St-Merri, 75004* (metro: *Châtelet, Les Halles*); open Wed–Mon 1000–2200; Sat, Sun and public holidays 1200–2200; modern art museum till 1800; 2200 Fri (Fr.30, free on Sun 1000–1400).

This inside-out construction of see-through escalators, pipes and tubes houses a library, a music and acoustic research institute, an architecture and design institute and a modern art museum – the big draw for tourists. This riveting collection includes works by Picasso, Giacometti, Miró, Dalì, Klee and just about every other major (and minor) force in 20th-century art.

To bear homage to the remains of Parisians past visit the huge **Cimetière du Père-Lachaise**, *blvd de Ménilmontant, 75020*, (metro: *Gambettta, Philippe Auguste*). Tombs of all shapes, sizes and designs include the graves of Jim Morrison, Delacroix, Edith Piaf, Oscar Wilde and many others. Get a map at the gate. Open daily 0900–1730.

Back down the river at **Trocadéro**, *pl. du Trocadéro, 75016* (metro: *Trocadéro*) is the vast colonnaded **Palais de Chaillot**. Created for the Universal exhibition in 1937 it houses the **Musée du Cinéma**, Fr.25, the **Musée National des Monuments Français**, Fr.21, the **Musée de la Marine** (Naval Museum; Fr.31) and the **Musée de l'Homme** (Musem of Mankind; Fr.25). The **Musée Marmottan**, *2 r. Louis Boilly, 75016* (metro: *La Muette*) has an intimate collection of Impressionist works, especially Monet's, in a 19th-century town house. Open Tues–Sun 1000–1730, Fr.35. The **Musée du Vin**, *5 sq. Charles Dickens, 75016* (metro: *Passy*) traces the history of the sacred fluid and ends with a free tasting.

Nothing grates on the French ego as much as someone robbing their rhubarb, so call at the **Musée de la Contrefaçon** (Forgery), *16 r. de la Faisanderie, 75016* (metro: *Dauphine*) to marvel at the quality, or lack thereof, of captured counterfeit merchandise. Admission free.

The Left Bank (La Rive Gauche)

Though less grandiose than the Right Bank, the Left Bank is arguably richer in charm. More residential in character, it is more intimate and in keeping with the traditional image of Paris. Its narrow streets also mean you have to fight for a parking space.

It also has Paris's best known landmark: the **Eiffel Tower** (*Tour Eiffel*), *Champ de Mars, 75007* (metro: *Bir Hakeim, Trocadéro*), open 0930–2300 (Sept–Jun), 0900–2400 (July–Aug); Fr.12 by stairs to the second floor; Fr.20, Fr.38 and Fr.55 to the first, second and third levels respectively, by lift. The tower was built by Gustave Eiffel for the Universal Exhibition of 1889 and was only meant as a temporary structure. Saved from demolition in 1910, it now attracts more than four million visitors each year.

Following the river upstream, you reach the 17th-century **Hôtel des Invalides**, *espl. des Invalides, 75007* (metro: *Varenne, Latour Maubourg*); open 1000–1645 (winter), 1000–1745 (summer). This complex was conceived by Louis XIV as a home for retired soldiers, and includes the 'soldiers' church' **St Louis des Invalides** and the sumptuous Cour d'Honneur (courtyard). The **Musée de l'Armée**, *pl. Vauban, 75007* (metro: *Varenne*), is open 1000–1700 (summer), 1000–1800 (winter) and is closed on public holidays. The collection covers just about every facet of military paraphernalia right up to modern times. The Fr.34 ticket for the Invalides complex also covers **Napoleon's tomb** in the **Église du Dôme des Invalides**. On the eastern side of the Invalides is the **Musée Rodin**, *Hôtel Biron, 77 r. de Varenne, 75007* (metro: *Varenne*), open Tues–Sun, 0930–1745 (summer), 1000–1700 (winter), Fr.27; Fr.7 for the garden only.

Works on display span the sculptor's career, with several, including *The Kiss* and *The Thinker* outside in the beautiful garden. Continue east along the river to reach the former railway station that now houses the **Musée d'Orsay**, *1 r. de Bellechasse, 75007* (metro: *Solférino*); open Tues–Sun 0900–1800 (summer), 1000–1800 (winter, except Sun from 0900); open till 2145 Thur; Fr.36; Fr.24 on Sun. This gallery, worth visiting for the building alone, displays fine art from the 1840s to 1914, including works by Delacroix, Gaugin, Cézanne and the Impressionists. Be sure not to miss Théodore Gaultier's fabulous model of the Paris opera house.

Further east is **St-Germain des Prés**, the heart of Paris's artistic life, with small galleries and cafés lining the *r. de Seine* and anyone who's anyone, and many who aren't, drinking endless coffees and people-watching in the **Deux Magots** or **Café Flore** on *blvd St-Germain*. This leads on into the **Latin Quarter**, home of the **Sorbonne**, *r. de la Sorbonne*, where Latin-speaking scholars once ruled the roost, and where as recently as 1968 students threatened the very existence of the French state. The peaceful streets with their cafés and shops are wonderful for exploring and soaking up the atmosphere. The **Musée de Cluny**, *6 pl. Paul Painevé, 75005* (metro: *Cluny, St-Michel*), delves into medieval history and is built around antique **Roman baths** (*Les Thermes*). Exhibits in this vast treasure house range from furniture, fine art and jewellery to stained glass and the superb **Dame de la Licorne** tapestries. Look out for concerts held at lunch time. Open Wed–Mon 0915–1745, Fr.27; Fr.18 on Sun.

Two large parks skirt the edge of the Latin Quarter. The **Jardin du Luxembourg** is attached to the Palais du

Luxembourg, *15. r. Vaugirard, 75006* (metro: *Luxembourg*). Garden and palace were created in the 17th century for Marie de Médicis, the widow of Henry VI, who wanted an Italianate design to remind her of her native land. The tree-lined avenues, boating pond and strategically placed iron seats make it a great favourite for Parisian lovers. Honey from the park's own bees is sold during summer at the apiary (*la ruche*) and you can even take bee-keeping lessons. On the far side of St-Michel is the **Jardin des Plantes**, *57 r. Cuvier, 75005* (metro: *Gare d'Austerlitz*), open 0800–2000 (summer), 0800–1730 (winter), which houses a zoo and a botanical garden founded by Louis XIII in 1626.

France's strong Arab heritage is represented by the **Grande Mosquée de Paris**, *pl. du Puits de l'Hermite, 75005* (metro: *Monge*), where mint tea can be taken in a quiet courtyard café, whilst Arab culture from man's beginnings to the present day is explored at the fascinating **Institut du Monde Arabe**, *1 r. Fossés St Bernard, 75005* (metro: *Jussieu, Cardinal-Lemoine*).

The lower-numbered arrondissements are residential in character and are dominated by the incongruous **Tour Montparnasse**, *33 av. du Maine, 75015* (metro: *Montparnasse Bienvenüe*), a 210-m high skyscraper that struck horror into the hearts of Parisians when it was built. The views from the 59th floor are none the less breathtaking. Open 0930–2330 (summer), 1000–2230 (winter); Fr.40 for the viewing floor, Fr.32 for the 56th floor and a film about Paris.

The **Panthéon**, *r. Clothilde, 75005* (metro *Cardinal-Lemoine*), Fr.24, shelters the remains of many of France's greats, such as Voltaire, Hugo, Rousseau and Zola, beneath a leaking neo-classical cupola; the **Cimetière Montparnasse**, *3 blvd Edgar Quinet, 75014* (metro: *Edgar Quinet*) has provided the final answer for existentialist heart throbs Jean-Paul Sartre and Simone de Beauvoir, *Gitane*-puffing Serge Gainsbourg, Baudelaire and many others.

The Îles

Between the Right and Left Banks, in the middle of the Seine, are the city's two *Îles* (islands). The **Île St-Louis**, where chic has a capital C, is mainly composed of 17th-century town houses, boutiques and restaurants. Several impressive monuments are squeezed onto the **Île de la Cité**, starting with the Gothic church of **Notre Dame**, *parvis de Notre Dame, 75004* (metro: *Cité*). Built between 1163 and 1345 and conceived by Maurice de Sully, the vast interior contains some 37 medieval chapels and its stained glass is considered one of the high points of the Gothic style. Climb the tower for a closer look at the gargoyles and sculpture decorating the façade. Open daily 0800–1900, Sun till 2000. Guided tours, Fr.31, are conducted 0930–1830 (1 Apr–15 Sep), 0930–1730 (16 Sep–31 Oct) and 1000–17000 (1 Nov–31 Mar).

Try a delicious **Berthillon ice cream**, the best in Paris. Made on the Île St-Louis, it is available in several cafés and at **Berthillon**, *31 r. St-Louis en l'Île, 75004* (afternoons and evenings only). Wander up to the north end of the island where the **Palais de Justice**, *4 blvd du Palais, 75001* (metro: *Cité*), shelters another Gothic gem, the 700-year-old **Ste-Chapelle** (Holy Chapel; Fr.26). Built in only three years, its chief attraction is the dazzling series of stained glass windows, over 600 square metres in all, depicting over a thousand biblical scenes.

A more sinister air pervades the Capetian **Conciergerie**, *1 quai de l'Horloge,*

232

75001 (metro: *Cité, St Michel, Châtelet*), open 0930–1800 (summer), 1000–1630 (winter), closed public holidays; Fr.26. It became the city's first prison in 1391 and gained infamy during the French revolution when half its 4000 inmates (including Marie-Antoinette) were guillotined.

Further Out

North of the river, **Montmartre** (metro: *Abbesses, Anvers, Lamarck-Caulaincourt*) overlooks the city with the best views in Paris. Despite the tourist onslaught the **pl. du Tertre** and surrounding streets manage to preserve the bohemian aspect that drew artists here during the *Belle Epoque*. The **Musée de Montmartre**, *12 r. Cortot, 75018*, charts the quarter's history while in Oct *bonheur* (happiness) overflows at the harvesting of Paris's last **vineyard**, corner *r. St Vincent/r. de Daules, 75018*.

Out on the north-eastern edge of the city is the **Parc de la Villette** (metro and périph. exit: *Porte de la Villette*). The park has two concert halls, **La Zénith** and **la Cité de la Musique**, and the popular **Cité des Sciences et de l'Industrie**, which will keep stressed-out children amused for several hours. With its hands-on scientific gadgets, planetarium and panoramic cinema, they might even learn something in the process!

La Grande Arche, *parvis de La Défense, 92040* (metro: *Grande Arche de La Défense*), at the very western edge of Paris was the last of President Mitterrand's *grands projets* and critics say it is symbolic of his rule – expensive and hollow. The view from the top towards central Paris leads the eye back to the Louvre and exposes the **Voie Triomphale** (Triumphal Way) in all its glory. Open 0900–1900; Sat, Sun and public holidays till 2000 (summer); 0900–1800, Sat, Sun and public holidays till 1900 (winter); Fr.40.

OUT OF TOWN

There is a multitude of attractions outside Paris and a car allows quick and easy access to them.

The big event of recent years has been the opening of **Disneyland Paris** at *Marne La Vallée (autoroute A4 30 mins; périph. exit Porte de Bercy)*. After an extremely painful start, Disney's theme park seems to be heading for success. Reduced entrance fees and new rides such as *Space Mountain* and *Indiana Jones* have attracted larger crowds and bigger smiles. *Festival Disney* has several themed bars and restaurants drawing punters from Paris for an evening of good old American escapism. Entrance to the park: Fr.195 (children Fr.150); Festival Disney: free.

To the north of Paris is **Parc Astérix** (*autoroute A1 25 mins; périph exit: Porte de la Chapelle*), a home-grown theme park that has been a long-running success. Larger than life cartoon characters inhabit this Roman, or rather Gaulish, village. Open daily 1000–1900 8 Apr–6 Sept (Sept, Oct open Wed, Sat Sun only); Fr.160 (Children 3–11 years Fr.110).

Also to the north is the town of **Chantilly** (*autoroute A1; exit Chantilly*). France's greatest horse race, *Le Prix du Jockey Club* takes place in mid-June, and the equestrian theme continues at the **Musée Vivant du Cheval**, where horsy artefacts and the beasts themselves are on show. The largely rebuilt Renaissance **Château de Chantilly** is set amongst forest and formal gardens, with lakes adding a picturesque touch. The entrance fee includes the large collection of Renaissance paintings and a guided tour of the château in French; the sublime *Très Riches Heures du Duc de Berry*, an illuminated medieval manuscript, is the highlight of the visit.

Senlis (*autoroute A1; exit: Senlis*) a

233

lovely old town, with several good restaurants and a civilised provincial air, makes an excellent lunch stop on the way to, or back from, Chantilly.

To the west of Paris is the town of **Versailles** (*autoroute A13; périph exit: Porte d'Auteuil*), which is dominated by the 17th-century **Château de Versailles**, erstwhile residence of Louis XIV, *le Roi Soleil* (the Sun King). Open Tues–Sun, 0900–1830 (May–Sept), 0930–1730 (Oct–Apr), closed public holidays, Fr.42 (Fr.28). In this enormous city of a palace, with its 53 hectares of rooms, the breathtaking power and wealth of the French monarchy becomes strikingly apparent. Guided tours (for an extra fee) daily till 1530. The musical fountains in the gardens only operate on Sun, 1530 (7 May–8 Oct, Fr.21).

In modest (all things are relative) and restrained contrast is the earlier 17th-century **Château Vaux-le-Vicomte**, by the same architects and painters: Louis Le Vaux, Charles Le Brun and André Le Nôtre. The visit is an emotive one, especially during a **candle-lit tour** (each Sat, May–Sept; Fr.75/65) with a full script of 17th-century jealousy and intrigue. The gardens are a pleasure to visit and the château is less inundated than its younger sister at Versailles. The château (*77950 Maincy; tel: (1) 64 14 41 90);* is open daily 1000–1700 (Apr–Oct), 1100–1700 (Feb–Apr); Fr.30 (Fr.24); the fountains work the second and last Sun of each month. To get there follow the route to Fontainebleau (see below), turning off to **Melun**, then follow signs to the château, or take autoroute A4 (*périph: porte de Bercy*) leaving at Melun; follow the N36, then D215 to the château (journey time 45 mins).

Fontainebleau, to the south (*autoroute A6, exit Fontainebleau; 45 mins; périph.: Porte d'Italie, Porte d'Orléans*) has another royal château with a luxurious mish-mash of architectural styles; open Wed-Mon, 0930–1230, 1400–1700; Fr.31; gardens free. The **Forest of Fontainebleau** is a recreation ground for thousands of Parisians each weekend who come to rock climb, mountain bike, ramble or just breathe clean air. Mountain bikes can be hired from **À La Petite Reine**, *32 r. Sabots; tel: (1) 60 74 57 57;* Mon–Sat Fr.50 half day, Fr.80 full day; Sat–Sun, Fr.90 half day, Fr.100 full day. The **Tourist Office** at *31 pl. Bonaparte; tel: 64 22 25 68,* can furnish maps of the forest and lists of events in the town.

To the east of Paris is the medieval town of **Provins**; 20 minutes outside Paris (*autoroute A4, exit Provins, périph: Porte de Bercy*), Provins has some impressive ramparts and a lovely old town. It is an excellent lunch stop on the way to **Champagne**.

The *maisons de champagne*, vineyards, and the possibility of a *dégustation* (tasting) are the principal attractions of the region (*autoroute A4, exits Reims/Epernay 1.5 hrs, périph. Porte de Bercy*). Whilst **Épernay** is home to the famous houses of **Moët et Chandon**, **Mercier** and **Pol Roger**, all grouped on the *av. de Champagne*, **Reims** (Rheims) is host to **Veuve Clicquot**, **Mumm** and **Piper-Heidseck**, not to mention one of France's greatest Gothic masterpieces, the cathedral of **Notre Dame de Reims**, site of the coronations of the French monarchy from Charlemagne to their demise. The Champagne houses charge a small entrance fee for an enlightening tour and some hefty PR, but are generally an amusing and improving experience.

For details of tours and attractions contact the **Tourist Office**, *7 av. de Champagne, 51200, Epernay; tel: 26 55 33 00*; **Tourist Office**, *2 r. Guillaume de Machault, 51100, Reims; tel: 26 77 45 25*.

QUIMPER

The beautiful old city of Quimper is the capital of Cornouaille and a strong bastion of Breton traditions. Museums, buildings and old districts testify to the town's rich architectural and cultural heritage, enhanced by the picturesque setting of the Odet River. Quimper's moderate size and leisurely pace of life make it a pleasure to stroll along the quaintly sinuous streets, from one tiny square to the next, and to gaze at the clear waters of the Odet from one of the low bridges decorated with a colourful array of flowers. Join in the general merrymaking during the summer Festival de Cornouaille when the energy and pride of the Breton people is fully expressed.

TOURIST INFORMATION

Tourist Office: *pl. de la Résistance, 29000 Quimper; tel: 98 53 04 05, fax: 98 53 31 33.* Open Mon–Sat 0830–2000, Sun 0930–1230, 1500–1800. A smaller office at *pl. St-Corentin* (summer). Two general information brochures are available, *Quimper en Cornouaille* and *Quimper Magazine*, as well as a practical information leaflet which includes a list of hotels and campsites (assistance in booking accommodation if required). A **passeport culturel**, giving access to the main sights (guided tours of the town included) costs Fr.50 for three visits or Fr.100 for six.

Declin, *34 r. de Douamenez, 29000 Quimper; tel: 98 55 83 83* (open Mon afternoon, Tues, Wed and Fri all day), is the local branch of the *Association Départementale d'Information des Jeunes* (A.D.I.J., Young People's Information Centre).

ARRIVING AND DEPARTING

Airport
The **Aéroport de Quimper Cornouaille** is located 7 km from the town centre, on the D785. There are no international flights, but several daily flights to and from Paris.

By Car
Quimper is linked to Brest, Lorient, Vannes, Nantes and Rennes by the fast N165 dual carriageway (take the exit signposted *Quimper Centre*).

Other roads converging on Quimper make it easily accessible from anywhere in Finistère, in particular from the Crozon Peninsula, Cap Sizun, the south coast, Morlaix and the Montagnes Noires.

There is a fee-paying car park (except 1200–1400) in front of the Tourist Office. Free car parks are available outside the perimeter of the old town, for instance in *pl. de la Tour d'Auvergne* on the west side and *pl. du Champ de Foire* to the north.

GETTING AROUND
Quimper can only be toured on foot. The old town is quite compact and streets are narrow, so everything can be looked at quite closely: corbels leaning precariously, carved beams on the façades of houses and a profusion of interesting details. Should you feel tired, there is always a pavement café waiting to welcome you.

235

The **Musée de la Faïence** and the **Faïenceries HB Henriot** (see p. 237), on the banks of the Odet south of the centre, are easily reached by car and there is free parking outside.

To call a **taxi** any time of the day or night, *tel: 98 90 21 21*.

STAYING IN QUIMPER

Accommodation

There are a couple of fairly expensive hotels in the old town: **Gradlon**, *30 r. de Brest; tel: 98 95 04 39*, and **La Tour d'Auvergne**, *13 r. des Réguaires; tel: 98 95 08 70*. Cheaper ones are to be found near the station; otherwise, all the chain hotels (*Ba, BB, Ca, Ct, Cl, F1, Ib, Nv, NH* and *PC*) are located out of town, on the roads to Brest, Nantes and Bénodet.

HI: The **youth hostel**, *6 av. des Oiseaux* (south-west along *quai de l'Odet*); *tel: 98 55 41 67*, is open Apr–Sept.

There is a splendid **campsite**, **Orangerie de Lanniron**, *tel: 98 90 62 02*, with swimming-pool and tennis courts on the banks of the Odet River, on the way south to Bénodet.

The Tourist Office provides a list of classified holiday homes and Bed and Breakfast accommodation in and around Quimper.

Eating and Drinking

Restaurants in the old town usually offer more than just a meal: setting and atmosphere are no doubt worth a little extra to most visitors. There are a couple of fairly expensive restaurants, both in *r. Elie-Fréron*, which fit into this category: **L'Ambroisie**, *tel: 98 95 00 02*, and **Le Clos de la Tourbie**, *tel: 98 95 45 03*. A cheaper alternative can be found nearby in the *pl. au Beurre* and *r. Verdelet* where there are two excellent *crêperies*: **Au Vieux**

Quimper, *tel: 98 95 31 34* and **La Krampouzerie**, *tel: 98 95 13 08*. There are also some moderately priced restaurants near the station.

Les Halles (covered market), located just west of the Cathedral, is the place to buy fresh fruit and vegetables as well as *charcuterie* and bread for picnics. Nearby, in the *r. St-François*, **Au Régal**, *tel: 98 95 01 14*, is a delicatessen selling Breton specialities such as the famous *Filet Bleu* biscuits, traditionally served with champagne.

Communications and Money

The main **post office** (PTT), *37 blvd de Kerguélen; tel: 98 64 28 28*, offers change facilities Mon–Fri 0800–1830, Sat 0800–1200. Most banks are open Tues–Sat except **Crédit Agricole** and **BNP** which are open on Mon and closed on Sat.

ENTERTAINMENT

In summertime, the emphasis is on outdoor entertainment: excursions, boat trips (see sightseeing) and sport in the day time, cultural, folk and traditional events round the clock (see events). Spectator sports include windsurfing on the Odet River, cycle races, show-jumping and tennis (details given in *Quimper Magazine*).

There are several cinemas in the town centre; one of them, **Le Chapeau Rouge**, *r. du Chapeau Rouge* (near the Église St-Mathieu); *tel: 36 68 03 07*, shows films in English.

Events

The climax of the summer season is the **Festival de Cornouaille** (July), one of the main expressions of Breton culture. It is a popular event with music, dancing and singing, Celtic games, exhibitions, traditional tales, costumed parades and general rejoicing throughout the town. For more information, *tel: 98 55 53 53*.

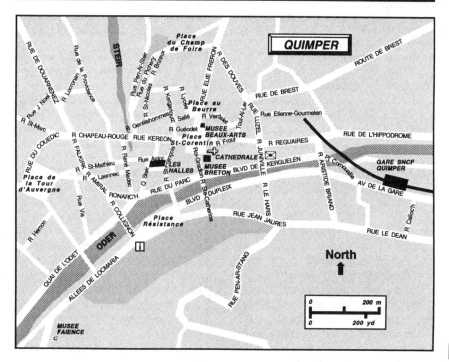

The **Semaines Musicales** is a festival of classical music which takes place in Aug with some ten concerts usually programmed round a common theme.

SHOPPING

Quimper earthenware stands apart from other Breton specialities, for it is truly original (see box, p.238). It can be bought from the main manufacturer, **HB Henriot**, r. Haute; tel: 98 90 09 36, or from several shops in the town centre: **La Civette**, 16 bis r. du Parc; tel: 98 95 34 13, and **L'Art de Cornouaille**, pl. de la Cathédrale; tel: 98 95 39 24. For linen to go with it, try **François Le Villec**, 4 r. du Roi Gradlon; tel: 98 95 31 54.

Breton clothing, derived from traditional sailing garments, is usually of excellent quality but fairly expensive: try **Heoligou**, 16 r. du Parc; tel: 98 95 13 29

and **Le Glazik**, 9 r. du 19 mars 1962; tel: 98 52 29 28. Lovers of Breton and Celtic music will find a choice of CDs and cassettes at **Ar Bed Keltiek**, 2 r. du Roi Gradlon; tel: 98 95 42 82.

SIGHTSEEING

Quimper certainly deserves an extended visit and it is also the ideal starting point of excursions to central and south Finistère, in particular the picturesque Bigouden country (see p. 84).

Conscious of the importance of its architectural heritage, Quimper has undertaken to preserve it and to improve its urban environment. This is being done with financial help from the state: the **Caisse Nationale des Monuments Historiques et des Sites** (National Fund for Historic Sites and Monuments) is in charge of restoration work and provides competent guides to help the public discover Quimper's picturesque old town. Guided tours start from the Tourist Office, daily (May–Sept); commentary in English Tues 1400 (July and Aug).

The Gothic **Cathédrale St-Corentin**, the largest cathedral in Brittany, was built between the 13th and 15th centuries, but the spires were added in the mid-19th century. It is dedicated to St-Corentin, a hermit whom King Gradlon made first bishop of Quimper in the 5th century.

A statue of the king on horseback stands between the towers high above the façade. Some years ago, the remarkable flying buttresses showed signs of weakness and had to be reinforced. Inside, notice that the nave, built two centuries after the chancel, is not in alignment with it.

To tour the **old town**, walk north from the *pl. St-Corentin* up the *r. Elie-Fréron* and explore the side streets on the left, in particular *r. du Sallé, pl. au Beurre, r. du Lycée* (Jesuit Chapel), *r. de Kergariou, r. du Guéodet* (Maison des Cariatides), *r. Kéréon* lined with boutiques, *Pont Médard* and the picturesque bartizan (overhanging turret) overlooking the Steïr River, *r. des Gentilshommes.*

Museums

Housed in the former Bishops' Palace, next to the cathedral, the **Musée Départemental Breton**, *tel: 98 95 21 60*, contains substantial regional collections from the prehistoric and Gallo-Roman periods as well as costumes, furniture, Quimper earthenware and other objects representing various aspects of Breton culture. Open daily 0900–1800; admission Fr.25, (Fr.12).

The main asset of the recently refurbished **Musée des Beaux-Arts** (Museum of Fine Arts), *pl. St-Corentin; tel: 98 95 45 20*, is its remarkable collection of Breton

---

Faïence de Quimper

A young craftsman from Moustiers in Provence settled in Quimper in 1690 and founded the first pottery workshop in Locmaria, close to the Odet River where manufacturing still takes place. During the 18th century, craftsmen from Nevers and Rouen brought their own technique with them and gradually a unique style emerged, which soon made Quimper pottery famous all over the world. Breton traditions and costumes were used as motifs, entirely painted by hand with a brush stroke which became the trade mark of *la faïence de Quimper*. Today, each piece is still decorated by hand and signed by the artist. In 1984, the HB Henriot workshops were taken over by an American company which has ensured production continues (visits Mon–Fri 0900–1115 and 1330–1415, Fri 1500).

---

paintings of the 19th and 20th centuries. Landscapes, seascapes, scenes of daily life, *pardons,* legends and weddings – all the main Breton themes are illustrated. Beside a number of lesser known artists inspired by Brittany, there are some famous names such as Sérusier, Bernard, Meyer de Haan, who were friends of Gauguin, and also Delaunay, Lemordant, Marquet, Derain and Bazaine. Open daily except Tues 1000–1900; Fr.25, (Fr.15).

The **Musée de la Faïence** (Museum of Ceramics), *14 r. JB. Bousquet; tel: 98 90 12 72*, offers a fascinating journey back in time through 300 years of earthenware manufacture. The unique collection of 2000 pieces, exhibited in rotation, illustrates changing fashions, tastes, artistic trends and lifestyles, as well as manufacturing techniques. Open mid-Apr–Oct Mon–Sat 1000–1800; Fr.26, (Fr.15).

QUIMPER-MORLAIX

This route meanders through the Parc Naturel Régional d'Armorique, an area of austere landscapes, where eroded peaks rise above moors and marshes. The heart of Finistère is a land of mystery, of folk tales and legends, but also a land of deep religious fervour where a highly original style of architecture blossomed in the 16th century and produced the *endos* *paroissiaux* (parish closes). This drive can be done in a day, but allow two days so that you may fully appreciate the scenery and soak up the atmosphere.

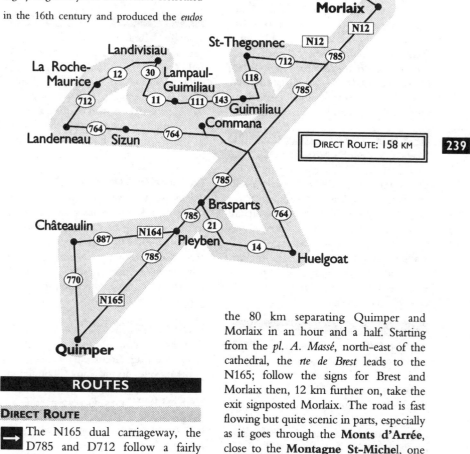

St-Malo–Brest, page 288

DIRECT ROUTE: 158 KM 239

the 80 km separating Quimper and Morlaix in an hour and a half. Starting from the *pl. A. Massé*, north-east of the cathedral, the *rte de Brest* leads to the N165; follow the signs for Brest and Morlaix then, 12 km further on, take the exit signposted Morlaix. The road is fast flowing but quite scenic in parts, especially as it goes through the **Monts d'Arrée**, close to the **Montagne St-Michel**, one of the highest 'peaks' of the whole range.

ROUTES

DIRECT ROUTE

→ The N165 dual carriageway, the D785 and D712 follow a fairly straight line and make it possible to cover

SCENIC ROUTE

This 158-km scenic route goes through several typical river towns and mountain villages of inland Finistère. Follow the *rte de Brest* as above but, instead of joining the N165, carry on along the D770 to **Châteaulin**. From Châteaulin, drive along D887 then N164 to **Pleyben** and turn left onto D785 to **Brasparts**. D21 going east joins D14 after 4 km; turn left towards **Huelgoat** via Lannédern, Loqueffret and St-Herbot. From Huelgoat, join D764 and drive to **Landerneau** through **Commana** and **Sizun**. Leave Landerneau on D712 to **La Roche-Maurice** and continue along D12, which follows the Elorn Valley to **Landivisiau**. From there drive east along D11, D111, D143 and D118 to St-Thégonnec via **Lampaul-Guimilau** and **Guimilau**, then turn right onto D712 to Morlaix.

QUIMPER TO CHÂTEAULIN

The **Chapelle Notre-Dame de Quilinen** stands in a secluded spot, 12 km from Quimper; nearby is an unusual calvary with a triangular base, dating from the mid-16th century. Five km further on, just off the main road, stands another chapel with a similar calvary, dedicated to **St Venec**. According to legend, his mother, St Gwen, had three nipples so that she could feed him and his two brothers, St Guénolé and St Jacut.

CHÂTEAULIN

Tourist Office: *quai Cosmao; tel: 98 86 02 11*; open all year; has information on guided walks, boat trips, and canoeing.

Le Chrismas, *33 Grand Rue; tel: 98 86 01 24,* is a reasonably priced hotel and restaurant; there are also a couple of cheaper ones and a municipal **campsite**, *tel: 98 86 32 93.*

The canalised **Aulne River** meanders

lazily past Châteaulin on its way to the Brest roadstead. Inaugurated in 1858 by Emperor Napoleon III, the Guilly-Glaz lock in Port-Launay, 2 km down river, marks the end of the Nantes-Brest canal, once vital to the Breton economy but now only used by cabin cruisers and converted barges. Châteaulin is a peaceful holiday resort, sought after by keen fishermen. Built on a hillock where a castle once stood, the 18th-century **Chapelle Notre-Dame** overlooks the town and the Aulne valley.

PLEYBEN

Tourist Office: *pl. du Gén. de Gaulle; tel: 98 26 71 05*; open Mon–Sat 1000–1230 and 1430–1800 mid-June–mid-Sept. It has information about the *Fête bretonne* (festival of music and dancing) and several *pardons* (religious festivals), marked footpaths and various outdoor activities. It is also possible to watch *crêpes* and fine chocolates being made: the Tourist Office has details.

ACCOMMODATION AND FOOD

There are a couple of *crêperies* and two unclassified *hôtels-restaurants* on the main square, including **La Croix Blanche,** *tel: 98 26 61 29*. The nearest campsite is at **Pont-Coblant** on the banks of the Aulne, 4 km from Pleyben, and the nearby **Club Nautique** has accommodation for young people, *tel: 98 73 34 69.*

SIGHTSEEING

The plain village houses are grouped round the magnificent **parish close** (see p. 244), one of the most imposing in Brittany. Free guided visits are provided by the SPREV, a national organisation for the preservation of ancient religious buildings (in front of the church July–Aug daily except Sun 1000–1300, 1430–1900).

The half-Gothic, half-Renaissance

church has a distinctive tower surmounted by a lantern and four pinnacles as well as two Gothic steeples. Inside, notice the beautiful vaulting, the original stained glass and the altar with its panelled altarpiece. The carved figures on the monumental calvary are lifelike and graceful. The 16th-century ossuary (charnel-house) houses a small museum open in summer.

BRASPARTS

Tourist Office: *Chapelle Ste-Anne; tel: 98 81 47 06*; open July and Aug. It has details of outdoor activities, traditional events, and excursions.

The **church** looks impressive with its beautifully carved porch, while the less ornate calvary displays a very moving *pietà* in a striking rustic style.

⤴ SIDE TRACK FROM BRASPARTS

The D785 continues northwards to the **Montagne St-Michel** (8 km); from the summit, crowned with a tiny chapel, there is a remarkable view of the vast peat bog known as Yeun Elez (the 'Gate of Hell' according to an ancient legend) and of the heath-covered Monts d'Arrée and Montagnes Noires. On the way back, stop by the **Maison des Artisans**, a traditional farm which displays the work of over 200 Breton craftsmen. ⤴

BRASPARTS TO HUELGOAT

From Brasparts, follow the D21 and the D14 eastwards to Huelgoat. The villages of **Lannédern** and **Loqueffret** each have their own parish close in picturesque surroundings. Four km further on, take a right turn to the **Chapelle St-Herbot** (a chapel dedicated to the patron saint of cattle), dating from the 14th century, built in Flamboyant Gothic style with an elegant

square tower; the interior is decorated with a beautiful roodscreen carved in oak and a set of ornate choir stalls.

HUELGOAT

Tourist Office, *pl. A. Penven, 29690 Huelgoat; tel: 98 99 72 32* (summer), *98 99 71 55* (winter), has a list of classified holiday homes; also map of marked footpaths in the Forêt d'Huelgoat and riding trips across the heaths of the Monts d'Arrée.

ACCOMMODATION AND FOOD

The family **Hôtel-Restaurant du Lac,** *tel: 98 99 71 14*, overlooks the lake which offers fishing and canoeing; in addition, there are several *crêperies* in the village. Close to the hôtel is the **Camping Municipal du Lac,** *tel: 98 99 78 80*; the other campsite is in the forest: **La Rivière d'Argent,** *tel: 98 99 72 50*.

SIGHTSEEING

Huelgoat means 'high forest' in Breton language and indeed the village is ideally situated between an attractive lake and picturesque woodland sloping down to the **rivière d'Argent** (Silver River). The forest is strewn with huge granite boulders weighing up to 100 tonnes (**Roche Tremblante**), sometimes piled on one another in striking formations (**Chaos du Moulin**), obstructing the river bed. The presence of these curiously eroded rocks has given rise to various legends, hence the names given to some of them, for instance **la Grotte du Diable** (the Devil's Cave).

HUELGOAT TO SIZUN

Leave Huelgoat towards the north-west and join the D764 which crosses the **Monts d'Arrée** from east to west. This part of the route is particularly picturesque and should be driven at a leisurely pace as numerous signposts on the roadside suggest things to see and do in this protected area of the Parc Naturel Régional d'Armorique. You can learn all about Breton horses and admire some splendid specimens at the **Domaine de Ménez Meur**, you can visit a typical 18th-century farm at **St-Rivoal** or make a detour to the **Barrage du Drennec** (Drennec Dam) where trout fishing is quite an art as you will discover if you visit the **Maison du Lac**.

Follow the D764 until you reach a major crossroads 14 km from Huelgoat; turn left onto the D785; about 1.5 km further on, a path leads to **Roc Trévezel,** the highest peak of the Monts d'Arrée.

Continue for 2.5 km and turn right onto the D11 to rejoin the D764. Almost immediately, you will see a sign for **Commana**. Within the parish close, the 17th-century church has a remarkable Renaissance south porch. Across the main road, at **Mougau-Bian** there is an interesting prehistoric passage grave.

Moulins de Kérouat, 5 km further on, is an ancient hamlet dating back to the 17th century. About 15 granite buildings in all – houses, mills, bread ovens – illustrate the life of a family of millers over the past 200 years (open daily July and Aug).

SIZUN

Tourist Information: Office du Tourisme des Monts d'Arrée, *pl. de l'Abbé-Broc'h, 29450 Sizun; tel: 98 68 88 40;* open daily July and Aug, closed Sun June and Sept. It has information about walks, mountain bike tours, riding, water sports, fishing, cultural guided tours, pardons and traditional events, holiday homes etc.

ACCOMMODATION

The two *LF* hotels are good value for money: **Hôtel des Voyageurs,** *tel: 98 68 80 35* and **Les Quatre Saisons,** *tel: 98 68*

Folk tales and legends

A highly imaginative people, the Bretons traditionally sought mystery and magic on the heaths and in the forests, in the wild seas and in the still lakes, even in the strange shapes of the rocks which suddenly come to life. They have created their own fantasy world, peopled by elves and fairies, giants and mermaids, saints and magicians, and orchestrated by the fearsome Ankou, the personification of Death. In this mythical world, Good and Evil often fight epic battles in which Man is but a pawn, a representation, no doubt, of the fragility of Man in the 'real' world. One of the most famous legends is that of King Arthur, who lies asleep in the Forêt de Brocéliande, now the Forêt de Paimpont (see p. xxx),

There are also larger than life but otherwise quite 'human' giants such as Gargantua, Rannou and Hok-Braz. Tales abound about how they threw rocks about the place and erected the megaliths. Elves and fairies are the expression of the Bretons' poetic vein and of their aspiration for a life in total harmony with nature: thus the Golfe du Morbihan was formed by the tears of unhappy fairies and the islands within the gulf appeared where they threw their crowns of flowers into the water!

---

80 19. Both have a wide choice of menus. **Camping du Gollen** on the banks of the Elorn River, *tel: 98 24 11 43.*

SIGHTSEEING

Sizun is a pleasant holiday resort and the main tourist information centre for the area. A superb three-arched monumental gate, surmounted by a calvary, leads into the **parish close** (see p. 244) which comprises an ossuary (now housing a small

242

local museum) and a very interesting church. Inside, there is a carved wooden beam running all the way round the top of the walls, several beautiful altarpieces and a 17th-century organ by Thomas Dallam.

Just outside Sizun, an old water-mill has been turned into a river museum illustrating the importance of the quality of water in the preservation of the region's natural fish resources (**Maison de la Rivière, de l'Eau et de la Pêche,** *Moulin de Vergraon, tel: 98 68 86 33*).

LANDERNEAU

Tourist Office: *Pont de Rohan, BP 164, 29800 Landerneau; tel: 98 85 13 09*, has details of boat trips, mountain bike tours, outdoor activities and traditional events.

There is an *Ib* chain hotel and another hotel, **Le Clos du Pontic,** *r. du Pontic, tel: 98 21 50 91*. The choice of restaurants covers a wide price range.

Situated deep inside the Elorn estuary, **Landerneau** is a thriving market town linking inland and coastal Finistère. From its prosperous past in the canvas trade, the city has retained a famous 16th-century bridge lined with picturesque houses, the **Pont de Rohan,** and an interesting church, **St-Thomas-de-Cantorbéry** with a striking three-tiered square tower.

Leave Landerneau on the D712 and stop briefly at **La Roche-Maurice** to admire the ossuary dating from 1640: above the outside stoup stands a personification of Death threatening a group of humans with the words *Je vous tue tous* (I kill you all).

LANDIVISIAU

Tourist Office: *14 av. Foch; tel: 98 68 03 50*; open all year, closed Sun in summer, weekend in winter. Information leaflet (*L'Estivant*) published regularly between June and Sept. Details of guided coach tours, mountain bike tours, riding trips, maps of marked footpaths, etc.

Landivisiau is a convenient centre from which to explore the surrounding area, and there is a wide choice of accommodation and restaurants. The **church** was rebuilt in 1865, but it has retained a magnificent 16th-century porch – partly Gothic, partly Renaissance – and a very high steeple. The nearby **Fontaine St-Thivisiau** is decorated with a flamboyant Gothic low relief.

LANDIVISIAU TO MORLAIX

Follow the D11 to **Lampaul-Guimiliau,** where you can see the first of three impressive parish closes, situated within a few km of one another. The bright interior of **Lampaul-Guimiliau Church** is a hymn to the Resurrection with a remarkable *pietà* carved out of one single block, an elegant font, a splendid gilt altarpiece depicting the Passion and a brightly coloured rood-beam held by two dragons and decorated with lively biblical scenes.

Continue on the D111 to **Guimiliau.** Over 200 characters are displayed round the base of the monumental calvary, while the south porch of the **church** is decorated with a profusion of small statues; inside, note the magnificent baptistery in carved oak and also the pulpit and the three altarpieces.

The third close is at **St-Thégonnec,** 7 km along the D118. The calvary looks relatively modest and one's attention is drawn instead to the ossuary with its slim Corinthian columns and to the elegant steeple of the **church**; inside, the pulpit and the retables (ornatmental panels behind the altar) are worthy of a cathedral.

MORLAIX

Tourist Office: *pl. des Otages, 29203 Morlaix Cedex; tel: 98 62 14 94*; open

243

Parish Closes and Calvaries

Particularly concentrated in and around the Elorn valley, parish closes represent a rich cultural legacy, assembled over a period of 200 years and illustrating the unique qualities of a highly individual people. A combination of deep religious fervour and favourable economic conditions made it possible for this original art form to blossom in Brittany at a time when the Renaissance was sweeping across Europe with extraordinary vigour. These impressive granite buildings showed both the spiritual and practical qualities of the Breton people. Around the church, which was the focal point of social life, they built an enclosure including a graveyard, an ossuary in the shape of a small chapel and a calvary, (usually a crucifixion scene) very often of monumental size. The originality of this type of architecture lies mainly in the profusion of ornamentation both outside and inside. Elegant lanterns and pinnacles, beautiful porches and elaborate calvaries depict scenes from the Bible with as many as 200 characters carved in granite. The interior of churches are decorated with intricately carved rood-beams, ornate oak pulpits and baldachined (canopied) fonts, gilt altarpieces and delicately carved organ lofts which testify to the astonishing mastery of the local craftsmen.

daily 0900–1900, Sun 1000–1230 (July–Aug); open Mon–Sat 0900–1200, 1400–1800 (Sept–June). It provides an accommodation booking service within the region, guided tours of the town Thurs 1430, Fr.20, and; dramatised guided tours with live performances Tues and Fri 2030 Fr.25; and mapped walking tours.

ACCOMMODATION AND FOOD

There are two chain hotels on the outskirts: *BB* and *Ca*. Otherwise there is a good choice of two-star hotels (middle price range) in the city centre. Cheaper ones can be found in the old town with restaurants attached. There are several *crêperies* and a selection of reasonably priced restaurants where traditional French cuisine is served.

SIGHTSEEING

Traditional events include weekly demonstrations of Breton dancing, while *Les Arts dans la rue* is an outdoor art festival with shows, street concerts, comedies and circus performances, taking place in the old town every Wed from mid-July to mid-Aug.

The tall viaduct carrying the main Paris–Brest railway line casts a dark shadow on the compact city confined within the narrow valley of the Jarlot and Queffleuth rivers. There is a feeling of austerity in the air, underlined by the slate covered façades of the old houses lining the narrow streets known as *venelles*. Easily defended, Morlaix was, like St-Malo, a corsair stronghold until the late 18th century. Famous privateers based in Morlaix protected the maritime trade routes on which the town's prosperity depended and occasionally captured the odd English ship.

The brochure *Circuit des Venelles*, available at the Tourist Office, makes it easier to explore old Morlaix and to appreciate its historic buildings. Notice in particular the **Maison de la Reine Anne** (Queen Anne's House) overlooking the *pl. Allende* and the **Église St-Mélaine** almost beneath the viaduct. Housed in a former church, the **Musée des Jacobins** contains archaeological collections, furniture and paintings, including works on Breton themes. Open all year, closed Tues in winter; admission Fr.24, (child Fr.12).

QUIMPER–VANNES

The south coast of Brittany is famous for its sunny beaches, opulent seaside resorts and megalith. It is also popular for the variety of its unspoilt scenery which, over a hundred years ago, fascinated Gauguin and his friends. Distinctive coastal features include picturesque estuaries called rias where the succulent Bélon oysters are bred, fish-abounding rivers and attractive islands, in particular the largest of them, appropriately called Belle-Île. The coastal route links two ancient cities with a definite southern flavour, Quimper and Vannes. Allow at least three days to sample life on the sunny south coast.

DIRECT ROUTE: 120 KM

245

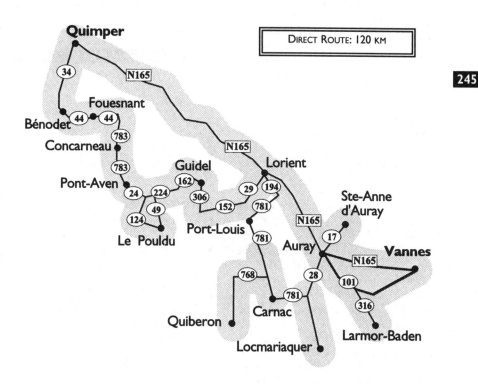

ROUTES

DIRECT ROUTE

➡️ The 120 km separating the two towns can easily be covered in an hour and a half. The N165 dual carriageway by-passes all the towns but there are exits for Concarneau, Pont-Aven, Lorient, Carnac and Auray. Leave the centre of Quimper eastwards along the south bank of the Odet and carry straight on following signs for Rennes and Lorient. After Lorient, ignore Rennes and follow signs for Vannes.

SCENIC ROUTE

➡️ This route is nearly three times as long but well worth the extra driving.

Leave the town centre in the opposite direction (westwards) and follow signs for Fouesnant and Bénodet, eventually joining the D34, which leads to **Bénodet**.

From Bénodet, take the D44 eastwards to **Fouesnant**. Continue to La Forêt-Fouesnant and take the right fork to **Concarneau**. Follow the D783 to **Riec-sur-Bélon**, then turn right on the D24 leading to **Clohars-Carnoët** via Moëlan-sur-Mer. Turn right towards the coast along the D124 to **Le Pouldu**. Drive north on the D49 for 4 km and turn right, following the D224, then the D162, to **Guidel**.

Leave Guidel on the D306 towards the coast. The road continues as the D152 and D29 to **Lorient**. Drive round the Lorient roadstead along the D194, then the D781, which goes through **Port-Louis** and turns south-east to **Carnac**.

Continue on this road through **La Trinité-sur-Mer** across the Pont de Kérisper, then follow the D28 northwards to **Auray**. Leave Auray on the D101 for Vannes.

Station Kid

In 1992 it was offically decided to recognise efforts made by certain *municipalités* to provide holiday villages, children's menus, baby-sitters and nurseries, greater safety in the streets and a protected environment. In Brittany, three resorts have been awarded this distinction and been labelled *Station Kid*: **Perros-Guirec** on the north coast; **Arzon** in the Golfe du Morbihan; and **Fouesnant**, where children from the age of four have the choice of several beach clubs and an aqua park, **Les Balnéides**, *allée de Loc'hilaire; tel: 98 56 18 19*, which has the longest slide in Brittany (75 m). In addition various competitions are organised on the beach and in the sea.

BÉNODET

Tourist Office: *pl. du Gén. de Gaulle, 29950 Bénodet; tel: 98 57 00 14;* open daily 0900–1900, Sun 1000–1300 (summer); 0900–1230 and 1400–1800, closed Sat afternoon and Sun (winter). Accommodation booking service, plus details of daily excursions, boat trips, maps of suggested walks.

ACCOMMODATION

Hotel prices are slightly higher than elsewhere in this fashionable resort. **Hostellerie Abbatiale**, *av. de l'Odet; tel: 98 57 05 11*, where Sarah Bernhardt once stayed, overlooks the harbour, while the **Eurogreen**, *Golfe de l'Odet; tel: 98 82 84 86*, is the obvious choice for golfers. There are several first class campsites by the sea with mobile homes to let.

EATING AND DRINKING

Restaurants offering regional specialities are fairly expensive. Try **l'Alhambra**,

Corniche de l'Estuaire; tel: 98 57 16 00, for seafood or **La Ferme du Letty**, tel: 98 57 01 27, on the edge of the lagoon, for a choice of Breton dishes. There are also several crêperies and snack bars along the seafront.

ENTERTAINMENT

Regattas, cultural guided tours and lectures take place throughout the summer; in addition, **Les quinzaines estivales de Bénodet** stage regular concerts and shows. Otherwise night entertainment is provided by the **Casino**, Corniche de la Plage; tel: 98 57 04 16, and a discotheque, **Yannick club**, tel: 98 57 03 99.

SIGHTSEEING

A half-hour tour of Bénodet in the small **tourist train** (every 40 mins from 1030 onwards, departure by the church overlooking the harbour) will enable you to get your bearings. After that it is a question of exploring the surrounding area: the **Pont de Cornouaille** over the Odet River offering a stunning view, **la Mer Blanche**, a picturesque lagoon edged with dunes, **Ste-Marine** across the estuary via the foot-passenger ferry, not forgetting the **Glénan Islands**; admire the protected sea flora and fauna of this archipelago aboard a catamaran specially fitted for underwater observation (**Vedettes de l'Odet**, tel: 98 57 00 58).

FOUESNANT

Tourist Office: 5 r. Armor, 29170 Fouesnant; tel: 98 56 00 93, outdoor activities for children and teenagers; guided walks.

There is a good choice of moderately priced hotels in Fouesnant and at Beg-Meil and Cap Coz on the edge of the Baie de la Forêt. Try the peaceful and cosy **Hôtel de Bretagne**, Beg-Meil; tel: 98 94

98 04, or, for a memorable experience, choose the 16th-century **Manoir du Stang**, 29940 La Forêt-Fouesnant; tel: 98 56 97 37. Campsites abound all round the bay.

Traditional events include the **Fête des Pommiers** in July, which celebrates cider-making.

Take advantage of a free guided visit of the lovely Romanesque **church** and of the **Chapelle Ste-Anne** and enjoy one of the safe beaches inside the bay, between **Kerleven** and **Beg-Meil**.

CONCARNEAU

Tourist Office: quai d'Aiguillon, BP 529, 29185 Concarneau Cedex; tel: 98 97 01 44. Open daily 0900–2000 July and Aug; otherwise 0900–1200 and 1400–1800, closed Sun. Guided tours, boat trips, walks; brochures on the 'Painters' Route'.

ACCOMMODATION

Hotels cover a wide price range from the expensive **Hôtel de l'Océan**, Plage des Sables Blancs; tel: 98 50 53 50, overlooking the beach, to the reasonably priced **Renaissance**, 56 av. de la Gare; tel: 98 97 04 23. The **HI: Auberge de Jeunesse** is on the seafront, quai de la Croix; tel: 98 97 03 47 and there are several **campsites** within easy reach of the town centre.

EATING AND DRINKING

Seafood restaurants are at the harbour and inside the Ville-close (walled town). **Le Buccin**, 1 r. Duguay Trouin; tel: 98 50 54 22, is popular with the locals, but for a cheaper meal, try **L'Assiette du Pêcheur**, 12 r. St-Guénolé, Ville-close; tel: 98 50 75 84 or one of the crêperies in the Ville-close.

SIGHTSEEING

Follow the picturesque corniche along the

247

seafront and park your car in front of the Tourist Office: the **Ville-close** and the **harbour** are within easy reach.

Concarneau today is the third largest fishing port in France; it is possible to go aboard a trawler, visit a cannery, watch the unloading of the fish and the auction sale (ask at the Tourist Office).

Facing the harbour is the fortified town dating back to medieval times. Stroll along the narrow cobbled streets, visit the **Musée de la Pêche** (fishing museum) and climb to the top of the walls for splendid views of the harbour and the bay.

The town's two main events are the **Festival International de la Baie** (international folk festival) in July and the **Fête des Filets Bleus** (Breton festival) in Aug.

PONT-AVEN

Tourist Office: *5 pl. de l'Hôtel de Ville BP 36, 29930 Pont-Aven; tel: 98 06 04 70.* Open all year Mon–Sat 0900–1230 and 1400–1830, Sun and public holidays 1030–1230 and 1500–1830; closed 1930 July and Aug, closed Sun and public holidays Nov–Mar. It has a hotel-booking service and change facilities Sun Mon and holidays (June–Sept), information on guided tours and visits, walks and cycle tours.

ACCOMMODATION

Particularly attractive are the **Moulin de Rosmadec,** *Venelle de Rosmadec; tel: 98 06 00 22* (book well in advance), a converted 15th-century water-mill, and **Roz-Aven,** *11 quai Th-Botrel; tel: 98 06 13 06,* an 18th-century thatched cottage overlooking the harbour. Both are expensive.

There is a choice of cheaper hotels, bed and breakfast and holiday homes in and around Pont-Aven; campsites are on the coast between Raguenès and Port-Manech.

EATING AND DRINKING

Strictly for gourmets are **Le Moulin de Rosmadec** (see above) and **La Taupinière,** *Croissant St-André, tel: 98 06 03 12* (on the Concarneau road, expensive). Several cafés and brasseries serve snacks and salads.

SIGHTSEEING

Guided tours of the town and museum start from the Tourist Office (Tues–Sat, Fr.35). Also available are mapped walks in the footsteps of the Pont-Aven painters and boat trips up and down the Aven and Bélon estuaries (*tel: 98 71 14 59*).

The **Fête des Fleurs d'Ajoncs** (Gorse Flower Festival) in Aug is a lively folk festival during which local women wear the graceful Pont-Aven *coiffe* (head-dress).

The peaceful riverside town of Pont-Aven took on a new dimension when, over a hundred years ago, Paul Gauguin and his friends decided to settle there, hoping to find new inspiration and new means of expression. And they did – the authentic life they shared with the local population provided the inspiration which led to a new style of painting called *synthétisme*, the golden rule being for the artist to paint what he saw and not what was there.

Inaugurated in 1986 for the hundredth anniversary of Gauguin's arrival in Pont-Aven, the **Musée Municipal** (open daily mid-Feb–Dec 1000–1230 and 1400–1830, Fr.25) houses a permanent collection of paintings by the Pont-Aven group and holds three temporary exhibitions every year. Take a stroll in the **Bois d'Amour** along the Aven, the painters' favourite haunt, and visit the **Chapelle de Trémalo** and the **Église de Nizon** which inspired two of Gauguin's famous paintings, *Yellow Christ* and *Breton Calvary or Green Christ*.

PONT-AVEN TO LORIENT

The D24 between **Riec-sur-Bélon** and **Moëlan-sur-Mer** follows the sinuous estuary of the Bélon River, famous for its delicious oysters. For tours of oyster-breeding farms: contact the **Tourist Office**, *29124 Riec-sur-Bélon; tel: 98 06 97 65.*

Manoir de Kertalg, *rte de Riec-sur-Bélon, 29350 Moëlan-sur-Mer; tel: 98 39 77 77,* is a romantic castle hotel (very expensive). There are cheaper hotels on the coast at Kerfany, Doëlan and Le Pouldu **(Le Panoramique**, *29360 Le Pouldu; tel: 98 39 93 49).* A complete list of accommodation in the area and guided nature walks is available from the **Tourist Office:** *r. des Moulins BP 26, 29350 Moëlan-sur-Mer; tel: 98 39 67 28.* This lively market town possesses an architectural gem, the 16th-century **Chapelle St-Philibert-St-Roch,** with a rustic calvary and fountain nearby.

Le Pouldu, on the coast, has a lovely sheltered beach, but is mostly famous for the **Maison Marie-Henry,** a faithful reconstruction of the inn where Gauguin and some of his friends settled in 1889 after leaving the 'overcrowded' Gloanec boarding-house in Pont-Aven (guided tours mid-June–mid-Sept, Fr.20).

Across the Laïta River, **Guidel** is a pleasant resort with a beautiful beach **(Tourist Information: Centre Culturel Brizeux,** *r. Cap. Quillien; tel: 97 65 01 74).*

The coastline between Guidel and Lorient has retained its natural beauty, its fine sand beaches, wild dunes and tiny fishing ports, the perfect setting for an 18-hole golf course overlooking the sea.

LORIENT

Tourist Office: *quai de Rohan, 56100 Lorient; tel: 97 21 07 84* (information), *97*

Brittany and the Celts

Brittany was so deeply influenced by the Celts that it still bears the marks of their ancient civilisation and stands apart from other French regions, feeling in many ways closer to other Celtic areas like Wales or Cornwall. To explain this, one must go back 2500 years when wave after wave of Celtic tribes arrived from northern Europe and settled in Gaul. Their civilisation soon flourished, particularly in Brittany where it readily absorbed the culture of the previous occupants, noted for their megalithic monuments (see box on p. 251). Both practical and highly imaginative, the Celts were competent traders and craftsmen, endowed with a strong artistic sense which led them to worship nature and confuse myth with reality. They shared a common language with Celts from across the Channel who, quite naturally, landed in Brittany when they were chased out of Britain by the Angles and the Saxons. Deeply religious, these 'Bretons' came as missionaries and Brittany became the land of parishes and monastic villages, echoes of which remain today.

249

84 97 97 (accommodation-booking service, closed weekends). Open Mon–Fri 0900–1900, Sat closed lunchtime, Sun and holidays 1000–1200 and 1400–1700 July–Aug; the rest of the year it closes lunchtime and an hour earlier.

ACCOMMODATION AND FOOD

There is a large selection of hotels in the medium-price range, all very much alike since the town was completely rebuilt after World War II. book well ahead for accommodation in Aug. (see 'Sightseeing'). Hotel chains include *Ib, IH, Mc* and *Nv*.

HI: youth hostel at *41 r. V. Schoelcher, 56100 Lorient; tel: 97 37 11 65*.

Regional cuisine is found at **Le Jardin Gourmand**, *46 r. J. Simon; tel: 97 64 17 24* (meat dishes); and **La Compagnie des Indes**, *45 r. J. Legrand; tel: 97 64 43 31* (seafood).

SIGHTSEEING

Occupying a sheltered position inside the combined estuaries of the Blavet and the Scorff, Lorient is France's second largest fishing port (guided tours of the harbour) and an important naval base. Rebuilt in record time after World War II, the town boasts a homogenous architectural style typical of the 1950s. Guided tours include a wartime air raid shelter situated beneath *pl. Alsace-Lorraine*, recently reopened and turned into a **Mémorial de la ville détruite** (Memorial to the destroyed city).

The **Centre Nautique de Kerguelen** (*tel: 97 33 77 78*) at Larmor-Plage offers sailing and diving as well as day cruises and special activities for children. Contact the Tourist Office for a day's fishing at sea with professionals.

In Aug, Lorient is host to an international event, the **Festival Interceltique** (*tel: 97 21 24 29*), a great gathering of artists from all the Celtic countries, which attracts more than 200,000 spectators. In addition there are outdoor concerts at the harbour throughout the summer.

There is a wide choice of boat trips round the roadstead, to the sunny island of Groix or up the Blavet estuary to the walled town of **Hennebont** and its national stud.

The course of the two rivers also offer many possibilities for motor tours: along the wooded valley of the placid Blavet River to the charming ancient village of **Poul Fetan**, or up the green valley of the untamed Scorff River, famous for its salmon.

LORIENT TO CARNAC

The **Port-Louis Citadel** has for the past 300 years guarded the entrance to the Lorient roadstead; today it houses the **Musée de la Compagnie des Indes** (Museum of the India Company) which, during the 17th and 18th centuries, controlled the Far Eastern trade based in Lorient (*Orient* meaning east). Open 1000–1900 Apr–Sept, open afternoons, closed Tues (Oct–Mar except July, Aug); Fr.26 (Fr.17).

The D781 to Carnac crosses the Rivière or **Ria d'Etel,** a wide river valley scattered with islands, where landscapes change with the tides and oyster-breeding is a way of life.

> **SIDE TRACK TO QUIBERON**
>
> Before going on to Carnac, make a detour to the **Presqu'île de Quiberon** which juts out into the ocean like a spindly arm stretched towards the large island of **Belle-Île.** Once an island itself, it is now linked to the mainland by a narrow sandbank 22 m wide. The east coast is lined with sheltered beaches in total contrast with the windswept cliffs of the west coast. At the tip of the peninsula, **Quiberon** is a lively resort with a famous hydrotherapy centre, a sunny south-facing beach and a busy harbour, Port Maria. The activity is provided by the frequent ferries to Belle-Île, Houat and Hoëdic and by the coming and going of sardine trawlers. A traditional cannery can be visited; enquire at the **Tourist Office**, *7 r. de Verdun BP 97, 56170 Quiberon; tel: 97 50 07 84.*

(accommodation is rather expensive and advance booking is recommended). 🖪

CARNAC

Tourist Information: Office de Tourisme de Carnac-Plage, *74 av. des Druides BP 65, 56342 Carnac Cedex; tel: 97 52 13 52.* Open Mon–Sat all year; Sun afternoon as well July and Aug. An office in Carnac-Ville is open June–early Nov.

ACCOMMODATION AND FOOD

The large number of hotels shows how sought-after this attractive seaside resort is, with its sheltered beaches and superb hydrotherapy centre. Hotel chains include *BW, Ib* and *Nv.* Prices tend to be expensive. Holiday homes are plentiful and **campsites** extremely comfortable. The choice of restaurants covers a wide price range.

SIGHTSEEING

Throughout the world, the name of Carnac is synonymous with megaliths and rightly so for this small unassuming town on the coast of Morbihan is literally surrounded by hundreds of these enigmatic standing stones known in Brittany as *menhirs.*

The **Musée de la Préhistoire,** *10 pl. de la Chapelle; tel: 97 52 22 04,* newly inaugurated in 1985, retraces the evolution of mankind from the palaeolithic to the neolithic periods. Open 1000–1830 July–Aug, otherwise closed Wed; Fr.32 (Fr.12). North of the town, nearly 3000 standing stones are arranged in rows stretching 4 km in a south-west–north-east alignment; the most important group is the **Alignements du Ménec,** situated just north of the town centre; near the car park, the **Archéoscope de Carnac** offers a trip back to neolithic times with the help

---

Megaliths

The Morbihan *département* has one of the highest concentrations of megaliths in the world; these 'large stones', as they were so rightly called, were left behind by neolithic Man between 5000 and 2000 BC. Scientists have come to the conclusion that only a well-organised society could have undertaken the erection of such huge monuments but their exact function remains a mystery.

Menhirs (standing stones) can be as high as 20 m (*Grand Menhir brisé* in Locmariaquer); some stand isolated in the middle of a field, others are grouped in rows (*alignements de Carnac*), in the shape of a circle or a horse-shoe (*cromlec'h du Ménec, Carnac*). *Dolmens* consist of large slabs resting on standing stones, usually buried under a stone mound. They served as burial chambers accessible via a passage (*Table des Marchands* in Locmariaquer) and some are decorated with carvings (Locmariaquer and Gavrinis). The graves contained various objects which are now exhibited in museums in Carnac and Vannes.

Excavations are still being carried out and archaeologists are hoping that one day they will be able to answer the question 'why?'.

251

---

of spectacular special effects (in English, open daily in summer). A small train goes round Carnac, the beaches and the megaliths.

CARNAC TO AURAY

From the **Pont de Kerisper** there is a magnificent view of the Crach estuary and of the beautiful marina at **La Trinité-sur-Mer,** a picturesque seaside resort and an important oyster-breeding centre

(Tourist Office: *Cours des Quais; tel: 97 55 72 21).*

Follow the D781 to **Locmariaquer** where there is an extremely interesting group of megaliths (well signposted).

Go back to the crossroads and follow the D28 to Auray.

AURAY

The ancient city of **Auray** is situated at the head of a deep *ria* (estuary) opening out into the Golfe du Morbihan. The **Tourist Office:** *20 r. du Lait; tel: 97 24 09 75* is on the right bank of the river, while the medieval town and once busy harbour, known as **St-Goustan**, is on the left bank, across a picturesque stone bridge.

The **Hôtel Le Marin,** *1 pl. du Rolland; tel: 97 24 14 58,* simple but full of atmosphere, is situated a stone's throw from the quai Benjamin Franklin named in honour of the American politician who landed here in 1776 on his way to negotiate a treaty with France.

⚡ SIDE TRACK
FROM AURAY

One of the most famous *pardons* (see feature box) in Brittany takes place at the end of July in the village of **Ste-Anne d'Auray**, 6 km north of Auray. It started in 1623 when a farmer had a vision of Ste-Anne, the mother of Mary, and a chapel was built on the spot where a statue of the saint was found buried. A splendid basilica has replaced the modest chapel and today some 35,000 people from all over Europe follow the procession. ▨

AURAY TO VANNES

Drive south to **Larmor-Baden** where you can take a boat trip (Vedettes Blanches

Armor, *tel: 97 57 15 27)* to the island of **Gavrinis** famous for its cairn. A covered passage leads to a large funeral chamber; the carvings decorating the stone slabs suggest the grave might have been intended for a chieftain.

Continue along the D316 and rejoin the D101 which leads to Vannes (see p. 334).

Pardons

A *pardon* is a highly original mixture of religious celebration and folk festival. The religious side of it is an expression of the Bretons' strong religious feelings and of their ancestral need either to beg for forgiveness or ask a favour from one of the numerous saints whom they traditionally revere. The folkloric side of *pardons* stems directly from the ancient Celtic gatherings which had music, dancing and games on their menu.

The most colourful ceremony is the procession which follows the same route every year: the statue of the saint to whom the *pardon* is dedicated is carried in front, followed by the local people, some of them in regional costume and holding colourful banners. Next come the devout followers from other areas and the undisciplined crowd of onlookers. The festivities which ensue usually last part of the night.

There are a great number of *pardons* throughout Brittany, each parish boasting its local saint, sometimes not officially recognised by the church. Some of the *grands pardons*, however, are of national and even international interest (see Ste-Anne d'Auray). Two of the most picturesque are the *Grande Troménie* in Locronan (July, see Brest to Quimper p. 78) and the *Grand Pardon* in Ste-Anne-la-Palud (Aug, see Brest to Quimper route).

RENNES

Rennes is an expanding and dynamic regional metropolis, which has retained a substantial and varied architectural heritage worthy of the historic capital of Brittany. Far from spoiling the general appearance of the town, the contrasting styles underline the impression of careful planning which gradually turned this aristocratic city into the political and economic centre of Brittany. Economic prosperity has led the town to play an increasingly important role as the guardian of Breton traditions and culture, not only through its university, where the Breton language is taught, but also through its numerous cultural events, such as the Festival des Tombées de la Nuit (Nightfall Festival) in July, which reconciles tradition with innovation and promotes artistic creation in the whole region.

TOURIST INFORMATION

Tourist Office: *Pont de Nemours BP 2533, 35025 Rennes Cedex; tel: 99 79 01 98.* Open all year weekdays 0900–1800, closed Mon morning. **Accueil Gare** (station), *pl. de la Gare; tel: 99 53 23 23.* Open all year Mon–Fri 0800–1900, Sat Sun and public holidays 1000–1300 and 1500–1800. It provides a booking service for accommodation, guided visits and tours, excursions etc.

Comité Régional du Tourisme, *74 bis r. de Paris; tel: 99 28 44 30,* provides information about Brittany as a whole.

Comité Départemental du Tourisme, *4 r. J. Jaurès; tel: 99 78 47 47,* has information about the *département* of Ille-et-Vilaine.

Centre Information Jeunesse Bretagne (Young People's Information Service), *6 cours des Alliés, 35043 Rennes Cedex; tel: 99 31 47 48.*

Maison de la Randonnée (Touring Information Office), *9 r. des Portes Mordelaises; tel: 99 31 59 44,* has information, itineraries, guidebooks on walks, drives etc., throughout Brittany.

The magazine *Le Rennais* (July and Aug edition), available at the Tourist Office, has a section entitled *le guide de l'été* which lists things to see and do in and around Rennes.

ARRIVING AND DEPARTING

Airport

The **Aéroport de Rennes-St-Jacques**, *35136 St-Jacques de la Lande; tel: 99 29 60 00,* is located 7 km south-west of the town centre along the D177. There are weekly direct flights to and from Cork, and several flights a week to and from London Gatwick via Le Havre or Caen.

By Car

Whatever direction you come from, follow signs for *Centre ville* (town centre). Once there, head for one of the free parking areas at *pl. St-Mélaine* or *av. A. Briand.* Additional parking spaces (maximum stay two hours) are found at *pl. Ste-Anne* and *pl. Hoche.* Long term car parks, open 24 hours, are located near the station, south of the Vilaine River.

253

GETTING AROUND

The historic centre of Rennes surrounds the *pl. de la Mairie* and *pl. du Parlement de Bretagne*. All the main sights can easily be reached on foot. However, there is an efficient bus service called **S.T.A.R.**, information at *pl. de la République* or *tel: 99 79 37 37*. To call a **taxi** anytime seven days a week, *tel: 99 30 79 79*.

STAYING IN RENNES

Accommodation

There are numerous hotels in town and in the suburbs, the majority being reasonably priced. Only one or two are located in the city centre: **Hôtel des Lices**, *7 pl. des Lices; tel: 99 79 14 81*, in the medieval district is moderately priced. **Auberge St-Martin**, *230 r. de St-Malo; tel: 99 59 80 80*, north of the *pl. Ste-Anne*, is further away but inexpensive. There is a wider choice south of the river, including the **Anne de Bretagne**, *12 r. de Tronjolly; tel: 99 31 49 49*, one of the best hotels in Rennes (fairly expensive), and the **St-Brieuc**, *35 av. Janvier* (near the station); *tel: 99 31 69 11*, which is very good value for money. A cheaper choice would be the **Venezia**, *27 r. Dupont des Loges* (near the river); *tel: 99 30 36 56*.

Hotel chains in the Rennes conurbation include *Ba, Ct, CI, F1, Ib, Mc, PC*.

HI: the **Centre International de Séjours Auberge de Jeunesse** (Youth Hostel), *10-12 Canal St-Martin; tel: 99 33 22 33* is situated north of the centre.

There is a **campsite** within the city boundaries, to the north: **Camping Municipal des Gayeulles**, *Parc des Bois; tel: 99 36 91 22*.

Eating and Drinking

Rennes has an amazing number of **gastronomic restaurants**. They offer a choice of several menus but most of them are expensive, such as the **Auberge St-Sauveur**, *6 r. St-Sauveur; tel: 99 79 32 56*, in an authentic 15th-century house, and the **Four à Ban**, *4 r. St-Mélaine; tel: 99 38 72 85*, in a rustic 18th-century setting. A couple of establishments, situated south of the river, are more reasonably priced: **Chouin**, *12 r. d'Isly; tel: 99 30 87 86*, specialises in seafood, and **La Toque Rennaise**, *9 r. E. Souvestre; tel: 99 30 84 25*, provides quick service at lunchtime, rather unusual for a gastronomic venue.

There are also many traditional restaurants and *crêperies* offering a wide price range, the highest concentration being on *pl. Ste-Anne* and *r. St-Michel;* **La Maison de la Galette**, *6 pl. Ste-Anne; tel: 99 79 01 43*, and **Crêperie Ste-Anne**, *5 pl. Ste-Anne; tel: 99 79 22 72*, are both housed in picturesque timber-framed buildings.

The most colourful open market takes place on Sat on the *pl. des Lices* at the heart of the medieval district – the locals are proud to say that it has been called the 'finest market in France'. A daily market is held at the **Halles Centrales** (main covered market), *pl. H. Commeurec*, just south of the river. In both these places you will find all you need for a picnic.

Communications

The main **post office** is located near the station, *27 blvd du Colombier, 35032 Rennes Cedex; tel: 99 01 22 11*. Open Mon–Fri 0900–1900, Sat 0900–1200. Letters may be addressed to a person (name in block capitals), Poste Restante, La Poste Recette Principale, at the above address.

There is another office closer to the old town, along the south bank of the river.

Money

On average banks are open Mon–Fri 0900–1700 (with an interruption of one or

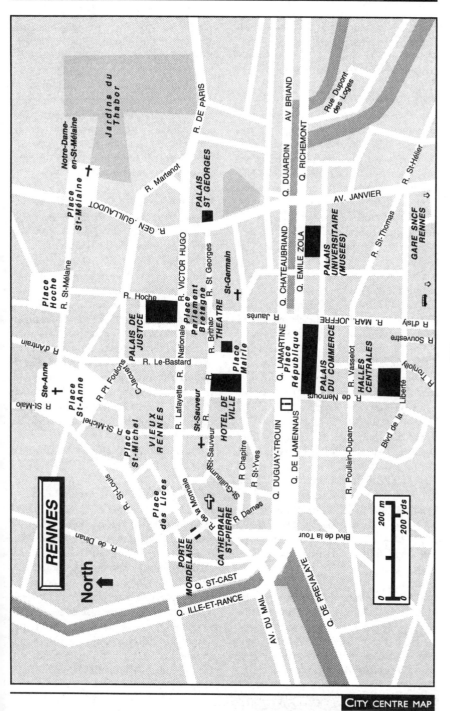

two hours for lunch) and Sat 0900–1200. The **Youth Hostel** (see address p. 254) offers change facilities Sat, Sun and public holidays 0800–1000 and 1800–2300.

ENTERTAINMENT

The town assigns 14 per cent of its budget to cultural activities, a fact that is not surprising if judged by the programme called *Spectacles Infos*, which is published every three months by the Tourist Office. This lists thematic visits of the city, exhibitions, classical music concerts, opera, ballet and theatre performances, jazz evenings, variety shows, special shows for children, lectures, spectator sports, antique fairs and festivals.

Other forms of entertainment on offer include films. Two cinemas show films in *V.O. (version originale)*, foreign productions with their original soundtrack, usually in English: **Cinéma L'Arvor**, *29 r. d'Antrain; tel: 99 38 72 40*, and **Ciné TNB**, *1 r. St-Hélier; tel: 99 30 88 88*.

There are two piano bars with live music and cabaret shows on *pl. St-Michel*, **Le Cox**, *tel: 99 78 25 15*, and **Le Métropolitain**, *tel: 99 78 11 69*.

Discos usually cater for all ages, either together in the same hall at the same time, like the **Charleston**, *1 quai d'Ille et Rance; tel: 99 59 22 56*, or separately, in different hall or on different days and times, like the **Pym's Club**, *27 pl. du Colombier; tel: 99 67 30 00*. **Pub Satori**, *3 r. Liothaud; tel: 99 33 90 52* is a pub and a disco all in one with music from the 1960s to today.

Events

Main events during the summer season include: **Les Soirées du Thabor**, free evenings of music and Breton dancing in the kiosk of the Thabor gardens; free concerts of classical music given by the resident **Orchestre de Bretagne** in Aug;

various activities at the open-air farm museum on the outskirts of the town; and, above all, **Les Tombées de la Nuit** in July, the capital's summer nightfall festival. Its aim is to show the public what present-day Brittany is like through contemporary artistic creation, including new plays and contemporary dance shows, and at the same time to focus on the main architectural heritage in order to underline the link between past and present.

SHOPPING

Elegant boutiques line the *pl. du Parlement* and adjacent streets. Quite a few sell exclusive clothes but **Ti Breiz**, *tel: 99 79 17 83*, has a choice of Breton specialities: clothing, HB Henriot pottery (see Quimper chapter, p. 235), table linen, embroidery, jewellery and handicraft.

In total contrast, the lively **centres commerciaux**, shopping precincts usually on several storeys, containing more than a 100 boutiques, offer a more relaxed approach to shopping in a pedestrianised area. In **Colombia**, *pl. du Colombier; tel: 99 35 17 77*, you can buy furniture, sport equipment, clothes, food, cameras etc or simply window-shop – and, if you're feeling homesick, even call into McDonald's for a quick meal.

SIGHTSEEING

Rennes is at the heart of eastern Brittany, usually referred to as *Haute Bretagne*, where French influence was more deeply felt than in the rest of Brittany, yet it has managed to remain typically Breton and the elegance of its historic centre has no equal. Moreover it is surrounded by several towns of great interest such as Dinan, Combourg, Fougères and Vitré, by impressive châteaux like Caradeuc and Montmuran and it is reasonably close to the legendary Paimpont Forest. These provide excellent reasons for staying in Rennes for a few days.

Rennes itself has a lot to offer the curious visitor since its architecture clearly reflects the colourful episodes of its development from medieval times until today. Its moderate size lends itself to strolling or cycling along 110 km of suitably adapted roads; parking areas reserved for cycles are also available and it is possible to hire a bike on *pl. de la République*, in front of the Palais du Commerce (*tel: 99 79 63 72*, daily 0900–1900, Fr.15 for up to 4 hours and Fr.25 for the day).

Guided Tours

The comprehensive programme of guided visits organised by the Tourist Office makes it possible to discover the various facets of Rennes, in turn picturesque and stately. During July and Aug there is a daily guided tour of the town beginning at 1030 (Thur by night at 2100) in front of the **Cathedral**.

In addition there are tours of the town based on different themes, starting daily at 1500 from various places: for instance on Tues the theme is the medieval district and timber-framed architecture and the tour starts in front of the Cathedral; on Wed the theme is parliament and the law, therefore the tour starts in front of the **Parlement de Bretagne** (Breton Parliament); on Fri the theme chosen is royal squares and 18th-century architecture and the tour starts in front of the **Hôtel de Ville** (Town Hall). Tours cost Fr.35 (Fr.15 children, free to under 7s).

Some tours, organised in the form of a game (Tues and Thur 1500 in front of the Cathedral), are specially designed for children aged 6–12; the aim is to rouse young children's interest in beautiful buildings and to enable their parents to enjoy their own guided tour in peace.

Old Rennes

Until the end of the 17th century, the city consisted of timber-framed buildings, some of them decorated with beautiful carvings. Part of this essentially medieval town survived the terrible fire which devastated Rennes in 1720. Today, the narrow streets surrounding the Cathedral are still lined with 15th- and 16th-century corbelled houses which contrast with the stone-built mansions dating from the 18th century.

Walk along *r. St-Guillaume* behind the Cathedral: no. 3 is one of the most attractive medieval houses in Old Rennes. Carry on along *r. de la Psalette* which leads into *r. du Chapitre* where the elegant mansion at no. 6 is now an administrative building. Follow *r. St-Yves* and *r. des Dames* to the **Cathédrale St-Pierre**, rebuilt in the mid-19th century after part of it collapsed: inside, notice the splendid Flemish retable (the ornate screen-like structure behind the altar) in a chapel on the south side. The **Porte Mordelaise** nearby is all that remains of the 15th-century town walls.

During the Middle Ages, tournaments took place on *pl. des Lices*, north of the Cathedral, later surrounded by private mansions when Rennes became the seat of the Breton Parliament. Carry on further north through *pl. St-Michel* to *pl. Ste-Anne*, a lovely shaded square, lined with many picturesque timber-framed houses now mostly turned into *crêperies* and restaurants. Walk back towards *pl. de la Mairie* along the lively *r. du Pont à Foulons* and *r. du Champ-Jacquet*.

Palaces

The 'new' town built after the 1720 fire was centred around two monumental squares. The rectangular *pl. de la Mairie* has, at one end, the magnificent **Hôtel de**

Ville built by Gabriel between 1734 and 1743 (open weekdays 0900–1700). The more austere *pl. du Parlement de Bretagne* is dominated by the sober façade of the **Palais du Parlement** (now the **Palais de Justice** or Law Courts), the work of Salomon de Brosse who built the Palais du Luxembourg in Paris (see p. 232). This superb example of 17th-century classical architecture was spared by the great fire of 1720 only to be severely damaged recently by an unexplained fire which swept through the roof (closed indefinitely for major restoration work). Nearby, another palace, formerly belonging to St-George's Benedictine Abbey, has been turned into an administrative building.

The tradition of building palaces continued during the 19th century. The **Palais Universitaire,** which now houses two museums, was built on the south bank at the beginning of the 19th century, followed at the end of the century by the impressive and richly decorated **Palais du Commerce et des Communications,** facing the Hôtel de Ville across the Vilaine River. The *pl. de la Mairie* was completed with the building of the **Théâtre** in 1832.

Museums

The **Musée des Beaux-Arts** (Fine Arts Museum) and the **Musée de Bretagne** (Breton Museum) are both housed in the former university palace (see above).

The rich collections of paintings, drawings and sculpture of the **Musée des Beaux-Arts,** *20 quai E. Zola; tel: 99 28 55 85* cover the 14th–20th centuries, all the great masters being represented: Veronese, Rubens, Chardin, Sisley, Gauguin and Picasso to name but a few. *Le Nouveau Né* by Georges de la Tour, with its unique contrast of light and darkness, is one of the masterpieces owned by the museum. The archaeological collections illustrate various aspects of Egyptian and Greco-Roman civilisations. Open daily except Tues and holidays 1000–1200 and 1400–1800; Fr.15 (Fr.7.5).

The ambitious **Musée de Bretagne,** *tel: 99 28 55 84* retraces the evolution of Brittany from prehistoric times until today. In addition, the museum organises regular temporary exhibitions, lectures, debates and concerts. Open daily except Tues and holidays 1000–1200, 1400–1800; Fr.15 Fr.7.5.

Gardens

Covering an area of 10 hectares, the **Jardin du Thabor** – the former gardens of **St-Mélaine Benedictine Abbey** – were landscaped during the 19th century and include French-style gardens (laid out according to a strict symmetrical design), an English-style park, a rose garden and a small waterfall.

The **Ecomusée du Pays de Rennes,** *Ferme de la Bintinais, rte de Châtillon-sur-Seiche; tel: 99 51 38 15,* is situated 8 km south of the town. Take *r. du Mar. Joffre* from the town centre and then follow the signs. On a 15-hectare estate, it is a fascinating open-air museum which illustrates daily life on a Breton farm in the past and depicts traditional activities and ancient customs. Open daily except Tues and public holidays 0900–1200 and 1400–1800, closed Sat and Sun morning, admission Fr.22.

Nearby, the **Parc Ornithologique de Bretagne,** *53 blvd Pasteur, 35170 Bruz; tel: 99 52 68 57,* houses more than 1000 exotic birds in a beautiful environment where flowers and birds offer a wonderful display of colours (open Mar–mid-Nov 1000–1200 and 1400–1900; otherwise weekend afternoons).

RENNES–LE MANS

DIRECT ROUTE: 153 KM

This route passes through three départements, Ile-et-Vilaine, Mayenne and Sarthe, much of it through largely rolling countryside. Several large fortresses are included among the sights, and there is a popular family excursion towards the end.

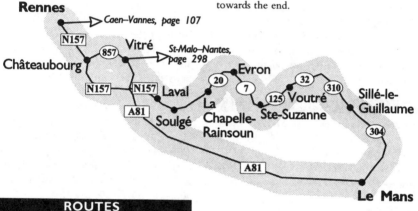

ROUTES

DIRECT ROUTE

Leave Rennes via the *quai de Richemont*, joining the D157 and then N157 dual carriageway. At **La Gravelle**, south-east of **Vitré**, the high-speed route becomes the A81 motorway, which continues to the outskirts of **Le Mans**, where it joins the A11 motorway.

Turn right at junction 8 to enter **Le Mans** via the N157 from the west or left to junction 7 to enter via the N138 from the north. Total distance from centre to centre is 153 km. Driving time is about 1 hr 30 mins.

SCENIC ROUTE

Take the same route out of Rennes, but about 12 km after joining the

N157 take the **Chateaubourg** exit onto the D857 to **Vitré**. Continue on the D857 until the major intersection at **La Gravelle**, then carry on along the N157 into **Laval**. Beyond Laval stay on the N157 as far as **Soulgé-sur-Ouette**, then turn left onto the D20, passing through **La Chapelle-Rainsoun**, which has a notable church, en route to **Evron**. From Evron, take the D7 to **Ste-Suzanne**, leaving on the D125. Just beyond **Voutré**, turn right on the D310 to **Sillé-le-Guillaume**. The D304 completes the route to Le Mans.

Distance is 165 km and driving time approximately 2 hrs 30 mins.

259

CHÂTEAUBOURG

Though scarcely worth a second glance, Châteaubourg does have an excellent three-star hotel, the **Hôtel Ar Milin**, *30 r. de Paris; tel: 99 00 30 91*. A former mill on the River Vilaine, it occupies a picturesque setting on the town's eastern edge and has rooms ranging in price from moderate to expensive. Prices in the restaurant, which specialises in fish and fowl, fall into similar categories. Another three-star hotel worth investigating is the modern **Hôtel Pen'Roc**, *La Peinière-en-St-Didier; tel: 99 00 33 02*, complete with swimming pool, sauna and fitness room, a short distance east of Châteaubourg, just off the D857. Moderate to expensive.

VITRÉ

Tourist Office: *promenade St-Yves, 35500 Vitré; tel: 99 75 04 46*. Open daily 1000–1900 July and Aug.

Vitré also features on the St-Malo to Nantes route, pp. 298–301.

ACCOMMODATION AND FOOD

This a good value place to stay and even the most expensive hotel falls into the moderate category. This is the **Minotel**, *47 r. Poterie; tel: 99 75 11 11*, a modern, two-star hotel in the heart of the pedestrian area. It has no restaurant, but there is a good *crêperie* opposite. The **Hôtel du Château**, *5 r. Rallon; tel: 99 74 58 59*, also two-star, is in a quiet street beneath the ramparts of the castle. Exceptional value and with a traditional French feel to it is the one-star **Hôtel Le Chêne Vert**, *2. pl. de Gén. de Gaulle; tel: 99 75 00 58*. The restaurant is also good value.

The two-star municipal **campsite**, **Camping St-Etienne**, *rte d'Argentré du Plessis; tel: 99 75 25 28*, is close to the racecourse on the southern edge of town.

There is a choice of traditional restaurants and *crêperies* along *r. Notre-Dame* and *r. d'En Bas*.

SIGHTSEEING

There is a good view of **Vitré** on the approach from Rennes. One of the best-preserved medieval towns in Brittany, its position on a spur above the River Vilaine is dominated by its **château**, *pl. du Château; tel: 99 75 04 54*, open daily 1000–1230 and 1400–1815 (July–Sept); Wed–Fri 1000–1200 and 1400–1730, Sat–Mon 1400–1730 (Oct–Mar); Wed–Mon 1000–1200 and 1400–1730 (Apr–une), admission Fr.26 adults (Fr.16 children). Inside the château, which dates from the 13th, 14th and 15th centuries and has fairy-tale witches' hat towers, there are two **museums**, one with relics of the old town, the other on the natural history of the area. The chapel in the **Tour de l'Oratoire** has a triptych decorated with 32 Limoges enamel plates, while the **Tour de Montafilant** gives good views over the town.

Below the castle, the **Musée St-Nicolas**, *r. du Rachapt; tel: 99 75 04 54*, open daily 1000–1230 and 1400–1815 (July–Sept); Wed–Fri 1000–1200 and 1400–1730, Sat–Mon 1400–1730 (Oct–Mar); Wed–Mon 1000–1200 and 1400–1730 (Apr–June), admission Fr.26 (Fr.16), housed in a 15th-century chapel, has displays of religious art. The town itself has some delightful old cobbled streets lined with granite and half-timbered houses with picturesque pointed gables, once the homes of rich cloth merchants. Particularly worth exploring are *r. de la Baudrairie*, *r. d'En Bas* and *r. Poterie*, which has attractive arcaded shops. The best sections of the ramparts lie to the north and east of the old town, along the *promenade du Val*.

On the way out of town via the *blvd de*

Châteaubriant, is an unusual museum, the **Musée de l'Abeille Vivante** (Museum of the Living Bee), *18 r. de la Briqueterie; tel: 99 75 09 01,* open Mon 1400–1800, Tues–Sat 0800–1800 (Mar–Oct), admission Fr.15 (Fr.10). Here, visitors can find out about beekeeping, watch the activities of bee colonies from behind the safety of glass panels, and taste products of the beehive in the shop.

About 6 km south of Vitré, via the D88, stands the 15th-century **Château des Rochers-Sévigné;** *tel: 99 75 04 54,* open daily 1000–1230, 1400–1815 (July–Sept); Wed–Fri 1000–1200, 1400–1730, Sat–Mon 1400–1730 (Oct–Mar); Wed–Mon 1000–1200, 1400–1730 (Apr–June), admission Fr.26 (Fr.16), the Breton residence of Madame de Sévigné, whose writings provided vivid pictures of the region in the 17th-century. The château contains some of her personal possessions.

Note: just **one ticket** permits entry to the Château des Rochers-Sévigné, the Château de Vitré and the Musée St-Nicolas.

LAVAL

Tourist Office: *allée du Vieux St-Louis, 53000 Laval; tel: 43 49 46 46.*

ACCOMMODATION

Most of Laval's hotels are located east of the River Mayenne, particularly along *av. Robert Buron,* which leads to the railway station. The top hotel is the three-star **Hôtel Les Blés d'Or,** *83 r. Victor Boissel; tel: 43 53 14 10,* but other useful options are the two-star **Grand Hôtel de Paris,** *r. de la Paix; tel: 43 53 76 20,* which has many more rooms but no restaurant (there is one next door), the **Hôtel St-Pierre,** *95 av. Robert Buron; tel: 43 53 06 10,* which has a two-star restaurant to match the accommodation, and the **Hôtel**

L'Imperial, *61 av. Robert Buron; tel: 43 53 55 02,* also two stars but no restaurant.

One of the few hotels west of the Mayenne, the **Hôtel La Bonne Auberge,** *170 r. de Bretagne; tel: 43 69 07 81,* has one of the best restaurants of any hotel in the town.

A two-star **campsite, Camping du Potier,** *chemin St-Pierre Cumont; tel: 43 53 68 86,* is located next to the river about 10 minutes' drive south of the town centre. Open Apr–Sept.

SIGHTSEEING

The capital of Mayenne, Laval is a pretty town on the River Mayenne. Its **Vieux Château** (Old Castle), *pl. de la Trémoille; tel: 43 53 39 89,* which looks down on the river, dates mainly from the 13th and 15th centuries and contains the **Musée d'Art Naïf** (Museum of Naive Art), open Tues–Sun 1000–1200 and 1400–1600, admission Fr.16 (Fr.10). As well as displaying naive art from various countries around the world, the museum contains a reconstruction of the studio of Henri Rousseau, who lived in Laval and was considered the father of *Art Naïf.* The museum also contains two of his works. A short walk from the castle, the **Jardin de la Perrine** (La Perrine Gardens), *r. du Douanier Rousseau,* also has fine views on the river. Within the gardens stands the neo-Greek **Musée des Sciences;** *tel: 43 56 91 17,* open Tues–Sat 1000–1200 and 1400–1800, Sun 1400–1800, admission Fr.15 adults, Fr.10 children, containing archaeological finds and a good example of a 19th-century astronomical clock. Also in the gardens is a replica of the **Fire-Crest,** the cutter in which Alain Gerbault, another inhabitant of Laval, sailed singlehanded round the world between 1923 and 1929.

An unusual sight on the river below the

gardens is the **Bateau-Lavoir St-Julien** (St-Julian Washing Stage), *quai Paul Boudet*, open Tues–Sun 1400–1800 (July–Aug), one of several public wash-houses that once lined the quay. Just upstream is the **Pont Vieux**, a 13th-century bridge which leads to the narrow streets of the old town. Among the churches worth visiting are the **Cathédrale St-Trinité** (St Trinity Cathedral), *r. de Curés*, which has some 17th-century Aubusson tapestries and a 16th-century triptych, the **Basilique de Notre-Dame d'Avesnières** (Basilica of Our Lady of Avesnières), *quai d'Avesnières*, an attractive mixture of Romanesque and Gothic-Renaissance, and the **Église Notre-Dame des Cordeliers**, *r. de Bretagne*, and **Église St-Vénérand**, *r. du Pont de Mayenne*, which both have exceptional altar-pieces.

EVRON

Tourist Office: *pl. de la Basilique, 53600 Evron; tel: 43 01 63 75.*

ACCOMMODATION

The **Hôtel de la Gare**, *pl. de la Gare; tel: 43 01 60 29*, a moderately priced two-star LF opposite the railway station, has been attractively modernised, complete with double-glazed windows to reduce the sound of high-speed trains. It also has a moderately-priced restaurant. There are two fairly basic but economically priced hotels, the **Hôtel Le Pilori**, *13 pl. du Pilori; tel: 43 01 60 45*, which is ideal for the centre, and the **Hôtel La Mignon-ette**, *r. de l'Image; tel: 43 01 60 51*, which is a little further out but has a restaurant with a *menu du jour* at a price to match that of its rooms.

The municipal **campsite**, the three-star **Camping du Parc des Loisirs**, *blvd du Maréchal Juin; tel: 43 01 65 36*, is

located on the western fringes. Open all year.

SIGHTSEEING

The **Basilique Notre-Dame-de-l'Epine** (Basilica of Our Lady of the Thorn), *pl. de la Basilique*, open Tues–Fri 1000–1200 and 1500–1730, Sat 1030–1200 and 1300–1730, dominated by its 11th-century square tower, is considered one of the finest churches in the Mayenne *département*. Presently undergoing extensive restoration, it is attached to abbey buildings dating from the 18th century, but the *pièce de résistance* is the chapel on the north side. Built in the 12th century by a returning crusader, it contains several works of art, including a statue of the Notre-Dame in solid oak laminated with silver and four Aubusson tapestries.

STE-SUZANNE

Tourist Office: *pl. Ambroise-de-Lore; tel: 43 01 43 60.* Bicycles are available for hire from the office.

ACCOMMODATION

Ste-Suzanne's one hotel stands outside the village walls. The **Hôtel Beausejour**, *4 r. de la Libération; tel: 43 01 40 31*, has two stars and 14 rooms ranging in price from economic to moderate. Specialities in the restaurant include trout and duck.

Camping Les Sports; *tel: 43 01 43 60*, is a small two-star **campsite** open Mar–Oct.

SIGHTSEEING

Perched on a steep promontory, Ste-Suzanne is a delightful walled village with extensive views over the surrounding countryside to the hills of the Coëvrons. A footpath, the *promenade de la Poterne*, encircles the walls. Within, stands the 11th-century **donjon** (keep), *r. du Château;*

with, next to it, the **château**; *tel: 43 01 40 77*, open daily 1000–1900 (June–Sept); 1400–1800 (Apr–June and Sept–Oct), admission Fr.15 (Fr.6), built in the early 17th century by Guillaume Fouquet de la Varenne, France's first postmaster general. At the **Musée de l'Auditoire**, *7 Grande Rue; tel: 43 01 42 65*, open daily 1400–1900 (June–Aug); Tues–Sun 1400–1800 (Apr–June and Sept), admission Fr.15 (Fr.8), housed in the old courtroom, there are various tableaux depicting Ste-Suzanne's eventful history. One such event took place between 1083 and 1086 when William the Conqueror besieged Ste-Suzanne. He set up camp 800 m from the walls and the earthworks of the **Camp de Guillaume le Conquérant** can still be seen. Follow the signs along the D143 towards Assé-le-Béranger. About 2 km further along the same road is the 6000-year-old **Dolmen des Erves**, one of the oldest megaliths in Mayenne.

SILLÉ-LE-GUILLAUME

Tourist Office: *13 pl. du Marché, ; tel: 43 20 10 32.*

ACCOMMODATION

The **Hôtel du Pilier Vert**, *pl. du Marché; tel: 43 20 10 68*, is a comfortable one-star LF with a good, though pricey, restaurant specialising in seafood. Economical to moderate. With similarly priced rooms, the two-star **Hôtel de Bretagne**, *1 pl. de la Croix-d'Or; tel: 43 20 10 10*, has a restaurant with a more economical menu. For all-round economy try the **Hôtel de Paris**, *12 pl. de la Gare; tel: 43 20 11 38.*

There are two lakeside **campsites** in the Forêt de Sillé north of the town, the three-star **Camping Les Mollières**; *tel: 43 20 16 12*, open Apr–Aug, and the two-star **Camping de la Forêt**; *tel 43 20 11 04*, open Apr–Oct.

SIGHTSEEING

The main attraction in the town is the 15th century **château**, *pl. des Minimes*, built on ruins of another fortress sacked by the English in the Hundred Years' War.

A favourite spot outside town is the **Lac de Sillé** (follow the signs for Plage via the D203), where boating, windsurfing and swimming are possible in the forest lake. There are bars and restaurants, bikes can be hired and boat rides can be taken aboard the *Silius*, Fr.20 (Fr.10).

LE MANS

For details of the city, see p. 170.

LE MANS 24-HR RACE

One of the most famous motor races in the world, the Le Mans 24-hr race was first run in 1923. In that year drivers Lagache and Léonard won at the wheel of a Chenard-Walcker, completing over 2000 km at an average speed of 92 kph. These days, the cars cover more than 5000 km at average speeds of 220 kph or more.

In the early years the 'Bentley Boys' took the race by storm, but then other marques came to the fore, such as Alfa Romeo and Mercedes-Benz. After World War II, Ferrari and Jaguar had their turns, followed by Ford, Porsche and Renault. Among the most successful drivers have been Jacky Ickx, Henri Pescarolo, Derek Warwick and Derek Bell.

In 1955, the worst accident in motor racing history took place during the race when a Mercedes-Benz driven by Pierre Levegh collided with a slower car in front of the pits. One of the cars somersaulted into the crowd of spectators and more than 80 were killed.

ROUEN

The capital of Upper Normandy meticulously recreated its 'medieval' centre after its devastation in World War II, and even now Rouen's streets are busy with restoration projects. The heart of the city, on the Seine's right bank, offers a maze of narrow streets, pedestrianised squares, and some of the most impressive architecture in France.

TOURIST INFORMATION

Tourist Office: *25 pl. de la Cathédrale, 76000 Rouen; tel: 35 71 41 77*. Open Mon–Sat 0900–1900, Sun 0930–1230 and 1430–1800 (May–Sept); Mon–Sat 0900–1230 and 1400–1830, Sun 1000–1300 (Oct–Apr). Maps and information are available on the city and Normandy.

ARRIVING AND DEPARTING

Airport
Aéroport de Rouen-Vallée de Seine, *tel: 35 79 41 00*, 10 km south-east of the city centre on the N14 at Boos, has regular flights to London.

By Car
Access by road to Rouen is excellent, with motorway links with Paris, Le Havre and Caen (A13), Abbeville (A28) and the A15/A1501 quick-access link with the N27 to Dieppe. Other major routes entering Rouen are the N31 from Beauvais, the N14 from Paris, the N15 linking Paris with Le Havre, the N138 from Le Mans and N175 from Caen.

GETTING AROUND

Buses
The *gare routière* (bus station) is at *25 r. des Charrettes* (near the river); *tel: 35 71 23 29*. **CNA**; *tel: 35 71 81 71*, operates regular services from here to a wide number of destinations across Normandy. **TCAR**, *Centre les Deux Rivières, 15 r. de la Petite Chartreuse; tel: 35 25 52 00*, operates the local **Métrobus** network, which has 37 routes linking the suburbs with the city centre, as well as two underground/overground metro tram lines running from Boulingrin, just north of the city centre, to Georges-Braque in the southern outskirts A branch line runs south of the river from St-Sever to Hôtel de Ville-Sotteville. Tickets are valid for both the bus and metro and various options are available. A basic ticket costs Fr.7 which allows unlimited use for an hour after the ticket has first been validated (when you board). A carnet of 10 tickets costs Fr.56. The **Découverte** ticket is available for one, two or three days unlimited travel and costs Fr.20, Fr.30 and Fr.40 respectively. Tickets can be bought from bus drivers, automatic ticket dispensers (*billetteries*) at metro stations and TCAR offices at **Espace Métrobus** at the bottom of *r. Jeanne d'Arc*, the **Hôtel de Ville** in *pl. du Gén de Gaulle* and at the **Gare Rive-Droite** (railway station) at the top of *r. Jeanne d'Arc*, as well as 130 shops, mainly *tabacs* (tobacconists) and *librairies* (bookshops), around Rouen. A map and information detailing the services can be obtained from any of the addresses above or the Tourist Office.

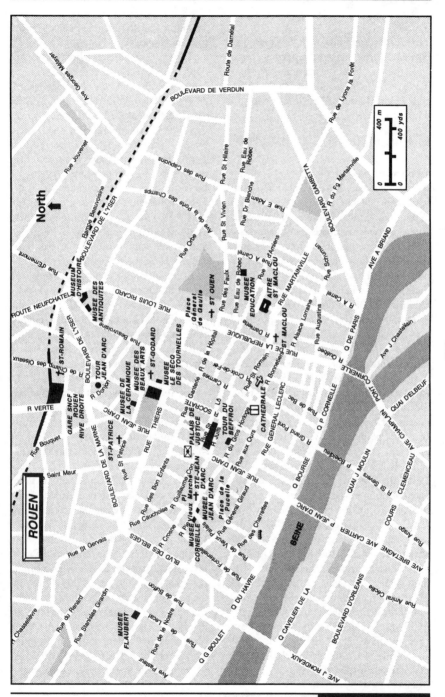

Taxis

There are numerous taxi ranks around Rouen. If you need to telephone for a taxi, there are two companies, **Radio-Taxis**, *67 r. Jean Lecanuet; tel: 35 88 50 50*, and **Taxis Blancs**, *52 r. St-Julien; tel: 35 61 20 50*.

STAYING IN ROUEN

Accommodation

Affordable hotels are easy to find around *pl. du Vieux Marché, pl. de la Cathédrale* and *r. des Juifs*. Overall there is an excellent choice of two-star hotels, both in the city and around the periphery. One-star hotels are reasonably well represented, as are non-classified ones, but of three-star hotels there are only a handful in the centre, with a similar number in the outskirts.

Hotel chains in Rouen include *BW, Ca, CI, Ct, F1, Ib, IH, Mc, Nv, RS*.

One of the best is the modern **Colin's Hotel**, with entrances at *33 r. du Vieux Palais* and *15 r. de la Pie; tel: 35 71 00 88*. Its 48 rooms are expensively decorated and this is reflected in its high prices. There is no restaurant, but the hotel stands at the corner of *pl. du Vieux Marché* so there are plenty to choose from within just a few yards. It has its own garage parking. The **Hôtel de Dieppe**, right opposite the railway station in *pl. Bernard Tissot; tel: 35 71 96 00*, (moderate-expensive), has its own restaurant but no garage. Very close to the cathedral is the similarly priced **Hôtel Mercure**, *7 r. Croix-de-Fer; tel: 35 52 69 52*, which provides modern comforts though no restaurant. A larger **Hôtel Mercure** overlooking the Seine to the east of the centre on *av. Aristide Briand; tel: 35 52 42 32*, does offer that option. Both Mercures have garage parking. The **Hôtel Le Dandy**, *93 r. Cauchoise; tel: 35 07 32 00*, is much smaller than the others with 18 rooms and no restaurant, but it is more moderately priced.

Two two-star hotels close to but on opposite sides of the **cathedral** are the **Hôtel Cardinal**, *1 pl. de la Cathédrale; tel: 35 70 24 42*, and the 16th-century **Hôtel de la Cathédrale**, *12 r. St-Romain; tel: 35 71 57 95*, which are both moderately priced. Parking at the latter, however, is awful, though its leafy courtyard may prove soothing compensation. A two-star hotel that does have its own car-park is the **Hôtel Québec**, *18-24 r. de Québec; tel: 35 70 09 38*, which is just off the main road that runs along the right bank of the Seine, but is still only a short walk from the cathedral. Again, moderate prices.

In the more economic price range, the **Hôtel St-Ouen**, *43 r. des Faulx; tel: 35 71 46 44*, is pleasant enough and faces the garden behind the Église St-Ouen. Several others are located south of the Seine and a little distant from the main sights. If you want a really cheap room, try the **Hôtel Normandy**, *47 r. du Renard; tel: 35 71 13 69*, on the right bank, but some way from the main attractions.

HI: Auberge de Jeunesse youth hostel: **Centre de Séjour**, *118 blvd de l'Europe; tel: 35 72 06 45*, on the left bank.

There are four **campsites** within a reasonable distance of Rouen, all of them classified two-star. The two nearest, within about 4 km of the centre, are **Camping Municipal**, *r. Jules Ferry, Déville-Lès-Rouen; tel: 35 74 07 59*, on the N27 Dieppe road west of the centre, and **Camping de l'Aubette**, *23 r. Vert Buisson, St-Léger-du-Bourg-Denis; tel: 35 08 47 69*, on the eastern outskirts. A little further out are **Camping de la Forêt de Roumare**; *tel: 35 33 80 75*, in the forest of the same name west of Rouen, and **Camping les Terrasses**, *2 r. de Rouen, Igoville; tel: 35 23 08 15*, near the Seine, south of the city.

Eating and Drinking

You should have no difficulty at all finding a place to eat out in Rouen – the range of food is so wide, from cheap fast food to gourmet meals. If you want to wander around a little before making your choice, head for the *pl. du Vieux-Marché*, where you'll find plenty of restaurants on offer, all with set-price menus. Rouen's speciality is duck.

In addition to a wide choice of traditional French restaurants, there are several offering Chinese, Vietnamese, Caribbean, Italian and Tex-Mex menus.

Self-service and fast food restaurants near the centre include **Flunch**, *60 r. des Carmes; tel: 35 71 81 81*, **Quick**, *84 r. du Gros-Horloge; tel: 35 88 51 20*. and **Jumbo**, *11 r. Guillaume le Conquérant; tel: 35 70 35 88*. A couple of *crêperies* worth considering, are **La Tarte Tatin**, *99 r. de la Vicomté; tel: 35 89 35 73*, and **La Tour de Beurre**, *20 quai Pierre Corneille; tel: 35 71 95 17*, while two good pizzerias are **Pizza Pai**, *60 r. des Carmes; tel: 35 07 73 94*, and the **Taormina**, *18 r. de Vieux-Palais; tel: 35 70 94 06*.

Around *pl. du Vieux-Marché*, some of the options include **Les Maraîchers**, *(no. 37); tel: 35 71 57 73*, which has a terrace outside and turn-of-the-century Parisian decor inside (moderate), and **La Couronne**, *(no. 31); tel: 35 71 40 90*, the oldest restaurant in Rouen, which though quite pricey is well worth it. More middle-of-the-road pricewise are **Le Maupassant**, *(no. 39); tel: 35 07 56 90*; **La Mirabelle**, *(no. 3); tel: 35 71 58 21*; and **La Toque d'Or**, *(no. 11); tel: 35 71 46 29*, while a couple of cheaper options in the square are **Le Pub au Bureau**, *(no. 2); tel: 35 98 68 68*, and **La Taverne de Maître Kanter** *(no. 9); tel: 35 71 22 92*.

If you want something special try **Les Nympheas**, which is just off the *pl. du Vieux-Marché* at *7-9 r. de la Pie; tel: 35 89 26 69*, one of the most fashionable restaurants in Rouen. It is certainly one of the prettiest, and, though expensive, the food is superb. If, however, it is the *crême de la crême* you seek then it is to the **Gill**, *9 quai de la Bourse; tel: 35 71 16 14*, that you should make your way. Not just the top restaurant in Rouen, this favourite is rated the best in Normandy, but it has a price to match, menus ranging from Fr.195 to Fr.370 and *à la carte* topping out at Fr.450. Among its specialities are caviar, pan-fried langoustine and *pigeon à la rouennaise*. Naturally, it also has an excellent wine-list.

Communications

The main **post office** is at *45 r. Jeanne d'Arc; 35 08 73 73* (open Mon–Fri 0800–1900, Sat 0800–1200; public holidays 0900–1200). Facilities include poste restante, phones (phonecards are sold here) and Minitel information screens with an English language option.

Money

All the major banks are represented in Rouen, each having several branches, most with automatic cash dispensers. Almost all have branches on *r. Jeanne d'Arc*. There is also a branch of **Barclays** at *15 r. Jeanne d'Arc; tel: 35 71 70 63*. There is a **bureau de change** at *9 r. des Bonnetiers; tel: 35 88 00 65*, open Mon–Sat 1000–1900.

ENTERTAINMENT

For the latest news on happenings in Rouen, the Tourist Office is your best bet, where the free *Cette Semaine à Rouen* (This Week in Rouen) should put you in the picture. An extremely useful publication to invest in, especially if you plan to stay in Rouen for more than a couple of days, is the annual *Le P'tit Normand*, which for

Fr.49 lists all centres of entertainment in the city, along with many other useful and not so useful names, addresses and telephone numbers. This, too, can be bought at the Tourist Office, or at bookshops and newsagents.

The city has several theatres, both north and south of the river: **Théâtre des Arts-Opéra de la Normandie**, *quai de la Bourse; tel: 35 71 41 36*; puts on opera, ballet and concerts; **Théâtre des Deux-Rives**, *48 r. Louis-Ricard; tel: 35 70 22 82*, presents plays by writers like Chekhov, Beckett and Feydeau; **Théâtre de la Ville**, *16 pl. de la Verrerie, Centre St-Sever; tel: 35 62 31 31*; puts on more avant-garde productions of theatre, dance and concerts; **Théâtre Charles Dullin**, *allée des Arcades, Le Grand-Quevilly; tel: 35 68 48 91*, has plays, dance, operettas and comedy; and the **Théâtre Maxime Gorki**; *24 r. Joseph Lebas, Petit-Quevilly; tel: 35 72 67 55*, has a programme of traditional French music.

For those who prefer other forms of music, jazz is performed at the **Cave à Jazz**, *39 r. aux Ours; tel: 35 70 31 30*, while rock and blues make regular appearances at **Le Bateau Ivre**, *17 r. des Sapins; tel: 35 70 09 05*, **L'Exo 7**, *13 pl. des Chartreux, Petit-Quevilly; tel: 35 03 32 30*, and **Rock'n'Roll Circus**, *177 rte de Paris, Amfreville-la-Mivoie; tel: 35 07 40 30*. Details of concerts and temporary art exhibitions in the city can be found in hotels or at the Tourist Office, while tickets for many performances can be booked through **fnac**, *37 r. Ecuyère; tel: 35 52 72 17*, a well-stocked book and CD store.

For visitors wishing to expend energy at discotheques, both L'Exo 7 and Rock'n'Roll Circus double in this respect. One of the closest clubs to the centre is **Le Jules**, *29 blvd des Belges; tel 35 07 76 20*, while **Le Queen**, *2 r. de Malherbe; tel: 35 03 29 36*, has a largely gay clientele. If you prefer to dance the night away to more classical disco music, perhaps even the odd waltz, try the **Bagatelle**, *124 blvd du 11 Novembre, Petit-Quevilly; tel: 35 72 03 93*.

Mainstream movies are shown at the **UGC Les Clubs** cinema (four screens), *75 r. du Gén. Leclerc* (near the cathedral), *tel: 35 71 37 76* or *35 07 15 15* (answerphone), the **Gaumont** (seven screens), *28 r. de la République; tel: 35 98 40 22* or *36 68 75 55* (answerphone), and **Les Cinémas St-Sever** (seven screens), *Centre St-Sever; tel: 35 73 58 23 and 36 65 70 09* (answerphone). The **Melville**, *12 r. St-Etienne-des-Tonneliers; tel: 35 98 79 79* (answerphone), sometimes shows foreign films in their original language. There is a bowling alley at **Grand Bowling International**, *130 r. de Constantine; tel: 35 71 24 47*, open daily 1430–0200, which is located some way west of the city centre.

As far as spectator sports are concerned, Rouen hosts two important powerboat races on the Seine: a 24-hr event in late Apr or early May and a grand prix in late Sept or early Oct.

Events

The **Fêtes Jeanne d'Arc** takes place in late May, while an organ festival is held at Église St-Maclou through July and Aug.

SHOPPING

The shopping area in the city centre takes in *r. du Gros-Horloge, r. Jeanne d'Arc* and some of the pedestrian streets near the cathedral. An excellent covered market in the *pl. du Vieux Marché* sells fruit, meat and vegetables. South of the river, there is a modern multi-storey shopping complex at **St-Sever** which has budget stores. An antique and bric-à-brac market is held in the *pl. des Emmurées* nearby. Rouen's speciality is decorated *faïence* (ceramics) and there are a number of shops selling it.

SIGHTSEEING

Rouen has the greatest concentration of medieval buildings of any town in Normandy and no matter where you wander in the centre you can hardly fail to catch at least a glimpse of old Rouen. The *pl. du Vieux-Marché* is a good place to see a number of half-timbered buildings all in one place, but there are many more around the **cathedral** and the **churches of St-Ouen** and **St-Maclou**. The *r. Eau de Robec*, with its narrow river running along it is especially interesting. Guided tours of Rouen's historic areas leave the Tourist Office Sat, Sun and bank holidays (Apr–June) and daily in July and Aug (Fr. 30). The **Tourist Office** itself is worth closer study, particularly outside, since it is housed in an elegant Renaissance building dating from 1510 which served as the **Bureau des Finances** (House of the Exchequer). For a striking overall panorama of the city, go to **Côte Ste-Catherine** (St Catherine's Hill) in the suburb of Bonsecours, and you'll have some idea why Rouen became known as the 'city of a hundred spires'. At **Bonsecours**, the Neo-Gothic **Basilica** at Mount Thuringe, which dates from the mid 1800s, is a popular place of pilgrimage and another place for good views along the Seine.

At the heart of the town centre is the **Cathédrale de Notre-Dame**, *pl. de la Cathédrale* (open Mon–Sat 0800–1900, Sun and public holidays 0800–1800), whose west façade was portrayed by Monet in a series of more than 30 paintings (most of them exhibited in the Musée d'Orsay in Paris) representing the varying light. Dating mainly from the early 13th century, the cathedral suffered badly during World War II, and its lacy exterior still has a battered look. Several effigies, including Richard the Lionheart's (whose heart is entombed here), are stored in the ambulatory (40-min tours of the ambulatory, crypt and Chapelle de la Vierge are conducted between 1000 and 1700). The building is illuminated at night until 0100.

The *r. St-Romain* runs alongside the cathedral and the gutted bishop's palace, where the Church condemned **Joan of Arc** as a witch in 1431, and where it changed its mind 25 years later. The road, which has some beautiful old half-timbered houses dating back to the 15th century, leads to the **Église St-Maclou**, *pl. Barthélemy*, open daily 1000–1200 and 1400–1730, a superb church built in Flamboyant Gothic style between 1437 and 1521. An alleyway leads to its half-timbered cloisters, the **Aître St-Maclou**, *186 r. Martainville*, open daily 0800–2000, admission free, which was used as a burial ground for 16th-century plague victims and is still surrounded by grotesque wooden carvings of skulls and other morbid subjects, including a dance of death. Since the 18th century the cloister and its galleries have been enclosed and the building now serves as Rouen's **École des Beaux-Arts** (Fine Arts School).

From St-Maclou, the *r. Damiette*, lined with half-timbered houses and antique shops runs to the twin-towered **Abbatiale St-Ouen**, *pl. du Gén. de Gaulle,* open Wed–Mon 1000–1230 and 1400–1800 (Apr–Oct); Wed, Sat and Sun 1000–1230 and 1400–1630 (Nov–Mar), which is nearly as imposing as the cathedral. Built between the 14th and 16th centuries in a unity of Gothic style, the church, which has one of the largest organs in France and some fine 14th-century stained glass windows, is set in small gardens where Rouen's boules players gather. In the *pl. du Vieux Marché*, which isn't exactly what

269

it looks, since some of the medieval buildings were brought from other parts of the city during the restoration work after the war, the **Église Ste-Jeanne d'Arc**, open daily (except Fri and Sun morning) 1000–1230 and 1400–1800, is a memorial to Joan of Arc, who was burned at the stake in the square in 1431. A 65ft high cross, the **Croix de la Réhabilitation** (Cross of the Rehabilitation) marks the actual spot nearby. Designed by Louis Arretche and completed in 1979, the controversial church has a pointed, twisted roof said to represent flames leaping heavenwards. The interior is far more beautiful, with a polished timber ceiling like an upturned boat and a huge tapestry of a stained glass window incorporating 16th-century glass from the church of St-Vincent, destroyed in 1944. In front of the church can be seen the remains of the Église St-Sauveur, which was destroyed during the Revolution.

Other churches in Rouen include the 15th-century **Église St-Godard**, *24 r. Charles Lenepveu*, the Gothic **Église St-Patrice**, *22 r. St-Patrice*, and the 17th-century former Carmelite chapel **Église St-Romain**, *17 r. du Champ des Oiseaux*, all of which have splendid stained glass windows dating from the 15th, 16th and 17th centuries.

Just off *pl. du Vieux-Marché* is one of Rouen's most famous, and oldest, mansions, the **Hôtel de Bourgtheroulde**, *15 pl. de la Pucelle*, a mix of Gothic and Renaissance architecture. The courtyard is decorated with a bas-relief representing the Field of the Cloth of Gold, the 16th-century summit meeting between François I and Henry VIII. A short walk east of *pl. du Vieux-Marché* is the marvellous 15th-and early 16th-century Renaissance **Palais de Justice** (Law Courts), *r. aux Juifs*, where the Normandy parliament used to

meet. Only its ornate façade was left standing at the end of World War ll, but a remarkable restoration has returned it to its original grandeur, with the main building and its two wings enclosing a courtyard. During excavations in the courtyard, the 11th-century **Monument Juif** (Jewish Monument) was discovered.

To the south is the *r. du Gros-Horloge*, the commercial centre of Rouen in the Middle Ages and still a lively street today, where the **Gros-Horloge**, a gatehouse with its 14th-century one-handed clock spans the street; carvings of Christ and his flock decorate the underside of the arch. The belfry next to it, the **Tour du Beffroi**, is where the clock was originally displayed (open Wed–Mon 1000–1300 and 1400–1800 , admission Fr.10 (Fr.6 children). There are excellent views from the top. The **Tour Jeanne d'Arc** (Joan of Arc Tower), *r. du Donjon; tel: 35 98 16 21*, open Wed–Mon 1000–1200 and 1400–1700, admission Fr.6, is all that remains of the château built by Philippe Auguste in the early 13th century and in which Joan of Arc was imprisoned and tortured. On display is a copy of a manuscript relating to her trial and other information about her life.

Museums

Rouen has an impressive selection of museums. The main one is the **Musée des Beaux-Arts** (Museum of Fine Arts), *sq. Verdrel; tel: 35 71 28 40*, open Wed–Mon 1000–1800, admission Fr.20 (Fr.13), which has an art collection ranging from the 15th to the 20th centuries and includes Impressionist works by Monet and Renoir. Although the museum is undergoing extensive renovations which will take several years to complete, all its major works will remain on display. A 'passport' can be bought here giving reduced admission to the fine arts museums in Dieppe, Fécamp, Le Havre and Honfleur.

Next door, housed in the 15th century **Église St-Laurent**, is the quirky **Musée de Ferronnerie le Secq des Tournelles** (Wrought-Ironwork Museum), *r. Jacques Villon; tel: 35 88 42 92*, (open Wed–Mon 1000–1200 and 1400–1800, Wed 1400–1800, admission Fr.13 (children free), the only museum of its kind in France. Its ironwork displays of some 15,000 items ranging from the 3rd to the 19th centuries include a Louis XV bannister, shop signs like manic doodles, and orthopaedic corsets. Housed in the elegant **Hôtel d'Hocqueville** mansion, which dates from 1657, the **Musée de la Céramique** (Ceramics Museum), *1 r. Faucon; tel: 35 07 31 74*, open Wed–Mon 1000–1300 and 1400–1800, admission Fr.13 (Fr.9), traces the history of Rouen's *faïence* industry through the 16th–19th centuries and in addition has ceramic exhibits from other towns in France, as well as from elsewhere in Europe.

Further north, regional archaeological discoveries, tapestries, Roman mosaics, including the 4th-century Lillebonne mosaic (one of the largest discovered in France) and collections from more ancient cultures are exhibited at the **Musée des Antiquités**, *198 r. Beauvoisine; tel: 35 71 78 78*, open Mon and Wed–Sat 1000–1230 and 1330–1730, Sun 1400–1800, admission Fr.10. Nearby is the **Muséum d'Histoire Naturelle, Ethnographie et Préhistoire** (Museum of Natural History, Ethnography and Prehistory); *tel: 35 71 41 50*, open Tues–Sat 0945–1200 and 1345–1730, Sun 1400–1900, admission Fr.13 (Fr.9), has scenes of wild animals of Normandy in their natural habitat and botanical collections.

Not surprisingly, given the city's history, there is a **Musée Jeanne d'Arc** (Joan of Arc Museum), *33 pl. du Vieux-Marché; tel: 35 88 02 70*, open daily 0930–1830 (May–Sept), Tues–Sun 1000–1200 and 1400–1800 (Sept–Apr), admission Fr.22 adults, Fr.11 children. Among its displays are tableaux of wax models depicting various episodes of her life, a model of the castle in which she was confined and a reconstruction showing the *pl. du Vieux-Marché* as it was in 1431.

In spite of it being so far from the sea, Rouen (which is the main port for Paris) is the fifth busiest port in France, indeed, the principal European port for the export of cereals, and the **Musée Maritime Fluvial et Portuaire**, *Hangar Portuaire, 13 blvd Emile Duchemin; tel: 32 10 15 51*, open Mon–Fri 0830–1730, Sat 1430–1800, admission free, tells the story of maritime life in Rouen and on the Seine. A Seine barge, the *Pompon Rouge*, can also be visited. A tour of the port is possible aboard the motorboat, the *Cavelier-de-la-Salle*. Bookings can be made through the Tourist Office.

Gustave Flaubert's father was a surgeon in the 18th-century **Hôtel Dieu** (now being restored), where the writer was born in 1821. This is now the **Musée Flaubert et d'Histoire de la Médecine**, *51 r. de Lecat; tel: 35 15 59 95* (open Tues–Sat 1000-1200 and 1400–1800; ring doorbell for free admittance), which contain mementos of his life, including a stuffed parrot, and 19th-century hospital life. The **Musée Corneille**, *4 r. de la Pie; tel 35 71 63 92*, open Thur–Mon 1000–1200 and 1400–1800, Wed 1400–1800, admission Fr.5, the birthplace and home for 56 years of Pierre Corneille, the celebrated writer of tragic plays (*Le Cid* was among his works), contains some 17th-century furniture plus engravings recalling his life and the Rouen of the time.

271

ROUEN–CHARTRES

The two routes here reflect two very different aspects of this part of France; the fast, direct route heading across the open vistas of the plain-like landscape, the slower, scenic route largely following the green and picturesque meanderings of the River Eure.

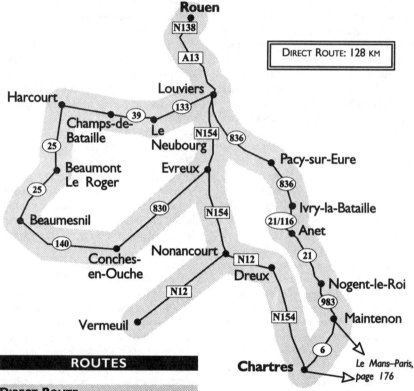

DIRECT ROUTE: 128 KM

272

ROUTES

DIRECT ROUTE

Join the A13 south of Rouen and head in the direction of Paris as far as junction 19, exiting on to the N154 to **Louviers**. From there, continue on the N154 south to **Evreux** and then **Nonancourt**, where you join the N12 to **Dreux**. At Dreux rejoin the N154 to Chartres. Distance is 126 km, journey time around 1 hr 30 mins.

SCENIC ROUTE

Take the same route from Rouen to Louviers, but from there follow the D164 and then D836 along the Eure Valley via **Autheuil-Authouillet**, **Chambray**, **Cocherel** and **Pacy-sur-Eure** to **Bueil**, where, just south of the village the D836 forks right and crosses the

Eure to **Garennes-sur-Eure** and then **Ivry-la-Bataille**. Depart Ivry on D21 and immediately after crossing the Eure again, turn right onto the D116 alongside the river to **Anet**. Leave Anet on the D21 and follow it via **Rouvres, Bû, Marolles** and **Broué** to **Coulombs** and then turn right on the D983 into **Nogent-le-Roi**. Stay on the D983 south to **Maintenon** and from there follow the D6 along the Eure via **St-Prest** to the D906 on the northern outskirts of Chartres and turn left into the city centre. Driving time for the 133-km journey is around 2 hrs 15 mins.

LOUVIERS

Tourist Office: *10 r. du Mar. Foch, 27400 Louviers; tel: 32 40 04 41.*

ACCOMMODATION

The three-star **Hôtel La Haye-le-Comte**, *rte de La Haye-le-Comte; tel: 32 40 00 40*, is a 16th-century manor house in a 12-acre park, with rooms ranging from moderate to expensive. Another three-star hotel, **Hôtel Pré-St-Germain**, *7 r. St-Germain; tel: 32 40 48 48*, is modern with expensive rooms and a restaurant. More moderate are the two-star **Hôtel Hostellerie de la Poste**, *11 r. des Quatre-Moulins; tel: 32 40 01 76*, and **Hôtel de Rouen**, *11 pl. Ernest Thorel; tel: 32 40 40 02*. A three-star campsite, **Camping Le Bel Air**, *rte La Haye-Malherbe; tel: 32 40 10 77*, located 3 km from the town on the D81, is open Apr–Sept.

SIGHTSEEING

Largely industrial, Louviers, a former drapery town, stands on the Eure and its tributaries. There are a number of old houses, particularly around the *r. du Quai* and the *r. Pierre Mendès-France*. The Tourist Office is housed in a lovely timber-framed mansion. At the northern end of the *r. du Mar.*

Foch is the **Église Notre-Dame**, a 13th- and 16th-century church noted for its porch, lavish interior and works of art. Just across the Eure from the church are the remains of the 17th-century Franciscan **Couvent des Pénitents**, *r. des Pénitents*, the only monastery in Europe to be built on a bridge. An unusual museum in the town is the **Musée des Décors de Théâtre, d'Opéra, et de Cinéma** (Museum of Theatre, Opera and Film Sets), *pl. Ernest Thorel; tel: 32 40 22 80*, open daily 1000–1200, 1400–1800 (July–Sept); Wed–Mon 1000–1200, 1400–1800 (Oct–June), with 150 backdrops painted by Georges Wakhévitch between 1930 and 1984.

SIDE TRACK FROM LOUVIERS

Leave Louviers on the D133, which goes directly to **Le Neubourg**, an important market town with an impressive church, the 16th-century **Église St-Paul**, and the ruined walls of an old castle. The town has the two-star **Hôtel au Grand St-Martin**, *68 r. de la République; tel: 32 35 04 80*, (economic to moderate), the two-star **Hôtel de Soleil d'Or**, *29 pl. du Château; tel: 32 35 00 52* (moderate), and the economic one-star **Hôtel de la Gare**, *pl. de Mar. Leclerc; tel: 32 35 05 61*.

The town is a useful base for visiting several châteaux in the area. About 5 km north-west by way of the D39 is the recently restored **Champ de Bataille**; *tel: 32 34 84 34*, open Tues–Sun 1000–1200, 1400–1830 (Apr–Oct), admission Fr.30, one of the most sumptuously decorated and furnished châteaux in Normandy, which dates from around 1655. A little farther west, via Ste-Opportune-du-Bosc, are the 12th- and 13th-century towers of

273

the **Château d'Harcourt**; *tel: 32 45 07 11*, grounds open daily 1000–1900 (July–Aug); Wed–Mon 1000–1900 (Mar–June); Wed–Mon 1400–1900 (Sept–Oct) which stand in the middle of an arboretum boasting more than 400 tree species. From Harcourt, the D25 heads south through **Beaumont-le-Roger**, a charming small town on the River Risle with ruins of a 13th-century priory, to **Beaumesnil** and its elegant **château**; *tel: 32 44 40 09*, open Wed–Mon 1430–1800 (July–Aug); Fri–Mon 1430–1800 (May–June, Sept), admission Fr.35. One of the most outstanding châteaux to be built during Louis XIII's reign in the 17th century, it is mirrored in the waters of the moat. Inside, it is noted for its Louis XV furniture and a library containing a collection of 17th- and 18th-century bound books as well as further displays on the history of bookbinding.

From Beaumesnil, the D140 heads south-east to **Conches-en-Ouche**, an attractive little town which lies on a rocky promontory all but surrounded by a loop in the River Rouloir. Another useful place to stay while exploring off route, it has two hotels, the **Hôtel Le Cygne**, *36 r. du Val; tel: 32 30 20 60*, a two-star *LF* with moderately priced rooms and restaurant, and the unclassified **Hôtel Grand'Mare**, *13 av. Croix de Fer; tel: 32 30 23 30* (economical). Campers and caravanners will find **Camping La Forêt**, *pl. de Coubertin; tel: 32 30 22 49*, a two-star municipal campsite, has ample pitches.

In the **Jardin de l'Hôtel de Ville** (Town Hall Garden) stands the ruined, moat-encircled **donjon** (keep) of the 11th-century castle. From the terrace, there are good views of the Rouloir Valley. Nearby is the **Église Ste-Foy**,

a 16th-century church containing some excellent stained-glass windows of the Renaissance period. To return to the main route at Evreux, leave Conches on the D830. 🏛

ÉVREUX

Tourist Office: *1 pl. de Gaulle, 27000 Évreux; tel: 32 24 04 43*.

ACCOMMODATION

No hotel shortage in this, the capital of the Eure *département*. The centre's top hotels are the three-star **Hotel Normandy**, *37 r. Edouard Feray; tel: 32 33 14 40*, and **Hôtel de l'Orme**, *13 r. des Lombards; tel: 32 39 34 12*, both offering moderately priced rooms, though the latter is better value. Around the same price, another three-star option, the **Hôtel Mercure**, *blvd de Normandie; tel: 32 38 77 77*, is on the town's ring road. A two-star *LF* with a good restaurant is the **Hôtel de France**, *29 r. St-Thomas; tel: 32 39 09 25*, (moderate), but better value is the economically priced **Hôtel de la Biche**, *9 r. Joséphine; tel: 32 38 66 00*. The town has a two-star **Camping Municipal**, *chemin d'Harrouard; tel: 32 39 43 59*, on the banks of the River Iton. Open Apr–Oct.

SIGHTSEEING

Évreux has been destroyed many times in its history, by Vandals, Vikings, the English and French in the Middle Ages, the Germans in 1940, and Allied forces in 1944, so it is remarkable that the **Cathédrale Notre-Dame**, *r. Charles Corbeau*, has survived so well. Worth seeing are the 14th-century stained glass windows and the carved wooden screens. Also worth seeing is the **Église St-Taurin**, *pl. St-Taurin;* which is built on the burial site of St Taurin, the first bishop of Évreux. The church contains St Taurin's shrine, made of decorated gold-plated silver in the form of a miniature chapel. Next to the cathedral is the **Musée Municipal**, *6 r. Charles Corbeau; tel: 32 3152 29*, open Tues–Sat 1000–1200, 1400–1800, Sun 1400–1800 (Apr–Sept); Tues–Sat 1000–1200, 1400–1700, Sun 1400–1700 (Oct–Mar), which contains many art treasures from Gallo-Roman times as well as displays devoted to local history and paintings of the 17th and 18th centuries. An attractive way to enjoy a town centre visit is to walk the footpaths that follow the line of the old ramparts beside the River Iton, leading to a colourful floral square containing the town hall, theatre and an elegant 15th-century clock tower.

NONANCOURT

Tourist Office: *Maison Mouret, Grande-Rue, 27320 Nonancourt; tel: 32 58 01 90.*

Moderate prices prevail at the **Hôtel du Grand Cerf**, *17 r. Grande; tel: 32 58 15 27*, but for those with economy in mind the **Hôtel Au Rendez-vous des Pêcheurs**, *117 av. Victor Hugo; tel: 32 58 03 54*, is a better bet.

This old town was founded by Henry I of Beauclerc as one in a line of fortified towns defending Normandy from the French. It has managed to preserve some of its picturesque character, with several half-timbered houses around the *pl. Aristide Briand*. The **Musée de la Laiterie** (Dairy Museum), *11 r. de l'Hôtel-Dieu; tel: 37 58 22 73*, open Sat 1400–1800, Sun 1000–1800 (June–Nov), admission Fr.20, has more than 1000 items used in dairy production.

⬑ SIDE TRACK FROM NONANCOURT

VERNEUIL-SUR-AVRE

From Nonancourt, the dualled N12 leads directly to Verneuil (**Tourist Office:** *129 pl. de la Madeleine; tel: 32 32 17 17*). Top hotel in the town is the four-star **Hostellerie du Clos**, *98 r. de la Ferté-Vidame; tel: 32 32 21 81*, a 19th-century manor house with expensive rooms and a top quality restaurant. The moderately priced **Hôtel du Saumon**, *89 pl. de la Madeleine; tel: 32 32 02 36*, a two-star *LF*, has an excellent restaurant. Not such an attractive proposition, the two-star **Hôtel de la Gare**, *160 av. Victor Hugo; tel: 32 32 12 72*, is good value nevertheless and has six rooms, ranging from economical to moderate, plus a restaurant.

An attractive medieval town, Verneuil was built, like Nonancourt, in the 12th century by Henry I of Beauclerc to defend Normandy from the French, and has managed to preserve many of its old buildings and fortifications. There are several impressive churches, the most notable being the **Église Notre-Dame**, *pl. Notre-Dame*, a Romanesque church with ornate woodwork, and the **Église de la Madeleine**, *pl. de la Madeleine*, which has a magnificent tiered tower and numerous statues. ⬑

DREUX

Tourist Office: *4 r. Porte-Chartraine, 28100 Dreux; tel: 37 46 01 73.*

ACCOMMODATION

Two town centre hotels worth considering are the two-star **Hôtel Le Beffroi**, *12 pl. Métézeau; tel: 37 50 02 03*, and the much larger **Hôtel Arcade**, *8 pl. Mézirard; tel: 37 42 64 10*. The two-star **Hôtel Au Bec Fin**, *8 blvd Pasteur; tel: 37 42 04 13*, is further out, but has a restaurant. Room prices range from economical to moderate.

SIGHTSEEING

Most outstanding sight in Dreux is the **Chapelle Royale St-Louis** (St-Louis Royal Chapel), *2 sq. d'Aumale; tel: 37 46 07 06*, open daily 0900–1130, 1400–1820 (Apr–Sept); 0900–1130, 1400–1615 (Oct–Dec and Feb–Mar), guided tours only, with English text, admission Fr.29 adults, (Fr.12 children). Amid the ruins of the former château, it was completed in 1848 as a tomb for the Orléans family and contains 26 sculptured recumbent figures by famous artists of the time. In addition, there are some impressive stained-glass windows. Another building of significance in the town is the magnificent **Beffroi** (Belfry), *Grande Rue Maurice Viollette*, a 16th-century Renaissance structure partially designed by local architect Clément Métézeau. A short walk away is the **Musée Marcel Dessal**, *7 pl. du Musée; tel: 37 50 18 61*, open Mon, Wed–Fri 1400–1800, Sat–Sun 1000–1200, 1400–1800 (July–Aug); Wed 1400–1800, Sat–Sun 1000–1200, 1400–1800 (Sept–June), admission free, an art and history museum housed in a former chapel, with paintings by Monet, Vlaminck and Valtat, plus many items connected with local history. A second museum, the **Musée du Vin Flora Gallica** (Museum of Wine), *68 r. St-Thibault; tel: 37 46 01 73*, open Wed–Thur 1400–1800, Fri–Sat 1000–1200 and 1400–1800 (all year), admission Fr.15 (children free), has displays about the area's wine production prior to the last century.

PACY-SUR-EURE

Tourist Office: *pl. Dufay, 27120 Pacy-sur-Eure; tel: 32 26 18 21*.

Moderately priced hotels to choose from include the two-star **Hôtel de l'Etape**, *1 r. Isambard; tel: 32 36 22 74*, and the **Hôtel Altina**, *rte de Paris; tel: 32*

36 13 18. A slightly cheaper option is the one-star **Hôtel l'Espérance**, *39 r. Isambard; tel: 32 36 01 22*. For a taste of real luxury, the **Hôtel Château de Brécourt**; *tel: 32 52 40 50*, is 6 km northeast via the D181 and D75, expensive, with two restaurants.

A lively market town, Pacy makes a good base for exploring the Eure valley. This area has strong links with the great politician Aristide Briand, who was several times premier of France between 1909 and 1929, and his statue stands at the entrance to the town. The **Église St Aubin** in Pacy is a 13th-century Gothic church and has some excellent statues inside.

IVRY-LA-BATAILLE

Tourist Information: Syndicat d'Initiative, *Ezy-sur-Eure; tel: 37 64 77 36*.

ACCOMMODATION

The refurbished **Hôtel Au Grand St-Martin**, *9 r. d'Ezy; tel: 32 36 41 39*, is rated two-star and is moderately priced, though guests are obliged to take the evening meal. **Camping Les Îles**, *chemin du Roi; tel: 37 64 55 77*, provides four-star camping and caravanning on a large site close to the river and a lake. Open Feb–Nov. Rather smaller, **Camping du Petit Point**, *r. Docteur Bihorel; tel: 32 36 40 90*, is a two-star municipal site by the Eure. Open all year.

SIGHTSEEING

Originally built as Ivry in Norman times, the town's 'la-Bataille' suffix was added after Henri IV's victory over the Duke of Mayenne and the Catholic League in 1590. There are still a number of medieval houses, including one at *5 r. de Garennes* where Henri is said to have stayed on the eve of the battle. Other sights include the remains of the ancient fortress and the

Église St-Martin, which was founded by Diane de Poitiers in the early 16th century. North-west of the town via the D833 and D163 stands an **obelisk**, which was erected by Napoleon in 1804 to commemorate the Battle of Ivry.

ANET

Tourist Information: Syndicat d'Initiative, *8 r. Delacroix, 28260 Anet; tel: 37 41 49 09.*

ACCOMMODATION

The largest of Anet's hotels is the two-star **Hôtel La Dousseine**, *rte de Sorel; tel: 37 41 49 93*, which has 20 moderately priced rooms but no restaurant. Also moderate in price but slightly cheaper, the **Hôtel l'Auberge de la Rose**, *6 r. Charles Lechevrel; tel: 37 41 90 64*, is a one-star *LF* with a two-star restaurant where menus range from moderate to expensive. More economically priced, the unclassified **Hôtel du Château**, *9 r. Diane de Poitiers; tel: 37 41 92 50*, has just five rooms and no restaurant. The one-star **Camping Municipal**, *r. des Cordeliers; tel: 37 41 42 67*, provides pitches for 80 caravans and tents on the banks of the River Eure.

SIGHTSEEING

Upon its completion, Anet's **château** was considered the finest Renaissance château in France; *tel: 37 41 90 07*, open Mon–Sat 1430–1830, Sun 1000–1130, 1430–1830 (Aug); Mon, Wed–Sat 1430–1830, Sun 1000–1130, 1430–1830 (Apr–July, Sept–Oct); Sat 1400–1700, Sun 1000–1130, 1400–1700 (Nov–Mar), admission Fr.36 (Fr.20). Built in the middle of the 16th century for Diane de Poitiers, the favourite mistress of Henri II who held great influence over the court, it was almost lost for ever after the Revolution when more than half of it was demolished.

The restored remains include Diane's bedroom, the guardroom, the main stairway, the Salle de Faïences (where the crockery was kept), the dining room, the magnificent gateway complete with clock tower surmounted by a stag and baying hounds, and the funerary chapel of Diane de Poitiers in which she was laid to rest on her death in 1566.

NOGENT-LE-ROI

Tourist Information: Syndicat d'Initiative, *Mairie; tel: 37 51 42 88.*

SIGHTSEEING

This is another town with a history going back a thousand years. There are picturesque parts with half-timbered houses dating from the 15th and 16th centuries, particularly in the centre and on the banks of the River Roulebois. Of the same period, the Gothic **Église St-Sulpice**, open daily 0900–1800 (all year), has an interesting collection of stained-glass windows. On the edge of the town the **château park**; *tel: 37 51 42 88*, open daily 0900–2000 (July–Aug); Sat–Mon 0900–2000, Wed 1400–2000 (May–June); Sat–Mon 0900–1830, Wed 1400–1830 (Oct–Apr), admission free, has some 200 deer wandering freely.

Just south of the town, on the D104, the **Manoir de Vacheresses** (Vacheresses Manor), *Vacheresses-les-Basses; tel: 37 82 71 46*, open daily 1400–1800 (July–Aug); Sat–Sun 1400–1800 (Apr–June and Sept–Nov), admission Fr.20, dates from the late 14th century and has an unusual collection of brides' crowns from the period 1820–1920. Also on show are the works of the artist Michèle Battut, who is one of the manor house's present owners.

MAINTENON

For details, see p. 178–179.

ROUEN–PARIS

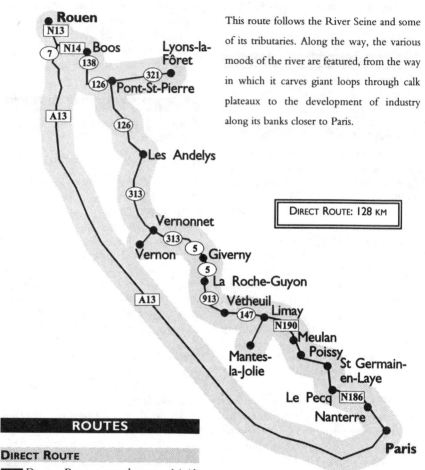

This route follows the River Seine and some of its tributaries. Along the way, the various moods of the river are featured, from the way in which it carves giant loops through calk plateaux to the development of industry along its banks closer to Paris.

DIRECT ROUTE: 128 KM

ROUTES

DIRECT ROUTE

Depart Rouen on the *av. Aristide Briand* (N15) towards Paris, and at **Le Port St-Ouen** bear right on the D7 to join the A13 at **Tourville-la-Rivière**. Head in the direction of Paris and stay on the road through **Mantes-la-Jolie** to join the capital's *blvd Périphérique* south of the **Bois de Boulogne**. Time for the 80-mile (128-km) journey is approximately 1 hr 30 mins, subject to traffic volume.

SCENIC ROUTE

Again, leave Rouen via the *av. Aristide Briand*, but at **Bonsecours** bear left on the N14 towards Paris. In about 8 km bear right at **Boos** on the D138, then D126 to **Pont St-Pierre**. On leaving Pont St-Pierre, turn right on the continuing D126 and follow this down into the Seine Valley to **Les Andelys**. From there, take the D313 through **Port-Mort** to **Vernonnet**, where you turn right and cross the Seine to enter **Vernon**. Retrace your tracks across the Seine and turn right on D5 through **Giverny** and **La Roche-Guyon**, from where D913 continues to **Vétheuil**. Continue alongside the Seine for a short distance, now on D147, and then head via **St-Martin-la-Garenne** to **Limay**. Turn right across the Seine to **Mantes-la-Jolie**. Return to Limay and turn right on the N190 to **Meulan** and then cross the Seine into **Poissy**. Stay on N190 to **St-Germain-en-Laye**. Cross the Seine to **Le Pecq** and then take N186 through **Nanterre**, re-crossing the Seine at **Neuilly-sur-Seine** and joining the *blvd. Périphérique* at the Porte Maillot. Distance is around 140 km, driving time about 2 hrs 30 mins.

PONT ST-PIERRE

There is little to detain you in Pont St-Pierre, but it acts as the starting point for a side-track through the Forêt de Lyons.

⚑ **SIDE TRACK FROM PONT ST-PIERRE**

FORÊT DE LYONS

Take the D321 towards Lyons-la-Forêt passing en route the ruins of the 12th-century Cistercian abbey, **Abbaye de Fontaine-Guérard**, *tel: 32 49 03 82*, open Tues–Sun 1400–1800 (Apr–Nov), admission Fr.10, standing on the banks of the River Andelle. **Lyons-la-Forêt** (**Tourist Office:** *r. de l'Hôtel de Ville; tel: 32 49 31 65*) is a charming village at the heart of the Forêt de Lyons with traditional half-timbered houses and a small 15th-century covered market. The village is popular with film companies; most recently

Madame Bovary was filmed here. There are two hotels overlooking the market square: the three-star **Hôtel de la Licorne**, *pl. Benserade; tel: 32 49 62 02*, a modernised 17th-century inn with a good restaurant has moderate to expensive rooms; two-star **Hôtel Le Grand Cerf**, *pl. de la Halle; tel: 32 49 60 44*, is an unusual half-timbered building with slightly more moderate rooms and restaurant. **Hôtel Domaine St-Paul**, *rte de Forges-des-Eaux, tel: 32 49 60 57*, is a two-star *LF* on the D321 just north of the village with moderately priced rooms, though the restaurant is rather expensive. Sights on the fringe of the forest include the 12th-century Cistercian **Abbaye de Mortemer**; *tel: 32 49 54 34*, open daily 0900–1200, 1400–1800 (Apr–Oct); Sun 1400–1800 (Nov–Mar), admission Fr.35 adults (Fr.25 children), the 17th-century red-brick **Château de Fleury-la-Forêt**; *tel: 32 49 63 91*, open daily 0900–1200, 1400–1800 (Apr–Oct); Sun 1400–1800 (Nov–Mar), admission Fr.35 (Fr.25), and the **Château de Vascoeuil**, *tel: 35 23 62 35*, open daily 1100–1900 (July–Aug); 1430–1830 (Apr–June, Sept–Oct), admission Fr.35 (Fr.25), which contains a museum devoted to the historian Michelet. It also holds regular art exhibitions. ⚑

LES ANDELYS

Tourist Office: *1 r. Philippe Auguste, 27720 Les Andelys; tel: 32 54 41 93.*

ACCOMMODATION

Top place to stay is the three-star **Hôtel La Chaine d'Or**, *27 r. Grande; tel: 32 54 00 31*, a delightful 18th-century hotel. Rooms are expensive, as is the restaurant which looks out on the River Seine. Just along the road, the two-star **Hôtel**

Normandie, *1 r. Grande; tel: 32 54 10 52,* offers more modest accommodation in a similar location, though at the moderate prices. Guests are obliged to eat at the restaurant. Moderate options away from the river include the **Hôtel Moderne**, *8-10 r. G. Clémenceau; tel: 32 54 10 41,* the **Hôtel de Paris**, *10 av. de la République; tel: 32 54 00 33,* and the **Hôtel au Soleil Levant**, *2 av. Gén. de Gaulle; tel: 32 54 23 55.*

A large three-star municipal campsite, **Camping L'Isle des Trois Rois**, *chemin de Halage; tel: 32 54 23 79,* is located beside the Seine at the foot of Château Gaillard.

SIGHTSEEING

Les Andelys is two towns in one, **Petit-Andely**, which is beside the Seine, and **Grand-Andely**, which occupies the valley running inland. Petit-Andely has a number of half-timbered houses, especially around *pl. St-Sauveur*. Its most impressive sight is the ruined 12th-century **Château Gaillard**, *chemin de Château-Gaillard; tel: 32 54 04 16,* open Thur–Mon 0900–1200, 1400–1800, Wed 1400–1800 (Apr–Oct), which occupies a chalk promontory overlooking a bend in the Seine. It was built in less than a year by Richard the Lionheart to protect Normandy from the French king, but was eventually captured after an eight-month siege. The views over the town and river are magnificent.

The **Musée Nicolas Poussin**, *r. Ste-Clotilde; tel: 32 54 10 50,* open Wed–Mon 1400–1800 (all year), has a collection of paintings, sculptures and Regency and Louis XV furniture, the centrepiece being Poussin's famous painting, *Coriolanus*. The **Musée Normandie-Neimen**, *r. Raymond Phelip; tel: 32 54 49 76,* is open Wed–Mon 1400–1800 (Apr–Sept); Wed, Fri–Sun 1400–1800 (Oct–Mar), admission Fr.15 (Fr.5), which relates the exploits of a fighter squadron created by Gen. de Gaulle in 1942. At the entrance is a full-size Mirage jet.

Two churches worthy of a visit include the Gothic **Église St-Sauveur**, *pl. St-Sauveur,* and **Église Notre-Dame**, *r. du Gén de Fontanges-de-Couzan,* a former collegiate church with an interesting collection of stained glass. At the **Galerie Tuffier**, *22 r. Marcel Lefèvre* and *3 r. Grande; tel: 32 54 09 57,* open Tues–Sat 0900–1215, 1400–1900, Sun 1030–1215, 1430–1830, paintings by the Rouen and Normandy schools are exhibited.

VERNON

Tourist Office: *36 r. Carnot, 27200 Vernon; tel: 32 51 39 60.*

ACCOMMODATION

The three-star **Hôtel Normandy Soleil d'Or**, *1 av. Pierre Mendès; tel: 32 51 97 97,* has moderate to expensive rooms plus a restaurant. Better value is the moderately priced **Hôtel d'Evreux**, *11 pl. d'Evreux; tel: 32 21 16 12,* with a good restaurant.

SIGHTSEEING

Situated on the south bank of the Seine, Vernon was founded in the 9th century by Rollo, the first Duke of Normandy. There are a number of medieval houses in the town, especially around *r. Potard* and *r. Carnot,* and a tower, the **Tour des Archives**, *r. Potard,* the former keep of a 12th-century castle. In recent years the town has seen a growth in high-tech industries. **Musée Alphonse Georges-Poulain**, *12 r. du Pont; tel: 32 21 28 09,* open Tues–Fri 1100–1300, 1400–1800, Sat–Sun 1400–1800 (Mar–Oct); Tues–Sun 1400–1730 (Nov–Feb), admission Fr.15 (children free), is arranged in buildings dating from the 15th–19th centuries and has collections of local history and works of art. There is a good collection of animal art but also paintings showing the development of art through to Impressionism. Artists represented include Monet and Bonnard. The **Église Notre-Dame**, r. Carnot, dates from the 12th century and has a splendid façade.

On the northern side of the Seine are the remains of a medieval bridge complete with a half-timbered house. On the shore nearby stand the remaining watch towers of the **Château des Tourelles**. Further afield, just 2 km south on the D181 to Pacy, stands the 18th-century **Château de Bizy**; tel: 32 51 00 82, open Tues–Sun 1000–1200, 1400–1800 (Apr–Oct); Sat–Sun 1400–1700 (Nov–Mar), admission Fr.20, which was owned by Louis XV and Louis-Philippe. The rooms contain tapestries and souvenirs of the First Empire while the grounds are noted for their English-style terraced gardens and water garden. The outbuildings hold a collection of horse-drawn carriages.

GIVERNY

Tourist Office: as Vernon, p. 280.

ACCOMMODATION

The two-star **Hôtel La Musardière**, 123 r. Claude Monet; tel: 32 21 03 18, is an attractive ivy-covered building but rooms are expensive, as is the restaurant. The hotel's crêperie is more reasonable.

SIGHTSEEING

Since 1980, visitors have flocked to Giverny to see the Impressionist artist **Claude Monet's house and gardens**, r. Claude Monet; tel: 32 51 28 21, open Tues–Sun 1000–1800 (Apr–Oct), admission Fr.35 (Fr.20). The pink house was the artist's home from 1883 until his death in 1926. Each room has its own colourful charm and most are decorated with his

collection of Japanese engravings. Monet's studio, next to the house contains a shop selling Monet memorabilia. There are two gardens, the **Clos Normand**, with archways of climbing plants just behind the house, and, via a tunnel under the road, the famous **Water Garden**, formed by diverting a tributary of the River Epte, with its Japanese Bridge, weeping willows, wistarias, azaleas and water lilies which were featured so frequently in his paintings. No Monet originals are exhibited at the house.

Nearby, the **Musée Américain** (American Museum), 99 r. Claude Monet; tel: 32 51 94 65, open Tues–Sun 1000–1800 (Apr–Oct), admission Fr.35 (Fr.15), contains the works of American artists who visited France seeking inspiration from the French Impressionists. Among the artists exhibited are Theodore Butler, Mary Cassatt, Frederick Friesecke, Samuel Morse, Lilla Cabot Perry, Theodore Robinson and James Whistler.

281

LA ROCHE-GUYON

Tourist Information: Syndicat d'Initiative; tel: 34 79 72 84.

This small village developed alongside the Seine at the foot of chalk cliffs skirting the Vexin plateau. Beneath the crumbling 13th-century fortress that stands on the cliffs is a 15th-century **château**; tel: 34 79 74 42, open Mon–Fri 1000–1800, Sat–Sun 1000–1900 (Apr–Oct), admission Fr.25 (Fr.15). It underwent alterations in the 18th century and during World War II became the German Headquarters of Field Marshal Rommel.

Just north of the village on the D37 towards Amenucourt is the **Arboretum de la Roche**, where different tree groupings represent each département of the Ile-de-France. Plane trees at the centre represent Paris.

MANTES-LA-JOLIE

Tourist Office: *5 pl. Jean XX111, 78200 Mantes-la-Jolie; tel: 34 77 10 30.*

ACCOMMODATION

This large town has a number of moderately priced two-star hotels to choose from, among them the **Hôtel Les Acacias**, *blvd du Mar Juin; tel: 30 33 05 67*, which is located on the busy N13 through the town, and the **Hôtel Ibis**, *allée des Martinets; tel: 30 92 65 65*, on the D928 to the south of the town. Close to the centre, the **Hôtel du Commerce**, *11 pl. de la République; tel: 34 77 00 17*, has rooms at more economical prices.

SIGHTSEEING

This busy town on the Seine reached its peak in the Middle Ages when its main trade was in wine. Its name, 'Pretty Mantes' was rendered less accurate after World War II damage.

Nevertheless, the 12th-century **Collégiale Nôtre-Dame** (Collegiate Church of Our Lady), *pl. Jean XXIII*, draws comparison with many of the country's cathedrals including the Nôtre-Dame in Paris. It was built with a gift from William the Conqueror to atone for his sins after he was fatally wounded during the sacking of the town in 1087. Within, the Navarre Chapel, a shrine to the kings of Navarre, is worth seeing.

Other medieval remains in the town include the **Tour St-Maclou**, *pl. St-Maclou*, a tower dating from the 14th and 15th centuries, and the remains of the 18th-century **Pont de Limay**, which once linked the Île aux Dames with the north bank of the Seine.

POISSY

Tourist Office: *132 r. du Gén. de Gaulle, 78300 Poissy; tel: 30 74 60 65.*

ACCOMMODATION

Close to the centre and ideal for the RER rail station which links the town with central Paris, the two-star **Hôtel Arcade**, *97 av. Maurice Berteaux; tel: 39 65 56 10*, has moderately priced rooms but no restaurant. Further out of town are the two-star **Hôtel Balladins**, *Parc d'Activités de la Grange St-Louis; tel: 39 22 00 50*, and the **Hôtel Relais Bleus**, *Parc d'Activités de la Grange St-Louis; tel: 39 11 62 25*, which both have restaurants and plenty of rooms. Prices at both are moderate though they tend to be lower at the Balladins.

SIGHTSEEING

Poissy was a royal residence until the château was demolished by Charles V in the 14th century. Later, it became the site of France's largest livestock market and today is known for its motor industry. Its **Collégiale Nôtre-Dame** (Collegiate Church of Our Lady), *r. St-Louis*, open daily 0800–1200 and 1400–1900, is largely Romanesque and dates from the 11th and 12th centuries, with side chapels added in the 15th century. There is a superb 16th-century Burial of Christ in one of the chapels. Near the church is the former **Prieuré St-Louis**, *r. de la Tournelle*, which hosted the Poissy Symposium, in which Catholics and Protestants aired their differences in 1561, prior to the Wars of Religion. The fortified entrance to the abbey now houses the **Musée du Jouet** (Toy Museum); *tel: 39 65 06 06*, open Wed–Sun 0930–1200, 1400–1730, admission Fr.10 (Fr.5), which contains a range of toys and games dating up to the 1950s. Opposite the Nôtre-Dame is the **Musée d'Art et d'Histoire** (Art and History Museum), *12 r. St-Louis; tel: 39 65 06 06*, open Wed–Sun 0930–1200, 1400–1730, admission Fr.10 (Fr.5), which outlines Poissy's history from Merovingian times until the 20th century. An unusual sight is the **Villa Savoye**, *62 av. Blanche de Castille; tel: 39 66 01 06*, open Wed–Mon 1000–1200, 1330–1730 (Apr–Oct); 1000–1200, 1330–1630 (Nov–Mar), a futuristic work of architecture created in 1929 by Le Corbusier.

ST-GERMAIN-EN-LAYE

Tourist Office: *38 r. au Pain; tel: 34 51 05 12.*

ACCOMMODATION

The most famous hotel in St-Germain is the four-star **Hôtel Pavillon Henri IV**, *21 r. Thiers; tel: 39 10 15 15*, formerly part of the château. It became a hotel in 1836 and was a meeting place of writers and artists of the time. Alexandre Dumas wrote *The Three Musketeers* and *The Count of Monte Cristo* there. It has expensive rooms, plus an equally expensive restaurant. Slightly smaller and slightly less expensive, the four-star **Hôtel La Forestière**, *1 av. Prés. Kennedy; tel: 39 73 36 60*, is located in the forest north of the town. This, too, has an expensive restaurant. Moderate two-star alternatives include the modern **Hôtel Campanile**, *rte de Mantes; tel: 34 51 59 59*, and the **Hôtel Le Papillon Bleu**, *pl. Guynemer; tel: 34 51 08 64*.

SIGHTSEEING

St-Germain, at the southern edge of an extensive forest, stands on the side of a hill overlooking the Seine and was chosen as the site of a stronghold by Louis VI in the 12th century. Despite restoration work following the Hundred Years War, François I found it wasn't grand enough and he had it rebuilt, though it wasn't until Henri IV's reign that it was finally completed. Louis XIV was born there and lived at the château until the court was moved to Versailles in 1682. James II of England died there seven years later and his tomb can be seen in the **Église St-Germain** (Church of St Germain) opposite the château. Today, although largely closed to the public, the château houses the **Musée des Antiquités Nationales** (National Museum of Antiquities); *tel: 34 51 53 65*, open Wed–Mon 0915–1715 (all year), admission Fr.20, which was created by Napoleon III in 1837 to contain exhibits relating to early French history. It includes a copy of one of the prehistoric painted caverns at Lascaux and the Lady of Brassempouy, which, dating back to 20,000 BC, is the oldest representation of the human face ever discovered. Other exhibits date back to Egyptian, Gallo-Roman and Merovingian periods. Also worth seeing at the château is Ste-Chapelle, a small church built in the early 13th century and similar to Ste-Chapelle in Paris, though lacking the latter's magnificent stained-glass. Behind the château, extensive gardens lead to the tree-lined **Grand Terrace**, which stretches for more than 2 km, from where there are fine views over the Seine towards central Paris.

To the south of the town, the **Musée du Prieuré** (Priory Museum), *2 r. Maurice Denis; tel: 39 73 77 87*, open Wed–Fri 1000–1730, Sat–Sun 1000–1830 (all year), Fr.25 (Fr.15), was built as a priory in 1678, but was owned at one time by Maurice Denis, leader of the Nabis art movement. The museum contains examples of the movement's work, as well as paintings by Gauguin and Toulouse-Lautrec. Another cultural figure associated with the town is the composer Claude Debussy, who was born there in 1862. His house, **Maison Debussy**, *38 r. au Pain; tel: 34 51 05 12*, open Mon–Sat 0900–1830 (Apr–Oct); 0900–1230, 1430–1830 (Nov–Mar), now contains the Tourist Office. Mementoes of his life can be seen on the first floor.

283

ST-MALO

St-Malo is one of the most visited towns in Brittany. Its legendary fame rests on its turbulent past as a privateer stronghold and home to a prosperous seafaring people, proudly claiming to be neither French nor Breton, whose explorers, shipowners and corsairs doggedly braved the dangers of the sea to look for new territories and trade routes. However, 12 centuries of maritime history were almost entirely wiped out during World War II, which reduced the town to ruins. Once again the people of St-Malo rose to the challenge, and saved their unique architectural heritage rebuilding the walled city stone by stone. The municipality gradually absorbed the nearby towns of Paramé, Rothéneuf and St-Servan, and today St-Malo is the main port on the northern coast of Brittany. Passenger traffic, particulary between Britain and France, is on the increase. The harbour facilities have been extended to include a marina, and St-Malo has become a pleasant seaside resort with several lovely beaches, a luxury hydrotherapy centre which offers sea water treatments, and a choice of activities linked with the sea.

TOURIST INFORMATION

Tourist Office: *Esplanade St-Vincent, 35400 St-Malo* (in front of the marina, just below the city walls); *tel: 99 56 64 48.* Open Mon–Sat 0900–1200, 1400–1900, closed Sun (Sept–June); Mon–Sat 0830–2000, Sun 1000–1900 (July–Aug). There is no accommodation booking service.

ARRIVING AND DEPARTING

Airport
The **Aéroport de Dinard/Pleurtuit/St-Malo**, *tel: 99 46 18 46,* is located 14 km south-west of St-Malo along the D168. There are frequent flights to and from London, Jersey and Guernsey.

By Car
When arriving from the south and west, follow the N137 to the town centre. The coastal road and the D155 from the east lead straight to the walled town. Parking is available in *Esplanade St-Vincent* nearby and in various places around the harbour.

By Ferry
Brittany Ferries *(tel: 99 40 64 41)* has regular crossings to and from Portsmouth, Poole and Cork. Other ferry companies deal with passenger traffic between the Channel Islands and Brittany; **Condor Ferries** *(tel: 99 20 03 00)* run daily crossings to and from Weymouth (via Guernsey and Jersey) Apr–Oct.

GETTING AROUND
Once close to the walled town, you can proceed on foot and enjoy strolling along the narrow streets or the top of the town's walls. However, transport is needed to reach some of the sights outside the walled town. They are easy to find and parking is available nearby (though this is restricted in Aug). There is an efficient bus service

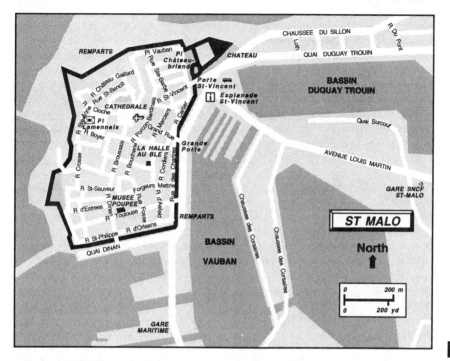

called **St-Malo Bus,** which links the out-lying districts of Rothéneuf and St-Servan via the harbour (*Esplanade St-Vincent; tel: 99 56 06 06*). A day ticket costing Fr.20 can be bought at the information centre or from the bus drivers.

Allo Taxis Malouins, *tel: 99 81 30 30* are on call 24 hrs, seven days a week.**Taxis Persehaye,** *tel: 99 40 02 02* have seven-seater vehicles.

STAYING IN ST-MALO

Accommodation

There is a large number of hotels, with and without restaurants. Within the walled town, prices are moderate to expensive; try the elegant **Hôtel France et Chateaubriand,** *pl. Chateaubriand BP 77* (in front of the château) *35412 St-Malo Cedex; tel: 99 56 66 52,* or the refined

Hôtel Elizabeth, *2 r. des Cordiers; tel: 99 56 24 98.* Outside the walled town, there is a high concentration of hotels along the seafront, which include cheaper establish-ments. The most prestigious is the **Grand Hôtel des Thermes,** *100 blvd Hébert; tel: 99 40 75 75,* (expensive) which forms part of the hydrotherapy centre.

Two of the most charming hotels in St-Malo are to be found in St-Servan, just south of the walled town and close to the harbour and the beach. **La Korrigane**, *39 r. Le Pomellec; tel: 99 81 65 85,* offers refinement and comfort in attractive sur-roundings; **Le Valmarin**, *7 r. Jean XXIII; tel: 99 81 94 76;* is an authentic *mal-ouinière,* in the past a wealthy *Malouin's* (inhabitant of St-Malo) country house; both hotels are expensive.

Hotel chains in St-Malo include *F1, Ib* and *IH.* Several **youth centres** offer full board, half board or accommodation only: **Centre de Rencontres Internationales**, *37 av. du R.P. Umbricht BP 108, 35407 St-Malo Cedex; tel: 99 40 29 80*; **Centre International d'Accueil**, *15 blvd Chateaubriand; tel: 99 56 01 72.*

There are 8 **campsites** offering varying degrees of comfort and, in most cases, a view of the sea, mainly in Panamé, Rothéneuf and St-Servan.

Eating and Drinking

The influence of the sea on gastronomy is nowhere more evident than in St-Malo as most restaurants offer their own mouthwatering seafood speciality: grilled lobster, roast salmon, home-made smoked salmon, mussels from the nearby Mont-St-Michel Bay. For a cheaper meal, try a *brasserie* or a *crêperie*. There is a good selection of all three types of establishments inside the walled town.

A market is held in **La Halle au Blé** (Corn Market, inside walled town) on Tues and Fri mornings.

Communications and Money

Main **post office**; *1 blvd de la Tour d'Auvergne* (just behind the *Grande Plage*); *tel: 99 20 51 78.* Also inside the walled town at *pl. des Frères Lamennais; tel: 99 40 89 90.*

Change facilities: **Bureau de Change St-Vincent**, *2 r. St-Vincent; tel: 99 40 21 10* (open seven days a week).

ENTERTAINMENT

Outdoor leisure activities are mainly connected with the sea: sailing is a tradition in the **Baie de St-Malo** where a number of **regattas** take place throughout the summer, among them the Cowes-St-Malo and the Triangle de Cherbourg, both in July. Details from **Société Nautique de la Baie de St-Malo**, *quai du Bajoyer; tel:*

99 40 84 42). Windsurfing is also very popular and the new 'fun board' is the latest craze – spectacular competitions take place close to the beach.

Corsairs and their adventures are no longer confined to history books, for it is now possible to sail in an exact replica of a privateer cutter, **Le Renard** (daily, Fr.210–360, *tel: 99 40 53 10*).

Loisirs Quotidiens des Jeunes organises various activities for children above the age of 8, including hang-gliding (*10/13 r. du Grand Passage; tel: 99 81 51 69*); **Centre Allende**, *r. des Acadiens; tel: 99 82 13 70,* has similar activities for 13–18-year-olds

There are three cinemas in town; one of them, **Solidor,** *35 r. Jean XXIII, St-Servan; tel: 99 81 90 98* shows films in V.O. (original sound-track, usually English).

There are several piano bars and night clubs/discos in St-Malo but, like all self-respecting fashionable resorts, the town has its own casino firmly established along the seafront: dancing and gambling go on into the early hours of the morning; in addition there is a pizzeria, a brasserie and a separate discotheque on the premises .

Events

Two main festivals take place during the summer. The **Festival de Musique Sacrée** (Festival of Sacred Music), lasting one month from mid-July to mid-Aug, offers a varied programme from Gregorian Chant to modern works by Duruflé and Jolivet. The **Festival du Clos Poulet** is an international folk festival which stages performances in the open, during a week in July.

Various concerts of classical and popular music are scheduled throughout the summer in the Cathedral, Église Ste-Croix, in public gardens and other venues. For details apply to the Tourist Office.

SHOPPING

Elegant boutiques within the walled town are mostly located along the *Grande Rue* and adjacent streets. Confectioners offer authentic Breton earthenware filled with delicious regional specialities. Glassblowers show their delicate work in the **Atelier-Galerie Baquère**, *2 r. des Lauriers*, and you can admire a collection of mother-of-pearl and coral objects in **Via Natura**, *3 r. St-Vincent*. Regional ceramics, including **HB Henriot** (see Quimper, p. xxx), can be purchased from **Faïencerie Malouine**, *6 r. Porçon de la Barbinais*. Traditional fishing and sailing garments have inspired new lines of fashionable clothes found at **Bleu Marine**, *6 r. St-Vincent*, and **Marin-Marine**, *5 Grande Rue*.

SIGHTSEEING

The city of St-Malo is divided into the walled town (known as *Intra-muros* or i.m. for short) and the rest, which includes the districts of **St-Servan**, **Paramé** and **Rothéneuf**.

Since the settlement was transferred from the Aleth peninsula (now St-Servan) in the 12th century to its present location on a barren rock jutting out into the sea, St-Malo has been a fiercely independent city relying for survival on its prosperous maritime activities and powerful fortifications. Boat trips around the bay offer a good overall view of the strategic position of St-Malo and of the two rocky islands: **Fort National** (fortified by the 17th-century military architect Vauban to protect St-Malo) and **Grand Bé**, where the Romantic poet Chateaubriand is buried. Both islands are accessible by foot at low tide.

There are regular guided tours of the walled town in July and Aug, and a small train takes tourists round the old town in 30 mins, starting from **Porte St-Vincent**, in English, Fr.25 (Fr.20), *tel: 99 40 49 49*.

Begin with a tour of the **ramparts** from Porte St-Vincent, and walk past impressive bastions and towers – the view all round the bay is magnificent. Follow the marked itinerary leading from *pl. Chateaubriand* to the most interesting sights: the **Cathedral**, **5 r. du Pélicot** (the last remaining 17th-century house), ancient **chapels** and imposing 18th-century **mansions** built by the wealthy shipowners.

There is a comprehensive **Musée de la Poupée et du jouet** (Doll and Toy Museum) at *13 r. de Toulouse*, open July and Aug, Fr.25 (Fr.15). The massive château guarding the entrance to the city now houses the town hall and two museums. The **Musée d'Histoire de la Ville**, provides fascinating information on the development of the town through the centuries, in particular on its careful rebuilding after World War II. Open daily 1000–1200 and 1400–1800; Fr.19 (Fr.9.5); and **Quic-en-Groigne**, where you can see wax figures of famous Malouins, starting with Jacques Cartier, open daily 0930–1200 and 1400–1800, Fr.19 (Fr.9).

Jacques Cartier, the explorer who discovered Canada in 1534, lived in **Limoëlou** manor, *r. MacDonald Stewart*, *Rothéneuf*. This has been turned into a museum recalling his lifestyle and his travels; open all year, guided tours in English July and Aug 1000–1130 and 1430–1800, Fr.20 (Fr.15); *tel: 99 40 97 73*.

An impressive medieval keep in St-Servan, **Tour Solidor,** houses the **Musée International du Long-Cours Cap-Hornier**, *tel: 99 40 71 58,* retracing the perilous journeys of long-distance sailing ships which regularly rounded Cape Horn. Open daily 1000–1200 and 1400–1800, Fr.20 (Fr.10).

ST-MALO–BREST

This 585-km route along the northern coast of Brittany offers many opportunities to sample the best of the region. Contrasts in colour from the deep emerald green of the sea, lapping the golden sands of Sables-d'Or-les-Pins or breaking against the cliffs of Cap Fréhel, to the lovely shades of pink along the Côte de Granit Rose are a feast to the eye. And if sophisticated seaside resorts like Dinard or Perros-Guirec are undeniably attractive, the wild Côte des Légendes west of Roscoff has a fascination all of its own. The deep estuaries of the Rance and the Rivière de Morlaix add another dimension to this beautiful drive which should take about five days or more if island trips tempt you.

DIRECT ROUTE: 238 KM

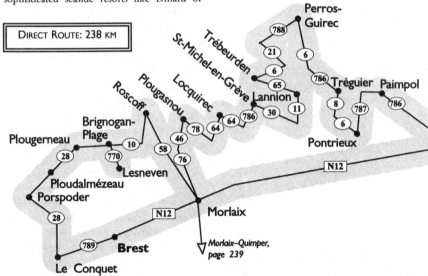

N176 which joins the N12 just before Lamballe; from there it's dual carriageway all the way to Brest (follow signs for *Centre Ville*).

ROUTES

DIRECT ROUTE

The distance between the two historic cities of St-Malo and Brest is only 238 km; leave St-Malo towards Rennes and follow the N137 for 14 km then turn right towards St-Brieuc on the

SCENIC ROUTE

This sinuous 585-km route follows the coast as closely as possible with a few incursions inland; leave St-Malo as above but turn right onto the D168 to

Dinard. The road crosses the Rance estuary over a 750-m long dam: the **Usine marémotrice de la Rance** uses the force of tidal currents both ways to produce electricity (free visit daily 0830–2000).

From Dinard drive westwards on the D786 through St-Lunaire, St-Briac-sur-Mer, Lancieux and Ploubalay; 2.5 km beyond Ploubalay, turn right onto D26 to St-Jacut-de-la-Mer. Rejoin the D786 at Le Guido and turn right. Four km further on, turn right onto D19 to **St-Cast-Le-Guido**. Leave St-Cast on D13 to Matignon and turn right, following D786 for 6.5 km. Turn right on the D16A to

Fort-la-Latte, then turn west on D16 to **Cap Fréhel**. From there, drive along D34A through Sables-d'Or-les-Pins until it joins D786 leading to **Le Val-André** through Erquy. Follow D34 to Les Marais, then the D80 for 3.5 km and turn right to **St-Brieuc**.

Leave St-Brieuc on D24, keeping close to the coast and rejoin D786 after Rosaires. Turn right and follow the Côte du Goëlo to **Paimpol**. From there, drive west for 5 km, rejoin D786 and, almost immediately, turn south on D787 to **Pontrieux**, then west again on D21 to Runan and north on the D8 to **Tréguier**.

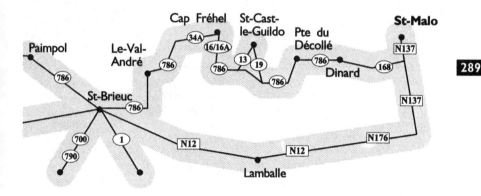

289

D786 and D6 take you to **Perros-Guirec**. Leave Perros-Guirec along the coast road D788 through Ploumanc'h and Trégastel-Plage, turn left at Penver on D21 to Pleumeur-Bodou then right onto D6 to **Trébeurden**. D65 leads to **Lannion**. Drive south on D11 and turn right after 7.5 km onto D340 to **St-Michel-en-Grève**. Turn left and follow the coast to **Locquirec** (D786, D42, D64). Continue on D64 for 8.5 km and

turn right onto D78 to St-Jean-du-Doigt, then on to the Pointe de Primel on D46. From there, follow the D46A and D76 along the Rivère de Morlaix estuary south to **Morlaix**.

Leave Morlaix towards Carantec on the D769, D73 and D33 along the west bank of the estuary. Continue on the D58 to St-Pol-de-Léon and **Roscoff**. Retrace your steps for 6 km and turn right on the D770 to **Brignogan-Plages**. Rejoin the D10

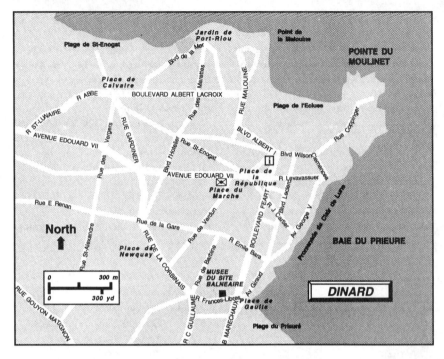

and turn right towards **Plouguerneau**. Fom there D13 and D28 lead to **Ploudalmézeau**. Follow D168 out of the town to the coast, then take the picturesque D27A and D27 coast roads through Porspoder to Aber Ildut and the D28 south to **Le Conquet**. Drive to Brest along the D789.

DINARD

Tourist Office: *2 blvd Féart, 35802 Dinard Cedex; tel: 99 46 94 12.* Open all year, it has details of excursions, boat trips and a multilingual guide service. For details of flights and ferry crossings: see St-Malo p. 284.

ACCOMMODATION AND FOOD

The **Grand Hôtel**, *46 av. George-V; tel: 99 88 26 26* symbolises the refined luxury Dinard stands for. There are more reason-

ably priced hôtels close to the sea (**Printania,** *tel: 99 46 13 07*) and cheaper ones further away. Hotel chains include *Ct, F1, IH* and *Nv.*

Restaurants offer a wide range of menus from Fr.50 upwards, with the emphasis on fish and seafood. For a gastronomic meal try the **Altaïr,** *blvd Féart; tel: 99 46 13 58.*

SIGHTSEEING

Sumptuous villas, exclusive clubs and hotels, an elegant casino and the romantic **Promenade du Clair de Lune**, lined with flowers and palm trees, contribute to maintain the incomparable Belle-Époque atmosphere which brought international fame to Dinard in the 1880s. The development of the resort from the mid-19th century is illustrated in the **Musée du Site Balnéaire** (Seaside Resort Museum), *r.*

des Français-Libres; open Easter–Oct 1000–1200, 1400–1800, closed weekends.

DINARD TO ST-CAST-LE-GUILDO

The **Chemin des Peintres en Côte d'Émeraude** is a marked itinerary following in the footsteps of Renoir, Signac, Picasso and others, with reproductions of their paintings displayed on the spots which inspired them. A brochure *Regards d'Emeraude* is available in English from Tourist Offices. The indented coastline offers a succession of small peninsulas with splendid panoramas from St-Malo to Cap Fréhel, the most breathtaking being from **Pointe du Décollé** in St-Lunaire. Lively seaside resorts, all with beautiful beaches and picturesque harbours, are dotted along the way: St-Lunaire, St-Briac-sur-Mer, Lancieux, St-Jacut-de-la-Mer and above all **St-Cast-le-Guildo**, a family resort with a wide choice of accommodation, beach clubs for children, varied outdoor activities (**Centre Nautique**, *tel: 96 41 86 42,* open all year) and entertainment (**Tourist Office:** *pl. C. de Gaulle; tel: 96 41 81 52.* Open all year, July and Aug 0900–1930; boat trips, excursions, walks, cycle tours).

ST-CAST-LE-GUILDO TO ST-BRIEUC

Facing St-Cast across the Baie de la Frénaye, **Fort La Latte** is a medieval fortress built on top of a 60-m cliff and accessible across two succesive drawbridges spanning impressive crevasses (guided tours daily June–Sept). Nearby, **Cap Fréhel** juts out defiantly into the sea: spectacular cliffs of pink sandstone, a protected nesting ground for large colonies of sea birds.

Continue along the scenic D34A across heathland and woodland through **Sables-** d'Or-les-Pins** with its fine golden sand beach to **Cap d'Erquy** from where the view extends over the whole wide bay of St-Brieuc, as far as Bréhat Island when the weather is clear (pleasant walks across the heath).

The D786 to **Le Val-André** passes near the **Château de Biénassis**, built in pink sandstone between the 15th and the 17th centuries and still inhabited (open mid-June–mid-Sept daily).

Pléneuf-Val-André consists of the old village of Pléneuf and the attractive seaside resort of Val-André, organised in an orderly fashion along the *Promenade de la Digue* bordering a magnificent beach, one of the safest in Brittany (**Tourist Office,** *r. W. Churchill; tel: 96 72 20 55;* boat trips to Bréhat Island, list of reasonably priced accommodation).

ST-BRIEUC

Tourist Office: *7 r. St-Gouéno, 22008 St-Brieuc Cedex; tel: 96 33 32 50.* Open Mon–Sat 0900–1200 and 1400–1800 (1900 and Sun morning in July and Aug). It has change facilities on Mon, details of guided tours and excursions.

ACCOMMODATION AND FOOD

Hotel prices are cheap to moderate. In the old town try *r. du Gouët* or *pl. de la Poste;* otherwise *r. de Brest* and *r. de la Gare.* Hotel chains include *Ca, CI, F1, Ib, NH* and *PC.* **HI:** youth hostel, *Manoir de la ville Guyomard, Les Villages; tel: 96 78 70 70.* Open all year. There is a **campsite**: **Les Vallées**, *tel: 96 94 05 05.*

Regional cuisine (*menu terroir*) is on offer at **Aux Pesked**, *59 r. du Légué; tel: 96 33 34 65. Brasseries* are cheaper.

SIGHTSEEING

Daily guided tours start from the Cathedral. The massive fortified **Cathédrale St-Éti-**

enne looks anything but elegant and the harmonious proportions of the interior come as a surprise. Stroll along the *r. Fardel, pl. au Lin, r. Quinquaine,* and *r. du Gouët* lined with several splendid specimens of timber-framed corbelled houses from the 15th and 16th centuries.

SIDE TRACKS FROM ST-BRIEUC

The two small historic cities of **Moncontour** and **Quintin,** located 23 km (D1) and 20 km (D700 and D790) south of St-Brieuc are worth a detour for both have retained an exceptionally rich architectural heritage: ramparts, old houses, churches, private mansions and castles. ▣

CÔTE DU GOËLO

Tourist Information: as for Paimpol (p. 292). Other tourist information centres are found along the coast.

The west coast of the Baie de St-Brieuc, known as the Côte du Goëlo, is lined with picturesque fishing ports, seaside resorts and ancient villages against a background of fine beaches framed by high cliffs.

Drive northwards from St-Brieuc along the coast road then the D786 to St-Quay-Portrieux. It is hard to believe that the picturesque seaside resort of **Binic** was once engaged in fishing for cod off the coast of Newfoundland and Iceland. Today fishermen unload their local catch (mainly scallops) at the modern harbour of St-Quay-Portrieux, where it is sold by auction. The road goes past the magnificent **Plage des Godelins**, the main beach of yet another family resort, Étables-sur-Mer.

With its five beaches, beach clubs for children and teenagers, casino, discotheque and piano bars, **St-Quay-Portrieux** is the main tourist centre along

---

Breton Saints

Pardons (religious festivals) express the fervent devotion of the Bretons for their saints (see box, p. 252). Some, like St Yves (born in Trégier), are recognised by the Church and attract followers from all over Brittany, France and sometimes from other countries. Among these larger than life mystic figures, St Anne rouses deep veneration for she is the patron saint of Brittany. As the grandmother of Christ she symbolises Breton religious fervour. As the beloved Duchesse Anne she embodies Breton national pride, and as the namesake of the Celtic goddess Ana she reminds the Bretons of their strong ties with their pagan past. In contrast, local saints are treated more like friends people turn to when they need advice or a favour. There are those who cure diseases, offer protection from the raging elements, help young girls find a husband and even look after cattle and horses. They form part of the local community and cohabit harmoniously with sirens, fairies and facetious *korrigans* (elves).

---

this stretch of coastline. Its modern harbour with facilities for pleasure boats is accessible at any time of the day.

Continue along the D786, turning right at Plouha towards **Port-Moguer** then **Plage Bonaparte**, both surrounded by some of the highest cliffs in Brittany. The latter was the rendezvous point for Allied airmen shot down over France – the path they followed to get to the beach is now freely accessible.

PAIMPOL

Tourist Office: *Mairie de Paimpol, r. P. Feutren; tel: 96 20 83 16.* Open daily 0900–1930, Sun 1000–1300 (summer),

0900–1200 and 1400–1700 (winter); boat trips, maps of footpaths and cycle tracks, good choice of accommodation within a 5-km radius (**HI**: youth hostel, **Château de Kéraoul,** *tel: 96 20 83 60*).

SIGHTSEEING

The **Fête des Terre-Neuvas et Islandais** in July celebrates the long-standing tradition of fishing off the coasts of Newfoundland and Iceland, which brought prosperity and fame to the town at the cost of many fishermen's lives. Pierre Loti's *Pêcheur d'Islande,* written in 1886, is set in Paimpol. Near the harbour, the **Musée de la Mer,** *r. de Labenne; tel: 96 22 02 19,* illustrates the seafaring past of Paimpol (open 1000–1200 and 1500–1900 Easter–Sept).

Pl. du Martray, in the town centre, is lined with austere 16th-century granite houses. The beautiful ruins of the **Abbaye de Beauport,** dating from the 13th and 14th centuries, stand overlooking the sea (off D786; guided tours June–Sept daily).

Boat trips to **Bréhat Island,** famous for its pink rock formations and its Mediterranean vegetation, start from the **Pointe de l'Arcouest,** 5 km north of Paimpol (July and Aug daily every hour, crossing 10 min).

PAIMPOL TO PERROS-GUIREC

At Lézardrieux, 5 km west of Paimpol, turn south on the D787. The **Château de la Roche-Jagu,** overlooking a bend of the Trieux River, is a splendid example of late medieval architecture, fortified on the river side and residential on the land side (Apr–Oct daily). Further south, **Pontrieux** is a picturesque riverside town with a wealth of 15th- to 18th-century domestic architecture, a granite fountain, ancient wash-houses along the river and flowers everywhere. The 15th-century church in **Runan** has a richly decorated southside and porch (mid-June–mid-Sept daily except Sun morning).

Drive north to **Tréguier,** a prestigious ecclesiastical centre during the Middle Ages and the birthplace of St Yves, known all over Europe as the advocate of the poor. The beautiful Gothic **Cathédrale St-Tugdual** has survived the test of time remarkably well (guided tours July and Aug daily except Sun morning). Built in the local pink and grey granite, it incorporates earlier Romanesque elements; inside note St-Yves's grave (a copy of the medieval one) and a group in carved wood representing St-Yves between the poor and the rich; the Flamboyant cloisters are splendid. Take a stroll through the old town nestling round the cathedral.

PERROS-GUIREC

Tourist Office: *21 pl. de l'Hôtel de Ville, 22700 Perros-Guirec; tel: 96 23 21 15.* Open Mon–Sat 0900–1930, Sun and holidays 1000–1230 and 1600–1830 (summer); otherwise closed Sun and lunchtime. Information on walks, cycle tours and boat trips to bird sanctuaries.

ACCOMMODATION AND FOOD

More than 30 hotels covering a wide price range from the expensive but exceptionally well-situated **Manoir du Sphinx,** *chemin de la Messe; tel: 96 23 25 42* to the cheap but charming **Les Violettes,** *r. du Calvaire; tel: 96 23 21 33.*

In addition there are several **campsites,** bed and breakfast and holiday homes. Contact the Tourist Office for details.

Seafood is on all menus in restaurants, brasseries and *crêperies.* A good address for a gastronomic meal is **Hôtel des Rochers,** *Port de Ploumanac'h; tel: 96 91 44 49.*

Côte de Granit Rose

Stretching from Bréhat Island to Trébeurden, the Pink Granite Coast is at its best between Perros-Guirec and Trégastel, a mere 7 km of coastline that is a feast to the eye through the sheer harmony of form and colour of the pink rock formations lining the seashore. They are particularly striking in Ploumanac'h and Trégastel. Their strange shapes, caused by erosion, have worked on the imagination of the Bretons who have given them evocative names. The geological formation of these huge boulders is explained in the **Maison du Littoral**, *chemin des Douaniers, Ploumanac'h* (mid-June–mid-Sept daily 1030–1900; admission free).

SIGHTSEEING

One of only three *Stations Kid* in Brittany (see p. 246), Perros-Guirec is, with its beach clubs, marina, hydrotherapy and fitness centre, casino, discotheques and entertainment for all ages, the ultimate in seaside resorts, ideally situated along one of the most picturesque coastal areas, the Côte de Granit Rose. Excursions aboard the 'Little Train' start from the marina every afternoon in July and Aug. The pink granite **church** is a curious mixture of Romanesque and Gothic styles.

PERROS-GUIREC TO LANNION

From Perros-Guirec, the D788 follows the coast closely to **Ploumanac'h.** Walk down to the harbour: on your right, a path skirts the shoreline of the tiny peninsula, strewn with pink boulders, and affords breathtaking panoramas of this unspoilt protected environment.

Further west, **Trégastel-Plage** is a superb seaside resort with no fewer than 12 beaches framed by pink rock formations and a string of small pink islands. There are many possibilites of exciting walks and cycle tours in the area and an interesting aquarium beneath huge rocks (July and Aug daily 0900–2000. **Tourist Office:** *pl. Ste-Anne; tel: 96 23 88 67;* open all year).

Continue on the D788 to Penvern; a road on your right leads to **Île Grande** famous for its birdwatching centre linked by video cameras to the **Sept Îles** and Rouzic bird sanctuaries. Turn left towards **Pleumeur-Bodou** and its telecommunications centre (July and Aug daily).

The D6 leads to **Trébeurden**, an important resort with a great variety of landscapes: high cliffs, pink rock formations, sand dunes and heaths. The wide choice of accommodation includes an **HI youth hostel** open all year (**Tourist Office**, *pl. de Crec'h Héry; tel: 96 23 51 64;* boat trips to islands and nature trails).

Situated deep inside the Léguer estuary, **Lannion** is a lively market town which has retained many timber-framed houses along its narrow paved streets. With its eight hotels, four **campsites**, bed and breakfast, holiday homes and and **HI youth hostel**, Lannion is the ideal starting point for excursions in the area (**Tourist Office**, *Les Quais; tel: 96 46 41 00*).

LANNION TO MORLAIX

Drive south on the D11. Set among trees, the lovely 15th-century **Chapelle de Kerfons** has Flamboyant and Renaissance features which contrast with the austere appearance of the fortified **Château de Tonquédec** nearby (July and Aug daily 1100–2000). Further south, the **Château de Kergrist** offers a happy mixture of Gothic and 18th-century styles (June–Sept 1400–1830).

The D30 leads to **La Lieue de Grève**,

294

a magnificent bow-shaped 4-km long beach. Follow the picturesque **Corniche de l'Armorique**, past the **Grand rocher** (fine view) and the **Chapelle St-Efflam** dedicated to the hermit from Ireland.

Locquirec is a small fishing port and peaceful family resort on the border of Côtes d'Armor and Finistère. Local fishing provides a wonderful variety of fresh seafood served in almost all restaurants (**Tourist Office**, *pl. du Port; tel: 98 67 40 83*). West of Locquirec, the small village of **St-Jean-du-Doigt** owes its name to the relic of St John the Baptist's finger. According to legend, the finger was brought to the local chapel and this started a popular pilgrimage. The more spacious present church, set within an impressive parish close, replaced the original building but its treasury still contains the saint's relic.

From the **Pointe de Primel**, reminiscent of the Côte de Granit Rose, the road follows the east coast of the Rivière de Morlaix overlooked by the 6000-year old **Cairn de Barnenez** (open all year). This imposing prehistoric monument consists of two burial stone mounds covering several dolmens.

The D76 leads to Morlaix at the head of the estuary

MORLAIX

For details, see p. 243–244.

MORLAIX TO ROSCOFF

Carantec is a small family resort with several fine beaches, picturesquely situated on a peninsula jutting out into the Baie of Morlaix and surrounded by dozens of islands, the largest being **Île Callot** accessible at low tide only. (**Tourist Office:** *4 r. Pasteur; tel: 98 67 00 43*. July and Aug daily 0900–1900; maps of footpaths, excursion booking service). Accom-

---

Seaweed

The seabed off the Côte des Abers is predominantly rocky and particularly favourable to the growth of seaweed. Huge fields, which have been farmed for centuries, lie offshore in the Plouguerneau area. The seaweed is gathered at sea or simply collected after it has been washed ashore by storms. Nowadays, Plouguerneau owns the largest fleet of seaweed gatherers in Finistère. It sails as far as Molène Island to bring back the precious crop which was and still is mainly used as fertilizer or burnt to produce kelp. However, other uses are being introduced gradually along with the development of new species.

---

modation is very reasonably priced; try **Le Pors-Pol**, *7 r. Surcouf; tel: 98 67 00 52* for its relaxed atmosphere.

There are daily boat trips round the islands, some of them bird sanctuaries, and the **Château du Taureau** guarding the access to Morlaix.

Continue northwards towards Roscoff; **St-Pol de Léon** (**Tourist Office**, *pl. de l'Évêché; tel: 98 69 05 69*) is a small market town at the heart of the Ceinture Dorée, which produces early vegetables. Its two splendid religious buildings testify to its long-standing prosperity: the elegant 77-m high steeple of the **Chapelle Notre-Dame du Kreisker**, a magnificent example of 15th-century tracery denoting the influence of English Perpendicular and Norman styles, was used as a model throughout Brittany. Nearby, the Gothic **cathedral**, now a basilica, is built in white stone from Caen instead of granite, but the style is undoubtedly Breton, a subtle mixture of sober design and refinement (free guided visits).

295

ROSCOFF

Tourist Office: *46 r. Gambetta, 29680 Roscoff; tel: 98 61 12 13.* Open July and Aug 0900–1230 and 1330–1900, Sun 0930–1230. It has a booking service for accommodation, excursions and boat trips, particularly to the 'exotic' Île de Batz. Information on everything to see and do is in the weekly brochure *L'Estivant* (The Holidaymaker).

Until the 1960s, many Bretons nicknamed 'Johnnies' crossed the Channel from Roscoff, their bicycles loaded with onions they hoped to sell in the south of England and Wales. Today, Roscoff is mostly known as one of the main ferry ports, handling thousands of holidaymakers travelling between Britain and France; however, a stroll through the town centre will enable you to discover **Old Roscoff**, a granite city with lots of character. Moreover, there are interesting discoveries to be made about marine life off the coast of Brittany at the **aquarium** of the **Station Biologique** (Marine Biology Research Centre, open daily), *pl. G. Teissier; tel: 98 29 23 25,* and **Thalado,** *2 av. V. Hugo; tel: 98 69 77 05,* a fascinating permanent exhibition devoted to seaweed.

ROSCOFF TO BRIGNOGAN-PLAGES

The coastal fringe west of Roscoff is a prosperous agricultural area, producing high quality early vegetables, in particular artichokes. Inland there are impressive castles like the 15th-century **Château de Kérouzéré** and ancient market towns like **Plouescat** with its splendid covered market also dating from the 15th century.

The shoreline is a succession of rocky creeks and sand beaches sheltered by dunes. The sea is dotted with reefs as far as the eye can see. This is the beginning of the **Côte des Légendes**: its inhabitants

had the sinister reputation of deliberately provoking shipwrecks, by tying lanterns to the horns of their cattle in order to attract ships close to the treacherous reefs.

Past the old granite village of Goulven, turn right to **Brignogan-Plages**.

BRIGNOGAN-PLAGES

Tourist Office: *6 r. de l'Église; tel: 98 83 41 08).* Brignogan-Plages is the main resort along this stretch of coastline. There is a reasonably priced comfortable hotel/ restaurant, **Ar Reder Mor,** *av. Gén. de Gaulle; tel: 98 83 40 09,* and a two-star campsite as well as a selection of holiday homes.

> ↙ **SIDE TRACK FROM BRIGNOGAN-PLAGES**
>
> **Lesneven** lies 11 km south of Brignogan along the D770; its cattle fairs were once famous all over Brittany and the town has retained some 15th- and 16th-century houses (**Tourist Office,** *14 pl. Le Flô; tel: 98 83 01 47).* One of the most important *pardons* in Brittany takes place in Sept in the 15th-century basilica at **Le Folgoët,** 2 km south of Lesneven. Inside, the rood-screen is a fine example of Flamboyant granite tracery. ⌂

BRIGNOGAN-PLAGES TO PLOUDALMÉZEAU

Inhabited since prehistoric times, this part of northern Finistère is known as **Pays des Abers** because the coast is deeply indented by three shallow estuaries, Aber Wrac'h, Aber Benoît and Aber Ildut. There is a drastic change of scenery at low tide when the sea drains away and boats are left stranded on the murky flats.

Tourist Information: Association Pays des Abers–Côte des Légendes, *BP 35 29830 Ploudalmézeau; tel: 98 48 10*

79. It provides a comprehensive list of accommodation, mapped walks, topical information.

Reefs, which render navigation so difficult, are favourable to the development of seaweed and **Plouguerneau (Tourist Office:** *pl. de l'Europe; tel: 98 04 70 93)* is the traditional centre of seaweed gathering (see box, p. 295). The **Musée des Goémoniers** (Seaweed Gatherers' Museum), *rte de St-Michel BP 35; tel: 98 04 60 30,* open July and Aug 1000–1200 and 1400–1800, otherwise afternoons only, illustrates the various aspects of this ancient profession and explains the dangers and the economic impact on the whole region. The **Fête du Goémon** (Seaweed Festival) takes place in Aug.

An excursion to the **Phare de l'Île Vierge,** the tallest lighthouse off the French coast, offers wonderful views of the rock-strewn shoreline. There are also interesting boat trips from Port de Paluden on the south bank of **Aber Wrac'h** to the mouth of the **Aber** and the **Dunes de Ste-Marguerite,** covered in seaweed laid there to dry in the sun.

PLOUDALMÉZEAU TO LE CONQUET

Further south, **Ploudalmézeau** is at the heart of another picturesque area between Aber Benoît and Aber Ildut (**Tourist Office:** *pl. de l'Eglise; tel: 98 48 11 88).* The region has several hotels, a choice of seaside campsites and many holiday homes.

One of the most striking megaliths in the area is the **Dolmen du Guilliguy,** on top of a promontory ovelooking Portsall Creek. Great navigational skills are needed to get past the fearsome **Roches de Portsall** on which the *Amoco Cadiz* ran aground in 1978, releasing 220,000 tonnes of crude oil along 300 km of coastline.

The picturesque road which runs south to Aber Ildut offers a wonderful overall view of the rocky coastline and its tiny coves sheltering small resorts like **Porspoder.**

The road skirts the north bank of the beautiful **Aber Ildut** before turning south towards Le Conquet.

LE CONQUET TO BREST

Like many traditional fishing ports in Brittany, **Le Conquet** has developed into a pleasant seaside resort with a choice of beaches including the superb 2.5-km **Plage des Blancs Sablons.** At the same time, it has retained 15th- and 16th-century houses and fishermen's cottages with picturesque outside staircases. Footpaths along the coast offer lovely views of the harbour and of the islands in the distance (**Tourist Office:** *Parc Beauséjour; tel: 98 89 11 31*).

Regular boat trips to **Molène** and **Ouessant Islands** are scheduled by **Compagnie maritime Pen Ar Bed,** *Port de Commerce; tel: 98 80 24 68* (crossing: 1½ hours, tickets from the Tourist Office).

Reefs, strong currents and spectacular storms have, in the past, inspired spine-chilling tales about Ouessant. However, today the island offers unspoilt natural beauty, breathtaking scenery and two fascinating museums; the **Ecomusée du Niou Huella** consists of two fully furnished typical Ouessant homes while the **Centre d'Interprétation des Phares et Balises** retraces the history of lighthouses and their keepers (**Tourist Office:** *tel: 98 48 85 83*).

Before heading for Brest on the D789, drive south to the **Pointe de St-Mathieu** for panoramic views of the entrance of the Brest roadstead, the Crozon Peninsula and the Pointe du Raz.

297

ST-MALO–NANTES

Meandering over a distance of 342 km from the Channel to the Atlantic along the ancient border of the duchy of Brittany and guarded by impressive castles, this route takes you on a journey through history to a time when two rival cities, Rennes and Nantes, fought for the privilege of being the capital of Brittany. Allow at least two days for this trip.

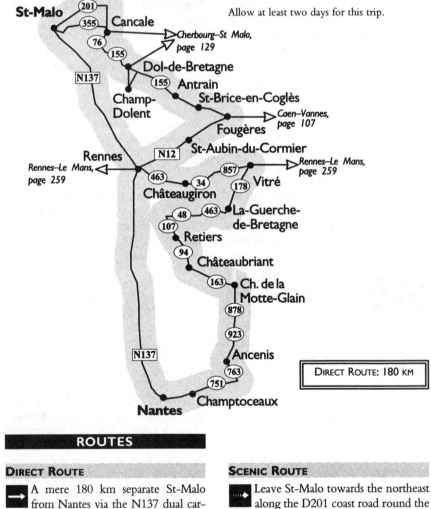

298

DIRECT ROUTE: 180 KM

ROUTES

DIRECT ROUTE

➡️ A mere 180 km separate St-Malo from Nantes via the N137 dual carriageway which by-passes Rennes.

SCENIC ROUTE

➡️ Leave St-Malo towards the northeast along the D201 coast road round the **Pointe du Grouin** which offers a won-

Cancale, capital of oyster-breeding

For several centuries Mont St-Michel Bay provided phenomenal quantities of 'wild' oysters, up to 20,000 tonnes a year. Eventually, oyster-gathering was restricted to certain times of the year when dozens of boats like *La Cancalaise* (see under Cancale) would go out into the Bay and bring back as many oysters as they could. Supplies continued to diminish and, during the 1920s, oyster-breeding was introduced. Today oyster-beds around Cancale cover an area of 400 hectares and produce 6000 tonnes of oysters a year. It takes several years for oysters to mature under careful supervision, but oyster-breeders don't complain as theirs have the reputation of being the finest. Try them for yourself: Cancale oysters are available at the harbour, next to the lighthouse.

derful overall view of Mont St-Michel Bay. From **Cancale**, drive along D76 and D155 to Le Vivier-sur-Mer and turn south towards **Dol-de-Bretagne**. Leave Dol on D795 to the Menhir de Champ-Dolent, go back to the junction with D4 and turn right, then right again at La Boussac on the D155. Go through **Antrain** and follow signs for Bonne-Fontaine and Tremblay, where you turn left to rejoin D155 leading to Fougères via **St-Brice-en-Coglès**. From **Fougères**, follow N12 to Rennes via **St-Aubin-du-Cormier**.

Leave Rennes on D463 to Châteaugiron; bear left onto D334 and drive for 10 km before turning left onto D95 to Châteaubourg then right on the D857 to **Vitré**. Drive south on D38, D48 and D178 to La Guerche-de-Bretagne, turn right on D463 for 5.5 km, then bear left on to D48 to La Roche-aux-Fées via

Marcillé-Robert. From there, D341, D41, D94 and D178 lead to **Châteaubriant** via Martigné-Ferchaud. Drive south-east along D163 to La Chapelle-Glain, then turn south on D878 to Ancenis, past the **Château de la Motte-Glain**. Once in **Ancenis**, cross the Loire and turn right onto D751, which follows the river to Nantes.

CANCALE

Tourist Office: *44 r. du Port, 35260 Cancale; tel: 99 89 63 72.*

Most hotels are located near the harbour, including three LF. Amongst the others **La Houle**, *18 quai Gambetta; tel: 99 89 62 38*, is moderately priced. For delicious local seafood, try **Bistrot de Cancale**, *2 quai Gambetta; tel: 99 89 92 42*.

Situated on high ground overlooking Mont St-Michel Bay, the town dominates the picturesque harbour at the foot of the cliff. A marked footpath winds round the coastline to the **Pointe du Grouin**, offering good views of the oyster beds lying offshore. Visit an oyster-breeding farm, **la Ferme Marine**, *tel: 99 89 69 99* or take a boat trip aboard *La Cancalaise*, a traditional oyster-fishing boat. Oyster-breeding techniques are shown at **Musée de l'Huître et du Coquillage**; *tel: 99 89 69 99*, open daily 1030–1800 (June–Sept); 1430–1700 (Feb–June, Sept–Oct), admission Fr. 38 adults (Fr.18 children).

CANCALE TO DOL-DE-BRETAGNE

Mont St-Michel Bay is on UNESCO's worldwide list of unique ecosystems; walks, cycle and riding tours are organised by the **Centre d'Animation de la Baie du Mont Saint-Michel**, *Gare Maritime, Le Vivier-sur-Mer; tel: 99 48 84 38*. Discover mussel-breeding (*mytiliculture*) aboard the **Sirène de la Baie**, an amphib-

299

ian vehicle based in **Le Vivier** (*tel: 9948 82 30*). Rows and rows of wooden posts covered with mussels can be seen across the Bay which produces 10,000 tonnes of these molluscs every year.

Turn southwards on the D155 and climb to the top of **Mont-Dol** for panoramic views.

DOL-DE-BRETAGNE

Tourist Office *tel: 99 48 15 37* (open 0930–1230 and 1430–1930 July and Aug) is located in *Grande Rue*, a street lined with old houses.

Dol-de-Bretagne has a good LF, the Hôtel de Bretagne, 17 pl. Chateaubriand; tel: 99 48 02 03. Moderate, with some economically priced rooms.

Dol is an ancient ecclesiastical centre which has retained a good deal of its medieval character and a remarkable 13th-century cathedral. Massive from outside, the **Cathédrale St-Samson** is lofty and elegant inside. In the treasury opposite, the **Musée de Dol,** *tel: 99 48 33 46*, open daily 0930–1800, retraces the history of the town.

DOL-DE-BRETAGNE TO FOUGÈRES

On the outskirts of Dol along the D795, the **Menhir de Champ-Dolent** stands 9.5 m high in the middle of a field. The D155 to Fougères goes through the **Forêt de Villecartier**, a lovely forested area ideal for picnics. In Antrain, turn right towards the 16th-century **Château de Bonnefontaine**, typical of the transitional style of that period, residential yet still fortified (outside only). Visit the Romanesque church of **Tremblay,** if you have time. In Brice-en-Coglès make a detour to the **Château du Rocher-Portail**, a harmonious building in dark granite, dating from the beginning of the 17th century.

Châteaux of Inland Brittany

Brittany's great wealth of château is especially rich in the east. Breton history provides a simple explanation: during the Middle Ages and particularly during the Hundred Years War, the region needed to defend itself against neighbouring France. Successive dukes and powerful barons therefore built impressive fortresses like Fougères, Combourg, Vitré, Châteaugiron and many more. However, once the Treaty of Union was signed, the east developed closer contacts with France and became more prosperous than the rest of Brittany. Château building reflects these changes: in the the Renaissance period, châteaux retained some defensive features – as in the Château de Bonnefontaine near Antrain – purely for aesthetic reasons, while the classical style did away with them altogether and beautiful residential palaces like Caradeuc near Bécherel were built by wealthy members of the Breton parliament.

FOUGÈRES

For details, see Caen–Vannes p. 110.

FOUGÈRES TO VITRÉ

The N12 to Rennes goes through **St-Aubin-du-Cormier**: the ruined keep of the 13th-century castle stands as a reminder of the battle which took place in 1488 between French and Breton forces, ending in the defeat of the Duke of Brittany. The road continues through the pleasant **Forêt de Rennes** and enters the capital from the north-east (see Rennes p. 253). Leave by the D463 towards **Châteaugiron**. This ancient feudal town still nestles round its mighty castle which has retained one of the most impressive keeps in Brittany (Guided tours of the castle and the town daily in July and Aug, *tel: 99 37 41 69*).

VITRÉ

Tourist Office: *pl. St-Yves, 35500 Vitré; tel: 99 75 04 46.*

Les Fêtes du bocage vitréen is a July festival offering concerts as well as theatre and dance performances in and around Vitré. For further details of the town, see Rennes to Le Mans route, p. 260.

VITRÉ TO CHÂTEAUBRIANT

Just south of Vitré, the charming **Château des Rochers-Sévigné** was the home of the Marquise de Sévigné, famous for her sensitive and witty correspondence with her daughter, which reveals a lot about 17th-century society (daily 1000-1230 and 1400–1815 June–Sept).

Drive south to **La Guerche-de-Bretagne**, an ancient trading centre which has a lively weekly market, watched over by the tall steeple of the **Basilique Notre-Dame** (**Tourist Office:** *pl. C. de Gaulle; tel: 99 96 30 78*).

Turn west on the D463 then left past the pleasant Marcillé lake to **La Roche-aux-Fées**. This superb prehistoric monument set among trees consists of 41 blocks of purple schist weighing between 5 and 40 tonnes each. According to legend, it was built around 2500 BC with the help of local fairies who carried the blocks inside their aprons.

CHÂTEAUBRIANT

Tourist Office: *22 r. de Couéré; tel: 40 28 20 90.* Open 0930–1200 and 1400–1800 except Mon morning and Sun. It organises guided tours of the old town.

Le Pont St-Jean, *5 r. Denieul et Gastineau; tel: 40 28 04 54* is a moderately priced, centrally situated hotel. Restaurants are plentiful and include *crêperies* and pizzerias.

Châteaubriant was once a border town defended by a strong medieval **château** partly destroyed in 1488; the square keep now faces the arcaded Renaissance wing built by Jean de Laval, first governor of Brittany (mid-June–mid-Sept guided tours FFr.12 and FFr.8). The **Église St-Jean-de-Béré** has a very early Romanesque chancel and crossing, and contains some remarkable 17th-century altarpieces.

CHÂTEAUBRIANT TO NANTES

Two more châteaux complete the line of defences of the ancient border of Brittany. The **Château de la Motte-Glain**, 20 km south-east of Châteaubriant, is set in beautiful surroundings on the edge of a small lake; rebuilt in 1496 in the Renaissance style, it has nevertheless retained several defensive features of an earlier age (*tel: 40 55 52 01*; open mid-June–mid-Sept 1430–1830, closed Tues).

Built on the north bank of the Loire, the **Château d'Ancenis** dates from the 15th century, but there had been other castles on this strategic site. The unusual gatehouse is obviously designed to slow down a possible attack. Note the fine residential building in Renaissance style (open daily 1500–1800 July and Aug). Take a stroll through Ancenis's old town from *pl. du Millénaire* along *r. des Tonneliers, r. du Gén. Leclerc* and *quai de la Marine.* (**Tourist Office:** *pl. du Millénaire; tel: 40 83 07 44*). Ancenis also feature as a diversion on the Nantes–Angers route, p. 189. A scenic road follows the south bank of the Loire, dotted with picturesque islands, the result of the gradual silting up of the river. Cross over to the north bank to reach the centre of Nantes (see p. 182).

ST-MALO–QUIMPER

From the Channel coast in the north-east to Cornouaille in the south-east, this route runs through the heart of Brittany, a region with no spectacular scenery but with a charm all of its own. It displays a subtle harmony between man and nature, a mellowness of form and colour, as you will discover when you see Josselin Castle reflected in the still waters of the Oust River or the wooded banks of Guerlédan Lake. The countryside of inland Brittany is as peaceful as the coastline can be wild. Proceed at a leisurely pace and allow three days.

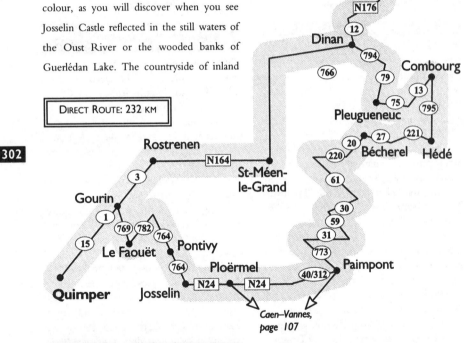

DIRECT ROUTE: 232 KM

Caen–Vannes, page 107

DIRECT ROUTE

There is no straight fast road going diagonally through central Brittany nor are there any large or even medium-sized towns along the route and it is possible to by-pass small ones as well.

The shortest distance between St-Malo and Quimper is 232 km. Leave St-Malo heading towards Rennes and follow the N137 for 16 km then turn right towards **St-Brieuc** on the N176; after 21 km, turn south on the D766. At **St-Méen-le-Grand**, take the N164 going west and follow it until you reach **Rostrenen**; 4 km beyond that town, take the D3 to **Gourin** and finally the D15 to Quimper.

SCENIC ROUTE

This 311 km-long route meanders slowly southwards along minor roads, crossing the **Canal d'Ille-et-Rance** and going through the **Forêt de Paimpont.**

From St-Malo, head for Rennes and turn right after 5 km towards La Passagère. Follow the east bank of the Rance, crossing at Port St-Hubert (D366). Turn left at Plouer-sur-Rance and drive along the D12 to **Dinan.** Leave Dinan on the D794 and, after 10 km, turn right on to D79 to **Pleugueneuc,** then left to La Chapelle-aux-Fitzméens and left again on D13 to **Combourg.** Leave Combourg to the south on D795; after 11 km turn left towards **Hédé.** Continue on the same road and cross the N137. Turn right on the D221 to Les Iffs; carry on until the road joins the D27 and turn right to **Bécherel.** Leave Bécherel on D20 towards the south-west, continue on D220 to Médréac and turn left onto D61 through Montauban in Iffendic. Bear right on D30 and proceed along D59 until you reach the **Forêt de Paimpont.** Turn right to the Tombeau de Merlin and the Fontaine de Jouvence, then left on the D31 to the Château de Comper; turn left again almost immediately on to D773 to **Paimpont** and right onto D40 which continues as the D312 and joins the old N24 leading to **Ploërmel.** Drive along N24 to **Josselin,** then continue westwards on D764 to Pontivy. Carry on along D764 for another 11 km, then bear left onto D782 to **Le Faouët** through Guéméne-sur-Scorff and Kernascléden. The D769 leads from Le Faouët to **Gourin.** Take D1 and D15 41 km south-west to Quimper

THE RANCE ESTUARY

Follow the scenic route, taking the minor road to La Passagère. The **Château du Bos** on the left is a typical 18th-century *malouinière,* a name given to manor houses belonging to wealthy shipowners from St-Malo (Guided visits daily in July and Aug).

Continue along the east bank of the Rance, a fjord-like estuary, 20 km deep, with small harbours, boatyards and tide mills; cross over at **Pont St-Hubert** where there are excellent views. Sea water does not penetrate beyond the lock known as the **Ecluse du Chatelier,** built across the narrowest part of the estuary.

DINAN

Tourist Office: *6 r. de l'Horloge BP 261, 22105 Dinan Cedex; tel: 96 39 75 40.* Open July and Aug 0900–1900, otherwise 0830–1230, 1400–1800; details of guided tours, bookings for boat trips and events. Purchase *Passeport pour l'Eté* (Summer Passport) a combined ticket which gives admission to various sights and includes a guided tour of the town: Fr.40.

ACCOMMODATION AND FOOD

The Tourist Office holds a long list of hotels, covering a wide price range including **Arvor,** *5 r. Pavie; tel: 96 39 21 22,* housed in an 18th-century stone building (moderate); **La Duchesse Anne,** *10 pl. Du Guesclin; tel: 96 39 09 63* (cheap).

For traditional cuisine, try **Le Jacobin,** *11 r. Haute-Voie; tel: 96 39 25 66* or **Le Pélican,** *3 r. Haute-Voie; tel: 96 39 47 05.* If you like grilled fish or meat and seafood, try **L'Aventure Grill,** *78 r. du Petit Fort* (by the harbour); *tel: 96 39 56 34.*

SIGHTSEEING

There are themed guided tours of the walled city July and Aug 1000 and 1500 except Sun and holidays.

From the top of the 15th-century **Tour de l'Horloge,** *r. de l'Horloge,* the former belfry and town hall, there is a

303

splendid view of the town; price Fr.14 adults (Fr.8 children). Corbelled houses with pointed gables, dating from the 15th and 16th centuries, line the narrow streets which have retained their medieval names, reflecting the city's prosperous cloth trade. The most remarkable houses can be seen round *pl. des Cordeliers* and *pl. des Merciers* and along adjacent streets. *R. de l'Ecole*, on the other hand, is lined with elegant 17th- and 18th-century mansions. Nearby is the **Couvent des Cordeliers**, now a college, with its 15th-century gate and cloisters. The **Église St-Malo** next door is a late Gothic church, while the **Église St-Sauveur** is partly Romanesque and partly Gothic. In the north transept, Du Guesclin's tomb contains the heart of this native of Dinan, a great military figure of the Hundred Years' War, who was buried in St-Denis Abbey next to the kings of France. Incorporated into the 3-km-long city walls, the **Château de Dinan** is an impressive oval keep housing the **Musée de Dinan,** which illustrates the history of the town (June–mid-Oct daily 1000–1830). The steep *r. du Jerzual* and *r. du Petit Fort* lead to the harbour, today almost exclusively used by pleasure boats. Across the old bridge, a tow path on the right follows the river to **Léhon** (2 km) where there is a splendid abbey and a ruined castle.

DINAN TO COMBOURG

Follow D794 towards Combourg for 10 km and turn right on D79 to Pleuguen-jeuc. The **Château de la Bourbansais** was built in the late 16th century by members of the Breton Parliament. It has beautiful French-style gardens, zoo; guided tours daily June–Aug.

COMBOURG

Tourist Information: Syndicat d'Initiative, *Maison de la Lanterne, pl. A. Parent, 35270 Combourg; tel: 99 73 13 93.* Open June–mid-Sept. List of holiday homes on request. Other accommodation ion the town includes four hotels (moderate) and one campsite.

The **Château de Combourg**, also known as Chateaubriand's Castle, is one of the best preserved medieval fortresses in Brittany. Admirably situated among dark trees overlooking a peaceful lake, it seems particularly awe-inspiring and enigmatic, an impression which is no doubt strengthened by the memory of the young François-René Chateaubriand who spent part of his lonely childhood there and later became one of the most eloquent Romantic poets (Apr–Oct daily except Tues 1400–1730, park open all day).

COMBOURG TO BÉCHEREL

Leave Combourg on the D795 to Rennes then turn left towards Hédé; traffic on the Ille-Rance Canal has to go through 11 locks in succession in order to negotiate a drop of 22 m. Go through the hilltop village of **Hédé** with its ruined castle. **Les Iffs** has one of the loveliest Gothic churches in the area: magnificent stained-glass windows, altarpieces and christening fonts. Just outside, the **Château de Montmuran** is a well-preserved defensive castle of the 13th and14th centuries with two drawbridges in working order (open daily 1400–1900 Easter–Oct).

BÉCHEREL

Tourist Information: Syndicat d'Initiative, *pl. A. Jéhanin; tel: 99 66 75 23.* Open mid-June–mid-Sept. otherwise *Mairie* (town hall), *tel: 99 66 80 55.*

Bécherel is another hilltop village. Note the fine old granite houses surrounding the market square

The speciality of Bécherel is books:

there are 13 bookshops, a bookbinder, and a monthly book market (for connoisseurs).

West of the village stands the **Château de Caradeuc**, often called the 'Breton Versailles' because of its classical style and beautiful park decorated with statues (Apr–mid-Sept 0900–1900, park only).

FORÊT DE PAIMPONT

The Paimpont Forest, covering 7000 hectares, is all that is left of the ancient **Forêt de Brocéliande**, birthplace of the legend of King Arthur. Various sights inside the forest are connected with characters such as Merlin, Viviane the enchantress, Lancelot and the scheming Morgane. These include the **Val Sans Retour** (the Valley of No Return) a delightful wooded valley, reached only on foot, where Morgane Le Fay imprisoned those who strayed off course.

Arriving from the north-east along the D59, turn right to the **Tombeau de Merlin** (Merlin's Tomb), decorated with a holly bush, and the **Fontaine de Jouvence** (Fountain of Youth) which brings eternal youth. Continue along the D31, on the edge of the forest to the **Château de Comper**, beside a lake, where Lancelot du Lac was brought up by Viviane. Turn left towards **Paimpont**, at the heart of the forest (**Tourist Information Centre**, next to the abbey, tel: 99 07 84 23; June–Sept daily; guided walks through the forest). For further details of Paimpont, see p. 111.

PLOËRMEL

For details of the town, see p. 112.

JOSSELIN

Tourist Information: Syndicat d'Initiative, *pl. de la Congrégation, 56120 Josselin; tel: 97 22 36 43.* Open July and Aug 1000–1200 and 1400–1800, other-

wise afternoons only. Hotels are reasonably priced and the campsite, located on the banks of the Oust is comfortable.

Josselin is rightly famous for its **Château des Rohans**, both massive and elegant, with its lofty medieval towers and Renaissance wing. The **Musée de Poupées** (Doll Museum) is housed in the stables (guided tours July and Aug 1000–1800; June, Sept afternoons only).

The old town is sandwiched between the castle and the hillside; in its centre stands the **Basilique Notre-Dame du Roncier**. Every year in Sept an important *pardon* celebrates the discovery by a humble farmer, in about 800, of a statue of the Virgin Mary beneath a bramble bush. The present church dates from the late 12th century. The **Festival Médiéval**, a medieval pageant involving about 1500 costumed participants, takes place in July.

PONTIVY

Tourist Information: Maison du Tourisme, *61 r. du Gén. de Gaulle, 56300 Pontivy; tel: 97 25 04 10.* Open June–Sept 1000–1800, otherwise closed for lunch. **Été Musical**, a classical summer music festival is held here in July and Aug.

ACCOMMODATION AND FOOD

Moderately priced hotels include **Le Porhoet**, *41 r. Gén. de Gaulle; tel: 97 25 34 88* and the cheaper **Napoléon**, *r. de la Butte; tel: 97 25 13 58.* The **HI** youth hostel is situated on Récollets Island; *tel: 97 25 58 27.* Most restaurants offer regional cuisine with a few variations. Try **Robic**, *2-4 r. J. Jaurès; tel: 97 25 11 80.*

SIGHTSEEING

Guided tours of the town leave from the Maison du Tourisme: July and Aug Tues Thur Sat 1000 and 1500.

Pontivy is two cities in one: the old

town which developed in the shadow of the mighty 15th-century **Château des Rohan** (July–Sept 1030–1900); and the 'new town' built by order of Napoleon Bonaparte when the Blavet River was canalised, and named Napoléonville. What remains of the old town is concentrated round the **Église Notre-Dame-de-Joie**, built in the 16th century in Flamboyant style.

⮒ SIDE TRACK
FROM PONTIVY

The **Lac de Guerlédan** lies 17 km north of Pontivy on D767 to Mur-de-Bretagne. Although the lake was artificially created in 1929, it has great natural beauty with its forested banks, picturesque creeks, old locks and ruined abbey. The south bank (take D35 from Mur-de-Bretagne to St-Aignan and turn right) is the most attractive (**Tourist Information**: *pl. Pobéguin, Cléguérec; tel: 97 38 00 15; pl. de l'Église, Mur-de-Bretagne; tel: 96 28 51 41*). ⬧

PONTIVY TO GOURIN

The route cuts across the green valleys of the Scorff and Ellé rivers, offering many possibilities of walks through unspoilt countryside (**Tourist Information: Syndicat d'Initiative**, *Mairie, Guémené-sur-Scorff; tel: 97 51 20 23*. There is also a Tourist Office in Le Faouët and *Syndicat d'Initiative* in Gourin, see below).

Leave Pontivy towards Guémené-sur-Scorff and **Kernascléden** where the **Église Notre-Dame** is a masterpiece of Flamboyant Gothic architecture. The decoration is light, elegant and not excessively rich; note in particular the south porches, rose windows, delicate pinnacles and gables. Inside, the vaulting and walls are decorated with frescos including a *Danse Macabre*, an illustration of Hell.

Further west, the **Chapelle St-Fiacre,** was built at the same time. The steeple surmounting the west front, flanked by two slim turrets, is remarkable. But the jewel of the chapel is its rood screen, in delicately carved wood, illustrating biblical scenes on the nave side and the seven deadly sins on the choir side.

An imposing 16th-century covered market stands in the main square of **Le Faouët** (**Tourist Office** *1 r. de Quimper; tel: 97 23 23 23*). The small town of **Gourin**, 16 km northwest, at the heart of the Montagnes Noires, is famous for its **Fête de la Crêpe** in July: three days in which to discover Breton traditions and to enjoy sweet and savoury pancakes (**Syndicat d'Initiative**, *24 r. de la Libération; tel: 97 23 66 33*).

Galettes and crêpes

These delicious snacks served in *crêperies* but also in the open for every festive occasion are not just another tourist attraction. They belong to a long-standing culinary tradition which goes back to the days when, accompanied by a bowlful of cider or *lait ribot* (a delicious slightly sour milk), they made up the usual Friday meal. *Galettes* are fairly thick and traditionally made from buckwheat, a cereal which disappeared for 25 years and is now making a comeback. Served with a filling of bacon, eggs, ham, cheese, tomatoes, even seafood, they are a complete meal in themselves. *Crêpes* are thin, sometimes so much so that they look like lace (*crêpes-dentelles*). Made from more refined wheatflour, they were considered a luxury in the majority of homes. Today they are served with a variety of sweet fillings and accompanied by a glass of *chouchenn*, an alcoholic drink made from honey, very much appreciated by ancient druids!

SAUMUR

Of the major Loire towns, Saumur, with its square-towered, hilltop château thrusting into the sky, presents the most charming silhouette. Around it is tree-fringed greenery and below it a huddle of red-roofed houses and the slender spire of St Peter's church. The fairy-tale look is completed by white limestone buildings gleaming in the sunlight and glowing in the night illuminations. Famous for its sparkling wines and its horse-riding school, the town is small, population 19,000, and boasts a number of interesting museums.

TOURIST INFORMATION

Tourist Office: *pl. de la Bilange 49418 Saumur; tel: 41 51 03 06.* Open Mon–Sat 0915–1900, Sun 1030–1230, 1530–1830 (June–Sept); Mon–Sat 0915–1230, 1400–1800, Sun 1000–1200 (Oct–May), with a selection of English information and bureau de change, open daily. It books hotels and *chambres d'hôtes* for a fee (Fr.5; outside Saumur, Fr.10; rest of France, Fr.25.).

ARRIVING AND DEPARTING

The N147 that links Angers and Poitiers passes through the town. To approach Saumur from Tours and the east, take N152 straight in to meet *av. de Gaulle*, turn left to cross over on the bridge (*Pont Cessart*) to *pl. de Bilange* for the Tourist Office and parking.

GETTING AROUND

The town centre is the area around *pl. de*

la Bilange so it is best to explore on foot. From nearby *pl. St. Pierre*, the hub of the old quarter, steep, picturesque streets, lead up to the château (*Montée du Fort*). By car, the road skirts around the historic core to reach the château car park at *r. des Moulins*.

Bus Saumur, *19 r. F. Roosevelt; tel: 41 51 11 87.* A single ticket is Fr.7.50. The town centre is so compact it is easier to walk, and there is no bus to the château.

STAYING IN SAUMUR

Accommodation

Although small, busy Saumur has a reasonable selection of two-star hotels and three which are three-star. Some are located on the riverside. Hotels near the rail station are well away from the centre and reached by crossing two bridges. There are a couple on the *Île d'Offard* (island). Booking ahead recommended because of the popularity of many equestrian events. Hotel chains include *IH*.

There is a **youth hostel** at *Île d'Offard; tel: 41 67 45 00.* **Camping**: *r. de Verden; tel: 41 67 45 00* (next to the youth hostel; they share the swimming pool).

Eating and Drinking

There is a wide choice of town-centre restaurants, many in the reasonably priced and cheaper ranges, including pizzerias, *crêperies* and burger bars. Mostly French cuisine is on offer; but Italian and Chinese is also available.

A bar/brasserie which is open daily is **La Bourse**, *1 pl. Bilange; tel: 41 51 02 05.* It stays open late, until 0030 (June–Oct). Leading away from the wide avenue of *pl.*

307

Bilange is the restaurant-packed, pretty *r. St-Nicholas*. The *pl. St-Pierre*, with its spired church and half-timbered houses, is a pleasant background for another busy restaurant area.

For food with views, there are three restaurants beside the château. Drive up the steep *av. du Peton* to get to the unpretentious **Restaurant du Château**, *r. des Moulins-Parking du Château; tel: 41 67 21 79*. It also has a souvenir shop and outdoor seating with stunning views. There are picnic tables. A short bridge walkway leads to the château entrance on the neigbouring hill. In the grounds is the smart **Délices du Château**; *tel: 41 67 65 60*, and next door, the informal **L'Orangerie**, *tel: 41 67 12 88* (closed Sun evening and Mon). It stages musical evenings in July and Aug.

A splendid pâtisserie and *salon de thé* is **La Duchesse Anne**, *22 r. F. Roosevelt; tel: 41 51 07 50*. Look for horse-shaped icing designs on chocolates, called *courbettes*, and gold-wrapped round ones cheekily called *crottins de cheval* (horse droppings), and a smartly turned-out chocolate ice-cream cake, called *glace cadre noir*, named after the horse-riding school's *élite*. Other chocolates resemble wine bottle corks or mushrooms

For food shopping, **Les Halles** (central market), *pl. St-Pierre*, is open Tues–Fri 0800–1230, Sat 0700–1300, 1500–1930; Sun 0900–1230. Inside, the **Spar** supermarket is open Mon–Sat 0800–2030; Sun 0800–1200.

Park benches for impromptu picnics are not plentiful but try the *Jardin des Plantes*, and *Jardin de Verdun*.

Communications

Main **post office** is at *r. Volney*. Open Mon–Fri 0800–1830; Sat 0800–1200, it has bureau de change and poste restante.

Money

Banks and bureaux de change are closed Sun, Mon. One exception is the **Banque de France**, *r. Beaurepaire*. Open Mon–Fri 0845–1200, 1345–1530.

ENTERTAINMENT

There a few late-night music bars in the streets around *pl. de la Bilange* which is also the site of the **theatre**; *tel: 41 51 01 41*. On summer evenings, *r. St-Nicholas* has bands playing outdoors to entertain diners at the many restaurant terraces. The **cinema**, *13 quai Carnot*, has French films only.

Events

Animations Saumur et sa région is a free brochure, French only, listing events and exhibitions, Apr–Oct. Classical concerts, jazz, ballet and theatrical events are staged at the château (mid-June–mid-Sept); Fr.30. There are many equestrian events. The **Cadre Noir**, a display team from the national riding school, give demonstrations of classical, academic riding at *pl. du Chardonet* and at neighbouring St-Hilaire-St-Florent (see Angers–Saumur, p. 53). The musical *Reprise,* described as 'airs above the ground', takes place in Apr, May, June, Sept; days vary. Reservations; *tel: 41 53 50 66*.

SHOPPING

The main shopping street is *r. Franklin Roosevelt*, which contains the department stores **Printemps** and **Monoprix** and many clothes shops.

Some local wines have labels with a horsey motif. Saumur is famous as a sparkling white wine region, with 20 million bottles produced annually. Besides selling the full range of regional wines, **Maison du Vin**, *25 r. Beaurepaire; tel: 41 51 16 40,* has display boards listing the ratings of the vintage years and information

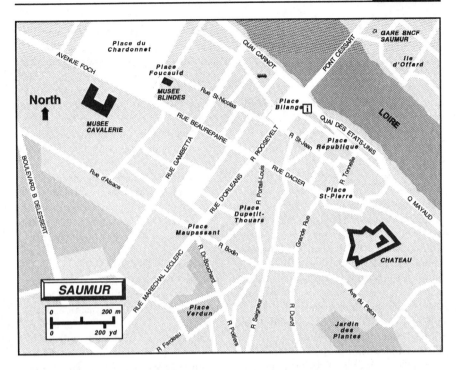

about vineyards which welcome visitors. Open Mon–Sat 0900–1230, 1400–1830 (June–Sept); Tues–Sat 0900–1230, 1400–1830 (Oct–May).

Fruit-based liqueurs, such as the orange-based *triple sec* and the multi-blended *Royal Combier*, are sold in the traditional shop of the **Distellerie Combier**, *48 r. Beaurepaire; tel: 41 51 27 90.* It recently opened to the public for behind-the-scene guided tours, including in English. Open 1000–1200, 1400–1800 (June–Sept). Fr.15 (Fr.12 children).

SIGHTSEEING

Walking tours in French explore *vieux Saumur* (old town), Tues 1500, 2100; Thur 1500 (July–Sept); Fr.25. Horse and carriage drives, 40 mins, take place Mon–Fri 1500, 1900 (July–Aug); Fr. 32. A cruise on the Loire leaves Tues–Sat

1500, 1700 (July–Aug). Fr.30. The 1-hr cruise is on a large, homely wooden boat, with commentary in French. The *Jean-Charlotte, tel: 41 67 55 29*, leaves from a mooring in front of the town hall. In case of low tide, it leaves from the marina at St-Hilaire-St-Florent.

For its views of Saumur, the large **Île d'Offard** makes a fine stroll and has some shops and houses. There are watersport centres such as **Club Samaurois Canoë Kayak**; half-day canoe hire is Fr.60.

Le Château de Saumur; *tel: 41 41 30 46.* stands fortress-like, on a steep hill overlooking the Loire. The château is mostly 14th century, built on the foundations of a 12th century castle. Its romantic look appealed to the 15th century artist who illustrated it for the manuscript *Les Très Riches Heures du Duc de Berri*. In turn, it affords romantic views of the Loire from its open windows especially at sunset during evening tours. The château houses two main museums.

Museums

The **Musée des Arts Décoratifs** has wonderful collections of porcelain, ceramics, enamel work, furniture and tapestries, from the 14th–16th centuries. On the upper floors is the **Musée du Cheval** (horse museum), laid out in grand halls with timbered ceilings. It provides a fascinating look at the history of the horse's place in man's world including Asia, Africa and America. Modern displays focus on Californian cowboys as well as Mexican and Argentinian gauchos.

Both museums are open daily 0900–1800; also evening tours Wed, Sat, 2000–2230 (June–Sept); daily 0930–1200, 1400–1730 (Oct, Apr, May); Wed–Mon 0930–1200, 1400–1730 (Nov–Mar); Fr.30. Guided visits only, English possible during the day (French only in the evening). The château courtyard provides a romantic setting to many summer events including musical concerts (featuring jazz, choral singing or classical quartets). There are also readings of works by French authors such as Rabelais.

Within the château's former gunpowder factory is **Le Musée de la Figurine-Jouet** (model museum); *tel: 41 67 39 23.* This privately run museum displays 20,000 figures including model soldiers. Open 1400–1800 (mid-June–mid-Sept). Fr. 12.

Saumur's famous **École de Cavalerie** (cavalry school) developed from 1763. Its crack riding teams came to be called the *Cadre Noir* because of their black uniforms, edged in gold, topped with two-cornered headgear. The school, now based in St-Hilaire-St-Florent, (see Angers–Saumur route, p. 53) trains the *élite* of the French cavalry and the officers for the armoured

regiments. Its jewelled swords, uniforms, medals and photographs are on display at the **Musée de la Cavalerie**, *av. Mar. Foch; tel: 41 83 93 06.* Open Tues–Thurs, Sun, public holidays 0900–1200, 1400–1700; Sat 1400–1700. Admission free (passport must be presented at the entrance). The musuem faces *pl. du Chardonnet*, the large sandy arena used for equestrian displays. Nearby is the **Musée des Blindés** (museum of the armoured corps), *pl. Charles de Foucauld; tel: 41 67 20 96.* The displays show armoured vehicles, with tanks from 12 countries. Open daily 0900–1200, 1400–1800. Fr.20 (Fr.15).

> ### ⬏ SIDE TRACKS
> ### FROM SAUMUR
>
> Saumur is the meeting point of several long-distance walking paths and the towns near it are good bases for pleasant walks. A set of walking route leaflets in English, the best produced in the Loire Valley, is sold at the Tourist Office. Fr.44. Called *Around Saumur*, it describes 22 walks, devised as circular routes, with good parking places at the starting points which include Cunault, Fontevraud and Saint-Georges-des-Sept-Voies. Depending on the length of the walk, it may be practicable to stay overnight at or near a starting point, such as the delightful château village of **Montreuil-Bellay** (18 km from Saumur). From here there are two walks, one following yellow markers, (2 hr 30 min, 8 km), which takes in the **River Thouet**, the other following blue markers, (5hr, 14.5 km), which crosses vineyards and the Brossay forest. **Montreuil-Bellay Tourist Office:** *r. Marché; tel: 41 52 32 39* (open May–Sept); in winter, the town hall; *tel: 41 52 33 86.* There is a *LF* hotel. ⬏

SAUMUR–TOURS

Highlights of this tour include the poignantly simple resting place of English kings at Fontevraud Abbey, the dream-like charms of the fairy-tale castle at Ussé and the delightful nocturnal promenades at romantic Azay-le-Rideau, the contrasting homes of the writers Rabelais and Balzac, the lively fortress town of Chinon and the outstanding gardens at Villandry. Along the way, the rivers Vienne and Indre add their own majesty to the river vistas of the Loire Valley.

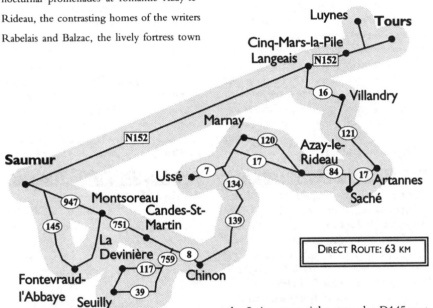

311

DIRECT ROUTE: 63 KM

ROUTES

DIRECT ROUTE

Cross the bridge and follow the N152 along the north bank of the Loire, 63.5km, which nevertheless takes in the château at Langeais.

SCENIC ROUTE

This 150 km route stays mostly south of the Loire. Take D947 alongside the Loire, turn right onto the D145 past Champigny to **Fontevraud**. Then take the D947 to **Montsoreau**, then the D751 to **Candes-St-Martin** where the merging of the Loire and Vienne is striking. Continue on D751 past **St Germain-sur-Vians** and **Thizay**, turn right onto D759 , then first right on D117 to **La Devinière**. The continue making first left into **Seuilly**, after the abbey turn right onto D224 to join D39 to rejoin D759 towards Chinon. Immediately after crossing the river turn right on D8 to Chinon. Then take D751, turn left on D139 past

St. Benoit-la-Fôret, turn left on D134 to Rigny-Ussé and turn left on D7 to the château. Take D7 back past **Rivarennes**, turn right onto D17 to cross the River Indre to **Azay-le-Rideau**. Alternatively, continue on D7 to D20, turn right for **Marnay** and its museum in the wood, then continue on D120/D57 to **Azay-le-Rideau**.

After Azay-le-Rideau, take D84 via the bridge crossing to Saché, then continue on D17 past Pont de Ruan. Turn left at **Artannes-sur-Indres** on the D121 towards Druyé. Keep following the D121 which turns right towards **Villandry**. From Villandry take the D16 to the bridge on D57, turn right to cross the river to Langeais. Then take N152 to Cinq-Mars-la-Pile. Then follow N152 to Tours, but take a 1 km detour to the lovely town of Luynes about half way along.

Sept); 0930–1200, 1400–1800 (third Sunday in Sept–Oct); daily 0930–1230, 1400–1730 or nightfall (Nov–first week in April). Fr.27; (Fr.10). From June to Sept there are guided tours in English, at 1100, 1400 and 1700; otherwise visits are self-guided with an English leaflet. A must-see site, this atmospheric monastic complex has royal funerary effigies, still showing vestiges of bright paint on their robes and strikingly serene in the empty, plain 12th-century abbey church. Here lie Henri II, his wife, Eleanor of Aquitaine, their son Richard III and their daughter-in-law, Isabel of Angoulême (who had been married to King John). There is some parking in the streets 50m from the abbey and at *Place du 8 Mai*, about 400 m from the abbey. There are summer concerts; for information and bookings, contact **Centre Culturel de l'Ouest**; *tel: 41 51 73 52.*

FONTEVRAUD

Tourist Office: *Chapelle Ste Catherine 49590 Fontevraud; tel: 41 51 79 45.* Open Mon–Sat 1000–1200, 1430–1830; also Sun, public holidays 1430–1830 (June–Sept). It is in a 13th-century chapel from which various guided tours leave (June–Sept), most are Fr.20. It arranges accommodation and has mostly French leaflets.

ACCOMMODATION

The pleasant town has some small hotels, both pricey and reasonable. Surprisingly, there is a very smart hotel and restaurant in the abbey grounds – the **Hôtellerie du Prieuré-St-Lazare** *BP 14, 49590 Fontevraud-l'Abbaye; tel: 41 51 73 16.*

SIGHTSEEING

Abbaye Royale de Fontevraud, *tel: 41 51 71 41.* Open Daily 0920–1230, 1400–1830 (second week in April–May); daily 0900–1900 (June–third Sunday in

MONTSOREAU

Tourist Office: *Île Verte 49730; tel 41 51 70 22.* Open 1000–1300, 1500–1900 (mid-May–June); 1000–1300, 1430–1900 (July–Aug); 1000–1300, 1700–1800 (Sept until the third week). For off-season tourist information, contact the town hall; *tel: 41 51 76 60.*

ACCOMMODATION

There are a couple of hotels and several *chambres d'hôte* and a campsite, *tel: 41 51 76 60*, right next to the Tourist Office. This charming town has streets lined with 15th- and 16th-century houses.

SIGHTSEEING

Château de Montsoreau, *49739 Montsoreau; tel: 41 51 70 25.* Open Wed–Mon 1000–1200, 1400–1830 (May–Sept). Wed–Mon 1330–1730 (Mar, Apr, Oct, Nov). Fr.27; (Fr15 children). This creamy, tall building looms importantly at the edge of the wide confluence of the rivers Loire and Vienne, where there are sandy beaches and a few fishing boats. There is also a **military museum** about the French conquest of Morocco, featuring the *goums* (knights), the cavalry units who fought for their conquerors. Alexandre Dumas wrote his novel *La Dame de Montsoreau* based on Françoise, one of the occupant's unfaithful wife, who caused her lover's murder when her husband forced her to make an assignation.

CANDES-ST-MARTIN

Just one and a half km from Montsoreau, the two rivers meet at this lovely, cobbled village, where vineyards fringe the river banks. St Martin of Tours, a Roman soldier who became a Christian missionary, died here on 8 Nov 397. The event is marked by his effigy in the chapel of Candes **church**, built in the 11th and 12th centuries. From the hilltop is a splendid view of the confluence of the rivers.

SEUILLY

La Devinière à Seuilly, *37500 Seuilly; tel: 47 95 91 18*. Open Wed–Mon 0900–1200 1400–1700 (Feb–mid-Mar, Oct–Nov); daily 0900–1200, 1400–1800 (mid-Mar–Apr); daily 1000–1900 (May–Sept). Fr.20 (Fr.14). Parking is in a field facing the museum, about five mins walk. The bawdy French satirist and philosopher François Rabelais was born around 1490 in this hamlet, in his parents' humble stone house which has a huge dovecote. Stone steps lead to his room and a small museum exploring the creation of his hero *Gargantua*. His education began at the nearby abbey of Seuilly, which is now used for tourist accommodation. It is open for viewing Apr–Sept by appointment. **Abbaye de Seuilly**, *37500 Seuilly; tel: 47 75 93 15*.

CHINON

Tourist Office: *12 r. Voltaire 37500 Chinon tel: 47 93 17 85*. Open Mon–Sat 0900–1900, Sun 0900–1230 (mid-June–mid-Sept). Mon–Sat 0900–1215, 1400–1830; also Sun from Easter (mid-Sept–mid-June. Tourist information also available on the *rte de Tours* beside the château Sun 1000–1830 (July–Aug). There are many small hotels, some in fine converted old houses. The main office arranges hotels, *chambres d'hôtes* and there are leaflets in English plus details of boat rides and the many wine festivals, special markets and *son et lumière* events. The château and town are intertwined to create a dramatic skyline setting and a lively, pretty place with pedestrianised streets and many cafés, bars and restaurants.

Château de Chinon, *tel: 47 93 13 45*. Open daily 0900–1800 (mid-March–June; Sept); daily 0900–1900 (July–Aug); daily 0900–1700 (Oct). Open daily (closed Wed in Dec, Jan) 0900–1200, 1400–1700 (Nov–mid-March). Fr.23. Guided tours in English are available as well as an English leaflet. The château has wonderful views over the old turreted houses and the River Vienne, plus wax-figure tableaux of the town's historical highlights. The one-way system and narrow streets prevent cars from venturing too far into the centre of town, which has many 15th- 16th- and 17th-century houses. Henry II of England died here, so did his mortally wounded son Richard the Lionheart in 1199. The dauphin, later Charles VII, came to meet Joan of Arc for the first time here. Even though he tried to mingle with the crowd, she recognised him and announced her divine mission to save his kingdom. Tastings of the ruby coloured fragrant Chinon wine are part of the visit to the **Musée Animée du Vin et de la Tonnellerie** (museum of wine-making

313

and cooperage), *12 r. Voltaire; tel: 47 93 25 63.* Open daily 1000–1230, 1400–1900. Fr.20; (Fr.15). Mechanical figures relate the story of wine-making; there are recorded commentaries in English. **Musée du Vieux Chinon et de la Batellerie** is a museum of town history and canal industry, *44 r. St. Maurice tel: 47 93 18 12.* Open daily 1000–1230, 1400–1930 (Easter–mid-Nov). Fr.20; (Fr.15).

RIGNY-USSÉ

Château d'Ussé *37420 Rigny-Ussé;tel: 47 95 54 05.* Its cluster of turrets look even more charming from the bridge or from the banks of the Loire, and it is easy to see how the writer Charles Perrault, who wrote such children's stories as *Little Red Riding Hood,* based his 1697 masterpiece *Sleeping Beauty* on this castle. Certainly Disney's castle echoes this silhouette. Inside, the wax-figure tableaux seem stilted in the otherwise lushly decorated rooms hung with Flemish tapestries. The château boasts a lovely Gothic chapel. Open 1000–1200, 1400–1730 (Feb–mid-Mar; last-week of Sept-second week Nov); 0900–1200, 1400–1800 (mid-Mar–Easter); 0900–1200, 1400, 1845 (Easter–mid-July; first three weeks in Sept); 0900–1830 (mid-July–Aug); 0900–1200. Fr.57 Helicopter rides leave from Château Ussé for excursions to various sites including Chinon, Langeais, Azay-Le-Rideau, Villandry and Fontevraud., with prices ranging from Fr.400 per person, for a 12-min ride to Chinon to Fr.1120 for a 35-min multi-site flight. **Heli 37,** *37420 Rigny-Ussé; tel: 47 95 43 38,* or ask at the château.

AZAY-LE-RIDEAU

Tourist Office: *pl de l'Europe; Azay-le-Rideau 37190; tel: 47 45 44 40.* Open Mon–Thur 0900–1300, 1430–1830, Fri

0900–1300, 1430–1900, Sat–Sun 1000–1300, 1400–1900 (Easter–Sept); Tues–Sat 1500–1800 (Oct–Easter) The little village has some family hotels and a selection of restaurants. Thanks to its stunning château, many riverside views, pleasant narrow streets and old houses as well as a 12th-century church, it gets busy so parking can be difficult.

SIGHTSEEING

Château d'Azay-Le-Rideau, *tel: 47 45 42 04.* Open daily 0930–1800, (Mar–June, Sept–Oct); 0900–1900 (July–Aug); 0930–1800 (first two weeks of Nov); 0930–1230, 1400–1730 (15 Nov–Feb). Fr.32 (Fr.21). Tours can be self-guided (with English leaflet) or guided (French only) This highly decorative château, always used as a summer residence since it was built in the early 16th century, makes the most of its pretty riverside setting with its annual **Les Imaginaires d'Azay-le-Rideau,** a type of *son et lumière* performance staged as a nocturnal promenade between the park and the château. Individuals take the route at their own pace. Open 2230–0030 (May–July) 2200–0030 (Aug–Sept) Last admission midnight. Fr.60; (Fr.35). Tickets sold at the door and during château opening hours. Outside the town of Marnay is the **Musée Maurice Dufresne,** *Marnay 37190 Azay-le-Rideau; tel: 47 45 36 18.* Open daily 0915–1800 (Mar–Dec). Closed Jan–Feb. In a large woodland site, the museum shows 2000 antique machines of all sort – motorcycles, cars and weaving looms. A working mill, snack bar and a picnic area are also on site. Fr.48; (Fr.25).

SACHÉ

Demeure de Balzac, *37190 Saché tel: 47 26 86 50.* Open daily 0930–1200, 1400–1800 (mid-Mar–June; Sept); 0930–1830

314

(July–Aug); Wed–Mon 0900–1200, 1400–1700 (Oct–Nov); 1000–1200, 1400–1700 (Feb–mid-Mar). Closed Dec, Jan. Fr.21; (Fr.17). English leaflet for self-guided tour. Guided tours in French. The elegant, simple decoration reflects the calm which the industrious novelist, Honoré de Balzac, 1799–1850, sought at this delightful house where there are manuscripts, letters and original editions.

VILLANDRY

Château de Villandry *37510 Villandry* tel: *47 50 02 09*. Open daily 0900–180 (June–mid-Sept); 0930–1730 (mid-Feb–June; mid-Sept–mid Nov). Gardens open daily 0830–2000 (June–mid-Sept); 0900–1900 or nightfall (mid-Sept–May). English leaflet for self-guided tour. Château and gardens Fr.40. Gardens only Fr.27. The amazing gardens are a wonder. The vast expanse is stunningly laid out on three levels, the first with an ornamental lake, the second with flowers planted between box hedges, and the third a decorative vegetable, or kitchen, garden. A slide-show of the garden changing during the four seasons is on view inside the elegantly furnished château, which was completed in 1536 by Jean Le Breton, a finance minister of François I. Through the windows, the extravaganza of geometric and heart shapes in the flower beds continues to attract the eye on tours of the château. It is near the Cher, another branch of the Loire.

LANGEAIS

Tourist Office: *La Mairie. 37130 Langeais; tel: 47 96 58 22*. Open Mon–Sat 0900–1700, Sun 1000–1230, 1430–1800 (third week June–Sept); 0900–1200, 1500–1800 (Oct–Easter) Also Sun 0900–1230, (May–June, Oct–Nov). Arranges accommodation in hotels, *chambres d'hôte* and *gîtes*. A very busy town bristling with

traffic, it has a selection of hotels and restaurants. It takes on a rural charm during its Sunday market, where the wares on sale include the melons which appear on its coat of arms.

Château de Langeais, *37139 Langeais; tel: 47 96 72 60*. Open daily 0900–1830 (mid-Mar–mid-July; Sept–Oct); 0900–2200 (mid-July–Aug); 0900–1200, 1400–1700 (Nov–mid-March). Fr.35; (Fr.17). Guided tours in French are available with English notes provided. This fortified 15th-century château glories in its one spectacular moment of history, the marriage of Charles VIII and Anne of Brittany in 1491. The event is recreated in a wax-figure tableau in a room with fine Flemish and Aubusson tapestries. The building is all the more remarkable for being relatively unchanged since first built as a fortress with drawbridge and portcullis, in just six years in the mid-15th century. The very late closures in summer allow for the treat of sunset watching over the Loire valley from the formal, pretty gardens.

315

CINQ-MARS-LA-PILE

On top of a hill in this quiet hamlet, there is a mysterious solid *pile* (tower) topped with four small pyramids. One theory of its origin is that it was a mausoleum built in the second century AD. **Château de Cinq-Mars** *37130 Langeais; tel: 47 96 40 49*. Open Tues–Sun 0900–1200, 1400–1900 Mar–Oct. Closed last two weeks Feb and last week Oct, first week Nov. Fr.12; guided tour in French, Fr.20. Two medieval towers, with three rooms each, survive from the old château of the Marquis Cinq-Mars. Unexpectedly there are two *chambres d'hôte* in the garden wing. Advance booking required. There are sweeping views of the Loire Valley and the gardens are romantically pleasant.

TOURS

This pleasant city, population 160,000, exudes a lively metropolitan confidence, boasts a central location within the Loire Valley and is very well-organised in showing off its attractions to visitors. It lacks a grand château but has an interesting 13th-century cathedral with a flamboyant façade, two picturesque enclaves – the cathedral quarter and the 'old town' – to explore, fine museums and pretty parks. Although it is located between the Loire and Cher, neither river features prominently on today's tourist scene, yet they made Tours an important trade centre and crossroads in the Roman era. Tours also became a pilgrimage stop, thanks to St Martin who was much venerated from the 4th century onwards and whose tomb is in the basilica.

TOURIST INFORMATION

Tourist Office: *78–82 r. Bernard Palissy* (facing the rail station), *B.P. 4201, 37042 Tours; tel: 47 70 37 37.* Open Mon–Sat 0830–1830, Sun, public holidays 1000–1300 (May, Sept); Mon–Sat 0830–1830, Sun, public holidays 1000–1230 and 1500–1800 (June–Aug); Mon–Sat 0900–1230, 1330–1800; Sun, public holidays 1000–1300 (Oct–Apr). There is a high proportion of English-speaking staff and the office has many leaflets, including walking route maps in English and organises regular walking tours, some in English. It will make hotel bookings in the city and the region. There is a bureau de change open on Sun and Mon when banks are closed.

ARRIVING AND DEPARTING

The A10 from Paris passes just east of the city centre. To approach Tours from Blois and the east, follow N152 along the River Loire to *quai Paul Bert*, turn left to cross the bridge, *Pont Wilson*, to *pl. Anatole France.* There is parking either side of the square.

GETTING AROUND

The **r. Nationale** is the backbone of the city, defining three distinct areas for visitors that are easy to explore by foot. Firstly, the road itself leads to the Loire, ending in a cluster of attractions. On its east side is the **cathedral**, on its west the **'old town'** quarter. There are ten car parks (the one beside the banks of the Loire is free), which are clearly marked on the free maps given at the Tourist Office.

FilBleu, *3 r. de la Dolve,* off *pl. Jean Jaurès, tel: 47 66 70 70,* is the information office for the efficient bus service. Open Mon–Fri 0730–1900; Sat 0900–1830. Free route maps and timetables available. Most buses go down *r. Nationale*, with *pl. Jean-Jaurès* the main terminal. A single ticket, valid one hour, is Fr.6.50. Tickets available in booklets of five and ten, Fr.28; Fr.54. Night service lines, N1 and N2, start around 2130 and end about half an hour after midnight.

STAYING IN TOURS

Accommodation

There is a wide choice of two- and three-star hotels plus two four-star hotels. Many,

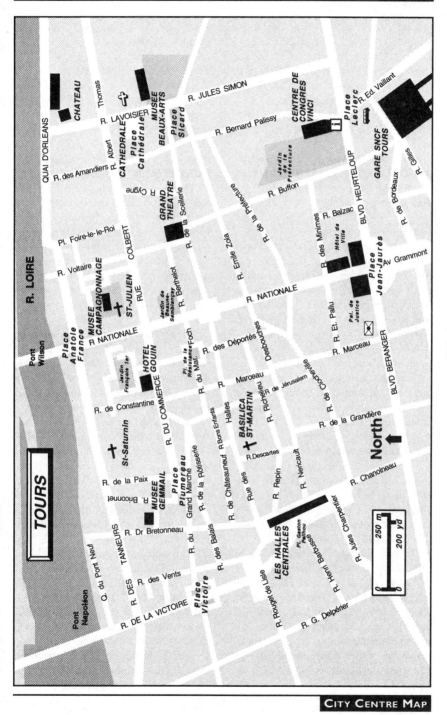

including some of the chain hotels, are found in *r. Edouard Vaillant* beside the rail station. Others are in pleasant streets near just north of the station (*r. V. Laloux, r. B. Palissy*). The cathedral quarter and the old town also have a good selection.

Hotel chains in Tours include *Ba, BW, Ca, Ct, F1, Hd, Ib, Mc, Nv, Pr, RC* and *RS*.

HI: youth hostel at *av. d'Arsonval, parc de Grandmot; tel: 47 25 14 45*. **Camping Municipal Edouard Peron**; *N152-quai Paul Bert; tel: 47 54 11 11*.

Eating and Drinking

The best choice of eating places in all price ranges is in the town's *vieux ville* (old town) quarter where every other building is a brasserie, bistro, *crêperie*, pizzeria, or restaurant, especially at *pl. Plumereau* and the streets radiating from it – *r. du Commerce, r. du Change* and *r. Grand Marché* – where, in the summer, there are street musicians.

Among the cuisines represented in the city are American, Mexican, Chinese, Vietnamese, Indian, Italian, Portuguese, Spanish and Greek.

The cathedral side is less bustling, but has smarter restaurants especially on *r. Colbert*. Again there is cuisine from several nationalities. A reasonably-priced restaurant in a 16th-century building is **Le Franglais**, *27 r. Colbert, tel: 47 61 62 44,* influenced by French and English cuisines (closed Sun).

A third busy area of restaurants is *pl. Jean Jaurès* (at the southern end of *r. Nationale*) and the wide *av. de Grammont* leading away from it. This area exudes the lively air of big city boulevards, busy with traffic but also with plenty of outdoor seating on the terrace fronts, ideal for people-watching. Open daily until late is **Brasserie de l'Univers**, *8 pl. Jean Jaurès;*

tel: 47 05 50 92, with food served until midnight. Specialising in seafood is **La Chope**, *25 bis av. de Grammont; tel: 47 20 15 15,* open daily until 0100.

Local specialities include *rillons* (small chunks of breast of pork) as a starter, *rillettes* (potted shredded pork or goose), *porc aux pruneaux* (pork with prunes in a cream and white wine sauce), *charbonée* (pork stew in red wine sauce) and *andouilletes* (grilled spicy tripe sausages).

There are many *charcuteries, pâtisseries* and *confiseries* for buying ready-to-eat snacks for informal picnics on park benches. For picnic sites try the willow-fringed bank of the Loire (take the steps down at *pl. Anatole France*) or the prettily-landscaped parks (*sq. Francois Sicard,* the informal half of the Musée des Beaux Arts garden and Mirabeau park) and *pl. de la Cathédrale*.

In the confectionery shops, look for *pruneaux farcis* (prunes stuffed with almonds). They are sold at **La Livre Tournois**, *6 r. Nationale; tel: 47 66 99 99,* which offers guided visits. It is also a *salon de thé,* one of several along the street.

Bread baked in wood-fired ovens is available at **Au Vieux Four**, *7 pl.des Petites Boucheries* (behind the cathedral); *tel: 47 66 62 33,* open Tues–Sat. It offers behind-the-scenes visits with commentary, in French, and breakfast. Fr.38.

For grocery shoping, there is a super-market (within the **Monoprix** department store), open Mon–Sat 0900–1900. There is a small supermarket beside the rail station, **ATAC**, *pl. Gen. Leclerc,* open Mon–Sat 0830–2000; Sun 0930–1230. The covered **Les Halles Centrales** (central market) is open daily,although some of the merchants close Sun morning and others close Mon morning. On the lower level of the building is the excellent cheese shop, **France Fromage**, *tel: 47 38 65 39,* which features seasonal cheeses such as *gaperon*. Other cheese shops of note are **Parfum de Buerre**, *2. r. Marceau; tel: 47 64 23 36*. Open Mon 1430–2030, Tues–Sat 0830–1245 and1500–2030; Sun 0930–1330.

Markets are held Tues–Sun in various streets, such as *pl. St-Paul* (Tues-Fri), *Les Fontaines* (Wed-Sat) and *pl. Velpeau* (Thurs, Fri afternoon, Sun)

In the old town quarter, **La Comtesse du Barry**, *24 r. Charles-Gilles; tel: 47 61 31 24*, is a gourmet must, selling *foie gras*, *grand cru* wines, preserves and ready-to-eat specialities. Open Mon 1430–1930, Tues–Sat 0930–1230 and 1430–1930.

Communications
The main **post office** at *1 blvd Béranger* is open Mon–Fri 0800–1900 and Sat 0800–1200. It has *poste restante* facilities and a bureau de change open the same hours.

Money
Banks and bureaux de change are closed Sun and Mon. There are two exceptions. The bureau de change kiosk at the rail station is open daily (including Sun and public holidays), 0730–1900; *tel: 47 20 00 26*. **Crédit Agricole** (beside the rail station), *10 r. E. Vaillant*, is open Mon, Tues, Thurs 0900–1230, 1330–1715; Wed 0930–1230, 1330–1715; Fri 0900–1230, 1330–1615 (closed Sat, Sun).

Consulates
Belgium: *6 r. d'Entraigues; tel 47 66 47 98*.
Netherlands: *36 pl. G. Pailhour; tel: 47 61 30 49*.

A twice-yearly magazine, in French, *Le chaînon*, listing musical, theatrical, cine-matic and artistic programmes, is available free at the Tourist Office.

At the **Grand Théâtre**, *34 r. de la Scellerie; tel 47 05 37 87*, opera, operettas, drama and classical concerts take place inside a rococo interior. A repertory company is based at the **Théâtre Louis Jouvet**, *12 r. Léonard-de-Vinci; tel: 47 64 50 50*. Also used for theatre and concerts is the modern **Centre de Congrès Vinci**, *26 blvd Heurteloup; tel: 47 70 70 70*.

There are several cinemas. Located behind the cathedral, the six-screen **Les Studios**, *2 r. des Ursulines; tel: 47 05 22 80*, always show some films which are marked V.O. for *version originale* (original language version) of foreign films. A cinema season of classic French and foreign films (in original language) is organised by **Cinémathèque de Tours**, *7 r. des Tanneurs; tel: 47 39 04 97*. Showings are on Wed, 1000 and 2000 at the **Olympia cinema**, *r. de Lucé; tel: 47 05 71 62*, or at the **Rex**, *47 r. Nationale; tel 47 05 71 62*.

Discotheques are found mainly in the streets around *pl. Plumereau*, including *r. de la Monnaie*, usually opening around 2200 and closing at 0400. With 28,000 university students around, the bars and pubs in the same area are very lively. The pub ambiance is popular, and regulars flock to **Le Sherlock Holmes**, *13 r. du Grand Marché; tel: 47 20 02 02*. Nearby is the Irish pub **Buck Mulligan's**, *37 r. du Grand Marché; tel: 47 39 61 69*.

Events
Annually there is a two-week **Florilège Vocal de Tours** (choral singing festival), held late May/early June; the **Fêtes Musicales en Touraine** (chamber music festival), takes place in mid-June; a three-week **Semaines Musicales de Tours** (classical musical festival) is held in July and there is the two-month **Les Feuilles**

319

d'Automne (jazz festival) Oct–Nov. Tickets for many events are available at the record and bookshop called **fnac** (on the first floor of the **Galeries National**), 72 r. National; tel: 47 31 27 00. Open Mon–Sat 1000–1900.

SHOPPING

The main shopping street is the r. Nationale which has department stores (**Monoprix, Galeries National**) as well as a wide selection of clothes shops. Many are closed Mon (or Mon morning). Antique shops are found in the r. Colbert area, including English furniture and knick-knacks at **Antiquités Anglaises**, 33 r. de Cygne; tel: 47 61 26 26. A bric-à-brac/antiques market is held at pl de Victoire, Wed and Sat mornings.

SIGHTSEEING

Walking tours (in French and English) leave daily from the Tourist Office, 1000 (mid-June–mid-Sept). An introductory walk, in French and English, leaves Sat–Tues, Thurs. There are two themed walks: the Renaissance, Wed at 1000; and the St-Martin neigbourhood Fri, 1000. A greater variety of themed walks are held in Apr–June, Oct (days vary), covering subjects that include the Roman period, 18th-century architecture, churches and stained glass. Fr.30 (Fr.25).

A brochure Tours – the Loire Valley, in English, describes the museums and attractions and has a simplified map. There are well-produced walking routes with maps, in English, free. Tours – A City of Art and History includes the cathedral area and the old town quarter. Tours – The Royal City takes in royal connections from Louis XI to Henri IV. Tours – Gardens of France gives historical and botanical details about the public gardens.

A **carte mult-visites** (multi-visit card) allows admission to the municipal museums and includes one guided tour; Fr.50.

The no. 12 bus is a city centre minibus following a circular route, which goes past the main attractions such as the cathedral, château, basilica and theatre. Mon–Sat 1330–1924.

It is best to explore the city area by area and on foot. At the River Loire end of the r. Nationale is the 13th-century abbey church of **St-Julien**. In its cloisters is the **Musée du Campagnonnage** (trade guild and journeymen museum), 8 r. Nationale; tel: 47 61 07 93. It displays masterpieces that craftsmen produced in the last stages of their apprenticeships to prove their dexterity and to gain admittance to their craft guilds. Also on display are illustrations, written documents and the tools used by the journeymen since 1840. Open Wed–Mon 0900–1200, 1400–1700 (Jan–Mar, mid–Sept–Dec); Wed–Mon 0900–1200, 1400–1800 (Apr–mid-June); daily 0900–1830 (mid–June–mid-Sept). Fr.20 (Fr.12). In St-Julien's cellars is the **Musée des Vins de Touraine** (Touraine wine region museum), 16 r. Nationale (the entrance is at the side of the church); tel: 47 61 07 93. Open Wed–Mon 0900–1200, 1400–1700 (Jan–Mar; Oct–Dec); Wed–Mon 0900–1200, 1400–1800 (Apr–Sept). Possible closures in Jan, Feb. Self-guided tour; Fr.10 (Fr.5).

Cathedral Quarter

The charming r. Colbert leads to the cathedral quarter. It was once the main commerical street. Number 39 has a plaque about Joan of Arc's visit. At Number 17, go into the narrow Passage du Coeur Navré (Broken Heart Passage) to look up at the half-timbered walls and ceilings. It leads into a pretty square with a fountain, called pl. Foire Le Roi, once a market place.

Nearby are the remaining wings of the

Château Royal de Tours, *25 quai d'Orléans*, now housing an aquarium and a waxworks museum. The **Aquarium Tropical**; *tel: 47 64 29 52*, displays 220 species of fresh- and salt-water fish. Open Mon–Sat 0930–1200, 1400–1800, Sun 1400–1800 (Apr–June, Sept–mid-Nov); daily 0930–1900 (July–Aug); daily 1400–1800 (mid-Nov–Mar). Fr.28, (Fr.17). The waxworks, **Historial de Touraine-Musée Grevin**; *tel: 47 61 02 95*, is open daily 1400–1730 (Jan–mid-Mar, Nov–Dec); daily 1400–1800 (mid-Mar–June; Sept–Oct); 0900–1830 (July–Aug). Fr.33 (Fr.20). There are 31 tableaux of the city's historical events with 165 wax figures, impressively costumed, with sound and smell effects. English information boards.

Cathédrale St-Gatien, dating to the 13th century, has an ornate front in Flamboyant style and twin lantern towers, built on the foundations of previous churches and a Roman arena and named after the first bishop of Tours. There is always some scaffolding due to the major restoration programme. Stained glass windows, some dating to the 13th century, include one depicting the life of **St-Martin**, the hero-saint of the Touraine region. One shows the episode which led to his religious calling when, while a soldier, he gave half of his cloak to a beggar – he could only give this portion as the other half belonged to the army. There are English noticeboards. The most interesting effigies are those of Charles VIII's children, dressed resplendently. The cathedral is open daily 0830–1200, 1400–2000 (summer); 0830–1200, 1400–1730 (winter) The **Cloître de la Psalette** (cloister) is open daily 0900-1200, 1400–1700 (Oct–Mar); 0900–1200 and 1400–1800 (Apr–Sept). Fr.14.

Behind the cathedral is the former archbishop's palace, now the **Musée des Beaux Arts** (Museum of Fine Arts), *18 pl. Francois Sicard; tel: 47 05 68 73*. It has a rich collection of 18th-century furniture, paintings from the Middle Ages to the 20th century and a lovely garden. Open Wed–Mon 0900–1245, 1400–1800. Fr.30 (Fr15).

A link with the pioneer history of Canada is found nearby at **Chapelle St-Michel-Centre Marie del'Incarnation** (St-Michael's chapel and the Mary of the Incarnation centre), *2 r.du Petit Pré; tel: 47 66 65 95*. Open daily 1500–1800 (mid-June–mid-Sept); hours can vary. Free. English leaflet. There is an exhibition about Marie, an Ursuline nun, mystic and missionary who took part in the settlement of Québec in the 1600s. Further down the *r. des Ursulines* is the **Jardin des Murs Romains** (garden of the Roman walls), tucked behind a modern apartment block, which has extensive excavations on view.

Old Town

From *r. Nationale*, the *r. du Commerce* leads to the 'old town' quarter and the **Basilica de St-Martin**, *7 r. Baleschoux; tel: 47 05 63 87*. Open daily 0800–1900 (Easter–Oct); 0800–1200, 1400–1845 (Oct–Easter). Free. Built between 1887 and 1924, the basilica houses the tomb of St Martin, who died in 397 and was originally buried in an older church, whose dramatic tower ruins are next door. Its carved stone remnants are in the nearby chapel of **St-Jean** which is the **Musée St-Martin**, *3 r. Rapin; tel: 47 64 48 87*. Open Wed–Sun 0930–1230, 1400–1730 (mid-Mar–mid-Nov). Fr.15 (Fr.7.50).

The *r. du Commerce* demonstrates how Tours could have become an unremarkable city following the great destruction of its buildings in the war. At first, the street has ordinary post-war rebuilding, done before the city fathers made the decision to use traditional methods in restoring the old quarter. Once the street becomes cobbled and pedestrianised, there are many half-timbered, brick buildings, helping to recreate the charming streetscapes of the Middle Ages. It is impossible to imagine this area, now buzzing with activity, as the urban slum it was until the late 1960s. A remarkable survivor of World War II bombings is the ornate, Renaissance façade of the **Hôtel Goüin**, *25 r.du Commerce; tel: 47 66 22 32*. Its rooms were rebuilt to house archaeological finds, including prehistoric, Gallo-Roman, Merovingian, medieval and Renaissance. English information available. Fr.18 (Fr.12). Off *r.de la Paix* are Gallo-Roman excavations on view at *pl. St-Pierre-le-Peullier*, which in the evening is a quiet spot to appreciate the fragments of music and the happy din of the nearby streets.

Other attractions include the **Musée du Gemmail et sa chapelle souterraine** (museum and underground chapel), *7 r. du Murier; tel: 47 61 01 19*. Modern stained-glass works glow in the main church; the underground chapel dates from the 12th century. Open Tues–Sun 1000–1200, 1400–1830 (mid-Mar–mid-Oct). Fr.30 (Fr.20). English information. **Musée des Equipages Militaires et du Train** (army service corps museum), *60 r. de Plat d'Etain; tel: 47 77 20 35*. It has a collection of arms, uniforms and vehicles from 1807 onwards. Open Mon–Fri 1000–1200, 1400–1700. English information. Free.

Out of Town

Near Tours, late evening *son et lumière* shows abound at grand châteaux. To see them without the worry of driving at night, there are bus excursions organised by SNCF (French Railways). These leave from platform 6 at the rail station. The

---

Fishing on the Loire

Solitary fishermen casting from the shore or sitting in flat-bottomed boats are a familiar sight along the Loire. *Gardon* (roach), *brème* (bream) and *goujon* (gudgeon) are plentiful. Other good catches include *brochet* (pike) and *sandre* (zander). Also caught in abundance are *anguilles* (eels), particularly in the Sologne region. Although freshwater fish are one of the gourmet glories of the Loire, migratory sea fish which return to spawn in the river include shad, salmon and lampreys.

There has been an extensive cleaning and replenishing programme of the Loire Valley waterways. The larger Tourist Offices generally have information on fishing breaks. Local fishing tackle shops sell a *carte de pêche* giving regulations about fishing (in French) and sell any necessary permits for angling on nearby lakes or canals.

---

price includes the bus journey and the entrance fee. To **Azay-le-Rideau** (25 km), Tues, late June–mid-Sept, leaving at 2130 until end of July, then at 2100; Fr.115. To **Le Lude** on the Loir river (40 km), Fri, second week July–mid-Aug; Sat third week June–mid Aug. Departures are 2100 until end of July, then 2030 onwards; Fr.145. To **Amboise** (25 km), Wed second week July–Aug. Departures are from 2130 to end of July, then 2100; Fr.125.

SNCF also offer half-day and day tours by bus which include châteaux, wine caves and other attractions, from the third week Apr–Sept, days vary. The day tours have commentaries in French and English. Information and bookings at the Tourist Office and at **Bureau Circuits Châteaux de la Loire** at the rail station. Open Mon–Sat 0800–1100, 1530-1900; Sun, public holidays 0800–1100 (Apr–Sept).

TOURS–BLOIS

After a look at the vineyard countryside at Vouvray on the north banks of the Loire, this route stays south of the river to take in a clutch of châteaux including one in the delightful town of Amboise and one on top of the steep hill at Chaumont, both overlooking wide views of the Loire. Other very contrasting châteaux include intimate Troussay, lavish Cheverny and portrait-packed Beauregard, which is a veritable history lesson about French royalty. The route includes three forests, typical of the Sologne terrain, as well as the tributaries of the Brenne, Bièvre and most grandly, the Cher.

DIRECT ROUTE: 58 KM

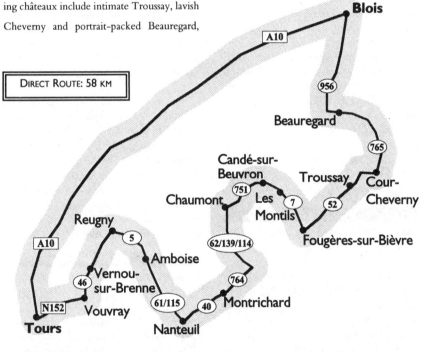

ROUTES

DIRECT ROUTE

➡ On the north side of Tours take the A10 motorway, which has toll booths, the 58 km to Blois.

SCENIC ROUTE

➡ This 125.5-km route starts north of the river. Take the ring road from Tours to join D29 to cross the bridge to join N152, turn right, follow N152 along the river to **Vouvray**. Leave Vouvray on

D46 which turns north towards Vernou-sur-Brenne, another wine village. Rejoin D46 and just past Chançay, turn right to cross the bridge for Valmer, its gardens and views. Again, rejoin D46 and drive to **Reugny**, turn right to cross the bridge to join D5, continue on D5 to **Amboise**, cross the bridge for the main town centre. Then take D61/D115 through the forest of Amboise to **Nanteuil**, turn left onto D40 to Montrichard. Take D764 through the forest of **Montrichard**, turn left onto D62 and follow the road (the road numbers change to D139 and D114) to **Chaumont-sur-Loire**. Follow D751 towards Blois but turn right at Candé-sur-Beuvron to join the D7 through Les Montils to **Fougères-sur-Bièvre**. After, turn left onto D52 to Troussay (just left off D52). After, rejoin D52 and at first right turn for **Cheverny**. Take D102 to **Cour-Cheverney**. Turn left on D765 which goes through the forest of Russy, turning left for the signpost to **Beauregard**. Follow the forest road to Celettes, turn right onto D956, passing St-Gervais-le-Forêt, to Blois.

VOUVRAY

Tourist Office: *152 r. Nationale 37210;. tel: 47 52 68 73.* Open Mon–Sat 0900–1300, 1400–1830, Sun 0900–1300 (Apr–May, Oct–Nov); Mon–Sat 0830–1300, 1400–1830, Sun 0900–1300 (July–Sept). An unprepossessing village with a famous name for white wine, Vouvray is set in sloping vineyard countryside and has several hotels and restaurants. The Tourist Office will book accommodation.

SIGHTSEEING

At the **Espace de la Vigne et du Vin** (exhibition of wine and vineyards), there is a video about the local wine made from Chenin grapes, and wine-tasting is part of the visit. It is at *30 r. Victor Herault; tel: 47 52 76 00.* Open daily 1000–1900. Fr.28 (Fr.22 children).

Some wine merchants will give tours of the wine stored in the caves, such as **Huet, Le Manoir du Haut-Lieu,** *11–13 r. Crois-Busée; tel: 47 52 78 87.* Tours possible in July–Aug; the premises are open for wine tastings and the purchase of wine, Mon–Sat 0900–1200, 1400–1800.

Further along the route is **Vernou-sur-Brenne**, another village surrounded by vineyards and with its hillsides dotted with caves. The Vouvray area vineyards extend over 1850 hectares and include eight villages along the **Route de Vouvray**. There are many wine fairs, most notably on the first weekend of Feb, the last weekend in May and around 15 Aug.

Further down the road there are good views over the vineyards from the terraces of the Italian-influenced **Valmer** park and gardens, *Chançay 37210; tel: 47 52 93 12.* Open Sat–Mon 0900–1300, 1400–1900 (first weekend in June, third weekend in Sept); Tues–Sun, 1400–1900 (July–Aug); Fr.25 (Fr.20). English leaflet. There are guided tours (some English possible) on May and June weekends.

AMBOISE

Tourist Office: *quai du Gén. de Gaulle 37402 Amboise; tel: 47 57 09 28.* Open Mon–Sat 0900–1230,1400–1830, Sun 1000–1200 (May–mid-June, mid Sept–Oct); Mon–Sat 0900–2030, Sun 1000–1200. 1600–1900 (mid-June–mid-Sept); Mon–Sat 0900–1230, 1500–1800 (Nov–Mar). It books accommodation and is next door to a bureau de change.

ACCOMMODATION AND FOOD

There is a good range of small hotels and lots of restaurants. Chain hotels: *Ib, Nv.*

There is a campsite on the **l'Île d'Or** (Golden Island) opposite the town; *tel: 45 57 23 37.*

It is best to explore the busy, pretty town on foot. Parking is in the bays in the wide avenue by the river where the Tourist Office is located. Amboise sems to have it all, from discotheques to off-beat museums to pleasant local wine.

Château Royal; *tel: 47 57 00 98.* Open daily all year but times vary. 0900–1200, 1400–1700 (Dec–Mar); 0900–1830 (Apr–June); 0900–2000 (July–Aug); 0900–1800 (Sept–Oct); 0900–1200, 1400–1730 (Nov). Fr.33 (Fr.23). Guided tours in English and English leaflet available.

Historically important as a royal residence for five kings, it also gets the credit for spreading the influence of the Renaissance when Charles VIII refurbished the feudal building on the site, following the Italian style. This enlightment continued with François I who became the patron of Leonardo da Vinci. As court painter, architect, engineer and ingenious entertainer, he created extravagant spectacles and firework displays. Now the town residents take part in the 420-member cast of the *son et lumière* shows on the theme of *A la cour du Roy François* (In the court of King Francis) Wed, Sat 2200 (third week June–Aug). Fr.70, *tel: 47 57 14 47.*

Leonardo da Vinci lived for the last four years of his life at the **Manoir du Clos Lucé**, *2 r. du Close-Lucé; tel: 47 57 62 88.* Open daily 0900–1800 (mid-Nov–Dec; Feb–third week Mar) daily 0900–1900 (third week Mar–mid-Nov). Fr.35 (Fr.26). There is a storybook look to the façade of this townhouse which neatly displays slick models of Leonardo's impressive mechanical inventions. The 40 models, reconstructed by computer from his drawings, include the first aeroplane, helicopter, parachute, tank, machine gun, swing-bridge and self-propelled vehicle. The brick-walled hall, salon rooms and the bedroom where he died, aged 67, on 2 May 1519, are furnished. There is an Italian Renaissance rose-garden in a shady park with a stream and a finely-decorated chapel as well as a *crêperie* and *salon de thé*.

Musée de la Poste et des Voyages (museum of postal transport), *6 r. de Joyeuse; tel: 47 57 00 11.* Open Tues–Sun 0930–1200, 1400–1830 (Apr–Sept); Tues–Sun 1000–1200, 1400–1700 (Oct–Dec, Feb–Mar). Fr.20 (Fr.10). English leaflet. In a 16th-century mansion is a collection of stagecoaches as well as uniforms, badges, letters, the first stamp printed in France and other artefacts associated with postal deliveries over the centuries.

La Maison Enchantée (the enchanted house), *7 r. du Gén. Foy; tel: 47 23 24 50.* Open Tues–Sun 1000–1200, 1400–1800 (Apr–Sun), daily 1000–1900 (July–Sept); Tues–Sun 1000–1200, 1400–1730 (Oct–Dec; Feb–Mar). Fr.25 (Fr.20). A bit twee for some tastes but charming for fans of the miniature, the 25 mini-tableaux here star 250 costumed figures portraying historical scenes such as da Vinci painting the *Mona Lisa*.

Just a few miles along the D431 is **Pagode de Chanteloup** (Chanteloup pagoda); *tel: 47 57 20 97.* Open daily all year but times vary: 1000–1800 (Apr–May); 1000–1900 (June, Sept); 0930–2000 (July–Aug); 1000–1200, 1400–1800 (Oct–mid-Nov, mid-Feb–Mar). This odd little building is all that is left of the château and park which was destroyed in 1823. Old maps, plans, engravings and paintings show how the estate would have looked. The pagoda was built in 1775, reflecting a Chinese influence.

325

MONTRICHARD

Tourist Office: *2 r. Pont 41400 Montrichard; tel: 54 32 05 10.* Open Tues–Sat 0900–1200, 1400–1800, Sun 0900–1200 (Easter–Sept). Tourist information the rest of the year (same hours) at *Mairie; tel: 54 32 00 46.* Neither office makes hotel bookings but has hotel information.

SIGHTSEEING

This busy, hilly market town has a sandy beach and its old walls still shape the layout of the picturesque streets and fine old houses (*r. de la Juiverie, r. Pont, r. Porte-aux-rois*). Brooding over the town is the **Donjon** (the keep) which is three attractions in one. A good viewpoint for a panoramic look over the Cher, it has 11 galleries about local themes including archaeology, paleontology, costumes and bygones. Birds of prey in flight displays take place. The keep and galleries are open daily 0930–1145, 1400–1815 (Easter–Sept). Fr.20 (Fr.16). It is more expensive in the afternoons due to the birds of prey display daily at 1530 and 1700 (mid-May–Sept); *tel: 54 32 01 16.* Fr.40 (which includes the galleries). The square keep is a gaunt reminder of violent days when a feudal lord, Fulk Nerra, built it in 1010.

CHAUMONT-SUR-LOIRE

This one-street hamlet on the banks of the Loire is overlooked by a hill with wide views and the **Château de Chaumont**; *tel: 54 20 98 03.* Open daily 0930–1800 (mid-Mar–Sept); 1000–1630 (Oct–mid-Mar). Fr.27 (Fr.18). English leaflet. Guided visits available in French or self-guided with English text. Parking is at the bottom of the hill by the riverside and it is a steep climb to the wind-swept top and the 15th-century fortress château, with moat and drawbridge. Diane de Poitiers was forced to accept after it being ousted

from her beloved Chenonceau by Catherine de Medici, who sought revenge – she had always wanted Chenonceau but her husband had bestowed it on his mistress, Diane, instead. Austere outside, but pleasant within, it has sxome Renaissance furnishings and tapestries from the 15th–19th centuries.

For a time it attracted cultural and high society, when the writer Mme de Staël held a salon after being exiled here by Napoléon in 1810. There was more entertaining when Marie Say took possesion; her wealthy, indulgent father bought it for her. She later married the prince Amadée de Broglie who spent her money, but she outlived the prince and married into the Spanish royal family. The château is now state-owned. A walking trail leads into the forest from the fine stables.

There is a **Festival International des Jardins** (garden festival) at the château's show farm garden of flowers and vegetables. Open 0900–nightfall (July–mid-Oct). Fr.40 (Fr.30). English leaflet; *tel: 54 20 00 24.*

There are one-and-a-half-hour river cruises daily aboard the **Leonard de Vinci** at 1500, 1700 (July–Aug); Sun, public holidays 1500, 1700 (Apr–Oct). Fr.50. Tickets sold on board.

FOUGÈRES-SUR-BIÈVRE

Set amid nursery gardens and asparagus fields, this charming village boasts the small but formidable **Château de Fougères-sur-Briève** *41120; tel: 54 20 27 18.* Open daily 0930–1200, 1400–1800 (Apr–Sept); 1000–1200, 1400–1630 Wed–Sun (Oct–Mar). Fr.21 (Fr.14). Self-guided tour with an English leaflet. A small, fortified 15th-century building with many conical turrets and Renaissance additions, it has a picturesque courtyard with covered arcades

TROUSSAY

On the road to Cheverney is the **Château de Troussay**; *tel: 54 44 29 07*. Open daily 1000–1900 (June–Aug); daily 1030–1300, 1400–1800 (Sept); Sun, public holidays 1030–1230, 1400–1730 (Oct–Nov); daily 1030–1230, 1400–1830 (mid-Apr–mid-May); Sun, public holidays 1030–1230, 1400–1830 (last two weeks May). Fr.22 (Fr.14). Self-guided visit with English leaflet. More intimate than the big châteaux on the route, this manor house was furnished by a historian, Louis de la Saussaye, in the 19th century with artefacts from now-gone historic houses of the region.

CHEVERNY

Château de Cheverny *41700; tel: 54 79 96 29*. Open daily 0915–1845 (June–mid-Sept); daily 0930–1200, 1415–1800 (last two weeks Sept) 0930–1200, 1415–1730 (Oct); 0930–1200,1415, 1700 (Nov–Feb); 0930–1200,1415–1730 (Mar); 0915–1200, 1415–1830 (Apr–May). Fr.30 (Fr.20). Self-guided visit with English leaflet. On the edge of the Sologne forest, this white-fronted building with a slate roof looks splendidly elegant facing neat swathes of lawn. Inside it is lavishly decorated, reflecting the taste of the original owner, Count Henri Hurault de Cheverny, who built it between 1604 and 1634, and whose descendants still live in the château.

They keep up the tradition of *la chasse* (the hunt) in the forest each winter. The pack of 70 English hunting hounds is fed beside the large kennels at 1700 daily. Besides the grand rooms, including the King's bedroom, private apartments are open. The village church has many family coats of arms. A *son et lumière* takes places in the park July, Aug at 2230. Days vary. Fr.80. For information and booking, *tel: 54 42 69 03*.

BEAUREGARD

Château de Beauregard *41129 Celettes; tel: 54 70 40 05*. Open daily 0930–1130, 1400–1800 (Apr–June); daily 0930–1800 (July–Aug); daily 0930–1130, 1400–1800 (Sept); Thur–Tues 0930–1130, 1400–1630 (Oct–Mar). Fr.25 (Fr.18). A 'who's who' portrait gallery of French kings, queens and their courts is the highlight of this handsome, 17th-century, privately-owned château built on the site of a former hunting lodge of François I. A financier, Paul Ardier, who bought the château in 1631, put in the collection of more than 350 historical portraits, arranged by reign, from the first Valois Philippe VI to Louis XIV. Dates and painted emblems are also on display and help to make sense of much French history by putting faces to names.

The huge 16th-century kitchen is on show and the **Cabinet des Grelots** is a charming study with gilded wood panelling and paintings on wood and an ornate ceiling. The golden-stone, classical château façade looks splendid at sunset.

327

Sologne

Sologne is the name of the large flat-lands area of the Loire Valley, stretching from the Cher to as far north as Orléans. It is a widespread plain with many little lakes and water meadows as well as thick forests, still popular for hunting. Its remote, rural and placid air makes touring a pleasure, with a feeling of having stepped back in time. Wildlife is abundant with many types of birds, butterflies and flowers. The many hamlets and old farms are as delightful to come across as the occasional grand château such as Chaumont, Cheverny and Beauregard.

TOURS–BOURGES

Getting away from the River Loire, this route includes the château of Chenonceau, despite the crowds, a must-see sight, as well as the medieval quarter and formidable castle at Loches. Both places have heroines at the heart of their histories. In contrast to Talleyrand's lavish château at Valençay, there is the sleepy village of Montrésor and the romantic ruins at Mehun-sur-Yèvre. Much of the route runs through pastoral landscape and tiny agricultural hamlets, with views enhanced by the tributaries of the Cher, Indre and Yèvre

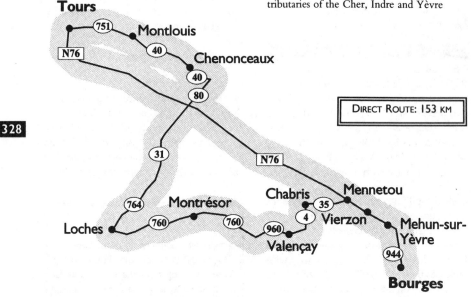

DIRECT ROUTE: 153 KM

328

ROUTES

DIRECT ROUTE

There is no motorway. Leave Tours on N76, which runs south of the River Cher. Continue on N76, which heads north of the river to Vierzon. Continue on N76 until the right turn to follow D944 into Bourges, 153 km.

SCENIC ROUTE

This is a 189.5 km route. Take D751 to **Montlouis-sur-Loire**, then continue on D751 to turn right onto D40 to St-Martin-le-Beau. Continue on D40 to **Chenonceaux** village and the château of

Chenonceau (which omits the letter x in its name). Continue along the D40 to turn right onto D80 going past St-Quentin-sur Indrois, and continue on D31 through the forest of Loches to the D764 to **Loches**. Leave Loches to cross the river onto D760 through Chartreuse du Liget to **Montrésor**. Leave the town on D760 passing Nouans-les Forêts, continuing on D960 to **Valençay**. From here, take D4 to Chabris, turn right onto D35 to la Chapelle Montmartin, continuing on D51 to St-Loup-sur-Cher. Leave by D100 to cross the river to **Mennetou-sur-Cher**. Turn right onto N76, going past Châtres-sur-Cher to go into **Vierzon,** then continue on N76 to **Mehun-sur-Yèvre**, and take the D944 into Bourges.

MONTLOUIS-SUR-LOIRE

A great rival to Vouvray across the other side of the river, the town's river frontage is lined with wine-producing merchants' premises set into the hillside caves, with parking just outside. **Cave des Producteurs de Vins de Montlouis**, *2 rte de St. Aignan; tel: 47 50 80 98*, open daily 0800–1130, 1400–1830; daily 800–1130, 1400–1730 (Sept–June). Free. **Cave Touristique de Montlouis**, *2 pl. Courtemanche; tel: 47 45 18 19*. Open daily 100–1200, 1400–1900 (June–Oct); Sat, Sun, public holidays 1000–1200, 1400–1900 (Nov–Dec, mid-Mar–May). Free. An exhibition about local flora and fauna is at **La Maison de la Loire**, *60 quai Albert Baillet; tel: 47 45 16 31*. Open daily 1400–1700 (Apr–mid-Oct). Fr.20 (Fr.15 children).

CHENONCEAUX

Tourist Office: *r. Chateau 37150 Chenonceaux; tel: 47 23 94 45*. Open Mon–Sat 1000–1200, 1400–1800, Sun 1000–1200 (Easter–Oct). It has English information and will book accommodation.

ACCOMMODATION

The village has seven hotels and a campsite, **Camping Municipal 'La Fontaine des Pres'**, *Chemin de l'Arabe 37150 Chenonceaux; tel: 47 23 90 13*.

SIGHTSEEING

The village is next to the grand **Château de Chenonceau**; *tel: 47 23 90 07*. Open daily all year but times vary in the winter, 0900–1700 (first two weeks Feb); 0900–1730 (last two weeks Feb); 0900–1800 (first two weeks Mar); 0900–1800 (mid-Mar–mid-Sept); 0900–1830 (last two weeks Sept); 0900–1800 (first two weeks Oct); 0900–1730 (last two weeks Oct); 0900–1700 (Nov–mid-Dec); 0900–1630 (mid-Dec–Jan). Fr.40 (Fr.25).

There are throngs of visitors and many tour buses to the château, which is easily the masterpiece of the Loire valley. Get there when it opens to avoid the worst of the crowds. Self-guided. English leaflet. Parking in the large car park is included in the entry cost.

The château gracefully spans the river Cher with a five-arched bridge, first commissioned by Diane de Poitiers, mistress of Henri II, and then completed by his widow, Catherine de Medici, who kicked out the mistress in 1599 after the king's death. She also built the splendid stables. They both laid out formal gardens. Catherine's was used for decadent court entertainments. Inside the **Bâtiment des Domes** is a wax museum about the French court. Fr.10. The six women who shaped the building are the theme of the *son et lumière*, called *Au Temps des Dames De Chenonceau* (In the times of the Ladies of Chenonceau) staged from the third week in June to the first few days of Sept

329

at 2215. Fr.40 (Fr.25). For information and bookings, telephone the château.

The other women featured are Catherine Briçonnet, who oversaw its building in 1521 when her husband, a tax collector, purchased the property; Louise de Lorraine, widow of Henri III; Mme Dupin, who held a salon for intellectuals here; and Mme Pelouze, who restored it in the last century. It is owned by the Menier family, who are in the chocolate business.

LOCHES

Tourist Office: *pl. de Wermelskirchen 37601 Loches; tel: 47 59 07 98.* Open Mon–Sat 0930–1230, 1400–1800 (Apr–June; also Sun morning in May); daily 0900–1900 (July–Sept); Mon–Sat 1000–1230, 1400–1700 (Oct–Mar). It has leaflets in English and will book accommodation.

ACCOMMODATION AND FOOD

There is a small selection of hotels in the town and several restaurant. **Camping Municipal de la Citadelle**, *av. A. Briand, Loches 37600; tel: 47 59 05 91.*

SIGHTSEEING

Because of the city walls and narrow streets, use the car parks at *mail de la Poterie* and *mail du Donjon* and walk up. There is also a large car park by the rail station.

The town is dominated by a formidable keep and the grim **Château de Loches** *37600 Loches; tel: 47 59 01 32.* Open daily 0900–1200, 1400–1800 (mid-Mar–June); daily 0900–1800 (July–Aug); daily 0900–1200, 1400–1800 (Sept); Thur–Tues 0900–1200,1400–1700 (Oct–Nov); Thurs–Tues 0900–1200, 1400–1700 (Feb–mid-March). The **Donjon** (keep), *tel: 47 59 07 86,* opens and closes a half-hour later than the château. One entry fee

for both is Fr.26 (Fr.19). Both buildings are either self-guided or guided (in French with some English possible).

The two buildings are on either side of the **Cité Médiévale** (medieval city quarter) within the city walls. In between is **St Ours** church, unusual for its domed nave and twin sets of towers. The unfurnished rooms of the château add to the gaunt atmosphere but it has royal connections with Charles VII and his mistress, Agnès Sorel, who lived here and is buried here. Her alabaster effigy shows her with her hands piously in prayer and with loving angels hovering by her head. The château has copies of the two famous portraits of her in which her modest pose is belied by her exposing her left breast, a fashion she set during her heyday at court before dying at 28, possibly by poisoning.

After her great victory at Orléans, Joan of Arc came to the great hall here in 1429 to convince Charles that he should go to be crowned at Rheims cathedral. The chapel of Anne of Brittany, another resident, is adorned with her emblem, the silver ermine. The keep is an impressive shell, with three floors missing – although the fireplaces can still be seen. In its **Martelet Tower** are extensive dungeons, with many gruesome stories. There is a steep staircase to the top for views of the town, the Indre Valley and the Loches forest. A *son et lumière* show takes place Fri, Sat 22.30 (second week July–third week Aug). Fr.70. For bookings, phone the Tourist Office.

In the intact medieval city quarter above the modern city and the river, there are fine Renaissance houses (*r. St-Ours*). A walk along the perimeter of the three-tier city walls will take around three-quarters of an hour.

Paintings by Emanuel Lansyer, 1835–93, a local artist of the Impressionist school, are on display along with local crafts and folklore at the the **Musée Lansyer et du Terroir** (Museum of Lansyer and the Countryside), *r. Lansyer; tel: 47 59 05 45.* Open daily 0900–1130, 1400–1630 (last two weeks Mar); daily 0900–1130, 400–1530 (Apr–Sept); Thur–Tues 0900–1130, 1400–1530 (Oct–mid-Mar). Fr.15 (Fr.5). Guided tours only (some English possible). An English leaflet is available. It has a reconstruction of a local house interior and gives visitors a view into the **Porte Royale** (royal gate).

Off the hurly-burly of the main châteaux trail, Loches residents enjoy daily life, which is especially evident during the jolly Wed and Sat markets and the **Marché Clair de Lune** (moonlight market) in mid-July which sells hand-made products.

MONTRÉSOR

The tiny, pretty, peaceful village, with stone houses and steep, narrow streets, is topped with the 16th-century **collegiate church** of St John the Baptist and is tucked into a loop of the River Indrois. Looming over the village is the square, solid-looking **Château de Montrésor**, *37460; tel: 47 92 60.* Open daily 1000–1200, 1400–1800 (Apr–Oct). Fr.32 (Fr.25). Exterior only Fr.17. English leaflet available. An earlier fortress was built by Fulk Nerra in the 11th century and some of the ramparts and towers remain. From the shady terraces are pastoral views of the lazy river, water meadows and cows placidly chomping in the verdant countryside.

The present building dates back to the 15th century and was restored in 1849 by a Polish nobleman, Count Xavier Branicki, who fought in the Crimean War with Napoléon III. His military medals and hunting trophies are on display along with many paintings by 19th-century French and Polish painters, as well as artefacts which had belonged to the 17th-century Polish king, Jan Sobieski. The count's descendants live in a 16th-century house in the grounds.

VALENÇAY

Tourist Office: *rte de Blois 36600 Valençay; tel: 54 00 04 42.* Open daily 1000–1230, 1500–1900 (mid-June–mid Sept); tourist information at the *Hôtel de Ville; tel: 54 00 14 33.* Open 0930–1200, 1400–1730. There are three hotels and a few restaurants in the small village.

SIGHTSEEING

Château de Valençay, *36600 Valençay; tel: 54 00 10 66.* Open daily 0900–1200, 1400–1900 or nightfall (mid-March–mid-June, mid-Sept–mid Nov); daily 0900–1900 (mid-June–mid-Sept). Fr.40 (Fr.32). The park is open daily 0900–1200, 1400–1800 or nightfall (Mar–Nov); daily 1400–1800 or nightfall (Dec–Feb). Entry to the park alone is Fr.8. Entry to the **Musée Automobile** (car museum) and the park is Fr.18 (Fr.16). There is an extra charge for visiting the kitchen, wine cellars and dining room Fr.12 (Fr.10). Guided tours only of the château. English leaflet.

Although strikingly beautiful, the building's silhouette against the wide sky has an odd look about it due to the asymmetrical contrast of its slate-roofed towers. These include massive classical domes at one end, small pepperpot-shaped ones at the other, and with a massive square keep sporting even smaller conical turrets. It was begun in 1540 by a local man, Jacques d'Estampes, using the château at Chambord as inspiration, but not completed until the 17th century.

It was the home for 35 years of Napoléon's great foreign minister, Comte

331

Charles Maurice Talleyrand de Périgord, later Prince de Bénévant, who died here in 1838. It is sumptuously furnished in First Empire style. There is an exhibition about his achievements. He was obliged by the emperor to house the exiled Spanish princes in 1808 for six years until the treaty of Valençay ended the Spanish War in 1813. The park has wide terraces, strutting peacocks, plodding ducks, graceful deer and a small zoo with llamas, kangaroos and zebras among the animals.

The car museum shows off more than 60 cars from 1898 onwards, all in working order. A *son et lumière* show with a cast of 900 uses the theme of love and chivalry and is performed the last week of July and in Aug (days vary) at 2200. Fr.70. Phone the Tourist Office for bookings.

MENNETOU-SUR-CHER

It is a delight to come across sleepy medieval villages like this. Its main attraction is the village itself, with its steep twisting streets, ancient houses (in *Grande Rue*), drawbridge and 13th-century defence walls, all set in lovely scenery. It is possible to drive around the ramparts which have three towers and three town gates. On the old keep is a plaque marking Joan of Arc's march through in 1429 on the way to Chinon and her first encountered the dauphin.

On the road from here, there are views of the **Canal du Berry** which flows alongside the Cher.

VIERZON

Tourist Office: *Hôtel de Ville, pl. Maurice-Thorez 18100 Vierzon; tel: 48 52 65 24.* There is a range of moderately-priced hotels and restaurants.

Vierzon is a commercial town but significant for being the meeting point of three rivers – the Cher, Arnon and the Yèvre. There is an old town quarter high on a hill dominated by a Gothic **belfry** (almost all that remains of the town's château), and some half-timbered houses (*r. Galilée, r. Mar. Joffré, pl. des Banc*). Leaving the wide views on top, the downhill roads lead to the romanesque **Nôtre-Dame** church.

MEHUN-SUR-YÈVRE

Tourist Office: *pl. 14-Juillet; tel: 48 57 35 51.* Open Mon–Fri 0830–1200, 1430–1800, Sat 1000–1215, 1400–1645 (June–Sept); Mon–Fri 0830–1200, 1345–1715, Sat 1000–1215, 1400–1645 (Oct–May). There are a handful of hotels, several *chambres d'hôtes* and restaurants.

SIGHTSEEING

This is a low key town which nevertheless has an important history. It offers pleasant walks along the river Yèvre and the Berry canal. Across a drawbridge is the **Château de Charles VII et le Jardin de Jean de Berry**; *tel: 48 57 30 25*, which contains an exhibition about the history of the site. Open daily all year; Fr.12. Two ruined towers in a sylvan riverside setting are all that is left of the château which inspired the famous *Très Riches Heures du Duc du Berry*, an illuminated manuscript depicting medieval life.

During the duke's time, the château was an important intellectual centre. It was also an alternative royal court for a time. Joan of Arc was ennobled here in 1429. Charles VII was declared king in the nearby ancient Nôtre-Dame church and he died in the village in 1461. An exhibition about him is in the **Musée Charles VII**, *pl. du Gén. Leclerc; tel: 48 57 30 25*. Open daily 1430–1830 (last week June–first few days of Sept); Sun, public holidays 1430–1830 (rest of year). Fr.10 (Fr.5).

Wines of the Loire Valley

Although wine is produced along the length of the 1000 km River Loire, there are four areas particularly known for wine production. To the far west is the Muscadet region, in the centre are the Anjou-Saumur and Touraine regions, while to the east is the Sancerre area.

Although all types of wine – dry, semi-sweet, sweet, white, pink, red – are produced, the Loire Valley is basically known as white wine country, admirably filling the medium-priced, medium-quality niche in the wine lover's world.

Each of the main regions has mini-divisions within it. For instance, the **Touraine** wine region, with Tours at its centre, consists of six valleys whose limestone slopes thrive in the temperate climate of many sunny days and regularly-paced rainfall. The famous **Vouvray** vineyards include eight villages, while **Amboise** has nine villages separated from each other by the river. Opposite Vouvray, known for its sparkling wines, are the **Montlouis** vineyards around three villages – Montlouis-sur-Loire, St-Martin-le-Beau and Lussault. Their wines were labelled as Vouvray until a court decision in 1938. The Montlouis winemakers use the same type of grape, the chenin blanc, but their wines are generally cheaper. Red wines, made from the Cabernet France grape, are the speciality around **Chinon** and **Bourgueil**.

The smaller **Sancerre** region is known for its tangy dry wine from the Sauvignon grape and is at its best when young. Just across the river, the famous **Pouilly Fumé** wines, known for their slightly smoky flavour, are made at Pouilly-sur-Loire.

Saumur uses the *méthode champenoise* from Chenin grapes to produce lively wines with a hint of apple. The **Anjou** white wines are among the cheapest of France's dry white wines. Locally, Anjou rosé wines are popular for everyday drinking.

Muscadet, the large wine-making region centred around Nantes, produces the light Muscadet wines. The best wine comes from between two Loire tributaries and is called Muscadet de Sèvre-et-Maine. Look for the words 'sur lie' on the label as this indicates the wine in this area was made using the sediment left from the fermentation process, giving it a pleasant yeasty flavour and a slight fizz.

Throughout the Loire Valley, the ubiquitous *dégustation gratuite* sign outside the wine merchants' shops and caves and the wine producers' vineyards means free tastings are on offer but inevitably the hope is that a bottle or two will be sold. Sometimes cellar tours are possible as at the **Caves Monmousseau et Musée des Confreries Europeanées,** *71/75 rte de Vierzon, Montrichard 41400; tel: 54 32 56 09.* (on the road towards St Aignan). The winemakers and vineyards which welcome visitors usually have their leaflets distributed widely at Tourist Offices and hotels and have large signs outside their estates. It is a good idea to visit the vineyards whose wines you already know and have enjoyed, ether at home or in local restaurants.

Wine fairs take place in the Loire Valley throughout most of the year. At Amboise the wine fair is held at Easter and on 15 August; at Azay-le-Rideau it is the last Saturday in Feb; in Chinon it is held on the second Saturday in March ; at Montlouis on the fourth Saturday in April and on 15 Aug; Vouvray, the last Sat in Jan and the last weekend in May, as well as on 15 Aug; and at Montrichard the wine festival takes place from 3–5 November.

VANNES

Founded 2000 years ago on the shores of the Golfe du Morbihan, Vannes has always played an active part in the major episodes of Breton history. It began as the capital of the powerful *Veneti*, a great seafaring people, then became one of the first bishoprics in Brittany, relying on maritime trade for its economic prosperity whilst its influence over the rest of the country was steadily growing. Chosen as the capital of the Duchy of Brittany at the end of the Middle Ages, it was the seat of the Breton Parliament during the 17th century and the Treaty of Union with France was signed within its walls by King François I in 1532. The past has left its mark and today Vannes is one of the best-preserved and most attractive historic cities in Brittany. It is also one of the fastest expanding medium-sized towns in France, yet its wealth no longer comes from the sea but from the development of high technology, from its important role as administrative centre of the Morbihan *département*, and from its cultural aura as a lively university town.

TOURIST INFORMATION

Tourist Office: *1 r. Thiers, 56000 Vannes; tel: 97 47 29 49.* Open Mon–Sat 0900–1900, Sun 1000–1300 and 1500–1900 (July–Aug); Mon–Sat 0900–1200 and 1400–1800, closed Sun (Sept–June).

During high season, change facilities and accommodation booking service are available. A general information brochure on Vannes and the Golfe du Morbihan is published annually by the Tourist Office.

Bureau d'Information Jeunesse (Young People's Information Centre); *19 bis r. du Pot d'Etain; 97 54 13 72.*

ARRIVING AND DEPARTING

By Air

For direct flights to and from Paris use **Lorient Airport**, one hour away by **Air-Inter-Bus** (Air Inter office at the marina, tel: 97 54 05 64).

By Car

Vannes is linked to Lorient, Quimper and Brest as well as to Nantes by the N165 dual carriageway and to Rennes by the N166 and N24. When approaching, look out for *Centre Ville*. Once there, head straight for the harbour: there is a vast car park on both sides of the long and narrow marina. If you stand with your back to it, the Tourist Office is on your left.

GETTING AROUND

All major sights are within walking distance from the centrally situated *pl. Gambetta*, at the head of the harbour, near the car park. The walled town lies beyond the *porte St-Vincent*, further north is the old **St-Patern** district and to the east, up the *r. A. Le Pontois*, is the charming **Jardin de la Garenne.**

For a taxi, *tel: 97 54 34 34* any time of day and night (**Radio Taxis Vannetais**, *pl. de la Gare*).

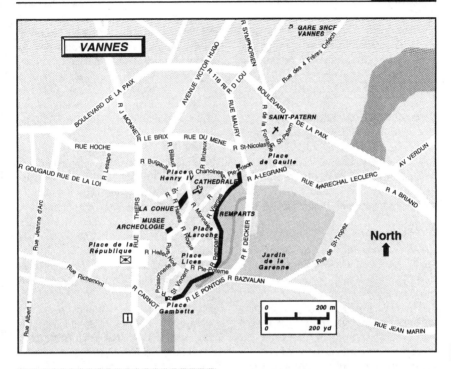

STAYING IN VANNES

Accommodation

There is a wide choice of hotels in and around Vannes, particularly in the cheap-to-reasonably-priced bracket: **Le Marina**, *4 pl. Gambetta; tel: 97 47 22 81*, overlooks the harbour while **Le Bretagne**, *36 r. du Mené; tel: 97 47 20 21*, is situated just outside the north section of the town walls. Among the more expensive, **Le Roof**, *tel: 97 63 47 47*, stands at the extremity of the Conleau peninsula (south-west of the town centre and jutting out into the Golfe du Morbihan) and **La Marébaudière**, *4 r. A.Briand; tel: 97 47 34 29*, is an attractive building in typical local style, surrounded by a garden.

Hotel chains in Vannes include *Ca, Ct, F1, Ib* and *PC*.

One of the best **campsites** is also situated on the Conleau peninsula, *tel: 97 63 13 88*. There is a **youth hostel** on the edge of the Golfe at *rte de Moustérian; tel: 97 66 94 25*.

Eating and Drinking

There are quite a few restaurants and *brasseries* on the *pl. Gambetta* and around the harbour. There is a fine *crêperie*, **La Taupinière**, *9 pl. des Lices; tel: 97 42 57 82*, inside the walled town, and a good seafood restaurant, **La Marée Bleue**, *8 pl. Bir-Hakeim; tel: 97 47 24 29*. Gourmets will gladly drive 4 km to St-Avé to sample the imaginative cuisine served at **Le Pressoir**, *7 r. de l'Hôpital; tel: 97 60 87 63*.

If you are self-catering, you might like to try some typical local products such as *les huîtres du golfe* (oysters from the Golfe du Morbihan), *charcuterie*, honey and *pâtisseries* (cakes), slightly salted butter and *lait ribot* (sour milk). These can be purchased at the market (Wed and Sat morning) and from various shops in and around the walled town. Try **Argenta**, *pl. des Lices,* and **Au Bec Fin**, *17 r. Hoche.*

Communications and Money

The main post office is situated *pl.de la République; tel: 97 01 33 33.*

Most banks provide change facilities weekdays 0900–1200 and 1400–1700; the Tourist Office offers a similar service during longer hours and on Sun (July–Aug).

ENTERTAINMENT

Spectator sports include regattas, rowing round the Golfe du Morbihan, nautical games, show-jumping, cycle races, parachute-jumping etc.

There is a wide choice of sporting activities (enquire at the Tourist Office) and the safe waters of the Golfe du Morbihan are particularly suitable for a variety of water sports including canoeing.

Situated on the edge of the Golfe, 10 mins away from the *pl. Gambetta* along the west side of the harbour, the **Parc du Golfe** is an exciting leisure centre which houses one of the finest aquariums in France, a superb collection of automata, a hot house full of beautiful butterflies, a gymnasium, a fleet of excursion boats, a nautical club, various indoor games and an exhibition hall. The Tourist Office can supply full details of opening times and admission charges.

Every night from mid-June to Sept, the floodlit ramparts enhance the lively atmosphere of the town which has three cinemas, five discotheques and several pubs and piano bars.

Events

The summer months are packed with festivities for all tastes and ages: there are the colourful **Fêtes Historiques** (Historical Festival) in July, the **Nuits Musicales du Golfe** (Musical Evenings, classical music) in July and Aug, the **Festival de Jazz** at the end of July and the **Fêtes d'Arvor** (Folk Festival) in Aug. Further information is available from the Tourist Office.

SHOPPING

If you feel like experiencing weekly shopping the French way, go to the **Continent shopping centre**, near the N165 dual carriageway, on a Fri or Sat afternoon. The hypermarket is surrounded by some 50 boutiques offering a wide range of goods.

Specialised shopping in town includes pottery and ceramics at **Pierrette and J.P. Soulet**, *6 r. Carnot; tel: 97 47 56 08,* marine objects at **Clipper**, *16 r. St-Salomon; tel: 97 54 17 24,* and delicious chocolates at **Les Chapeaux Bretons**, *9 r. St-Vincent; tel: 97 47 40 07.*

SIGHTSEEING

There are regular guided tours of the old town Wed and Sat 1500 (May, June and Sept); daily except Sun 1030 and 1500 (July and Aug); mid-July–late Aug *L'été des 6-12 ans* Tues and Thur 1500 (special guided tour for 6–12-year olds). Departure from **Musée de la Cohue**, *pl. St-Pierre* (opposite the cathedral); 1½ hours on foot, Fr.25 (Fr.15 children).

The **Petit Train Touristique** (little tourist train) takes passengers round the old town for a 30-min tour, daily (except Wed and Sat morning) 1030–1230 and 1400–1930 (Easter–Sept); for reservations *tel: 97 24 06 29.*

Recent excavations have revealed remains of a Gallo-Roman city beneath the old houses gathered round **St-Patern Church** and its fountain, a favourite haunt of artists and students.

Pleasure boats have replaced the old merchant ships in the **harbour**, but the area is still a centre of activity and a place where the townspeople like to meet. The quaysides lined with trees are ideal for strolling and every Wed in summer the bandstand resounds with live music.

Walled Town

Vannes has retained a 600-m-long section of its medieval fortifications, between the **Porte Prison** and the **Porte St-Vincent**. Reinforced at regular intervals by towers and fortified gates, these ramparts form a very picturesque setting with the Marle River running below.

Note in particular the imposing 15th-century **Tour du Connétable** near the old timber-framed wash-house and the bridge over the river. There is a lovely overall view of this part of the old town from the **Jardin de la Garenne** rising eastwards from the river.

Inside the walls, the long **pl. des Lices** was the usual venue for tournaments in medieval times. The narrow streets radiating from it are lined with a wealth of beautifully preserved timber-framed houses decorated with elegant and sometimes humourous carvings such as *Vannes et sa femme* (Vannes and his wife), a stone couple grinning at passers-by on the corner of *r. Noé* and *r. Rogue*.

At the heart of the walled city, the old covered market, known as **la Cohue**, houses the permanent collections of painting and sculpture of the **Musée des Beaux Arts** (Fine Arts Museum) which also holds temporary exhibitions (*tel: 97 47 35 86*); open daily 1000–1200 and 1400–1800, closed Tues and Sun morning in winter; Fr.25 (Fr.15). The building opens onto the *pl. St-Pierre*, opposite the cathedral. Dating mainly from the 15th century, the **Cathédrale St-Pierre** was remodelled several times. One of its most remarkable features is the round chapel on the north side, a rare example of Italian Renaissance style, dating from around 1530. It contains the tomb of St-Vincent Ferrier, a Spanish monk who preached during the early 15th century, died in the city in 1419 and was later canonised.

South of the *pl. St-Pierre*, in the *r. Noé*, there is a fine 15th-century house known as **Château Gaillard**, where the Breton Parliament used to meet; it houses the **Musée d'Archéologie**, *tel: 97 42 59 80*; open weekdays 0930–1200 and 1400–1800, closed in the morning in winter; Fr.20 (Fr.15), and its comprehensive prehistoric collection from various megalithic sites in the area, such as Carnac and Locmariaquer.

The *r. St-Vincent* leading south towards the harbour is lined with stone mansions built in the 17th century for members of the Breton Parliament in striking contrast with the medieval style of domestic architecture predominant in the old town.

OUT OF TOWN

Boat trips on the Golfe du Morbihan are the best way to appreciate all the riches of this unique expanse of water; for details see Vannes to Nantes route, p. 338.

A small guide published by the Tourist Office provides details and maps of some twenty walks in the surrounding area. Furthermore, guided walks are planned throughout the season by various organisations; the Tourist Office has details.

Radio-Taxis Vannetais suggest half-day excursions in the area. For information *tel: 97 54 34 34*.

There is also a choice of all day coach trips round the area and to other parts of Brittany, departuring from *pl. de la Libération*; information from **Tourisme Verney**, *2 r. J. Le Brix; tel: 97 42 40 54*.

337

VANNES–NANTES

The coastal area lying between Vannes and the lower reaches of the Loire is a region of picturesque river valleys, deep bays, vast marshlands and wide estuaries with fascinating features. These include the Golfe du Morbihan and the Parc Naturel Régional de Brière,

lovely old towns and villages like Rochefort-en-Terre and Redon, and the internationally famous resort of La Baule which boasts one of the most beautiful beaches in France. This route joins two historic cities and former capitals of the Duchy of Brittany. Allow two or three days, more if boat trips appeal to you.

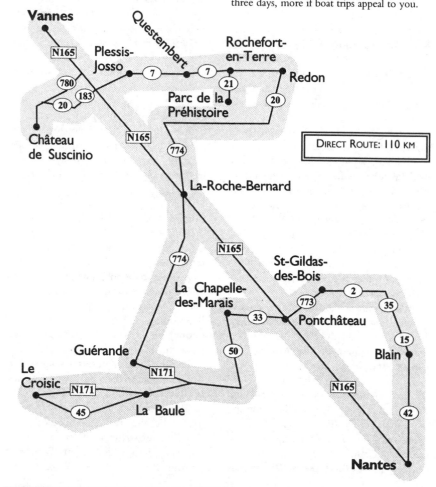

DIRECT ROUTE: 110 KM

ROUTES

DIRECT ROUTE

➡️ The 110 km separating Vannes from Nantes can be driven in just over an hour along the N165 dual carriageway. From *pl. Gambetta*, follow the general direction for Nantes (*r. A. Le Pontois* and *r. J. Martin*).

SCENIC ROUTE

➡️ The 278-km drive follows a picturesque route which meanders partly along the coast and partly inland.

Leave Vannes eastwards on D779, turn right onto the D780 and after 12 km bear left towards the **Château de Suscinio**. Return to D780 and turn right, bearing right almost immediately on the D20, then left at Surzur onto D183 to the **Château de Plessis-Josso**. Drive on for 2 km and turn right on the D7 to **Questembert**. Continue on D7 and D777 to **Rochefort-en-Terre**.

Leave Rochefort towards Malansac and after 2.5 km, turn left on the D134 and continue on D138 and D764 to **Redon**. From there, drive south on D775 and take the D20 on the left: 11 km further on turn left onto D148 to **La Roche-Bernard**. Continue southwards along D774 to **Guérande** on the D99 to La Turballe and turn left after 1 km to join the D92; turn left again. The road runs through an area of salt marsh to Saillé. Turn right onto D45 to **La Baule**. Leave La Baule eastwards on D92 and, 6 km beyond Pornichet, turn left on to D492. Continue on N171 for 6 km, then leave on the D50 going north through the **Grande Brière** to **La Chapelle-de-Marais**; turn right on the D33 to **Pontchâteau** and left onto D773. Follow D773 then the D2, D35 and D15 to **Blain**. From Blain the D42 leads the 33 km south to Nantes.

VANNES TO REDON

Follow the D780 along the eastern shore of the Golfe du Morbihan then bear left towards the Rhuys Peninsula and the **Château de Suscinio**, a splendid medieval fortress facing the ocean, once the favourite summer residence of the dukes of Brittany (open 1000–1900 July, Aug). Return to D780 and turn right onto D20 towards the **Château du Plessis-Josso**, a fortified manor-house in typical Breton style (open 1000–1900 July and Aug).

Drive on for 2 km and turn right onto D7 to **Questembert** (**Tourist Office:** *15 r. des Halles; tel: 97 26 56 00*). The town has a choice of accommodation and restaurants and a campsite by Célac lake. The 15th-century covered market has a remarkable wooden structure. There are several elegant granite houses nearby, including **Hôtel Belmont** housing the Tourist Office.

Continue eastwards to **Rochefort-en-Terre** (**Tourist Office:** *pl. des Halles; tel: 97 43 33 57*): the high street is lined with 16th–18th-century granite houses enhanced by a profusion of flowers. A few turrets and an old well add a quaint note to this picturesque setting. Two km east on D21, in the **Parc de la Préhistoire**, a series of reconstructed prehistoric scenes unfold before your eyes in a beautiful setting of wild woodland (Apr–mid-Oct 1000–2000). Proceed to Redon along D764; at St-Vincent-sur-Oust, you can detour left towards the Oust River and its famous beauty spot, **Île-aux-Pies**.

REDON

Tourist Office: *pl. du Parlement, 35600 Redon; tel: 99 71 06 04*. Open 1000–1900 (summer); 1000–1200, 1500–1800, closed Sun (winter).

ACCOMMODATION AND FOOD

Hotels are very reasonably priced; **Le**

339

Golfe du Morbihan

The Golfe du Morbihan (meaning 'small sea' in Breton) is a vast, almost enclosed lagoon formed by the recent (geologically speaking) subsidence of several river basins. A charming legend gives a more poetic explanation: the Golfe was filled with the tears of unhappy fairies who then threw into it their crowns of flowers. These immediately changed into 365 islands, three of which drifted out to sea. The water level varies with the tides and the scenery changes dramatically twice a day: at high tide gentle ripples glittering in the sun lap the shores of the numerous wooded islands, while at low tide large mud-flats emerge, revealing a complex network of narrow channels. The whole area enjoys a mild sunny climate. The Golfe du Morbihan is a bird sanctuary of international importance. Brent geese take up their winter quarters here together with ducks and cormorants, peacefully cohabiting with all sorts of waders including ringed plovers and sandpipers. The **Réserve de Falguérec** on the Séné peninsula is open daily in summer (*tel: 97 66 92 76*). The Golfe is also a paradise for sailing enthusiasts who appreciate its calm waters, sheltered moorings and well-appointed harbours, and also enjoy navigating among the islands. Many of these are privately owned, a few are inhabited and the most visited are the **Île d'Arz** and **Île-aux-Moines**. A number of islands contain megaliths: some of them, like the *cromlec'h* (stone circle) on **Er Lannic**, are only visible from a boat while others like the *cairn* (burial mound) on **Gavrinis Island** are regularly visited (Mar–Oct from Larmor-Baden, *tel: 97 42 63 44*). There is a great choice of boat trips: trips around the Golfe from Vannes and ports along the shores, shuttle services to several islands, and round tours aboard *sinagots* (traditional boats). It is also possible to rent a sailing boat or a cabin cruiser (information from the Tourist Office, Vannes, *tel: 97 47 24 34*).

340

France, *30 r. Du Guesclin; tel: 99 71 06 11* is in the town centre. There are some sixty holiday homes (list from the Tourist Office), an **HI** youth hostel (*2 r. Chantebel; tel: 99 72 14 39*), and a campsite along the river (*tel: 99 72 14 39*). Several restaurants offer traditional cuisine: **La Bogue**, *3 r. des Etats; tel: 99 71 12 95*, has fish and seafood; **L'Ile aux Grillades**, *15 r. d'Enfer; tel: 99 72 20 40* , prepares open fire grills.

SIGHTSEEING

This attractive riverside town was once an important religious centre and a prosperous maritime ports. The rich merchants' houses still line the *quai Duguay-Trouin* backed by impressive warehouses, but the bridges and locks are now decorated with flowers and pleasure boats glide peacefully along the Vilaine and the Nantes-Brest Canal. The Romanesque **Abbaye St-Sauveur** stands in the town centre next to its 14th-century steeple, separated from the church when a fire destroyed part of the nave. The **Musée de la Batellerie de l'Ouest,** *quai J. Bart; tel: 99 72 30 95,* depicts the life of mariners in the past (1000–1200 and 1500–1800).

LA ROCHE-BERNARD

Tourist Office: *pl. du Pilori; tel: 99 90 67 98*. Open Mon–Sat 0930–1230, 1430–1900; Sun 1000–1230, 1500–1900 July, Aug; otherwise the *Mairie, tel: 99 90 60 51*.

The picturesque **Auberge des Deux Magots**, *pl. du Bouffay; tel: 99 90 60 75*, at the heart of the old district, is the ideal choice for a short stay.

La Roche-Bernard gets its name from the Viking chieftain Bern-Hart ('as strong as a bear') who settled in 919 on a rock spur overlooking the Vilaine River. The city prospered from a thriving maritime trade, illustrated at the **Musée de la Vilaine Maritime** housed in **Château des Basses-Fosses** (*tel: 99 90 83 47*; open 1030–1230 and 1430–1900 July–mid-Sept). The old town has retained its narrow streets and cobbled lanes radiating from the central *pl. du Bouffay.*

LA ROCHE-BERNARD TO LA BAULE

Drive south from La Roche-Bernard to **Guérande,** an authentic medieval town still completely surrounded by its well preserved fortifications (**Tourist Office:** *1 pl. du Marché au Bois; tel: 40 24 96 71*).

Between Guérande and the coast lies a fascinating area of salt marshes, which produces high quality salt. Learn all about it at the **Maison des Paludiers** (Museum of the Salt Marsh Workers) in **Saillé** (*tel: 40 62 21 96*) and join a guided tour round a salt marsh. There is an interesting **Musée**

Salt

Sea salt is produced by a long and complicated process which has hardly changed since the 9th century. The sea penetrates along a narrow channel into a succession of shallow basins, leaving behind unwanted deposits so that, when it is finally allowed into the *oeillets* (small rectangular basins) at the heart of the salt marsh, it is purified and its salt content is very high. Each *oeillet* can yield up to 50 kg of salt a day; once the water has evaporated, the *paludier* (salt marsh worker) gathers the salt with a wide wooden rake and later stores it in the *salorges* (salt warehouses). Salt from the Guérande area, low in sodium and high in magnesium, has a taste which is appreciated by connoisseurs.

---

des Marais Salants (Museum of the Salt Marsh) in **Batz-sur-Mer,** *29 bis r. Pasteur; tel: 40 23 82 79,* (on the D45 west of La Baule) which retraces the history of salt production in the area (open daily June–Sept).

LA BAULE

Tourist Office: *8 pl. de la Victoire, 44504 La Baule Cedex; tel: 40 24 34 44.* Open all year, closed Sun in winter.

ACCOMMODATION AND FOOD

Hotels are generally more expensive than in other resorts. For traditional comfort in secluded surroundings 100 m from the sea, try the **St-Christophe,** *pl. Notre-Dame; tel: 40 60 35 35.* A cheaper choice is the **St-Bernard,** *6 av. des Evens; tel: 40 60 32 02,* also close to the beach. Restaurants also tend to be expensive, but the choice is vast and the ultimate luxury is to be able to have a meal without leaving the beach.

SIGHTSEEING

As in most fashionable resorts, entertainment is mainly focused on the **Grand Casino,** *Esplanade L. Barrière; tel: 40 11 48 28* which has its own restaurant. Outdoor activities available in La Baule include water sports, cycling, golf and horse-riding as well as fitness courses and salt-water cures at the hydrotherapy centres. The town's main feature is, of course, the 7-km-long beach of fine golden sand backed by luxury apartments and hotels. If you don't feel like walking, take a ride on the little **train** which runs from Pornichet to Le Pouliguen, which has stops en route.

◤ SIDE TRACK FROM LA BAULE

Situated 10 km west of La Baule and facing Guérande across a maze of salt marshes, **Le Croisic** is a picturesque

341

fishing port and fashionable resort (**Tourist Office,** *pl. de la Gare; tel: 40 23 00 70).* The **Océarium,** *av. de St-Goustan; tel: 40 23 02 44* is an aquarium with a difference: a see-through tunnel winds its way beneath a huge water tank where fish can be observed from various angles (July and Aug 1000–2200). Return to La Baule along the D45 scenic road which follows the **Côte Sauvage.** ▣

GRANDE BRIÈRE

This area of marshland north-east of La Baule, which harbours a unique and fragile ecosystem, is at the centre of the **Parc Naturel Régional de Brière** created in 1970 and covering 40,000 hectares, spread over 18 *communes* (municipalities).

Traditional economy was based on farming, hunting and fishing while local peat was used for fuel. Today the local population works in the nearby towns, and the flat boats carry visitors along the complex network of canals (**Tourist Information: Maison du Tourisme,** *38 r. de la Brière, 44410 La Chapelle-des-Marais; tel: 40 66 85 01).* Walks and cycle tours are available with or without guides.

Driving north along the D50 to La Chapelle-des-Marais, visit the **Maison de l'Eclusier** (Lock-keeper's House) in **Rozé** which illustrates marshland fauna and flora (open daily). A little further north, on the **Île de Fédrun, la Chaumière briéronne** is a traditionally furnished thatched cottage typical of the area *(tel: 40 91 17 80),* while the **Maison du Sabotier** in **La Chapelle-des-Marais** is a clog-maker's workshop (open June–Sept).

LA CHAPELLE-DES-MARAIS TO BLAIN

From La Chapelle-des-Marais, follow D33

to Pontchâteau then turn left onto D773 to **St-Gildas-des-Bois** where there is a fine 12th-13th-century former Benedictine abbey church. Continue on D2 to Plessé then turn right on the D35 which goes through the lovely **Forêt du Gâvre** and leads to **Blain.**

BLAIN

Tourist Office: *2 pl. J. Guihard; tel: 40 87 15 11.* Open all year Tues–Sat 1000–1200, 1400–1800, it has details of mapped walks.

La Gerbe de Blé, *pl. de l'Eglise; tel: 40 79 10 50* is a country style hotel in the town offering traditional cuisine.

Blain has been a thriving market town since Roman times. The **Musée des Arts et Traditions Populaires,** housed in the same building as the Tourist Office, is devoted to local history. One room contains Gallo-Roman remains and several shops have been reconstructed in 1900 style (open daily except Mon 1430–1730).

Across the canal stand the impressive ruins of the 14th-15th-century **Château de la Groulais** (Apr–Sept 1000–1200 and 1400–1800 except Mon).

Parcs Naturels Régionaux

These are inhabited rural areas where a delicate balance has to be maintained (with financial and practical help from the region) between the need for development and the will to preserve natural and cultural assets. There are two such parks in Brittany, the **Parc Naturel Régional d'Armorique** (see Quimper to Morlaix p. 239), by far the largest, and the **Parc Naturel Régional de Brière.** In France there are 27 parks covering 9% of the French landscape.

DRIVING DISTANCES AND TIMES

These distances between main centres generally follow autoroutes and Routes Nationales, not necessarily the most direct routes. Timings are approximate and assume good driving conditions.

	Km	Miles	Hours
Brest to . . .			
Calais	755	472	9½
Cherbourg	545	341	7
Nantes	297	186	4
Paris	593	371	7½
Rennes	244	153	3
Tours	485	303	6
Calais to . . .			
Brest	755	472	9½
Cherbourg	450	281	5½
Nantes	610	381	7½
Orléans	420	263	5
Paris	293	183	4
Rennes	511	319	6½
Rouen	212	133	3
Tours	520	325	6½
Cherbourg to . . .			
Brest	545	341	7
Calais	450	281	5½
Nantes	408	255	5
Orléans	391	244	5
Paris	342	214	4
Rennes	301	188	4
Rouen	238	149	3
Nantes to . . .			
Brest	297	186	4
Calais	610	381	7½
Cherbourg	408	255	5
Paris	384	240	5
Rennes	107	67	1½
Tours	204	128	2½

	Km	Miles	Hours
Orléans to . . .			
Calais	420	263	5½
Cherbourg	391	244	5
Paris	127	79	1½
Rouen	202	126	2½
Tours	112	70	1½
Paris to . . .			
Brest	593	371	7½
Calais	293	183	4
Cherbourg	342	214	4½
Nantes	384	240	5
Orléans	127	79	1½
Rennes	349	218	4½
Rouen	139	87	2
Tours	227	142	3
Rennes to . . .			
Brest	244	153	3
Calais	511	319	6½
Cherbourg	301	188	4
Nantes	107	67	1½
Paris	349	218	4½
Rouen	299	187	4
Tours	241	151	3
Rouen to . . .			
Calais	212	133	3
Cherbourg	238	149	3
Orléans	202	126	2½
Paris	139	87	2
Rennes	299	187	4
Tours	268	168	3½
Tours to . . .			
Brest	485	303	6
Calais	520	325	6½
Nantes	204	128	2½
Orléans	112	70	1½
Paris	227	142	3
Rennes	241	151	3
Rouen	268	168	3½

343

HOTEL CODES
AND CENTRAL BOOKING NUMBERS

The following abbreviations have been used throughout the book to show which chains are represented in a particular town or city. Most chains have a centralised worldwide-reservations system in every country where they have hotels. Most telephone calls are either completely free (usually incorporating 800) or charged at the rate for a local call (e.g. 0345 in the UK). (Aus=Australia, Can=Canada, Ire= Ireland, NZ=New Zealand, SA =South Africa, UK=United Kingdom, USA=United States of America.)

Accor
This encompasses Ibis, Mercure, Novotel and Sofitel, with central reser vation nos that cover them all
Aus (1 800) 642 244
Can/USA (800) 221 4542
UK (0171) 724 1000

Ba **Balladins**
France (1) 64 46 49 00
UK   (0171) 287 3171

BB **B&B**
contact individual hotels

BW **Best Western**
Aus (1 800) 222 422
Can/USA (800) 528 1234
Ire (1 800) 709 101
NZ (09) 520 5418
SA (011) 339 4865
UK (0800) 393130

Ca **Campanile**
France (1) 64 62 46 46
UK (0181) 569 6969

Cl **Comfort Inn**
Aus (008) 090 600
Can (800) 221 2222
France (05) 908536
Ire (1 800) 500 600
NZ (0800) 808 228
UK (0800) 444444
USA (800) 228 5150

Cn **Concorde**
Can (800) 888 4747
UK (0800) 181591
USA (800) 888 4747

Co **Confort**
France (1) 43 36 17 00

Ct **Climat de France**
Can (514) 845 1236
France (05) 11 22 11
UK (0171) 287 3181
USA (800) 332 5332

Dm **Demeure**
France (1) 48 97 96 97

Ex **Excelsior**
UK (0345) 40 40 40

FI **Formule 1**
contact individual hotels

GT **Golden Tulip**
Aus (008) 221 176
Can/USA (800) 344 1212
Ire (01) 872 3300
NZ (0800) 656 666
SA (011) 331 2672
UK (0800) 951 000

Hd **Holiday Inn**
Aus (800) 221 066
Can/USA (800) 465 4329
Ire (1 800) 553 155
NZ (0800) 442 222
SA (011) 482 3500
UK (0800) 897121

HI **Hostelling International**
France (1) 44 89 87 27
UK (0171) 248 6547

Hn **Hilton**
Aus (1 800) 222 255
Can/USA (800) 445 8667
NZ (0800) 448 002
SA (011) 880 3108
UK (0345) 581595

Hy **Hyatt**
Aus (1 800) 131 234
Can/USA (800) 233 1234
Ire (1 800) 535 500
NZ (0800) 441 234
SA (011) 773 9888
UK (0345) 581 666

Ib **Ibis**
France (1) 60 77 27 27

IH **Inter Hotel**
France (1) 42 06 46 46
UK (0171) 287 3231

LF **Logis de France**
France (1) 45 84 83 84

Mc **Mercure**
Can/USA (800) MERCURE
France (1) 60 77 22 33
UK (0181) 741 3100

Md **Méridien**
Aus (008) 331 330
Can/USA (800) 543 4300
NZ (0800) 445 577
UK (0171) 439 1244

NH **Nuit d'Hôtel**
contact individual hotels

Nv **Novotel**
Can/USA (800) NOVOTEL
France (1) 60 77 51 51
UK (0181) 748 3433

PC **Première Classe**
contact individual hotels

Pu **Pullman Hotels**
see Ibis

Ql **Quality Inn**
USA (0800) 228 5151
see also Comfort Inn

RC **Relais & Chateaux**
Aus (02) 957 4511
France (1) 45 72 90 00
UK (0171) 287 0987
USA (212) 856 0115

Rm **Ramada**
Aus (1 800) 222 431
Can (800) 854 7854
Ire (1 800) 252 627
NZ (0800) 441 111
UK (0800) 181737
USA (800) 854 7854

RS **Relais du Silence**
France (1) 44 49 90 00
UK (1) 44 49 90 00

Sf **Sofitel**
Can (800) SOFITEL
UK (0181) 741 9699
USA (800) SOFITEL

TH **TimHôtel**
France (1) 44 15 81 15

LANGUAGE

Although some English is spoken in most tourist locations – hotels, tourist offices, etc. – in the main towns, this will not necessarily be the case in smaller places. Wherever you are, however, not only is it more courteous to at least attempt to speak some French, but you will undoubtedly find that the effort is appreciated, and may even elicit a reply in perfect English!

The following is a very brief list of some useful words and phrases, with approximate pronunciation guides. For drivers' vocabulary, see p. 32.

The *Thomas Cook European Travel Phrasebook* (£4.95/$7.95) lists more than 300 travel phrases in French (and in 11 other European languages).

GENERAL

Hello/Goodbye Bonjour/Au revoir *Bawngzhoor/Ohrenvwahr*
Good evening/Goodnight Bonsoir/ Bonne nuit *Bawngswahr/Bon nwee*
Yes/No Oui/Non *Wee/Nawng*
Please S'il vous plaît *Seel voo play*
Thank you (very much) Merci (beaucoup). *Mehrsee (bohkoo).*
I'm sorry, I don't understand Pardon, je ne comprends pas *Pahrdawng, zher ner kawngprawng pah.*
Do you speak English? Vous parlez anglais? *Voo pahrlay ahnglay?*
Can you please write it down? Pouvez-vous l'écrire, s'il vous plaît? *Poovehvoo laycreer seelvooplay?*

AT THE TOURIST OFFICE

Do you have a map of the town/ area? Avez-vous une carte de la ville/ région? *Ahveh-voo ewn cart der lah veel/rehzhawng?*

Can I reserve accommodation here? Puis-je réserver un logement ici? *Pweezh rehzehrveh ang lozhmahng eessee?*
Do you have a list of accommodation? Vous avez une liste d'hôtels? *Vooz ahveh ewn leesst dohtehl?*

ACCOMMODATION

I have a reservation in the name of . . . J'ai fait une réservation au nom de . . . *Zheh feh ewn rehsehrvahssyawng o nawng der . . .*
I wrote to/faxed/telephoned you last month/last week. Je vous ai écrit/faxé/ téléphoné le mois dernier/la semaine dernière. *Zher voozeh ehkree/faxeh/tehlehfoneh ler mwah dehrnyeh/lah sermayn dehrnyair.*
Do you have any rooms free? Vous avez des chambres disponibles? *Voozahveh deh shahngbr deesspohneebl?*
I would like to reserve a single/double room with/without bath/ shower. Je voudrais réserver une chambre pour une personne/pour deux personnes avec/sans salle de bain/douche. *Zher voodray rehsehrveh ewn shahngbr poor ewn pehrson/poor dur pehrson avek/sawns sal der banne/doosh.*
I would like bed and breakfast/(room and) half board/(room and) full board. Je voudrais le petit-déjeuner/la demi-pension/la pension complète. *Zher voodray ler pewtee-dehjewneh/lah dermee-pahngsyawng/lah pahngsyawng kawngplait.*
How much is it per night? Quel est le prix pour une nuit? *Khel eh ler pree poor ewn nuwy?*
Is breakfast included? Est-ce que le petit-déjeuner est compris? *Ehsker ler pertee dehjerneh eh kawngpree?*

May I see the room? Puis-je voir la chambre? *Pweezh vwahr lah shahngbr?*
I would like to take the room. Je prends la chambre. *Zher prahng lah shangbr.*
I would like to stay for . . . nights. Je voudrais rester . . . nuits. *Zhe voodray resteh . . . newyh.*
At what time/where is breakfast served? A quelle heure/où servez-vous le petit-déjeuner? *Ah khel ur/ooh serveh-voo ler perteedehjerneh?*
Do you accept travellers' cheques/Eurocheques/credit cards? Vous acceptez les chèques de voyage/les Eurochèques/les cartes de crédit? *Voos aksepteh leh sheck der vwoyazh/laze eurosheck/leh kart der krehdee?*
May I have the bill please? Pouvez-vous me donner la note, s'il vous plaît? *Poovehvoo mer doneh lah nott seelvooplay?*

EATING AND DRINKING

346

I would like a cup of/two cups of/another coffee/tea. Je voudrais une tasse de/deux tasses de/encore une tasse de café/thé. *Zher voodray ewn tahss der/der tahss der/oncaw ewn tahss der kafeh/teh.*
I would like a bottle/glass/two glasses of mineral water/red wine/white wine, please. Je voudrais une bouteille/un verre/deux verres d'eau minérale/de vin rouge/de vin blanc, s'il vous plaît. *Zhe voodray ewn bootayy/ang vair/der vair doa mynehral/der vang roozh/der vang blahng, sylvooplay.*
Do you have any matches/cigarettes/cigars? Avez-vous des allumettes/des cigarettes/ des cigares? *Ahveh-voo dehz ahlewmaitt/deh cigaraytt/deh sigar?*
I would like a table for two. Je voudrais une table pour deux personnes. *Zher voodray ewn tabl poor der pehrson.*
Do you have a non-smoking area? Vous avez une zone non-fumeurs? *Voozahvah ewn zohn nong fewmur?*

Do you have any vegetarian dishes, please? Avez-vous des plats végétariens, s'il vous plaît? *Ahvehvoo der plah vehgehtahryang, sylvooplay?*
Could I have it well-cooked/medium/rare please? Je le voudrais bien cuit/à point/saignant. *Zher ler voodray beeang kwee/ah pwahng/saynyang.*
May I have some/some more bread/water/coffee/tea? Puis-je avoir du pain/encore du pain/de l'eau/du café/du thé? *Pweezh ahvoar dew pang/ahngkor dew pang/der lo/dew kafeh/dew teh?*
May I have the bill, please? L'addition, s'il vous plaît! *Laddyssyawng, sylvooplay!*
Where is the toilet (restroom), please? Où sont les toilettes, s'il vous plaît? *Oo sawng leh twahlaitt, sylvooplay?*

ASKING THE WAY

Excuse me, can you help me please? Excusez-moi, vous pouvez m'aider s'il vous plaît? *Ekskewzaymwah, voo poovay mahyday seelvooplay?*
I am looking for the . . . . Je cherche . . . . *Zher shaersh . . . .*
. . . the hotel/the tourist information office/the castle/the cathedral/the old town/the city centre. . . . l'hôtel/l'office de tourisme/le château/la cathédrale/la vieille ville/le centre ville. . . . *lohtel/lohfeece de tooreezm/ler shatoh/la kahtehdrahl/lah veeay veel/ler sahngtr veel.*
How far is it to . . . from here? . . . c'est loin d'ici? . . . *say looahng deesee?*
Thank you for your help. Merci pour vottre aide. *Mehrsee poor votrayd.*

SHOPPING

How much does it/this cost? Quel est le prix? *Kehl eh ler pree?*
I would like that one/a (half-)kilo of . . ., please. Je voudrais cela/un (demi-)kilo de . . ., s'il vous plaît. *Zher voodray serlah/ang (dermee)keelo der . . ., seel voo play.*

CONVERSION TABLES

DISTANCES (approx. conversions)
I kilometre (km) = 1000 metres (m) I metre = 100 centimetres (cm)

Metric	Imperial/US	Metric	Imperial/US	Metric	Imperial/US
I cm	3/8ths in.	10 m	33 ft (11 yd)	3 km	2 miles
50 cm	20 in.	20 m	66 ft (22 yd)	4 km	2½ miles
I m	3 ft 3 in.	50 m	164 ft (54 yd)	5 km	3 miles
2 m	6 ft 6 in.	100 m	330 ft (110 yd)	10 km	6 miles
3 m	10 ft	200 m	660 ft (220 yd)	20 km	12½ miles
4 m	13 ft	250 m	820 ft (275 yd)	25 km	15½ miles
5 m	16 ft 6 in.	300 m	984 ft (330 yd)	30 km	18½ miles
6 m	19 ft 6 in.	500 m	1640 ft (550 yd)	40 km	25 miles
7 m	23 ft	750 m	½ mile	50 km	31 miles
8 m	26 ft	I km	5/8ths mile	75 km	46 miles
9 m	29 ft (10 yd)	2 km	1½ miles	100 km	62 miles

24-HOUR CLOCK
(examples)

0000 = Midnight	1200 = Noon	1800 = 6 p.m.
0600 = 6 a.m.	1300 = 1 p.m.	2000 = 8 p.m.
0715 = 7.15 a.m.	1415 = 2.15 p.m.	2110 = 9.10 p.m.
0930 = 9.30 a.m.	1645 = 4.45 p.m.	2345 = 11.45 p.m.

TEMPERATURE
Conversion Formula: $°C \times 9 \div 5 + 32 = °F$

°C	°F	°C	°F	°C	°F	°C	°F
-20	-4	-5	23	10	50	25	77
-15	5	0	32	15	59	30	86
-10	14	5	41	20	68	35	95

347

WEIGHT
Ikg = 1000g 100 g = 3½ oz

Kg	Pounds	Kg	Pounds	Kg	Pounds
I	2¼	5	11	25	55
2	4½	10	22	50	110
3	6½	15	33	75	165
4	9	20	45	100	220

FLUID MEASURES
I litre(l) = 0.88 Imperial quarts = 1.06 US quarts

Litres	Imp.gal.	US gal.	Litres	Imp.gal.	US gal.
5	1.1	1.3	30	6.6	7.8
10	2.2	2.6	35	7.7	9.1
15	3.3	3.9	40	8.8	10.4
20	4.4	5.2	45	9.9	11.7
25	5.5	6.5	50	11.0	13.0

MEN'S CLOTHES

UK	Europe	US
36	46	36
38	48	38
40	50	40
42	52	42
44	54	44
46	56	46

MENS' SHOES

UK	Europe	US
6	40	7
7	41	8
8	42	9
9	43	10
10	44	11
11	45	12

LADIES' CLOTHES

UK	France	Italy	Rest of Europe	US
10	36	38	34	8
12	38	40	36	10
14	40	42	38	12
16	42	44	40	14
18	44	46	42	16
20	46	48	44	18

MEN'S SHIRTS

UK	Europe	US
14	36	14
15	38	15
15½	39	15½
16	41	16
16½	42	16½
17	43	17

LADIES' SHOES

UK	Europe	US
3	36	4½
4	37	5½
5	38	6½
6	39	7½
7	40	8½
8	41	9½

INDEX

349

READER SURVEY

If you enjoyed using this book, or even if you didn't, please help us improve future editions by taking part in our reader survey. Every returned form will be acknowledged, and to show our appreciation we will give you £1 off your next purchase of a Thomas Cook guidebook. Just take a few minutes to complete and return this form to us.

When did you buy this book? _____

_____

Where did you buy it? (Please give town/city and if possible name of retailer)

_____

When did you/do you intend to travel in Normandy, Brittany and the Loire Valley?

For how long (approx.)? _____

How many people in your party? _____

Which cities, towns and other locations did you/do you intend mainly to visit?

_____
_____
_____
_____

Did you/will you:
- ☐ Make all your travel arrangements independently?
- ☐ Travel on a pre-arranged package?

Please give brief details: _____

_____

Did you/do you intend to use this book:
- ☐ For planning your trip?
- ☐ During the trip itself?
- ☐ Both?

Did you/do you intend also to purchase any of the following travel publications for your trip?

Thomas Cook Travellers: Normandy/Brittany/Loire Valley/Paris
A road map/atlas (please specify) _____
Other guidebooks (please specify) _____

_____

Have you used any other Thomas Cook guidebooks in the past? If so, which?

_____

Please rate the following features of On the Road around Normandy, Brittany and the Loire for their value to you (Circle VU for 'very useful', U for 'useful', NU for 'little or no use'):

The 'Travel Essentials' section on pages 15–24	VU	U	NU
The 'Driving in France' section on pages 25–32	VU	U	NU
The 'Touring Itineraries' on pages 39–44	VU	U	NU
The recommended driving routes throughout the book	VU	U	NU
Information on towns and cities etc	VU	U	NU
The maps of towns and cities, etc.	VU	U	NU
The colour planning map	VU	U	NU

Please use this space to tell us about any features that in your opinion could be changed, improved, or added in future editions of the book, or any other comments you would like to make concerning the book:

Your age category: ☐ 21-30 ☐ 31-40 ☐ 41–50 ☐ over 50

Your name: Mr/Mrs/Miss/Ms
(First name or initials)
(Last name)

Your full address: (Please include postal or zip code)

Your daytime telephone number: _____

Please detach this page and send it to: The Project Editor, On the Road around Normandy, Brittany and The Loire Valley, Thomas Cook Publishing, PO Box 227, Peterborough PE3 8BQ, United Kingdom.

We will be pleased to send you details of how to claim your discount upon receipt of this questionnaire.